RESEARCH HANDBOOK ON SUSTAINABILITY REPORTING

RESEARCH HANDBOOKS ON ACCOUNTING

This new and exciting series brings together authoritative and thought-provoking contributions on the most pressing topics and issues in accounting. *Research Handbooks* in the series feature specially commissioned chapters from eminent academics, and are each overseen by an editor internationally recognized as a leading name within the field. Chapters within the *Research Handbooks* feature comprehensive and cutting-edge research, and are written with a global readership in mind. Equally useful as reference tools or high-level introductions to specific topics, issues, methods and debates, these *Research Handbooks* will be an essential resource for academic researchers and postgraduate students.

For a full list of Edward Elgar published titles, including the titles in this series, visit our website at www.e-elgar.com.

Research Handbook on Sustainability Reporting

Edited by

Gunnar Rimmel

Chair in Accounting and Sustainability Reporting, Aalborg University Business School, Denmark

Güler Aras

Professor of Finance, Accounting and Sustainability, Chair of the Center for Finance Governance and Sustainability (CFGS), Yildiz Technical University (YTU), Turkey

Diogenis Baboukardos

Associate Professor of Accounting, Audencia Business School, France and Athens University of Economics and Business, Greece

Joanna Krasodomska

Associate Professor of Accounting, Krakow University of Economics, Poland

Christian Nielsen

Department of Management Computer Science and Engineering, University of Bologna, Italy

Frank Schiemann

Professor of Management Accounting, University of Bamberg, Germany

RESEARCH HANDBOOKS ON ACCOUNTING

Edward Elgar PUBLISHING

Cheltenham, UK • Northampton, MA, USA

Published by
Edward Elgar Publishing Limited
The Lypiatts
15 Lansdown Road
Cheltenham
Glos GL50 2JA
UK

Edward Elgar Publishing, Inc.
William Pratt House
9 Dewey Court
Northampton
Massachusetts 01060
USA

A catalogue record for this book
is available from the British Library

Library of Congress Control Number: 2024941108

This book is available electronically in the **Elgar**online
Economics subject collection
https://dx.doi.org/10.4337/9781035316267

Printed on elemental chlorine free (ECF)
recycled paper containing 30% Post-Consumer Waste

ISBN 978 1 0353 1625 0 (cased)
ISBN 978 1 0353 1626 7 (eBook)

Printed and bound in the USA

Contents

v

Editors

Prof. Dr Gunnar Rimmel is the Chair in Accounting and Sustainability Reporting and Head of the Accounting Research Group at Aalborg University Business School. He is currently also a visiting professor at Henley Business School, where he was previously Chair in Accounting and Corporate Reporting and the founder and director of the Henley Centre for Accounting Research & Practice (HARP). Previously he worked in Sweden as full Professor in Accounting at Jönköping International Business School and Gothenburg Research Institute at the University of Gothenburg. He received his PhD in 2003 for the thesis "Human Resource Disclosures" from the School of Business, Economics and Law at Gothenburg University.

During the past 15+ years, he has been leading research programmes funded by the Handelsbanken research foundations as well as NASDAQ OMX Nordic Foundation. His current research project, "The Impact of Mandatory Sustainability Reporting on Swedish Reporting", is affiliated with the Gothenburg Research Institute and has received funding from the Handelsbanken Research Foundation.

He is active in a number of associations, notably in the European Accounting Association (EAA). He was Secretary General of the EAA's 28th Annual Congress in Gothenburg in 2005, and has been on the EAA management board as well as being Co-Chair and Chair of the Conference Committee. He is currently a member of the EAA Stakeholder Reporting Committee.

He has published articles in international academic journals such as the *Accounting, Auditing & Accountability Journal*, the *Journal of Accounting and Public Policy*, the *Social and Environmental Accountability Journal* and *Accounting Forum*. He has edited and contributed more than 30 book chapters and international books. For many years he has been an active researcher with a wide network. Until 2023, he was an executive board member of the Center for Social and Environmental Accounting Research (CSEAR), and an advisory board member of the British Accounting and Finance Association – Financial Accounting and Reporting Special Interest Group (FARSIG). He is also an editorial board member of *Accounting Forum*, the *Accounting, Auditing & Accountability Journal* and the *Journal of Business Models*. He is affiliated with EFRAG, where he is part of the project task force for the project on reporting of non-financial risks and opportunities and linkage to the business model (PTF-RNFRO) and worked on the team drafting EFRAG's implementation guideline for the new European Sustainability Reporting Standards (ESRS) of the European Commission.

Prof. Dr Güler Aras is an academic, civil society leader, and researcher who leads key studies on finance, corporate governance, corporate sustainability, and integrated reporting. She is a professor of finance and accounting at Yildiz Technical University in Istanbul, where she served as the Dean of the Faculty of Business and Dean of the Graduate School for many years. She spent a year as a visiting professor at Georgetown University McDonough School of Business in Washington DC. Founder of the Center for Finance Governance and Sustainability (CFGS), she is known as an ambassador of governance and sustainability. Professor Aras, who is a member of the Integrated Reporting and Connectivity Council – IRCC, the advisory body to the IFRS Foundation Trustees, the IASB, and the ISSB, pioneered a global initiative with the Integrated Reporting Association Turkey (ERTA), of which she is the founding chair.

Professor Aras is the author of more than 25 international books. She has contributed to more than 300 articles in international journals and conferences and has carried out numerous grant-funded international projects. Professor Aras is the founder and board member of numerous national and international professional and academic organizations and is a member of the Accountancy Europe Corporate Governance Task Force. She has spoken extensively at professional and academic conferences and has served as a consultant to several governmental and commercial organizations such as the Ministry of Development, the Ministry of Finance, the Treasury, and the Ministry of Labour and Social Security Employment in Turkey. She also serves as a board member of the Turkish Capital Markets Association.

Dr Diogenis Baboukardos is an associate professor of accounting at Audencia Business School, France and Athens University of Economics and Business, Greece. He is a visiting research fellow at the Essex Business School, University of Essex and a research affiliate of the Adam Smith Observatory of Corporate Reporting Practices at the University of Glasgow. His research interests lie in the broad field of corporate reporting with a particular focus on issues related to sustainability and climate change reporting. His research has been published in various academic journals (such as the *Journal of Accounting & Public Policy*, *British Accounting Review*, *Accounting Forum* and *Regional Studies*) and it has been funded by professional bodies and regulators (such as the UK Financial Reporting Council, the Association of Chartered Certified Accountants, and the Institute of Chartered Accountants of Scotland). He has also worked in consultancy projects in relation to the application of the UN's Sustainability Development Goals in local councils. He is the secretary of the BAFA Financial Accounting Reporting Special Interest Group and an editorial board member of the *Sustainability Accounting, Management and Policy Journal*, the *Journal of Accounting in Emerging Economies* and the *European Management Journal*. He is a fellow of the Higher Education Academy of the UK.

Dr Joanna Krasodomska holds the position of associate professor within the Department of Financial Accounting at Krakow University of Economics in Poland. Her primary research interests focus on sustainability reporting and its assurance and stakeholder engagement. Her contributions have been published in many academic journals including the *Accounting, Auditing & Accountability Journal*, *Accounting Education*, *Accounting in Europe*, the *Journal of International Financial Management and Accounting*, *Meditari Accountancy Research*, *Organization & Environment*, and the *Sustainability Accounting, Management and Policy Journal*. Joanna is a member of the European Accounting Association (EAA) Stakeholder Reporting Committee, and is Poland's Representative on the EAA Board. She serves as an editorial board member for *Accounting in Europe*, *Accounting Forum* and the *Journal of Accounting and Management Information Systems*. Joanna holds the role of Vice President for Administration within the Executive Committee of the International Association for Accounting Education & Research (IAAER). Additionally, she is a member of the Accountants Association in Poland's Committee for Foreign Cooperation.

Christian Nielsen is an adjunct professor at the University of Bologna and works as a sustainability advisor focusing on net-zero transition plans and due diligence. He is a global thought leader in designing disruptive and scalable business models and works with sustainability reporting and ESG performance measurement. Christian has a substantial number of international publications to his record and his work combines business model design with corporate performance and benchmarking and reaches into collaborative forms of organization and second-track processes. He is also the founding editor of the *Journal of Business Models* and an editorial board member of the *Accounting, Auditing & Accountability Journal* and the *Journal of Behavioural Economics and Social Systems*.

Frank Schiemann is Professor of Business Administration, especially Management Accounting, at the University of Bamberg. He received his PhD at the Technische Universität Dresden. He has been a visiting researcher at Macquarie University, Sydney, National Taiwan University, Taiwan and Auckland University of Technology, Auckland. His research focus is on sustainability reporting and accounting, development and consequences of (mandated) corporate climate-related reporting and materiality in the context of sustainability disclosures. His research has been published in international academic journals, including *Business & Society*, *European Accounting Review*, the *Journal of Accounting and Public Policy*, the *Journal of Business Ethics*, the *Journal of Business Finance and Accounting*, *Organization & Environment*, and *Organizational Research Methods*. Frank serves as an editorial board member for *Accounting Forum, European Accounting Review*, and the *Social and Environmental Accounting Journal*. He is a member of the Sustainable Finance Research Platform (WPSF), the Sustainable Disclosure Working Group of the Deutsche Vereinigung für Finanzanalyse und Asset Management (DFVA), and the EAA Stakeholder Reporting Group.

Contributors

Maizatulakma Abdullah is an assistant professor at the Faculty of Economics and Management, Universiti Kebangsaan Malaysia. She is a member of the editorial board of *Jurnal Pengurusan* (*UKM Journal of Management*). Her research areas include risk management reporting and environmental, social and governance reporting. Her articles have been published in international academic journals such as the *Journal of Applied Accounting Research* and the *Journal of Cleaner Production*. She is currently a member of the Centre for Social and Environmental Accounting Research (CSEAR), St Andrews, UK.

Hammed Afolabi is a lecturer in accounting and finance at Leeds Trinity University, UK. His previous work experience includes working as an accountant and forensic auditor. He holds a PhD in accounting and financial management from Henley Business School, University of Reading, UK, and an MSc in forensic audit and accounting from the University of South Wales, UK. Also, he is a Fellow of the Higher Education Academy, UK, Certified Fraud Examiner, Certified Public Accountant, and Certified Forensic Accountant, and a member of both the European Accounting Association and the British Accounting and Finance Association. Hammed's research resonates around accountability, corporate reporting, sustainability accounting, and extinction accounting. Within these areas, he has published in different international peer-reviewed academic journals. Furthermore, he is an active ad hoc reviewer for top academic accounting journals such as the *Sustainability Accounting, Management and Policy Journal* and the *International Journal of Emerging Markets*.

Syed Mahfujul Alam is a PhD candidate at the Department of Economics and Management, University of Trento, Italy. He obtained bachelor's and master's degrees in accounting and finance from the universities of Derby and Northampton, UK. He is an affiliate of the Association of Chartered Certified Accountants (ACCA). He is currently undertaking research in climate change accounting and disclosure and exploring the roles of accountants. He is also interested in governance and sustainability practices in different contexts. He is a member of the Centre for Social and Environmental Accounting Research (CSEAR) networks and his papers have been accepted at international conferences.

Cătălin-Nicolae Albu is Professor of Accounting with the Bucharest University of Economic Studies, Romania. Cătălin's research focuses on the application of Western models in emerging economies and was published in the *Accounting, Auditing and Accountability Journal*, *Critical Perspectives on Accounting*, *Accounting Forum*, and *Accounting and Business Research*, among others. Cătălin serves as associate editor of the *Journal of International Accounting, Auditing and Taxation* and as a member of the editorial board of *Accounting Forum*, among others.

Nadia Albu is Professor of Accounting with the Bucharest University of Economic Studies, Romania. She focuses her research on the institutional factors influencing the implementation of global standards and models in emerging economies. Nadia's research has recently been published in the *Accounting, Auditing and Accountability Journal*, *Critical Perspectives on*

Accounting, Accounting Forum, and *Accounting in Europe,* among others. Nadia serves as associate editor of *Accounting in Europe* and editor in chief of *Accounting and Management Information Systems.*

Maria Aluchna, PhD, is Professor of Management, Head of Department of Management Theory, and Chair of the Management Faculty Board, all at Warsaw School of Economics. She specializes in corporate governance, ESG reporting and strategic management. Maria is the author of academic articles and monographs. She teaches MBA, PhD, MA and BA studies. Maria is a member of the European Corporate Governance Institute, the International Corporate Governance Society, Finance Watch, the European Academy of Management (EURAM), the International Society for Business, Economics and Ethics (ISBEE), the Academy of Management (AOM), the Academy of International Business (AIB) and the editorial committees of the *International Journal of Corporate Social Responsibility,* the *European Journal of Economics and Management,* the *Journal of Knowledge Globalization, Przegląd Organizacji* and *e-Mentor.* She publishes in Polish and in English – including *Corporate Governance in Central Europe and Russia, Women on Corporate Boards: An International Perspective,* and *The Dynamics of Corporate Social Responsibility: A Critical Approach to Theory and Practice*), over 70 articles and conference papers, and takes active part in international conferences.

Simone Aresu is an associate professor of accounting at the University of Cagliari, Italy. His main research interests are related to impression management in corporate reporting, sustainable corporate governance, and accounting for sustainable development. Currently, he teaches management accounting at the undergraduate level and advanced management accounting at MSc level. He has published in top-tier accounting and management journals, such as the *Journal of Management,* the *Journal of Business Ethics* and *Critical Perspectives on Accounting.* In 2019, he received the best paper award for the *Journal of Applied Accounting Research* for the paper "Does graphical reporting improve risk disclosure? Evidence from European banks". Simone Aresu is a member of the Italian Society of Accounting Professors (SIDREA), the European Accounting Association (EAA), and the Centre for Social and Environmental Accounting Research (CSEAR).

Laura Bini is an associate professor of accounting in the Department of Economics and Management, University of Florence. Her main research interests are in the areas of non-financial disclosure to financial markets, including non-financial disclosure regulation, narrative disclosure quality and sustainability disclosure.

Sirle Bürkland is an associate professor at Aalborg University Business School in Denmark. She obtained her PhD degree at the University of Vaasa in Finland. Her research involves accounting and information technologies (e.g., enterprise resource planning systems), calculative and traceability infrastructures, social value accounting and sustainability. She has formerly worked as a forensic accountant in the public sector and as head accountant and financial manager in the biotechnology industry.

Dannielle Cerbone is an associate professor at the School of Accountancy, University of the Witwatersrand and a registered Chartered Accountant (South Africa). Dan teaches auditing and integrated reporting to undergraduate and postgraduate students. His research interests include value creation, materiality determination, business model development and integrated thinking. Dan completed his internship at PricewaterhouseCoopers and served as an audit manager until 2019. He has published numerous journal articles, books and book chapters. Notable articles are published in the *Australian Accounting Review*, the *British Accounting Review* and *Meditari Accountancy*.

Charles H. Cho is Professor of Sustainability Accounting and the Erivan K. Haub Chair in Business & Sustainability at the Schulich School of Business, York University, Canada. He holds a Bachelor of Science in Accounting, a Master of Science in Accounting, and a PhD in Business Administration (Accounting Track) from the University of Central Florida. He also worked for KPMG LLP and other public accounting firms for several years in auditing and taxation. His research interests include social and environmental accounting; corporate social responsibility (CSR); and accounting and the public interest. Professor Cho has published his work in leading academic journals such as the *Accounting, Auditing and Accountability Journal*, *Accounting, Organizations and Society*, *Critical Perspectives on Accounting*, the *European Accounting Review*, and the *Journal of Business Ethics*. He currently serves as an editor of *Accounting Forum*; the accounting and business ethics section co-editor of the *Journal of Business Ethics*; and as an associate editor of *Business & Society*.

Jesper Lindgaard Christensen, PhD, is an associate professor in industrial dynamics at Aalborg University Business School, Denmark. His current research interests cover climate-related risks and reporting, SME development and entrepreneurial finance, economic geography, innovation systems, low-tech industry studies, and innovation policy. He has considerable (25 years) experience in policy analyses and advice, including work for the EU Commission, the Nordic Council, the Swedish and Danish governments, as well as Danish regions. Dr Christensen has published in journals such as *Small Business Economics*, the *European Journal of Innovation Management*, *Structural Change and Economic Dynamics*, *European Planning Studies*, and *Regional Studies*, among others. His most recent book is on small country innovation systems in transition.

Michela Cordazzo is an associate professor of financial accounting in the Department of Management, Ca' Foscari University of Venice. She has been visiting scholar at the Faculty of Economics, University of Melbourne, and at the China Europe International Business School (Shanghai). Her research interests concern comparative and international accounting, market-based accounting, corporate reporting, financial statement analysis and evaluation. She is the author of several books and papers in national and international journals.

Ericka Costa (PhD in Business Economics, University of Udine, Italy) is Professor of Accounting, University of Trento. She has been a visiting scholar at the Centre for Social and Environmental Accounting Research, University of St Andrews. UK, University of Burgos, Spain, and at the Centre of Excellence in Accounting & Reporting for Co-operatives (CEARC), Sobey Business School in Halifax, Canada. She is a council member at the Centre for Social and Environmental Accounting Research (CSEAR) networks and director of CSEAR Italy. Her research interests focus on investigating sustainability accounting and corporate social responsibility for for-profit and non-profit organizations. She has written a number of book chapters, articles and papers that have been accepted for national and international journals. Her research has appeared in international publications, including the *Accounting, Auditing & Accountability Journal*, *Critical Perspectives on Accounting*, *Accounting and Business*

Research, the *Journal of Business Ethics*, *Service Business* and the *Sustainability Accounting and Management Journal*.

Mathias Cöster is an associate professor in the Department of Business Studies, Uppsala University Campus Gotland. He researches how organizations develop management control practices for realizing sustainability strategies. He also researches the impact of digitization on industries, organizational business models and price models. In his research he prefers to engage with case studies that have a multidisciplinary character. He has been published in several high-ranking international journals and he has co-authored a number of books. He is also a much-appreciated and frequently hired lecturer in various educational contexts.

Chiara Crovini is an associate professor at Aalborg University Business School in Denmark. She obtained her PhD in 2017 from the University of Torino in Italy. Her main research interests are risk management, risk reporting, business model reporting, intellectual capital, sustainability reporting and the accounting profession. She is also a chartered accountant and a statutory auditor.

Nabyla Daidj, PhD, HDR, is an associate professor (Strategy & Information Systems for Management) at Institut Mines-Telecom Business School. Her research interests are internal audit, business–IT alignment strategy and business models. Since 2015, she has published several books including: *The Digital Transformation of Auditing and the Evolution of the Internal Audit*; *Cooperation, Coopetition and Innovation*; *Value Creation in Management Accounting and Strategic Management*; *Strategy, Structure and Corporate Governance: Expressing Inter-Firms Networks*; *Developing Strategic Business Models and Competitive Advantage in the Digital Sector*. Several of her papers have been published in international journals (the *Information Resources Management Journal*, the *Journal of Research in Marketing and Entrepreneurship*, the *International Journal of Entrepreneurship and Small Business*, the *Journal of High Technology Management Research*, the *Journal of Media Business Studies*, the *Journal of Media Economics*, the *Digiworld Economic Journal*, *Leadership*, and the *Journal of Business Ethics*). She teaches strategic management, strategic IT alignment and evolution of business models in the context of digital transformation in graduate programmes.

Dorota Dobija is Professor of Accounting, Governance and Society at Kozminski University, Poland. Her research focuses on the topics at the intersection of accounting and governance, performance management and sustainability in the private and public sectors. Dorota was a Fulbright Scholar and held a series of visiting professorships internationally. She has published articles in the *Accounting, Auditing and Accountability Journal*, the *European Management Journal*, *Organization & Environment*, *Government Information Quarterly* and the *Public Performance and Management Review*, among others. She was also invited to co-edit special issues for the *Accounting, Auditing and Accountability Journal* as well as for *Qualitative Research in Accounting and Management*. She serves as the editorial board member of *Accounting Forum* and the *European Management Journal*.

Federica Doni, PhD, is an associate professor in business administration and accounting and the Scientific Director of the master's degree in Sustainability in Law Finance and Management (SiLFiM) at the Department of Business and Law, University of Milano-Bicocca, Milan, Italy. Her primary research interests over the past 15 years have been international accounting, financial reporting, intangibles and intellectual capital, corporate governance, ESG and integrated reporting, the SDGs, climate change and biodiversity issues. She is the Principal Investigator of the Jean Monnet Module "Sustainability Disclosure in Corporate Reporting. Improvement and harmonization of best practices in European Union", which was selected for EU support (2019–2022). She has more than 100 scientific publications. She has had papers published in the *Accounting Auditing and Accountability Journal*, the *Journal of Cleaner Production*, the *Journal of Intellectual Capital*, the *Journal of Environmental Management, Business Strategy and the Environment*, and the *Journal of Business Ethics*.

Mădălina Dumitru is professor of accounting at the Bucharest University of Economic Studies, Romania. Her research interests are sustainability accounting, management accounting and accounting education. She has been published in the *Journal of Accounting and Public Policy, Information Systems Management, Accounting in Europe*, and *Accounting Education*, among others. Mădălina serves as an associate editor of *Accounting and Management Information Systems* and is a member of the editorial board of *Amfiteatru Economic*.

Joanna Dyczkowska, PhD, is an associate professor in the Department of Cost Accounting, Taxes Management and Controlling at the Wroclaw University of Economics and Business in Poland. Her research interests include non-financial and integrated reporting, stakeholder management and stakeholder capitalism. She has authored a monograph on non-financial disclosures in the R&D area in biopharmaceutical companies. She has published her research works in many journals, including the *Accounting, Auditing & Accountability Journal, Meditari Accountancy Research*, the *Accounting and Management Information Journal*, and the *International Journal of Intellectual Property Management*. In 2018, she received a mini-grant directed to young researchers from CEECs funded by ACCA Global and another grant under the MINIATURA 2 programme from the National Science Centre in Poland to implement the research on the concept of an integrated reporting model in the light of the pragmatic constructivism paradigm. In 2019–2022, she was a Polish leader of the INTEREST project (INTEgrated REporting for SMEs Transparency).

Dusan Ecim is a senior lecturer at the University of the Witwatersrand's School of Accountancy. His research interests include auditing, corporate governance, integrated reporting and sustainable development. Dusan has published several journal articles, book chapters and technical reports. He teaches a range of undergraduate and postgraduate courses informed by his practical experience and research. Before joining academia, Dusan served at Deloitte. He is a member of the South African Institute of Chartered Accountants.

Christoph Feichtinger works as a project risk manager in the field of infrastructure. He holds a PhD in management accounting from the University of Bamberg (Germany). His research areas are digitalization, big data, start-ups, agile management, agility, corporate management and management accounting. Christoph has published several journal articles and book chapters. He is also currently a lecturer at the University of Bamberg and Aalen University in the fields of strategy, sustainability management and management accounting, with a track of records as a research assistant at the University of Bamberg for eight years, During this period, he gained teaching experience in cost management, management accounting, project management and business management.

Maria-Silvia Fota is an assistant professor of accounting at Bucharest University of Economic

Studies, Romania. Maria's research focuses on financial and non-financial reporting in emerging economies and has been published in *Amfiteatru Economic*, and the *Journal of Accounting and Management Information Systems*, among others.

Ozlem Kutlu Furtuna is an associate professor at Yıldız Technical University (YTU), Faculty of Economics and Administrative Sciences. Her fields of interest include Business Finance, Corporate Sustainability and Sustainable Finance. She has participated in local and multinational projects such as "Cooperation for Integration under Financial Inclusion of Current Refugees and Newcomers" (funded by the European Union), "An Alternative Model Suggestion in the Measurement of the Corporate Sustainability Performance: An Application on Turkish Banking Sector" (funded by TUBITAK, the Scientific and Technological Research Council of Türkiye), and "Generating Sustainable Development Goals Relevance and Impact Indices for Financial Institutions to reinforce Sustainable Financial System and Economy", also funded by TUBITAK. She received the best paper award for "Insights from Corporate Cash Holdings in Emerging Markets" at the seventh European Business Research Conference in 2016 and for "Comparison of Corporate Sustainability Performance of Turkish Conventional and Participation Banking" at the International Conference on Business, Economics and Finance (ICBEF) in 2017. Ozlem is a vice president of the Center for Finance Corporate Governance and Sustainability Research (CFGS) at YTU, and she has been the academic mentor of the YTU's CFA Research Challenge Team since 2020.

Silvia Gaia is a professor of accounting at Essex Business School (EBS), University of Essex. She holds a PhD in accounting from the University of Roma Tre (Italy). Silvia's research focuses on the interplay between financial and non-financial reporting, social and environmental issues and corporate governance. Silvia is currently the Chair of the Special Interest Group on Financial Accounting and Reporting (FARSIG) of the British Accounting and Finance Association (BAFA). She has published in several international journals, including the *Accounting, Auditing and Accountability Journal*, *Accounting Forum*, the *British Accounting Review*, the *Journal of Business Ethics* and *Regional Studies*. She is an associate editor for *Accounting Forum* and the *Journal of International Accounting, Auditing and Taxation* and an editorial board member of the *Journal of Accounting in Emerging Economies*.

Raluca Gina Guşe is an associate professor of accounting at Bucharest University of Economic Studies, Romania. Her research focuses on integrated reporting, accounting education and digitalization and was published in international journals such as *Amfiteatru Economic*, the *Journal of Accounting and Management Information Systems*, and *Accounting in Europe*. Raluca serves as an associate editor of the *Amfiteatru Economic* journal.

Md Alamgir Jalil is a PhD fellow at the University of Essex (Essex Business School), UK, under the Prime Minister's Fellowship of Bangladesh. He is also an assistant professor in accounting employed by the Government of Bangladesh to teach graduate students at the National University of Bangladesh. He has been undertaking PhD research at Essex Business School on the extent and nature of corporate water narratives to investigate how transparently water disclosures are presenting water performance and contributing to the sustainable development goals (SDG 6 and 14). Before starting his PhD research, he joined the government education service of Bangladesh in 2008 as a lecturer in accounting. For professional development, he completed an MSc in Sustainability at the University of Leeds, UK in 2015. After that, he was promoted to assistant professor in accounting.

Evrim Hacıoglu Kazak is a research assistant at Yıldız Technical University (YTU) Department of Business Administration, and holds a bachelor's degree in mathematics, a master's degree in business administration, and a PhD in finance. She conducted her doctoral studies in the fields of corporate sustainability and machine learning. She is a board member at YTU Center for Finance Governance and Sustainability (CFGS). She is also a trainer in the corporate sustainability training programme organized by CFGS for the business world, academia, the public, and NGOs. She has taken part in many projects and research conducted by CFGS in the fields of finance, corporate sustainability, and integrated reporting. One of the projects, entitled "An Alternative Approach for Corporate Sustainability Performance Measurement: An Application on Turkish Banking Sector", has been hailed by TUBITAK (Scientific and Technological Research Council of Turkey) as a success story.

Mariem Khalfaoui is a PhD student in accounting and business administration at the Department of Economic and Business Science at the University of Cagliari. Her main research interests are corporate governance, directors' compensation, accounting and corporate reporting. Her PhD project was awarded Best Project at the Doctoral Colloquium in the 25th Financial Reporting and Business Communication Conference organized by the Financial Reporting Special Interest Group (British Accounting and Finance Association).

Paul Klumpes is an associate professor of accounting at Aalborg University. He was previously Professor of Accounting at Abu Dhabi University, Nottingham Business School, Imperial College and the University of Nottingham. He holds a PhD in accounting, and is a fellow of CPA Australia and an honorary fellow of the UK Institute and Faculty of Actuaries. He regularly contributes to academically refereed journals, including the *Journal of Accounting, Auditing, and Finance*, other professional journal publications, book chapter contributions and research manuscripts. His current research interests cover the inter-relationship of financial sector institutions' voluntary reporting practices with emerging risks related to climate, nature-related financial risks, and cyber-related risk.

Blerita Korca is a postdoctoral researcher at the Chair of Management Accounting at the University of Bamberg in Germany. She received her PhD at the University of Trento in Italy. She has been a visiting scholar at the Essex Business School in the UK and Schulich School of Business in Toronto, Canada. Her research focuses on the role of regulations to improve sustainability reporting, and firms' performance changes due to mandatory sustainability reporting. She also explores topics such as comparability and materiality in sustainability reporting. Her research has been published in international academic journals such as *Accounting in Europe*, *Accounting Forum*, and the *Sustainability Accounting and Management Journal*. Additionally, she has contributed to a number of policy briefs on sustainability reporting topics.

Martina Macpherson, FICRS, PhD (c.) is Head of ESG Product Strategy and Management at SIX Financial Information, the Exchange Group that operates the Swiss and Spanish Stock Exchanges. She has over 20 years of sustainable finance experience, in industry and academia, and is an award-winning ESG influencer, researcher, and entrepreneur. Martina has an MBA certificate in finance and business from London School of Business and Finance in the UK, and an MA in law and human sciences from the University of Frankfurt in Germany. She is a fellow of the Institute for Corporate Responsibility and Sustainability (ICRS) UK. She is currently undertaking a part-time PhD at the University of Cardiff, UK, in sustainable accounting and finance. Martina is an academic lecturer, writer and public speaker in sustainable investing and has co-authored a range of ESG and Fintech books. For her work in sustainable finance and leadership, she was recognized as a one of the "Top 50 Women in Finance" by the World Finance Forum (WFF) in 2022.

Warren Maroun is a professor at the University of the Witwatersrand's School of Accountancy, South Africa and Leeds University Business School, UK. He has published numerous academic papers dealing broadly with financial accounting, assurance, sustainability reporting and corporate governance. Warren is a member of the South African Institute of Chartered Accountants and the Chartered Institute of Management Accountants. He is the joint editor of *Meditari Accountancy Research*. Before joining academia, he served in different capacities at PricewaterhouseCoopers. He retains close ties with commerce and industry, consulting on a range of accounting- and governance-related matters. He serves on working groups of the Integrated Reporting Committee of South Africa, the Independent Regulatory Board of Auditors and the International Auditing and Assurance Standards Board.

Łukasz Matuszak, PhD, is an assistant professor in the Department of Financial Accounting and Audit at the Poznań University of Economics and Business (PUEB) in Poland. His research interests include non-financial, integrated reporting and sustainability reporting. He co-authored a monograph on the consequences of the non-financial reporting directive (NFRD) in Poland. His studies have been presented at numerous academic conferences and published in international journals, including the *Journal of Accounting in Emerging Economics* and the *Sustainability Accounting, Management and Policy Journal*. He received a mini-grant in the ACCA and IAAER programme addressed to young researchers from CEECs. He was an Erasmus+ participant in Bulgaria, the Czech Republic, the United Kingdom and Croatia. He also serves as a reviewer for international journals. His current project delves into the quality of sustainability reporting. Additionally, since 2013, he has been the head of postgraduate studies in accounting at PUEB.

Andrea Melis, PhD, is Professor of Accounting and Corporate Governance at the University of Cagliari, Italy. He is currently editor-in-chief of the *Journal of Management and Governance*, and screening editor of *Corporate Governance: An International Review*. He also serves (or has recently served) as an editorial board member for *Accounting and Business Research*, the *Journal of International Accounting, Auditing and Taxation* and the *Journal of International Financial Management & Accounting*. His main research areas are in corporate governance, performance measurement and reporting.

Christian Ott is an associate professor of finance, accounting, and control at EM Strasbourg Business School and a member of the LaRGE research center at the Université de Strasbourg, France. He received his PhD from the Technische Universität Dresden, Germany. His research focuses primarily on the corporate disclosure environment. He is interested in the provision of non-financial information (e.g., climate-related information) in voluntary and mandatory corporate disclosures and its evaluation by shareholders and other stakeholder groups. Additionally, he explores the planning, management, and control of non-financial information. Christian Ott publishes in various academic journals, including the *Accounting, Auditing & Accountability Journal*, *Accounting and Business Research*, the *Journal of Accounting and Public Policy*, and the *Journal of Business Finance & Accounting*.

Silvia Panfilo, PhD, is an assistant professor in accounting at Venice School of Management (VSM), Ca' Foscari University of Venice. Her research interests include risk disclosure, enterprise risk management, sustainability accounting, and corporate governance. She is a member of many national (AIDEA and SIDREA) and international (European and American Accounting Association, European Risk Research Network) associations and she has published in many top journals including the *Journal of Accounting and Public Policy*, *Risk Analysis: An International Journal*, the *Journal of Management and Governance*, *Business Strategy and the Environment*, and *Accounting in Europe*. She is also co-founder of the Sustainability Lab at VSM and a member of its Technical Scientific Committee.

Emre Parlakkaya is a postdoctoral research fellow in accounting and financial management at Henley Business School, University of Reading. Emre holds a PhD and an MSc in accounting and financial management and has professional experience in financial services. His research is rooted in the fields of social and environmental accounting and corporate sustainability reporting. He is particularly interested in integrating innovative methods and tools into his research. Emre's approach aims to incorporate insights from linguistics into the analysis of accounting and accountability-related corporate narratives. Through this approach, he aspires to facilitate a more comprehensive and insightful understanding of corporate narratives and their broader societal implications.

Christoph Pelger is a professor of accounting and auditing and holds the Chair of Accounting and Auditing at the University of Passau, Germany. He is an adjunct professor at the Norwegian School of Economics (NHH) in Bergen and a part-time professor at the University of Innsbruck. His research interests lie in international accounting and standard setting, the enforcement of IFRS and qualitative financial accounting research. Christoph is the section editor for financial accounting and reporting of *Qualitative Research in Accounting and Management* and an associate editor of *Accounting and Business Research*.

Simone Pizzi, PhD, is an assistant professor in accounting at the University of Salento, Lecce, Italy. He is also an associate editor for the *Journal of Applied Accounting Research*. Simone has published his research in different international journals, such as *Accounting Forum*, *Accounting in Europe*, *Sustainability Accounting*, *Management and Policy Journal* and *Meditari Accountancy Research*. His research interests relate to the emerging issues of social and environmental accounting research, such as standard settings, materiality and impact assessments and sustainability reporting regulation.

Ronita Ram is an associate professor in accounting at Henley Business School, University of Reading, UK. Ronita holds a PhD in accounting from the University of Sydney and is a member of Chartered Accountants Australia and New Zealand. She is also a member of the UKEB's Academic Advisory Group and a member of the UKEB's Sustainability Working Group. Ronita has over 15 years of teaching experience at tertiary level. Her research interests include international financial reporting, IFRS, accounting for SMEs, and sustainability and environmental reporting. Ronita has published her research in different international journals, such as *Abacus*, *Accounting and Finance*, and the *Sustainability Accounting, Management and Policy Journal*. Ronita is also a reviewer for various international accounting journals.

Luigi Rombi, PhD, is a lecturer in accounting at the University of Cagliari, Italy. His research interests include corporate governance, directors' compensation, and the adoption of management accounting systems in start-ups. His teaching activity focuses on business economics, accounting, and corporate governance at undergraduate and master's levels.

Ewa Różańska, PhD, is an assistant professor in the Department of Financial Accounting and Audit at the Poznań University of Economics and Business in Poland. Her research interests lie in the field of sustainability reporting with the focus on regulations. She acted as an editor of a handbook on disclosure and assurance of non-financial information and co-authored a monograph on the consequences of the non-financial reporting directive (NFRD) in Poland. Her studies have been presented at numerous academic conferences and published in international journals, including the *Journal of Accounting in Emerging Economies* and the *Sustainability Accounting, Management and Policy Journal*. She received a mini-grant in the ACCA and IAAER programme addressed to young researchers from CEECs. She was an Erasmus+ participant in Bulgaria, the Czech Republic, Lithuania and Croatia. She is a member of the EAA. Additionally, she serves as a reviewer for international journals. Her current project delves into the quality of sustainability reporting.

Emmeli Runesson, PhD, is a senior lecturer at the University of Gothenburg. Her research and teaching interests within financial accounting are broad. Much of her work has been on the determinants and consequences of the International Financial Reporting Standards (IFRS) in the EU, including the effect of allowing discretion in accounting for credit losses in banks, and pay-performance sensitivity around IFRS adoption. Recent interests extend to any and all narratives in corporate reports, such as the qualitative aspects of sustainability reporting and the impact of top management tone on accounting choices. She has co-authored books on the challenges of IFRS, financial accounting theory, and financial statement analysis.

Niuosha Samani, PhD, is a senior lecturer at the University of Gothenburg. In her research, she focuses on the usefulness of financial and non-financial disclosures in assisting the decision-making of capital market users as well as the company's internal decision-making and governance. In her current research projects, she examines the significance of various governance mechanisms, including voluntary audits in private firms and the presence of employee representatives on the boards of listed firms. Her research interests also encompass the implications of recent sustainability reporting requirements among Swedish public and private firms. She envisions a future where disclosures serve not only as words for the sake of impression management but as a gateway towards more sustainable practices in corporations.

Thorsten Sellhorn is a professor of accounting and auditing and Director of the Institute for Accounting, Auditing and Analysis at the LMU Munich School of Management, Germany. Thorsten's research interests focus on IFRS, the role of accounting information in capital markets, and sustainability reporting. He advises the IFRS Foundation (IFRS Advisory Council), the European Securities and Markets Authority (ESMA), and EFRAG (Academic Panel and Expert Working Group on European Sustainability Reporting Standards). He is a co-founder of the Sustainability Reporting Navigator platform.

Chaoyuan She, PhD, joined the Essex Business School in January 2020 as a lecturer in accounting. Prior to his post at Essex, he was a doctoral student in accounting at the University of Exeter. He also holds master's and bachelor's degrees in accounting and finance from the University of Exeter. His research interests include social media engagement, corporate social responsibility, social and environmental accounting and reporting, and corporate governance.

He has publications in *Critical Perspectives on Accounting, Accounting Forum, Organization & Environment* and *Corporate Governance*. He serves as an editorial board member for *Accounting Forum* and as ad hoc reviewer for journals such as the *Journal of Business Ethics*, the *Accounting, Auditing and Accountability Journal, Critical Perspectives on Accounting, Accounting Forum*, the *Sustainability Accounting, Management and Policy Journal*, and the *Social and Environmental Accounting Journal*.

Lorenzo Simoni is an assistant professor of accounting at the Department of Economics and Business Studies, University of Genoa. He has also been a visiting professor at Aarhus University (Denmark). His interests revolve around financial accounting, business model reporting, risk reporting, intellectual capital, sustainability disclosure, key performance indicator disclosure, earnings quality, accounting choices, and goodwill accounting.

Matti Skoog is a professor in the School of Business and Economics and head of the "Accounting and Control" subject at Åbo Akademi University. He has a history of doing research in multidimensional accounting research with a focus on the interaction between financial and non-financial accounting and control logics within both private and public organizations. Methodologically he mostly engages himself in case studies and has over the years published in high-ranking international research journals as well as contributing several book chapters and books with an interdisciplinary perspective on accounting and control. Currently his research focus is mainly directed towards the implementation challenges regarding management accounting and control of sustainability aspects in different organizational settings.

Renata Stenka is an associate professor in accounting at Henley Business School, Reading, UK. She completed her PhD at the University of Liverpool in the UK and, before moving to Henley Business School, she held her first academic position at Keele University, UK. Prior to that, she studied at the University of Szczecin in Poland and the University of Odense in Denmark. Her novel interdisciplinary scholarly work integrates cognitive sociolinguistic and quantitative corpus-based analytical paradigms to study corporate and regulatory discourses. Her research explores discursive pathways of institutionalization of professional and regulatory practices. Her current research focuses on issues considering the implementation of the social and environmental corporate reporting innovations. Renata's work has been published in the top international journals such as *Accounting, Organizations and Society, Critical Perspectives on Accounting*, and *Accounting and Business Research*. She is also a recipient of awards from the British Academy for her research projects.

Diego Toscani is CEO and Head of the Board of Directors of several companies, some of which are listed on the Italian stock market, and the member of the Board of Directors of AssoNext, which is the Italian association of listed SMEs. He serves as a guest speaker in national and international conferences on the topics of corporate governance, sustainability, listing on financial markets, SMEs, loyalty value, marketing, and brand advocacy. He collaborates with the University of Milano-Bicocca on training courses, teaching activities and research projects on sustainability and corporate governance issues. He has published several articles on loyalty, marketing and sustainability.

Wayne van Zijl, CA(SA), is an associate professor at Wits University's School of Accountancy and is the Assistant Dean of Research for his faculty. Wayne completed his articles at Deloitte and then joined Wits in 2015. He teaches on a wide range of accounting courses from undergraduate to master's level. Wayne is a dedicated qualitative cross-disciplinary corporate reporting researcher, with a primary focus on IFRS, the evolution of accounting, the operationalization of accountability, and the co-evolution of society and accounting. His influential work has been published in reputable journals, including *Accounting Forum*, the *Australian Accounting Review*, the *British Accounting Review*, and *Critical Perspectives on Accounting*. Wayne's editorial roles include serving as the section and associate editor of the *South African Journal of Economic and Management Sciences* and *Meditari Accounting Research*. Wayne serves as the Deputy Chair of Wits' Center for Critical Accounting & Auditing Research (CCAAR) and sits on both the university and faculty research committees.

Victor Wagner is a doctoral student at the Institute for Accounting, Auditing and Analysis at the LMU Munich School of Management, Germany. In his dissertation, Victor follows the establishment of the International Sustainability Standards Board and the European Sustainability Reporting Standards. He conducts qualitative studies about organizations' reporting practices and quantitative research on the evolution of the sustainability-related information environment. He is a co-founder of the Sustainability Reporting Navigator platform.

Katharina Weiß is an assistant professor at the Institute for Accounting, Auditing and Analysis at the LMU Munich School of Management, Germany. Katharina's research interests focus on the determinants and consequences of financial and sustainability reporting regulation.

Frederik Zachariassen is an associate professor at Aalborg University Business School in Denmark. He obtained his PhD at the University of Southern Denmark in Denmark. His research interests include total cost of ownership (TCO), supply chain management, enterprise resource planning systems, accounting for social value and sustainability reporting.

Ewelina Zarzycka is an associate professor at the University of Lodz. Her research interests focus on performance management, management control, corporate social responsibility, and social and environmental accounting and reporting. She has published in accounting and management journals such as *Organization & Environment, Business Ethics, Environment & Responsibility*, the *Journal of Management Control*, the *Journal of Applied Accounting Research, Qualitative Research in Accounting & Management*, the *Journal of Accounting and Organizational Change*, and *Sustainable Development*. From 2023, she has been an editorial board member of *Accounting Forum*. She is part of an international research project, "Corporate Social Practices and Related Disclosures: The Role of Stakeholders' Engagement", the aim of which is to develop nascent insights into sustainability reporting and communication, business ethics and stakeholder engagement.

Abbreviations

AAAJ	*Accounting, Auditing and Accountability Journal*
AAR	*Australian Accounting Review*
ABR	*Accounting and Business Research*
AF	*Accounting Forum*
AI	artificial intelligence
AIGCC	Asia Investor Group on Climate Change
AJG	Academic Journal Guide
AM	asset manager organizations
AO	asset owner organizations
AOS	*Accounting, Organizations and Society*
ARJ	*Accounting Research Journal*
BAR	*British Accounting Review*
BFFP	Break Free From Plastic
BICS	Bloomberg Industry Classification Standard
BIST	Borsa Istanbul
BSC	balanced scorecard
BVA	blended value accounting
CA100+	Climate Action 100+
CapEx	capital expenditure
CDP	Carbon Disclosure Project
CDSB	Climate Disclosure Standards Board
CEE	Central and Eastern Europe
CEO	Chief Executive Officer
CMB	Capital Markets Board of Turkey
CoC	cost of capital
CoD	cost of debt
CoE	cost of equity
COP26	26th Conference of the Parties
COSO	Committee of Sponsoring Organizations of the Treadway Commission
CPA	*Critical Perspectives on Accounting*
CPCS	corporate governance principles compliance score
CRD	Corporate Reporting Dialogue
CSDDD	Corporate Sustainability Due Diligence Directive
CSR	corporate social responsibility
CSRD	Corporate Sustainability Reporting Directive

EAR	*European Accounting Review*
EC	European Commission
ED	exposure draft
EFRAG	European Financial Reporting Advisory Group
EPCS	environmental principles compliance score
ESG	environmental, social and governmental
ESRS	European Sustainability Reporting Standards
EU	European Union
EUDR	EU Deforestation Regulation
FASB	Financial Accounting Standards Board
FFB	fresh fruit bunches
FSB	Financial Stability Board
GAAS	generally accepted auditing standards
GDPR	General Data Protection Regulation
GHG	greenhouse gas (emissions)
GOF	Group of Five
GPCS	general principles compliance score
GRI	Global Reporting Initiative
HCS	high carbon stock
HCV	high conservation value
IASB	International Accounting Standards Board
ICAEW	Institute of Chartered Accountants in England and Wales
IFAC	International Federation of Accountants
IFRS	International Financial Reporting Standards
IFRS SDS	International Financial Reporting Standards Sustainability Disclosure Standards
IFRS S2	IFRS Sustainability Disclosure Standard S2
IGCC	Investor Group on Climate Change
IIGCC	The Institutional Investors Group on Climate Change
IIRC	International Integrated Reporting Council
IJDG	*International Journal of Disclosure and Governance*
IMF	International Monetary Fund
IOSCO	International Organization of Securities Commission
IPSF	International Platform on Sustainable Finance
IR	integrated reporting
IRQ	integrated reporting quality
IS	information system
ISSB	International Sustainability Standards Board
IT	information technology
JAAR	*Journal of Applied Accounting Research*

JAEE	*Journal of Accounting in Emerging Economies*
JAPP	*Journal of Accounting and Public Policy*
JBFA	*Journal of Business Finance and Accounting*
JSE	Johannesburg Stock Exchange
KPI	key performance indicator
LDA	latent Dirichlet allocation
MAJ	*Managerial Auditing Journal*
MCCG	Malaysian Code on Corporate Governance
MCP	management control process
MCS	management control system
MNCs	multinational corporations
MPOB	Malaysian Palm Oil Board
MPOCC	Malaysian Palm Oil Certification Council
NFRD	Non-Financial Reporting Directive
NGO	non-governmental organization
NLP	natural language processing
NPO	non-profit organization
OECD	Organisation for Economic Co-operation and Development
OpEx	operating expenditure
PEG	price–earnings–growth model
PIEs	public interest entities
PMS	performance management system
PRI	principles of responsible investment
RDT	resource dependency theory
REQ	Requirements of the Climate Disclosure Standards Board (CDSB REQ – 01)
RISS/SRI	The JSE Socially Responsible Development Index (SRI) index
ROA	return on assets
ROE	return on equity
RPA	robotic process automation
RSPO	Roundtable on Sustainable Palm Oil
SA	sustainability assurance
SAMPJ	*Sustainability Accounting, Management and Policy Journal*
SASB	Sustainability Accounting Standards Board
SB	sustainability budget
SD	sustainable development
SDGs	Sustainable Development Goals
SEBC	Social Enterprise Balanced Scorecard
SEC	Securities and Exchange Commission
SES	social entrepreneurship

SFDR	Sustainable Finance Disclosure Regulation
SLR	systematic literature review
SM	social media
SMEs	small and medium-sized enterprises
SPCS	social principles compliance score
SR	sustainability reporting
SROI	social return on investment
SRQ	sustainability reporting quality
SSM	Stakeholder Salience Model
TAI	Thinking Ahead Institute
TAR	*The Accounting Review*
TCFD	Task Force on Climate-Related Financial Disclosures
TCS	total compliance score
TRI	toxic release inventory
TRWG	Technical Readiness Working Group
UN	United Nations
UNCTAD	United Nation Conference on Trade and Development
USDA	United States Department of Agriculture
VRF	Value Reporting Foundation
WACC	weighted average cost of capital
WBCSD	World Business Council for Sustainable Development
WEF	World Economic Forum
WFE	World Federation of Exchange
WWF	World Wildlife Fund
ZSL	Zoological Society of London

PART I

INTRODUCTION

1. Multifaceted, complex, and multilayered aspects of sustainability reporting research: an introduction

Gunnar Rimmel, Güler Aras, Diogenis Baboukardos, Joanna Krasodomska, Christian Nielsen and Frank Schiemann

PART I: INTRODUCTION

Although the recent media attention and regulatory developments in sustainability reporting might portray it as a 'new trend' in accounting, sustainability reporting is not a new topic as such. Sustainability reporting has a dynamic history that has evolved alongside societal shifts, changing attitudes towards corporate responsibility, and increasing awareness of environmental and social impacts (Rimmel, 2020a).

The roots of sustainability reporting can be traced back to the early 1970s when companies began to disclose environmental information voluntarily (Rimmel, 2020a). These early reports mainly focused on pollution prevention and resource conservation (Gray, 2010). One key milestone in the development of sustainability reporting was the 1987 'Brundtland Report'. The World Commission on Environment and Development, chaired by Gro Harlem Brundtland, introduced the concept of sustainable development in the landmark report titled *Our Common Future* (World Commission on Environment and Development, 1987). This report laid the groundwork for considering economic, social, and environmental dimensions in business practices.

The 1990s witnessed a paradigm shift with the introduction of the triple bottom line (TBL) concept, emphasizing the need for businesses to report not only financial performance but also social and environmental impacts. This holistic approach is aimed at capturing a company's overall contribution to society (Elkington, 1998). The foundation of the Global Reporting Initiative (GRI) in 1997 marked a pivotal moment in the standardization of sustainability reporting. Since then, a growing number of companies across the world have adopted GRI as their framework for reporting on economic, environmental, and social dimensions, making GRI the global standard (Luque-Vílchez et al., 2023).

The early 2000s witnessed a surge in the adoption of sustainability reporting, driven by increased stakeholder demands, regulatory developments, and a growing recognition of corporate responsibility. Many multinational corporations started publishing annual sustainability reports (Afolabi et al., 2022; 2023). In 2006, the United Nations Principles for Responsible Investment (PRI) initiative was launched, encouraging investors to incorporate environmental, social and governance (ESG) factors into their decision-making processes (Principles for Responsible Investment, 2022). This further catalysed the integration of sustainability considerations into corporate reporting. In 2010, the International Integrated Reporting Council (IIRC) was founded to promote integrated reporting, aiming to provide a more comprehensive view of a company's value creation by incorporating financial and non-financial aspects in a single report (Rimmel, 2020b).

In 2014 an important development occurred at the European Union (EU) level. The European Commission (EC) highlighted the necessity for legislative reform to improve companies' disclosure of social and environmental information by introducing Directive 2014/95/EU, commonly known as the Non-Financial Reporting Directive (NFRD). The NFRD required companies to include non-financial statements in their annual reports or in a separate filing from 2018 onwards, including information on environmental protection, social responsibility and treatment of employees, respect for human rights, anti-corruption and bribery, and diversity on company boards. The NFRD has led to important changes in accounting regulations in EU member states and has also drawn attention to the role of the accounting profession in the pursuit of sustainable development (Krasodomska et al., 2020).

In 2015, the United Nations (UN) General Assembly formulated the 17 Sustainable Development Goals (SDGs), which set unique targets that aim to create a world where economic growth and human well-being are achieved in a way that is environmentally sustainable, socially just, and economically inclusive. The UN SDGs provided a globally recognized framework for companies to align their sustainability efforts. Many organizations began to incorporate SDG-related targets into their reporting, and it became an enabling role for accounting research (Bebbington and Unerman, 2018).

Two years later, the Task Force on Climate-Related Financial Disclosures (TCFD) was established to develop recommendations for disclosing climate-related financial risks and opportunities. This marked a significant step in acknowledging the materiality of climate-related information in corporate reporting for financial decisions, shifting the focus of sustainability accounting from impacts to risks and dependencies (O'Dwyer and Unerman, 2020).

The EU Green Deal, launched in 2019, unveiled a comprehensive strategy to transform the EU region into a sustainable and resilient economy. Its transformative agenda aims to achieve climate neutrality by 2050 and stands as a landmark initiative with far-reaching implications (European Commission, 2019). The EU Green Deal encompasses various policy measures aimed at decoupling economic growth from environmental degradation and places sustainability reporting at the forefront of the bloc's strategy, recognizing the pivotal role of transparent and standardized disclosure in tracking progress and fostering accountability (European Commission, 2019). In 2021, the EU further enhanced its reporting regulation by introducing Directive 2022/2464/EU, called the Corporate Sustainability Reporting Directive (CSRD). The new CSRD attempts to expand and standardize sustainability reporting requirements for companies operating within the EU, reflecting a continuous commitment to advancing transparency and accountability (Luque-Vílchez et al., 2023). In reaction to the EU sustainability reporting standard setting, notable entities from the financial reporting realm, including the IFRS Foundation/International Sustainability Standards Board (ISSB), the European Financial Reporting Advisory Group (EFRAG), and the Securities Exchange Commission (SEC) in the USA, have actively engaged in the field of sustainability reporting standard setting. Their involvement aims to play a role in standardizing sustainability practices, especially concerning sustainable development (Abela, 2022; Afolabi et al., 2022; 2023).

The history of sustainability reporting reflects an ongoing evolution, which is shaped by a combination of voluntary international initiatives, regulatory developments, and the increasing recognition of sustainability as a fundamental aspect of corporate accounting and governance. As businesses continue to navigate complex global challenges, sustainability reporting remains a crucial tool for communicating their impact and progress towards a more sustainable future. Research on sustainability reporting is inherently interesting for several compelling reasons, reflecting its multidimensional nature and its intersection with various academic disciplines.

The intention of the *Research Handbook on Sustainability Reporting* is to show the multifaceted, complex, and multilayered aspects of research on sustainability reporting, which is done in the handbook's seven parts and 28 chapters by 59 researchers from 14 countries around the world. The book's chapters touch upon the important moments in the historical development and evolution of sustainability reporting presented above, addressing specific issues, and they also offer insights into potential avenues for future research in this field.

The chapters are arranged in themes. Part I, 'Introduction', sets the scene for the sustainability reporting developments. The chapter considers how sustainability reporting practice has developed and the key influences in that development. Part II, 'Frameworks and Standard Setters', contains six chapters that consider the evolution of the sustainability reporting arena and the important role of reporting standard setters within it. Part III, 'Sustainability Reporting within the Company', consists of four chapters focusing on the rather underexplored issue of sustainability reporting in management control and internal audit. Part IV, 'Sustainability Reporting and Capital Markets', has four chapters that examine the capital market consequences of sustainability reporting, and the role of sustainability reporting regulation. Part V, 'Governance', is comprised of three chapters that focus on the interplay between corporate governance and sustainability reporting. The five chapters in Part VI, 'Sustainability Reporting – Around the World', emphasize the multidimensional aspects of sustainability reporting across the world today. The final part, Part VII, 'Sustainability Reporting – Methods, Theories and Outlook', contains four chapters that shed light on different methodological and theoretical aspects applied in sustainability reporting research. Drawing from all chapters, the concluding chapter of the *Research Handbook on Sustainability Reporting* attempts to provide an outlook of future research avenues in sustainability reporting.

PART II: FRAMEWORKS AND STANDARD SETTERS

Chapter 2 is written by Wayne van Zijl, Dannielle Cerbone and Warren Maroun from the University of the Witwatersrand in South Africa. This chapter shows that corporate reporting is crucial for the efficient operation of capital markets, and integrated reporting is gaining attention for its ability to succinctly convey a company's value creation narrative. While existing research often views integrated reporting as a neutral communication tool, this conceptual chapter introduces memetic evolution theory as a novel perspective to understand its evolution. The chapter explores the application of memetic evolution to integrated reporting and suggests potential areas for future research within this framework.

Chapter 3, by Hammed Afolabi, Ronita Ram and Gunnar Rimmel, investigates the convergence of sustainability reporting standards and the role of key institutions in this process. It explores whether these institutions truly contribute to achieving convergence and assesses their impact on sustainable development. Using a Stakeholder Salience Model (SSM) and qualitative content analysis, the chapter categorizes salient institutions and examines their role in the convergence of sustainability reporting standards. The findings suggest a self-centred approach in influential international institutions, motivated by political and profit considerations rather than a genuine understanding of the concept of sustainability.

Chapter 4, by Blerita Korca, Ericka Costa and Frank Schiemann, employs a building block approach to assess sustainability reporting standards, exploring various frameworks used by companies. It highlights differences in target audience, disclosure content, and materiality among these standards, influencing how reports are presented and understood. The building blocks – Scope, Disclosure Content, Materiality, Assurance, and Disclosure Channel – are described with reference to recent state-of-the art research findings and provide a 'reading lens' of two prominent frameworks to the European Sustainability Reporting Standards (ESRS) and the IFRS Sustainability Disclosure Standards (IFRS SDS).

Chapter 5, by Silvia Panfilo, Simone Pizzi and Joanna Krasodomska, explores the evolution of sustainability reporting regulation in the EU, focusing on the transition from voluntary corporate social responsibility (CSR) disclosures to mandatory sustainability reporting following the introduction of Directive 2014/95/EU. The study employs bibliometric analysis tools to examine the academic debate surrounding this Directive. The analysis identifies key contributors, influential publications, and the conceptual structure of the scientific discourse, providing a synthesis of current knowledge on the role of Directive 2014/95/EU in shaping sustainability reporting in the EU.

Chapter 6, by Ewa Różańska, Łukasz Matuszak and Joanna Dyczkowska, compares the Global Reporting Initiative (GRI) Standards with the International Integrated Reporting (IR) Framework. Both serve as foundations for high-quality non-financial disclosure. The analysis focuses on materiality, reporting principles, and content elements to assess reporting quality. The comparative results highlight core differences, alignment, and complementarity between the GRI Standards and the IR Framework, as well as whether organizations have implemented these standards and how they influence disclosure quality based on previous research. This chapter discusses the evolving role of GRI Standards and the IR Framework in the global sustainability reporting landscape.

Victor Wagner, Thorsten Sellhorn, Katharina Weiß and Christoph Pelger investigate, in Chapter 7, the creation of the International Sustainability Standards Board (ISSB) by the IFRS Foundation, which marks a significant development in global sustainability reporting. It analyses constituent reactions through comment letters, comparing them with the Foundation's conclusions. The chapter explores how these discussions influence the drafting of the ISSB's climate change reporting standard, emphasizing the concept of 'exposure' to sustainability-related risks and opportunities. This chapter contributes insights into stakeholder responses to the IFRS Foundation's consultation, complementing existing literature on sustainability reporting standard setters and adding to the debate on the Foundation's role in setting sustainability reporting standards.

PART III: SUSTAINABILITY REPORTING WITHIN THE COMPANY

Chapter 8, by Matti Skoog and Mathias Cöster, draws from the outcomes of an action research project conducted within a public organization in Sweden. Despite having a strong sustainability focus in its strategic goals for several years and incorporating various sustainability aspects into long-term planning documents, the translation of these strategic aspirations into practical and operational organizational activities has proven to be challenging. Existing research on management control and sustainability emphasizes that without active enforcement by organizations, sustainability objectives may remain mere aspirations. The findings suggest that the management control system and processes play diverse moderating roles in the transformation process from sustainability goals to organizational actions.

Chapter 9, by Chiara Crovini, Sirle Bürkland and Frederik Zachariassen, proposes perspectives for management control systems by outlining various ways in which sustainability goals manifest in management and reporting procedures. It explores three perspectives – compliance, critical and managerial – under which the integration of sustainability into organizational accounting has been examined. These perspectives represent distinct approaches to framing sustainability narratives and management control practices within organizations. The chapter describes how these perspectives impact the realization of sustainability agendas in accounting practices and shape managerial reporting and sustainable development overall.

Nabyla Daidj discusses, in Chapter 10, the evolving role of the internal audit function in response to changes in global business practices, particularly in the context of digital transformation and a rapidly changing regulatory landscape. The impact of digitalization on audit environments, internal audit practices, risk management, and information systems is explored. The chapter emphasizes the integration of environmental, social and governmental criteria compliance into internal audit practices, along with the challenges posed by the increasing volume of available data and emerging management issues.

In Chapter 11, Christoph Feichtinger provides a literature review of the growing interest in social entrepreneurship from an academic and policy perspective, emphasizing its impact on social and economic development. He shows that the majority of relevant literature is conceptual in nature, with empirical research predominantly utilizing case study methodology. Notably, accounting and performance management have received limited attention. The findings in this chapter hold theoretical implications for advancing literature on social entrepreneurship, performance measurement systems, and management accounting.

PART IV: SUSTAINABILITY REPORTING AND CAPITAL MARKETS

In Chapter 12, Michela Cordazzo, Laura Bini and Lorenzo Simoni review the literature on the economic outcomes linked to sustainability disclosure, specifically focusing on its relationship to firms' stock prices and cost of capital. Analysing papers published from 2000 to 2023, the review generally supports the idea that sustainability disclosure is value relevant, although some studies indicate a neutral or negative investor reaction to the release of such information. Notably, challenges related to measuring sustainability disclosure may hinder both comparability and generalizability of findings.

Chapter 13, by Martina Macpherson, evaluates and compares current policy and regulatory developments in Europe, focusing on their impact on the investment value chain. Key considerations include the EU's Sustainable Finance Action Plan, Sustainable Finance Disclosure Regulation, Green Taxonomy, Markets in Financial Instruments Directive (MiFID) II, and impending ESG ratings regulation across European jurisdictions. This chapter aims to highlight implications for the investment value chain, examining the potential of harmonizing and standardizing rules, specifically through interoperability of different frameworks, to address fragmentation challenges.

Christian Ott examines, in Chapter 14, the existing literature concerning how capital market participants perceive climate-related disclosure. The empirical findings in the literature indicate varied effects on capital markets, influenced by factors such as the type and extent of climate-related disclosure and the overall disclosure environment. Consequently, the chapter proposes potential avenues for future research to further investigate the capital market effects of climate-related disclosure.

Fresh insights into the motivations of globally significant asset owners and asset management organizations to adopt the UN-sponsored Principles for Responsible Investment (PRI) are presented in Chapter 15, authored by Paul Klumpes and Jesper Lindgaard Christensen. Major institutional investors, with substantial influence over global carbon emissions through their equity portfolios, demonstrate a commitment to responsible investment practices by becoming PRI signatories. However, the chapter emphasizes the contrasting incentives faced by asset managers, who prioritize short-term performance for clients, and asset owners, bound by fiduciary responsibilities to act in the long-term interests of their members. This chapter illustrates the distinct factors influencing globally large asset managers and asset owners in becoming PRI signatories, considering legitimation versus institutional-based accountability considerations.

PART V: GOVERNANCE

Chapter 16, by Federica Doni and Diego Toscani, highlights new trends in the European Union that place corporate governance under increased scrutiny. Commitment to sustainable corporate governance is being examined by various stakeholders, including governments, supervisory authorities, financial markets, social spheres, and the media. The European Commission's approval of the European Sustainability Reporting Standards (ESRS) has prompted significant changes in governance and business integrity. In Italy, the corporate governance code plays a crucial role in promoting ethical values and good corporate governance practices, although SMEs face challenges in integrating ESG issues into their governance structures, as shown in this chapter.

Chapter 17, by Syed Mahfujul Alam and Ericka Costa, delves into the critical role of boards in governing and disclosing climate change-related information, garnering attention from academics, stakeholders, and investors. It emphasizes the need to theorize climate change governance and disclosure to improve sustainability reporting. Drawing on various theories such as agency, institutional, legitimacy, stakeholders, resource dependency, and signalling, the chapter explores the significance of factors such as gender diversity, independence, external expertise, and board tenure in enhancing boards' capabilities for climate change governance and disclosure.

Chapter 18, by Andrea Melis, Simone Aresu, Luigi Rombi and Mariem Khalfaoui, explores key mechanisms of sustainable corporate governance designed to ensure responsible governance with a focus on the long-term social, environmental, and economic impact of a company's activities. Specifically, it examines four crucial incentive, advisory, and monitoring mechanisms: integrating sustainability criteria into executive remuneration contracts; establishing a sustainability-related committee; third-party auditing for sustainability-related information assurance; and having sustainable owners in a company's shareholding structure. The chapter outlines the roles, main antecedents, and consequences of each mechanism, drawing on evidence from prior academic empirical literature, current data on their practical development, and anecdotal case studies from real-life companies.

PART VI: SUSTAINABILITY REPORTING – AROUND THE WORLD

In Chapter 19, Güler Aras, Ozlem Kutlu Furtuna and Evrim Haciolglu Kazak focus on the evaluation of voluntary sustainability compliance disclosures over the years 2015 to 2020 among Turkish firms listed in the Borsa Istanbul (BIST) 100 Index. They shed light on the determinants of sustainability reporting compliance in developing countries. This empirical study employs content analysis to identify disclosure levels and to explore the relationship between overall sustainability disclosure scores and financial indicators.

Chapter 20, by Maizatulakma Abdullah and Gunnar Rimmel, examines the adoption of a sustainability reporting model within the Malaysian palm oil industry. This chapter explores the forms, channels, and scopes of the reports used by entities to communicate information to stakeholders. Employing a qualitative approach, this chapter reveals the complexity of the sustainability reporting model in the Malaysian palm oil industry, which can be understood through the lens of complex adaptive system theory.

In Chapter 21, Dusan Ecim and Warren Maroun use an integrated thinking scheme to assess the extent and quality of sustainability-related reporting within South African listed companies. The chapter explores potential determinants of integrated thinking, such as levels of financial and extra-financial risk, financial performance, and the existence of a separate sustainability committee. Results suggest that companies are not merely engaged in impression management, but they vary in their progress toward operationalizing integrated thinking.

An overview of sustainability reporting practices in Central and Eastern Europe is provided in Chapter 22 by Cătălin Albu, Nadia Albu, Mădălina Dumitru, Raluca Gina Guşe and Maria-Silvia Săndulescu. The region is characterized by the coexistence of Western-based formal institutions and remnants of its communist past. The chapter delves into the impact of the context on the advancement or hindrance of sustainability reporting practices, drawing on prior research in the region. Additionally, it explores the organizational-level implementation of sustainability reporting, including the involvement of various professional groups in coordinating reporting and the communication channels employed.

In Chapter 23, Md Alamgir Jalil, Silvia Gaia and Chaoyuan She investigate how companies communicate their commitment to achieving water-related Sustainable Development Goals (SDGs) by analysing both the quantity and quality of narrative disclosures in corporate sustainability reports. Focusing on a sample of 143 international companies between 2016 and 2020, operating in sectors with high or medium operational sensitivity to water, they find limited engagement of corporations with SDG water-related disclosures. Furthermore, their analysis suggests a bias in the disclosures, with companies highlighting more positive aspects of their water-related performance that are complex and challenging to understand.

PART VII: SUSTAINABILITY REPORTING – METHODS, THEORIES AND OUTLOOK

In 24 Chapter, Emmeli Runesson and Niuosha Samani conduct a comprehensive bibliometric analysis of accounting publications related to sustainability reporting and stakeholders, highlighting prominent journals, methods, and theories in the field. Using computerized topic modelling, nine major topics are identified, with CSR and valuation emerging as dominant and increasingly popular. The analysis categorizes papers based on their focus on various stakeholder groups, revealing that investors and valuation are heavily featured, representing a continuously expanding area of research. Additionally, due to regulatory developments, policymakers and the topics of assurance and audits are gaining traction.

Emre Parlakkaya and Renata Stenka introduce, in Chapter 25, the underutilized corpus linguistics approach, which originates in the field of linguistics but has been underutilized in accounting research. This innovative methodology holds potential to enhance existing discourse studies in accounting. This chapter offers an overview of prevalent methodologies in accounting literature that examine language use, namely quantitative and qualitative approaches, outlining their strengths and limitations. This chapter illustrates the potential of corpus linguistics to contribute to language studies in accounting, with a specific focus on corporate sustainability reporting.

Chapter 26, by Dorota Dobija, Ewelina Zarzycka, Chaoyuan She and Charles H. Cho, discusses the evolution and pervasive adoption of the Internet and social media, which have significantly transformed corporate communication practices. This shift is particularly pronounced in the context of sustainability reporting, where the increased scrutiny of sustainability information has amplified engagement and interaction with stakeholders. This chapter explores how different types of organizations leverage new media to communicate sustainability information. It provides a comprehensive overview of the strategies employed by the private sector, public sector organizations, and NGOs in reporting on sustainability through various online platforms.

The aim of Chapter 27, by Maria Aluchna, is to examine how EU regulations have enhanced sustainability disclosure. This chapter provides an overview of the legislative framework, encompassing the Non-Financial Reporting Directive (NFRD), the Sustainable Finance Disclosure Regulation (SFDR), and the Taxonomy Regulation. Additionally, it discusses the Corporate Sustainability Directive (CSRD) alongside the European Sustainability Reporting Standards (ESRS) and the Corporate Sustainability Due Diligence Directive (CSDDD). The chapter analyses EU regulations, drawing on prior studies and integrating theory, empirical evidence and policy recommendations.

Drawing on all the previous chapters, the concluding chapter of the *Research Handbook on Sustainability Reporting*, Chapter 28, is intended to provide an outlook over future research avenues in sustainability reporting.

The chapters in this *Research Handbook on Sustainability Reporting* display a large array of this vibrant research field, focusing on the intersection of accounting and sustainability, elucidating the primary drivers of developments, critiquing these advances, summarizing research findings on crucial themes, proposing avenues for further research, and presenting evidence-based solutions for practice and policy. It is intended to narrow the historical division between accounting and sustainability reporting research streams. Traditional accounting research has long been centred around financial reporting and compliance with generally accepted accounting principles (GAAP). Sustainability reporting, on the other hand, emerged as a response to broader societal and environmental concerns, shifting the focus from purely financial aspects to non-financial indicators and impacts. However, it is important to note that this division is gradually fading out as sustainability reporting becomes more integrated into corporate practices and regulatory frameworks. The recognition of the interconnectedness between financial and non-financial performance is leading to greater collaboration and convergence between accounting and sustainability reporting research. The emphasis is on informed negotiation and interpretation, guided by evidence, challenging the notion that these aspects are in conflict with each other. The overarching goal of this *Research Handbook on Sustainability Reporting* is to inspire accounting researchers to play a transformative role by understanding that solutions emerge from evidence-based critique and research on sustainability reporting.

REFERENCES

Abela, M. (2022). A new direction? The 'mainstreaming' of sustainability reporting, *Sustainability Accounting, Management and Policy Journal*, 13(6), pp. 1261–1283.

Afolabi, H., Ram, R. and Rimmel, G. (2022). Harmonization of sustainability reporting regulation: analysis of a contested arena. *Sustainability*, 14(9), p. 5517.

Afolabi, H., Ram, R. and Rimmel, G. (2023). Influence and behaviour of the new standard setters in the sustainability reporting arena: implications for the Global Reporting Initiative's current position. *Sustainability Accounting, Management and Policy Journal*, 14(4), pp. 743–775.

Bebbington, J. and Unerman, J. (2018). Achieving the United Nations Sustainable Development Goals: an enabling role for accounting research. *Accounting, Auditing, and Accountability Journal*, 31(1), pp. 2–24.

Elkington, J. (1998). Accounting for the Triple Bottom Line. *Measuring Business Excellence*, 2(3), pp. 18–22.

European Commission (2019). Communication from the Commission – Guidelines on non-financial reporting (methodology for reporting non-financial information). Official Journal of the European Union, Communication from the Commission to the European Parliament, the European Council, the Council, the European Economic and Social Committee and the Committee of the Regions the European Green Deal, COM/2019/640 final.

Gray, R. (2010). Is accounting for sustainability actually accounting for sustainability … and how would we know? An exploration of narratives of organisations and the planet. *Accounting, Organizations and Society*, 35(1), pp. 47–62.

Krasodomska, J., Michalak, J. and Świetla, K. (2020). Directive 2014/95/EU: Accountants' understanding and attitude towards mandatory non-financial disclosures in corporate reporting. *Meditari Accountancy Research*, 28(5), pp. 751–779.

Luque-Vílchez, M., Cordazzo, M., Rimmel, G. and Tilt, C.A. (2023). Key aspects of sustainability reporting quality and the future of GRI. *Sustainability Accounting, Management and Policy Journal*, 14(4), pp. 637–659.

O'Dwyer, B. and Unerman, J. (2020). Shifting the focus of sustainability accounting from impacts to risks and dependencies: researching the transformative potential of TCFD reporting. *Accounting, Auditing and Accountability Journal*, 33(5), pp. 1113–1141.

Principles for Responsible Investment (2022). *Annual Report 2021*. UN Principles for Responsible Investment.

Rimmel, G. (2020a). Chapter 1: 'Accounting for sustainability – historical development of the field', in Gunnar Rimmel (ed.), *Accounting for Sustainability*, Abingdon, UK: Routledge.

Rimmel, G. (2020b). Chapter 8: 'Integrated Reporting, in Gunnar Rimmel (ed.), *Accounting for Sustainability*, Abingdon, UK: Routledge.

World Commission on Environment and Development (1987). *Our Common Future*, Oxford: Oxford University Press.

PART II

FRAMEWORKS AND STANDARD SETTERS

2. Integrated reporting – a memetic evolutionary perspective

Wayne van Zijl, Dannielle Cerbone and Warren Maroun

1 INTRODUCTION

Prior studies on sustainability reporting focus on its patterns (Gray et al., 1995; Buhr et al., 2014), motivation (Windolph et al., 2014; Cerbone and Maroun, 2019) and response to significant events (Hill and Maroun, 2015). To explain integrated reporting's progression, the literature primarily deploys legitimacy, stakeholder and neo-institutional theory (see, for example, Gray et al., 1995; Edgley et al., 2015; Cerbone and Maroun, 2019). These approaches lack a unifying framework to understand integrated reporting's evolution holistically. To this end, this chapter adopts an innovative framework by viewing integrated reporting through a memetic evolutionary lens. In doing so, this conceptual chapter sheds new light on the underlying mechanisms of integrated reporting's evolution that complements existing literature, focusing on key changes and events. It aims to inspire a research agenda which takes a holistic approach to explaining the broader evolution of corporation reporting. In doing so, it makes an important contribution. Firstly, by adopting a novel framework, it provides a new perspective from which to view integrated reporting. Secondly, it provides a summary of the core theoretical elements required to take this line of inquiry further. Finally, the chapter illustrates the application of memetic evolution to integrated reporting. In doing so, it explains why a person's historicity impacts their acceptance or rejection of new reporting practices. It also provides insight into accounting's early focus on economic wealth accumulation as a key driver of accounting practices.

The chapter begins with a broad overview of the non-financial corporate reporting landscape. Selected key events are considered to allow the discussion section to apply the novel memetic evolution framework to integrated reporting's development. Section 3 provides an overview of memetic evolution while Section 4 illustrates memetic evolution in the non-financial corporate reporting context. The chapter concludes with suggestions for future research drawing on a memetic evolutionary lens.

2 A BRIEF HISTORY OF SUSTAINABILITY REPORTING

Corporate reporting has evolved extensively over the last 10,000 years (Brown, 1905; Hopwood, 1987; Mattessich, 1998) in four distinct eras. The first era is known as the agricultural era and is distinguished by single- and then double-entry accounting. This was followed by financial reporting in the industrial era and sustainability reporting in the information era (Bray and Ridehalgh, 2020). The current era is defined by a multi-capital approach. It is characterised by "business models and competitive edges dominated by innovation, intellectual property, technology, customer relationship management and satisfaction, and the engagement and strategic alignment of an organisation's people" (Bray and Ridehalgh, 2020, p. 70).

The shift from traditional financial statements to integrated reports is not as recent as it appears and is characterised by waxing and waning interests depending on prevailing socio-economic conditions (Buhr et al., 2014). Non-financial information has been included in annual reports from before the beginning of the 19th century, with early forms of social reporting addressing employee-related issues. US Steel and BHP reported on dwellings built for workers, worker safety, employee mortgage assistance and community development as examples (Guthrie and Parker, 1989). Early social reporting tended to report *about* employee issues and transitioned to reporting *to* employees after 1919 (Buhr et al., 2014).

The 1960s and 1970s saw interest in what had come to be known as social reporting rise and fall with societal factors both in the United Kingdom and North America. Environmental issues were still reported but social reporting took precedence (Buhr et al., 2014). The reporting landscape enabled corporations to decide what social factors they considered material from an economic or legitimacy-management perspective (Patten, 2002). By the end of the 1970s, social reporting was declining.

The next stage of sustainability reporting emerged in the late 1980s and can be traced to the Bhopal (1984) and *Exxon Valdez* oil spill (1989) disasters (Buhr et al., 2014; Rupley et al., 2017). The environmental disasters resulted in calls by investment funds and environmental groups for greater disclosure of environmental risks. Renewed interest in environmental responsibility and reporting led to a proliferation of environmental reports, codes, principles and regulations. For example, the 1987 Brundtland Report established the notion of sustainable development (World Commission on Environment and Development, 1987). The Coalition for Environmentally Responsible Economies (CERES) was formed soon after the *Valdez* oil spill and released the Valdez Principles.[1] But, due to numerous deficiencies in the principles (see Sanyal and Neves, 1991), the Valdez Principles were not well received (Pava and Krausz, 1996).

After the Valdez Principles' poor reception, the 1990s again saw renewed interest in environmental reporting and saw significant developments. Several attempts were made to address the need to integrate financial and non-financial information (de Villiers and Alexander, 2014), including internal performance measurement tools such as the Balanced Scorecard in 1990 (Kaplan and Norton, 1996), Triple Bottom Line reporting in 1994 (Elkington, 1998), and the Global Reporting Initiative's Sustainability Reporting Guidelines (GRI, 2000). These developments occurred in tandem with advances in codes on corporate governance. In 1992, the Cadbury Report and the Code of Best Practices were released in the UK and numerous other codes have been developed internationally (Maroun and Cerbone, 2020).

By the early 2000s, companies began preparing separate sustainability or sustainable development reports. These reports included measurable environmental, economic and social aspects of corporate performance but still did not *integrate* them with financial information. Numerous corporate scandals[2] in the late 1990s and early 2000s highlighted significant deficiencies in financial reporting for which investors and the public required further transparency (White, 2005). Corporate scandals also brought into question whether non-financial reporting "is safe in the hands of business" on a voluntary basis, or requires government intervention (Gray and Milne, 2002, p. 67). Several codes of governance were updated and new regulations implemented, such as the Sarbanes-Oxley Act, to prevent future corporate scandals. The demand for enhanced disclosure and transparency resulted in companies integrating environmental and social aspects with financial performance and one of the first "integrated" reports was released in 2004 by Novo Nordisk (White, 2005). In 2004, the Prince of Wales's Accounting for Sustainability (A4S) was formed to assist companies in operationalising integrated reporting (de Villiers et al., 2014).

The Global Financial Crisis of 2008 intensified the need to address deficiencies in corporate reporting practices by emphasising the need to integrate financial and non-financial disclosures (Mio et al., 2016; de Villiers et al., 2017; Bray and Ridehalgh, 2020; Topazio et al., 2020). South Africa became the first country to recommend the preparation of an integrated report through its codes on corporate governance. While the country stopped short of mandating integrated reporting, the Johannesburg Stock Exchange's[3] listing requirements called on listed companies to comply with governance codes or provide reasons for not doing so (Maroun and Cerbone, 2020).

In 2010, the A4S project, in collaboration with the GRI and the International Federation of Accountants (IFAC), established the International Integrated Reporting Council (IIRC) to develop and promote an integrated and connected approach to corporate reporting (de Villiers et al., 2014; Dumay et al., 2016; A4S, 2021). Subsequently, the International Integrated Reporting Framework (IIRF) was issued in December 2013 (IIRC, 2014; Flower, 2015) which included concepts such as materiality to aid in the filtering of disclosure items to improve the understandability of corporate reports.

Integrated reporting is an extension of the need "to ensure that [humanity] meets the needs of the present without compromising the ability of future generations to meet their own needs" (World Commission on Environment and Development, 1987, p. 16). Integrated reporting aims to address the lack of sustainability issues addressed by conventional financial accounting (Burritt and Schaltegger, 2010; IIRC, 2011). This is achieved by explaining the interconnections between financial and non-financial information in a way that enables users to make more informed decisions (Eccles and Krzus, 2010; IIRC, 2013; Lai et al., 2016; Mervelskemper and Streit, 2017; Maroun and Cerbone, 2020). The IIRC define an "integrated report" as "a concise communication about how an organization's strategy, governance, performance and prospects, in the context of its external environment, lead to the creation of value over the short, medium and long term" (IIRC, 2013, p. 7).

The multi-capital disclosures are used to assess an organisation's risks and sustainability more comprehensively than financial reports alone. These disclosures have gained popularity and are increasingly important to institutional investors and other stakeholders (Deegan and Rankin, 1997; Dawkins, C. and Ngunjiri, 2008; Atkins and Maroun, 2015; García-Sánchez et al., 2020). The movement toward integrated reporting is largely driven by the needs of stakeholders for better information and transparency. By preparing an integrated report, it is hoped that companies will internalise integrated thinking, become better corporate citizens and take accountability for their impact on environmental and social matters (King and Atkins, 2016; de Villiers and Maroun, 2017).

Since the IIRC's formation, integrated reporting has gained prominence under a mainly voluntary adoption regime. For example, integrated reports are prepared voluntarily by companies in Japan, the Netherlands, Germany, France, the UK, Italy, South Korea, Sri Lanka, India and the United States (Zhou et al., 2017; Gibassier et al., 2019). Nevertheless, integrated reporting has not become a universally accepted basis for explaining how different capitals are being managed to generate value and achieve sustainable development. This is, in part, a result of practical and technical challenges. For example, the accounting infrastructure has been focused on financial reporting with the result that the systems and processes for collecting and reporting on non-financial data are underdeveloped in comparison (Hopwood, 1983; de Villiers et al., 2014; Maroun, 2017). Similarly, governance structures and the internal controls necessary for ensuring high quality integrated reports have not kept pace with the rapid development of integrated reporting frameworks and the complexity of modern business (Cohen and Simnett, 2015; Maroun and Atkins, 2015; Simnett and Huggins, 2015). Often the themes reported by companies are what the reports' authors perceive society as valuing most and, more broadly, could be seen as a response to public pressure and an attempt to manage legitimacy (Guthrie and Parker, 1989; Deegan et al., 2002).

In its first discussion paper after the Covid-19 pandemic, the IIRC emphasised a shift toward a proactive view of multi-capital opportunities that assesses how the capitals can collectively and simultaneously contribute to the primary goal of value creation (Value Reporting Foundation (VRF), 2022). Subsequently, in June 2021, the Sustainability Accounting Standards Board in the United States and the IIRC merged to form the VRF, with a renewed emphasis on enterprise value reporting. The VRF's aim is twofold. Firstly, to enhance internal and external decision making for companies and investors, respectively, through the adoption of integrated thinking and corporate reporting; and secondly, to unlock insights into performance and holistically assess the factors that affect long-term value creation (VRF, 2022). The VRF has now been consolidated into the IFRS Foundation with its International Sustainability Standards Board (ISSB).

The ISSB issued its first two standards about the general requirements for disclosing sustainability-related financial information (IFRS S1) and climate-related disclosures (IFRS S2) in 2023 (IFRS Foundation, 2023a).

3   THEORETICAL FRAMEWORK – MEMETIC EVOLUTION

Evolution is the study of how organisms evolve to become more complex and diverse over time (Darwin, 1859; Dawkins, R., 2016). Darwin is considered the pioneer of evolution by natural selection. His work in the mid 1800s sought to describe and explain the processes at work that lead simple organisms to evolve into more diverse and complex ones (Darwin, 1859). Around the same time, Mendel's experiments discovered the idea of heritable genes and helped to explain their impact on future generations. Fisher combined Darwin and Mendel's work to form the start of modern genetics (Fisher, 1930; de Beer, 1964; Müller-Wille, 2021).

Put simply, evolution arises where future generations are better suited to their environment than their parents. Variations in offsprings' genes that provide an advantage are selected and become prominent within a population while gene variations that are disadvantageous die out. This process can be categorised into three highly interrelated processes, being those of inheritance, two-step accumulation and selection (Darwin, 1859; Dawkins, R., 1986; Vincent and Brown, 2005; Dawkins, R., 2016).

Memetic evolution is the application of Darwinian evolution concepts to non-biological systems. The idea that non-biological systems may also evolve according to the principles of inheritance, two-step accumulation and selection was introduced by Dawkins in 1976. Since then, memetic evolution has been used in various disciplines including, for example, sociology, religion, project management, law and economics (Roe, 1996; Heylighen, 1997; 1998; Blackmore, 2001; Hodgson, 2002; Whitty, 2005; Dawkins, R., 2016).

In biology, genes are the inheritable building blocks that make up organisms. In non-biological systems, the building blocks are referred to as memes and are defined as any unit of information that "survives intact long enough to be subject to selection pressures", can be replicated by new hosts and whose fitness in a given environment determines its propagation success (Blackmore, 2001, p. 231; Vincent and Brown, 2005; Dawkins, R., 2016). Tunes, fashion and architecture are examples of systems that evolve according to memetic evolution (Dawkins, R., 2016). These systems are made up of many different memes that are related and are co-beneficial to one another. A small collection of co-beneficial memes is called a memeplex. For example, while each note is a meme, musical chords are each memeplexes. Memeplexes that are co-beneficial are called a high memeplex, such as the chorus of a popular tune. All high memeplexes form a grand memeplex. Rock and roll, pop and classical are all examples of types of musical grand memeplexes with their own memeplexes and high memeplex (adapted from Rutherford, 2020).

Just as in Darwinian evolution, memetic evolution arises because information can be inherited or copied with variation. Due to people's limited ability to retain information (see Basu and Waymire, 2006), memes compete for people's attention, retention and expression (Heylighen, 1997; Blackmore, 2001; Dawkins, R., 2016). What attracts a person's attention and encourages them to retain a meme is extremely complex and highly subjective. This is because, for example, a person's upbringing and experiences impact what draws their attention. In addition, their existing knowledge base will impact how difficult it is to retain new technical memes and express them (see Heylighen, 1997; Blackmore, 2001; Dawkins, R., 2016).

Memes, like genes, do not wish to change – they selfishly wish to be copied by as many people as possible for as long as possible. But, ironically, change is fundamental to evolution. The more opportunities there are for memes to be inherited and modified, the more rapidly the discipline they are a part of can evolve. To illustrate, picture an isolated farming family. With no exposure to other farming techniques, tools and experiences, generation after generation will primarily replicate their forefathers' methods with few adaptations. Those that do arise mainly do so by chance due to incorrect inheritance. There may be very limited active modification. However, when farmers from different countries interact, they can share their memes and experiences. This allows more memes to be compared and *useful* aspects of different memes combined to form new memes at a much quicker rate (Dawkins, R., 2016).

The processes of inheritance, two-step accumulation and selection are highly interrelated but are discussed separately below. This allows the nuances of each process to be understood more easily.

3.1   Inheritance

Memes are units of information that selfishly "wish"[4] to be copied as many times as possible, as accurately as possible and for as long as possible. This highlights the key qualities that successful memes possess. Firstly, memes that can replicate more quickly than others will be more successful. To illustrate, if Meme A can replicate ten times a day, while Meme B can only replicate five times per day, Meme A will soon outnumber Meme B. This trait is called fecundity, where a higher fecundity is more advantageous. Secondly, the accuracy with which memes can be copied affects their success. For instance, memes that have error rates of one in 100 will be more successful than memes with error rates of one in ten as the latter will result in fewer overall copies and more competition from the mis-copied memes. This trait is referred to as copy-fidelity. Lastly, memes that have longevity will be more successful as they are in existence in the same form (intact) for longer, providing them with more opportunities to copy themselves. This trait is referred to as longevity (Dawkins, R., 2016).

Fecundity and copy-fidelity result in successful memes being small and less complex units of information. This is because, intuitively, smaller units can be copied more quickly than longer units. In addition, the longer and more complex a piece of information is, the more difficult it is to copy accurately (Dawkins, R., 2016). For instance, people can easily remember parts of songs with great accuracy but often don't accurately remember entire songs. Consequently, people can only sing along to discrete parts of songs. In essence, a "song" can be understood as a collection of memes and not one meme in itself (Dawkins, R., 2016).

Memes can either be stored in people's memory or exist in more permanent formats – such as in books and electronic media (Blackmore, 2001; Finkelstein, 2008). The relative ease with which humans can copy a meme has led to memes being analogised to "viruses of the mind" (Dawkins, R., 1993) and is where the popular term "meme" for "viral" pictures and video clips comes from. Advances in technology continue to facilitate the rapid spread and evolution of memes across the globe (Finkelstein, 2008).

Memes are inherited by, or transferred to, new hosts by imitation (Blackmore, 2001). These processes are not perfect and give rise to opportunities for variation. Variations (new memes) may be due to copy errors during initial inheritance; inaccuracies that arise over time as memes fade from memory (Blackmore, 2001; Basu and Waymire, 2006) or from active modification as people recombine and alter existing memes in an iterative process (Blackmore, 2001; Finkelstein, 2008; Dawkins, R., 2016). Research is an example of memetic evolution where both copy errors and active modification affect how researchers internalise, apply and develop new memes. Technology and globalisation are important accelerators of memetic evolution. They facilitate memes from different jurisdictions, cultures, and environments being compared and recombined by different people and for different reasons (such as cross-disciplinary research) (Walker, 2006; Finkelstein, 2008). In addition, the cost of transmitting memes across the globe is now negligible, facilitating the rapid dissemination and modification of memes (Finkelstein, 2008).

3.2   Two-Step Accumulation and Selection

Like living organisms, memetic systems do not become complex overnight (single-step evolution). Instead, small changes constantly arise and are either selected and aggregated with other memes or rejected. To illustrate the power of two-step accumulation, picture trying to solve a four-digit password in a single step – correctly guessing the password is almost impossible. If, on the other hand, correct digits in the correct place are kept and only incorrect digits are revised after each attempt, the password can be cracked in as few as ten attempts[5] (Dawkins, R., 1986).

Systems become more diverse and complex over time via the two-step accumulation of memes. Which memes people inherit is complex and impacted by each person's upbringing, experiences, knowledge and job (collectively called a person's historicity). Meme selection can be broken down into three stages: assimilation, retention and expression (Heylighen, 1997). Assimilation refers to how easily a meme can be inherited. In order to be assimilated, memes must be noticeable as something worth imitating or copying (Heylighen, 1997; Rutherford, 2020). They must be understandable and acceptable or believable. Memes that are more precise (or formally documented) and that are from an authoritative source have a selection advantage (Heylighen, 1997; 1998; Blackmore et al., 2000; Blackmore, 2001; Dawkins, R., 2016).

In stage 2, memes must be retained in memory so that they can be used by hosts. The longer a meme is retained, the longer it has to be expressed by the host and inherited by other hosts, and is what Dawkins (2016) calls longevity. Meme retention is difficult, with many being retained temporarily before being forgotten (Heylighen, 1997). A meme's complexity is negatively associated with its fecundity and copy-fidelity. Similarly, the less a meme requires pre-existing knowledge to build onto, the greater its selection advantage (see Heylighen, 1997; Illeris, 2009). Because people become conflicted when they hold contradictory memes, the greater a meme's coherence with other memes retained by a host, the greater its selection advantage. The more a meme is expressed, the greater its retention (recurrence) and hosts are more likely to exert more effort remembering memes with greater utility (Heylighen, 1997; Blackmore, 2001; Dawkins, R., 2016). A meme's likelihood of retention is significantly dependent on each host's personal circumstances and historicity. Consequently, meme selection is highly subjective (Heylighen, 1997; 1998) and this may explain why a meme's selection and inheritance success is different for each person.

The last stage is expression. Expression can take a variety of forms including actions, pictures and speech. Memes that are frequently expressed are constantly reinforced, reducing their degradation over time (Heylighen, 1997). Table 2.1 provides a summary of selection's three stages and the factors impacting them.

Table 2.1   *Selection stages and factors*

Stage	Key selection factors
Assimilation	Noticeability Acceptability/believability Precision/formality Authority
Retention	Fecundity (complexity) Copy-fidelity (complexity) Reliance on pre-existing memes Longevity Coherence Recurrence Utility
Expression	Expressivity

Source: Adapted from Heylighen, 1997; 1998; Blackmore, 2001; Dawkins, R., 2016.

Each meme is unlikely to, figuratively speaking, score high in respect of all selection factors. Instead, selection can be viewed as a game where memes with higher net scores are more likely to be selected over competitors (Heylighen, 1997; 1998). The emphasis on different selection factors gives rise to different strategies that memes play in order to be selected (Blackmore, 2001; Dawkins, R., 2016). For example, a meme may focus on maximising acceptability, fecundity, copy-fidelity and reliance on pre-existing memes and forgoing utility. Its utility may be lower as it over-simplifies complex issues, but its "simplicity" strategy is that its lower utility score is compensated for with higher scores on the other factors. By contrast, a meme may adopt a strategy of providing high utility at the cost of fecundity and copy-fidelity.

In order for a meme to increase its survival, memes and genes must co-evolve. Blackmore (2001) argues that this co-evolution resulted in humans having large brains that are highly adept at *selecting* which memes to imitate. For instance, inheriting memes to create long spears help people to protect themselves and hunt. People who inherit these memes will have an advantage and increase within a population – benefiting both the spear memes and those hosts' genes. However, memes can exploit gene–meme coevolution. To illustrate, hosts with genes that are predisposed to selecting spears based on the greatest length can be fooled by memes adopting a strategy that focuses on increasing length at all costs. Put differently, because hosts selecting long spear memes have been successful, their dependents' genes use spear length to decide which memes to imitate and which to reject. Memes can take advantage as any modified memes for a longer spear will be selected. But, eventually, the spear length will diminish its utility, decreasing the host's survival and, consequently, reproductive prospects. Accordingly, genes that supported the development of increasingly complex brains that can "selectively [copy] the most useful memes, while not copying the useless, costly or harmful ones" prosper in the gene pool (Dawkins, R., 1999; Blackmore, 2001, p. 246).

In line with gene–meme co-evolution, memes that impact mate selection are crucial (Blackmore, 2001; Vincent and Brown, 2005; Dawkins, R., 2016). Animals look for mates who will have the resources (food, shelter and strength) to ensure the successful upbringing of their offspring – because this will ensure their selfish genes will prosper. Flamboyant feathers and well-constructed nests are examples of indicators used to demonstrate to prospective mates that they are so strong they do not fear being highly visible to predators or are capable of building good homes, respectively (Blackmore, 2001; Dawkins, R., 2016). In a human context, evolutionary psychologists consider wealth to be an important indicator of success and, consequently, mate selection (Blackmore, 2001; Hou et al., 2020). Financial resources mean that the prospective mate can provide food, shelter, protection and a good education for their offspring. Expensive cars, homes and clothing are important displays to signal wealth and attract mates. Accordingly, memes that facilitate financial wealth accumulation prosper.

In the context of this chapter, people can accumulate wealth by, inter alia, keeping their job or by making good buy, hold or sell decisions in capital markets. A person's current job is important for determining which meme strategies will be more advantageous to each person. In addition, what strategies successful memes employ is not static. As society, technology and the global environment change, so, too, may the strategies successful memes deploy.

Ultimately, selection is about new meme variants engaging other memes in a game. The memes are the players, which each have a set strategy in order to achieve greater selection.[6] While memes are the players, the game must be understood from the perspective of the people who will either select or reject them based on the factors in Table 2.1. For this chapter, that is the accountants and investors who prepare or use corporate reporting.

The next section provides an introductory application of memetic evolution to integrated reporting. Section 5 provides closing remarks and presents a research agenda using the memetic evolutionary lens to extend our understanding of corporate reporting in its entirety.

4 APPLICATION OF MEMETIC EVOLUTION TO INTEGRATED REPORTING

This section uses the different eras discussed in Section 2 to illustrate the applicability of memetic evolution to integrated reporting. To provide maximum impact, different aspects of the usefulness of memetic evolution are highlighted in different eras.

In the context of non-financial corporate reporting, a meme is an idea, concept, practice or disclosure. Examples include the amount of water used and carbon emissions generated. A memeplex would encompass the memes dealing with a particular issue – such as the identification, recording and disclosure of water usage. A high memeplex would be all the memeplexes dealing with, for example, environmental issues and a grand memeplex would encompass all the respective high memeplexes. The GRI and IIRC are each distinct grand memeplexes in their own right (adapted from Rutherford, 2020).

4.1 Agricultural and Industrial Eras

We cannot know what the first corporate reporting meme was. We can speculate that a meme to count quantities of grain and livestock is a likely candidate (Brown, 1905; Mattessich, 1998). This simple meme would evolve into an increasing number of diverse memes, leading to memeplexes of increasing complexity. Examples include memes that dealt with the cost of goods, recording barter transactions and, later, facilitating trade via tokens (such as shells) that represent value and, eventually, money. Evolution was likely slow due to the limited extent of interactions between different groups of people (Finkelstein, 2008). As society expanded and technology developed to make travelling and communicating easier, people would be exposed to memes from different contexts more frequently. Consequently, the rate at which memes were compared and modified would also increase (Dawkins, R., 2016).

The industrial era would likely have been one of the first periods of significant meme competition and also caused new spin-off disciplines (high memeplexes) to emerge. Hopwood (1987, p. 207) emphasises the fact that accounting has "been called upon to serve an ever greater variety of different and changing purposes". While initial accounting memes facilitated internal decision making and control (what we may now call management accounting), the socialisation of capital required a new type of accounting – external reporting. Memes that provided useful information about the summarised *financial* performance and position of a company were highly successful. This may be due to the co-evolution of genes and memes. Wealth and displays thereof are important mate selection indicators (see Section 3.2) and may explain the early focus on and selection of memes that provide useful financial information and incentivise short-term profit-seeking behaviour. Social and environmental information did not affect a company manager's bonus nor help to make better buy, hold or sell decisions and short-term financial success.

The early 1900s saw companies including information about employee issues and community involvement in annual reports. Employee grievances and strike action can have significant financial implications. These may have prompted corporations to try to legitimise their businesses and practices. This may have led corporations to modify memes related to typical financial corporate reporting to deal with non-financial matters. For example, they modified the memes to report on the number of assets a company controls to report the number of houses built for employees. Those memes may then have been further modified (via two-step accumulation) to report qualitative information about what has been done to develop communities impacted by the company, improve worker safety and assist employees to purchase their own homes (see Guthrie and Parker, 1989).

From a selection perspective, the new memes to report on employee-related information would compete with memes that aimed to maintain corporate privacy or the status quo. Both memes have relatively equal scores for most factors from Table 2.1 except recurrence, longevity and utility. The meme not to report non-financial information has greater longevity (being then the norm) and recurrence. This meant displacing this meme for those that require non-financial information to be reported is difficult. Utility, in the form of maximising financial performance and position, would have been an important determining factor. Companies with a high risk of strike action or threats to their legitimacy may gain greater utility from reporting on employee-related information than those that do not. This helps to explain why some companies reported whilst others resisted and did not. In addition, companies that sought to differentiate themselves from other companies may also perceive great utility in reporting employee-related information and adopt the employee-reporting memeplex.

Environmental issues were not high on society's priority list at the time. Accordingly, any memes that did arise to report on a company's environmental impact would have low utility and be easily dismissed. This would continue until society changed and the utility of environmental memes increased or the technology to identify and report environmental issues developed to make their other selection factor scores (see Table 2.1) low enough to encourage selection.

4.2   Information and Multi-Capital Eras

The information era is characterised by its significant generation and consumption of information, aided by rapid technological developments (Bray and Ridehalgh, 2020). In addition, the significant size of multinational companies meant that companies have significant and visible effects on the environment either directly or indirectly (van Zijl et al., 2017). Several environmental crises played a key role in the demand for, and utility provided by, environmental sustainability reporting and corporate accountability (World Commission on Environment and Development, 1987; Sanyal and Neves, 1991). In particular, the Bhopal and *Exxon Valdez* disasters of the 1980s received significant public scrutiny. Importantly, while activists had played the leading role in demanding corporate environmental disclosures, they had little ability to encourage or demand their selection. However, the environmental crises and their financial impact[7] led to investors joining forces with activists to demand environmental information (see, for example, World Commission on Environment and Development, 1987; Sanyal and Neves, 1991; Hellier, 2015). While activists can be important agents for change, capital providers have greater power and influence over companies' actions because of their financial support and voting rights.

While memes for environmental disclosures existed, they had not achieved great success (frequency) in the corporate grand memeplex. Their strategy of improving the transparency of companies' non-financial impacts aligned with activists' interests but did not clearly align with the interests of investors and company executives. Activists had little power to influence the utility and selection of environmental reporting memes. Companies are not heavily reliant on activists to purchase their goods or services nor do they provide material financial capital support to companies. But the disasters revealed just how important environmental disclosures are for understanding the risks a firm is exposed to and determining firm value (see, World Commission on Environment and Development, 1987; Sanyal and Neves, 1991; Hellier, 2015; Yu et al., 2018). As discussed in Section 3.2, the better memes are at helping a person accumulate financial wealth, the more successful they, their genes and memes will be (Blackmore, 2001). This may explain why investor support was so crucial to change the corporate reporting grand memeplex and why the environmental memes became "winners" and aggregated into the corporate reporting grand memeplex – they enhanced economic decision making and wealth generation.

Due to the significance of the disasters, several new memes were likely created alongside the existing memes created by activists. To demonstrate a possible game, assume the following memes engaged one another: memes calling for environmental information to be incorporated into the existing financial statements; a quantification of environmental risks being disclosed; and separate qualitative environmental reporting to be prepared and published by companies. A key issue facing the first meme was the lack of supporting memes to achieve it. In other words, while a meme requiring environmental information to be recognised in financial statements may have high utility, it required other acceptable memes that provided the procedures to operationalise it (see Finkelstein, 2008; Dawkins, R., 2016). As memes detailing what to recognise and how to measure environmental impacts were missing, the meme to recognise environmental information in financial statements was easily defeated in the game and did not become a part of the non-financial reporting memeplex.

Quantifying the environmental risks is possible with some aspects of environmental reporting, but not all (McNally et al., 2017). Similarly, only relying on qualitative environmental information diminishes its credibility as it is too easy to engage in de-coupling, where the information presented is not a true reflection of the operations and activities of the entity (de Villiers and Maroun, 2017) and represents greenwashing (see Delmas and Burbano, 2011; de Freitas Netto et al., 2020). The result was a mixture of the two latter memes with quantification of the factors that can be quantified and qualitative disclosures for other aspects (Eccles and Saltzman, 2011; Owen, 2013).

The surge in research (active modification of memes) around non-financial corporate reporting resulted in a myriad of voluntary codes, frameworks and regulations. These aimed to assist and regulate how companies prepared and reported non-financial information and to enhance corporate accountability. At this stage, several similar memes were acceptable and had varying levels of success depending on a variety of factors, including jurisdiction and prevailing legal and exchange regulations. For instance, there was the Balanced Scorecard (Kaplan and Norton, 1996), Triple Bottom Line reporting (Elkington, 1998), and the GRI (GRI, 2000).

The IFRS, with which over 166 countries currently require compliance to prepare financial statements (IFRS Foundation, 2023b), still does not provide a means to recognise social and environmental assets and liabilities in financial statements. Consequently, environmental and sustainability reporting is still largely published in separate reports to financial statements and is often seen as being supplementary to financial statements. While financial reporting has been tightly regulated for decades, the separate environmental, social and sustainability reports are still largely unregulated. The key obstacle to regulating non-financial reporting is the sheer diversity of non-financial aspects that can be reported and the difficulty of trying to create a framework that can be applied by all industries in all countries to all relevant non-financial aspects (Wang et al., 2019; Landau et al., 2020; Lange, 2020). These memes are simply missing at present despite the efforts of many practitioners, academics and regulators to create them (GRI, 2020; IIRC, 2021; VRF, 2022).

In keeping with the central idea of memetic evolution that memes selfishly wish to survive and thrive, memes took advantage of the unregulated non-financial reporting arena. Memes with strategies of pacifying stakeholder calls for transparency and non-financial reporting without substantive change were highly successful. These memes' strategy was to provide non-financial information that presented the company in the best light and was difficult to dispute. Non-financial information is not audited (Maroun, 2018; Maroun, 2019a) and is often qualitative, making it inherently subjective. This type of reporting became known as *greenwashing* and destroyed some of the legitimacy of non-financial reporting (Delmas and Burbano, 2011; de Villiers and Maroun, 2017). The decreased usefulness of these greenwashing memes was eventually identified and our highly developed brains began rejecting memes with a strategy of greenwashing or pacifying stakeholders with superficial non-financial reporting information in favour of demanding more useful ones (de Villiers and Maroun, 2017).

The increasing rejection of greenwashing memes may have caused a shift towards the current multi-capital era that followed. Memes with strategies of reporting "poor environmental performance [with] positive communication about environmental performance" (Delmas and Burbano, 2011, p. 65) decreased the usefulness of these disclosures for investors and their ability to general wealth. The existing memes were modified to overcome this weakness by adopting a multi-capital approach and preparing integrated reports (IIRC, 2021). By providing more detailed information about how the six capitals (financial, manufactured, intellectual, human, social and relationship, and natural) are used by a business, it makes it more difficult to engage in greenwashing, improving the credibility and usefulness of integrated reports.

An interesting idea also emerged. Due to the lack of existing technologies to recognise environmental and social assets and liabilities in financial statements, integrated reporting's meme may also have adopted the strategy of asserting that its adoption would change management's business approach towards *integrated thinking* as a compromise or substitute for the lack of recognition in financial statements. This, the meme's strategy contended, would ensure management incorporates the six capitals into their day-to-day thinking and planning. Doing so would lead to the environmental and social risks and rewards being evaluated and responded to by those with the most information and who are in the best position to use that information profitably – management. Consequently, stakeholders could rest assured and decrease demands for more detailed environmental and social reporting.

Novo Nordisk is acknowledged as having produced one of the first integrated reports that combined financial and non-financial information into a single report (White, 2005). The integrated reporting meme initiated the development of entirely new memeplexes related to, inter alia, the balance between good and bad news within integrated reports (Roberts et al., 2020), using integrated reports to foster a culture of integrated *thinking* by management (King and Atkins, 2016; de Villiers and Maroun, 2017; Maroun et al., 2023), being environmentally and socially responsible (de Villiers and Maroun, 2017), how to enhance the credibility of integrated reporting through assurance mechanisms (Maroun and Atkins, 2015; Maroun, 2019b) and creating systems designed (proactively) to gather and monitor non-financial information that can then be used to prepare high quality integrated reports (Zhou et al., 2019; Prinsloo and Maroun, 2020). Integrated reporting also highlights the possibilities of speciation. Certain jurisdictions, such as South Africa, have regulations requiring the preparation of integrated reports, while other jurisdictions, such as Japan, the Netherlands, Germany and France, still allow the publication of separate environmental, social and sustainability reports (Zhou et al., 2017; Gibassier et al., 2019).

Regardless of whether non-financial reporting is standardised or not, the three principles of memetic evolution are still relevant (Rutherford, 2020). Variant memes will still arise either by error or active modification. Those memes with higher net selection factor scores (see Table 2.1) will still be selected, allowing non-financial reporting to evolve via the two-step accumulation of "winning" memes. The presence of standardising bodies (for example the ISSB and GRI) may accelerate the rate at which memes are actively modified. This is because their due processes usually require consultations with global constituents and various different stakeholders in order to be accepted as a legitimate standardising body (see, for example, Bamber and McMeeking, 2016; Wingard et al., 2016; De Freitas et al., 2023).

Standardising bodies may also alter the selection environment. For example, a body that prioritises conceptual validity as opposed to pragmatism impacts how each selection factor will score. Standardising bodies also accelerate the inheritance of selected memes by enhancing the selected memes' authority and allowing education institutions to focus on helping students inherit them correctly and efficiently. This will have knock-on consequences for future meme games as those memes with greater longevity have a selection advantage (see Rutherford, 2020). Finally, standardising the non-financial reporting landscape can have important implications for their assurance. Without suitable criteria, auditors cannot conduct efficient and effective audits to provide their opinions about whether reports comply with underlying frameworks and should be relied upon (Farooq and de Villiers, 2017; Braam and Peeters, 2018; Prinsloo and Maroun, 2020; Roberts et al., 2020).

5   CONCLUSION AND AREAS FOR FUTURE RESEARCH

Accounting has evolved significantly from its primitive beginnings as marks on tokens (Mattessich, 1998) to the sophisticated IFRS and, more recently, integrated reports. As Hopwood (1987, p. 207) noted, accounting has "a tendency to become what it was not". Too many academic papers accept accounting (including integrated reporting) as a neutral and progressive means of communicating information to users. But the mechanics of its evolution are often overlooked (Hopwood, 1987). To this end, this chapter proposes that non-financial corporate reporting evolves according to the principles of memetic evolution. The chapter explains how accounting and human evolution are inextricably linked through the co-evolution of genes and memes (Blackmore, 2001). This should open a new research agenda aimed at exploring the nuances of this relationship and improve our understanding of the forces at work in accounting and integrated reporting's evolution. For example, a memetic evolutionary perspective suggests that accounting's early short-term profit focus may be due to gene–meme co-evolution and is not due to a blatant disregard of social values and the importance of environmental protection.

The chapter provides an overview of memetic evolution and used the four eras associated with non-financial corporate reporting's evolution to illustrate memetic evolution's application. Memes, being pieces of information capable of being imitated or replicated by human hosts, are actively modified by human intellect (Blackmore, 2001; Finkelstein, 2008). The discipline evolves via the two-step accumulation of selected memes over time. Which memes are selected is a complex function of the strategies memes play and how well they score on key selection factors. How well meme strategies score is subjective and is affected by environmental, social and technological factors (Heylighen, 1997; Blackmore, 2001; Dawkins, R., 2016).

There is evidence of speciation, where memes evolve slightly differently across different jurisdictions as the factors affecting the success of different meme strategies are different in each context. As the world has become a small place where memes are not strictly bound to any one jurisdiction, memes from different jurisdictions will continue to engage one another and this may reduce, but not eliminate, the effects of speciation.

This chapter makes an important contribution by reflecting on how a novel framework can improve our understanding of how integrated reporting, as an important form of corporate reporting, has evolved and may evolve. The framework helps to illustrate why there is resistance to integrated reporting's adoption, the impact of people's historicity on meme selection and why early accounting focused on maximising economic wealth.

Future research should investigate what strategies are associated with different memes in anticipation of conducting more detailed research into the types of games played between memes. While quantitative illustrations of integrated reporting's memetic evolutionary games may be elusive (see Rutherford, 2020), research should consider this seriously as it could provide greater insights into the evolution of different memetic strategies and their pay-offs.

Detailed research, drawing heavily on game theory, will be especially valuable. Research into the role of gender and corporate reporting's evolution is crucial. Adopting a memetic evolutionary lens may help to extend research that considers the role of, for example, testosterone and risk-taking and aggressive reporting practices (see, for example, Apicella et al., 2008; Parker, 2008; Jia et al., 2014). Finally, memetic evolution may shed new light on alternate forms of social and environmental reporting such as pictorial accounts (Haslam and Gallhofer, 1996; Atkins and Maroun, 2020), emancipatory accounting (Haslam and Gallhofer, 1996; Atkins and Macpherson, 2022) and "nature diaries" (see Sullivan and Hannis, 2017; Büchling and Atkins, 2020; Buchling and Maroun, 2023).

NOTES

1. The Valdez Principles were modelled on the Sullivan Principles, which had been developed to discourage investment in South Africa to protest against apartheid.
2. Corporate scandals such as Enron, WorldCom and Tyco in the US, and Ahold, Parmalat and ABB in Europe.
3. The Johannesburg Stock Exchange is the main stock exchange in South Africa and is the largest stock exchange in Africa.
4. The word "wish" in this context is not used to imply that replicators have a consciousness and inherent desires. It is a convenient word to express the notion that replicators exist to replicate themselves.
5. Assume the password is 1580. Assume attempt one is "0000". The last "0" is retained and only the first three digits are revised. Assume the second attempt is "5550". The second and last digits ("x5x0") are retained and only the remaining two digits are revised. There are only eight possibilities for each of the remaining digits (adapted from Dawkins, R., 1986).
6. Memes cannot change their strategy. Doing so would be tantamount to creating a new meme that would compete with the "original" for selection.

7. Dow Chemicals paid $470 million as a settlement for the Bhopal incident while Exxon paid $4.5 billion in damages for its oil spill in Alaska (Hellier, 2015).

REFERENCES

A4S. 2021. *Navigating the Reporting Landscape: An Introduction to Sustainability-Related Reporting for Finance Professionals*. London: A4S Accounting Bodies Network.

Apicella, C. L., Dreber, A., Campbell, B., Gray, P. B., Hoffman, M. & Little, A. C. 2008. Testosterone and financial risk preferences. *Evolution and Human Behavior*, 29, 384–390.

Atkins, J. & Macpherson, M. 2022. *Extinction Governance, Finance and Accounting: Implementing a Species Protection Action Plan for the Financial Markets*. Abingdon, UK: Taylor & Francis.

Atkins, J. & Maroun, W. 2015. Integrated reporting in South Africa in 2012: perspectives from South African institutional investors. *Meditari Accountancy Research*, 23, 197–221.

Atkins, J. & Maroun, W. 2020. The Naturalist's Journals of Gilbert White: exploring the roots of accounting for biodiversity and extinction accounting. *Accounting, Auditing & Accountability Journal*, 33(8), 1835–1870.

Bamber, M. & McMeeking, K. 2016. An examination of international accounting standard-setting due process and the implications for legitimacy. *The British Accounting Review*, 48, 59–73.

Basu, S. & Waymire, G. B. 2006. Recordkeeping and human evolution. *Accounting Horizons*, 20, 201–229.

Blackmore, S. 2001. Evolution and memes: the human brain as a selective imitation device. *Cybernetics & Systems*, 32, 225–255.

Blackmore, S., Dugatkin, L. A., Boyd, R., Richerson, P. J. & Plotkin, H. 2000. The power of memes. *Scientific American*, 283, 64–73.

Braam, G. & Peeters, R. 2018. Corporate sustainability performance and assurance on sustainability reports: diffusion of accounting practices in the realm of sustainable development. *Corporate Social Responsibility and Environmental Management*, 25, 164–181.

Bray, M. & Ridehalgh, N. 2020. The fourth wave is integrated reporting, in C. De Villiers, P.-C. Hsiao & W. Maroun (eds), *The Routledge Handbook of Integrated Reporting*. Abingdon, UK: Routledge, pp. 67–83.

Brown, R. 1905. *A History of Accounting and Accountants*. London: Ballantyne, Hanson & Co.

Büchling, M. & Atkins, J. 2020. Reporting on more than just natural capital, in C. De Villiers, P.-C. Hsiao & W. Maroun (eds), *The Routledge Handbook of Integrated Reporting*. Abingdon, UK: Routledge, pp. 440–455.

Büchling, M. & Maroun, W. 2023. Biodiversity reporting practices of the South African national parks. *Social Responsibility Journal*, 19(1), 138–165.

Buhr, N., Gray, R. & Milne, M. J. 2014. Histories, rationales, voluntary standards and future prospects for sustainability reporting, in J. Bebbington, J. Unerman, J. and B. O'Dwyer (eds), *Sustainability Accounting and Accountability*. 2nd edn. Abingdon, UK: Routledge, pp. 51–71.

Burritt, R. L. & Schaltegger, S. 2010. Sustainability accounting and reporting: fad or trend? *Accounting, Auditing & Accountability Journal*, 23, 829–846.

Cerbone, D. & Maroun, W. 2019. Materiality in an integrated reporting setting: insights using an institutional logics framework. *The British Accounting Review*, 100876.

Cohen, J. R. & Simnett, R. 2015. CSR and assurance services: a research agenda. *Auditing: A Journal of Practice & Theory*, 34, 59–74.

Darwin, C. 1859. *The Origin of Species by means of Natural Selection, or the Preservation of Favoured Races in the Struggle for Life*. London: John Murray.

Dawkins, C. & Ngunjiri, F. W. 2008. Corporate social responsibility reporting in South Africa: a descriptive and comparative analysis. *Journal of Business Communication*, 45, 286–307.

Dawkins, R. 1986. *The Blind Watchmaker: Why the Evidence of Evolution Reveals a World without Design*. New York: WW Norton.

Dawkins, R. 1993. Viruses of the mind, in Bo Dahlbom (ed.), *Dennett and His Critics: Demystifying Mind*. Oxford: Blackwell, pp. 13–27.

Dawkins, R. 1999. *The Extended Phenotype*. New York: Oxford University Press.

Dawkins, R. 2016. *The Selfish Gene*. Oxford: Oxford University Press.

De Beer, G. 1964. Mendel, Darwin, and Fisher (1865–1965). *Notes and Records of the Royal Society of London*, 19, 192–226.

De Freitas, M. T., Van Zijl, W., Ram, A. J. & Maroun, W. 2023. Stakeholder and jurisdictional influence over IFRS 10's development. *South African Journal of Accounting Research*, 1–23.

De Freitas Netto, S. V., Sobral, M. F. F., Ribeiro, A. R. B. & Da Luz Soares, G. R. 2020. Concepts and forms of greenwashing: a systematic review. *Environmental Sciences Europe*, 32, 1–12.

De Villiers, C. & Alexander, D. 2014. The institutionalisation of corporate social responsibility reporting. *The British Accounting Review*, 46, 198–212.

De Villiers, C. & Maroun, W. 2017. *Sustainability Accounting and Integrated Reporting*. Abingdon, UK: Routledge.

De Villiers, C., Rinaldi, L. & Unerman, J. 2014. Integrated reporting: insights, gaps and an agenda for future research. *Accounting, Auditing & Accountability Journal*, 27, 1042–1067.

De Villiers, C., Venter, E. R. & Hsiao, P. C. K. 2017. Integrated reporting: background, measurement issues, approaches and an agenda for future research. *Accounting & Finance*, 57, 937–959.

Deegan, C. & Rankin, M. 1997. The materiality of environmental information to users of annual reports. *Accounting, Auditing & Accountability Journal*, 10(4), 562–583.

Deegan, C., Rankin, M. & Tobin, J. 2002. An examination of the corporate social and environmental disclosures of BHP from 1983–1997: a test of legitimacy theory. *Accounting, Auditing & Accountability Journal*, 15, 312–343.

Delmas, M. A. & Burbano, V. C. 2011. The drivers of greenwashing. *California Management Review*, 54, 64–87.

Dumay, J., Bernardi, C., Guthrie, J. & Demartini, P. 2016. Integrated reporting: a structured literature review. *Accounting Forum*, 40(3), 166–185.

Eccles, R. G. & Krzus, M. P. 2010. Integrated Reporting for a Sustainable Strategy. Available at: http://www.financialexecutives.org/KenticoCMS/Financial-Executive-Magazine/2010_03/Financial -Reporting-Feature--March-2010.aspx#axzz48iuAkAHV (Accessed 26 November 2012).

Eccles, R. G. & Saltzman, D. 2011. Achieving sustainability through integrated reporting. *Stanford Social Innovation Review*, Summer, 56–61.

Edgley, C., Jones, M. J. & Atkins, J. F. 2015. The adoption of the materiality concept in social and environmental reporting assurance: a field study approach. *The British Accounting Review*, 47, 1–18.

Elkington, J. 1998. Accounting for the triple bottom line. *Measuring Business Excellence*, 2(3), 18–22.

Farooq, M. B. & De Villiers, C. 2017. Assurance of sustainability and integrated reports, in C. de Villiers & W. Maroun (eds), *Sustainability Accounting and Integrated Reporting*. Abingdon, UK: Routledge, Chapter 12.

Finkelstein, R. 2008. *A Memetics Compendium*. Potomac, MD: Robotic Technology Inc.

Fisher, R. A. 1930. *The Genetical Theory of Natural Selection: A Complete Variorum Edition*. Oxford: Oxford University Press.

Flower, J. 2015. The International Integrated Reporting Council: A story of failure. *Critical Perspectives on Accounting*, 27, 1–17.

García-Sánchez, I.-M., Hussain, N., Khan, S.-A. & Martínez-Ferrero, J. 2020. Do markets punish or reward corporate social responsibility decoupling? *Business & Society*, 60(6), 1431–1467.

Gibassier, D., Adams, C. A. & Jérôme, T. 2019. *Integrated Reporting and the Capitals' Diffusion*. Report published by the French Accounting Standard Setter (Autorité des Normes Comptables).

Gray, R. & Milne, M. 2002. Sustainability reporting: who's kidding whom? *Chartered Accountants Journal of New Zealand*, 81, 66–70.

Gray, R., Kouhy, R. & Lavers, S. 1995. Corporate social and environmental reporting: a review of the literature and a longitudinal study of UK disclosure. *Accounting, Auditing & Accountability Journal*, 8(2), 47–77.

GRI. 2000. *Sustainability Reporting Guidelines on Economic, Environmental, and Social Performance*. Boston, MA: Global Reporting Initiative.

GRI. 2020. Consolidated set of GRI sustainability reporting standards (2019). Available at: https:// www.globalreporting.org/standards/gri-standards-download-center/?g=ae2e23b8-4958-455c-a9df -ac372d6ed9a8 (Accessed 13 January 2021).

Guthrie, J. & Parker, L. D. 1989. Corporate social reporting: a rebuttal of legitimacy theory. *Accounting and Business Research*, 19, 343–352.

Haslam, J. & Gallhofer, S. 1996. Accounting/art and the emancipatory project: some reflections. *Accounting, Auditing and Accountability Journal*, 9, 23–44.

Hellier, D. 2015. Corporate scandals and how (not) to handle them. *The Guardian*, 26 September.

Heylighen, F. 1997. Objective, subjective and intersubjective selectors of knowledge. *Evolution and Cognition*, 3, 63–67.

Heylighen, F. 1998. What makes a meme successful? Selection criteria for cultural evolution. *Proc. 16th Int. Congress on Cybernetics (Association Internat. de Cybernetique Namur)*, 423–418.

Hill, N. & Maroun, W. 2015. Assessing the potential impact of the Marikana incident on South African mining companies: an event method study. *South African Journal of Economic and Management Sciences*, 18, 586–607.

Hodgson, G. M. 2002. Darwinism in economics: from analogy to ontology. *Journal of Evolutionary Economics*, 12, 259–281.

Hopwood, A. G. 1983. On trying to study accounting in the contexts in which it operates. *Accounting, Organizations and Society*, 8, 287–305.

Hopwood, A. G. 1987. The archaeology of accounting systems. *Accounting, Organizations and Society*, 12, 207–234.

Hou, J., Shu, T. & Fang, X. 2020. Influence of resources on cue preferences in mate selection. *Frontiers in Psychology*, 11.

IFRS Foundation. 2023a. *IFRS Sustainability Standards Navigator*. Available at: https://www.ifrs.org/issued-standards/ifrs-sustainability-standards-navigator/ (Accessed 6 October 2023).

IFRS Foundation. 2023b. *Use around the world*. Available at: https://www.ifrs.org/use-around-the -world/use-of-ifrs-standards-by-jurisdiction/ (Accessed 18 December 2023).

IIRC. 2011. "Towards Integrated Reporting. Communicating Value in the 21st Century". Discussion Paper.

IIRC. 2013. *The International Integrated Reporting Framework*. London: International Integrated Reporting Council.

IIRC. 2014. IIRC Stakeholder Feedback Survey. Available at: http://integratedreporting.org/wp-content/uploads/2016/12/IIRC-Stakeholder-Survey-Report-Findings.pdf (Accessed 15 August 2016).

IIRC. 2021. *The International Integrated Reporting Framework*. London: International Integrated Reporting Council.

Illeris, K. 2009. A comprehensive understanding of human learning, in K. Illeris (ed.), *Contemporary Theories of Learning: Learning Theorists ... in Their Own Words*. Abingdon, UK: Routledge, pp. 7–20.

Jia, Y., Lent, L. V. & Zeng, Y. 2014. Masculinity, testosterone, and financial misreporting. *Journal of Accounting Research*, 52, 1195–1246.

Kaplan, R. S. & Norton, D. P. 1996. Using the balanced scorecard as a strategic management system, in R. S. Kaplan and D. P. Norton, *Focusing Your Organization on Strategy—with the Balanced Scorecard*. 2nd edn. Boston, MA: Harvard Business School Publishing, pp. 2–18.

King, M. & Atkins, J. 2016. *The Chief Value Officer: Accountants Can Save the Planet*. Austin, TX: Greenleaf Publishing.

Lai, A., Melloni, G. & Stacchezzini, R. 2016. Corporate sustainable development: is "integrated reporting" a legitimation strategy? *Business Strategy and the Environment*, 25, 165–177.

Landau, A., Rochell, J., Klein, C. & Zwergel, B. 2020. Integrated reporting of environmental, social, and governance and financial data: does the market value integrated reports? *Business Strategy and the Environment*, 29(4), 1625–1808.

Lange, Y. 2020. Practical insights into implementing integrated reporting, in C. de Villiers, P.-C. Hsiao & W. Maroun (eds), *The Routledge Handbook of Integrated Reporting*. Abingdon, UK: Routledge, pp. 322–338.

Maroun, W. 2017. Assuring the integrated report: insights and recommendations from auditors and preparers. *British Accounting Review*, 49(3), 329–346.

Maroun, W. 2018. Modifying assurance practices to meet the needs of integrated reporting: the case for "interpretive assurance". *Accounting, Auditing & Accountability Journal*, 31, 400–427.

Maroun, W. 2019a. Future of the audit profession, in M. Büchling, D. Cerbone, M. Kok, W. Maroun, G. Marque & T. Segal, *Assurance, Risk and Governance an International Perspective*. Cape Town: Juta, Chapter 15.

Maroun, W. 2019b. Does external assurance contribute to higher quality integrated reports? *Journal of Accounting and Public Policy*, 38, 106670.

Maroun, W. & Atkins, J. 2015. *The Challenges of Assuring Integrated Reports: Views from the South African Auditing Community*. London: The Association of Chartered Certified Accountants.

Maroun, W. & Cerbone, D. 2020. *Corporate Governance in South Africa*. Berlin: Walter de Gruyter.

Maroun, W., Ecim, D. & Cerbone, D. 2023. Refining integrated thinking. *Sustainability Accounting, Management and Policy Journal*, 14, 1–25.

Mattessich, R. 1998. Recent insights into Mesopotamian accounting of the 3rd millennium BC—Successor to token accounting. *Accounting Historians Journal*, 25, 1–27.

McNally, M.-A., Cerbone, D. & Maroun, W. 2017. Exploring the challenges of preparing an integrated report. *Meditari Accountancy Research*, 25, 481–504.

Mervelskemper, L. & Streit, D. 2017. Enhancing market valuation of ESG performance: is integrated reporting keeping its promise? *Business Strategy and the Environment*, 26, 536–549.

Mio, C., Marco, F. & Pauluzzo, R. 2016. Internal application of IR principles: Generali's internal integrated reporting. *Journal of Cleaner Production*, 139, 204–218.

Müller-Wille, S. 2021. Gregor Mendel and the history of heredity, in M. R. Dietrich, M. E. Borrello & O. Harman (eds), *Handbook of the Historiography of Biology*. Cham: Springer, pp. 105–126.

Owen, G. 2013. Integrated reporting: a review of developments and their implications for the accounting curriculum. *Accounting Education*, 22(4), 340–356.

Parker, L. D. 2008. Strategic management and accounting processes: acknowledging gender. *Accounting, Auditing & Accountability Journal*, 21, 611–631.

Patten, D. M. 2002. The relation between environmental performance and environmental disclosure: a research note. *Accounting, Organizations and Society*, 27, 763–773.

Pava, M. L. & Krausz, J. 1996. The association between corporate social responsibility and financial performance: the paradox of social cost. *Journal of Business Ethics*, 15, 321–357.

Prinsloo, A. & Maroun, W. 2020. An exploratory study on the components and quality of combined assurance in an integrated or a sustainability reporting setting. *Sustainability Accounting, Management and Policy Journal*, 12(1), 1–29.

Roberts, L., Van Zijl, W. & Cerbone, D. 2020. The Integrated Reporting Committee of South Africa: on the balance of integrated reporting, in C. De Villiers, P.-C. Hsiao & W. Maroun (eds), *The Routledge Handbook of Integrated Reporting*. Abingdon, UK: Routledge, pp. 37–66.

Roe, M. J. 1996. Chaos and evolution in law and economics. *Harvard Law Review*, 109, 641–668.

Rupley, K. H., Brown, D. & Marshall, S. 2017. Evolution of corporate reporting: from stand-alone corporate social responsibility reporting to integrated reporting. *Research in Accounting Regulation*, 29, 172–176.

Rutherford, B. A. 2020. Are accounting standards memes? The survival of accounting evolution in an age of regulation. *Philosophy of Management*, 19, 499–523.

Sanyal, R. N. & Neves, J. S. 1991. The Valdez principles: implications for corporate social responsibility. *Journal of Business Ethics*, 10, 883–890.

Simnett, R. & Huggins, A. L. 2015. Integrated reporting and assurance: where can research add value? *Sustainability Accounting, Management and Policy Journal*, 6, 29–53.

Sullivan, S. & Hannis, M. 2017. "Mathematics maybe, but not money": on balance sheets, numbers and nature in ecological accounting. *Accounting, Auditing & Accountability Journal*, 30(7), 1459–1480.

Topazio, N., McCaffry, R., Farrar, M., Spence, P., Simons, P. & Selby, I. 2020. The management accounting perspective of a professional accounting body, in C. De Villiers, P.-C. Hsiao & W. Maroun (eds), *The Routledge Handbook of Integrated Reporting*. Abingdon, UK: Routledge, pp. 84–92.

Van Zijl, W., Wöstmann, C. & Maroun, W. 2017. Strategy disclosures by listed financial services companies: signalling theory, legitimacy theory and South African integrated reporting practices. *South African Journal of Business Management*, 48, 73–85.

Vincent, T. L. & Brown, J. S. 2005. *Evolutionary Game Theory, Natural Selection, and Darwinian Dynamics*. Cambridge: Cambridge University Press.

VRF. 2022. *The Value Reporting Foundation: Home.* Available at: https://www.valuereporting foundation.org/ (Accessed 9 February 2022).

Walker, R. G. 2006. *Consolidated Statements: A History and Analysis.* Sydney: Sydney University Press.

Wang, R., Zhou, S. & Wang, T. 2019. Corporate governance, integrated reporting and the use of credibility-enhancing mechanisms on integrated reports. *European Accounting Review*, 29(4), 1–33.

White, A. L. 2005. New wine, new bottles: the rise of non-financial reporting. A Business Brief by Business for Social Responsibility.

Whitty, S. J. 2005. A memetic paradigm of project management. *International Journal of Project Management*, 23, 575–583.

Windolph, S. E., Harms, D. & Schaltegger, S. 2014. Motivations for corporate sustainability management: contrasting survey results and implementation. *Corporate Social Responsibility and Environmental Management*, 21, 272–285.

Wingard, C., Bosman, J. & Amisi, B. 2016. The legitimacy of IFRS: an assessment of the influences on the due process of standard-setting. *Meditari Accountancy Research*, 24, 134–156.

World Commission on Environment and Development. 1987. *Our Common Future*. Oxford: Oxford University Press.

Yu, E. P. Y., Guo, C. Q. & Luu, B. V. 2018. Environmental, social and governance transparency and firm value. *Business Strategy and the Environment*, 27, 987–1004.

Zhou, S., Simnett, R. & Green, W. 2017. Does integrated reporting matter to the capital market? *Abacus*, 53, 94–132.

Zhou, S., Simnett, R. & Hoang, H. 2019. Evaluating combined assurance as a new credibility enhancement technique. *Auditing: A Journal of Practice & Theory*, 38, 235–259.

3. Convergence of sustainability reporting standards for sustainable development: are salient institutions obliging?

Hammed Afolabi, Ronita Ram and Gunnar Rimmel

1   INTRODUCTION

In recent years, there has been a growing urgency to address pressing environmental, social and governance (hereafter ESG) challenges, driven by the recognition of sustainable development as a global imperative (O'Dwyer and Unerman, 2020; United Nations, 1987). Importantly, the recognition of sustainable development as a global concern has prompted organisations, governments, and stakeholders to commit more attention to the business impact on people, planet, and society at large (Hamad et al., 2023; Lee et al., 2020). As a result, sustainability reporting has emerged as a powerful tool for businesses to measure, disclose, and manage their ESG performances (Stolowy and Paugam, 2018). However, the proliferation of sustainability reporting institutions and standards has created a fragmented landscape, resulting in confusion, inefficiencies, and limited comparability of reports (Humphrey et al., 2017; ICAEW, 2020). Institutions that develop and provide sustainability reporting standards and guidelines include the Global Reporting Initiative (GRI), the Climate Disclosure Standards Board (CDSB), the World Resources Institute, the Task Force on Climate-Related Financial Disclosure (TCFD), and the Value Reporting Foundation (VRF).[1] Thus, the sustainability reporting terrain has been conceptualised as a contested arena due to the plethora of the sustainability institutions and diversity in their behaviour (Afolabi et al., 2022).

Consequently, the demand for the convergence of sustainability reporting standards has garnered substantial momentum over the last decade (Adams and Abhayawansa, 2022). In particular, the push for the convergence is most driven by influential and international organisations like the World Bank, the International Federation of Accountants (IFAC), the Impact Investing Institute, and the World Economic Forum, among others. These international organisations advocate a unified framework to enhance comparability, consistency, and transparency in the sustainability reporting terrain (see Barker and Eccles, 2018; Eumedion, 2020a; 2020b; Accountancy Europe, 2020; Impact Investing Institute, 2020). The focal point of the discussions among these international organisations predominantly revolves around issues pertaining to materiality, scope, core priorities, audience, and the purpose of reporting (IFAC, 2020a; Accountancy Europe, 2020). In response, prominent standard-setting bodies from the financial reporting sphere, such as the IFRS Foundation / International Sustainability Standards Board (ISSB), the European Financial Reporting Advisory Group (EFRAG), and the Securities Exchange Commission (SEC) in the USA (with a focus on climate-related disclosure), have intervened in the sustainability arena to contribute to its standardisation, particularly for sustainable development (Abela, 2022; Afolabi et al., 2022).

However, the entry of these two influential standard-setting entities (IFRS Foundation and EFRAG) into the sustainability arena has been observed to exacerbate the existing confusion and intricacies within this domain. For instance, Afolabi et al. (2023) demonstrate that the actions taken by the IFRS Foundation/ISSB and EFRAG in the sustainability arena stem from the interest of specific international organisations, and their strategic behaviour is aimed at influencing the direction of regulatory norms to align with the preferences of those international organisations. This therefore underscores the pivotal role that certain international organisations, such as IFAC, the World Bank, the World Economic Forum, and others, can play in regulating sustainability reporting, and how their perceptions are influential in shaping the convergence of sustainability standards and guiding the actions of standard setters. Furthermore, this highlights how they can significantly impact the direction of business behaviour concerning sustainable development.

Nonetheless, a considerable body of research has investigated the activities of various sustainability institutions, exploring their frameworks, guidelines, and governance structures (e.g., Afolabi et al., 2022; Adams, 2015; Flower, 2015; Tweedie and Martinove-Bennie, 2015). Additionally, other scholars have examined the critical behaviour of emerging sustainability standard-setting bodies like the IFRS Foundation/ISSB, EFRAG, and the European Commission (see Abela, 2022; Afolabi et al., 2023; Giner and Luque-Vilchez, 2022). Further, Adams and Mueller (2022) have scrutinised the engagement of academics with the IFRS Foundation Trustee's consultation paper on sustainability reporting. However, this chapter takes a unique perspective by delving into the intricacies of the convergence process regarding sustainability reporting standards for sustainable development. It primarily focuses on the active involvement and impact of influential international organisations, like IFAC, the World Bank, the International Organization of Securities Commissions (IOSCO), the International Monetary Fund (IMF), the Organisation for Economic Co-operation and Development (OECD) and others, which, while not standard setters themselves, play a significant role in pushing for this convergence. In particular, this chapter extensively explores whether these influential international organisations contribute positively to the pursuit of convergence in sustainability reporting standards.

Consequently, through the examination of the challenges and contributions of the above influential organisations in driving the convergence of sustainability reporting, this chapter aims to make a valuable contribution to the ongoing discussion regarding the establishment of unified sustainability reporting standards. Additionally, it aims to scrutinise the influence exerted by international organisations that, while not standard setters themselves, play a significant role and hold salient stakeholders' positions in this realm. Importantly, our recognition of these international organisations as salient stakeholders is rooted in their diverse sources of influence, which encompass the capacity to steer and impact the decisions and initiatives of standard-setting bodies within the sustainability domain (Afolabi et al., 2023; Giner and Arce, 2012). Therefore, we contend that this chapter makes a significant contribution because these international organisations have influence to either endorse or reject the convergence of sustainability reporting standardisation, leveraging their inherent capacity to promote the acceptance of specific decisions that align with their own objective in this context (Camfferman and Zeff, 2007; 2018).

The remainder of this chapter is structured as follows. Section 2 presents the case for convergence issues in the sustainability arena and the role of salient institutions. Section 3 introduces the theoretical framework, the stakeholder salience model, which underpins the main argument of this chapter. Section 4 outlines the research methodology employed, and Section 5 presents the analysis and findings. Finally, Section 6 concludes the chapter and suggests future directions for research.

2   CONVERGENCE OF SUSTAINABILITY REPORTING FOR SUSTAINABLE DEVELOPMENT: CHALLENGES AND ROLE OF THE SALIENT INSTITUTIONS

In 1987, the United Nations World Commission on Environment and Development drew attention to the urgent requirement for comprehensive measures to safeguard both people and the environment (United Nations, 1987). Further, the Commission argued that sustainable development should possess certain overarching characteristics, as well as a broad strategic framework for its achievement (United Nations, 1987, p.1). Consequently, in 2015, the United Nations General Assembly established 17 Sustainable Development Goals (SDGs), which represent a set of distinct targets aimed at fostering a world where economic growth and human well-being are attained in an environmentally sustainable, socially equitable, and economically inclusive manner (United Nations, 2022). These targets encompass a wide range of activities and significant issues, including SDG 13 (climate action) and SDG 7 (clean energy), among others. As a result, sustainable development has increasingly become ingrained as a fundamental component of global endeavours to address the challenges posed by climate change, environmental degradation, and social inequality.

Consequently, given the heightened prominence of sustainable development as a global concern, the necessity for companies to disclose their impact on sustainability has emerged as a central topic of discussion in corporate reporting (Adams, 2017). Importantly, there has been a notable surge in policy initiatives and scrutiny pertaining to companies' responsibility for their contributions to sustainable development megatrends, such as climate change, biodiversity, human rights, inequality, and responsible consumption and production, among others (see Oelze et al., 2016; Hamad et al., 2023). In turn, the convergence of sustainability reporting has garnered significant attention in recent years, as organisations, policymakers and stakeholders recognise the need for a unified and globally accepted framework to measure and disclose ESG performance for sustainable development (Hamad et al., 2023). However, whilst there are multitudes of institutions and frameworks like the GRI, each framework has its own unique approach, reporting requirements, and target audiences, reflecting varying stakeholder interests and geographical contexts (Afolabi et al., 2022). Importantly, their differences have given rise to inconsistencies in reporting methodologies' metrics, and in disclosure requirements. Consequently, organisations face challenges in deciding which framework to adopt and how to ensure the relevance and reliability of their sustainability disclosures. Further, previous studies have long argued that the diversity hinders stakeholders' ability to assess and compare organisational sustainability performance (Giner and Luque-Vilchez, 2022).

Consequently, the concept of convergence is seen as a potential solution to streamline sustainability and address this challenge by establishing common reporting principles and metrics, facilitating meaningful comparisons across organisations and sectors (Adams and Abhayawansa, 2022). The goal is to establish a common language for sustainability reporting that transcends geographical boundaries, facilitates comparability, and enhances the usefulness of reporting information (Accountancy Europe, 2020). However, certain influential institutions, such as standard-setting bodies, regulatory authorities, and international organisations have been conceived to have a significant role to play in shaping the convergence of accounting standard setting (Camfferman and Zeff, 2018), which can also be extended to the sustainability arena. This is because these various institutions possess the power to influence the standard-setting process and acceptance through the development of guidelines, mandates, and recommendations. For instance, the IFRS Foundation and EFRAG have recently expanded their focus to include sustainability reporting, signalling a shift towards integrating financial and non-financial information (Afolabi et al., 2023). In this vein, the influence of these various institutions can be observed in multiple ways.

Firstly, non-state sustainability standard-setting bodies, like the GRI and IIRC, actively engage in dialogue with stakeholders to refine reporting frameworks and align them with evolving sustainability challenges (Humphrey et al., 2017). In fact, in furthering this commitment, five standard-setting institutions of international significance, the Carbon Disclosure Project, the Sustainability Accounting Standards Board (SASB), the CDSB, the GRI and the IIRC, have co-published a shared vision of the elements necessary for more comprehensive corporate reporting and issued a joint statement of intent to drive towards this goal (Carbon Disclosure Project, 2023). Such institutions often rely on the expertise and feedback of multiple stakeholders, including businesses, investors, and civil society organisations, to ensure the credibility and relevance of the reporting standards (Afolabi et al., 2022). Secondly, regulatory authorities, both at national and international levels, have begun mandating or encouraging the adoption of specific reporting frameworks. For example, the European Union's Non-Financial Reporting Directive and the Corporate Sustainability Reporting Directive aim to harmonise sustainability reporting practices across member states (Kinderman, 2020). These regulatory interventions can act as catalysts for convergence, as organisations strive to comply with mandated standards and streamline their reporting processes.

Thirdly, whilst the roles of standard-setting bodies and regulatory bodies appear significant, the roles of influential international organisations, such as the World Bank, the International Monetary Fund (IMF), the International Organization of Securities Commission (IOSCO), and the big audit firms (KPMG, PwC, Deloitte, and Ernst and Young), are substantial in the direction of accounting standard-setting processes and the acceptance of accounting standards globally (see Alali and Cao, 2010; Dobler and Knospe, 2016). Moreover, academic scholars have long argued that accounting regulations, and standard setting and acceptance, are strongly influenced by political and economic factors (e.g., Ball, 2006; Camfferman and Zeff, 2007). For example, in the context of the IFRS Foundation, the development of the IFRS by the International Accounting Standards Board (IASB) necessitates the consideration of various stakeholders' concerns. These stakeholders include international organisations, global public authorities, audit firms, investment banks, and multinational organisations (Camfferman and Zeff, 2018). Consequently, previous research has consistently argued that the composition of the IFRS Foundation is significantly influenced by G20 countries (Dobler and Knospe, 2016). Further, Alali and Cao (2010) demonstrate the influence of international institutions such as the World Bank and the IOSCO in the promotion and adoption of IFRS. In the same vein, previous studies have also shown that the IASB's funding is provided by prominent audit firms, and the G8, including the European Commission (Dobler and Knospe, 2016).

Additionally, there is other substantial evidence concerning the reliance of the IASB on influential international organisations for endorsement, including financial support, raising serious concerns about the independence of the IFRS Foundation and the IASB in their establishment of accounting standards. For instance, Eroglu (2017) reveals the heavy reliance of the IFRS Foundation on influential institutions like the IOSCO and the World Bank for the endorsement and adoption of its standards. Moreover, there are instances of lobbying by influential institutions, including the Big 4 accounting firms, during the development of IFRS 2, which indicates that the Foundation is occasionally influenced by certain interest groups and international organisations (Giner and Arce, 2012). These assertions therefore reinforce the significance of the influence held by various international organisations and the relevance of their perspectives in the accounting standard-setting spectrum. Consequently, the following section presents the employed theoretical framework that establishes the connection and coherence of the discussed elements with the premise proposed in this chapter.

3   STAKEHOLDER SALIENCE THEORY

In this chapter, we adopt the stakeholder salience model (hereafter SSM) developed by Mitchell et al. (1997) and further refined by Gifford (2010). This model enhances stakeholder theory by providing a comprehensive understanding of how stakeholder importance is established and highlights its transient nature (Magness, 2008). According to Mitchell et al. (1997), stakeholder salience refers to the level or significance of being noticeable, important, or prominent in the eyes of decision-makers. Further, they propose that stakeholders with a high degree of salience are crucial stakeholders who possess three essential factors: power, legitimacy, and urgency.

Consequently, Mitchell et al. (1997) conceptualised the concept of power, drawing upon Etzioni's (1964) power typology, to denote the stakeholder's capacity to exert substantial influence on decision-makers through coercive, normative, or utilitarian methods. Coercive power encompasses the utilisation of force, violence, or constraints, such as the imposition of sanctions. Normative power relies on symbolic resources like reputation and media attention. Utilitarian power pertains to tangible assets, including financial support, investment and the influence wielded by shareholders.

Legitimacy is predicated on the perception that an organisation's actions conform to the socially constructed system of norms, definitions, values, and beliefs (Mitchell et al., 1997). Suchman (1995) further categorised legitimacy into three forms: pragmatic, moral, and cognitive. The pragmatic legitimacy is contingent upon an organisation's ability to convince its stakeholders that its actions serve their best interest. Moral legitimacy hinges on whether the organisation's activities contribute to societal well-being as defined by the socially constructed system embraced by the stakeholders. Cognitive legitimacy pertains to the extent to which an organisation's activities align with the beliefs and expectation of its audience.

The final component in Mitchell et al.'s (1997) SSM is urgency. This denotes the degree to which a stakeholder's claim necessitates immediate attention from the organisation. Expanding this, Agle et al. (1999) assert that urgency plays a pivotal role in achieving maximum salience for a stakeholder. As a result, Mitchell et al. (1997) and Agle et al. (1999) explain that urgency emanates from two sources: "time sensitivity and criticality". The "time sensitivity" arises from time constraints or pressures, and "criticality" is associated with the significance of the stakeholders' claims.

Moreover, Gifford (2010) extends the SSM by introducing three additional moderating factors. The first factor pertains to the relative economic size of the stakeholder, which posits that stakeholders holding a larger economic stake in an entity possess greater power and legitimacy. Consequently, they enjoy enhanced access and influence over the governance of the entity. For instance, investors with a substantial share in a company are expected to have more representation and sway in the company's decision-making processes. The second factor revolves around management values, which reflects the degree of alignment between the values held by decision-makers and the values advocated by stakeholders in their claims. This factor assesses the extent to which decision-makers embrace and incorporate stakeholders' values into their decision-making practices. Lastly, the third factor encompasses coalition building, which encompasses the process through which stakeholders pool their resources and legitimacy to bolster their claims against an entity. Gifford (2010) purports that this can take the form of shareholder coalitions or other collective efforts aimed at amplifying their impact and influence.

Based on the above discussion, our contention remains that certain international organisations, despite not being standard-setting bodies, wield considerable influence over activities within the sustainability sphere, particularly regarding the behaviour of businesses in relation to sustainability reporting. This influence stems from their prominence, authority, and ability to facilitate and endorse the acceptance and implementation of sustainability reporting frameworks and standards within specific jurisdictions. Additionally, drawing from the perspective put forth by Gifford (2010), and as discussed in Section 2, we assert that powerful groups with significant economic size and influence over specific standard setters have a greater impact on shaping the decisions and directions pursued by businesses in their ESG performance. For instance, the IOSCO possesses coercive power to sway the following of standards within the capital market. Therefore, it becomes crucial to identify specific international organisations that qualify as definitive stakeholders in the sustainability arena to grasp their perspectives on the convergence of sustainability reporting, including the key challenges encountered in achieving sustainable development. To accomplish this, we employ the attributes of the SSM, particularly focusing on "power, urgency, and economic size" to identify these definitive stakeholders, comprehend their significance, and explore the concerns raised within this chapter.

4   METHOD

This chapter employs a qualitative research approach due to its capacity to provide comprehensive explanations and valuable insights into the phenomenon being investigated (Bryman and Bell, 2015). This approach is particularly crucial considering the involvement of diverse global organisations in the convergence of sustainability reporting, as well as the complex issues that give rise to tensions and uncertainties in sustainability standardisation. Therefore, it is necessary to explore the perspectives of these organisations and their potential impacts on sustainable development. To accomplish this, the chapter utilises qualitative content analysis as the analytical method, aiming to accurately present international organisations' viewpoints in the sustainability terrain by identifying specific characteristics that are presumed to shape their preferred approaches to regulating sustainability reporting, particularly concerning the key issues involved. Further, the decision to use this approach is motivated by its reputation as a reliable method for systematically examining the attitudes, values, and behaviours of

individuals (Rimmel and Cordazzo, 2021), achieved by identifying objective textual characteristics that are relevant to the phenomenon under study (Beck et al., 2010).

4.1   Application of the SSM Elements to Classify Influential International Organisations as Definitive Stakeholders in the Sustainability Arena

This study focuses on a selected group of international organisations that play a crucial role
in shaping and advancing sustainability reporting towards convergence. The identification of
these salient stakeholders is based on insights from Mitchell et al. (1997) and Gifford (2010),
which are discussed in Section 2. These organisations are considered salient stakeholders in
the sustainability landscape due to their unique attributes, reinforcing the significance of their
perspective among policymakers and standard setters. Moreover, their selection stems from
a historical legacy and seminar contributions in standard setting, predominantly within the
financial accounting sphere, coupled with their distinctive sway and authority in shaping and
endorsing potential sustainability standards, such as the European national standard setters,
the big accounting firms, and United Nations organisations (see Armstrong et al., 2010;
Camfferman and Zeff, 2018; Gauman and Dobler, 2019; Jorissen et al., 2012). While we
acknowledge the presence of diverse stakeholder groups in the sustainability standard-setting
arena, the selected organisations stand out as exceptionally active and wield substantial influence, potentially steering the decisions and orientations of various sustainability institutions.

For instance, regulators such as the IOSCO are recognised as salient stakeholders in the
sustainability arena. This is because they possess coercive power, enabling them to determine
the acceptance of standards within specific jurisdictions and capital markets. Additionally,
their endorsement of the IASB's work in the past further solidifies their influential positions. Moreover, IOSCO holds normative power due to its global influence, particularly
in the capital market, as it represents over 95% of global securities regulators. Secondly,
international organisations like the World Bank, United Nations groups, the Organisation for
Economic Co-operation and Development (OECD), and the four major audit firms (Deloitte,
PwC, KPMG, and Ernst and Young) are also regarded as influential groups in the sustainability arena. These organisations possess significant normative power and have a historical
involvement in the standard-setting processes of the IFRS Foundation and within the European
context. Thus, they have gained legitimacy through their efforts to promote the global acceptance and implementation of the IFRS standards.

Further, the committees of international organisations and influential groups are composed
of members from various global commercial, political, social, and economic organisations.
This composition grants them substantial power and influence over the standard-setting processes (Eroglu, 2017). Thus, we contend that this also represents a form of coercive power,
as these committees have the potential to impede the widespread adoption of accounting
standards on a global scale. Similarly, the Big 4 accounting firms, being the largest and most
prominent firms globally, exert considerable influence. They hold significant representation
within the governance structure of the IFRS Foundation and have a track record of shaping the
Foundation's decision-making processes. Additionally, these firms make substantial annual
contributions towards the funding of the IFRS Foundation (Giner and Arce, 2012). Further,
the European Commission and European national standard setters hold significant power and
legitimacy because they propose laws and make sure that the European Union's (EU) laws are
properly applied and ensure that the EU agendas are achieved (Gauman and Dobler, 2019).

Table 3.1   *International organisations categorised as definitive stakeholders*

International and influential organisations identified	Category	Relevant SSM attributes
IOSCO	Regulators	Coercive and normative power; pragmatic legitimacy
International Monetary Fund (IMF) G20's Financial Stability Board (FSB) World Bank World Federation of Exchange (WFE) International Federation of Accountants (IFAC) Organisation for Economic Co-operation and Development (OECD) United Nations Conference on Trade and Development (UNCTAD) United Nations Principles for Responsible Investment (UNPRI) United Nations Development Programme (UNDP)	Global institutions	Coercive and normative power; pragmatic legitimacy
Big 4 (KMPG, Deloitte, Ernst and Young, PwC)	Leading global accounting firms	Utilitarian and normative power; pragmatic legitimacy High economic size

Source: Authors' elaboration.

Further, the European Commission is perceived as having a sense of urgency, especially considering its role in expediting the development of the European Sustainability Reporting Standards (see Afolabi et al., 2023). Table 3.1 presents a list of the international organisations categorised as salient stakeholders with their primary attributes in this context.

4.2   Method of Data Collection and Analysis

To explore the engagement of the selected influential international organisations in the sustainability arena, specifically regarding convergence efforts and the primary issues causing tension within this domain, we examined publicly accessible documents. These documents encompassed all materials published by the influential international organisations concerning their perspectives on ongoing matters in the sustainability terrain, including their responses to consultation papers from various sustainability standard setters and policymakers.[2] The collection of these documents was sourced directly from the official websites of each international organisation, ensuring their status as official and reliable information. Table 3.2 provides a list of the documents examined in this chapter. Our focus centred on these documents due to their ability to provide insights into the prevailing perspectives of influential international organisations regarding sustainability reporting convergence and their viewpoints on the key issues that give rise to tensions and uncertainties in the sustainability domain.

Moreover, our analysis encompassed documents published between January 2018 and March 2023. The rationale for selecting this time frame is twofold. Firstly, in 2018, the demand for sustainability reporting convergence and identification of primary uncertainties and issues in sustainability reporting gained significant prominence, with notable publications supporting these claims available during this period (see Barker and Eccles, 2018; Corporate Reporting Dialogue, 2019). Secondly, other influential standard setters, including the IFRS

Table 3.2   List of documents examined from salient stakeholders

Influential international organisations	Documents examined
IOSCO	• Sustainable finance and the role of securities regulators and IOSCO (IOSCO, 2020a) • IOSCO response to the IFRS Foundation consultation on sustainability reporting (IOSCO, 2020b) • IOSCO welcomes ISSB's publication of sustainability standards exposure draft (IOSCO, 2022)
IMF	• How strengthening standards for data and disclosure can make a greener future (IMF, 2021)
G20's Financial Stability Board (FSB)	Response to the IFRS Foundation's consultation paper
World Bank	Response to the IFRS Foundation's consultation paper Strengthening the organisation (World Bank, 2023)
World Federation of Exchanges (WFE)	Response: IFRS Foundation's consultation on sustainability reporting (WFE, 2020)
IFAC	• Enhancing corporate reporting: the way forward (IFAC, 2020a) • IFAC responds to IFRS Foundation sustainability reporting consultation (IFAC, 2020b)
OECD	• OECD Business and Finance Outlook: Sustainable and Resilient Finance (OECD, 2020a) • OECD Response to the IFRS Foundation consultation on sustainability reporting (OECD, 2020b) • OECD Guidelines for Multinational Enterprises on Responsible Business Conduct (OECD, 2023)
Chair, working group on Sustainable Development Goals (SDGs) delivery expert group on resource management (EGRM) UN Economic Commission for Europe	Response to the IFRS Foundation's consultation paper
United Nations Conference on Trade and Development (UNCTAD)	• Guidance on core indicators for entity reporting on contribution towards implementation of the sustainable development goals (UNCTAD, 2019) • Response to the IFRS Foundation's consultation paper (UNCTAD, 2020)
United Nations Principles for Responsible Investment	Response to the IFRS Foundation's consultation paper
KPMG	Response to the IFRS Foundation's consultation paper
Deloitte	Response to the IFRS Foundation's consultation paper
Ernst and Young	Response to the IFRS Foundation's consultation paper
PwC	Response to the IFRS Foundation's consultation paper

Source: Authors' elaboration.

Foundation and EFRAG, engaged in substantial activities related to sustainability within this time frame, including the issuance of various consultation papers on sustainability, to which most of the selected influential international organisations responded.

The authors carefully read through all the documents multiple times to ensure accuracy, acknowledging variations in wording and phrasing among the different influential international organisations. To facilitate the analysis, *NVivo 12* software was employed for coding purposes. The coding process primarily focused on capturing the institutions' perspectives on "convergence" and the key urgent issues and tensions outlined in the introduction. These issues encompassed aspects such as the "convergence of global sustainability standards, materiality, target audience, reporting purposes and scope, and relevance to sustainable development" (see Accountancy Europe, 2020; IFAC, 2020a; Impact Management Project, 2020). Additionally, comments that were relevant but did not directly address a specific theme were also coded. To ensure rigour, the analysis undertook further scrutiny through keyword searches and reviews of the original submissions. Thus, within the broader thematic framework, specific codes were identified based on the data.

5   FINDINGS

The findings of this chapter are structured in two stages, which are derived from the premise and questions raised in this study. As discussed in Section 1, this chapter aims to explore the inquiry of whether influential global organisations contribute positively to achieving convergence in sustainability reporting and influencing business behaviour towards sustainable development. In the first stage, the chapter presents the key problems identified and the proposed solutions put forth by influential international organisations concerning the regulation of sustainability reporting and convergence of global sustainability standards. The second stage delves into perspectives of these influential organisations regarding the ongoing debates and significant issues that create tensions in the sustainability reporting field. These issues encompassed aspects like "materiality, target audience, reporting purposes and scope, and relevance to sustainable development" (see Accountancy Europe, 2020; IFAC, 2020a). Additionally, their preferences on how sustainability reporting should be conducted are examined. This analysis also considers the implications of directing business behaviour towards sustainable development.

5.1   Convergence of Global Sustainability Reporting Regulations and Standards

This theme encompasses the perspectives of influential international organisations concerning the complexities and challenges surrounding the current state of sustainability reporting regulation. Several prominent groups, particularly those within the capital market and regulatory bodies like the IOSCO, emphasised that the primary challenges in the field of sustainability reporting are the absence of a unified legal framework and the fragmentation of reporting frameworks. Further, other institutions like the IFAC highlighted that a significant gap exists between financial reporting and sustainability reporting, which thus necessitates immediate global integration and clarification. In particular, IFAC propose that the establishment of a new, independent, sustainability standard setter, potentially affiliated with the IFRS Foundation, could play a pivotal role in achieving this objective.

To provide further insight, Table 3.3 presents a comprehensive overview of the specific problems identified by each international organisation, along with their recommended solutions. This compilation sheds light on the diverse perspectives and proposed approaches of these organisations in tackling the challenges associated with sustainability reporting.

Based on the analysis presented in Table 3.3, it can be deduced that all international organisations agree that the current state of regulating sustainability reporting lacks the capability to drive sustainability reporting behaviour among businesses. The main premise they raised is the need to enhance sustainability performance and disclosure that can facilitate informed

Table 3.3   *Key problems identified, and solutions proposed*

Influential international organisations	Problems identified	Solution proposed
IOSCO	The reporting on ESG matters is characterised by inadequate quality and lack of consistency. The ESG disclosure of public companies is not sufficient to meet the requirements and expectations of major asset managers and investors (IOSCO, 2020a)	"Establishing a global system architecture for sustainability reporting under the IFRS Foundation could help to promote consistency and comparability across borders and reduce the risk of fragmentation" and "could help to promote consistency and comparability across borders and reduce the risk of fragmentation" (IOSCO, 2020b, p.2)
IMF	"Investors and policy makers face a lack of forward-looking, granular, and verifiable data – especially on firms' effort to move to sustainable business models (e.g., by reducing their greenhouse gas emissions)" (IMF, 2021)	Better disclosure of climate information by households, firms, and financial institutions. Standardised and decision-useful information will be critical to help meet the large financing and investment needs associated with climate change mitigation and adaptation. Convergence toward more-standardised sustainability reporting should now be a priority (IMF, 2021)
G20's Financial Stability Board (FSB)	The multitude of initiatives has inundated stakeholders, posing a risk of "greenwashing" the system	A global standardised sustainability reporting framework would help avoid fragmentation, improve market confidence, and promote financial stability, while providing material and decision-useful information to investors and a broader audience to consider climate related risks in financing and investment (FSB, 2020)
World Bank Group World Economic Forum	There is a need for more comprehensive information that is consistent, comparable, reliable, and verifiable, which pertains to attracting capital, especially to emerging markets (World Bank Group, 2020) There is a serious need for enhanced transparency and alignment. Metrics need to be capable of verification (World Economic Forum, 2020a)	A global set of internationally recognised sustainability reporting standards guiding disclosure of environmental, social and governance (ESG) information will bring the long-needed harmonisation and result in reliable, comparable, consistent disclosure necessary to attracting capital, especially to emerging markets (World Bank, 2020, p.1) Reporting of 21 core "metrics" focusing primarily on activities within the organisation's own boundaries (World Economic Forum, 2020b)
World Federation of Exchange (WFE)	Lack of enhance transparency and alignment. No metrics to ensure verification (WFE, 2020, p.1)	Materiality should be interpreted in relation to the significant stakeholders and the company itself. There is a need for a global set of internationally recognised standards

Influential international organisations	Problems identified	Solution proposed
IFAC	Lack of consistent, comparable, reliable, and assurable information relevant to enterprise value creation, sustainable development (IFAC, 2020a, p.1)	IFRS Foundation should intervene "to create an International Sustainability Standards Board adopting a 'building blocks' approach drawing on existing frameworks/standards" (IFAC, 2020b)
OECD	Strong growth in sustainability-focused investing has encouraged a proliferation of disclosure frameworks, metrics, rating methodologies and investment approaches. Currently, these practices vary so widely that they lack clear alignment with financial materiality or with non-financial environmental and social objectives (OECD, 2020a)	Need for international guidance to facilitate a broad-based shift to low-carbon activities and, despite legitimate regional and jurisdictional differences, it is critical that common ground is found to ensure sufficient global consistency of sustainability reporting (OECD, 2020b, p.1)
Chair, working group on Sustainable Development Goals (SDGs) delivery expert group on resource management (EGRM) UN Economic Commission for Europe	Lack of deep and useful metrics and reporting mechanisms to achieve sustainable development	There is a need to explore the financial purposes for which sustainability standards would be required Need to agree the range and nature of both shareholder and stakeholder interests: investors, board of directors, employees, communities, suppliers and customers, industry associations, civil society
United Nations Conference on Trade and Development (UNCTAD)	There is serious lack and inadequate ESG information and lack of ESG reporting standards (UNCTAD, 2019)	The need to foster efforts and cooperation in all initiatives towards a single, coherent, and robust set of standards on sustainability reporting that would provide consistent and comparable data, facilitate the interconnectivity of integrated reporting, and ensure an equal footing of financial and sustainability reporting (UNCTAD, 2020, p.1)
United Nations Principles for Responsible Investment (PRI)	The lack of high quality, relevant and comparable corporate sustainability data remains one of the central challenges faced by investors seeking to integrate sustainability risks into their processes and increase their contribution to sustainability outcomes (PRI, 2020, p.2)	Sustainability reporting should: Provide current and forward-looking information to assess the full range of sustainability risks and opportunities Enable investors and other stakeholders to consistently assess and compare a company's sustainability performance and alignment in the context of long-term sustainability goals and thresholds Recognise the relevance of global and local sustainability objectives in contextualising and tracking a company's sustainability performance (PRI, 2020, p.3)

Influential international organisations	Problems identified	Solution proposed
KPMG	The existence of multiple reporting frameworks and standards that differ in metrics, definitions, and priorities The specific information requirements of ESG rating and ranking agencies No metrics to ensure verification	There is an urgent need for a global set of internationally recognised sustainability reporting standards. We believe that the IFRS Foundation has a key role to play in setting these standards considering its capital market focused mission, its expertise, know-how, due process, and governance structure (KPMG, 2020, p.3)
Deloitte	Divergent concerns in the interpretations regarding materiality Lack of clear assurance indicators	We support standard setting at a global level because global issues need global solutions. Businesses have global supply and value chains, face global risks, and have global investors. Issues such as climate change and achieving the UN Sustainable Development Goals require a global approach (Deloitte, 2020, p.1)
Ernst and Young	The existence of multiple reporting frameworks and standards that differ in metrics, definitions, and priorities Divergent concerns in the interpretations regarding materiality Lack of clear assurance indicators The very existence of multiple frameworks and methodologies with different perspectives contradicts the greater goal of global standards (EY, 2020, p.3)	There is urgent need to resolve the confusion in the sustainability reporting landscape and show a commitment to working towards a comprehensive corporate reporting system (EY, 2020)
PwC	The existence of multiple reporting frameworks and standards that differ in metrics, definitions, and priorities Divergent concerns in the interpretations regarding materiality Lack of clear assurance indicators	There is a need for urgent development of a single set of global sustainability reporting standards to address the needs for corporate reporting beyond financial reporting. We believe that this can be achieved by creating an Independent Sustainability Standards Board (SSB) within the sphere of the IFRS Foundation (PwC, 2020, p.1)

Source: Authors' elaboration.

decision-making among users. Moreover, there is a widespread consensus among these organisations that the proliferation of reporting frameworks and standards, which possess varying and conflicting metrics, definitions, and priorities, is the primary driver of the challenges faced by businesses in their pursuit of sustainable development.

However, notable differences emerge in the approaches recommended for regulating sustainability reporting. Certain groups advocate the involvement of new standard setters from the financial reporting domain, asserting that the existing challenges in the sustainability field cannot be adequately addressed without their intervention. This raises concerns regarding the underlying motivations behind the proposed solutions put forth by specific institutions like the IFAC, IOSCO, and the World Bank Group. This is because of their specific claim regarding the need for the IFRS Foundation, and lack of consideration of how the efforts of existing sustainability institutions like the GRI can be leveraged, and how different standards can be effectively utilised in combination to achieve substantial harmonisation of disclosure, metrics, and indicators. Therefore, this analysis prompts further explorations, which leads to the second theme, which examines the perspectives of influential international organisations regarding the primary issues that contribute to tensions and uncertainty in the sustainability arena. These perspectives will be examined with the consideration of the various solutions proposed by these organisations, shedding light on the complexities and potential paths forward in addressing these challenges and tensions.

5.2 Perspectives of Influential International Organisations on the Primary Issues Causing Tensions and Uncertainty in the Sustainability Arena

5.2.1 Scope and relevance to sustainable development

The importance of understanding and disclosing climate change risks is strongly emphasised by certain influential groups, given the ongoing escalation of global environmental damage and the lack of reliable data to assess the financial vulnerability of companies to climate-related risks. Particularly, global organisations such as the IFAC and the big audit firms, which represent some of the most influential accounting profession groups, urge key policymakers and emerging standard setters like the IFRS Foundation to prioritise the issue of climate change and its associated risks. They call for a comprehensive examination of how these risks can potentially impact an enterprise's ability to create value:

... the Foundation's initial focus on climate-related financial disclosures would be appropriate given the importance of global consistency in the actions that are already beginning to be taken by certain national and regional authorities. (FSB, 2020, p.1).

... the IFRS Foundation must position the SSB with a comprehensive mandate to address sustainability topics relevant to enterprise value creation with a clear intent. And ... a climate approach only will not provide a sufficiently robust global platform to support/accommodate jurisdiction-specific sustainability reporting initiatives such as the EU, where policy and legislative momentum appears to embrace the broad range of sustainability issues. (IFAC, 2020b, p.10)

... SSB should prioritise climate-related risk in the first sustainability standards issues, because of its urgency and market and prudential regulators and investors have made clear their expectation for transparency and high-quality information on climate-related matters in mainstream financial reports. (Deloitte, 2020, p.12)

... Climate change poses an existential challenge to humanity. Recognizing the impact of climate change on economic and financial stability and performance, we are in the process of mainstreaming

> climate-related issues in the IMF's monetary, fiscal, and financial sector policies ... standardizing climate-risk reporting at the global level will help achieve these objectives. (IMF, 2020, p.1)

> ... We believe that a global solution should be focused on promoting global standards that are relevant to long-term enterprise value creation as a baseline for wider corporate reporting. (KPMG, 2020, p.9)

Nevertheless, although the recognition of climate-related risks finds support among various European and UN institutions, such as the European Supervisory Authorities, the OECD, and the United Nations Conference on Trade and Development (UNCTAD), these institutions emphasise the crucial need to enhance consistency and comparability in sustainability reporting. They assert that improving these aspects of reporting is essential for effectively implementing the Sustainable Development Goals (SDGs) adopted in 2015. Further, by highlighting the importance of consistency and comparability, these organisations underscore the significance of standardised and reliable sustainability reporting practices. They further argue that such practices enable better assessment, monitoring, and comparison of organisations' environmental and social performance, facilitating informed decision-making and fostering progress towards achieving the SDGs. Following this, their premise remains that with consistent and comparable data, policymakers, investors, and stakeholders can more effectively evaluate sustainability efforts of businesses and identify areas where improvements are needed. In particular, the UNCTAD and WFE believe that this perspective aims to enhance the transparency and accountability of organisations, ultimately contributing to the collective pursuit of sustainable development:

> ... promote high-quality and comparable sustainability reporting by enterprises based on a limited number of core indicators common to all types of businesses aligned with the SDG monitoring framework. (UNCTAD, 2020, p.1)

> ... supports the IFRS Foundation's initial focus on climate-related disclosures, based on an initial broad definition of potential environmental factors, and it should endeavour to address environmental and other sustainability reporting issues after the climate-specific issues are addressed. (OECD, 2020b, p.7)

> ... the environmental issues are interdependent, and therefore, climate-related disclosures need to go hand in hand with the other environmental issues. (UNDP, 2020, p.3)

> ... it is important to ensure that a future sustainability standards board does not solely focus on climate. (European Supervisory Authorities (ESA), 2020, p.2)

> ... WFE acknowledges the urgency around climate-related financial disclosures ... this should not be allowed to hinder progress around the "S" and "G" (as well as non-climate related environmental issues) of ESG reporting. ... social and governance disclosures may be more salient, and an exclusive focus on climate-related financial disclosures could slow down progress on the broader ESG reporting agenda. (WFE, 2020, p.4)

> ... a key element to foster sustainable growth in economic activities enabling contributing to environmental, social and governance-related objectives, is to improve data availability, and there with the public disclosure of relevant metrics by reporting entities. (ESA, 2020, p.1)

5.2.2   Materiality

The concept of materiality is the subject of frequent discussion and high importance among influential groups who are actively proposing and deliberating on key ESG issues and risks that should be considered significant for disclosure. These groups generally advocate greater clarity and a broader scope in sustainability reporting, which encompasses the disclosure of impacts from all organisations, regardless of their jurisdiction, size, type, or industry. They argue that reporting should not be limited to climate risk of financial aspects alone. However, there are differing opinions among other significant definitive stakeholders. For instance, certain influential organisations within the United Nations group place emphasis on the concept of "double materiality". According to their perspective, it is essential to identify material issues that enhance enterprise value while also bridging the gap between financial materiality and the ESG impact associated with sustainable development.

> ... financial materiality cannot provide the entire picture. (EY, 2020, p.10)

> ... we recommend a planet–people–prosperity approach that respects basic human rights and needs as the founding assumptions, covering all the SDGs from the start. (Chair of the Working Group, UN Economic Commission EGRM, 2020, p.4)

> ... Double materiality is increasing in prominence, with initiatives such as the GRI and the EU's Non-Financial Reporting Directive using the concept. ... it may be more efficient to commence work on the broader concept of materiality. (WFE, 2020, p.8).

However, amidst these discussions, there are ongoing concerns regarding the prioritisation of either double materiality or financial materiality. Importantly, certain specific groups argue that it may be impractical to start with the concept of double materiality. Instead, they propose that efforts should be focused on understanding and addressing the aspects of "financial materiality", which revolve around key issues that can significantly impact an enterprise's ability to generate value:

> ... capital market development could benefit from widely accepted and consistent sustainability reporting standards. A global set of internationally recognized sustainability reporting standards guiding disclosure of ESG information will bring the long-needed harmonization and result in reliable, comparable, consistent disclosure necessary to attracting capital, especially to emerging markets. (World Bank Group, 2020, p.4)

> ... Addressing areas that impact enterprise value that are important to both investors and broader stakeholders is where the SSB should look to develop standards. (PwC, 2020, p.8)

> ... Sustainability reporting standards viewed through the lens of investors and capital market participants (i.e., materiality focused on enterprise value/financial materiality) will attract the broadest range of global support and promote the international consistency needed by global capital markets. (Deloitte, 2020, p.12)

5.2.3   Target audience

Prominent influential groups within accounting organisations and capital markets consistently emphasise, through various communications and published reports, the need for a focus on the most critical sustainability information that is relevant to investors and other market participants. Specifically, they emphasise the need to build on the existing momentum of sustainability institutions, such as IIRC and SASB, which primarily deal with financial risks and investors' interests, and demands for the IFRS Foundation to intervene following its historical focus on accounting standard setting:

> ... we agree with stakeholder sentiment that supports focusing on the importance of gaining legitimacy and acceptance with investors and market-focused public authorities, such as IOSCO ... the

SSB must determine, based on due process and analysis, which standards best serve the needs of investors – be they metrics or disclosure from SASB, GRI, or other initiatives. (IFAC, 2020b, p.12)

… Effective provision and allocation of green financing and investment depend on investors and other market players and stakeholders having access to material, standardized, and decision useful data and information. (IMF, 2020, p.1)

Nevertheless, influential groups, including salient stakeholders from the United Nations, have raised objections to the emphasis placed on prioritising the investor perspective and interests. These groups argue that a different starting point should be considered, characterised by:

… agreeing the nature of both shareholder and stakeholder interest addressed by these standards, such as investors, board of directors, employees, communities, suppliers and customers, industry associations, civil society. (Chair of the Working Group, UN Economic Commission EGRM, 2020, p.3)

6   DISCUSSIONS, CONCLUSIONS AND SUGGESTIONS FOR FUTURE RESEARCH

This chapter delves into the intricate process of achieving convergence in sustainability reporting standards for sustainable development, particularly the role played by influential international organisations in driving this convergence. The analysis also considers the question whether international organisations that are not directly involved in setting sustainability standards contribute positively to this endeavour. As presented in Section 5, there is a widespread desire among all the influential international organisations for urgent convergence, increased transparency, and relevance in sustainability reporting terrain. However, capital market participants, such as IOSCO and IFAC, argue that addressing the issue of fragmentation and complexity in the sustainability landscape specifically requires the intervention of the IFRS Foundation. Their argument is based on the belief that stakeholders, particularly investors, require a comprehensive understanding of how business risks and opportunities translate into long-term value creation, profitability, and their relationship to short-term financial performance. Consequently, we contend that the advancement of sustainability reporting is under the control of a double-edged sword, simultaneously reinforcing its traditional approaches, while also seeking to divert its focus from the primary tenets. This assumption would seem reasonable, considering relevant cases in this context.

Firstly, previous research has indicated that the push for harmonisation is driven by a desire to centralise control away from a multi-stakeholder process (Adams and Abhayawansa, 2022). Moreover, there is a perceived hegemony in the sustainability arena, which reinforces the practical challenges of achieving convergence in the sustainability landscape (Afolabi et al., 2022). Our findings confirm these conjectures. Further, by examining the perspectives of the selected influential international organisations in the sustainability terrain, this chapter reveals a self-centred approach among the organisations, driven by political and profit motives, influenced by a lack of understanding of the true essence of "sustainability". This lack of clarity is evident in the indecisiveness among certain groups regarding the definition and standardisation of "sustainability". Expanding on this, while there is a consensus that all relevant ESG issues are crucial for sustainable investment, transitioning to a greener economy, and safeguarding people and the planet, specific groups, particularly those from the capital market such as IOSCO, IFAC, IMF, the World Bank Group, and members of the Big 4 accounting firms, stress the importance of prioritising climate change and promote global standards that are align with long-term value creation as a foundational element for broader corporate reporting. Thus, the prevailing view among capital market participants is that sustainability reporting should prioritise climate change and global standards for long-term value creation. However, this view met only opposition and was contradicted by certain UN groups, such as UNCTAD, and other institutions like the OECD, who are the primary proponents and pioneers of sustainable development. This highlights the existence of political manoeuvring, empty rhetoric, and misguided beliefs within influential international organisations in the ongoing debate surrounding the convergence of sustainability reporting standards. Moreover, the capital market institutions' ability and influence to selectively choose which actions sustainability standards setters, like the IFRS Foundation, may take, further exacerbate the complexities of the debate.

Secondly, building upon the points above, we argue that the beliefs held by major capital market participants such as IOSCO, IFAC, IMF, and the World Bank Group are myths, marked by misconceptions and a lack of understanding regarding the true essence of sustainable development. Expanding on this, we assert that while sustainability metrics should undoubtedly align with financial materiality for reporting purposes, it is crucial to further explore the interplay between financial, environmental, social and governance materiality. Reporting entities, whether engaging in voluntary or mandatory reporting, must consider not only financial materiality but also environmental and social aspects (such as material risks posed by businesses to the environment, including biodiversity loss, climate change, fraud, child labour, etc.) in their disclosures. This points toward the concept of dynamic materiality highlighted in the white paper published by the World Economic Forum. According to the World Economic Forum (2020b), the financial significance and impact of environmental and social factors are dynamic and evolving. Certain environmental factors that were previously deemed non-financial may become financially material over time and contribute to long-term value creation. This is especially evident as the physical impacts of climate change become more prevalent, destructive, and costly.

Additionally, reputational risks, due diligence considerations, and the growing focus on environmental and social risks and opportunities all underscore the need for corporations to broaden the scope of their disclosures beyond immediate financial performance factors. This further highlights the misconception propagated by the belief that sustainability disclosure and performance should primarily revolve around investors and climate change risks. This perspective overlooks the comprehensive metrics that underpin the core principles of sustainable development, which served as the foundation for the emergence of sustainability reporting itself (see Enders and Remig, 2015). Thus, further research is needed to gain a more critical understanding of the perspectives and actions of influential international organisations in achieving the convergence of sustainability reporting, potentially employing alternative research approaches such as interviews. More importantly, this study has limitations in its scope, by focusing solely on salient institutions within a diverse pool of stakeholder groups in the sustainability sphere. Furthermore, the research only analysed published documents from the selected organisations, lacking the depth that may have been provided through interviews, which could uncover comprehensive insights into their decision-making rationale and pathways pursued.

Consequently, future studies can expand upon the findings of this chapter by exploring the following aspects:

- The perspectives of diverse stakeholders, including investors, regulatory bodies, non-governmental organisations (NGOs), and reporting entities, regarding the role played by international organisations in driving convergence and accountability in sustainability reporting. This exploration should encompass their expectations, challenges faced, and contributions made to the overall process.
- The effectiveness of capacity-building initiatives and knowledge-sharing efforts undertaken by international organisations to enhance the competencies of reporting entities and stakeholders in sustainability reporting.
- The roles and contributions of international organisations in addressing sector-specific challenges and variations in sustainability reporting practices across different industries or sectors.
- The interplay between international organisations and regulatory bodies in shaping sustainability reporting standards and disclosure requirements on both national and international scales. This research could scrutinise the dynamics, interactions, and potential conflicts of interest between these entities.
- The influence exerted by influential financial institutions, such as the IMF, World Bank Group, and development banks, in promoting convergence in sustainability reporting. The research could encompass the examination of their policies, guidelines, and support mechanisms aimed at encouraging reporting entities to adopt standardised sustainability practices.

NOTES

1. In June 2021, the Value Reporting Foundation was established through the merger of the International Integrated Reporting Council and the Sustainability Accounting Standards Board.
2. Like Pelger (2020), this chapter benefits from the involvement of two its authors in the European sustainability standard-setting process and the UK Endorsement Board (UKEB) Academic Advisory Group and Sustainability Working Group respectively. Their participation and membership lend valuable insights to the authors' decision-making regarding the inclusion of pivotal documents pertinent to the activities of the influential international organisations in this study. However, due to confidentiality concerns, the specific details of their participation and the privileged information they gained access to, which facilitated their comprehensive monitoring of publicly accessible data and information from influential international organisations, will not be disclosed.

REFERENCES

Abela, M. (2022). A new direction? The "mainstreaming" of sustainability reporting. *Sustainability Accounting, Management and Policy Journal*, 13(6), 1261–1283.
Accountancy Europe (2020). Follow-up paper: Interconnected standards setting for corporate reporting. Accountancy Europe, Brussels.

Adams, C.A. (2015). The International Integrated Reporting Council: a call to action. *Critical Perspectives on Accounting*, 27, 23–28.

Adams, C.A. (2017). The sustainable development goals, integrated thinking and the integrated report. London: International Integrated Reporting Council and the Institute of Chartered Accountants of Scotland.

Adams, C.A. and Abhayawansa, S. (2022). Connecting the COVID-19 pandemic, environmental, social and governance (ESG) investing and calls for "harmonisation" of sustainability reporting. *Critical Perspectives on Accounting*, 82, 102309.

Adams, C.A. and Mueller, F. (2022). Academics and policymakers at odds: the case of the IFRS Foundation Trustees' consultation paper on sustainability reporting. *Sustainability Accounting Management and Policy Journal*, 13(6), 1310–1333.

Afolabi, H., Ram, R. and Rimmel, G. (2022). Harmonization of sustainability reporting regulation: analysis of a contested arena. *Sustainability*, 14(9), 5517.

Afolabi, H., Ram, R. and Rimmel, G. (2023). Influence and behaviour of the new standard setters in the sustainability reporting arena: implications for the Global Reporting Initiative's current position. *Sustainability Accounting, Management and Policy Journal*, 14(4), 743–775.

Agle, B.R., Mitchell, R.K. and Sonnenfeld, J.A. (1999). Who matters to CEOs? An investigation of stakeholder attributes and salience. Corporate performance and CEO values. *Academy of Management Journal*, 42(5), 507–525.

Alali, F. and Cao, L. (2010). International financial reporting standards – credible and reliable? An overview. *Advances in Accounting*, 26(1), 79–86.

Armstrong, C., Barth, M.E., Jagolinzer, A. and Riedl, E. (2010). Market reaction to the adoption of IFRS in Europe. *The Accounting Review*, 85(1), 31–61.

Ball, R. (2006). International financial reporting standards (IFRS): pros and cons for investors. *Accounting and Business Research*, 36(1), 5–27.

Barker, R. and Eccles, R. (2018). Green paper: Should the FASB and IASB be responsible for setting standards for non-financial information? Available at: https://www.sbs.ox.ac.uk/sites/default/files/2018-10/Green%20Paper_0.pdf (accessed 10 April 2022).

Beck, A.C., Campbell, D. and Shrives, P.J. (2010). Content analysis in environmental reporting research: enrichment and rehearsal of the method in a British–German context. *British Accounting Review*, 42(3), 207–222.

Bryman, A. and Bell, E. (2015). *Business Research Methods*. 4th edn. Oxford: Oxford University Press.

Camfferman, K. and Zeff, S.A. (2007). *Financial Reporting and Global Capital Markets: A History of the International Accounting Standards Committee, 1973–2000*. Oxford: Oxford University Press.

Camfferman, K. and Zeff, S.A. (2018). The challenge of setting standards for a worldwide constituency: research implications from the IASB's early history. *European Accounting Review*, 27, 289–312.

Carbon Disclosure Project (2023). Five global organisations, whose frameworks, standards, and platforms guide the majority of sustainability and integrated reporting. Available at: https://www.cdp.net/en/articles/media/comprehensive-corporate-reporting (accessed 4 December 2023).

Corporate Reporting Dialogue (2019). Driving alignment in climate-related reporting: Year One of the Better Alignment Project. London: Integrated Reporting Foundation.

Deloitte (2020). Response to the IFRS Foundation consultation paper on sustainability reporting. Available at: https://www2.deloitte.com/bg/en/pages/audit/articles/deloitte-welcomes-the-role-of-the-ifrs-foundation-in-sustainability-standard-setting.html (accessed 3 February 2023).

Dobler, M. and Knospe, O. (2016). Constituents' formal participation in the IASB's due process: new insights into the impact of country and due process document characteristics. *Journal of Governance and Regulation*, 5(3), 50–66.

Enders, J.C. and Remig, M. (2015). *Research Handbook on Theories of Sustainable Development*. Abingdon, UK: Routledge.

Eroglu, Z.G. (2017). The political economy of international standard setting in financial reporting: how the United states led the adoption of IFRS across the world. *Northwestern Journal of International Law & Business*, 37, 459.

ESA (2020). IFRS Foundation's Consultation on Sustainability Reporting. European Supervisory Authorities. Available at: https://ifrs-springapps-comment-letter-api-1.azuremicroservices.io/v2/

download-file?path=570_27262_AlessandrodEriEuropeanSupervisoryAuthoritiestheESAs_0_E
SAsLettertoIFRSFoundationconsultationsustainabilityreporting.pdf (accessed 3 February 2023).

Etzioni, A. (1964). *Modern Organizations*. Englewood Cliffs, NJ: Prentice-Hall.

Eumedion (2020a). Feedback statement on Eumedion's green paper "towards" a global standard setter for non-financial reporting. Eumedion Corporate Governance Forum, The Hague.

Eumedion (2020b). Towards a global standard setter for non-financial reporting. Eumedion Corporate Governance Forum, The Hague.

EY (2020). Invitation to comment-IFRS Foundation consultation paper on sustainability report-ing. Available at: https://ifrs-springapps-comment-letter-api-1.azuremicroservices.io/v2/download -file?path=570_27420_LUCIWRIGHTEY_0_IFRSFoundationCPSustainabilityReportingco mmentletterDec222020.pdf (accessed 3 February 2023).

Flower, J. (2015). The international integrated reporting council: a story of failure. *Critical Perspectives on Accounting*, 27, 1–7.

FSB (2020). FSB response to the IFRS Foundation's Consultation Paper on Sustainability Reporting. Available at: https://ifrs-springapps-comment-letter-api-1.azuremicroservices.io/v2/download -file?path=570_27437_RupertThorneFinancialStabilityBoardFSB_0_ResponsetoIFRSpubliccon sultationpublication.pdf (accessed 4 February 2023).

Gaumann, M. and Dobler, M. (2019). Formal participation in the EFRAG's consultation processes: the role of European national standard setters. *Accounting in Europe*, 16(1), 44–81.

Gifford, J.E. (2010). Effective shareholder engagement: factors that contribute to shareholder salience. *Journal of Business Ethics*, 92(1), 79–97.

Giner, B. and Arce, M. (2012). Lobbying on accounting standards: evidence from IFRS 2 on share-based payments. *European Accounting Review*, 21(4), 655–691.

Giner, B. and Luque-Vilchez, M. (2022). A commentary on the "new" institutional actors in sustainabil-ity reporting standard-setting: a European perspective. *Sustainability Accounting, Management and Policy Journal*, 13(6), 1284–1309.

Hamad, S., Lai, F.W., Shad, M.K., Khatib, S.F.A. and Ali, S.E.A. (2023). Assessing the implementation of Sustainable Development Goals: does integrated reporting matter? *Sustainability Accounting, Management and Policy Journal*, 14(1), 49–74.

Humphrey, C., O'Dwyer, B. and Unerman, J. (2017). Re-theorizing the configuration of organizational fields: the IIRC and the pursuit of "Enlightened" corporate reporting. *Accounting and Business Research*, 47(1), 30–63.

ICAEW (2020). Non-financial reporting: Ensuring a sustainable recovery. Available at: non-financia l-reporting-ensuring-a-sustainable-global-recovery.ashx (icaew.com) (accessed 20 June 2023).

IFAC (2020a). Enhancing corporate reporting: The way forward. Available at: https://www.ifac.org/ knowledge-gateway/contributing-global-economy/discussion/enhancing-corporate-reporting-way -forward (accessed 20 January 2022).

IFAC (2020b). IFAC responds to IFRS Foundation sustainability reporting consultation. Available at: https://www.sustainability-reports.com/ifac-responds-to-ifrs-foundation-sustainability-reporting -consultation/#:~:text=The%20International%20Federation%20of%20Accountants%20%28IFAC %29%20submitted%20its,rationalize%20the%20current%20fragmented%20ecosystem%20for %20sustainability%20information (accessed 2 December 2022).

IMF (2020). IFRS Consultation paper on Sustainability Reporting. Available at: https://ifrs-springapps -comment-letter-api-1.azuremicroservices.io/v2/download-file?path=570_27865_Kristal inaGeorgievaInternationalMonetaryFundIMF_0_IFRSFoundation2020MDCoverLetterandRespon setoIFRSConsultation.pdf (accessed 3 February 2023).

IMF (2021). How strengthening standards for data and disclosure can make for a greener future. Available at: https://www.imf.org/en/Blogs/Articles/2021/05/13/how-strengthening-standards-for -data-and-disclosure-can-make-for-a-greener-future (accessed 10 April 2023).

Impact Investing Institute (2020). Reporting of environmental, social and economic outcomes. London: Impact Investing Institute.

Impact Management Project (2020). Reporting on enterprise value illustrated with a prototype climate-related financial disclosure standard. London: Carbon Disclosure Project, Climate Disclosure Standards Board, the Global Reporting Initiative, the International Integrated Reporting Council, and the Sustainability Accounting Standards Board.

IOSCO (2020a). Sustainable finance and the role of securities regulators and IOSCO. Available at: https://www.iosco.org/library/pubdocs/pdf/IOSCOPD652.pdf (accessed 12 May 2022).

IOSCO (2020b). IOSCO response to the IFRS Foundation consultation on sustainability reporting. Available at: https://www.iosco.org/library/comment_letters/pdf/IFRS-17.pdf (accessed 7 May 2024).

IOSCO (2022). IOSCO welcomes ISSB's publication of sustainability standards exposure drafts. Press release. Available at: https://www.iosco.org/news/pdf/IOSCONEWS638.pdf (accessed 7 May 2024).

Jorissen, A., Lybaert, N., Orensn, R. and Van der Tas, L. (2012). Formal participation in the IASB's due process of standard setting: a multi-issue/multi-period analysis. *European Accounting Review*, 21(4), 693–729.

Kinderman, D. (2020). The challenges of upward regulatory harmonization: the case of sustainability reporting in the European Union. *Regulation and Governance*, 14, 674–687.

KPMG (2020). IFRS Foundation-consultation paper on sustainability reporting. Available at: https://assets.kpmg.com/content/dam/kpmg/xx/pdf/2021/01/isg-comment-letter-ifrsf-consultation-paper-on-sustainability-reporting.pdf (accessed 3 February 2023).

Lee, K.H., Noh, J. and Khim, J.S. (2020). The blue economy and the United Nation's Sustainable Development Goals: challenges and opportunities. *Environment International*, 137, 105528.

Magness, V. (2008). Who are the stakeholders now? An empirical examination of the Mitchell, Agle and Wood Theory of stakeholder salience. *Journal of Business Ethics*, 83, 177–192.

Mitchell, R.K., Agle, B.R. and Wood, D.J. (1997). Toward a theory of stakeholder identification and salience: defining the principle of who and what really counts. *Academy of Management Review*, 22(4), 853–886.

O'Dwyer, B. and Unerman, J. (2020). Shifting the focus of sustainability accounting from impacts to risks and dependencies: researching the transformative potential of TCFD reporting. *Accounting, Auditing and Accountability Journal*, 33(5), 1113–1141.

OECD (2020a). *OECD Business and Finance Outlook 2020: Sustainable and Resilient Finance*. Paris: OECD Publishing.

OECD (2020b). OECD response to the IFRS Foundation consultation on sustainability reporting. Available at: https://ifrs-springapps-comment-letter-api-1.azuremicroservices.io/v2/download-file?path=570_27468_RobertPatalanoOrganisationforEconomicCooperationandDevelopmentOECD_0_OECDCommentLettertoIFRSFoundation_SustainabilityReporting_23Dec2020.pdf (accessed 3 February 2023).

OECD (2023) OECD guidelines for multinational enterprises on responsible business conduct. Available at: https://www.oecd-ilibrary.org/finance-and-investment/oecd-guidelines-for-multinational-enterprises-on-responsible-business-conduct_81f92357-en (accessed 15 June, 2023).

Oelze, N., Hoejmose, S.U., Habisch, A., Millington, A. (2016). Sustainable development in supply chain management: the role of organizational learning for policy implementation. *Business Strategy and the Environment*, 25, 241–260.

Pelger, C. (2020), The return of stewardship, reliability and prudence – a commentary on the IASB's new conceptual framework. *Accounting in Europe*, 17(1), 33–51.

PRI (2020). IFRS Foundation Consultation Paper on Sustainability Reporting. Available at: https://ifrs-springapps-comment-letter-api-1.azuremicroservices.io/v2/download-file?path=570_27306_RenvanMerrienboerUNPrinciplesforResponsibleInvestment_0_PRIresponseIFRSconsultationonsustainabilityreporting.pdf (accessed 4 February 2023).

PwC (2020). Consultation Paper on Sustainability Reporting. Available at: https://ifrs-springapps-comment-letter-api-1.azuremicroservices.io/v2/download-file?path=570_27430_HenryDaubeneyPricewaterhouseCoopersPwC_0_PwCresponsetoIFRSConsultationPaperonSustainabilityReporting.pdf (accessed 4 February 2023).

Rimmel, G. and Cordazzo, M. (2021). Deductive versus inductive content analysis: a methodological research note to disclosures studies in intellectual capital research, in J. Dumay, C. Nielsen, M. Lund and J. Guthrie (eds), *Research Handbook on Intellectual Capital and Business*. Cheltenham, UK and Northampton, MA, USA: Edward Elgar Publishing, pp. 109–124.

Stolowy, H. and Paugam, L. (2018). The expansion of non-financial reporting: an exploratory study. *Accounting and Business Research*, 48, 525–548.

Suchman, M.C. (1995). Managing legitimacy: strategic and institutional approaches. *The Academy of Management Review*, 20, 3, 571–610.

Tweedie, D. and Martinov-Bennie, N. (2015). Entitlements and time: integrated reporting's double-edged agenda. *Social and Environmental Accounting Journal*, 35(1), 49–61.

UN Economic Commission EGRM (2020). Response from: Chair, working group on sustainable development goals (SDG) delivery expert group on resource management (EGRM) UN Economic Commission for Europe. Available at: https://ifrs-springapps-comment-letter-api-1.azuremicroservices .io/v2/download-file?path=570_27957_JulianHiltonIndividual_0_CL562JulianHilton.pdf (accessed 3 February 2023).

UNCTAD (2019). Guidance on core indicators for entity reporting on contribution towards implemen-tation of the Sustainable Development Goals. Available at: https://unctad.org/system/files/official -document/diae2019d1_en.pdf (accessed 2 June 2023).

UNCTAD (2020). Response to IFRS Foundation Consultation Paper on Sustainability Reporting. Available at: https://ifrs-springapps-comment-letter-api-1.azuremicroservices.io/v2/download-file?path=570 _27798_TatianaKrylovaUnitedNationsConferenceonTradeandDevelopmentUNCTAD_0_Comm entletterontheIFRSFoundationConsultationPaperonSustainabilityReporting_17December2020.pdf (accessed 3 February 2022).

UNDP (2020). IFRS Consultation Paper on Sustainability Reporting. Available at: https://ifrs-springapps -comment-letter-api-1.azuremicroservices.io/v2/download-file?path=570_27543_MarcosNetoUni tedNationsDevelopmentProgramme_0_UNDP_Response_IFRS_Public_Consultation.pdf (accessed 12 February 2023).

United Nations (1987). *Our Common Future: Report of the World Commission on Environment and Development*. Available at: www.un-documents.net/ocf-02.htm (accessed 28 May 2022).

United Nations (2022). Sustainable Development Goals. Available at: www.un.org/sustainablede velopment/development-agenda/ (accessed 2 May 2022).

World Bank (2023). Strengthening the Organization. Available at: https://www.worldbank.org/en/about/ annual-report/strengthening-the-organization (accessed 10 February 2024).

World Bank Group (2020). Comments on Consultation Paper on Sustainability Reporting. Available at: https://ifrs-springapps-comment-letter-api-1.azuremicroservices.io/v2/download-file?path=570 _27501_SvetlanaKlimenkoWorldBankGroup_0_WBGIFRSSustainabilityComments.pdf (accessed 3 February 2023).

World Economic Forum (2020a). Toward Common Metrics and Consistent Reporting of Sustainable Value Creation. Geneva: World Economic Forum.

World Economic Forum (2020b). Embracing the New Age of Materiality: Harnessing the Pace of Change in ESG. Available at: https://www3.weforum.org/docs/WEF_Embracing_the_New_Age_of _Materiality_2020.pdf (accessed 6 December 2023).

World Federation of Exchanges (2020). Response: IFRS Foundation's Consultation on Sustainability Reporting. Available at: https://ifrs-springapps-comment-letter-api-1.azuremicroservices.io/v2/ download-file?path=570_27787_MushtaqAhmedWorldFederationofExchangesWFE_0_WFERes ponseIFRSSustainabilityReporting31122020.pdf (accessed 20 February 2023).

4. Research states and avenues in sustainability reporting: a building block approach

Blerita Korca, Ericka Costa and Frank Schiemann

INTRODUCTION

Sustainability reporting has been exercised by companies as a voluntary practice for a long time. Initially, companies published information about social aspects to complement conventional financial reporting. Subsequently, environment-related information was disclosed, and ultimately a more comprehensive approach, i.e., sustainability reporting, emerged. The Global Reporting Initiative (GRI), which represents the most frequently used reporting framework, provides the following definition for sustainability reporting:

> Sustainability reporting helps organizations to set goals, measure performance, and manage change in order to make their operations more sustainable. A sustainability report conveys disclosures on an organization's impacts – be they positive or negative – on the environment, society and the economy. In doing so, sustainability reporting makes abstract issues tangible and concrete, thereby assisting in understanding and managing the effects of sustainability developments on the organization's activities and strategy. (GRI, 2013, p. 3)

The definition above represents one of the earlier definitions of sustainability reporting provided by the GRI, which for more than two decades has developed and provided voluntary standards for sustainability reporting. According to a report of the International Platform on Sustainable Finance (IPSF, 2021), voluntary disclosure measures include frameworks, guidelines, or standards (hereafter reporting standards) that help companies identify, measure and report on relevant sustainability matters. The existing reporting standards have helped to institutionalize sustainability reporting over the years. While different reporting standards and frameworks generally aimed to assist companies in their reporting processes, there are some noteworthy differences between them. For instance, the standards and frameworks might differ in their target audience, disclosure content and level of details, or materiality definition. Those differences have implications as to how sustainability reports are published by companies and how report users read and understand the information provided. Considering that reporting standards have been used voluntarily by companies for a long time, research has found that they contain some drawbacks. Specifically, one of the limitations of voluntary sustainability reporting is considered to be the level of quality and information comparability (Jeffrey and Perkins, 2013; Korca *et al.*, 2021). Previous research characterized voluntary sustainability reporting as lacking objectivity and neutrality (Hibbitt and Collison, 2004; Jeffrey and Perkins, 2013) thus allowing companies a higher degree of freedom to decide what to report and how to report. To address the identified drawbacks of voluntary sustainability reporting, mandatory disclosure measures are being developed worldwide.

According to IPSF (2021), mandatory disclosure measures are on the rise and include laws or regulations (hereafter regulations), mandating certain firms to report on their sustainability matters. While reporting standards and regulations consider sustainability reporting as one enabling tool towards sustainable development, they differ in their motivations (Christensen *et al.*, 2021) and level of regulatory power. Reporting standards provide more or less detailed descriptions of what to disclose (e.g., specific disclosure items on a narrow or wide set of sustainability issues). Often, reporting standards are voluntary, meaning they merely provide guidance. Reporting regulations usually oblige a defined set of firms to engage in sustainability reporting, while often referring to one or several reporting standards for the specification of the disclosure content. Among the first regulations to mandate sustainability reporting is the Non-Financial Reporting Directive (NFRD) in the European Union (EU), issued in 2014 and in place from 2018. From 2024, the EU will implement the Corporate Sustainability Reporting Directive (CSRD), which will enlarge the scope of companies targeted and will request disclosure over a number of sustainability-related topics. In the United States (US) for instance, the Securities Exchange Commission (SEC) in March 2022 proposed a new rule to mandate climate-related disclosure for US-listed public companies (both domestic and foreign). Similar developments are occurring in other countries worldwide.

Currently, at the global scale, two main developments are taking place. First, following the emergence of the CSRD, the EU has tasked the European Financial Reporting Advisory Group (EFRAG) to develop the European Sustainability Reporting Standards (ESRS). The ESRS will mainly be required to be used by EU firms, and non-EU firms that are operating in the EU. Second, in parallel, but not directly linked to the development in the EU, the International Sustainability Standards Board (ISSB) is developing the IFRS Sustainability Disclosure Standards (IFRS SDS). Both reporting standards, the ESRS and IFRS SDS, are considered as crucial developments in the field of sustainability reporting because both aim to overcome the limitations of previous reporting standards by achieving higher reporting quality and comparability.

The outlined developments motivate accounting researchers to investigate determinants and consequences of disclosure regulation and disclosure standards. Therefore, in this chapter, we provide the building block approach as a framework for a systematic assessment of both research and disclosure regulation/standards across the five building blocks of disclosure mandate, disclosure content, materiality definition, assurance, and disclosure channel.

Below, an introduction of the building blocks of sustainability reporting measures is provided. In this section, we discuss the characteristics of disclosure measures and highlight the main research around them. We also offer a table outlining how both the ESRS and IFRS SDS stand across the disclosure building blocks. Considering that the ESRS and IFRS SDS are new disclosure measures, which are expected to impose significant changes on companies' disclosure, it is relevant that research analyzes these new measures across the building blocks. Therefore, we also provide a section with an in-depth discussion of research avenues based on both the current state of research and the current development of international sustainability disclosure measures.

BUILDING BLOCKS OF SUSTAINABILITY REPORTING REGULATIONS

In this section, we will explain five central building blocks, which can be used to describe and analyze sustainability reporting measures. To the best of our knowledge, the building block approach was first used in the IPSF report (IPSF, 2021), which presented seven building blocks: disclosure content, mandatory versus voluntary, materiality, scope, assurance, disclosure channel, reporting standard. For the purpose of this chapter, it seems useful to consolidate and consider five building blocks. Specifically, we combine the building blocks of 'mandatory versus voluntary' and 'scope' as both address the underlying question, which companies are mandated to disclose. Furthermore, we do not elaborate on the building block of 'reporting standards', which was included in the IPSF report to consider whether and how national legislation (i.e., disclosure regulation) explicitly referenced existing and internationally accepted disclosure standards as guidelines for corporate sustainability disclosure. For the purpose of this chapter, it seems more useful to focus on the underlying building blocks influenced by disclosure standards (e.g., disclosure content, materiality).

In the following, we will introduce and explain the resulting five building blocks, scope/mandate, disclosure content, materiality, assurance, and disclosure channel, in more detail. Thereby, we link each building block to relevant literature in order to map the state of research.

Building Block: Scope/Mandate

The first building block refers to the question, which organizations – if any – are subject to the reporting regulation. Of course, any organization not covered by a disclosure mandate can provide sustainability information on a voluntary basis. Indeed, voluntary sustainability disclosures were a common occurrence in the past, but recent years have seen an increase in disclosure mandates around the world. Some of these disclosure mandates have been analyzed in accounting research, for example the mandate on integrated reporting in South Africa (Baboukardos and Rimmel, 2016; Barth *et al.*, 2017), the introduction of a CSR disclosure mandate in China (Chen *et al.*, 2018), a disclosure mandate of the US SEC regarding mine accidents (Christensen *et al.*, 2017), the disclosure of direct carbon emissions to the EPA in the USA (Bauckloh *et al.*, 2022; Tomar, 2023), disclosure of direct carbon emissions in the UK (Downar *et al.*, 2021), or the introduction of the Non-Financial Reporting Directive in the EU (Korca *et al.*, 2021; Fiechter *et al.*, 2022). In general, results show significant improvements in sustainability performance after disclosure mandates were introduced. At the same time, some studies report negative impacts on the financial or operational performance of companies falling under sustainability disclosure mandates (e.g., Christensen *et al.*, 2017; Chen *et al.*, 2018).

Barth *et al.* (2017) investigated the link between disclosure quality and firm value by focusing on firms reporting sustainability-related information mandatorily. Specifically, the authors use data from South Africa where integrated reporting (IR) is mandatory. Results show that there is a positive association between reporting quality and liquidity, which supports the capital market channel. Furthermore, the authors do not find evidence of a relationship between IR quality and cost of capital but find a positive association with the expected future cash flows. Thus, the results highlight that higher disclosure quality, caused by the mandatory regime, has positive financial consequences. In other settings such as the US or European Union, research has explored real effects stemming from sustainability disclosure mandates. Christensen *et al.* (2017) explore the real effects of mandatory disclosure for SEC-registered mine owners who have to report on their mine safety in financial reports. Using as a comparison group those mine companies not registered as SEC issuers, the authors find that including mine safety information in financial reports on a mandatory basis has positive effects on mining-related citations and injuries. More recently, Fiechter *et al.* (2022) investigated the real effects of the NFRD, which mandates sustainability disclosure of firms in the EU. The authors conduct a difference-in-differences analysis to better understand if companies reporting on sustainability matters on a mandatory basis actually improve their behavior. The findings show that firms complying with the NFRD increase their CSR-related activities. Importantly, it is noted that firms did so even before the official entry into force of the NFRD. The effect is stronger for firms with low levels of sustainability reporting and activities prior to the regulation. Therefore, Fiechter *et al.* (2022) conclude that the specific introduction of the NFRD has documented some real effects in CSR. Downar *et al.* (2021), Bauckloh *et al.* (2022) and Tomar (2023) analyzed the effect of disclosure mandates specifically for carbon emissions in a UK and a US setting. The studies consistently found that disclosure mandates are connected to decreases in carbon emissions or intensity. While the overall effects are significant, it can still be argued that the achieved emission reductions are not, in themselves, large enough to achieve science-based targets.

Overall, the findings of a range of empirical studies strongly support the notion that disclosure mandates lead to measurable real effects. Additionally, some evidence shows that firms with previously low sustainability performance or sustainability reporting activities are affected by the disclosure mandate, where typically sustainability performance is improved, but financial performance can be negatively affected. From a regulator's perspective, it seems that disclosure mandates can be a tool to motivate rather bad or more laggard firms to put sustainability issues on their agenda. However, the overall effect of disclosure mandates on sustainability should not be overestimated, because the disclosure requirements do not contain clear performance targets that firms are supposed to achieve. For example, there is no evidence that emission reductions due to disclosure mandates are anywhere near the necessary reductions for a net zero target in line with a 1.5- or 2-degree scenario. Therefore, it is important to understand that disclosure mandates are a complement to environmental policy, but by no means a substitute.

Building Block: Disclosure Content

Disclosure content is concerned with two questions: First, which topics should companies' sustainability reports address? And second, which specific measures or indicators are required or suggested by the respective disclosure standard or regulation? Disclosure measures can differ between sustainability topics in terms of content and character. Measures can be qualitative or quantitative, and measures can contain a direct link to financial implications or refer to non-financial aspects. Additionally, the specificity of measures can differ. For instance, some measures capture broad sustainability-related topics (e.g., ESG ranking or information about the company's sustainability advisory board) while others focus on a specific disclosure topic (e.g., direct carbon emission, work force accidents). Thus, depending on the respective measure, disclosure content requirements might differ. These differences can also be observed regarding the level of detail for such disclosure content. Furthermore, measures can aim to capture a retrospective and forward-looking perspective. For example, while carbon emissions for Scope 1, 2 and 3 typically refer to the last fiscal year (i.e., retrospective), climate-related risk disclosure or disclosure of a net zero target provides forward-looking information. Lastly, while many disclosure measures directly focus on the reporting entity, disclosure requirements can transcend the company and extend to supply chain issues as well, thus covering a more comprehensive picture of companies' actions towards sustainability.

Following the emergence of sustainability reporting measures, researchers in the field have explored, for instance, the level of completeness of sustainability information (Melloni *et al.*, 2017), disclosure of forward-looking information (Sakhel, 2017; Schiemann and Sakhel, 2019), and reporting on sustainable supply chain practices.

Completeness of reporting: Melloni *et al.* (2017) explored the level of disclosure completeness of companies using integrated reports (IR). Specifically, the authors focus on the conciseness, completeness and balance in the IR, which are characterized as the high-quality characteristics of an IR. Drawing on impression management theory, the authors report that firms that have weak financial performance also have weaker IR (i.e., less concise, balanced or complete). The same holds for firms with poorer sustainability performance. Their reports are considered less complete and with a low quality of reporting. Thus, Melloni *et al.* (2017) emphasized that early adopters of IR provided more information in terms of volume, but that it is not necessarily high-quality information.

Supply chain reporting: Other studies have looked into the supply chain disclosure practices of companies. Antonini *et al.* (2020) focus on the sustainability reporting boundaries and how those affect the definition of social risks across the supply chain. The authors use the case of Inditex, operating in the ready-made garment industry, to better understand how their boundary setting in sustainability reporting takes place and to what extent it is influenced by sub-political drivers. Findings show that the definition of sustainability reporting boundaries influences the exclusion and abstraction of information.

Forward vs backward looking information / risk disclosure: Previous research has analyzed how different types of risk are perceived by firms (Sakhel, 2017) and the association of risk disclosure with information asymmetry (Schiemann and Sakhel, 2019). Sakhel (2017) focused on risk disclosure to better understand how firms perceive the different types of risk, such as regulatory, physical and market risk. Focusing on data obtained from the Carbon Disclosure Project, Sakhel (2017) shows that the majority of firms feel less exposed to physical and market risks, in comparison to regulatory risks. Furthermore, results show that firms in regulated industries (i.e., high-emitting firms) implement more actions to respond to regulatory requirements. The study also highlights that market or physical threats might be insufficient to drive change in corporate behavior for climate action. Schiemann and Sakhel (2019) explore the role of physical climate-risk disclosure on information asymmetry. The authors focus on an EU setting, which covers firms that are or are not mandated to disclose direct carbon emissions to the EU Emissions Trading System. Results show that disclosure of a higher exposure to physical risks is associated with lower information asymmetry for mandated firms, whereas for other firms the direction of the relationship reverses.

Overall, research on specific questions around disclosure content is rather sparse, especially empirical research focused on a more aggregate level, such as whether firms disclose any sustainability information or on ESG disclosure scores. However, the current development towards more disclosure mandates and more detailed disclosure requirements makes it possible and necessary to also analyze the challenges and consequences of reporting about specific disclosure items. Thereby, supply chain-related and forward-looking information is especially relevant as it poses challenges for preparers and readers.

Building Block: Materiality

In the context of sustainability reporting, materiality is concerned with the question of which sustainability issues can potentially impact firm-related decisions of a company's stakeholders. Accordingly, materiality can be understood as a prioritization tool, which companies apply to determine which information to report. The concept of materiality is deeply rooted in financial accounting, and in this context, it has a strong focus on (potential) investors and their investment decisions, although this focus does not necessarily translate to sustainability reporting, where a wider range of stakeholders can and should be considered. Of course, materiality also plays an important role in auditing, where the concept is applied to determine which errors exceed certain materiality thresholds and, accordingly, must be acknowledged by auditors and addressed by companies. Despite, or because of, the central importance of the materiality concept, there is no clear or agreed-upon guidance about specific threshold values. Even in financial accounting, rules of thumb are communicated with some ambiguity (e.g., information is material if it translates to at least 1–5% of total assets or to 5–10% of income).

In sustainability reporting, it can be argued that the ambiguity about the concept is even higher. First, many sustainability issues do not easily translate into financial terms, which makes it more problematic to formulate a financial threshold. Second, stakeholders other than investors are not necessarily relying on financial information for their decision-making. For example, people living in the near vicinity of a company's production facilities might be more interested in toxic emissions, noise, or water usage. In general, the understanding of materiality in sustainability reporting can be categorized into three groups.

The first group of materiality conceptions is referred to as financial materiality, and is very closely related to the understanding of materiality in financial accounting. Typically, it is focused on (potential) investors. Thereby, materiality refers to sustainability-related issues, which potentially influence a company's current or future financial performance. This conception follows an outside-in perspective, meaning it considers the impact of sustainability issues on the reporting company.

The second group of materiality conceptions is referred to as double materiality because it extends the outside-in perspective with an inside-out perspective. These conceptions consider a wider range of stakeholders and how companies' activities impact these groups. Accordingly, the inside-out perspective is also said to capture the impact materiality – meaning that double materiality considers both financial and impact materiality. In some cases, the (impact) materiality conceptions refer to specific stakeholder groups (such as employees, customers, general public, or governments). Often, companies initiate a materiality assessment to understand which sustainability issues are most relevant to different stakeholder groups. However, such assessments typically address stakeholders, which are able to directly communicate their opinions and views, but the inside-out perspective can also apply to stakeholder groups, which cannot express themselves (e.g., nature, future generations), and for which it is therefore difficult to identify material issues.

The third group aims to unify financial and double materiality through the concept of dynamic materiality. This follows the argument that any sustainability issue that is material from an inside-out perspective will eventually become financially material in the near or far future. For example, carbon emissions were not considered to be financially material in the 1980s or 1990s, but now – due to a better understanding of its impact on climate change, the introduction of carbon prices, and reputational effects – carbon emissions clearly are financially material for any high-emitting company. While the concept's approach to express the link between financial and double materiality is straightforward, it is not clear how quickly different sustainability issues can develop from inside-out material to outside-in material. This makes it difficult for companies to operationalize this materiality conception.

Standard setters can provide guidance about the materiality assessment process. For example, the SASB published its Materiality Map™, which indicates the industry-specific financial materiality for a range of sustainability issues. The GRI provided extensive explanations about the materiality assessment process to guide companies in identifying sustainability issues under the conception of double materiality. The ESRS also provides more detailed explanations about financial and impact materiality, and the EFRAG provides a guidance document for materiality assessment (EFRAG, 2023).

Researchers are increasingly focusing on materiality-related issues of sustainability disclosure. However, there seems to be a methodological divide, meaning that publications focusing on financial materiality are, in general, applying quantitative methods, while papers focusing on double materiality are more qualitative. Thereby, empirical evidence shows that the financial materiality indications of the SASB are valid (Khan *et al.*, 2016), are used by capital market participants (Spandel *et al.*, 2020; Bochkay *et al.*, 2021; Serafeim and Yoon, 2022) and even lead to changes in firm behavior (Goettsche *et al.*, 2023). The area of potential research for double materiality is much wider as more stakeholders are considered, and accordingly research in this regard seems more fragmented. For example, there is evidence about the different perception of sustainability issues from different assurers (Edgley *et al.*, 2015) and from different stakeholder groups (Reimsbach *et al.*, 2020).

Building Block: Assurance

Assurance is the building block that refers to the (potential) obligation of firms to receive a third-party verification of their disclosed information. Assurance is a traditional form of control which is well established in the financial accounting literature because it is used as a form of validation of the reported information. The assurance process is intended both for stakeholders and for the market, and therefore it is essential that the assurance process is developed by an independent third party.

In the sustainability reporting field, the assurance has been voluntarily applied by some companies to increase users' confidence and their perceptions of information credibility (Boiral *et al.*, 2019; Du and Wu, 2019). Therefore, voluntarily engaging in sustainability assurance is believed to reduce greenwashing (Lyon and Maxwell, 2011). Whilst assurance of sustainability reports is still at an early stage and there are some questions raised about its reliability (Farooq and de Villiers, 2019), studies suggest that assurance is essential to ensure a certain level of reliability, and stakeholders perceive the assured reports as more reliable than non-assured ones (Reimsbach *et al.*, 2018). The KMPG Survey of Sustainability Reporting (KPMG, 2022) and the World Business Council for Sustainable Development's *Reporting Matters* (WBCSD, 2022) both confirm the increasing role of external assurance in the sustainability reporting field.

With the CSRD, the assurance of sustainability reporting will become compulsory and it is referred to as sustainability assurance (SA). SA is defined as a disciplinary mechanism that certifies the report's reliability, contributing to its credibility (Simnett *et al.*, 2009). With the NFRD the commitment to the assurance process was fairly low. The NFRD had not included an assurance process requirement for non-financial statements, but only the possibility of verifying that such a document was developed, as a binary valuation of presence/absence, without any verification of the published data and information (NFRD, 2014).

The assurance process in both financial and sustainability reporting has specific impacts. Some of them are positive and some are negative. When it is on a voluntary basis, the choice to subject sustainability reporting to assurance is undertaken by companies when it emerges that the positive effects outweigh the costs (Simnett *et al.*, 2009; Kolk and Perego, 2010). While it is clear that the two major negative aspects are connected to cost-related and time-related issues of the appointed auditing firm, the positive impacts are broader (Unhee, 1997). The main determinants of SA could be found as follows:

- *Increase company's credibility.* Sustainability assurance by an independent third party can increase the company's credibility as regards sustainability reporting (Kolk and Perego, 2010).
- *Enhance shareholder perception and market value.* Sustainability assurance can lead to an increase in the shareholder's perceived value and to an increase in the share price. The benefit of assurance to the market is greater when a company has a high sustainability performance and is socially and environmentally committed (Coram *et al.*, 2009).
- *Increase stakeholder recognition and credibility.* Like shareholder and market values, sustainability assurance increases trust in the information published to all stakeholders. For instance, investors and financial analysts increasingly demand sustainability assurance to increase the accuracy of the data and information underlying their decisions (KPMG, 2017).
- *Better risk management and understanding of sustainability issues.* Thanks to sustainability assurance, companies carry out a critical reading of the situation and data collected, and therefore they properly manage the resulting risks in advance (Abdelfattah *et al.*, 2021).

The sustainability assurance can differ in its required depth, ranging from comprehensive audits ('full' or 'reasonable' assurance) to less comprehensive 'consistency checks'. The comprehensive audit that allows the auditor's opinion on the sustainability report can be either reasonable or limited:

Reasonable assurance reduces the risk of the engagement to an acceptably low level in the given circumstances. Reasonable assurance is comparable to the assurance process of the financial statements and leads the auditor to express a positive opinion that 'the information in the environmental and social report complies in all material respects with the identified criteria' (Hodge *et al.*, 2009). This positive form of expression states an opinion on the measurement of the subject matter against previously defined criteria. In the development of reasonable assurance, the understanding phase is expected to identify and assess the risks of significant errors and then plan procedures in response to the identified risks so as to acquire a reasonable degree of assurance to support its conclusion (IAASB, 2013). Furthermore, the auditor is expected to assess the configuration of relevant controls put in place by the company and whether they consider additional procedures. The controls aspect is relevant because it makes the process of data collection and management more structured and decreases the risk of errors, bringing the information processes of non-financial data closer to those of the economic–financial data that make up the financial statements.

Limited assurance engagements provide a lower level of assurance than reasonable assurance engagements. This is a verification activity with considerably less magnitude that leads the auditor to express an opinion on the report in negative terms, i.e., that 'nothing has come to his or her attention that indicates that the information is not fairly presented in accordance with the identified criteria' (Hodge *et al.*, 2009). Limited assurance is required to identify the areas/subject matter for audit where significant error is likely to occur and to plan audits of those areas.

It is possible for companies to opt for a mixed review, which provides limited assurance on the whole sustainability report and reasonable assurance on specific information or indicators. The mixed review allows companies to increase the level of audits performed and obtain a better-quality document and also to gain familiarity with the assurance process for approaching future obligations. The WBCSD (2022) *Reporting Matters* report shows that nearly 98% of sustainability reports have some form of assurance on their sustainability disclosures. However, the level of assurance can vary significantly. From their data it is clear that the majority of the report received a limited level of assurance on specific indicators and/or the reporting process (82%). Moreover, a combination of limited and reasonable assurance (11%) and reasonable assurance covering the whole report (6%) saw moderate use in 2022, similar to 2021. In Europe, the level of combined and reasonable assurance is higher (20%) than in North America (8%) and Asia (7%).

Building Block: Disclosure Channel

This building block refers to different reporting media, or channels where the sustainability information can be disclosed. The traditional channel of sustainability reporting is through hard copies of annual reports (Krasodomska and Cho, 2017). However, because sustainability reporting is conceived as any media/channels that corporate entities adopt to communicate with their stakeholders, channels can be formal and informal. Formal sustainability reporting occurs when the content of the sustainability report is well structured according to laid-down standards. Formal sustainability reports include annual reports, stand-alone reports, and integrated reports. The WBCSD report (2022) shows that the majority of companies tend to produce a combination of annual, integrated and stand-alone reports to communicate sustainability information. In detail, the majority of the companies (64%) produce a separate stand-alone sustainability report, 19% include the sustainability disclosure in the annual report and the remaining 16% produce a self-declared integrated report without making reference to a specific standard. Research shows that producing a stand-alone sustainability report has its benefits. The use of stand-alone sustainability reports is more likely to mitigate concerns that the linguistic features of sustainability information might affect or be affected by the financial information (Clarkson *et al.*, 2020). Moreover, stand-alone sustainability reports, on average, are longer and cover more sustainability issues than the sustainability information disclosed in the annual or integrated reports (Dhaliwal *et al.*, 2011).

If the content of a sustainability report is less or not structured following any widely accepted standard, it is possible to call it an informal sustainability report (Amoako *et al.*, 2022). Informal sustainability reporting includes a variety of different media, from meetings, emails, social media and notice boards. Both formal and informal reporting are powerful mechanisms for building trust and confidence by keeping in touch with several stakeholders, thus ensuring an interactive dialogue with stakeholders.

Previous research on sustainability reporting has mainly investigated the formal documents covering corporate environmental, economic and social policies, initiatives, objectives, and performance and they have highlighted the presence of a majority of formal channels of disclosure for disseminating sustainability information, especially in the Western countries (Amoako *et al.*, 2022). A recent study on Australian companies (Ardiana, 2019) has investigated the multiple forms of communication channels of 154 sustainability disclosures in both the annual and sustainability reports of large Australian companies. The study reveals that there are 12 communication channels, which can be classified into three groups: (1) conventional, such as a postal address, telephone, feedback forms enclosed in reports and SMS messaging; (2) internet-based, such as websites, emails and online/web-based feedback forms; (3) social media, such as Twitter, Facebook, YouTube, LinkedIn and Blog. In the largest Australian companies, the websites, where formal reports are uploaded and published, were the most popular communication channel. As the corporate sustainability reporting survey of KPMG (2022) indicates, multinational companies are increasingly adopting disclosure via websites to spread their sustainability performance as a result of the high rising number of internet users and the perceived benefits of the internet (Lodhia, 2018). Corporate websites serve as the platform for organizations to spread annual reports and supplementary non-financial information at a faster, cheaper and easier rate. The WBCSD report (2022) shows a significant increase in providing external links and complementary online material across different companies and countries. Most of the companies with an offline-first approach (98%) produce complementary online content.

At the European level, the CSRD will require the sustainability information to be disclosed within the annual report. In addition, the EU is discussing the so-called 'single access point' with the objective of providing one platform containing all corporate reports. Such approaches aim to improve the accessibility of information and increase information comparability, if more standardized disclosure is provided.

APPLYING THE BUILDING BLOCK APPROACH TO CURRENT DEVELOPMENTS

In the following, Table 4.1 provides an overview of CSRD/ESRS and IFRS SDS across those five building blocks. The table provides a short summary for each building block and allows a comparison between the current status of CSRD/ESRS and IFRS SDS. It becomes evident that there are some similarities between CSRD/ESRS and IFRS SDS, especially regarding the general structure of the disclosure requirements, with a focus on governance, strategy, risk management as well as metrics and targets. However, currently the IFRS SDS show a much narrower thematic focus, restricted to climate-related issues, while the ESRS already contain a wider range of thematic standards. Additionally, the materiality definition fundamentally differs, with IFRS SDS narrowly focusing on financial materiality, while the CSRD/ESRS explicitly references double materiality.

This example highlights the potential of the building block approach to quickly summarize reporting standards and to identify similarities and differences at an aggregated level.

Table 4.1   *Comparison of CSRD/ESRS and IFRS SDS across five building blocks*

Building Blocks	CSRD/ESRS	IFRS SDS
Scope/mandate	For fiscal years starting in: 2024: Large and listed entities in scope of the NFRD 2025: Other large companies if they meet two of the three requirements (i.e., more than 250 employees and/or €40 million in turnover and/or €20 million in total assets) 2026/2028: Listed SMEs 2028: Non-EU companies generating a net turnover of more than €150 million and having a subsidiary in the EU that follows the criteria applicable to the EU companies	An entity may apply IFRS Sustainability Disclosure Standards irrespective of whether the entity's related general purpose financial statements (referred to as 'financial statements') are prepared in accordance with IFRS Accounting Standards or other generally accepted accounting principles or practices (GAAP)
Overview of disclosure requirements	● Governance ● Strategy ● Impact, risk, and opportunity management ● Metrics and targets	● Governance ● Strategy ● Risk management ● Metrics and targets
Thematic disclosure requirements	● Climate change ● Pollution ● Water and marine resources ● Biodiversity and ecosystems ● Resource-use and circular economy ● Own workforce ● Workers in the value chain ● Affected communities ● Consumers and end users ● Business conduct	Currently only for climate change-related disclosure – IFRS S2 Climate-related disclosures
Materiality	Double materiality	Financial materiality
Assurance	Initially limited assurance is required. At a later stage, reasonable assurance will be mandatory	Not specified
Disclosure channel	Annual disclosure in the management report as required by the CSRD	As part of companies' general purpose financial reporting

Notes: This table was created based on the state of CSRD/ESRS and IFRS SDS in November 2023. For IFRS SDS some building blocks are not specified (yet). More specifically, the scope, assurance, and disclosure channel can be further specified by any national (or international) legislation specifying and/or mandating the application of IFRS SDS.

CHALLENGES AND AVENUES FOR FUTURE RESEARCH

This section provides a more in-depth discussion of avenues for future research based on both the current state of research and the current development of international sustainability disclosure regulation. The section on the building blocks has already revealed that the research focus is heterogeneously distributed across the building blocks. In addition, the significant development towards more mandatory disclosure regulation also adds new potential research settings, which have not been widely available in the past due to the great reliance on voluntary disclosure.

Building Block: Scope/Mandate

Considering that new regulations are being developed worldwide (IPSF, 2021; Michelon, 2021), research in the field is also evolving. While there are some previous studies looking at the effects of disclosure mandates, from both financial and non-financial perspectives, there remains high potential for future research on these effects.

For example, it is still not clear to firms subject to a disclosure regulation how different contextual factors influence their compliance and how (good vs bad) compliance is connected to real effects and subsequent financial performance (Korca *et al.*, 2021). For example, does voluntary sustainability reporting facilitate firms' compliance with a regulation? Or, when firms which are subject to a disclosure mandate have been reporting sustainability information on a voluntary basis, does this mean lower costs for them to comply with the new mandatory regulation and thus a non-deteriorated financial performance? Similarly, with sustainability performance: Does voluntary sustainability reporting help to further improve firms' sustainability performance when a disclosure mandate is introduced?

Additionally at the EU level, the development towards the CSRD raises the question of whether firms that were previously mandated to disclose under the NFRD are better prepared for the new disclosure requirements compared to firms that did not fall under the scope of the NFRD and which have to report under the CSRD. Previous research has highlighted that when companies must adapt to a regulatory regime, this can cause extra costs (Christensen *et al.*, 2021; Michelon, 2021). This raises the question of how to best prepare for new regulations and whether previous regulations act as a sort of training device, which decreases adaptation costs.

Building Block: Disclosure Content

Previous research in sustainability accounting and reporting has focused on disclosure volume (or quantity) and quality in both voluntary and mandatory regimes (Melloni *et al.*, 2017; Korca *et al.*, 2021; Agostini *et al.*, 2022). Additionally, other studies focus on forward looking disclosure, specifically related to risk disclosure (Sakhel, 2017; Schiemann and Sakhel, 2019) and supply chain disclosure (Antonini *et al.*, 2020). While research on disclosure volume and quality has matured, there is a need for more research related to forward-looking and supply chain-related disclosure. Following the increase in mandatory measures (IPSF, 2021; Michelon, 2021), companies are facing more requirements related to forward-looking and supply chain-related disclosure.

Accounting research on forward-looking disclosure has mainly analyzed the risk-perspective (Sakhel, 2017; Schiemann and Sakhel, 2019) or has used this type of disclosure to create a disclosure quality index (Agostini *et al.*, 2022). However, forward-looking disclosure is not limited to climate risk, but may also encompass disclosure related to targets. For instance, forward-looking disclosure may include climate-related targets that the reporting firm has adopted. According to the ESRS E1 on Climate Change, if the reporting organization has set GHG emission reduction targets, target values should be disclosed for the year 2030 and if available, for the year 2050 (EFRAG, 2022). Similarly, the IFRS S2 Climate-Related Disclosure outlines that the reporting firms shall disclose their climate-related targets in a detailed way, including the period for which the target applies (IFRS, 2022b). Both reporting standards, the ESRS E1 and IFRS S2, clearly highlight the need for and importance of forward-looking disclosure. In this regard, future research could analyze the extent to which companies report such forward-looking information. Furthermore, when forward-looking disclosure is mandated, and thus more firms are expected to report on their targets, future research could analyze whether the setting of sustainability-related targets by firms helps to improve their sustainability performance in the future, and whether companies are able to reach their targets or interim milestones. Answering questions like this could shed light on the role of regulating disclosure in improving firms' actions toward sustainability.

Similar to forward-looking disclosure, supply chain-related disclosure will be required by some disclosure measures. According to IPSF (2021), in the current measures worldwide there is a lack of disclosure requirements on supply-chain related issues. However, new standards, such as the ESRS, highlight that reporting firms shall also include information on the material impacts, risks and opportunities related to the firm's direct and indirect relationships in the upstream and/or downstream value chain (IFRS, 2022a). The more detailed requirements, such as the ESRS, might overcome the issues related to supply chain disclosure highlighted by Antonini *et al.* (2020). The authors find that the way in which boundaries are set can impact disclosure related to the supply chain. Future studies could analyze if more detailed requirements and guidance, such as the ESRS (or other upcoming reporting requirements) do increase transparency and facilitate firms' overall reporting on the supply chain.

Building Block: Materiality

Despite the recent increase in research on materiality, there are many avenues for future research. In general, research can be classified by its focus on financial or double materiality. For financial materiality, the SASB Materiality Map is a convenient approach for companies (as preparers) and investors or readers of sustainability reports, and it has been the subject of several publications (Khan *et al.*, 2016; Spandel *et al.*, 2020; Bochkay *et al.*, 2021; Serafeim and Yoon, 2022; Goettsche *et al.*, 2023). A similar indication on the perspective of impact materiality is not available, yet. Such an approach could be useful as it would save costs for companies, which would not need to invest in extensive materiality assessment procedures, and it would increase comparability of sustainability reports. In addition, such an approach would create a need for research on the validity, financial and real effects of such materiality indications. Therefore, the development of materiality indications for impact materiality provides an avenue for future research and for regulators.

Additionally, research on the interdependencies and differences between financial and impact materiality is both a challenge and avenue for future research. Currently, research is mostly focused on either financial or double materiality, but does not attempt to compare the two conceptions. As discussed by Spandel *et al.* (2023), there is a potential for future research by combining insights from research on financial and impact materiality, and comparing how these approaches impact companies and investors. Furthermore, an approach of problem-based cooperation would go beyond the field of accounting research and discuss challenges of corporate disclosure and its impact on ecological, social or economic aspects.

Finally, as discussed by Korca *et al.* (2023), how companies undertake their materiality assessments can have direct implications on the information comparability in sustainability reports. Considering that comparability creation is at the top of the agenda of policymakers, research exploring the interplay between materiality and comparability creation could shed light on the potential of sustainability information to become comparable.

Building Block: Assurance

Many studies have highlighted how assurance processes are implemented in sustainability reports (Mock *et al.*, 2007; Mock *et al.*, 2013; Junior *et al.*, 2014; Gillet-Monjarret and Rivière-Giordano, 2017; Alsahali and Malagueño, 2022; Yan *et al.*, 2022). From these studies three main challenges emerge for the future of assurance in sustainability reporting, which are described below.

First, the lack of specific standards at both firm and national levels, ambiguity in guidelines, and lack of norms in terms of social conduct are the main challenges of sustainability assurance. Compared with financial assurance, which is guided and restricted by explicit rules and laws, producing a high quality and reliable assurance statement for sustainability reports is much more difficult and subject to dispute (Junior *et al.*, 2014; Boiral *et al.*, 2019). At the worldwide level, sustainability assurance is a voluntary initiative in most jurisdictions, and the market is open to different types of assurance providers competing for market share (Farooq and de Villiers, 2019). The CSRD could represent a step forward for the European market and maybe set the benchmark for other worldwide jurisdictions.

Second, the interplay between different stakeholders and the lack of engagement of all of them may cause conflicting pressure. Farooq and de Villiers (2019) highlight that in the engagement between reporting firms and assurance providers, client pressure (i.e., managerial capture) and assurance practitioners' purpose of growing income (i.e., professional capture) may also affect the quality and reliability of an assurance statement.

Finally, with reference to the role of assurance providers, scholars and experts often categorize assurors into two groups: accounting firms and non-accounting firms (i.e., consultancies) (Farooq and de Villiers, 2019). Some argue that accounting firms (e.g., Big 4 auditing firms) have a relative advantage over consulting firms in terms of expertise in assurance, while others suggest that consultancies (e.g., environmentalists, biologists, ethicists) have an advantage in the field of sustainability knowledge (Farooq and de Villiers, 2019). Thus, there is little agreement on whom reporting firms should recruit to undertake assurance services and the scope of assurance.

Building Block: Disclosure Channel

Sustainability reporting media and channels are crucial for reporting content. Thus, the forms and channels through which sustainability reporting takes place are as important as the message (Lodhia, 2018). However, to date, not much attention has been paid to these issues in the literature. From previous academic studies and professional reports, we can highlight some potential issues to be considered in the changing regulatory framework.

First, future research could explore the sustainability reporting channels' practices in the light of the different and changing regulations that have been in practice at the European level. For example, it would be interesting to interview managers and other stakeholders to obtain their opinions with regard to this changing institutional environment and how they cope with meeting the regulatory framework by also considering their previous expertise.

Second, conventional web pages are the most adopted communication channels where companies publish their stand-alone sustainability reports. However, as many researchers have highlighted, websites tend to function as a medium of communication *to* stakeholders instead of a medium of communication *with* stakeholders. This is because websites do not enable two-way interaction and communication through dialogue, discussion and debate between reporting companies and their stakeholders (Manetti and Bellucci, 2016). Websites are only utilized as a medium for disseminating information on sustainability to stakeholders. Therefore, Ardiana (2019) suggests expanding internet-based communication channels through the adoption of emails along with a conventional communication channel postal address. Both email and postal mail allow stakeholders to send messages containing their opinions, suggestions and criticisms to reporting companies and they will therefore open a dialogue between the company and the stakeholders. Twitter, Facebook, or other social media channels can also be used to extend the bidirectional dialogue with the stakeholders. Indeed, they allow reporting companies to post information on sustainability issues, performance and agenda to their followers, and to receive comments from very different stakeholders.

Third, some studies in the emerging economies context (Amoako *et al.*, 2022) have highlighted that most of the stakeholders from the community they had interviewed were not aware and not interested in formal sustainability reports. On the contrary, the specific context that was analyzed used informal channels of communication, including meetings, and a verbal engagement with the local community and their representatives on sustainability matters. This form of informal disclosure was critical for gaining external legitimacy from the host community and other interest groups. Therefore, in emerging economies and maybe also for small and medium-sized entities (i.e., SMEs), where there are fewer resources (economic and personnel) to implement reliable formal sustainability disclosure, it is essential to consider more informal forms of sustainability reporting – alongside the formal channels – to engage many different stakeholders, and the local communities, and to address sustainability issues in a more collaborative way. Both formal and informal channels are powerful mechanisms for building trust and confidence by keeping in touch with several stakeholders, thus ensuring an interactive dialogue with stakeholders. Informal forms of reporting, such as dialogue via social media, can also create a genuine stakeholder engagement process based on a democratic solicitation of stakeholder opinion (Manetti and Bellucci, 2016).

Interconnections between Building Blocks

We highlighted research opportunities within each of the five building blocks in this section. A further opportunity lies in analyzing connections between building blocks. For example, it is a challenge for regulators to provide disclosure standards that deliver comprehensive, comparable and decision-useful information while, at the same time, keeping direct and indirect costs of disclosure low. This challenge is even greater when considering disclosure standards for SMEs, which typically have fewer resources and less expertise than large companies. At the same time, SMEs are very heterogeneous (e.g., fundamentally different business models, considerable differences in their local network of customers and suppliers). Therefore, coordinating the building blocks of scope/mandate and disclosure content is of high importance, especially when sustainable disclosure regulation extends to SMEs.

Another interesting connection lies in the way in which forward-looking information on net zero targets and milestones can be subject to assurance processes. While forward-looking information can be highly relevant to stakeholders, to better understand whether and how companies are able to decrease their carbon emissions in line with climate targets, such information can be regarded as subjective or of low credibility. Therefore, assurance can play an important role in increasing credibility and reachability of the proposed net zero target.

These examples highlight how connections between building blocks can create further research opportunities. Of course, it is not possible to discuss each of the many potential connections in detail, but as the examples show, specific combinations can be highly relevant and they can benefit from problem-based research.

CONCLUSION

In this chapter, we described five essential building blocks, which can be used to analyze sustainability reporting regulation in a systematic way. The building blocks are scope/mandate, disclosure content, materiality, assurance, and disclosure channel. We highlighted the state of related research for each building block and showed a comparison of the CSRD/ESRS and IFRS SDS, before explaining challenges and avenues for future research.

Overall, the state of research is heterogeneous across the building blocks, where we find a rather strong focus on the building block scope/mandate with literature analyzing financial and real effects of the introduction of disclosure mandates. While there is significant research on disclosure content, there are many open research questions on this building block, especially regarding the role and content of supply chain and forward-looking disclosures. Research on materiality has increased in recent years, mainly driven by the publication of the SASB Materiality Map. Here, future research can focus more strongly on the similarities and differences between financial and impact materiality. Furthermore, research on materiality could also explore issues such as its implications towards information comparability, which is one of the main objectives of disclosure regulations (Korca *et al.*, 2023). The building block assurance contains a range of further research opportunities regarding the effects of assurance mandates and different levels of assurance. Research on disclosure channels is extremely scarce, which is especially surprising considering that regulators have to consider in which way sustainability information should best be disclosed. Additionally, when stakeholder groups beyond investors are addressed by sustainability disclosure, the question arises as to how to assure accessibility of this information. Finally, there is further research potential for the analyses of combinations of building blocks. Insights into ways in which to assure supply chain or forward-looking information, or how to provide suitable disclosure standards for SMEs, by optimizing the required disclosure content with the respective scope of disclosure are just two of many potential research areas.

While we focused on the state of the research and potential future research based on the building block approach, this approach is also very useful for practitioners and standard setters. As our example on the comparison of CSRD/ESRS and IFRS SDS showed, the building block approach provides a straightforward and systematic comparison of disclosure regulation and disclosure standards. In connection with existing (and future) research, standard setters might be able to continuously improve sustainability disclosure standards based on the current state of research.

The development of sustainability disclosure measures provides many opportunities and challenges for companies, regulators, readers and researchers. The outline of a building block structure can help to systematize research areas and projects.

REFERENCES

Abdelfattah, T., Elmahgoub, M. and Elamer, A.A. (2021) 'Female audit partners and extended audit reporting: UK evidence', *Journal of Business Ethics*, 174(1), pp. 177–197. Available at: https://doi.org/10.1007/s10551-020-04607-0.

Agostini, M., Costa, E. and Korca, B. (2022) 'Non-financial disclosure and corporate financial performance under Directive 2014/95/EU: evidence from Italian listed companies', *Accounting in Europe*, 19(1), pp. 78–109. Available at: https://doi.org/10.1080/17449480.2021.1979610.

Alsahali, K.F. and Malagueño, R. (2022) 'An empirical study of sustainability reporting assurance: current trends and new insights', *Journal of Accounting & Organizational Change*, 18(5), pp. 617–642. Available at: https://doi.org/10.1108/JAOC-05-2020-0060.

Amoako, K.O. *et al.* (2022) 'Formal and informal sustainability reporting: an insight from a mining company's subsidiary in Ghana', *Journal of Financial Reporting and Accounting*, 20(5), pp. 897–925. Available at: https://doi.org/10.1108/JFRA-12-2020-0368.

Antonini, C., Beck, C. and Larrinaga, C. (2020) 'Subpolitics and sustainability reporting boundaries: the case of working conditions in global supply chains', *Accounting, Auditing & Accountability Journal*, 33(7), pp. 1535–1567. Available at: https://doi.org/10.1108/AAAJ-09-2019-4167.

Ardiana, P.A. (2019) 'Stakeholder engagement in sustainability reporting: evidence of reputation risk management in large Australian companies', *Australian Accounting Review*, 29(4), pp. 726–747. Available at: https://doi.org/10.1111/auar.12293.

Baboukardos, D. and Rimmel, G. (2016) 'Value relevance of accounting information under an integrated reporting approach: a research note', *Journal of Accounting and Public Policy*, 35(4), pp. 437–452. Available at: https://doi.org/10.1016/j.jaccpubpol.2016.04.004.

Barth, M.E. *et al.* (2017) 'The economic consequences associated with integrated report quality: capital market and real effects', *Accounting, Organizations and Society*, 62, pp. 43–64. Available at: https://doi.org/10.1016/j.aos.2017.08.005.

Bauckloh, T. *et al.* (2022) 'Under pressure? The link between mandatory climate reporting and firms' carbon performance', *Organization & Environment*, 36(1), pp. 126–149. Available at: https://doi.org/10.1177/10860266221083340.

Bochkay, K., Hales, J. and Serafeim, G. (2021) 'Disclosure standards and communication norms: evidence of voluntary disclosure standards as a coordinating device for capital markets', University of Miami Business School Research Paper [Preprint], Paper No. 3928979. Available at: http://dx.doi.org/10.2139/ssrn.3928979.

Boiral, O. *et al.* (2019) 'Ethical issues in the assurance of sustainability reports: perspectives from assurance providers', *Journal of Business Ethics*, 159(4), pp. 1111–1125. Available at: https://doi.org/10.1007/s10551-018-3840-3.

Chen, Y.-C., Hung, M. and Wang, Y. (2018) 'The effect of mandatory CSR disclosure on firm profitability and social externalities: evidence from China', *Journal of Accounting and Economics*, 65(1), pp. 169–190. Available at: https://doi.org/10.1016/j.jacceco.2017.11.009.

Christensen, H.B. *et al.* (2017) 'The real effects of mandated information on social responsibility in financial reports: evidence from mine-safety records', *Journal of Accounting and Economics*, 64(2), pp. 284–304. Available at: https://doi.org/10.1016/j.jacceco.2017.08.001.

Christensen, H.B., Hail, L. and Leuz, C. (2021) 'Mandatory CSR and sustainability reporting: economic analysis and literature review', *Review of Accounting Studies*, 26(3), pp. 1176–1248. Available at: https://doi.org/10.1007/s11142-021-09609-5.

Clarkson, P.M. *et al.* (2020) 'A textual analysis of us corporate social responsibility reports', *Abacus*, 56(1), pp. 3–34. Available at: https://doi.org/10.1111/abac.12182.

Coram, P.J., Monroe, G.S. and Woodliff, D.R. (2009) 'The value of assurance on voluntary nonfinancial disclosure: an experimental evaluation', *Auditing: A Journal of Practice & Theory*, 28(1), pp. 137–151. Available at: https://doi.org/10.2308/aud.2009.28.1.137.

Dhaliwal, D.S. *et al.* (2011) 'Voluntary nonfinancial disclosure and the cost of equity capital: the initiation of corporate social responsibility reporting', *The Accounting Review*, 86(1), pp. 59–100. Available at: https://doi.org/10.2308/accr.00000005.

Downar, B. *et al.* (2021) 'The impact of carbon disclosure mandates on emissions and financial operating performance', *Review of Accounting Studies*, 26(3), pp. 1137–1175. Available at: https://doi.org/10 .1007/s11142-021-09611-x.

Du, K. and Wu, S.J. (2019) 'Does external assurance enhance the credibility of CSR reports? Evidence from CSR-related misconduct events in Taiwan', *Auditing: A Journal of Practice & Theory*, 38(4), 101–130. Available at: https://doi.org/10.2308/ajpt-52418.

Edgley, C., Jones, M.J. and Atkins, J. (2015) 'The adoption of the materiality concept in social and environmental reporting assurance: a field study approach', *The British Accounting Review*, 47(1), pp. 1–18. Available at: https://doi.org/10.1016/j.bar.2014.11.001.

EFRAG (2022) *ESRS E1: Climate Change*. Available at: https://www.efrag.org/Assets/Download ?assetUrl=%2Fsites%2Fwebpublishing%2FSiteAssets%2F08%2520Draft%2520ESRS%2520E1 %2520Climate%2520Change%2520November%25202022.pdf.

EFRAG (2023) Implementation Guidance for the materiality assessment. Available at: https://www .efrag.org/Assets/Download?assetUrl=%2Fsites%2Fwebpublishing%2FMeeting%20Documents %2F2305101036110389%2F02-02%20Materiality%20Assessment%20Implementation %20guidance%20TEG%20231106%20clean.pdf.

Farooq, M.B. and de Villiers, C. (2019) 'The shaping of sustainability assurance through the competition between accounting and non-accounting providers', *Accounting, Auditing & Accountability Journal*, 32(1), pp. 307–336. Available at: https://doi.org/10.1108/AAAJ-10-2016-2756.

Fiechter, P., Hitz, J.-M. and Lehmann, N. (2022) 'Real effects of a widespread CSR reporting mandate: evidence from the European Union's CSR Directive', *Journal of Accounting Research*, 60(4), pp. 1499–1549. Available at: https://doi.org/10.1111/1475-679X.12424.

Gillet-Monjarret, C. and Rivière-Giordano, G. (2017) 'Sustainability assurance: a literature review', *Accounting Auditing Control*, 23(2), pp. 11–62.

Goettsche, M. *et al.* (2023) 'Materiality indications as a double-edged sword: real effects of sustainability disclosure standards'. [Preprint] Available at: http://dx.doi.org/10.2139/ssrn.4324667.

GRI (2013) *G4 Sustainability Reporting Guidelines*. Amsterdam: Global Reporting Initiative. Available at: https://www.globalreporting.org/how-to-use-the-gri-standards/gri-standards-english-language/.

Hibbitt, C. and Collison, D. (2004) 'Corporate environmental disclosure and reporting developments in Europe', *Social and Environmental Accountability Journal*, 24(1), pp. 1–11. Available at: https://doi .org/10.1080/0969160X.2004.9651708.

Hodge, K., Subramaniam, N. and Stewart, J. (2009) 'Assurance of sustainability reports: impact on report users' confidence and perceptions of information credibility', *Australian Accounting Review*, 19(3), pp. 178–194. Available at: https://doi.org/10.1111/j.1835-2561.2009.00056.x.

IAASB (2013) *ISAE 3000 (Revised), Assurance Engagements Other than Audits or Reviews of Historical Financial Information*. Available at: https://www.ifac.org/_flysystem/azure-private/publications/ files/ISAE%203000%20Revised%20-%20for%20IAASB.pdf.

IFRS (2022a) *[Draft] IFRS S1 General Requirements for Disclosure of Sustainability-Related Financial Information*. Available at: https://www.ifrs.org/content/dam/ifrs/project/general-sustainability-related -disclosures/exposure-draft-ifrs-s1-general-requirements-for-disclosure-of-sustainability-related -financial-information.pdf.

IFRS (2022b) *[Draft] IFRS S2 Climate-Related Disclosures*. Available at: https://www.ifrs.org/content/ dam/ifrs/project/climate-related-disclosures/issb-exposure-draft-2022-2-climate-related-disclosures .pdf.

IPSF (2021) *State and trends of ESG disclosure policy measures across IPSF jurisdictions, Brazil, and the US*. Available at: https://finance.ec.europa.eu/system/files/2021-11/211104-ipsf-esg-disclosure -report_en.pdf.

Jeffrey, C. and Perkins, J.D. (2013) 'Social norms and disclosure policy: implications from a comparison of financial and corporate social responsibility reporting', *Social and Environmental Accountability Journal*, 33(1), pp. 5–19. Available at: https://doi.org/10.1080/0969160X.2012.748468.

Junior, R.M., Best, P.J. and Cotter, J. (2014) 'Sustainability reporting and assurance: a historical analysis on a world-wide phenomenon', *Journal of Business Ethics*, 120(1), pp. 1–11. Available at: https://doi .org/10.1007/s10551-013-1637-y.

Khan, M., Serafeim, G. and Yoon, A. (2016) 'Corporate sustainability: first evidence on materiality', *The Accounting Review*, 91(6), pp. 1697–1724.

Kolk, A. and Perego, P. (2010) 'Determinants of the adoption of sustainability assurance statements: an international investigation', *Business Strategy and the Environment*, 19(3), pp. 182–198. Available at: https://doi.org/10.1002/bse.643.

Korca, B., Costa, E. and Farneti, F. (2021) 'From voluntary to mandatory non-financial disclosure following Directive 2014/95/EU: an Italian case study', *Accounting in Europe*, 18(3), pp. 353–377. Available at: https://doi.org/10.1080/17449480.2021.1933113.

Korca, B., Costa, E. and Bouten, L. (2023) 'Disentangling the concept of comparability in sustainability reporting', *Sustainability Accounting and Management Policy Journal*, 14(4), pp. 815–851. Available at: https://doi.org/10.1108/SAMPJ-05-2022-0284.

KPMG (2017) The Road Ahead: KPMG Survey of Corporate Responsibility Reporting 2017. Available at: https://assets.kpmg.com/content/dam/kpmg/xx/pdf/2017/10/kpmg-survey-of-corporate-responsibility-reporting-2017.pdf.

KPMG (2022) Big Shifts, Small Steps: Survey of Sustainability Reporting 2022. Available at: https://assets.kpmg.com/content/dam/kpmg/se/pdf/komm/2022/Global-Survey-of-Sustainability-Reporting-2022.pdf.

Krasodomska, J. and Cho, C.H. (2017) 'Corporate social responsibility disclosure', *Sustainability Accounting, Management and Policy Journal*, 8(1), pp. 2–19. Available at: https://doi.org/10.1108/SAMPJ-02-2016-0006.

Lodhia, S. (2018) 'Is the medium the message?', *Meditari Accountancy Research*, 26(1), pp. 2–12. Available at: https://doi.org/10.1108/MEDAR-08-2017-0197.

Lyon, T.P. and Maxwell, J.W. (2011) 'Greenwash: corporate environmental disclosure under threat of audit', *Journal of Economics & Management Strategy*, 20(1), pp. 3–41. Available at: https://doi.org/10.1111/j.1530-9134.2010.00282.x.

Manetti, G. and Bellucci, M. (2016) 'The use of social media for engaging stakeholders in sustainability reporting', *Accounting, Auditing & Accountability Journal*, 29(6), pp. 985–1011. Available at: https://doi.org/10.1108/AAAJ-08-2014-1797.

Melloni, G., Caglio, A. and Perego, P. (2017) 'Saying more with less? Disclosure conciseness, completeness and balance in integrated reports', *Sustainability Accounting, Reporting and Assurance*, 36(3), pp. 220–238. Available at: https://doi.org/10.1016/j.jaccpubpol.2017.03.001.

Michelon, G. (2021) 'Financial markets and environmental information', in J. Bebbington, C. Larrinaga, B. O'Dwyer and I. Thomson (eds), *Routledge Handbook of Environmental Accounting*. Abingdon, UK: Routledge, pp. 165–178.

Mock, T.J., Strohm, C. and Swartz, K.M. (2007) 'An examination of worldwide assured sustainability reporting', *Australian Accounting Review*, 17(41), pp. 67–77. Available at: https://doi.org/10.1111/j.1835-2561.2007.tb00455.x.

Mock, T.J., Rao, S.S. and Srivastava, R.P. (2013) 'The development of worldwide sustainability reporting assurance', *Australian Accounting Review*, 23(4), pp. 280–294. Available at: https://doi.org/10.1111/auar.12013.

NFRD (2014) Directive 2014/95/EU of the European Parliament and of the Council of 22 October 2014 amending Directive 2013/34/EU as regards disclosure of non-financial and diversity information by certain large undertakings and groups Text with EEA relevance. Available at: https://eur-lex.europa.eu/legal-content/EN/TXT/?uri=CELEX%3A32014L0095.

Reimsbach, D., Hahn, R. and Gürtürk, A. (2018) 'Integrated reporting and assurance of sustainability information: an experimental study on professional investors' information processing', *European Accounting Review*, 27(3), pp. 559–581. Available at: https://doi.org/10.1080/09638180.2016.1273787.

Reimsbach, D. *et al.* (2020) 'In the eyes of the beholder: experimental evidence on the contested nature of materiality in sustainability reporting', *Organization & Environment*, 33(4), pp. 624–651. Available at: https://doi.org/10.1177/1086026619875436.

Sakhel, A. (2017) 'Corporate climate risk management: are European companies prepared?', *Journal of Cleaner Production*, 165, pp. 103–118. Available at: https://doi.org/10.1016/j.jclepro.2017.07.056.

Schiemann, F. and Sakhel, A. (2019) 'Carbon disclosure, contextual factors, and information asymmetry: the case of physical risk reporting', *European Accounting Review*, 28(4), pp. 791–818. Available at: https://doi.org/10.1080/09638180.2018.1534600.

Serafeim, G. and Yoon, A. (2022) 'Which corporate ESG news does the market react to?', *Financial Analysts Journal*, 78(1), pp. 59–78.

Simnett, R., Vanstraelen, A. and Chua, W.F. (2009) 'Assurance on sustainability reports: an international comparison', *The Accounting Review*, 84(3), pp. 937–967. Available at: https://doi.org/10.2308/accr .2009.84.3.937.

Spandel, T., Schiemann, F. and Hoepner, A.G. (2020) 'Capital market reactions to ESG materiality classifications'. Available at: https://dx.doi.org/10.2139/ssrn.3694285.

Spandel, T. *et al.* (2023) 'Materiality as an essentially contested concept: pathways forward for sustainability disclosure research'. Available at: https://dx.doi.org/10.2139/ssrn.4323836.

Tomar, S. (2023) 'Greenhouse gas disclosure and emissions benchmarking', *Journal of Accounting Research*, 61(2), pp. 451–492. Available at: https://doi.org/10.1111/1475-679X.12473.

Unhee, K. (1997) *Environmental and Safety Auditing: Program Strategies for Legal, International, and Financial Issues*. Boca Raton, FL: Lewis Publishers.

WBCSD (2022) *Reporting Matters*. Available at: https://www.wbcsd.org/Programs/Redefining-Value/ Reporting-matters/Resources/RM2022.

Yan, M. *et al.* (2022) 'Assurance process for sustainability reporting: towards a conceptual framework', *Journal of Cleaner Production*, 377, p. 134156. Available at: https://doi.org/10.1016/j.jclepro.2022 .134156.

5. (R)evolution of sustainability reporting regulation in the European Union

Silvia Panfilo, Simone Pizzi and Joanna Krasodomska

INTRODUCTION

Significant advances in corporate social responsibility (CSR) regulations were originally made in the United States, stemming from social and environmental concerns that emerged in the late 1960s and early 1970s (Latapí Agudelo *et al.*, 2019). Yet Europe is now seen as a leader when it comes to sustainability practices and reporting, including the regulatory landscape.

CSR has long been present in European Union (EU) policy. However, when it comes to CSR-related disclosures, the shift from a voluntary to a mandatory approach with the introduction of Directive 2014/95/EU is seen as a milestone in the (r)evolution of sustainability reporting regulation, and not only in the EU. The Directive posed a challenge not only to companies that fell within its scope and had very different prior experiences with voluntary sustainability disclosure but also to national standard setters and the accounting profession. Academic debate in accounting, finance, and management has blossomed around the compulsoriness of the CSR and sustainability reporting (Christensen *et al.*, 2021): the EU Directive represents the main pillar of the discussion about specific issues related to it, its relevance to reporting companies and their stakeholders and its effectiveness.

This chapter aims to synthesize current knowledge on the role of Directive 2014/95/EU in the ongoing process of regulating sustainability reporting in the EU by examining the related academic debate. More specifically, it aims to provide answers to the following questions:

> *RQ1: Which authors, academic institutions and journals have contributed to the debate over time?*
> *RQ2: Which publications have had the greatest impact?*
> *RQ3: What is the conceptual structure of the scientific discourse?*

In the next section of the chapter, we present the institutional setting by offering basic information on the development and implementation of Directive 2014/95/EU. Then we explain the main assumptions of the bibliometric analysis performed with the use of *VOSviewer* and *Bibliometrix* to provide answers to the above questions. After that, we offer the results of the analysis. The chapter concludes by summarizing its overall contribution and suggesting recommendations for future research.

INSTITUTIONAL SETTING: DIRECTIVE 2014/95/EU

In its Communication of October 25, 2011, the European Commission shared the renewed EU strategy 2011–2014 for CSR, which re-emphasized the need for legislative reform to improve companies' disclosure of social and environmental information. The EC communication defined CSR as 'the responsibility of enterprises for their impact on society' (European Commission, 2011, p. 6). In its previous 2006 definition, the EC presented CSR as 'a concept whereby companies integrate social and environmental concerns in their business operations and in their interaction with their stakeholders on a *voluntary* basis'. The lack of voluntariness in the new 2011 definition can be interpreted as a clear signal that the EU would move toward stricter regulation of CSR in the future. Indeed, in the same document, the EC officially announced that it 'will present a legislative proposal on the transparency of the social and environmental information provided by companies in all sectors' (European Commission, 2011, p. 12).

This legislative proposal came into force as Directive 2014/95EU on the disclosure of non-financial and diversity information by certain large undertakings and groups (European Union, 2014), which amended Directive 2013/34/EU (the so-called Accounting Directive). The aims of the Directive were to encourage companies to disclose relevant non-financial information to provide investors and other stakeholders with a more complete picture of their development, performance and position and of the impact of their activity, as well as to increase the relevance, consistency and comparability of information disclosed by certain large undertakings and groups across the EU.

Directive 2014/95/EU entered into force on December 5, 2014, and the deadline for its transposition to the law of EU Member States was December 6, 2016. The Directive was addressed to large public interest entities (PIEs) (with more than 500 employees) and required them to present (within the management report or as a separate document) non-financial disclosures related to four key areas: (1) environmental issues, (2) social and employee matters, (3) respect for human rights and (4) anti-corruption and bribery matters. It also introduced the following elements of the disclosures: (1) a description of the business model, (2) a description of the policies pursued in relation to non-financial matters, (3) the outcomes of those policies, (4) the principal risks related to non-financial matters and (5) non-financial key performance indicators (KPIs) relevant to the business. With respect to the guidelines companies should follow while preparing the disclosures, the Directive was flexible. Companies were free to choose from a wide range of international, European or national frameworks. Approximately 11,700 companies across the EU reported the above-presented information for the first time in 2018.

Since the disclosure requirements included in the Directive itself were quite vague and there were many reporting frameworks companies could follow, art. 2 of the Directive noted that the EC will issue non-binding guidelines to help companies draw up relevant, useful and concise non-financial statements according to the new requirements. The *Guidelines on non-financial reporting: Methodology for reporting non-financial information* (European Commission, 2017) were published in 2017 and the *Guidelines on non-financial reporting: Supplement on reporting climate-related information* (European Commission, 2019) two years later. The 2019 guidelines included the double-materiality concept, which described materiality for the first time from both perspectives, as environmental and social impacts which affect the company and the company's activities impacting the environment and society.

Even though Directive 2014/95EU was seen as a real game changer when it comes to non-financial reporting in Europe, its effects have been less than satisfactory. The EC committed itself to revise Directive 2014/95/EU in the European Green Deal (European Commission, 2019) as part of the strategy to strengthen the foundations for sustainable investment. Additionally, in the impact assessment (European Commission, 2020) published in

2020 the EC stated that non-financial information produced as a result of the Directive is not sufficiently comparable or reliable, disclosures required by stakeholders are often not reported, and when they are, they are difficult to find. This situation led to subsequent changes in the EU sustainability reporting regulatory landscape.

In December 2021, the EC published the final draft of the Corporate Sustainability Reporting Directive (CSRD), which will amend Directive 2013/34/EU (European Commission, 2021). The contribution of the CSRD will be relevant for the achievement of the standardization goal because of the introduction of stricter requirements about corporate reporting (KPMG, 2022). In detail, the CSRD will require the European undertakings to disclose their sustainability information considering the European Sustainability Reporting Standard (ESRS) developed by the EFRAG. Furthermore, the sustainability declarations will be embedded within the management reports to enhance the interlinkages between financial and sustainability information.

According to this evidence, the next few years will be interesting, due to an intense debate about the future of mandatory sustainability reporting in Europe. The comprehension of the main effects related to the transition from the principle-based approach proposed by Directive 2014/95/EU to the standardized approach required by the CSRD will represents a key issue for accounting scholars (Dinh *et al.*, 2023; Stolowy and Paugam, 2023). In this regard, many accounting scholars underlined the need to systematize the scientific knowledge about Directive 2014/95/EU to identify the main insights about the 'real' effects of Directive 2014/95/EU. Therefore, in the following section we will explore the first wave of studies about mandatory sustainability reporting in Europe to identify the main constraints and opportunities related to the transposition of Directive 2014/95/EU by the European Member States.

BIBLIOMETRIC ANALYSIS

The analysis consists of a bibliometric evaluation of the scientific debate about the effects related to the transposition of Directive 2014/95/EU by the Member States. The main goal of a bibliometric analysis is to quantitatively evaluate and analyze the scientific output and impact of research publications within a specific field or research area (Broadus, 1987). In detail, bibliometrics involves the application of statistical and mathematical methods to bibliographic data, such as the citations, authors, journals, and keywords to offer valuable insights for researchers, policymakers, funding agencies, and institutions seeking to understand the dynamics of scientific research and make informed decisions. The choice to adopt a bibliometric analysis is also consistent with previous studies published by accounting scholars about specific sub-fields of accounting studies (Baker *et al.*, 2022; Schaltegger *et al.*, 2013).

The bibliometric analysis was conducted through the identification of a research protocol by the authors. In particular, we developed a research protocol based on the following items: (a) data identification, (b) data processing and (c) data analysis. The data identification was conducted using Scopus, which represents the leading source for management scholars. In particular, the adoption of Scopus instead of other databases (e.g. Google Scholar, EBSCO) favored the identification of more reliable sources. In fact, the inclusion of a theoretical contribution in Scopus requires adherence to strict requirements such as the double-blind revisions. For our purposes, we defined the following search string (SS):

SS= (TITLE-ABS-KEY ('Directive 2014/95') OR TITLE-ABS-KEY ('Directive 95/2014') OR TITLE-ABS-KEY ('non financial directive') OR TITLE-ABS-KEY ('non-financial directive')) AND (LIMIT-TO (SUBJAREA , 'BUSI')) AND (LIMIT-TO (LANGUAGE , 'English')) AND (LIMIT-TO (SRCTYPE , 'j'))

Specifically, we identified those papers which include in their title, abstract or keywords a reference to the Directive. Furthermore, we considered only contributions published in scientific journals included in the 'Business and management' group. Our choice has been driven by the opportunity to exclude from our sample conference proceedings and book chapters, which are usually considered less informative than articles by bibliometric analysts (Caputo, A. et al., 2021). Finally, our last screening criteria is represented by the choice to consider only articles published in English. This choice is related to the need to consider a homogeneous sample of keywords. Following this search criterion, our final set consists of 86 articles published during the period between January 2015 and November 14, 2022.[1]

The data processing was conducted by combining the bibliometric software *VosViewer* (van Eck and Waltman, 2010) and *Bibliometrix* (Aria and Cuccurullo, 2017). The need to operate with different indicators is related to the opportunity to develop bibliometric research characterized by an adequate degree of objectivity. In fact, prior studies have suggested that combining two or more indicators will produce a more detailed representation of the field, avoiding any risk of bias caused by the analysis of a synthetic indicator (Caputo, A. et al., 2021; Marzi et al., 2017). Therefore, the adoption of the two types of software supported the development of a reliable and replicable bibliometric analysis.

Building on a multidimensional approach based on performance indicators and bibliometric evaluations, the final outcome of our research is represented by the identification of the conceptual structure of the field. Our approach allowed us to determine the development of the literature over time, the geographical and institutional backgrounds of the authors, and the scientific impact of their publications. Considering the authors' keywords, we generated a graphical representation of the main research clusters that characterized the introduction of Directive 2014/95/EU, thus identifying the main research topics analyzed within the articles.

RESULTS

The Development of the Literature over Time and the Geographical and Institutional Backgrounds of the Authors

We identified 86 documents that were published between 2015 and 2022 on the topic under study. The first contribution to the debate was published by Müller and Stawinoga (2015), which identified the main implications related to the transposition of Directive 2014/95/EU in Germany. Later, other authors tried to perform *ex ante* evaluations of the potential impacts related to Directive 2014/95/EU. In this regard, the analysis confirmed that the attention paid by accounting scholars to this topic has been relevant since the publication of the first draft in 2014. Furthermore, the development of the field has been favored by the launch of two special issues of *Meditari Accountancy Research* (La Torre et al., 2020) and *Journal of Applied Accounting Research* (Venturelli et al., 2022). In this regard, the attention paid by accounting scholars revealed the existence of a proactive approach that has favored the rapid growth of the field over the years.

The scientific debate has been characterized by an intense contribution provided by Italian (141), Polish (21) and Spanish (15) authors, with an overall incidence equal to 69% of the total. A relevant contribution has been also provided by German (14) and Romanian (12) scholars, while the contribution of non-European scholars has been limited (10). The limited contribution provided by non-European scholars could be related by the pivotal role taken by the European Commission in the debate about non-financial regulation. In this regard, the lack of similarities with other legal requirements did not favor the development of cross-country research by international scholars. It is also interesting to note the low presence of scholars from countries such as France (~3%), Denmark (~5%), and Sweden (~5%), which have been leading in the mandatory sustainability reporting regime in Europe since before EU Directive 95/2014. As recalled in Panfilo and Krasodomska (2022):

> France has a long tradition of social and environmental reporting, as the first law requiring such disclosures dates back to 2002 (The Nouvelles Régulations Economiques); in Sweden, state-owned companies have been required to publish annual sustainability reports in accordance with Global Reporting Initiative guidelines since the financial year starting on 1 January 2008 (Guidelines for external reporting by state-owned companies issued by the Ministry of Enterprise, Energy and Communications in 2007); and since 2009, the largest companies in Denmark have been required to provide environmental, social and governance disclosures (Danish Financial Statements Act adopted in 2008). (p. 248)

The most prolific institutions in terms of co-authorships (Table 5.1) that have contributed to the debate are the University of Salento (30), the Ca' Foscari University of Venice (14), followed by the Cracow University of Economics and the University of Naples 'Parthenope' (10 in both cases) and the University of Siena (8). Interestingly, only two papers included in the sample were published in collaboration between those institutions (Panfilo and Krasodomska, 2022; Venturelli *et al.*, 2022).

Table 5.1   Most prolific affiliations

Affiliations	Country	City	Co-authorships
Università of Salento	Italy	Lecce	30
Ca' Foscari University of Venice	Italy	Venice	14
Cracow University of Economics	Poland	Cracow	10
University of Naples 'Parthenope'	Italy	Naples	10
University of Siena	Italy	Siena	8

The Scientific Impact of Publications

The main aim of a performance analysis consists of the opportunity to shed light on the main actors involved in the debate (Caputo, A. *et al.*, 2021). The following section summarizes the main contributions provided by academic sources, articles, and authors to the scientific debate about Directive 2014/95/EU. For our purposes, we considered global and local citations as the main proxies for scientific impacts. In particular, global citation analysis contributes to our evaluation through quantitative insights about the overall impact of each item, while local citation contributes through more specific information about the interlinkages between each item and the other items included in our sample (Ferreira, 2018; Pizzi *et al.*, 2020).

The main sources that have contributed to the debate in terms of citations are *Meditari Accountancy Research* (215), *Business Strategy and the Environment* (177) and *Corporate Social Responsibility and Environmental Management* (112) (Table 5.2). However, an effective evaluation of the specific contribution provided by the three sources requires a preliminary overview of their contents. In fact, the contribution provided by *Meditari Accountancy Research* consists of specific insights about accounting implications, while many papers published in *Business Strategy and the Environment* and *Corporate Social Responsibility and Environmental Management* shed light on the managerial implications related to the disclosure of non-financial information. Interestingly, as Table 5.2 shows, leading journals in the field, such as *Accounting in Europe*, the *Journal of Applied Accounting Research* and the *Sustainability Accounting, Management and Policy Journal*, are not in the first position of the ranking. This evidence is related to their late entrance into the field, with many papers published after the year 2020. However, also investigating the journals' ranking according to the Association of Business Schools' Academic Journal Guide 2021 (ABS) it emerges that top accounting journals are not taking part at the debate on the Directive. On one side, the journal with the highest ranking in which papers on the topic under investigation have been published is *Business Strategy and the Environment* (ranked 3 out of 4/4*). Although it is not a journal dedicated to accounting, it publishes papers that are among the most cited in the field. On the other side, most of the accounting journals emerging from the performance analysis exhibited in Table 5.2 are only ranked 2 by the ABS (out of 4/4*).

Table 5.2   *Performance analysis of the main journals that have contributed to the development of the field*

Source (ABS ranking)	H-index	TC	NP	PY
Meditari Accountancy Research (1)	8	215	11	2018
Business Strategy and the Environment (3)	6	177	6	2020
Corporate Social Responsibility and Environmental Management (1)	6	112	8	2020
Accounting in Europe (2)	4	110	6	2017
Journal of Intellectual Capital (2)	2	95	2	2016
Administrative Sciences (n/a)	2	93	3	2018
Journal of Applied Accounting Research (2)	6	59	11	2020
Social Responsibility Journal (1)	1	58	1	2019
Sustainability Accounting, Management and Policy Journal (2)	3	53	3	2020
Journal of International Financial Management and Accounting (n/a)	2	37	2	2021

Notes: TC: total citation; NP: number of publications; PY: publication year of the first publication about Directive 2014/95/EU.

As regards the evaluation of the main articles (Table 5.3), we adopted a multidimensional approach in order to mitigate the effects related to articles' contents and time horizons. In this regard, we distinguished between global citations, local citations and normalized local citations.

The most relevant article about Directive 2014/95/EU has been published by La Torre *et al.* (2018), which represented one of the main research agendas considered by accounting scholars interested in exploring Directive 2014/95/EU. Other relevant contributions have been published by Pizzi *et al.* (2021a) and Dumay *et al.* (2019). Pizzi *et al.* (2021a) discussed the relationship between Sustainable Development Goals (SDGs) reporting and Directive

2014/95/EU and the theoretical implications related to the adoption of accounting framework in a mandatory institutional setting, while Dumay *et al.* (2019) focused on implications for intellectual capital and integrated reporting.

As regards the specific contribution to the development of studies about Directive 2014/95/EU according to local citations, the main articles are the contributions of Sierra-Garcia *et al.* (2018) and Dumitru *et al.* (2017). Both present findings on the transposition of the Directive during the period of its entry into force. Sierra-Garcia *et al.* (2018) focus on Spain and Dumitru *et al.* (2017) compare the situation in Romania and Poland.

However, citation analysis is influenced by the time span. In this regard, recent papers are usually characterized by fewer citations. To avoid this criticism, we integrated our analysis by considering normalized local citations. This methodological approach favored the identification of interesting contributions published by Zarzycka and Krasodomska (2022), Ottenstein *et al.* (2022) and Mio *et al.* (2020a). The three contributions are particularly relevant for accounting scholars interested in evaluating mandatory sustainability reporting because they analyzed complex and novel topics directly related to the new Corporate Sustainability Reporting Directive (CSRD).

Table 5.3   *Performance analysis of the main articles that have contributed to the development of the field*

Global citations		Local citations		Normalized local citations	
Article	#	Article	#	Article	#
La Torre *et al.* (2018)	99	La Torre *et al.* (2018)	33	Zarzycka and Krasodomska (2022)	6.2
Pizzi *et al.* (2021b)	71	Sierra-Garcia *et al.* (2018)	17	Ottenstein *et al.* (2022)	4.13
Dumay *et al.* (2019)	68	Dumitru *et al.* (2017)	15	Mio *et al.* (2020a)	3.94
Dumitru *et al.* (2017)	67	Venturelli *et al.* (2019)	14	Krasodomska and Zarzycka (2021)	3.93
Sierra-Garcia *et al.* (2018)	62	Aureli *et al.* (2019)	13	La Torre *et al.* (2018)	3.3

Furthermore, we evaluated the theoretical roots of the field, extracting from *Bibliometrix* the co-citation network. The co-citation analysis allows researchers to identify the intellectual structure of the observed research field. In this regard, co-citation favors the identification of the main sources considered by the authors in developing their research, such as pioneer studies, theoretical framework, and early contributions. The analysis revealed the existence of four independent research clusters considered by academics in their articles (Figure 5.1). The first cluster refers to contributions about the real impacts related to the transposition of Directive 2014/95/EU by the Member States while the second cluster consists of *ex ante* evaluation of the potential impacts related to its future transposition. In this regard, the first two clusters are different in terms of time horizon. The third cluster consists of papers about the enabling role covered by specific items on sustainability reporting practices, with a specific focus on corporate governance (Hahn and Kühnen, 2013) and regulation (Bebbington *et al.*, 2012). Finally, the fourth cluster considers theoretical framework and viewpoints about sustainability reporting and regulation.

THE CONCEPTUAL STRUCTURE OF THE SCIENTIFIC DEBATE

Although the effects related to the launch of Directive 2014/95/EU have been explored by considering theories and methodological approaches inspired by accounting traditions, the analysis confirmed the existence of a high degree of fragmentation caused by the alternative perspectives adopted by accounting scholars (Korca and Costa, 2020; La Torre *et al.*, 2020). According to this evidence, we evaluated the conceptual structure of the field using a keyword analysis, which represents a methodological approach particularly suitable for summarizing the main contributions about a specific topic (Caputo *et al.*, 2021). In this regard, using *VosViewer*'s co-occurrence analysis, we identified three potential research clusters able to summarize the main contributions about Directive 2014/95/EU published during the last few years.[2] In detail, the (1) *cluster A* refers to 'Regulation & Policy', the (2) *cluster B* consists of research papers about 'Accountability & Stakeholder engagement' while the (3) *cluster C* analyses 'Corporate Governance and Strategy' (Figure 5.1). In the following subsection, we present an overview of the main contents included in each cluster.

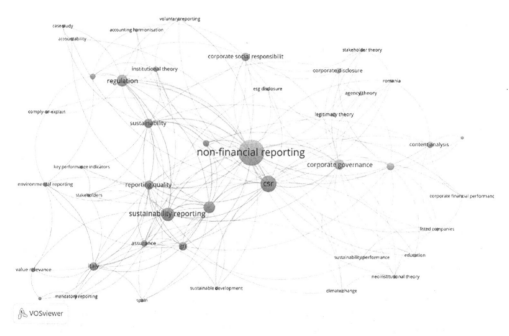

Note: References to 'cluster A' are to the top left-hand cluster, centered around the label 'regulation'; references to 'cluster B' are to the bottom left-hand cluster, centered around the labels 'sustainability reporting' and 'csr'; and references to 'cluster C' are to the right-hand cluster, centered around the labels 'non-financial reporting' and 'corporate governance'.
Source: Own elaboration based on *VOSviewer*.

Figure 5.1   *Co-occurrence analysis based on the authors' keywords*

1   Cluster A: Regulation & Policy

Cluster A provides specific insights about the attempts made by accounting scholars to conceptualize the enabling role covered by non-financial regulation on sustainability reporting.

The development of the sub-field has been driven by the wide adoption of the institutional theory, which represents the traditional accounting lens used by accounting scholars to evaluate the mechanisms related to the adoption of business practices on a mandatory basis. This topic is particularly relevant for social and environmental accounting scholars, as evidenced by Bebbington *et al.* (2012) in their early research on non-financial reporting regulation. In this regard, Mio *et al.* (2020b) first provide evidence that confirms that the intended outcomes of the European legislator have been met, at least in terms of the increase of the overall level of non-financial disclosure. They also found that two enforcement variables have been particularly effective in increasing such disclosure: content and auditors. This means that requirements of Member States that additional information be disclosed and that non-financial information be assured by an assurance provider produced greater incentives for companies to disclose. In a following study, Mio et al. (2021) empirically test the impact of different implementation strategies on non-financial information quantity and quality. They find that regulations providing incentives ('carrots') are more effective than regulations imposing costs ('sticks'). More specifically, while mandatory assurance and safe harbor have a positive impact on non-financial reporting quantity, fines do not. Korca *et al.* (2021) also found that the effects related to the transposition of Directive 2014/95/EU have been related to an increase in the overall quantity of information disclosed annually, while the qualitative effects were residual. This evidence was consistent with Pizzi *et al.* (2021a) and Panfilo and Krasodomska (2022), which underlined the existence of many criticisms related to the disclosure of environmental and climate information by companies. Institutional theory was also considered by Lambooy *et al.* (2018), which highlighted the lack of materiality of certain information for investors.

Another key issue in *cluster A* is accounting harmonization. Building on a critical reflection about the real effects related to the introduction of Directive 2014/95/EU, Aureli *et al.* (2019) identified the existence of differences between European countries. In this regard, the authors anticipated some of the main criticisms identified by the European Commission during the public consultations about the revision of Directive 2014/95/EU. A similar analysis was conducted by Stefanescu (2021), who adopted a quantitative approach to evaluate the main drivers that have impacted on non-financial reporting harmonization. Interestingly, the author did not identify the relationships with economic and financial pressures, which represent two of the main motivations considered by policymakers in their decision-making processes.

Finally, *cluster A* also provides interesting insights about voluntary reporting. The topic has been widely explored by academics because of the existence of many companies that were only aligned to the legal requirements identified by the European Commission. In particular, many studies considered the transition from voluntary to mandatory reporting in alternative institutional settings such as Italy (Doni *et al.*, 2019), Spain (Sierra-Garcia *et al.*, 2018), the United Kingdom (Venturelli *et al.*, 2019), Romania and Poland (Dumitru *et al.*, 2017), and at European level (Mio *et al.*, 2020b; 2021).

2 Cluster B: Accountability and Stakeholder Engagement

Accountability and stakeholder engagement have been two topics widely explored by academics because of the need to evaluate the effects related to the disclosure of sustainability information and the role of stakeholder engagement when it comes to the identification of relevant material topics by preparers. In fact, Directive 2014/95/EU was inspired by the harmonization principle, which did not require companies to align their reports to strict requirements. In this regard, many companies disclose their information using alternative forms of reporting standards and frameworks. Thus, academics developed conceptual and theoretical frameworks able to collect insights about the quality of the information disclosed by the European PIEs on a mandatory basis (Caputo *et al.*, 2020; Manes-Rossi *et al.*, 2018). Furthermore, other studies were developed using sets of standardized information in order to bridge the conceptual gap between qualitative and quantitative analysis (Zarzycka and Krasodomska, 2022). In this sense, the current scenario is characterized by the coexistence of alternative frameworks about sustainability reporting quality in Europe (Fiandrino *et al.*, 2021).

Stakeholder engagement represents one of the main principles considered by the main international standard setters. In fact, an effective engagement with stakeholders favors the identification of relevant material topics by businesses' non-financial report preparers (Baumüller and Sopp, 2021). At the same time, an unreliable engagement is often related to unethical practices such as greenwashing and impression management. In this regard, Mazzotta *et al.* (2020) conceptualized a framework to evaluate the identification of the reliability index of the information disclosed by the European PIEs. Furthermore, many studies have been developed to collect insights about specific sectors of activity such as the financial sector (Cosma *et al.*, 2021) and state-owned enterprises (Dragomir *et al.*, 2022).

Finally, the concept of reporting quality has been also connected to the value relevance of the information disclosed by the European PIEs. In particular, much research was developed considering alternative proxies for sustainability reporting quality. Considering risk disclosure, Veltri *et al.* (2020) found a positive relation with PIEs' market value. A similar result was identified by Paolone *et al.* (2021), which considered the specific effects related to environmental risks. Interestingly, Simoni *et al.* (2022) did not identify a significant relationship between business model disclosure and market value. The combination of those results confirms the central role covered by environmental and climate information on financial markets.

3   Cluster C: Corporate Governance and Strategy

Cluster C considers the relationship between corporate governance and sustainability reporting practices in Europe. This cluster is typically related to the legitimacy theory revised by Guthrie and Parker (1989), which underlined the existence of strategic implications related to the disclosure of information by companies. The rise of this research field has been also supported by the attempt made by the European Commission to include Directive 2014/95/EU within a set of rules about the adoption of more sustainable business models by European PIEs.

The adoption of the traditional quantitative approach favored the identification of potential interlinkages between corporate governance, Directive 2014/95/EU, and specific topics (Gerwing *et al.*, 2022). Building on a sample of Italian PIEs, Pizzi *et al.* (2021b) identified a positive relationship between SDG Reporting and independent directors. Nicolò *et al.* (2022) shed light on the enabling role taken by women directors on mandatory ESG reporting practices. This result is in contrast with Krasodomska *et al.* (2020), which did not identify any significant differences between the attitudes of male and female accountants toward mandatory CSR disclosures under the Directive. Furthermore, Cosma *et al.* (2022) underlined the central role covered by the CSR committee when it comes to providing disclosures in line with the recommendations of the Task Force on Climate-related Financial Disclosures (TCFD).

Finally, *cluster C* also considers the implications related to companies' business models. Di Tullio *et al.* (2019) highlighted that the disclosure of information about the business model can contribute to the legitimation processes conducted by managers. A similar perspective was also adopted by Cerrato and Ferrando (2020), which encouraged companies to foster accountability processes that would contribute to sustainable development. In the same vein, a recent paper published by Krasodomska *et al.* (2023) identifies a significant positive change in the share of companies providing a reference to SDGs prior to and after the implementation of Directive 2014/95/EU. In this regard, encouraging companies to disclose their sustainability information should be considered by policymakers as a way to indirectly encourage the adoption of more sustainable business models.

CONCLUSIONS

In line with the declaration of the European Green Deal, the European Commission conducted internal conceptual work on possible directions for changes to Directive 2014/95/EU in 2019. On December 16, 2022, the CSRD was published in the Official Journal of the EU. Starting from that date, member countries have 18 months to implement the CSRD in national legislation. In parallel, the EC permitted the European Financial Reporting Advisory Group (EFRAG) to develop the European Sustainability Reporting Standards (ESRS). Draft versions of the standards were published in April 2022 and adopted in November 2022. The European Commission adopted the ESRS with a Delegated Act on July 31, 2023.

Moreover, on the global level, in 2021 the International Financial Reporting Standards (IFRS) Foundation established the International Sustainability Standards Board (ISSB). In March 2022, the ISSB published two standards, *S1 General Requirements for Sustainability-Related Financial Disclosures* and *S2 Climate-Related Disclosures*, and subjected them to public consultation. The proposed standards, once finalized, are expected to provide a comprehensive global basis for sustainability-related disclosures aimed at meeting investors' information needs in assessing a company's value.

All these changes in the reporting landscape in the EU and beyond present new research opportunities. The current chapter, adopting a bibliometric analysis, identified the profuse and brand-new literature on Directive 2014/95/EU. The study highlights how researchers are interested in exploring the role of these new regulations and related policies for corporate sustainability reporting, the importance of stakeholder pressure and engagement for regulatory processes and subsequent reporting, and the impact of the new regulations on corporate strategies, with consideration of corporate governance mechanisms. A *fil rouge* emerging from the three main clusters identified is the theme of the real effects that the mandatory adoption of the Directive may have on companies' activities and practices. For instance, Fiechter *et al.* (2022) document that firms within the scope of the Directive respond by increasing their CSR activities and that they start doing so before the entry into force of the Directive. Furthermore, they found that these real effects are concentrated in firms with low levels of both CSR reporting and CSR activities before the introduction of the Directive. Nevertheless, this stream of literature is still in its infancy and requires more empirical investigation due to its practical implications.

The findings of this research show that the scientific debate has been characterized by an intense contribution provided mainly by Italian, Polish, and Spanish authors. In contrast, the contribution of non-European scholars has been limited. Since non-financial disclosure was found to be value relevant and associated with corporate accountability, and to have real effects on stakeholder engagement and corporate governance practices, future research may want to investigate it in non-mandatory contexts as well.

Furthermore, apart from a few exceptions, results highlight that accounting journals are not taking part in such a debate. Accounting scholars are therefore discussing sustainability accounting regulations, policies, and practices in management or sustainability journals. Journals in the accounting field should be more involved in the discussion, considering the real impacts related to sustainability reporting and the transposition of the CSRD, because of the professional implications that will take place not only at the European level. Accounting academia, on the other hand, plays a key role in developing theoretical frameworks and viewpoints about sustainability reporting and practices useful to policymakers and institutions for making informed decisions and contributing to the (sustainability) accounting harmonization process.

ACKNOWLEDGEMENTS

The chapter presents the results of the project financed by the subsidy granted to the Krakow University of Economics.

NOTES

1. Date of the data collection.
2. This figure appears in grayscale in the print version of this book. References to the 'blue cluster' are to the top left cluster, centered around the label 'regulation'; references to the 'red cluster' are to the bottom left cluster, centered around the labels 'sustainability reporting' and 'csr'; and references to the 'green cluster' are to the right-hand cluster, centered around the labels 'non-financial reporting' and 'corporate governance'.

REFERENCES

Aria, M. and Cuccurullo, C. (2017), 'Bibliometrix: An R-tool for comprehensive science mapping analysis', *Journal of Informetrics*, Vol. 11 No. 4, pp. 959–975, doi: 10.1016/j.joi.2017.08.007.

Aureli, S., Magnaghi, E. and Salvatori, F. (2019), 'The role of existing regulation and discretion in harmonising non-financial disclosure', *Accounting in Europe*, Vol. 16 No. 3, pp. 290–312, doi: 10.1080/17449480.2019.1637529.

Baker, H.K., Kumar, S., Pandey, N. and Kraus, S. (2022), 'Contemporary accounting research: a retrospective between 1984 and 2021 using bibliometric analysis*', *Contemporary Accounting Research*, doi: 10.1111/1911-3846.12779.

Baumüller, J. and Sopp, K. (2021), 'Double materiality and the shift from non-financial to European sustainability reporting: review, outlook and implications', *Journal of Applied Accounting Research*, Vol. 23 No. 1, pp. 8–28, doi: 10.1108/jaar-04-2021-0114.

Bebbington, J., Kirk, E.A. and Larrinaga, C. (2012), 'The production of normativity: a comparison of reporting regimes in Spain and the UK', *Accounting, Organizations and Society*, Vol. 37 No. 2, pp. 78–94, doi: 10.1016/j.aos.2012.01.001.

Broadus, R.N. (1987), 'Toward a definition of 'bibliometrics'', *Scientometrics*, Vol. 12 No. 5–6, pp. 373–379, doi: 10.1007/BF02016680.

Caputo, A., Pizzi, S., Pellegrini, M.M. and Dabić, M. (2021), 'Digitalization and business models: where are we going? A science map of the field', *Journal of Business Research*, Vol. 123, pp. 489–501, doi: 10.1016/j.jbusres.2020.09.053.

Caputo, F., Leopizzi, R., Pizzi, S. and Milone, V. (2020), 'The non-financial reporting harmonization in Europe: evolutionary pathways related to the transposition of the Directive 95/2014/EU within the Italian context', *Sustainability*, Vol. 12 No. 1, pp. 1–13, doi: 10.3390/SU12010092.

Cerrato, D. and Ferrando, T. (2020), 'The financialization of civil society activism: sustainable finance, non-financial disclosure and the shrinking space for engagement', *Accounting, Economics and Law: A Convivium*, Vol. 10 No. 2, pp. 1–28, doi: 10.1515/ael-2019-0006.

Christensen, H.B., Hail, L. and Leuz, C. (2021), 'Mandatory CSR and sustainability reporting: economic analysis and literature review', *Review of Accounting Studies*, Vol. 26, pp. 1176–1248, doi: 10.1007/s11142-021-09609-5.

Cosma, S., Leopizzi, R., Pizzi, S. and Turco, M. (2021), 'The stakeholder engagement in the European banks: regulation versus governance. What changes after the NF directive?', *Corporate Social Responsibility and Environmental Management*, Vol. 28 No. 3, pp. 1091–1103, doi: 10.1002/csr.2108.

Cosma, S., Principale, S. and Venturelli, A. (2022), 'Sustainable governance and climate-change disclosure in European banking: the role of the corporate social responsibility committee', *Corporate Governance*, Vol. 22 No. 6, pp. 1345–1369, doi: 10.1108/CG-09-2021-0331.

Di Tullio, P., Valentinetti, D., Nielsen, C. and Rea, M.A. (2019), 'In search of legitimacy: a semiotic analysis of business model disclosure practices', *Meditari Accountancy Research*, Vol. 28 No. 5, pp. 863–887, doi: 10.1108/MEDAR-02-2019-0449.

Dinh, T., Husmann, A. and Melloni, G. (2023), 'Corporate sustainability reporting in Europe: a scoping review', *Accounting in Europe*, Vol. 20 No. 1, pp. 91–119, doi: 10.1080/17449480.2022.2149345.

Doni, F., Bianchi Martini, S., Corvino, A. and Mazzoni, M. (2019), 'Voluntary versus mandatory non-financial disclosure', *Meditari Accountancy Research*, Vol. 28 No. 5, pp. 781–802, doi: 10.1108/medar-12-2018-0423.

Dragomir, V.-D., Dumitru, M. and Feleaga, L. (2022), 'The predictors of non-financial reporting quality in Romanian state-owned enterprises', *Accounting in Europe*, Vol. 19 No. 1, pp. 110–151, doi: 10.1080/17449480.2021.2018474.

Dumay, J., La Torre, M. and Farneti, F. (2019), 'Developing trust through stewardship: implications for intellectual capital, integrated reporting, and the EU Directive 2014/95/EU', *Journal of Intellectual Capital*, Vol. 20 No. 1, pp. 11–39, doi: 10.1108/JIC-06-2018-0097.

Dumitru, M., Dyduch, J., Guşe, R.G. and Krasodomska, J. (2017), 'Corporate reporting practices in Poland and Romania – an ex-ante study to the new Non-Financial Reporting European Directive', *Accounting in Europe*, Vol. 14 No. 3, pp. 279–304, doi: 10.1080/17449480.2017.1378427.

European Commission (2011), Communication from the Commission to the European Parliament, the Council, the European Economic and Social Committee and the Committee of the Regions. A renewed EU strategy 2011–14 for Corporate Social Responsibility, COM(2011) 681 final. Available at: https://eur-lex.europa.eu/LexUriServ/LexUriServ.do?uri=COM:2011:0681:FIN:en:PDF%20.

European Commission (2017), Communication from the Commission. Guidelines on non-financial reporting (methodology for reporting non financial information). Available at: https://eur-lex.europa.eu/legal-content/EN/TXT/?uri=CELEX%3A52017XC0705%2801%29.

European Commission (2019), Communication from the Commission. Guidelines on non-financial reporting: Supplement on reporting climate related information. Available at: https://eur-lex.europa.eu/legal-content/EN/TXT/PDF/?uri=CELEX:52019XC0620(01).

European Commission (2020), Inception impact assessment, proposal for a regulation as regards disclosure of nonfinancial information by certain undertakings and groups document ares(2020)580716. Available at: https://eur-lex.europa.eu/legal-content/EN/ALL/?uri=PI_COM:Ares(2020)580716.

European Commission (2021), Proposal for a Directive of the European Parliament and of the Council amending Directive 2013/34/EU, Directive 2004/109/EC, Directive 2006/43/EC and Regulation (EU) No 537/2014, as regards corporate sustainability reporting, COM(2021) 189 final. Available at: https://eur-lex.europa.eu/legal-content/EN/TXT/PDF/?uri=CELEX:52021PC0189.

European Union (2014), Directive 2014/95/EU of the European Parliament and of the Council of October 22, 2014 amending Directive 2013/34/EU as regards disclosure of non-financial and diversity information by certain large undertakings and groups. Available at: https://eur-lex.europa.eu/legal-content/EN/TXT/?uri=celex:32014L0095.

Ferreira, F.A.F. (2018), 'Mapping the field of arts-based management: bibliographic coupling and co-citation analyses', *Journal of Business Research*, Vol. 85, pp. 348–357, doi: 10.1016/j.jbusres.2017.03.026.

Fiandrino, S., di Trana, M., Tonelli, A. and Lucchese, A. (2021), 'The multi-faceted dimensions for the disclosure quality of non-financial information in revising directive 2014/95/EU', *Journal of Applied Accounting Research*, Vol. 23 No. 1, pp. 274-300, doi: 10.1108/JAAR-04-2021-0118.

Fiechter, P., Hitz, J.M. and Lehmann, N. (2022). 'Real effects of a widespread CSR reporting mandate: evidence from the European Union's CSR Directive', *Journal of Accounting Research*, Vol. 60 No. 4, pp. 1499–1549, doi: 10.1111/1475-679X.12424.

Gerwing, T., Kajüter, P. and Wirth, M. (2022), 'The role of sustainable corporate governance in mandatory sustainability reporting quality', *Journal of Business Economics*, Vol. 92 No. 3, pp. 517–555, doi: 10.1007/s11573-022-01092-x.

Guthrie, J. and Parker, L.D. (1989), 'Corporate social reporting: a rebuttal of legitimacy theory', *Accounting and Business Research*, Vol. 19 No. 76, pp. 343–352, doi: 10.1080/00014788.1989.9728863.

Hahn, R. and Kühnen, M. (2013), 'Determinants of sustainability reporting: a review of results, trends, theory, and opportunities in an expanding field of research', *Journal of Cleaner Production*, Vol. 59, pp. 5–21, doi: 10.1016/j.jclepro.2013.07.005.

Korca, B. and Costa, E. (2020), 'Directive 2014/95/EU: building a research agenda', *Journal of Applied Accounting Research*, Vol. 22 No. 3, pp. 401–422, doi: 10.1108/JAAR-05-2020-0085.

Korca, B., Costa, E. and Farneti, F. (2021), 'From voluntary to mandatory non-financial disclosure following Directive 2014/95/EU: an Italian case study', *Accounting in Europe*, pp. 1–25, doi: 10.1080/17449480.2021.1933113.

KPMG (2022), 'The new CSRD: What does this mean for you?' Available at: https://www.headvisor.it/sites/default/files/pdf/ie-esg-eu-reporting.pdf.

Krasodomska, J. and Zarzycka, E. (2021). 'Key performance indicators disclosure in the context of the EU directive: when does stakeholder pressure matter?' *Meditari Accountancy Research*, Vol. 29 No. 7, pp. 1–30.

Krasodomska, J., Michalak, J. and Świetla, K. (2020), 'Directive 2014/95/EU: accountants' understanding and attitude towards mandatory non-financial disclosures in corporate reporting', *Meditari Accountancy Research*, Vol. 28 No. 5, pp. 751–779, doi: 10.1108/MEDAR-06-2019-0504.

Krasodomska, J., Zieniuk, P. and Kostrzewska, J. (2023), 'Reporting on Sustainable Development Goals in the European Union: what drives companies' decisions?', *Competitiveness Review*, Vol. 33 No. 1, pp. 120–146, doi: 10.1108/CR-12-2021-0179.

La Torre, M., Sabelfeld, S., Blomkvist, M., Tarquinio, L. and Dumay, J. (2018), 'Harmonising non-financial reporting regulation in Europe: practical forces and projections for future research', *Meditari Accountancy Research*, Vol. 26 No. 4, pp. 598–621, doi: 10.1108/MEDAR-02-2018-0290.

La Torre, M., Sabelfeld, S., Blomkvist, M. and Dumay, J. (2020), 'Rebuilding trust: sustainability and non-financial reporting and the European Union regulation', *Meditari Accountancy Research*, Vol. 28 No. August, pp. 701–725, doi: 10.1108/MEDAR-06-2020-0914.

Lambooy, T.E., Maas, K.E.H., van 't Foort, S. and van Tilburg, R. (2018), 'Biodiversity and natural capital: investor influence on company reporting and performance*', *Journal of Sustainable Finance and Investment*, Vol. 8 No. 2, pp. 158–184, doi: 10.1080/20430795.2017.1409524.

Latapí Agudelo, M.A., Jóhannsdóttir, L. and Davídsdóttir, B. (2019), 'A literature review of the history and evolution of corporate social responsibility', *International Journal of Corporate Social Responsibility*, Vol. 4, p. 1, doi: 10.1186/s40991-018-0039-y.

Manes-Rossi, F., Tiron-Tudor, A., Nicolò, G. and Zanellato, G. (2018), 'Ensuring more sustainable reporting in Europe using non-financial disclosure – de facto and de jure evidence', *Sustainability*, Vol. 10 No. 4, p. 1162, doi: 10.3390/su10041162.

Marzi, G., Dabić, M., Daim, T. and Garces, E. (2017), 'Product and process innovation in manufacturing firms: a 30-year bibliometric analysis', *Scientometrics*, Vol. 113 No. 2, pp. 673–704, doi: 10.1007/s11192-017-2500-1.

Mazzotta, R., Bronzetti, G. and Veltri, S. (2020), 'Are mandatory non-financial disclosures credible? Evidence from Italian listed companies', *Corporate Social Responsibility and Environmental Management*, Vol. 27 No. 4, pp. 1900–1913, doi: 10.1002/csr.1935.

Mio, C., Fasan, M. and Costantini, A. (2020a), 'Materiality in integrated and sustainability reporting: A paradigm shift?', *Business Strategy and the Environment*, Vol. 29 No. 1, pp. 306–320, doi: 10.1002/bse.2390.

Mio, C., Fasan, M., Marcon, C. and Panfilo S. (2020b), 'The predictive ability of legitimacy and agency theory after the implementation of the EU Directive on non-financial information', *Corporate Social-Responsibility and Environmental Management*, Vol. 27 No.6, pp. 2465–2476, doi: 10.1002/csr.1968.

Mio, C., Fasan, M., Marcon, C. and Panfilo S. (2021), 'Carrot or stick? An empirical analysis of the different implementation strategies of the EU Directive on non-financial information across Europe',

Corporate Social-Responsibility and Environmental Management, Vol. 28 No.6, pp. 1591–1605, doi: 10.1002/csr.2124.

Müller, S. and Stawinoga, M. (2015), 'Stakeholder expectations on CSR management and current regulatory developments in Europe and Germany', *Corporate Ownership and Control*, Vol. 12 No. 4 (cont.), pp. 506–513, doi: 10.22495/cocv12i4c4p8.

Nicolò, G., Zampone, G., Sannino, G. and De Iorio, S. (2022), 'Sustainable corporate governance and non-financial disclosure in Europe: does the gender diversity matter?', *Journal of Applied Accounting Research*, Vol. 23 No. 1, pp. 227–249, doi: 10.1108/JAAR-04-2021-0100.

Ottenstein, P., Erben, S., Jost, S., Weuster, C.W. and Zülch, H. (2022), 'From voluntarism to regulation: effects of Directive 2014/95/EU on sustainability reporting in the EU', *Journal of Applied Accounting Research*, Vol. 23 No. 1, pp. 55–98, doi: 10.1108/JAAR-03-2021-0075.

Panfilo, S. and Krasodomska, J. (2022), 'Climate change risk disclosure in Europe: the role of cultural-cognitive, regulative, and normative factors', *Accounting in Europe*, Vol. 19 No. 1, pp. 226–253, doi: 10.1080/17449480.2022.2026000.

Paolone, F., Granà, F., Martiniello, L. and Tiscini, R. (2021), 'Environmental risk indicators disclosure and value relevance: an empirical analysis of Italian listed companies after the implementation of the Legislative Decree 254/2016', *Corporate Social Responsibility and Environmental Management*, Vol. 28 No. 5, pp. 1471–1482, doi: 10.1002/csr.2181.

Pizzi, S., Caputo, A., Corvino, A. and Venturelli, A. (2020), 'Management research and the UN Sustainable Development Goals (SDGs): a bibliometric investigation and systematic review', *Journal of Cleaner Production*, Vol. 276, p. 124033, doi: 10.1016/j.jclepro.2020.124033.

Pizzi, S., Rosati, F. and Venturelli, A. (2021a), 'The determinants of business contribution to the 2030 Agenda: introducing the SDG reporting score', *Business Strategy and the Environment*, Vol. 30 No. 1, pp. 404–421, doi: 10.1002/bse.2628.

Pizzi, S., Venturelli, A. and Caputo, F. (2021b), 'The "comply-or-explain" principle in Directive 95/2014/EU. A rhetorical analysis of Italian PIEs', *Sustainability Accounting, Management and Policy Journal*, Vol. 12 No. 1, pp. 30–50, doi: 10.1108/SAMPJ-07-2019-0254.

Schaltegger, S., Gibassier, D. and Zvezdov, D. (2013), 'Is environmental management accounting a discipline? A bibliometric literature review', *Meditari Accountancy Research*, Vol. 21 No. 1, pp. 4–31, doi: 10.1108/MEDAR-12-2012-0039.

Sierra-Garcia, L., Garcia-Benau, M.A. and Bollas-Araya, H.M. (2018), 'Empirical analysis of non-financial reporting by Spanish companies', *Administrative Sciences*, Vol. 8 No. 3, doi: 10.3390/admsci8030029.

Simoni, L., Schaper, S. and Nielsen, C. (2022), 'Business model disclosures, market values, and earnings persistence: evidence from the UK', Abacus, Vol. 58 No. 1, pp. 142–173, doi: 10.1111/abac.12233.

Stefanescu, C.A. (2021), 'Transposition of Directive 2014/95/EU – do macroeconomic determinants affect non-financial reporting harmonisation?', Journal of Financial Reporting and Accounting, Vol. 19 No. 5, pp. 861–884, doi: 10.1108/JFRA-07-2020-0193.

Stolowy, H. and Paugam, L. (2023), 'Sustainability reporting: is convergence possible?', Accounting in Europe, Vol. 20 No. 2, pp. 139–165, doi: 10.1080/17449480.2023.2189016.

van Eck, N.J. and Waltman, L. (2010), 'Software survey: VOSviewer, omputer program for bibliometric mapping', Scientometrics, Vol. 84 No. 2, pp. 523–538, doi: 10.1007/s11192-009-0146-3.

Veltri, S., De Luca, F. and Phan, H.T.P. (2020), 'Do investors value companies' mandatory nonfinancial risk disclosure? An empirical analysis of the Italian context after the EU Directive', Business Strategy and the Environment, Vol. 29 No. 6, pp. 2226–2237, doi: 10.1002/bse.2497.

Venturelli, A., Caputo, F., Leopizzi, R. and Pizzi, S. (2019), 'The state of art of corporate social disclosure before the introduction of Non-Financial Reporting Directive: ross country analysis', Social Responsibility Journal, Vol. 15 No. 4, pp. 409–423, doi: 10.1108/SRJ-12-2017-0275.

Venturelli, A., Fasan, M. and Pizzi, S. (2022), 'Guest editorial: Rethinking non-financial reporting in Europe: challenges and opportunities in revising Directive 2014/95/EU', Journal of Applied Accounting Research, Vol. 23 No. 1, pp. 1–7, doi: 10.1108/JAAR-02-2022-265.

Zarzycka, E. and Krasodomska, J. (2022), 'Non-financial key performance indicators: what determines the differences in the quality and quantity of the disclosures?', Journal of Applied Accounting Research, Vol. 23 No. 1, pp. 139–162, doi: 10.1108/JAAR-02-2021-0036.

6. Comparative analysis of the GRI Standards and the IR Framework and their impact on the quality of disclosures

Ewa Różańska, Łukasz Matuszak and Joanna Dyczkowska

INTRODUCTION

Reporting standards and frameworks are essential tools for companies to communicate their sustainability performance effectively. Thanks to them, companies can strengthen relations with stakeholders, identify business opportunities, reduce risk, enhance accountability and improve transparency. They also play a crucial role in the global reporting landscape by helping standardize reporting on such important issues as climate change, human rights, governance and social well-being across different industries and regions. In turn, this enables investors and other stakeholders to make informed decisions.

This chapter contrasts the Global Reporting Initiative (GRI) Standards and the Integrated Reporting (IR) Framework. It displays a comprehensive comparative analysis in relation to the materiality concept, reporting principles and content elements. The results of the analysis present not only the core differences between the GRI Standards and the IR Framework but also indicate how they are aligned and complement each other. The chapter also provides a systematic literature review from the last decade aimed at clarifying the potential of the GRI Standards and the IR Framework in enhancing sustainability reporting quality (SRQ) and integrated reporting quality (IRQ). Finally, we highlight the actions and efforts undertaken by both organizations, the GRI and the International Integrated Reporting Council (IIRC), in the context of the upcoming changes in the global sustainability reporting landscape. The chapter also includes implications for reporters and regulators and identifies areas for future research.

The structure of this chapter consists of four sections. Section 1 briefly describes the evolution of the GRI Guidelines/Standards and the IR Framework and links between the GRI and the IIRC. In section 2, the comprehensive comparative analysis of the GRI Standards and the IR Framework, and their practical implementation, is conducted. Section 3 undertakes an up-to-date systematic literature review on SRQ and IRQ and identifies research paths in which the GRI Guidelines/Standards and the IR Framework played a significant role. Finally, section 4 provides conclusions and future outlook.

6.1 Background Information

The GRI is an independent, international non-profit organization that was founded in Boston, USA, in 1997. In its early stages, the GRI had one major mission, which was to create standards and guidelines to support sustainability disclosures, but over the years, its focus has expanded to include ambitious goals such as harmonizing the sustainability landscape, becoming the central hub for sustainability reporting (SR), leading efficient and effective SR and driving effective use of sustainability information to improve performance (GRI, 2020) and lastly, creating a sustainable future (GRI, 2023).

The GRI has released six different guidelines and standards over the 20 years of the 21st century (Table 6.1). During this period, the GRI has sought to adapt and modify its guidelines and standards to make them widely available and help build consensus. This has been achieved through dialogue, feedback, roundtables and tests. The GRI published the first version of the GRI Guidelines (G1) in 2000. The initial GRI Guidelines (G1) have been extended and improved. In subsequent versions of the guidelines (G2, G3, G3.1 and G4, 2002–2013), they have evolved, mainly in terms of structure and content. In 2016, this process led to the setting of the first global standards for SR – the GRI Standards. The standards are structured as a set of modular, interrelated standards, including the Universal Standards, the Sector Standards and the Topic Standards, which deliver an inclusive picture of an organization's material topics, their related impacts, and how they are managed. The standards are constantly updated (e.g., revised Universal Standards in 2021) and supplemented by new Topic Standards and the continued roll-out of Sector Standards.

The IIRC is a global coalition of regulators, investors, companies, standard setters, the accounting profession, academia and non-governmental organizations (NGOs), which was formed in 2010. In 2021, the IIRC merged with the Sustainability Accounting Standards Board (SASB) to form the Value Reporting Foundation (VRF). In 2022, the VRF consolidated with the International Financial Reporting Standards (IFRS) Foundation into the IFRS Foundation.

The IIRC's long-term vision is a world in which integrated thinking is embedded within the mainstream business practices in the public and private sectors, facilitated by integrated reporting as the corporate reporting norm. The cycle of integrated reporting and integrated thinking, resulting in efficient and productive capital allocation, will act as a force for financial stability and sustainable development. (IIRC, 2021, p. 2)

Table 6.1   The background information

GRI (1997)	IIRC (2010)
Independent, international non-profit organization	Global coalition of regulators, investors, companies, standard setters, the accounting profession, academia and NGOs
GRI Guidelines: ●G1 (2000) ●G2, G3, G3.1, G4 (2002–2013) GRI Standards (2016): Universal Standards, the Sector Standards and the Topic Standards Updates of GRI Standards: revision of Universal Standards (2021) + new Topic Standards + the continued roll-out of Sector Standards	●Integrated Reporting <IR> Framework (2013) ●Revision of the <IR> Framework (2021) 2021: Merger of the IIRC with the SASB to form the VRF 2022: VRF consolidated with the IFRS Foundation

Source: Own elaboration.

In 2013, after a Pilot Program (IIRC, 2012), the IIRC published the first version of its International Integrated Reporting <IR> Framework, defining the guiding principles. Following a revision process, in 2021, the second improved version of the <IR> Framework was developed. Now, it is maintained under the auspices of the VRF.

When analyzing the evolution of SR and IR, it is worth paying attention to the strong links between the GRI and the IIRC. The GRI was one of the founders of the IIRC and expressed support for the development of the IR Framework. Over the past decade, the GRI and the IIRC have shared several joint initiatives.

Both organizations were members of the Corporate Reporting Dialogue (CRD), a platform launched in 2014 to promote greater consistency and comparability between frameworks, standards and related requirements. In 2019, the CRD published a document stating that major global standards and frameworks are closely aligned with the recommendations of the Task Force on Climate-Related Financial Disclosures (CRD, 2019). The GRI and the IIRC were also involved in a joint Corporate Leadership Group on IR, which explored the best ways to use the GRI Standards and the IR Framework in the reporting process (GRI, 2016).

In 2020, five leading organizations, including the GRI and the IIRC, came together to form the Comprehensive Reporting Group, signaling their intent to work towards a comprehensive framework with one set of global reporting standards. The group published a report that specifically highlights the integration of financial and sustainability data, public access to environmental, social and governance (ESG) information, and the assessment of long-term value creation as important features of an effective reporting framework (CDP et al., 2020).

Currently, the GRI Standards and the IR Framework are voluntary, but their application may be obligatory locally, such as for sustainability reporting in the United Arab Emirates (Regan, 2022) or integrated reporting in South Africa (Maroun and Atkins, 2015). Furthermore, both standard setters assist companies in complying with mandatory reporting requirements where they apply. For example, a reference to the GRI Standards was included in Directive 2014/95/ EU. Similarly, a reference to the IR Framework can be found in the EU Guidelines 2017/ C215/01 to Directive 2014/95/EU, published by the European Commission.

Compared to the IR Framework, the GRI Standards have a much broader application in the practice of organizations worldwide (Figure 6.1). Global research conducted by KPMG shows that the GRI has remained the most dominant SR standard over the past decade, with around

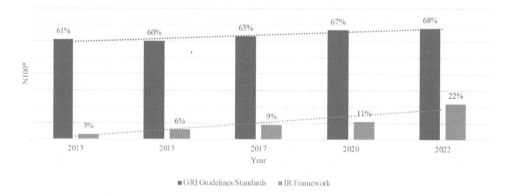

Note: N100* refers to the top 100 companies by revenue in each of the 41, 45, 49, 52 and 58 countries for 2013, 2015, 2017, 2020 and 2022, respectively.
Source: Own elaboration based on KPMG (2013, 2015, 2017, 2020, 2022).

Figure 6.1   Use of GRI Guidelines/Standards and IR Framework in 2013–2022

two-thirds of the N100 using them (see Note, Figure 6.1). While IR is becoming increasingly popular among the N100, it is still in the early stages of uptake, with approximately only one-fifth of N100 referring to its framework in 2022.

6.2   The Comparative Analysis of the GRI Standards and the IR Framework

6.2.1   The materiality concept in the GRI Standards and the IR Framework

Considering the intensive cooperation between the GRI and the IIRC, we ask what the compliance between the GRI standards and the IR framework has been so far and whether the updated version of the GRI Standards (2022a) is aligned with the latest IR Framework (2021). To answer these questions, we conducted a comprehensive comparative analysis of SR and IR in relation to their materiality concept, reporting principles and content elements.

The materiality concept is the cornerstone of accountancy (Frishkoff, 1970) and a useful starting point for reporting for companies of all sizes (KPMG, 2022). Materiality plays a key role in minimizing the risk of information overload, affects the flow of information from companies to external stakeholders, and forms the decision-making activity of managers (Mio et al., 2020a).

Both the IIRC and the GRI confer a central role in materiality. The IIRC (2021) stresses the importance of materiality since it is one of the seven Guiding Principles that underpin the preparation and presentation of an integrated report. In contrast, the GRI (2022a) lists materiality among the key concepts that lay the foundation for SR.

One of the most significant differences between IR and SR is the approach to materiality. The IIRC approach is based on a financially oriented definition. The IIRC (2021) requires an integrated report to disclose information on material matters that "substantively affect the organization's ability to create value over the short, medium and long term" (p. 7) – i.e., that are reasonably likely to impact the financial performance of a company. The IIRC (2021) specified that the intended IR users are the providers of financial capital, and the issues need to be material to them.

In contrast to the IR Framework, the GRI Standards' approach to materiality is based on an impact-oriented definition. The GRI Standards require the organization to prioritize reporting on material topics that reflect its most significant economic, environmental, and social impacts or the benefit of multiple stakeholders (GRI, 2022a). The GRI requires organizations to be involved in the materiality process governance body and expects regular engagement with relevant stakeholders and experts. Most of the impacts of an organization that have been identified through this process are or will eventually become financially material over time. Such impacts can have negative and positive consequences (operational or reputational) for the organization itself, thus providing input for identifying financial risks and opportunities and for financial valuation. Therefore, understanding these impacts is necessary to get a complete overview of material issues affecting the company and its long-term success. This, in turn, assists in making financial materiality judgments about what to include in the financial statements. The material topics and impacts that have been determined for SR are, therefore, crucial for financial and value-creation reporting. In addition, the GRI Standards point out that impact reporting is also highly relevant in its own right as a public activity for multiple stakeholders. The impacts of a company matter and, therefore, must be reported regardless of the consideration of their financial implications (GRI, 2022a).

To sum up, the approaches to the materiality concept of the GRI and the IIRC are different, but in our view, they are not competing but complementary forces. Different reporting frameworks have different purposes for different audiences. Thus, the IR Framework, with the sole purpose of informing investors, is built on a different concept from the GRI Standards that inform a broader group of stakeholders.

While both the IIRC and the GRI help organizations identify material issues and require organizations to provide information about the materiality determination process in their reports, there are concerns regarding the application of the materiality concept in practice (Farooq et al., 2021; Torelli et al., 2020; Mio et al., 2020; Machado et al., 2021; Lakshan et al., 2022). To address these concerns, GRI supports the double materiality concept under the European Sustainability Reporting Standards (ESRS) being created by the EU.

6.2.2 The reporting principles in the GRI Standards and the IR Framework

Both the GRI Standards and the IR Framework are fundamentally principle-based. The GRI reporting principles guide the organization in ensuring the quality and proper presentation of the reported information (GRI, 2022a), whereas the seven Guiding Principles of the IR Framework underpin the preparation and presentation of an integrated report, informing the content of the report and how information is presented (IIRC, 2021).

When comparing the principles in the GRI Standards and the IR Framework, there is substantial alignment, although minor differences can also be identified (Figure 6.2).

The reporting principles of the GRI Standards and the IR Framework show a different focus: sustainability versus strategic and future. While a sustainable report should be prepared "in the wider context of sustainable development" (*sustainability context*) (GRI, 2022a), an integrated

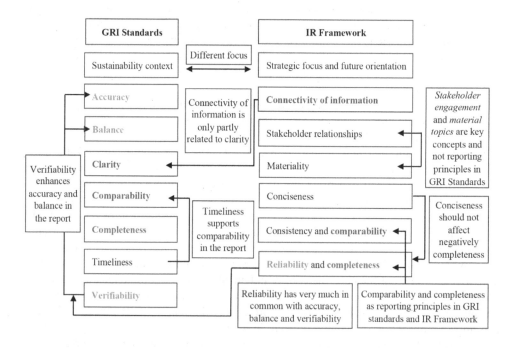

Source: Own elaboration.

Figure 6.2   Reporting principles – differences and interrelations

report "should provide insight into the organization's strategy and how it relates to the organization's ability to create value in the short, medium and long term and to its use of and effects on the capitals" (*strategic focus and future orientation*) (IIRC, 2021).

The comparability principle is a reporting principle desired by the GRI Standards and the IR Framework. To apply the *comparability* principle in the sustainability report, the organization should select, compile and present information consistently to enable comparison over time and to other organizations (GRI, 2022a). Similarly, such *consistency and comparability* of information are required in the integrated report (IIRC, 2021). It is worth noting that ensuring the comparability of information over time is affected by its *timeliness*. However, timeliness is a separate principle only in the GRI Standards and requires the organization to report on a regular schedule so that information is available in time for information users to make decisions (GRI, 2022a).

References to the principle of completeness are also included in the IR Framework and the GRI Standards. The IR Framework combines *reliability and completeness* in one principle; thus, a complete integrated report includes all material information, both positive and negative, presented in a balanced way and without material error (with appropriate accuracy). The IIRC notes that reliability is enhanced by various mechanisms, such as robust internal control or independent external assurance. Moreover, the organization needs to seek an equilibrium between *conciseness* (another principle) and the completeness of the integrated report (IIRC, 2021).

The GRI Standards present a convergent approach to these principles, postulating that the organization shall provide sufficient information in the sustainability report to enable an assessment of the organization's impacts during the reporting period (*completeness*). Moreover, this information should be correct and sufficiently detailed (*accuracy*), providing a fair representation of the organization's negative and positive impacts in an unbiased way (*balance*) (GRI, 2022a). It can be seen that the accuracy and the balance thus constitute reliability (often called faithful representation) to which the IR Framework refers. These principles are also enhanced by *verifiability*. This means that the organization should set up internal controls and organize documentation in such a way that the information can be examined by internal auditors or external assurance providers (IIRC, 2021). It should be mentioned that neither the GRI Standards nor the IR Framework obliges organizations to assure their reports externally, although they encourage them to do so (GRI, 2022a; IIRC 2021).

An important principle of the IR Framework, which seemingly has no direct equivalent in the GRI Standards, is the *connectivity of the information*. Within the meaning of the IIRC, it is interpreted quite broadly and on many levels. It concerns the connectivity between the content elements of the integrated report; past, present and future information; capitals; financial and other information; quantitative and qualitative information; management, board and externally reported information; information disclosed in the integrated report, in other company communication tools and from other sources. Moreover, the connectivity of information is enhanced when an integrated report is logically structured, well presented, written in clear, understandable and jargon-free language, and includes effective navigation tools (i.e. links, cross-referencing) (IIRC, 2021). The above is partly related to the principle of *clarity* referred to in the GRI Standards. To apply this principle, the organization should present information in a way that is accessible and understandable (GRI, 2022a).

In addition to the above, the IR Framework lists *materiality* (see section 6.2.1) and *stakeholder relationships* among its reporting principles, noting that it is important to understand, consider and respond to the legitimate needs and interests of stakeholders (IIRC, 2021). Similarly, the GRI Standards initially included materiality and stakeholders' inclusiveness under the principles for defining report content (GRI, 2020). However, after the last update of the standards effective from January 1, 2023, material topics and stakeholder engagement that help identify the most significant impacts are key concepts and not principles of sustainable reporting (GRI, 2022a).

To sum up, the IIRC and GRI reporting principles are convergent and aim to achieve similar reporting results. A more in-depth analysis of the principles reveals that the principles presented in the IR Framework and GRI Standards are largely consistent.

6.2.3   The contents of the report according to the GRI Standards and the IR Framework

Both the GRI Standards and the IR Framework provide guidance on the contents of the report (see Table 6.2). IR requires disclosures answering questions about organizational overview and external environment, governance, business model, risks and opportunities, strategy and resource allocation, performance, outlook and basis of preparation and presentation (IIRC, 2021). In contrast, SR provides quantitative and qualitative disclosures according to (1) the Universal Standards – about the organization, its activities, governance structure, strategy and policies and the process for determining and managing material topics; (2) the Sector Standards – applicable to specific sectors and; (3) the Topic Standards – for each material topic regarding economic, environmental and social categories (GRI, 2022a).

Table 6.2   *Comparison of the requirement regarding the content of the reports*

GRI Standards	IR Framework
Quantitative and qualitative disclosures according to:	Contents of the report:
● The Universal Standards – about the organization, its activities, governance structure, strategy and policies and the process for determining and managing material topics	● Organizational overview and external environment ● Governance ● Business model ● Risks and opportunities
● The Sector Standards – applicable to specific sectors	● Strategy and resource allocation ● Performance
● The Topic Standards – for each material topic regarding economic, environmental and social categories	● Outlook ● Basis of preparation and presentation

Source: Own elaboration

It can be seen that most of the IR elements have their counterparts in the SR. However, more discrepancies can be identified in the presentation of the main areas of disclosure. The main difference between the GRI Standards and IR Framework is that the *content elements* in IR are not intended to be a structure or a checklist of the integrated report, but rather, they are questions that management should consider when deciding on the content of the report (IIRC, 2021). In this sense, content elements in IR can be perceived more as a direction of thinking.

On the other hand, GRI Standards require disclosures to be made according to a specific list of content items, including detailed indicators. Moreover, the GRI provides a content index – an overview of the organization's reported information – and shows the location where information can be found. The content index also informs which GRI Standards and disclosures the organization has used (GRI, 2022a). However, this main difference creates the conditions in which the two may complement each other in such a way that the GRI Standards may be a fulfilment of the IR Framework. For example, the GRI qualitative and quantitative disclosures can be used in reporting company performance – one of the main elements of IR content – to answer the question of what its outcomes are in terms of effects on the capitals, such as financial, manufactured, intellectual, human, social and relationship and natural.

6.3   The systematic literature review on IRQ and SRQ

6.3.1   The course of the research study

Together, the concept of materiality, reporting principles and content elements adopted by the GRI and IIRC, respectively, constitute the foundations that play an important role in the preparation of high-quality non-financial disclosures. The study by Stuart et al. (2022) reveals that compliance with properly designed reporting standards/frameworks influences the quality of information disclosed. Given the core differences between the GRI Standards and the IR Framework in the approach to materiality, emphasis and terminology used in reporting principles, and the way content elements are presented, identified in the previous section, the question arises as to how they affect the quality of reporting.

Thus, in this section, we conducted a systematic literature review to analyze the role of the GRI Standards and the IR Framework in shaping the reports' disclosure quality. For this purpose, we searched the Scopus database for articles published between 2013 and 2022 related to IRQ or SRQ. We chose a ten-year research period in which both the GRI Guidelines/ Standards and the IR Framework were in force, and organizations could have voluntarily applied them to produce non-financial reports.

We narrowed our search to the following domain areas: (1) business, management and accounting, (2) social sciences, (3) environmental science, and (4) economics, econometrics and finance. We searched by titles, keywords and abstracts. We performed a sorting of the following combinations of terms: first "sustainability reporting" and "quality" and then "integrated reporting" and "quality". Searches of the first pair of terms yielded indications of 237 documents, while for the second pair of terms, the Scopus database indicated 165 documents. When we compared the results of the two compilations, we identified a common part of these collections comprising 37 documents. A total of 365 abstracts were included in the further content analysis. During this analysis, 11 abstracts whose subject matter did not justify their thematic link to the area of IR or SR quality were excluded, although the word "quality" appeared in these abstracts in contexts different to the one studied. One abstract was excluded because the publication was not written in English.

Tables 6.3 and 6.4 present the statistics on the number of papers published on the SR and IR topic. The data presented in Table 6.3 confirms an upward dynamic in the total number of publications on SRQ and IRQ from 2013 onwards, when the IR Framework was published, except for a minor fluctuation in 2017 and a larger one in 2021, which may have been due to the effects of the Covid-19 pandemic and lower publication activity.

Table 6.4 provides information on the most active journals in the Scopus database that published works, including IRQ or SRQ terms in the keywords or abstracts. Six journals prevailed in this regard, publishing more than ten articles that addressed IRQ or SRQ in their keywords or abstracts. The dynamic of this process is also interesting. Most articles (over 74%) appeared in the second half of the period studied, i.e., between 2018 and 2022.

Further investigation required a thorough thematic analysis of 354 selected abstracts. The analysis allowed us to identify four primary research paths that dominated academic works

Table 6.3   Number of articles on the quality of SR and IR in the Scopus database

Year	"SR"+"quality"	"IR"+"quality"	"SR"+"IR" +"quality"	Total	Correction	Total	Share
2022	42	39	9	90	−1	89	25.1%
2021	16	13	4	33		33	9.3%
2020	37	27	2	66	−4	62	17.5%
2019	22	19	6	47		47	13.3%
2018	19	6	7	32		32	9.0%
2017	18	6	1	25		25	7.1%
2016	17	8	2	27	−2	25	7.1%
2015	9	6	3	18	−1	17	4.8%
2014	10	3	2	15	−1	14	3.9%
2013	10	1	1	12	−2	10	2.8%
	200	128	37	365	−11	354	100%

Source: Own elaboration

Table 6.4   The most active journals with research works, including IRQ or SRQ terms in the keywords or abstracts

Names of journals with the highest number of articles on the researched topic	Number of articles	2013–2017, number of articles	2018–2022, number of articles
Sustainability	30	3	27
Corporate Social Responsibility and Environmental Management	22	6	16
Business Strategy and the Environment	20	1	19
Sustainability Accounting, Management and Policy Journal	17	2	15
Journal of Cleaner Production	15	8	7
Meditari Accountancy Research	12	1	11
Journal of Applied Accounting Research	8	0	8
Accounting, Auditing and Accountability Journal	8	3	5
Social Responsibility Journal	7	3	4
Journal of Business Ethics	6	2	4

Source: Own elaboration

between 2013 and 2022. They referred to testing IRQ/SRQ, examining determinants of IRQ/SRQ, investigating the effects of IRQ/SRQ, and analyzing the impacts of regulatory frameworks/guidelines on IRQ/SRQ. We also identified two smaller streams of literature that raised IRQ and SRQ issues in the context of assurance and materiality.

From the perspective of this chapter's aim, we focused on the research stream reflecting the impacts of regulatory frameworks/guidelines on IRQ/SRQ. Within this research path, the academics investigated not only the implementation and application of the GRI Guidelines/Standards or the IR Framework but also the Non-Financial Reporting Directive, corporate regulatory frameworks, governance codes and other regulations. It should be noted that significantly more studies concentrated on examining how GRI Guidelines/Standards influenced the quality of the reports (Buys and Van Niekerk, 2014; Knebel and Seele, 2015; Romolini et al., 2015; Dennis et al., 2015; Comyns, 2016; Cantele et al., 2018; Malola and Maroun, 2019; Safari and Areeb, 2020; Khan et al., 2021; Henriques et al., 2022; Tsalis et al. 2023; Maji,

2022) than what was the impact of the IR Framework (Liu et al., 2019; Adhikariparajuli et al., 2021; Herbert and Graham, 2021; Henriques et al., 2022, Hsiao et al., 2022; Aslanertik and Yardımcı, 2022). It may be explained by the fact that the GRI Guidelines have been on the market since 2000, whereas IIRC released its IR Framework in 2013.

6.3.2   Impact of the GRI Guidelines/Standards on the quality of non-financial reports

Applying the GRI Standards may improve the overall comparability and quality of the reports. Thus, such reports can underpin management in setting goals and targets and implementing policies and practices. In turn, stakeholders are supported in making informed decisions based on knowledge about the business's impacts and its contribution to sustainable development (GRI, 2022a). Bebbington et al. (2009) emphasized that the GRI exerted normative pressure on companies because the objectives of the guidelines were formulated along with how they should be achieved. Thus, the GRI Guidelines indicated how to proceed with the SR processes, how to respect the reporting principles and which indicators must be disclosed in the sustainability report.

Due to the detailed level of application guidance and broad use, the GRI Guidelines were supposed to contribute to the growth in the quantity and quality of disclosures (Malola and Maroun, 2019). The extent of voluntary disclosures may also have been influenced by management driven by "pragmatic legitimacy" (Suchman, 1995), and having self-interest interest in adopting only specific SR guidelines (Khan et al., 2021). The reason for this was the necessity of upholding social licences and pleasing essential stakeholders. However, all these efforts may have been disrupted when there was a lack of resources to adopt the GRI guidelines seamlessly. In this situation, organizations might have tended to "tick more GRI boxes", making their sustainability disclosures more symbolic than substantive (Khan et al., 2021) and indeed manipulating and distorting the stakeholders' perception (Hahn and Lulfs, 2014).

Symbolic sustainability disclosures are not the only objections to a questionable SRQ. Critics have questioned the process of preparing sustainability reports, considering it "defective" due to the lack of assured confidence in their content (Knebel and Seele, 2015). They have challenged accuracy, sincerity, and completeness (Doane, 2000; Adams and Zutshi, 2004) and the visual form of the sustainability reports, overwhelmed by numerous images obscuring their content (Bowers, 2010). Critics also undermined the optimistic rhetoric used in sustainability reports, which blurred responsibility for poorer performance (Cho et al., 2010) and the questionable credibility of the disclosed non-financial information (Adams, 2004; Moneva et al., 2006), which was caused by a lack of external audit and data verification. These allegations meant that sustainability reports could be seen as nothing more than public relations schemes without substance (Branco and Rodrigues, 2006; Diouf and Boiral, 2017; Baldassarre and Campo, 2016), impression management strategies (Cho et al., 2012; Diouf and Boiral, 2017) or just a kind of simulacrum – "an artificial and idealized representation which is disconnected from reality" (Boiral, 2013, p. 1037).

Other critical views on reporting sustainability information concerned the problems of "greenwashing", opportunistic attitude, lack of valiant attempts to change the internal reporting practices, lack of stakeholder engagement, and failure to meet users' expectations (Burritt and Schaltegger, 2010; Thorne et al., 2014; Leung et al., 2015; Cho et al., 2015; Chelli et al., 2019; Khan et al. 2021; Zharfpeykan, 2021).

These problems have given rise to questions about the role of regulatory frameworks. Over the last ten years, there have been several studies on the impacts of GRI Guidelines/Standards on the quality of non-financial reports. The researchers examined the level of compliance with the guidelines (Malola and Maroun, 2019). They explored the challenges related to SRQ (Knebel and Seele, 2015) and investigated the organizational self-perception of the compliance level (Buys and Van Niekerk, 2014). The studies also examined the motivations of the sustainability reports' preparers to observe GRI principles (Safari and Areeb, 2020).

Malola and Maroun (2019), for instance, investigated whether compliance with the GRI Guidelines was associated with the higher quality of reports. The study was conducted on the largest 40 companies listed on the JSE, and the review period covered 2015 and 2016 reporting year ends. Interestingly, the results indicated that applying the GRI Guidelines to inform the form and content of the integrated report was a poor predictor of the reports' high quality. Other authors – Buys and Van Niekerk (2014) – studied whether ten organizations from the financial services sector in South Africa referred to the GRI Guidelines in their 2012 and 2013 integrated reports. The authors stated that the analyzed entities successfully introduced the GRI Guidelines. All organizations reported on core indicators, but some did not disclose sector-specific indicators. Buys and Van Niekerk (2014) also examined the level of compliance of an organization's self-declared ratings with the ratings based on the disclosure analysis. It turned out that only in one case was the organization over-optimistic and assessed itself higher than would result from the assessment of disclosures.

On the other hand, Knebel and Seele (2015) quantitively tested the rigor of application of GRI G3.1 Guidelines in GRI A+ certified reports. They searched for how far GRI Guidelines contributed to the transparency and standardization of non-financial reporting. Noteworthy is that changes brought by GRI G3.1 Guidelines were evolutionary at that time, since such elements as application levels, a technical protocol, indicator protocol sets, and updates of performance indicators were introduced (GRI, 2011). Knebel and Seele (2015) evidenced challenges related to sustainability reports' completeness, accessibility and benchmarking. They claimed that the certification levels of the GRI did not reflect disclosure frequencies of mandatory core performance indicators, which was hard to accept in the case of the best-in-class reports externally assured as GRI 3.1 A+. In the face of variations in the standardized way of reporting sustainability using GRI guidelines, Knebel and Seele (2015) reflected on the need for mandatory non-financial disclosure processes, supported by government regulations.

Also, in this vein, Safari and Areeb (2020) conducted in-depth semi-structured interviews with individuals who had critical roles in preparing sustainability reports to investigate how they perceived and applied the GRI Principles, including accuracy, balance, clarity, comparability, reliability, and timeliness. The aim was to know the motivations and intentions of the preparers of the sustainability reports. The study was conducted during the transition period from the GRI G4 Guidelines to the new GRI Standards. The findings suggest that individuals preparing reports prioritized compliance with the GRI indicators over investing in stakeholder engagement techniques. These practices might reduce adherence to the GRI's ethos of disclosing sustainability information that meets the stakeholders' expectations and thus decrease the quality and usefulness of the reports.

There were also some other studies that examined the use of the GRI Guidelines for the assessment of the quality of sustainability reports in the context of specific disclosures (Dennis et al., 2015; Comyns, 2016; Cantele et al., 2018; Maji, 2022) or in specific industries (sectors) (Anguiano-Santos and Salazar-Ordóñez, 2024; Khan et al., 2021; Henriques et al., 2022; Romolini et al., 2015).

Finally, it must be stressed that some studies confirmed that following the GRI Guidelines did not always lead to developing a high-quality report (Malola and Maroun, 2019; Anguiano-Santos and Salazar-Ordóñez, 2024). Indeed, voluntary regulations have no direct legal force and can be applied symbolically (Malola and Maroun, 2019). Moreover, the quality construct is complex and is not only related to the disclosure quantity. Organizations should, therefore, not just tick off each element of the disclosure item but focus first and foremost on the attributes of high-quality information and related GRI principles that are fundamental to achieving high-quality SR.

6.3.3   Impact of the IR Framework on the quality of non-financial reports

There was much less research in the Scopus database during 2013–2022 on the impact of the IR Framework on non-financial reporting than on the impact of the GRI Guidelines. Liu et al. (2019) also confirmed a scarcity of research on implementing the IR Framework or assessing compliance with the IR Framework in its entirety. Nevertheless, the study by Henriques et al. (2022) investigated the association between the quality of non-financial reports and the application of the IR Framework and between the stakeholder engagement impact and the adoption of the materiality principle. The results confirmed that entities which followed the IR Framework also published higher-quality non-financial reports. Over the years, they have also given more attention to observing the materiality principle, which contributed to an increase in the quality of the reports.

Hsiao et al. (2022), in turn, conducted a broader study on the type of firms that voluntarily adopted the IR Framework and how markets responded to voluntary IR adherence. They offered a deep insight into the global debate on whether there is value in adopting the IR Framework. The authors emphasized that barriers to the broad adoption of the IR Framework existed in countries where IR was not mainstream. This is because organizations with poor social and environmental management are less inclined to adopt the IR Framework voluntarily. Moreover, without progress in accounting systems that underpin integrated thinking and information connectivity, the IR Framework's potential to enhance information quality may be limited in countries where IR is not a trending practice.

Interestingly, although the overall level of IRQ has been increasing over the years and enhancements have been observed in information connectivity, in the materiality determination process, and in the reliability and completeness of reports, these changes were more ceremonial than substantive and were introduced to achieve organizational legitimacy (Ahmed Haji and Anifowose, 2016). The results of Ahmed Haji and Anifowose's research (2016), which referred to the evidence drawn from integrated reports of large South African companies during 2011–2013, were confirmed by the studies of Pistoni et al. (2018) and Malola and Maroun (2019). Pistoni et al. (2018) investigated integrated reports from the "Getting Started" section of the website of IR examples. The study evidenced that even though a significant improvement of quality from 2013 to 2014 in certain areas could be observed, the overall quality of integrated reports was still quite limited, particularly concerning the content and background areas, and organizations gave more attention to the form than to the content of reports. Likewise, the study of Malola and Maroun (2019) found that while IR has become well established in South Africa, there is still considerable room for improvement as "most disclosures are qualitative and symbolic rather than quantified and substantive". Moreover, IR preparers have problems with the complete application of the IR Framework (Pistoni et al. 2018), and in particular, with the guiding principles, which "still have a long way to go, especially in relation to the principle of conciseness" (Ruiz-Lozano and Tirado-Valencia, 2016, p. 252).

6.4   Final Remarks and Future Outlooks

The purposes of this chapter were twofold. Firstly, it comprehensively compared the GRI Standards and the IR Framework, focusing on their similarities and differences in assumptions and their practical implementation. Secondly, based on the previous research on SRQ and IRQ, our study evidenced the roles of the GRI Guidelines/Standards and the IR Framework in shaping disclosure quality. Our research makes several contributions to the literature.

First, the comparative analysis showed a large overlap in the assumptions of the GRI Standards and the IR Framework, with the significant differences being in the concepts of materiality as described by the GRI and IIRC. While the GRI Standards refer to the concept of sustainability development, are addressed to multiple stakeholders, and their materiality concept is based on the most significant economic, environmental, and social impact, the IR Framework focuses on providers of financial capital and its materiality relies on value creation over the short, medium and long term. However, in our view, these differences are not competing but are complementary forces. In terms of reporting principles and content elements, while an emphasis on different principles and elements is diverse, we believe that, in essence, they are complementary and largely aligned. Although the terminology used in the principles differs slightly, both the GRI Standards and the IR Framework aim to achieve similar reporting results focusing on comparable, reliable, complete, and understandable information.

Second, based on the literature review, we explored whether the GRI Guidelines/Standards and the IR Framework were actually implemented in the reporting practice and analyzed their role in shaping the quality of disclosures. We noted that both voluntary regulation schemes had put pressure on organizations, resulting from normative isomorphism and a need for professionalization and diffusion of certain norms and practices. We also remarked that management might take a pragmatic approach to adopt certain solutions to uphold social license (coercive isomorphism) and please selected stakeholders (informal pressure). Interestingly, various researchers' investigations on alignment with the GRI Guidelines/Standards and the IR Framework provide ambiguous evidence. Some authors stressed that the application of the said standards and framework was not a good predictor of the quality of reports or that the existing reporting principles were not applied in practice. By contrast, other researchers evidenced that organizations which rigorously observed the GRI Standards and those that took care of relations with their stakeholders achieved higher levels of materiality and, thus, higher-quality reports. Similar results were obtained in reference to organizations which followed the IR Framework.

Third, the study also addressed a wave of criticism regarding SRQ and IRQ. Critics accused the preparers of the sustainability reports of providing too-optimistic rhetoric during periods of poor performance, using impression management strategies, and cultivating organizational narcissism reflected in self-praise monologues. Other problems regarded greenwashing practices and failed attempts to meet stakeholder expectations. Criticism has not escaped the preparers of the integrated reports either. The main allegations were made in terms of the scale of changes in the quality of the integrated reports. They were determined to be ceremonial or symbolic rather than substantive and qualitative.

The findings of the study have implications for report preparers. The GRI Standards and the IR Framework are largely aligned and complementary, so we believe that one reporting process can meet both the GRI and IIRC requirements. Thus, report preparers can use this study to develop a conceptual framework based on the IR and SR configuration. In addition, a more in-depth analysis suggests that ticking off more elements of report content may not be a practice sufficient to lead to higher reporting quality. Although both the GRI Standards and the IR Framework are principle-based, the mere existence of these principles does not guarantee that they will be applied thoroughly, particularly in the face of a lack of experience and resources to proceed smoothly with their application . Moreover, report preparers should be aware that non-financial reporting is not about the self-portrayal of organizations based on a monologue of self-praise. That process may result in the misperception of reality caused by images or symbols obscuring the actual situation and may lead to a lack of a balanced representation of certain aspects.

Finally, we remark that the problems with the practical and adequate use of the GRI Standards or IR Framework might be partly due to Directive 2014/95/EU (NFRD), which has not imposed the mandatory use of specific reporting frameworks or standards. The report preparers were only obliged to state which standards or frameworks they decided to apply in their non-financial statement. The voluntary choices of organizations in the EU could have led to inconsistent information being reported. In order to prevent such problems, Directive 2022/2464 (CSRD), which replaced the NFRD, aims to standardize sustainability information for EU reporters and thus enhance the overall quality of sustainability reports. The CSRD also introduces mandatory double materiality assessment with its two perspectives: "inside-out" (organization's impact on environment and society) and "outside-in" (sustainability risks affecting the organization itself). In addition, the CSRD requires the provision of limited assurance for sustainability information, primarily focusing on understanding the process of gathering information and pinpointing areas where a material misstatement is likely to arise. The next stage will be the implementation of reasonable assurance, which is the highest assurance level, and which is currently applicable in the audit of financial statements.

While CSRD establishes reporting requirements and obligations, the ESRS deliver a framework and methodologies for reporting sustainability issues for approximately 49,000 entities, which create about 75% of the total turnover of EU companies. The ESRS will cause sustainability reports in the EU to be more coherent, comparable, and reliable. It is worth noting that the ESRS will be aligned with existing standards and frameworks, including the GRI Standards or the recommendations of the Task Force on Climate-Related Financial Disclosures. Indeed, the GRI has been diligently involved in the development of the ESRS through collaboration with EFRAG (GRI, 2022b).

The GRI also cooperates with the IFRS Foundation to align multi-stakeholder standards and investor-focused sustainability disclosures for capital markets and provide a cohesive approach to sustainability reporting. The respective standard-setting boards of these bodies – the Global Sustainability Standards Board and the International Sustainability Standards Board (ISSB) – are working on coordinating their work programs, standard-setting activities, terminology and guidance. These efforts aim to reduce the reporting burden for organizations and harmonize the sustainability reporting landscape at an international level (IFRS, 2022). It is worth mentioning that the consolidation of the IFRS Foundation with the Climate Disclosure Standards Board and the VRF implies that these bodies represent a common position on sustainability reporting standardization. Moreover, the ISSB, formatted by the Trustees of the IFRS Foundation, obtained international support from the G7, G20, other institutions, finance ministers and central bank governors from more than 40 jurisdictions in developing cost-effective, decision-useful and market-informed standards for a global baseline of sustainability disclosure. The close cooperation of the ISSB with the International Accounting Standards Board will also ensure a high level of alignment, providing interconnectedness between IFRS Accounting Standards and IFRS Sustainability Disclosure Standards. Thus, the prospects for the future look interesting and will bring challenges not only for report preparers under the scope of new regulations or regulators but also for the researchers.

Due to changing reporting requirements for various entities and the longevity and complexity of these processes, many paths for future research may appear. The regulators will be searching for answers as to whether the adoption of new standards is running smoothly. They may also be interested in the trickle-down effect of requirements to report information on undertakings in the value chain and how new reporting regimes will affect organizations' competitiveness. The report preparers will focus on methodologies and practical aspects of developing sustainability reports. They will also be curious about the competitive position costs caused by the disclosure of sector-specific risks and opportunities (CEPS and Milieu, 2022). The report preparers will be monitoring the direct costs of implementing the ESRS with regard to the administrative and assurance spheres. In particular, the assurance costs are expected to increase due to more comprehensive assurance coverage. The academics will be investigating the drivers for quality of the sustainability reports prepared under the new standards and the effects of this process on specific areas. Interestingly, the application of the ESRS seems to drive many behavioral changes, especially in those organizations that have not been reporting sustainability information already (CEPS and Milieu, 2022). Thus, the change of corporate mindset will also be in the research interest of academics. The ongoing changes in the standardization of sustainability reporting also raise questions about the contributions of the GRI as one of the three influential institutions playing a role in the harmonization of sustainability reporting and how it will affect its position and future direction (Afolabi et al., 2023). There is also a call for research to understand the challenges the preparers and stakeholders of the reports may encounter while using GRI Standards with regard to comparability, materiality, assurance, and any interrelations between them (Luque-Vílchez et al., 2023). In particular, both the GRI and the IIRC were inefficient over time in providing a clear and complete explanation of "materiality", which might incline organizations to avoid reporting on negative issues, though they could have been material for stakeholders (Khan et al., 2021). Finally, it should be noted that although the assurance and materiality research paths are still embryonic, they will likely evolve in the context of the limited assurance requirement on companies for sustainability information and the double materiality concept under the CSRD.

REFERENCES

Adams, C.A. (2004), "The ethical, social and environmental reporting-performance portrayal gap", *Accounting, Auditing & Accountability Journal*, Vol. 17 No. 5, pp. 731–757.

Adams, C., and Zutshi, A. (2004), "Corporate social responsibility: why business should act responsibly and be accountable", *Australian Accounting Review*, Vol. 14 No. 34, pp. 31–39.

Adhikariparajuli, M., Hassan, A., and Fletcher, M. (2021), "Integrated reporting implementation and core activities disclosure in UK higher education institutions", *Administrative Sciences*, Vol. 11 No. 3, 86.

Ahmed Haji, A., and Anifowose, M. (2016), "The trend of integrated reporting practice in South Africa: ceremonial or substantive?", *Sustainability Accounting, Management and Policy Journal*, Vol. 7 No. 2, pp. 190–224.

Afolabi, H., Ram, R. and Rimmel, G. (2023), "Influence and behaviour of the new standard setters in the sustainability reporting arena: implications for the Global Reporting Initiative's current position", *Sustainability Accounting, Management and Policy Journal*, Vol. 14 No. 4, pp. 743–775.

Anguiano-Santos, C., and Salazar-Ordóñez, M. (2024), "Sustainability reporting as a tool for fostering sustainable growth in the agri-food sector: the case of Spain", *Journal of Environmental Planning and Management*, Vol. 67 No. 2, pp. 426–453.

Aslanertik, B.E., and Yardımcı, B. (2022), "The relationship between compliance level and value creation: evidence from integrated reports in Turkey", *Journal of Financial Reporting and Accounting*, Vol. ahead-of-print No. ahead-of-print.

Baldassarre, F., and Campo, R. (2016), "Sustainability as a marketing tool: to be or to appear to be?", *Business Horizons*, Vol. 59 No. 4, pp. 421–429.

Bebbington, J., Higgins, C., and Frame, B. (2009), "Initiating sustainable development reporting: evidence from New Zealand", *Accounting, Auditing & Accountability Journal*, Vol. 22 No. 4, pp. 588–625.

Boiral, O. (2013), "Sustainability reports as simulacra? A counter-account of A and A+ GRI reports", *Accounting, Auditing & Accountability Journal*, Vol. 26 No. 7, pp. 1036–1071.

Bowers, T. (2010), "From image to economic value: a genre analysis of sustainability reporting", *Corporate Communications: An International Journal*, Vol. 15 No. 3, pp. 249–262.

Branco, M.C., and Rodrigues, L.L. (2006), "Corporate social responsibility and resource-based perspectives", *Journal of Business Ethics*, Vol. 69 No. 2, pp. 111–132.

Burritt, R.L., and Schaltegger, S. (2010), "Sustainability accounting and reporting: fad or trend?", *Accounting, Auditing and Accountability Journal*, Vol. 23 No. 7, pp. 829–846.

Buys, P., and Van Niekerk, E. (2014). "The South African financial services industry's integrated reporting compliance with the global reporting initiative framework", *Banks and Bank Systems*, Vol. 9 No. 4, pp. 107–115.

Cantele, S., Tsalis, T.A., and Nikolaou, I.E. (2018), "A new framework for assessing the sustainability reporting disclosure of water utilities", *Sustainability*, Vol. 10 No. 2, 433.

CDP, CDSB, GRI, IIRC and SAS (2020), *Statement of Intent to Work Together Towards Comprehensive Corporate Reporting*. Impact Management Project, World Economic Forum and Deloitte. https://www.globalreporting.org/media/bixjk1ud/statement-of-intent-to-work-together-towards-comprehensive-corporate-reporting.pdf

CEPS and Milieu (2022), *Cost-benefit analysis of the first set of draft European Sustainability Reporting Standards*. Final report, November 2022. https://www.ceps.eu/ceps-publications/cost-benefit-analysis-of-the-first-set-of-draft-european-sustainability-reporting-standards/

Chelli, M., Durocher, S., and Fortin, A. (2019), "Substantive and symbolic strategies sustaining the environmentally friendly ideology", *Accounting, Auditing and Accountability Journal*, Vol. 32 No. 4, pp. 1013–1042.

Cho, C.H., Roberts, R.W., and Patten, D.M. (2010), "The language of US corporate environmental disclosure", *Accounting, Organisations and Society*, Vol. 35 No. 4, pp. 431–443.

Cho, C.H., Michelon, G., and Patten, D.M. (2012), "Impression management in sustainability reports: an empirical investigation of the use of graphs", *Accounting and the Public Interest*, Vol. 12 No. 1, pp. 16–37.

Cho, C.H., Laine, M., Roberts, R.W., and Rodrigue, M. (2015), "Organized hypocrite, organizational façades, and sustainability reporting", *Accounting, Organisations and Society*, Vol. 40, pp. 78–94.

Comyns, B. (2016), "Determinants of GHG reporting: an analysis of global oil and gas companies", *Journal of Business Ethics*, Vol. 136 No. 2, pp. 349–369.

CRD (2019), *Driving Alignment in Climate-Related Reporting*. https://www.globalreporting.org/media/5wuhv3u2/crd_driving-alignment-in-climate-related-reporting_2019.pdf

Dennis, P., Connole, H., and Kraut, M. (2015), "The efficacy of voluntary disclosure: a study of water disclosures by mining companies using the Global Reporting Initiative framework", *Journal of Legal, Ethical and Regulatory Issues*, Vol. 18 No. 2, pp. 87–106.

Diouf, D., and Boiral, O. (2017), "The quality of sustainability reports and impression manage-ment: a stakeholder perspective", *Accounting, Auditing & Accountability Journal*, Vol. 30 No. 3, pp. 643–667.

Doane, D. (2000), *Corporate Spin: The Troubled Teenage Years of Social Reporting*, New Economics Foundation, London.

Farooq, M.B., Zaman, R., Sarraj, D., and Khalid, F. (2021), "Examining the extent of and drivers for materiality assessment disclosures in sustainability reports", *Sustainability Accounting, Management and Policy Journal*, Vol. 12 No. 5, pp. 965–1002.

Frishkoff, P. (1970), "An empirical investigation of the concept of materiality in accounting", *Journal of Accounting Research*, Vol. 8 (Empirical Research in Accounting: Selected Studies), pp. 116–129.

GRI (2011), *GRI Sustainability Reporting Guidelines G3.1*, GRI, Amsterdam.

GRI (2016), *Forging a path to integrated reporting: Insights from the GRI Corporate Leadership Group on integrated reporting.* https://integratedreportingsa.org/ircsa/wp-content/uploads/2017/05/GRI-CLG_IntegratedReporting.pdf

GRI (2020), *Consolidated Set of GRI Sustainability Reporting Standards 2020.* https://www.globalreporting.org/how-to-use-the-gri-standards/gri-standards-english-language/

GRI (2022a), *Consolidated Set of the GRI Standards 2021.* https://www.globalreporting.org/pdf.ashx?id=12024

GRI (2022b), Interoperability between ESRS and GRI Standards good news for reporters. https://www.globalreporting.org/news/news-center/interoperability-between-esrs-and-gri-standards-good-news-for-reporters/

GRI (2023), *Our mission and history.* https://www.globalreporting.org/about-gri/mission-history/

Hahn, R., and Lulfs, R. (2014), "Legitimizing negative aspects in GRI-oriented sustainability reporting: a qualitative analysis of corporate disclosure strategies", *Journal of Business Ethics*, Vol. 123 No. 3, pp. 401–420.

Henriques, R., Gaio, C., and Costa, M. (2022), "Sustainability reporting quality and stakeholder engage-ment assessment: the case of the paper sector at the Iberian level", *Sustainability*, Vol. 14 No. 21, 14404.

Herbert, S., and Graham, M. (2021), "Application of principles from the International <IR> Framework for including sustainability disclosures within South African integrated reports", *South African Journal of Accounting Research*, Vol. 35 No. 1, pp. 42–68.

Hsiao, P.-C.K., de Villiers, C., and Scott, T. (2022), "Is voluntary International Integrated Reporting Framework adoption a step on the sustainability road and does adoption matter to capital markets?", *Meditari Accountancy Research*, Vol. 30 No. 3, pp. 786–818.

IFRS (2022), IFRS Foundation and GRI to align capital market and multi-stakeholder standards to create an interconnected approach for sustainability disclosures. https://www.ifrs.org/news-and-events/news/2022/03/ifrs-foundation-signs-agreement-with-gri/

IIRC (2012), *The Pilot Programme 2012 Yearbook. Capturing the experiences of global busi-nesses and investors.* https://www.integratedreporting.org/wp-content/uploads/2012/10/THE-PILOT-PROGRAMME-2012-YEARBOOK.pdf

IIRC (2021), *The International Integrated Reporting Framework.* https://www.integratedreporting.org/international-framework-downloads/

Khan, H.Z., Bose, S., Mollik, A.T., and Harun, H. (2021), "'Green washing' or 'authentic effort'? An empirical investigation of the quality of sustainability reporting by banks", *Accounting, Auditing & Accountability Journal*, Vol. 34 No. 2, pp. 338–369.

Knebel, S., and Seele, P. (2015), "Quo vadis GRI? A (critical) assessment of GRI 3.1 A+ non-financial reports and implications for credibility and standardization", *Corporate Communications: An International Journal*, Vol. 20 No. 2, pp. 196–212.

KPMG (2013), *Survey of Corporate Responsibility Reporting.* https://assets.kpmg.com/content/dam/kpmg/pdf/2013/12/corporate-responsibility-reporting-survey-2013.pdf

KPMG (2015), *Currents of change. Survey of Corporate Responsibility Reporting.* https://assets.kpmg.com/content/dam/kpmg/pdf/2015/12/KPMG-survey-of-CR-reporting-2015.pdf

KPMG (2017), *The road ahead. Survey of Corporate Responsibility Reporting.* https://assets.kpmg.com/content/dam/kpmg/be/pdf/2017/kpmg-survey-of-corporate-responsibility-reporting-2017.pdf

KPMG (2020), *The time has come. Survey of Sustainability Reporting*. https://assets.kpmg.com/content/dam/kpmg/pl/pdf/2020/12/pl-the-time-has-come-the-kpmg-%20survey-of-sustainability-reporting-2020.pdf

KPMG (2022), *Big shifts, small steps. Survey of Sustainability Reporting*. https://home.kpmg/xx/en/home/insights/2022/09/survey-of-sustainability-reporting-2022.html

Lakshan, A.M.I., Low, M., and de Villiers, C. (2022), "Challenges of, and techniques for, materiality determination of non-financial information used by integrated report preparers", *Meditari Accountancy Research*, Vol. 30 No. 3, pp. 626–660.

Leung, S., Parker, L., and Courtis, J. (2015), "Impression management through minimal narrative disclosure in annual reports", *The British Accounting Review*, Vol. 47 No. 3, pp. 275–289.

Liu, Z., Jubb, C., and Abhayawansa, S. (2019), "Analyzing and evaluating integrated reporting: insights from applying a normative benchmark", *Journal of Intellectual Capital*, Vol. 20 No. 2, pp. 235–263.

Luque-Vílchez, M., Cordazzo, M., Rimmel, G. and Tilt, C.A. (2023), "Key aspects of sustainability reporting quality and the future of GRI", *Sustainability Accounting, Management and Policy Journal*, Vol. 14 No. 4, pp. 637–659.

Machado, B.A.A., Dias, L.C.P., and Fonseca, A. (2021), "Transparency of materiality analysis in GRI-based sustainability reports", *Corporate Social Responsibility and Environmental Management*, Vol. 28 No. 2, pp. 570–580.

Maji, S.G. (2022). "Disclosure pattern of labour practices and decent work and its impact on corporate financial performance: evidence from Asia", *Global Business Review*, Vol. 23 No. 4, pp. 1054–1070.

Malola, A., and Maroun, W. (2019), "The measurement and potential drivers of integrated report quality: evidence from a pioneer in integrated reporting", *South African Journal of Accounting Research*, Vol. 33 No. 2, pp. 114–144.

Maroun W., and Atkins, J. (2015), *The Challenges of Assuring Integrated Reports: Views from the South African Auditing Community*, Association of Chartered Certified Accountants, London. https://www.accaglobal.com/content/dam/ACCA_Global/Technical/integrate/ea-south-africa-IR-assurance.pdf

Mio, C., Fasan, M., and Costantini, A. (2020a), "Materiality in integrated and sustainability reporting: a paradigm shift?", *Business Strategy and the Environment*, Vol. 29, No. 1, pp. 306–320.

Moneva, J.M., Archel, P. and Correa, C. (2006), "GRI and the camouflaging of the corporate unsustainability", *Accounting Forum*, Vol. 30 No. 2, pp. 121–137.

Pistoni, A., Songini, L., and Bavagnoli, F. (2018), "Integrated reporting quality: an empirical analysis", *Corporate Social Responsibility and Environmental Management*, Vol. 25 No. 4, pp. 489–507.

Regan, D. (2022), *A sign of things to come: mandatory sustainability reporting in the Middle East*. Deloitte Middle East. https://www2.deloitte.com/content/dam/Deloitte/xe/Documents/About-Deloitte/mepovdocuments/mepovissue36/a-sign-of-things-to-come_mepov36.pdf

Romolini, A., Fissi, S. and Gori, E. (2015), "Quality disclosure in sustainability reporting: evidence from universities", *Transylvanian Review of Administrative Sciences*, Vol. 11 No. 44, pp. 196–218.

Ruiz-Lozano, M., and Tirado-Valencia, P. (2016), "Do industrial companies respond to the guiding principles of the Integrated Reporting framework? A preliminary study on the first companies joined to the initiative", *Revista de Contabilidad – Spanish Accounting Review*, Vol. 19 No. 2, pp. 252–260.

Safari M., and Areeb A. (2020). "A qualitative analysis of GRI principles for defining sustainability report quality: an Australian case from the preparers' perspective", *Accounting Forum*, Vol. 44 No. 4, pp. 344–375.

Stuart, A.C., Fuller, S.H., Heron, N.M. and Riley, T.J. (2022), "Defining CSR disclosure quality: a review and synthesis of the accounting literature", *Journal of Accounting Literature*, Vol. 45 No. 1, pp. 1–47.

Suchman, M. (1995), "Managing legitimacy: strategic and institutional approaches", *Academy of Management Review*, Vol. 20 No. 3, pp. 571–610.

Thorne, L., Mahoney, L.S., and Manetti, G. (2014), "Motivations for issuing standalone CSR reports: a survey of Canadian firms", *Accounting, Auditing and Accountability Journal*, Vol. 27 No. 4, pp. 686–714.

Torelli, R., Balluchi, F., and Furlotti, K. (2020), "The materiality assessment and stakeholder engagement: a content analysis of sustainability reports", *Corporate Social Responsibility and Environmental Management*, Vol. 27 No. 2, pp. 470–484.

Tsalis, T.A., Terzaki, M., Koulouriotis, D., Tsagarakis, K.P., and Nikolao, I.E. (2023), "The nexus of United Nations' 2030 Agenda and corporate sustainability reports", *Sustainable Development*, Vol. 31 No. 2, pp. 784–796.

Zharfpeykan, R. (2021), "Representative account or greenwashing? Voluntary sustainability reports in Australia's mining/metals and financial services industries", *Business Strategy and the Environment*, Vol. 30 No. 4, pp. 2209–2223.

7. Global baseline: the path to IFRS Sustainability Disclosure Standards

Victor Wagner, Thorsten Sellhorn, Katharina Weiß and Christoph Pelger

1 INTRODUCTION

With the consequences of climate change manifesting themselves, the awareness that corporations must contribute to mitigating and adapting to the climate catastrophe has grown.[1] As commentators point out, accounting might have a role to play here. By providing a language for assessing the economic, environmental, and social trade-offs that firms face, Peter Bakker, the CEO of the World Business Council for Sustainable Development, recently reiterated his credo that "accountants will save the world" (ICAEW, 2021). From an academic point of view, the long-standing strand of social and environmental accounting research has been advocating "developing a social accounting that takes an accountability, community and environment-centered approach" (Gray, 1992, p. 400) for a long time. While sustainability reporting[2] has gained considerable traction over the years (KPMG, 2022), many point out that this form of (voluntary) reporting has not so far changed firms' substantive actions, and hence they consider it mere greenwashing (Milne & Gray, 2013), although recent studies find that firms anticipate mandatory reporting requirements and adapt accordingly (Fiechter et al., 2022; She, 2022).

Despite the criticism, there have been many attempts to create authoritative frameworks for sustainability reporting. While the Global Reporting Initiative (GRI) has been in place since the early 2000s, notable contestants and collaborators in the landscape were the International Integrated Reporting Council (IIRC), the Sustainability Accounting Standards Board (SASB), and the Taskforce for Climate-Related Financial Disclosures (TCFD), among others. Due to the wealth of acronyms employed, commentators began using the picture of an "alphabet soup" to describe the initiatives (Tett, 2020). While earlier efforts at coordination and consolidation had been unsuccessful (Rowbottom, 2023), in 2020 the IFRS Foundation entered the landscape with the vision of pulling together existing initiatives and creating the global standard setter for investor-oriented sustainability reporting. This chapter examines (1) how the constituents of the IFRS Foundation reacted to this move, (2) what conclusions the Foundation drew, and (3) what effects this had on the drafting of the ISSB standard on climate.

In September 2020, the Trustees of the IFRS Foundation elicited feedback from its constituents as to whether and how the Foundation should move into the field of sustainability reporting. Backed by its analysis of the comment letters, which it summarized as indicating "widespread support for the IFRS Foundation to play a role" (IFRS Foundation, 2021a, p. 3), the Foundation saw an "urgent need for action" (IFRS Foundation, 2021b, p. 3) and engaged in technical preparations. In November 2021, during the 26th UN Climate Change Conference ("COP26"), the Foundation presented the International Sustainability Standard Board (ISSB) as the consolidator of existing initiatives and new standard setter for investor-oriented sustainability reporting standards. Bringing the SASB and the IIRC under its auspices, it set out to create "the global baseline standards for sustainability disclosures" (IFRS Foundation, 2021a, p. 2). A more than year-long phase of consultation and technical preparation followed this announcement and eventually led to the first two IFRS Sustainability Disclosure Standards, which were published in June 2023.[3]

Against this background, we report on analyses that speak to three research questions. First, to examine how the IFRS Foundation's constituents responded to its move into sustainability reporting, we analyze the comment letters submitted to the initial September 2020 Consultation Paper. Second, to assess the Foundation's reception of this feedback, we summarize its conclusions from its comment letter analysis and compare it with our own comment letter analysis. These examinations expose the dynamics of the Foundation's rationale on creating the ISSB, as they provide a clear understanding of the Foundation's initial views as well as constituents' reactions and their interpretation by the Foundation. Having thus established the vision on which the Foundation based its future standard-setting work, third, we compare the main changes that the different versions of the climate standard underwent during the time of their drafting. It is important to understand how the general focus of the ISSB translates into its standards, because these standards will ultimately shape the content of sustainability reporting by companies adopting the IFRS Sustainability Disclosure Standards.

By examining the establishment of the ISSB, we complement literature that closely follows the development and positioning of other sustainability reporting standard setters. Given its long existence and relevance for corporate reporting practice, prior research, for example, investigated how the GRI was able to establish its strong presence (Brown et al., 2009a; Etzion & Ferraro, 2010; Levy et al., 2010), how the IIRC needed to make detours to cater to a specific audience (Humphrey et al., 2017; Rowbottom & Locke, 2016), and how the Corporate Reporting Dialogue failed to pave the way towards consolidation in sustainability reporting standards (Rowbottom, 2023). We extend studies that have outlined the trajectory leading to the creation of the ISSB (Giner & Luque-Vílchez, 2022; Afolabi et al., 2022) by tracing how key themes that came up in the initial public consultation about the move of the IFRS Foundation into sustainability reporting were reflected in the creation of the ISSB and the development of its standard on climate-related disclosures. The implications of our chapter's main finding of the IASB's consistent and sharpened focus on exposure materiality in its climate-related standard also add to recent reflections on the interoperability between jurisdiction-specific and international sustainability standards (Stolowy & Paugam, 2023; Wagenhofer, 2024).

The chapter is structured along our three research questions: the next section presents our analysis of the constituents' responses to the Consultation Paper. In the following section, we compare these results with the Trustees' own conclusions. Finally, we explore differences in the four phases of the standard drafting process. The last section summarizes our findings and provides avenues for further research.

2 CONSTITUENTS' RESPONSES TO THE IFRS FOUNDATION'S CONSULTATION

2.1 Background

On 30 September 2020, the Foundation published the "Consultation Paper on Sustainability Reporting" (IFRS Foundation, 2020). The Consultation Paper first lays out the rationale for the Foundation's engagement in this new area and frames the existing landscape as having "limited effectiveness and impact, a high risk of complexity and an ever-increasing cost" (IFRS Foundation, 2020, p. 6). This led to "several recent calls for the IFRS Foundation to become involved in reducing the level of complexity and achieving greater consistency" (p. 7). Having set the stage by framing the need for consolidation, the paper sets out the Trustees' vision for creating a new standard setter that envelops the existing initiatives. The Consultation Paper then features a proposal on the new standard setter's scope of work. While acknowledging the voices that called the Foundation to base their new standards on the concept of double materiality, i.e., adopting a perspective that includes an entity's impacts on people and planet in addition to its exposure to sustainability-related risks and opportunities, the paper advocates an investor-focused, exposure-materiality perspective. Citing its current remit and expertise in the financial reporting standard-setting domain, broadening its work in a multi-stakeholder direction could "substantially increase the complexity of the task and could potentially impact or delay the adoption" (IFRS Foundation, 2020, p. 14). The consultation closes with ten questions set out for comment.

2.2 Method and Data

In what follows, we approach our first research question by examining constituents' responses to three of the ten questions posed in the Consultation Paper.[4] We focus on the three most relevant questions, as the other questions mainly relate to procedural, governance, auditability and assurance issues. Specifically, we quantitatively and qualitatively summarize the responses about the role of the IFRS Foundation (Question 1), the need for a new standard-setting board with a climate-first approach (Questions 7 and 8) and an exposure-materiality, investor-focused perspective (Question 9). Out of the 577 comment letters, we exclude 11 that lack reference to the Consultation Paper's questions, leaving 566 responses in total.

We start by categorizing responses by constituent group,[5] namely users[6] (n = 86; 18%), regulators (n = 66; 14%), the accounting profession (n = 62; 13%), non-financial firms (n = 58; 12%), academics (n = 51; 11%), individuals (n = 41; 9%), NGOs (n = 39; 8%), providers of advisory and consulting services (n = 34; 7%), and the financial sector (n = 28; 6%). Following prior literature (e.g., Jorissen et al., 2006), we classified 102 "template users" (18% of the total responses), who followed the call of two academics to sign and submit a prewritten answer to the IFRS Foundation (Murphy & Leaver, 2020), as a single comment letter. This reduces our sample to 465 letters. Table 7.1 shows the distribution of comment letters per constituent group.

Table 7.1   Distribution of comment letters across constituent groups

Constituent group	Number of comment letters	Percentage
Users	86	19%
Regulators	66	14%
Auditors	62	13%
Preparers	58	13%
Academics	51	11%
Individuals	41	9%
NGOs	39	8%
Advisory and consulting services	34	7%
Financial services	28	6%
Total	465	100%

2.3   Role of the IFRS Foundation

The first question of the Consultation Paper elicits whether there is a need for "internationally recognised sustainability reporting standards" (IFRS Foundation, 2020, p. 15) and, if so, whether the IFRS Foundation should play a key role in setting them. Given the prominence and relevance of this question, nearly all responses (96%) address it. The majority of respondents (82%) see a need for the Foundation to set standards, but often links its approval to conditions. Among the disapproving respondents, the largest group is academics, of which 37% reject the Foundation's involvement.[7] As Adams and Abhayawansa (2022) and Adams and Mueller (2022) point out, this question assumes that there are no such "internationally recognised" standards currently. In fact, given the broad acceptance of the GRI standards (for example, KPMG, 2022), this statement seems at odds with the status quo of sustainability reporting. The GRI's position as a multi-stakeholder organization that sets standards with an impact materiality perspective, however, is not something that the IFRS Foundation set out to mirror. Disapproving responses often reiterate the dominant position of the GRI and the existence of an internationally renowned set of standards (for example, Submissions 190 [academic], 453 [academic], 508 [NGO]). In the view of these respondents, adding a new standard-setting body would not decrease, but actually increase the complexity of the sustainability-related standard-setting landscape:

> We question how the institution of another (Sustainability Standards) Board would not (logically) add more complexity. Surely, this creates a greater risk of fragmentation, or else reflects an assumption that all other standards and guidelines will lessen in importance if the IFRS steps into the standards arena. (Submission 190 [academic])

The conditions phrased by the approving responses reiterate some of the points already mentioned in the Consultation Paper. For example, many responses urge the Foundation to work with and build upon existing initiatives such as the "Group of Five"[8] organizations, which published a prototype climate-reporting standard in December 2020 (CDP et al., 2020b) and express their support for a joint initiative in a letter to IOSCO (CDP et al., 2020a). Constituents deem this important for ensuring that the standards of the new board could be developed quickly and would achieve broad acceptance (for example, Submissions 170 [auditor], 349 [preparer], 499 [user]).

Respondents also cite that due to the urgency of climate change, "standard development for new standards may be unable to keep pace" and that "the initial and primary focus of the IFRS Foundation should be on the integration and alignment of existing standards – rather than development of new ones" (Submission 334 [other], see also, for example Submission 511 [NGO]). Overall, the comment letters largely express support for the IFRS Foundation to become active and build their standards on existing initiatives. Where respondents oppose the Foundation's approach, reference to the GRI as the dominant framework is a common argument.

2.4 Prioritizing Climate

Questions 7 and 8 elicit stakeholders' responses about the new board's starting point of developing climate reporting standards with a focused definition of climate-related risks, rather than "broader environmental factors" (IFRS Foundation, 2020, p. 15). The Consultation Paper argues that climate-related information constitutes "the most pressing concern" (IFRS Foundation, 2020, p. 12), and that this topic is already on the agendas of preparers and regulators. While most of the responses agree with the pragmatic advantage of this "climate-first" approach, it is met with considerable backlash, with 49% of respondents to the question expressing their concerns about this focus. Groups that exhibit the highest rates of disapproval are, again, academics (67%), but also NGOs (54%), whereas regulators (55%) and financial services firms (71%) show support for the proposal.

On the one hand, constituents point towards the inherent connections between the larger group of social and environmental issues:

> We believe that climate-related issues cannot be looked at in isolation: Many of the "E" issues considered in ESG are intertwined with "S" and "G". For instance, if an entity that is trying to reduce its carbon footprint by shutting down factories and setting free workers, a focus merely on the (positive) impact this has on "E" would not tell the complete story. (Submission 331 [regulator])

The Intergovernmental Panel on Climate Change (IPCC) also frequently uses the concept of a "just transition" to denote the idea that essentially nobody will be left behind (Intergovernmental Panel on Climate Change, 2022, p. 36) in the transition to a carbon-neutral economy. This implies a fundamental acceptance of the fact that these interlocking aspects cannot be addressed in isolation. On the other hand, some argue that, while the risks induced by climate change require urgent responses, topics such as "climate tipping points" (Armstrong McKay et al., 2022; Lenton et al., 2019) also deserve at least as much and as urgent attention (for example, Submission 190 [academic]).

Others express the fear that a new board focused on setting standards only for climate-related matters would actually increase fragmentation, as this would "leave a gap" (Submission 49 [auditor]), leading other initiatives to "try to fill the void" (Submission 252 [user], see also Submission 71 [NGO]):

> … limiting the scope to "E" or focusing on "E", or even only on climate-related disclosures, for too long forces firms to apply one or more other standards to cover the other relevant sustainability matters, which contributes to maintaining the current high level of fragmentation and complexity of the reporting landscape as well as hinders global acceptance and relevance. (Submission 154 [preparer])

Overall, proponents express their preference for a clear timeline of when the new board will broaden its remit into other areas (for example, Submissions 200 [preparer], 491 [regulator], 506 [individual]), while focusing on a subset of topics should not hinder its progress (for example, Submissions 60 [regulator], 90 [NGO]).

2.5   Materiality and Audience

Question 9 is concerned with the new board's perspective on materiality. In the Foundation's view, focusing on the broader, multi-stakeholder concept of double materiality, which encompasses both an impact perspective and an exposure perspective on sustainability topics, would "substantially increase the complexity of the task and ... potentially impact or delay the adoption of the standards" (IFRS Foundation, 2020, p. 14). The Consultation Paper also notes that a focus on investors would fit better with the existing mandate and structure of the Foundation and, thus, would be preferable. The materiality concept, and the related question of which audience the standards should address, receive considerable attention in the public discourse. This attention also manifests in the 87% response rate to that question, of which only a slight majority (42%) favors the proposal (41% reject the proposal and 16% do not answer).

Corporate preparers, for whom one could assume an increased reporting burden in the case of double materiality, argue predominantly in favor of this broader, more inclusive perspective. One reason is the fact that the recent standard-setting activities of the EU via the European Financial Reporting Advisory Group (EFRAG) follow a double-materiality approach. Anticipating that these requirements, first by means of the Non-Financial Reporting Directive (NFRD) and, later, its successor, the Corporate Sustainability Reporting Directive (CSRD), will become mandatory, preparers urge the Foundation to also encompass this perspective. As the association of publicly listed European firms puts it, "[t]he majority of [our] members covered by the NFRD have adopted a wider approach to materiality based on the double materiality principle contained in the mentioned directive" (Submission 262 [preparer]), and "the European legislation requires the double-materiality perspective and ... the disclosure frameworks as well as the legislative requirements currently being developed in Europe will largely build on this notion" (Submission 308 [user]; see also Submissions 124 [user] and 153 [user]).

Investors, in particular, also stress the fact that both the exposure of a firm to sustainability risks and opportunities as well as its impacts on sustainability topics inform enterprise value and should be included in the standards, as only this

> captures all decision-useful information on how the performance and risk profile of the investment might be affected, including its potential impact on the environment and society that might have a material effect on the product's returns to investors. In our view, such double perspective ... is key for a complete depiction of an entity's position and performance in ESG terms. (Submission 262 [preparer]; see also Submission 127 [NGO], 190 [academic])

The reason why only a double-materiality perspective captures all decision-useful information is spelled out very clearly in this comment:

> An entity that is making an impact on the wider environment is exposed to the reputational, legal, fiscal and regulatory risk as well as increased cost for public goods like water and land. It could be

penalized for the impact of such risks at some point in [the] future, internalizing that external impact. (Submission 380 [user])

Others highlight that sustainability reporting, by definition, serves multiple groups of stakeholders, and that standards should therefore not be limited to an investor audience (for example, Submission 388 [regulator]). Nevertheless, some constituents highlight the pragmatic benefits of starting small, which would make standard setting easier and thus allow the new board to establish a name and develop more topics from there (Submission 34 [auditor]).

Overall, the distinction between the two materiality perspectives seems vague at best and infeasible at worst. As one European regulatory group states: "Besides [the importance of both perspectives], both approaches are intermingled" (Submission 100 [regulator]; see also Submission 281 [NGO]).

2.6   Interim Conclusion

In summary, the feedback received by the IFRS Foundation on its proposal to set up its own standard setter for sustainability reporting was primarily positive. Constituents see a clear need for harmonizing the different initiatives, but also respect the long tradition in this field. Furthermore, constituents argue that the Foundation should build upon the work of the investor-oriented standard setters. The proposal that the new standards would be limited to the exposure-materiality perspective, however, was not unambiguously supported. Because of existing regulatory initiatives, such as the EU's NFRD and CSRD, as well as the potential relevance of a firm's environmental and social impacts for its enterprise value, comment letters urge the Foundation to also incorporate an impact-materiality view. Given this feedback, we now turn towards the Trustee's own conclusions about the feedback received, our second analysis.

3   THE TRUSTEES' CONCLUSIONS

3.1   Role of the IFRS Foundation and Creation of a New Board

Four weeks after the comment letter deadline passed, the Trustees quickly announced in February 2021 that there would be a definitive proposal at the 26th Conference of the Parties (COP26) in November 2021 if the initially demonstrated "growing and urgent demand" of the responses further manifested in the comment letters (IFRS Foundation, 2021c). Concurrently, the Trustees installed a "Steering Committee" to oversee the subsequent steps. With the first tentative strategic decisions being outlined in two statements in March 2021, the Trustees officially announced the working group that would later be known as the Technical Readiness Working Group (TRWG).[9]

The Feedback Statement reflecting the official analysis of the comment letters to the Consultation Paper was published later, at the end of April 2021 (IFRS Foundation, 2021b). It contained a reference to the strategic decisions made earlier and formalized the creation of a new board. This decision was accompanied by an Exposure Draft necessary for changing the Constitution in order to accommodate the second board next to the existing IASB (IFRS Foundation, 2021e). Overall, the Trustees' analysis revealed "widespread support for the

IFRS Foundation to play a role" (IFRS Foundation, 2021b, p. 3), which encouraged the already ongoing preparations for a new board by COP26. This strategic direction reflects the statements published earlier, and, according to the IFRS Foundation, rests on four pillars: (a) pursuing an investor focus on enterprise value, (b) sustainability scope prioritizing climate, (c) following a building blocks approach, and (d) setting the global baseline. In what follows, we summarize the responses in the Feedback Statement and compare them with the findings from our own comment letter analysis.

With regard to the demand for the IFRS Foundation to become active, the Feedback Statement presents a diverse set of opinions. While constituents overall expressed "broad support" for the Foundation to play a role and "broad agreement" that a new board would contribute most effectively to this end, the document also notes that "some" respondents urged the standard setter to encourage and support already existing initiatives such as GRI and EFRAG. From this, the Trustees summarize a "growing and urgent demand" (IFRS Foundation, 2021b, p. 4). Our analysis finds that 82% of the comment letters back the Foundation's proposal to become active and 75% approve the decision to set up a new board, which is in line with the analysis in the Feedback Statement. The Trustees also highlight requirements of success for the new board, which are broadly in line with our findings. In their analysis, they specifically highlight the need to have sufficient expertise on sustainability topics in the new board, and that a second board next to the IASB would allow for interoperability with financial reporting.

3.2   Investor Focus on Enterprise Value

The Feedback Statement further finds "significant public interest" (IFRS Foundation, 2021b, p. 27) in the development of sustainability reporting standards that address investors' information needs and thus follow the exposure materiality perspective. Besides the support from the comment letters, the Foundation justifies this conclusion with the arguments that this focus would allow for synergies with the IASB, would align with the Foundation's (investor-centric) mission and expertise, and would not require a different governance structure (e.g., increasing the representation of public-interest stakeholders). These arguments are in line with the reasoning in the Consultation Paper but do not take up the feedback from many of the comment letters to consider double materiality, at least in the longer term.

We find that only a slight majority of the respondents agrees with the investor-focused, single-materiality perspective and that a diverse group of respondents rather urges the Foundation to also consider the stakeholder-focused, double-materiality perspective. While the arguments brought forward in the Feedback Statement seem to refer to the structural and pragmatic problem of integrating a more diverse lens on sustainability reporting, the agreeing constituents seem to favor the structural advantages of setting up a new board under the investor-focused governance structure of the IFRS Foundation. In the view of the disagreeing respondents, however, the double-materiality perspective followed in the preparatory work by EFRAG for European Sustainability Reporting Standards (ESRS) and in the already frequently used GRI Standards implies that having a standard setter solely for the investor perspective would add fragmentation.

The Foundation, however, does include the Group of Five's concept of "nested" and "dynamic" materiality (CDP et al., 2020b, p. 7). This concept argues that in a comprehensive framework for corporate reporting, information must pass multiple filters to be reported at different levels. At the broadest level, all significant (positive or negative) impacts of the organization would have to be reported, regardless of their influence on enterprise value. Applying the first filter, however, only those sustainability matters that increase or decrease enterprise value must be reported. Finally, aspects that already fulfil the criteria to be represented in monetary amounts in the financial statements pass the second filter. This latter distinction is crucial, since information about possible future expenses (such as a carbon tax) might already be factored into the enterprise value calculation of investors, while these expenses do not appear in the financial statements. The Feedback Statement sets out that the new standards would apply to the second layer, and thus reflect matters affecting enterprise value. Given the involvement of the GRI in this presentation of the nested concept of materiality, it will be interesting to see how the standards will be reconciled in practice.

3.3   Sustainability Scope: Prioritizing Climate

The climate priority set out in the Feedback Statement can also be traced back to the proposal in the Consultation Paper, although with the ambition to expand the scope into other topics more quickly. Absorbing the views from comment letters, where 58% of respondents preferred a broader approach from the outset, the Foundation now seems to be more inclined to address other environmental as well as social and governance topics. Indeed, the Trustees acknowledge that most sustainability topics are interlinked. They argue for the priority on climate because of the urgent need to address global heating, and because organizations' reporting on climate-matters is most advanced. This is in line with the views of constituents, who, however, prefer a clear timeline of when the new board will broaden its remit to other sustainability topics.

An effort to do so can be seen in the ISSB's new consultation on its agenda priorities, which opened on 4 May 2023. Based on research on the information needs for investors, the ISSB has identified four projects about which it requests information on factors such as importance to investors and deficiencies in the way companies currently disclose sustainability information. These four projects are (1) biodiversity, ecosystems, and ecosystem services, (2) human capital, (3) human rights, and (4) integration in reporting.

3.4   Building Blocks Approach

By consolidating the major initiatives that had been dominating the sustainability reporting space, the ISSB followed the constituents' demand to base its work on, or cooperate directly with, existing initiatives, such as the Group of Five. It acknowledged the proposal brought forward by the constituents to follow a building blocks approach in which the new board would seek the common denominator of the investor-focused organizations and start its work from there, integrating the TCFD's four pillar recommendations. Here, the TRWG plays a crucial role. In the Feedback Statement, the Foundation first refers to the working group as a vehicle "to facilitate the work of a new board", but also hints at a second purpose, namely "to review how technical expertise and content might be made available to the new board … *to facilitate consolidation*" (IFRS Foundation, 2021b, p. 17, emphasis added). While the official consolidations of the VRF (consisting of IIRC and SASB) and the CDSB were announced only at COP26 in November 2021, the Feedback Statement published in April of that year already hints at the TRWG's double role as not only gathering information on how to proceed with standard setting, but also as engaging in consolidatory work.

3.5   Global Baseline

Related to the concept of building blocks is the notion of the ISSB providing the "global baseline" of investor-focused sustainability standards. This phrase was first coined in the early March 2021 statement by the Trustees (IFRS Foundation, 2021h), which summarizes the status quo of their comment letter analysis and already hints at the strategic directions that would be later reflected in the Feedback Statement. Similar to the building blocks, following the concept of a global baseline, the future board would identify the commonly used requirements in the different jurisdictions and align its standard-setting work accordingly.

This approach has a threefold appeal to the Foundation. First, by providing a common set of internationally agreeable standards with a low "barrier to entry", the Foundation can gather jurisdictional support from a diverse set of countries – a prerequisite, given that the EU, which played a major role in the adoption of IFRS (Accounting Standards) around the world (Camfferman & Zeff, 2018), is concurrently preparing its own standards. Second, framing its ambitions in this way leaves open a potential partnership, endorsement, or collaboration with the EU, as the Foundation does not openly confront these activities but rather sets a different focus, i.e., in providing *global* rather than *local* standards. Third, with this approach, the Foundation can respond to constituents' concerns that another standard setter besides the EFRAG and the GRI could increase fragmentation. In a sense, this framing allows the ISSB to find a niche and position its ambitions to fit into the sustainability reporting landscape.[10]

To sum up, our analysis highlights some differences between the Foundation's deliberations as expressed in the Consultation Paper and their final strategic direction spelled out in the Feedback Statement. In part, this seems to stem from criticism articulated in the comment letters. In these, the constituents urge the Foundation to build on, and possibly extend, the work that has already been done by existing standard setters. With the TRWG, the Foundation directly engages in this content-related exchange and also, as we argue in the next section, prepares the consolidation of the other investor-focused initiatives. In contrast to the preference of constituents to expand into double materiality, the Foundation stays focused on its mission to focus only on a subset of stakeholders interested in sustainability information, namely investors. In the third part of our analysis, we follow the board's work program to derive investor-focused IFRS Sustainability Disclosure Standards by comparing the different phases of standard development.

4   SETTING THE SCENE FOR THE ISSB'S FIRST DRAFT STANDARDS

4.1   Preparing the Exposure Drafts

Turning to our third research question, we compare the main changes that the different versions of the drafts of a climate standard underwent during their preparations. This analysis reveals how the general focus of sustainability reporting established by the IFRS Foundation translates into specific standards.

Under the leadership of an external chairperson, CDSB, SASB and IIRC came together to "accelerate convergence … and undertake technical preparation for a potential sustainability reporting standards board under the governance of the IFRS Foundation" (IFRS Foundation,

2021d). It was first officially called the TRWG by the ISSB (IFRS Foundation, 2021f), and its work program consisted of preparations to strategically align the Foundation's approach with the existing initiatives, as well as operational and technical work to "prepare material to inform strategic discussions about the potential transfer of technical expertise and resources to the potential new board" (p. 1).

The TRWG's prototypes build directly on (or "enhance") the Group of Five's prototypes (CDP et al., 2020b, p. 18), which resulted from the collaboration between the leading sustainability standard setters.[11] The Group of Five had already issued its "intent to work together" at the beginning of September 2020, before the Trustees started their consultation. The "intent" (CDP et al., 2020c) comprises a more than 20-page elaboration on how a "comprehensive corporate reporting system" could be formed, borrowing existing concepts from financial reporting and integrating the participating organizations' frameworks and standards. The prototypes are structured around the four TCFD pillars: governance, strategy, risk management, and metrics and targets. The prototype presentation standard was modeled after IAS 1, thereby providing a direct reference to the Foundation's scope of work.

The two prototypes developed by the TRWG evolved into the two Exposure Drafts (ED), which were drafted by the ISSB and published for comment until March 2022. In June 2023, the ISSB released the final versions of both standards. In what follows, we compare the differences between the drafts in the four phases of development, i.e., (1) the December 2021 Group of Five (GOF) prototype, (2) the November 2021 TRWG prototype, (3) the March 2022 ISSB Exposure Draft, and (4) the final IFRS Sustainability Disclosure Standard S2.

Table 7.2 shows the four phases of development and their respective documents.

Table 7.2   Development towards the Exposure Draft in three phases

Phase	Author	Date	Documents	Citation
1	GOF	December 2020	Reporting on enterprise value: Illustrated with a prototype climate-related financial disclosure standard	GOF
2	TRWG	November 2021	Climate-Related Disclosures Prototype	TRWG
3	ISSB	March 2022	Exposure Draft [Draft] IFRS S2 Climate-Related Disclosures	ED
4	ISSB	June 2023	IFRS S2 Climate-Related Disclosures	IFRS S2

4.2   Development of the Climate Standard

Surprisingly, considering the almost three years it took the ISSB to release IFRS S2, the final standard strongly resembles the GOF's early and the TRWG's later adapted prototype. All four "versions" follow the initial structure of the Group of Five and contain disclosure requirements on governance processes, the effects of climate risks on strategy and business model, implemented risk management to identify, monitor and assess risks, as well as metrics and targets. Thereby, all versions match the TCFD's four pillar structure. While the ISSB added subtopics such as transition planning, it also changed wording issues and clarified constructs.

What is striking, however, is the fact that the ED and IFRS S2 exhibit a significantly more streamlined wording towards exposure materiality, i.e., the perspective that for an investor-focused sustainability reporting standard only the risks and opportunities that the enterprise value is exposed to should be material and, in consequence, be reported by the entity. This is directly evident in the first paragraph about the objective of the standard: in the first prototype by the GOF, the objective is centered around enterprise value reporting, where information about an entity's exposure is only one aspect next to information on management's usage of internal resources to respond and adapt its strategy and business model (GOF, para. 1(c)–(d)). In all three further documents, the focus of the first paragraph lies on the aim to generate information on an entity's exposure to climate-related risks and opportunities (TRWG, para. 1; ED, para. 1; IFRS S2, para. 1). In IFRS S2, the ISSB introduces the term "primary user", a term borrowed from its financial reporting standards, which also reflects this focus.

This change in the details demonstrates that the ISSB now more clearly distinguishes its exposure perspective from an impact perspective. As the initial prototype tries to articulate how the different standards and frameworks from the participants in the Group of Five could interoperate, the distinction between exposure and impact is not emphasized. The aim of the initial prototype, to demonstrate the possibility of one comprehensive reporting system to encompass both perspectives, led to a stronger focus on the connections and "filters" between enterprise value reporting and a reporting system that focuses on impacts. The ISSB, however, in its effort to position its standard, highlights its focus on exposure materiality more clearly by stating that its standards are intended to serve the investor community so that only information that changes the assessment of enterprise value is considered (ISSB, 2022).

This is further supported by the fact that the term "impact" is not mentioned at all in the ED and IFRS S2, while it appears more frequently in the Group of Five (11 times) and the TRWG prototype (nine times). In both the ED and IFRS S2, "impact" was replaced by the terms "effects on" or "affected by" to explicitly highlight the focus on the risks the entity is exposed to (for example, paragraphs 7–10 in GOF, TRWG, ED and IFRS S2). Whereas the first prototype speaks of an entity's "ability to *create* enterprise value" (para. 1b, emphasis added), the formulation in the ED is amended to the focus on the "*effects* of significant climate-related risks and opportunities *on* ... enterprise value" (ED, para. 1a, emphasis added). Interestingly, in IFRS S2, the ISSB removed the term "enterprise value" completely from the standard, referring to stakeholders' concerns about the concept as the main reason (ISSB, 2023).

Another hint to support our interpretation of a clearer focus on exposure materiality is how the TRWG's and ISSB's documents quickly turn the explication of climate-related risks into the two categories of physical and transition risks. Whereas the former result from physical events induced or exacerbated by climate change (such as floods, droughts, or hurricanes), the latter result from the world's transition towards a carbon-neutral and socially equitable economic system (such as bans on carbon-intensive technology or increased taxes on emissions). The usage of this distinction of climate risk in two categories, however, follows a perspective that climate change threatens (or, in case of opportunities, improves) first and foremost an entity's *financial* position and performance. This distinction would not make sense when discussing physical and transition risks to indigenous people or ecosystems.[12]

Two other changes in the ED merit highlighting. In the Group of Five prototype, two disclosure requirements refer to plans (GOF, para. 10f) and processes (GOF, para. 14d) that would "significantly contribute to climate change mitigation and adaptation". This formulation is borrowed from the EU's Taxonomy Regulation. which classifies economic activities according to their significant contribution towards six ecological goals (European Parliament, 2020). Neither the TRWG's prototype nor the ISSB's later documents feature this phrase. Because of its direct reference to achieving climate goals, i.e., having an impact on people and planet, it possibly did not fit the ISSB's focus anymore.

Similarly, the disclosure requirements for scenario analysis (GOF, para. 11; TRWG, para. 10; ED para. 15; IFRS S2, para. 22) and an entity's own targets (GOF para. 26; TRWG, para. 15; ED, para. 23; IFRS S2, para. 33) underwent changes. Whereas the prototype suggests that an entity should disclose "whether [the analysis] has been conducted against a range of climate-related scenarios including a 2 degree Celsius or lower scenario" (GOF, para. 11a), further refined by the TRWG prototype that asks about a "Paris-aligned scenario" (TRWG, para. 10a), the ED and IFRS S2 only require the information if "among its scenarios, [the entity has used] a scenario aligned with the latest international agreement on climate change" (ED, para. 15b(4); similar wording in IFRS S2, para. 22b(i)(4)). Whether the ISSB accepts that "1.5 degrees is dead" with this formulation (The Economist, 2022) and thus tries to make its standard more future proof in case there is another "international agreement on climate change" or to reduce the ambition for firms to report on their plans' alignment with the Paris goal, is an open question. Regarding the requirement for own climate targets, the reference in the first version to "2 degrees Celsius or lower" had already been dropped from the TRWG's prototype (see TRWG para. 15c, ED para. 23d and IFRS S2 para. 33b). From a structural perspective, the standards did not change very much. Slight, but important wording changes, however, followed the ISSB's proclaimed vision of an exposure-materiality targeted at investors.

5   CONCLUSION

This chapter descriptively traces the developments that led to the establishment of the ISSB and the publication of its first two IFRS Sustainability Disclosure Standards. Our first and second analyses examine the constituents' responses to the IFRS Foundation's September 2020 Consultation Paper and contrast it with the Foundation's own analysis. With the announcement that is was creating its own board for sustainability reporting standards, the IFRS Foundation entered an already existing field, in which the GRI and the IIRC, in particular, had strong footholds. In addition, the European Union's standard setter for financial reporting standards, EFRAG, was already preparing its own standards.

We find that most commenting constituents disapprove of the exposure (single) materiality perspective for future standards. Following this perspective, an entity would have to report only on those issues that might affect its enterprise value, thus potentially turning a blind eye to impacts on people and planet that do not (yet) manifest as enterprise value relevant. Regarding this issue, stakeholders frequently mention that the EU is currently pursuing its own standard-setting ambitions. As these follow the impact perspective, i.e., consider an entity's impacts on people and planet, stakeholders fear that a standard setter focusing only on exposure might make reporting more complex rather than harmonizing the existing landscape.

Our third analysis follows the three phases of standard development. When the ISSB was set up under the governance structure of the IFRS Foundation during COP26 in Glasgow in November 2021, significant preparatory work had been underway for more than a year. In early 2021, the Foundation set up the TRWG, which consisted of the relevant players in the sustainability standard-setting sphere – the Group of Five – which had already proposed two prototypes and was able to lay the foundation for the ultimate standards, as this chapter shows. While IFRS S2, on climate-related disclosures, enhanced and extended the earlier proposals, it did not differ significantly content-wise, but closely followed the disclosures proposed by the Group of Five. However, changes in the detailed wording over time make clear that the ISSB further sharpened its focus on exposure materiality in its standard.

Overall, this chapter contributes to our understanding of standard setters' agenda setting. Most directly, we complement the literature that has investigated how other standard setters have evolved over time and responded to outside pressures (Brown et al., 2009a; Etzion & Ferraro, 2010; Humphrey et al., 2017; Larrinaga & Bebbington, 2021; Levy et al., 2010; Rowbottom & Locke, 2016). Specifically, we follow the IFRS Foundation's ambitions, starting with their proposal to set up a new standard setter towards its standard on climate.

Following this, the chapter opens multiple avenues for further research. As our scope is limited to the time frame starting from the IFRS Foundation's consultation in late 2020, further research could analyze the way the IFRS Foundation came to the decision to set up the new standard setter. Arguably, the harmonization work that led to the ISSB had already been initiated by the Corporate Reporting Dialogue (CRD), as Rowbottom (2023) shows. The CRD consisted of the IIRC and the GRI as well as the IASB, the US-based Financial Accounting Standards Board (FASB) and the International Organization on Standardization (ISO) and "provided a means for different bodies to coalesce and legitimate specific visions of sustainability reporting" (Rowbottom, 2023, p. 903). Further research could examine how the idea of harmonizing different existing organizations is brought forward, negotiated, and pursued in an organizational field. As we provide initial evidence on the relevance of the existing players in shaping not only the standard-setting activities, but also the organizational development of the new standard setter, establishing the *ex ante* conditions of how the Foundation's move was possible should provide important insights. Given the relevance of the EU's ambitions to set its own standards, this research could also consider the multiple ways in which the organization made a case for its offering. From a legitimacy perspective, it is *ex ante* unclear how the standard setter could establish itself given the dominance of the existing institutions and the clear will of the European Commission to intervene.

Second, our analysis of the different phases of standard development could be extended by a data point-based investigation of how the standards changed over time. By breaking up a reporting standard into its "atomistic" components, this micro-level analysis could shed light on the small, but often relevant changes that occur in the process of drafting a standard and thus complement our chapter's macro-level view. Given the multiple "rounds" that the standards went through, the changes could be explained by differing motivations of the authors in the different phases, the compositions of the groups of authors, and the political discourses that shape standard setting (such as the striving to align the standards in the early stage and the need to distinguish itself from the other standard setters in the later stages). Irrespective of the outcomes, it will be interesting to see what these (political) processes will look like and can achieve in the future. Given that sustainability-related transparency is and will be used even more as a key regulatory tool in tackling the mitigation and adaptation challenges in the future, we need to understand how an effective response to the climate crisis can be achieved by this form of targeted transparency, what standard setters' motivations are and how we can ultimately leverage financial markets for good.

Acknowledgment

We gratefully acknowledge funding by the German Research Foundation (Project-ID 403041268 – TRR 266 Accounting for Transparency).

NOTES

1. See, for example the recent engagement by asset owners and regulators advocating decarbonization in the corporate sector (Fink, 2022; GFANZ, 2023; UNFCCC, 2022).
2. This chapter uses the term "sustainability reporting" to denote any voluntary reporting practices from an impact materiality and broader stakeholder-focused perspective as well as those following an exposure materiality and narrower, investor-focused perspective. For an overview and discussion, see Sellhorn & Wagner (2022).
3. For a timeline of the key events during the development of these draft standards, see Appendix A.
4. The following analysis builds upon and extends our previous work in Großkopf et al. (2021).
5. A list of all cited comment letter submissions with the name of the organization can be found in Appendix B. The comment letters are publicly available on the website of the IFRS Foundation: https://www.ifrs.org/projects/completed-projects/2021/sustainability-reporting/consultation-paper-and-comment-letters/#view-the-comment-letters
6. The group of users comprises financial analysts and investors.
7. While it seems that this figure is not in line with Adams and Mueller's (2022) findings, we note the difference in assessment method. We elicited the responses to the single questions while Adams and Mueller categorize responses as being "overall" supportive or opposed (p. 9).
8. The Group of Five comprised the following five sustainability reporting standard-setting organizations: CDP, CDSB, SASB, IIRC and GRI.
9. The term "Technical Readiness Working Group" was first used in a website entry in June 2021 (IFRS Foundation, 2021f).
10. Interestingly, in a LinkedIn comment, the current CEO of the GRI answered his own (rhetorical) question of why there was a need for a GRI with the new European and international standards being developed, by referring to the GRI Standards as the "existing global baseline for *impact* reporting [which] will remain so under ISSB and ESRS" (emphasis added).
11. Whereas the GRI was a member of the Group of Five, it was not part of the TRWG.
12. Of course, physical risks are the prime threat to people and planet. The point made here, however, refers to the explicit use of this dichotomy which does not occur in impact-oriented disclosure standards. The dichotomy makes the focus of the ISSB's standards clear by only viewing these exposure-focused risks as relevant. Neither the GRI 305 standard on emissions, nor the "Sustainable Development Goals Disclosure (SDGD) Recommendations" (Adams et al., 2020) uses the words "transition risk".

REFERENCES

Adams, C. A., & Abhayawansa, S. (2022). Connecting the COVID-19 pandemic, environmental, social and governance (ESG) investing and calls for "harmonisation" of sustainability reporting. *Critical Perspectives on Accounting*, *82*, 102309. https://doi.org/10.1016/j.cpa.2021.102309

Adams, C. A., & Mueller, F. (2022). Academics and policymakers at odds: the case of the IFRS Foundation Trustees' consultation paper on sustainability reporting. *Sustainability Accounting, Management and Policy Journal*, *13*(6), 1310–1333. https://doi.org/10.1108/SAMPJ-10-2021-0436

Adams, C. A., Druckman, P., & Picot, R. (2020). *Sustainable Development Goals Disclosure (SDGD) Recommendations.* https://www.integratedreporting.org/wp-content/uploads/2020/01/ICAS5045 _SDGD_Recommendations_A4_22pp_AW3-1.pdf

Afolabi, H., Ram, R., & Rimmel, G. (2022). Harmonization of sustainability reporting regulation: analysis of a contested arena. *Sustainability*, *14*(9), 5517. https://doi.org/10.3390/su14095517

Armstrong McKay, D. I., Staal, A., Abrams, J. F., Winkelmann, R., Sakschewski, B., Loriani, S., Fetzer, I., Cornell, S. E., Rockström, J., & Lenton, T. M. (2022). Exceeding 1.5°C global warming could trigger multiple climate tipping points. *Science*, *377*(6611), eabn7950. https://doi.org/10.1126/science .abn7950

Brown, H. S., de Jong, M., & Lessidrenska, T. (2009a). The rise of the Global Reporting Initiative: a case of institutional entrepreneurship. *Environmental Politics*, *18*(2), 182–200. https://doi.org/10.1080/ 09644010802682551

Camfferman, K., & Zeff, S. A. (2018). *Aiming for Global Accounting Standards: The International Accounting Standards Board, 2001–2011.* Oxford University Press.

CDP, Climate Disclosure Standards Board (CDSB), Global Reporting Initiative (GRI), International Integrated Reporting Council (IIRC), & Sustainability Accounting Standards Board (SASB) (2020a). *Open Letter to Erik Thedéen (IOSCO). Re: Working together to meet the needs of the capital markets.* https://29kjwb3armds2g3gi4lq2sx1-wpengine.netdna-ssl.com/wp-content/uploads/Open-Letter-to -Erik-Thedeen-Chair-of-the-Sustainable-Finance-Task-Force-of-IOSCO.pdf

CDP, Climate Disclosure Standards Board (CDSB), Global Reporting Initiative (GRI), International Integrated Reporting Council (IIRC), & Sustainability Accounting Standards Board (SASB) (2020b). *Reporting on enterprise value. Illustrated with a prototype climate-related financial disclosure standard.* https://29kjwb3armds2g3gi4lq2sx1-wpengine.netdna-ssl.com/wp-content/uploads/Reporting-on -enterprise-value_climate-prototype_Dec20.pdf

CDP, Climate Disclosure Standards Board (CDSB), Global Reporting Initiative (GRI), International Integrated Reporting Council (IIRC), & Sustainability Accounting Standards Board (SASB) (2020c). *Statement of Intent to Work Together Towards Comprehensive Corporate Reporting.*

Etzion, D., & Ferraro, F. (2010). The role of analogy in the institutionalization of sustainability reporting. *Organization Science*, *21*(5), 1092–1107. https://doi.org/10.1287/orsc.1090.0494

European Parliament (2020). Regulation (EU) 2020/852 of the European Parliament and of the Council of 18 June 2020 on the establishment of a framework to facilitate sustainable investment, and amending Regulation (EU) 2019/2088. http://data.europa.eu/eli/reg/2020/852/oj

Fiechter, P., Hitz, J., & Lehmann, N. (2022). Real effects of a widespread CSR reporting mandate: evidence from the European Union's CSR Directive. *Journal of Accounting Research*, *60*(4), 1499–1549. https://doi.org/10.1111/1475-679X.12424

Fink, L. (2022). *Annual 2022 Letter to CEOs.* BlackRock. https://www.blackrock.com/corporate/ investor-relations/larry-fink-ceo-letter

GFANZ (2023). *Glasgow Financial Alliance for Net Zero. About.* https://www.gfanzero.com/

Giner, B., & Luque-Vílchez, M. (2022). A commentary on the "new" institutional actors in sustainability reporting standard-setting: a European perspective. *Sustainability Accounting, Management and Policy Journal*, *13*(6), 1284–1309. https://doi.org/10.1108/SAMPJ-06-2021-0222

Gray, R. (1992). Accounting and environmentalism: an exploration of the challenge of gently accounting for accountability, transparency and sustainability. *Accounting, Organizations and Society*, *17*(5), 399–425.

Großkopf, A.-K., Sellhorn, T., Wagner, V., & Weiß, K. (2021). Globale Standards für Nachhaltigkeitsberichterstattung: eine kritische Analyse des Vorstoßes der IFRS-Stiftung. *Der Betrieb*, *30*, 1621–1629.

Humphrey, C., O'Dwyer, B., & Unerman, J. (2017). Re-theorizing the configuration of organizational fields: the IIRC and the pursuit of "Enlightened" corporate reporting. *Accounting and Business Research*, *47*(1), 30–63. https://doi.org/10.1080/00014788.2016.1198683

ICAEW (2021). *When Chartered Accountants Save the World.* https://www.icaew.com/insights/insights -specials/when-chartered-accountants-save-the-world

IFRS Foundation (2020). *Consultation Paper on Sustainability Reporting.* https://www.ifrs.org/content/ dam/ifrs/project/sustainability-reporting/consultation-paper-on-sustainability-reporting.pdf

IFRS Foundation (2021a). IFRS Foundation announces International Sustainability Standards Board, consolidation with CDSB and VRF, and publication of prototype disclosure requirements. https://www.ifrs.org/news-and-events/news/2021/11/ifrs-foundation-announces-issb-consolidation-with-cdsb-vrf-publication-of-prototypes/

IFRS Foundation (2021b). *IFRS Foundation Trustees' Feedback Statement on the Consultation Paper on Sustainability Reporting.* https://www.ifrs.org/content/dam/ifrs/project/sustainability-reporting/sustainability-consultation-paper-feedback-statement.pdf

IFRS Foundation (2021c). IFRS Foundation Trustees announce next steps in response to broad demand for global sustainability standards. https://www.ifrs.org/news-and-events/news/2021/02/trustees-announce-next-steps-in-response-to-broad-demand-for-global-sustainability-standards/

IFRS Foundation (2021d). IFRS Foundation Trustees announce working group to accelerate convergence in global sustainability reporting standards focused on enterprise value. https://www.ifrs.org/news-and-events/news/2021/03/trustees-announce-working-group/

IFRS Foundation (2021e). *Exposure Draft ED/20215: Proposed Targeted Amendments to the IFRS Foundation Constitution to Accommodate an International Sustainability Standards Board to Set IFRS Sustainability Standards.* https://www.ifrs.org/content/dam/ifrs/project/sustainability-reporting/consultation-paper-on-sustainability-reporting.pdf

IFRS Foundation (2021f). *Technical Readiness Working Group.* https://web.archive.org/web/20210621203012/https://www.ifrs.org/groups/technical-readiness-working-group/

IFRS Foundation (2021h). IFRS Foundation Trustees announce strategic direction and further steps based on feedback to sustainability reporting consultation. https://www.ifrs.org/news-and-events/news/2021/03/trustees-announce-strategic-direction-based-on-feedback-to-sustainability-reporting-consultation/

Intergovernmental Panel on Climate Change (2022). *Working Group III contribution to the Sixth Assessment Report. Mitigation of Climate Change.* https://www.ipcc.ch/report/ar6/wg3/

ISSB (2022). ISSB makes key announcements towards the implementation of climate-related disclosure standards in 2023. https://www.ifrs.org/news-and-events/news/2022/11/issb-cop27-progress-implementation-climate-related-disclosure-standards-in-2023/

ISSB (2023). *Feedback Statement on IFRS S1 and IFRS S2.* https://www.ifrs.org/content/dam/ifrs/project/general-sustainability-related-disclosures/feedback-statement.pdf

Jorissen, A., Lybaert, N., & Van de Poel, K. (2006). Lobbying towards a global standard setter – do national characteristics matter? An analysis of the comment letters written to the IASB. In G. N. Gregoriou and M. Gaber (eds), *International Accounting—Standards, Regulations, and Financial Reporting* (pp. 1–40). Elsevier.

KPMG (2022). *Big shifts, small steps: Survey of Sustainability Reporting 2022.* https://assets.kpmg.com/content/dam/kpmg/se/pdf/komm/2022/Global-Survey-of-Sustainability-Reporting-2022.pdf

Larrinaga, C., & Bebbington, J. (2021). The pre-history of sustainability reporting: a constructivist reading. *Accounting, Auditing & Accountability Journal, 34*(9), 131–150. https://doi.org/10.1108/AAAJ-03-2017-2872

Lenton, T. M., Rockström, J., Gaffney, O., Rahmstorf, S., Richardson, K., Steffen, W., & Schellnhuber, H. J. (2019). Climate tipping points—too risky to bet against. *Nature, 575*(7784), 592–595. https://doi.org/10.1038/d41586-019-03595-0

Levy, D. L., Szejnwald Brown, H., & de Jong, M. (2010). The contested politics of corporate governance: the case of the Global Reporting Initiative. *Business & Society, 49*(1), 88–115. https://doi.org/10.1177/0007650309345420

Milne, M. J., & Gray, R. (2013). W(h)ither ecology? The triple bottom line, the Global Reporting Initiative, and corporate sustainability reporting. *Journal of Business Ethics, 118*(1), 13–29. https://doi.org/10.1007/s10551-012-1543-8

Murphy, R., & Leaver, A. (2020). Accounting is the new frontline when it comes to the environment – and we need to take action on it by 31 December. https://www.taxresearch.org.uk/Blog/wp-content/uploads/2020/12/IFRS-submission-8-12-20.pdf

Rowbottom, N. (2023). Orchestration and consolidation in corporate sustainability reporting. The legacy of the Corporate Reporting Dialogue. *Accounting, Auditing & Accountability Journal, 36*(3), 885–912. https://doi.org/10.1108/AAAJ-06-2021-5330

Rowbottom, N., & Locke, J. (2016). The emergence of <IR>. *Accounting and Business Research, 46*(1), 83–115. https://doi.org/10.1080/00014788.2015.1029867

Sellhorn, T., & Wagner, V. (2022). The forces that shape mandatory ESG reporting. SSRN Scholarly Paper No. 4179479. https://doi.org/10.2139/ssrn.4179479

She, G. (2022). The real effects of mandatory nonfinancial disclosure: evidence from supply chain transparency. *Accounting Review, 97*(5), 399–425. https://doi.org/10.2308/TAR-2020-0178

Stolowy, H. & Paugam, L. (2023). Sustainability reporting: is convergence possible? *Accounting in Europe, 20*(2), 139–165. https://doi.org/10.1080/17449480.2023.2189016

Tett, G. (2020). "The alphabet soup of green standards needs a new recipe", *Financial Times*, 16 January. https://www.ft.com/content/b3fadc18-3851-11ea-a6d3-9a26f8c3cba4

The Economist (2022). "Say goodbye to 1.5°C", *The Economist*, 5 November. https://www.economist.com/weeklyedition/2022-11-05

UNFCCC (2022). *Race to Zero: Progress report.* https://climatechampions.unfccc.int/wp-content/uploads/2023/12/Race-to-Zero-2023-Progress-Report_29112023.-pdf.pdf

Wagenhofer, A. (2024). Sustainability reporting: a financial reporting perspective. *Accounting in Europe, 21*(1), 1–13. https://doi.org/10.1080/17449480.2023.2218398

APPENDIX A: TIMELINE OF KEY EVENTS

	2020
11 Sep	Group of Five (CDP, CDSB, GRI, IIRC, SASB) announces collaboration
30 Sep	IFRS Foundation Trustees publish *Consultation Paper* on Sustainability Reporting
12 Dec	Group of Five release prototype climate and presentation standards
	2021
2 Feb	Trustees publish first response to the Consultation Paper, indicating their plan to propose the setting up of a new board at COP26
8 Mar	Trustees announce strategic directions and further steps to set up a new board
22 Mar	Trustees announce a working group with TCFD, IIRC, SASB, CDSB and WEF
30 Apr	Trustees publish the *Feedback Statement* on the Consultation Paper and an Exposure Draft for an amended Constitution
21 Jun	TRWG is publicly mentioned for the first time in a blog post
3 Nov	At COP26 in Glasgow, Erkki Liikanen, Chair of Trustees announces the creation of the ISSB, the consolidation with IIRC, SASB, and CDSB, and the publication of the *TRWG climate prototype*
16 Dec	Emmanuel Faber is appointed to chair the ISSB
	2022
31 Jan	ISSB completes consolidation of the CDSB
2 Mar	IFRS Foundation signs a Memorandum of Understanding (MoU) to establish the ISSB in Frankfurt, Germany
24 Mar	IFRS Foundation and GRI sign an MoU to align their work program
31 Mar	ISSB publishes the first two *Exposure Drafts*, for IFRS S1 and IFRS S2
20 Jul	ISSB holds its inaugural board meeting in Frankfurt
1 Aug	ISSB completes consolidation of the VRF (consisting of IIRC and SASB)
	2023
4 May	ISSB publishes its first Consultation on Agenda Priorities
26 Jun	ISSB publishes the first two *IFRS Sustainability Disclosure Standards*

Note to Appendix A: This table lists relevant events during the period 2020–2023 that played a role in the development of the first two IFRS Sustainability Disclosure Standards. Key documents are shown in italics.

APPENDIX B: LIST OF COMMENT LETTER SUBMISSIONS CITED

ID	Author	Group
34	International Federation of Accountants (IFAC)	Auditor
49	Pan African Federation of Accountants (PAFA)	Auditor
60	Consejo Mexicano de Normas de Información Financiera (CINIF)	Regulator
71	Ellen MacArthur Foundation	NGO
90	Integrated Reporting Committee (IRC) of South Africa	NGO
100	ERICA Working Group ECCBSO	Regulator
124	Federated Hermes International	User
127	ShareAction	NGO
153	European Fund and Asset Management Association (efama)	User
154	Allianz	Preparer
170	The Institute of Chartered Accountants in England and Wales	Auditor
190	Accountability Sustainability and Governance Research Group at the School of Accounting and Finance of the University of Bristol	Academic
200	The Banking Association South Africa	Preparer
252	Institute of International Finance (IIF)	User
262	EuropeanIssuers	Preparer
281	Impact Economy Foundation	NGO
331	DRSC eV (ASCG)	Regulator
334	S&P Global	Other
349	Daimler AG	Preparer
380	International Actuarial Association (IAA)	User
388	IAA – GLASS	Regulator
453	Charles Cho	Academic
491	Nigeria Integrated Reporting Committee	Regulator
499	Fidelity International	User
506	Julia Seppä and Olga Marjasova	Individual
508	A4S Accounting for Sustainability	NGO
511	International Monetary Fund (IMF)	NGO

Note to Appendix B: This table lists the comment letter submissions cited in the chapter. The comment letters can be accessed at https://www.ifrs.org/projects/completed-projects/2021/sustainability-reporting/consultation-paper-and-comment-letters/.

PART III

SUSTAINABILITY REPORTING
WITHIN THE COMPANY

8.   Management accounting and control for sustainability – management control as a moderator when transforming sustainability ambitions into actions in a public organisation

Matti Skoog and Mathias Cöster

INTRODUCTION

Sustainable development is a global phenomenon and concept, with historical roots that extends back to the early 1960s (Pisani, 2006). Today, frameworks like the SDG 2030 (United Nations, 2021) and the planetary boundaries (Steffen et al., 2015) address the need for global action and activities, orchestrated by intergovernmental organisations such as the UN and the EU, as well as by nations. On an organisational level, the interpretation of sustainability and the integration of it into ongoing activities pose several challenges. One is to develop a management control system and processes that are aligned to the sustainability goals and strategies of the organisation (Bebbington and Thomsson, 2013; Beusch et al., 2022; Burrit et al., 2002). For public organisations in Sweden (and elsewhere) such management control practices are of particular interest as these organisations are supposed to lead the transition towards more sustainable societies (Guarini et al., 2022).

A Sustainability Budget in a Public Organisation's Administrative Department

Gotland is the largest Swedish island. Located in the middle of the Baltic Sea, it has around 61 000 inhabitants. During summertime the number of people spending time on the island increase to around 200 000, as Gotland attracts a large number of visitors from Sweden and abroad. On the island, Region Gotland is the public organisation responsible for public municipality services to the locals as well as to visitors. It has three main tasks: municipal operations, county council operations and regional development.

Region Gotland has an organisational structure consisting of ten political committees, which control six administrative departments. In one of these departments, Technical Services, the head of department and his management team decided that they needed to increase their ambitions regarding implementing sustainability in their everyday operations. On the one hand, because on a personal level they believed that it is the right thing to do; and on the other hand, because they, among others, have experienced that climate change affects their operations. For example, water supply challenges, storm water management, how roads cope with seasonal changes, etcetera. Therefore, the 11 people that constitute the department management team believed that discussions on sustainability, and above all ecological sustainability, had become central to management group meetings.

A focus on sustainability was also in line with Region Gotland's current regional development plan, which describes how the society will develop until the year 2040 (Region Gotland,

2023a). The plan clearly states that a sustainable region is dependent on the integration and support of initiatives and actions that address social, economic, and environmental goals. To accomplish regional sustainable development, a constant integration of different kinds of sustainability activities and goals is necessary in order to reach relevant and sustainable outputs and outcomes.

Although the ambitions in the management team of the Technical Services department were high regarding sustainability (and in accordance to the development plan), they experienced organisational obstacles that were hard to overcome. One such obstacle was the current management control system. It had three main formal components: a financial budget, a balanced scorecard, and an activity plan. In all of these, sustainability was hardly present and especially not in the financial budget. So how could they overcome this obstacle? One idea that appeared was to investigate if they could develop a sustainability budget to complement the existing management control system.

Formal and Informal Management Control Systems and Processes

The management team of the Technical Services department is an example of employees in an organisation who are regularly confronted with and influenced by organisational management control practices. That may not be the case for all employees; depending on, for example, the size of an organisation, there may be people who seldom reflect upon the existence of management control. Still, unawareness doesn't mean that employees are not also influenced at an operational level, which ultimately is a main purpose of management control. For example, Simons' broad definition of a management control system (MCS) emphasises that "management control systems are the formalized procedures and systems that use information to maintain or alter organisational activity" (Simons, 1990, p. 128). Besides maintaining or altering organisational activities, i.e. influencing employees, the definition also states that an MSC includes formalised procedures and systems. Langfield-Smith (1997) describes formal controls as the more visible, objective components of a control system, while informal controls are "not consciously designed. They include the unwritten policies of the organization and often derive from, or are an artefact of the organizational culture" (Langfield-Smith, 1997, p. 208). Complementary to this, Malmi and Brown (2008) present a typology that includes formal as well as informal controls, bundled as a package of MCS. Ferreira and Otley (2009) represent an even broader approach to MCS and instead label it a performance management system (PMS). Such a system includes, according to them, both the formal mechanisms, processes, systems, and networks used by organisations, as well as more subtle informal controls.

Altogether, management control can be described as a system of formal as well as informal controls (Langfield-Smith, 1997; Malmi & Brown, 2008; Ferreira and Otley, 2009). In the Malmi and Brown typology, formal controls are grouped into planning, cybernetic controls, rewards and compensations, and administrative controls. Complementary to these, the informal controls are labelled cultural controls. Additionally, the definitions of MCS in the section above also include and emphasise procedures and processes (Simons, 1990, Ferreira and Otley, 2009). Instead of only considering the control processes as part of the system, it is possible though, to place them on an equal footing with the control system. In that case, the MSC can be considered as a set of formal and informal control tools that enable an analysis of what the control consists of. The management control process (MCP), on the other hand, then becomes a description of how the control is carried out (Cöster et al., 2023). Such an MCP contains a variety of activities, practices and material arrangements (Ahrens & Chapman, 2007) that also can be divided between formal and informal.

Formal activities in an MCP are consciously designed and recurring during an operating year, e.g., on a monthly, quarterly, or yearly basis and they are primarily supported by formal parts of the MCS. Example of formal activities are planning, measurement, reporting, analysis, evaluation, and feedback. The formal activities are present at various organisational levels and managers at these levels are responsible for performing the activities (Cöster et al., 2023). Complementary to this, there also exist informal activities in the MCP. These activities are often spurred by the formal ones and are performed by a wider group of employees. The informal activities can be negotiations of, for example, strategies, budgets, and performance targets. Furthermore, discussions about ways of realising targets, giving and receiving advice, and taking corrective actions often end up in creative solutions (Ahrens & Chapman, 2007).

Depending on how the formal and informal parts of MCS and MCP are designed and used by employees, they influence interpersonal dialogues in, for example, a management team. Simons (1994) notes that managers may use formal control systems as levers of strategic change and renewal. According to him, in situations of strategic change – such as those changes initiated in Region Gotland's development plan – control systems are used by top managers to formalise beliefs, set boundaries for acceptable strategic behaviour, and define and measure critical performance variables. In addition, control systems also motivate debate and discussion about strategic uncertainties, i.e., the set of uncertainties that managers believe must be monitored personally for their organisation's strategy to be achieved (Simons, 1990; Cheng & Humphreys, 2016). For many organisations today, the interpretation and implementation of sustainability in its operations may definitely be considered as a strategic uncertainty. For example, which investments are necessary to reduce CO_2 emissions? How do we have to change operational activities to address and improve social sustainability aspects?

Research Question and Disposition

With the introduction above as a starting point, later on in this chapter we will focus on how management control can be used to moderate debates and discussions on sustainability as a strategic uncertainty. We will use the case of the Technical Services department at Region Gotland as an illustration; more specifically, how their discussions and dialogues regarding the need to develop more strategically grounded and sustainable operations was supported by the creation of a sustainability budget. We will do that by addressing the following question:

● What moderating roles can management control systems and processes have when an organisation aims to transform strategic sustainability ambitions into actions?

The next section introduces research on sustainable development and management control, followed by a presentation of research methods. Thereafter comes a description of the sustainability budget case at the Technical Services department. It is followed by a discussion on the moderating roles that management control may have in organisational interpersonal dialogues addressing sustainability as a strategic uncertainty. Finally, we present some concluding remarks.

SUSTAINABLE DEVELOPMENT AND MANAGEMENT CONTROL

Research on management control and sustainable development uses a variety of theoretical concepts. For example, management control systems as a package (Lueg & Radlach, 2016; Crutzen et al., 2017), sustainability control systems (Gond et al., 2012; Beusch et al, 2022), environmental management control systems (Guenther et al., 2016), environmental management accounting (Burrit et al., 2002) and levers of eco-controls (Journeault et al., 2016). No matter what theoretical framework used, research repeatedly highlights that a fundamental reason to study management control and sustainability is that unless organisations make efforts to enforce them, sustainability goals may only remain good intentions.

As noted in previous section, management control contains formal as well as informal MCS and MCP. Regarding formal MCS, sustainability has been represented in flexible budgeting systems that assess environmental indicators; balanced scorecards that include sustainability perspectives; and sustainability accounting and reporting (Burrit et al., 2002; Lueg and Radlach, 2016; Guenther et al., 2016). Furthermore, research indicates that long- and short-term sustainability planning can provide meaningful direction and that it may contribute to lowering employees' resistance towards adopting sustainability initiatives in their operational activities. The integration of sustainability in the planning process can fail though, if specific sustainability action plans are not established, or if strategic planning is not adapted to local circumstances (Guenther et al., 2016). Crutzen et al. (2017) observe that informal cultural control is represented mainly through sustainability initiatives, communications, and engagement by top management and employees. In the cultural controls, gradual inclusion of sustainability seems to be a way to avoid resistance from employees who may feel overwhelmed by radical change.

When addressing sustainability in the formal MCP, it is desirable that the results and lessons learned from analysis, evaluation, and feedback form the basis of forthcoming planning phases. Unfortunately, this is too rarely the case. Often organisations emphasise planning, execution, measurement and reporting and too little time is spent on the other activities. Accordingly, the consequence may be less organisational and individual learning (Johansson & Skoog, 2015). Nevertheless, the formal and informal activities in the MCP have potential to contribute to the shaping of organisational sustainability practices that influence employees' motivations and coordination of their actions.

It is now time to move on to the case of a formal sustainability budget and how it contributed to interpersonal dialogues in a management team. But first some words about the research methods used to generate the empirical material in this chapter.

METHOD

The case study is based on empirical material collected during a one-year action research project funded by Uppsala University. Using collaborative methods, the authors, together with the management team of the Technical Services department at Region Gotland, explored the possible content and structure of a so-called "sustainability budget" and how it could be aligned to existing management control systems and processes at Region Gotland. Collaborative methods enable creative interaction between researchers and practitioners and how they together seek answers to questions of mutual interest through, for example, dialogue and examination of knowledge (Pasmore et al., 2008). The purpose of collaborative research is not primarily to carry out research *for* practice, but instead *with* practice.

The research agenda was very explorative in the sense that neither the management team nor the researchers knew what a "sustainability budget" was or could be. But the head of department had a vison to create something that at least could be complementary to the existing financial budget system and process. By making the traditional budgeting process more sustainability oriented and precise, it would fit better with the overarching strategic ambitions in the regional development plan, which to a significant degree links directly to the Agenda 2030 framework.

The actual research process regarding different sustainability aspects of management control systems and processes started out some time before the case study on the Technical Services department began. Initially, the researchers' interest was to understand how an entire public organisation included sustainability in their strategic management control agenda. But, since the strategic level(s) of the organisation were quite vague and indirect in how they wrote and spoke about sustainability, we approached a unit on the operational level to get more detailed knowledge on how sustainability was, or could be, handled in more operational and tactical terms.

The actual research process consisted of four separate, three-hour thematic workshops with the management team at the department. The themes for the workshops were: (a) sustainability in Region Gotland's current management control system, (b) key ratios relevant in a sustainability budget, (c) how can a sustainability budget be integrated into Region Gotland's formal control processes, and (d) content and use of an extended sustainability budget.

Ahead of every workshop, the management team were individually given questions to reflect upon. The intention was that they should come up with answers or new questions that they could bring with them to the next workshop. Complementary to this, they had to complete assignments and prepare presentations individually or in groups.

During the workshops the researchers mostly acted as initiators and facilitators for the discussion and sometimes as "pathfinders" so that the group did not get lost in internal debate or disagreement. There was of course a pre-planned structure, but the structure was continuously adjusted to reflect what happened in each workshop.

All workshops were summarised and reflected upon by both the researchers and the management team in a collective document. Between the workshops, the research team communicated with members of the management team primarily via e-mail conversations. This communication included sharing and validating written research notes as well as the gradually emerging sustainability budget. At the end of the project, the members of the management team believed that they had been able to create a control tool mainly due to the support of the researchers. They also appreciated that the focus had been on exploring possible content, rather than a time pressure to establish the budget. Thus, it was believed that ideas that were generated in a better way could mature over time.

In the end a collective structure for sustainability accounting and control was created and an internal university report was written and delivered to Uppsala University, which financed the project. Since the project has finished, the collective structure in the form of a sustainability budget has been applied by the management team. They expressed that it has been of great value to them.

THE CREATION OF A SUSTAINABILITY BUDGET AT A TECHNICAL SERVICES DEPARTMENT

Motives – Why the Need for a Sustainability Budget?

As mentioned in the introduction of this chapter, in the department of Technical Services at the public organisation Region Gotland, the head of department and his management team decided they needed to increase their ambitions regarding implementing sustainability in their everyday operations.

Source: Region Gotland (2023b).

Figure 8.1   *The seven divisions at the Department of Technical Services*

The department is organised in seven divisions (see Figure 8.1). A division manager is responsible for the operations in each division and the Head of Department is responsible overall. Besides these eight persons, the management team also consists of a chief financial officer (CFO), a human resource manager (HR), and an information officer (IO).

A major challenge that the management team initially experienced was how they could get politicians in the political committee (those that allocated resources to the department and the divisions) to come up with decisions that were in line with the sustainability ambitions in the strategic development plan. They believed that a new control tool in the form of a sustainability budget (SB) could be of help. The head of the department stated that: "We need to set aside resources to achieve something, identify what it is we are going to do."

The resources that are mentioned in the quote are in the current control system and processes, formally controlled via the financial budget. This consists of two main parts, a yearly budget and a long-term investment budget. The experience of the head of department and the division managers was that the financial budgets gave little room for sustainability initiatives. Instead, the budgets had a strict financial logic and cost focus. Therefore, they believed there was a need for an SB that enabled action plans that was integrated into the control system and processes.

Furthermore, they thought that an SB could be used in the internal dialogue as a tool for creating awareness and knowledge on sustainability among the employees (around 600 individuals) within the department of Technical Services. Finally, an SB could be used as a tool to communicate about sustainability initiatives with the other departments and the political committees at Region Gotland, in order to establish the Technical Services department's sustainability work within the organisation.

So, what would the content of the sustainability budget be? It was decided early on that the division managers should try to come up with what they believed were critical sustainability key ratios. The reason for this was that dialogue on sustainability, even on a departmental tactical and operational level, easily become overarching and not very specific. Everyone may agree that "yes, sustainability is important to us", but what does it actually mean in everyday operations? Instead, when identifying a control tool such as a key ratio, it raises several questions that one has to try to answer. For example: what does it measure, why is it important to measure this, what data is needed, how can data be collected, and – most importantly – what control effects are desirable outcomes?

The conditions for coming up with key ratios and answers to the questions above varied among the seven departments. The head of the Department for Property Management stated that regarding measuring the CO_2 footprint, they already had data, but they were not sure how it could be used: "We are already measuring, so we have measurement data available. The question is, how do we break it down?"

Examples were available in an annual document called "CO_2 accounting – Property Management Department". But the question in the quote illustrates that operations in all of the divisions are diverse and sometimes it is hard to establish where the responsibility for the operations starts and where it ends. Regarding property, the major sustainability impact is how buildings are cooled and heated and if the electricity is generated from renewable sources. The manager for the Port Division expressed similar concerns: "It [the port] is a customer-driven business. How do we take care of it, how do we affect the emissions that the ships produce?"

One idea that the Port Division manager expressed was that control effects could be achieved through differentiated port tariffs. The aim of that should be to achieve more cargo volume per freighter unloading in the ports. He also noted that it is the politicians who decide on the Region's tariffs, so they must be involved in the process of establishing them. On a later occasion, he stated that the establishment of differentiated port tariffs had been paused at a national level. At the same time and in contrast to this, the EU had communicated that member states are to establish penalty taxes for ships powered by diesel fuel, which emits a high level of CO_2 emissions. This illustrates that public organisations, especially regarding sustainability, are affected by various political decisions, legislation and directives that take place national and transnational levels; processes that a single region or municipality has little or no influence on, but the outcome of which they are still expected to execute. Based on this, a conclusion the Port Division manager came up with was that it is important that the sustainability budget addresses activities that the employees in the division actually can influence.

The manager for the Water and Sewer Division stated that it is important that the key ratios reflect that water is a finite resource. Also, consumption of water on Gotland varies greatly depending on the seasons of the hospitality industry. For example, during summertime, the number of people consuming water is triple the amount of people living there all year around. As a start, the manager decided to use an existing external framework, Swedish Water's sustainability index, to identify possible key ratios. Based on recommendations in the sustainability index, she believed a key ratio called the water and sewer climate footprint – total litres per day divided by number of people – could be of use. Her estimate was that on average the consumption per day and per person was 140 litres, but the goal should be to reduce it to under 100 litres.

Altogether, a focus on key ratios spurred a dialogue in the management team. As each division manager was to establish and motivate why their specific key ratios were of interest

Table 8.1   *Excerpts from parts of the sustainability budget matrix at the Department of Technical Services*

	Property Division	Port Division	Water and Sewer Division
Key ratio	$\dfrac{CO2e}{m^2\,heating}$ $\dfrac{CO2e}{New\ constructions}$	$\dfrac{KwH}{passengers}$ $\dfrac{Tons\ of\ cargo}{Number\ of\,ships\ calling}$	Share of recovered phosphorus that goes to use on productive land $\dfrac{Litres\ of\ water}{per\ person\ and\ day}$
Data source	Energy consumption Climate data	Energy consumption port terminal and terminal area Tons of goods from shipping data and calls from port registers	From existing system, "person" is calculated based on the number of subscriptions
Activities	Solar cell installations Charging points Energy optimisation/ efficiency Requirements for climate declarations	Develop technology in the port terminal Differentiated port tariff	Collaboration with Federation of Swedish Farmers and optimisation of the biogas plant in Visby Influence politicians to decide on an assignment regarding water consumption
Control effects	Influencing choice of energy sources Influencing choice of material New project requirements	Reduced energy consumption in the terminal area Fewer calls to the cargo port, but the same, or increased, amount of cargo	Equal to or more than 60% Less than 100 litres per person per day, which according to Swedish Water's sustainability index is an acceptable level

and the desirable control effects, it was possible to critically discuss how and in what ways sustainability was part of each division's specific operations. Besides the discussions, the content of the sustainability budget was visualised in a budget matrix (see Table 8.1).

In Table 8.1, the key ratios, data sources, activities, and control effects from the Properties, Port, and Water and Sewer Divisions are highlighted. The same content was also presented by the department's additional four divisions. The Properties Division believed that focusing on heating of properties and new constructions would be a substantial contribution in the department's ambition to lower its CO_2 emissions. As noted above, it was a kind of easy picking as the data already existed. An activity such as energy optimisation connects quite well to the key ratios, while it wasn't equally logical how charging points would contribute. The control effects have an indirect character, as two of them were about "influencing". Regarding new projects, the requirements were intended to be used in dialogue with contractors, among others.

Integration with Existing Control System and Processes

Gradually, as the content in the sustainability budget emerged, members of the management team also expressed concern regarding the integration of the new control tool into existing control system and processes. One of the managers said: "The concept of budget can be problematic to use, because there is no organisational framework today, such as for the financial budget. However, this is because the organization in general has not come that far in this matter. What we do is a bottom-up initiative."

These concerns reflect worries about organisational hierarchical integration of the sustainability budget. If Technical Services are the only department in Region Gotland that operates a sustainability budget, of what use will it actually be? It was acknowledged that the department initially would have an overall responsibility for the budget, but who in the organisation should have it in the long run? The management team collectively expressed that they are, after all, operating within a politically controlled organisation and therefore formal administrative controls are dominant. For example, they had not yet expressed actual goals and targets that the budget should address. In order to come up with these, they needed the support of the political committee that sets the goals and allocates resources to the department.

Another integration that was seen as challenging was the time frame of the sustainability budget, as the existing control tools and processes address different time lines. There is the ten-year investment plan which is updated once a year. Additionally, they also operate a five-year investment plan that contains more detailed information. On top of that is the financial budget that on an annual basis states expected revenues and costs for the forthcoming year. In order to improve performance and to reach sustainability goals, resources need to be directed to prioritised activities (examples of which are illustrated in Table 8.1). These resources will show up as costs in the yearly financial budget, but how can they simultaneously be addressed in the investment budgets? Some sustainability activities may be low-hanging fruits that don't require extra financial resources, i.e., they can be performed by simple adjustments of existing practices; for example, more efficient planning of the department's transport can reduce the CO_2 emissions from this, while others may require substantial investment and long-term commitment.

Still, everyone in the management team agreed that the sustainability budget should be integrated into existing formal control processes. It was especially emphasised by the CFO: "We do not need to have our own process for the sustainability budget, it should be part of the regular management control process. For example, it can become its own tab in the decision support system."

The CFO's quote illustrates that besides existing control systems and processes, the IT systems that support them also have to be considered if integration is to have a chance of being successful. If the control tool isn't present as a "tab" in the organisation's enterprise resource planning and/or business intelligence systems, there is a risk that it will not be visible at all.

How the budget should be communicated within the department was also up for discussion. The IO expressed some concerns about this:

> We need to think through how the budget should be communicated in the organisation. If we now create a new concept, sustainability budget, it may require some explanation. There may be a risk that employees otherwise just perceive it as yet another administrative burden. It is therefore important that it is included in the employee dialogue.

If a control tool such as a sustainability budget (and others) are to have any control effects at all, communication regarding it is of very great importance. This communication has to be integrated into the ongoing formal MCP activities, such as evaluation and feedback. Such activities may in turn initate informal activities among the employees, so that, for example, in their interpersonal dialogues they more regularly give and receive advice on sustainability in their everyday operations, and based on that, take corrective actions. Each of these corrections may be considered as a small step towards more sustainable operations. But added together, they can over time contribute to the overall sustainable performance of the department. In the next section we will analyse how such interpersonal dialogue, with a focus on discussions on sustainability as a strategic uncertainty, can be moderated more consciously by a combination of MCS and MCP practices.

THE MODERATING ROLES OF MANAGEMENT CONTROL IN ORGANISATIONAL INTERPERSONAL DIALOGUES

In the introduction section of this chapter, we stated that formal and informal control tools in a MCS co-exists with formal and informal activities in the MPC. Such systems and processes may enable and support management control driven interpersonal dialogues and (hopefully) actions on sustainability. For example, the system and processes could influence how a management team in their discussions address sustainability as a strategic uncertainty. In this context, management control can play various moderating roles in the ongoing interpersonal dialogues.

In Figure 8.2, the MCS is represented by the vertical line, the ends of which represent emphasis on formal or informal control tools. Similarly, the MCP is represented by the horizontal line, which also emphasises either formal or informal process activities. Given the combination of formal and informal MCS and MCP, four moderating roles that management control may have within an organisation are identified: *safe guardian, the adaptor, active listener*, and *creative order creator*. The roles are reflected by and match four different interpersonal dialogues that employees in an organisation may experience: *steady state, organisational shoe chafing, muttering displeasure*, and *chaos and creation*. The content of the roles and dialogues, and how they are reflected in the case of the Technical Services department, are explained below.

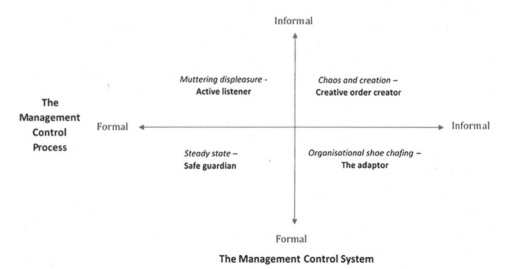

Figure 8.2   Four moderating roles of management control

In the *lower left corner* of Figure 8.2, the interpersonal dialogues are in a *steady state*. Primarily, this dialogue may be represented at a strategic level in the organisation. At Region Gotland, for example, this is represented by the political committees and the Regional Management Group,[1] which were not included in the case study. In the steady state, the dialogue emphasises formal parts of the management control system, e.g., long- and short-term plans, financial and non-financial key ratios, and organisational structures. The control process supporting the dialogue is also to a large extent formal and characterised by activities such as planning, measurement, reporting, and (hopefully) analysis, evaluation, and feedback. Overall, management control's moderating role in the ongoing interpersonal dialogue is to be a safe guardian that signals whether successes as well as failures are under way.

In the *upper left corner*, the interpersonal dialogues are characterised by a *muttering displeasure*. This dialogue may be represented primarily on a on a tactical and operative level in the organisation, for example the Technical Services department. Here the informal MCS, such as values and beliefs, is emphasised and fewer formal controls are practised. At the same time, the control process still emphasises formal activities that mainly address the formal parts of the control system. This may give rise to muttering displeasure, as the values and beliefs among employees of how and what the organisation should perform are not highlighted in the formal control process. This was not the case for the management team at the Technical Services department. On the contrary, the managers were very aware of and influenced by the formal MCS and they also interacted with it regularly through, for example, the writing of reports and analysis of how their divisions were performing.

To be able to find a better match between the control process and the control system, the management control moderating role is here to be an active listener. In this role the goal should be to turn the mutterings into clear speech in order to figure out what is causing the mismatch and what can be done about it.

In the *lower right corner*, the interpersonal dialogues can be described as *organisational shoe chafing* and management control's moderating role is to be an adaptor. The dialogue (just as muttering displeasure) is represented primarily on a on a tactical and operative level in the organisation. The formal parts of the management control system are emphasised in the dialogue, but the control process is dominated by informal activities. A consequence of this could be that when employees receive output from the formal control system, it may have a poor match to the informal process activities. For example, activities such as ongoing dialogues among employees regarding how well the part of the organisation they belong to, actually perform. In the case of the Technical Services department management team, there were signs of organisational shoe chafing.

The members of the team on a personal level believed that to develop more sustainable operations at the department was the right thing to do. Still, sustainability was only to some extent represented in the formal parts of the MCS, and not at all in the formal MCP. This led to informal MCP activities, such as discussions among the managers on ways of realising sustainability targets. In this context management control need to take a moderating role that enables the organisation to adapt and to pick up on thoughts and ideas that occur in the informal MCP activities. At the Technical Services department, the formal control tool sustainability budget became a tool that moderated the dialogue. As the case study was performed during one year, we don't know how well the sustainability budget in the long run help the management team to adapt their management control and operations. But in the empirical section above, it is illustrated that discussions on *what, how* and *when* to perform more sustainable operations occurred. Hopefully, the budget also spurred a development of existing control system and processes that better fit the internal views on, what, how and when the organisation should perform regarding sustainability.

In the *upper right corner*, the interpersonal dialogues are characterised by *chaos and creation* and this dialogue may be represented primarily on an operational level in the organisation. Both the control system and the control process are experienced by the employees as mainly informal. Here the employees have great influence on and can be creative regarding what and how to perform. At the same time, there is very little structured and recurring follow-up on how far employees' performances are actually in line with the organisational goals. This could be the case for the employees in the divisions of the Technical Services department. But, as the research only encompassed the management team, we do not know if that is in fact how the interpersonal dialogues at the operational level of the department can be described.

The moderating role of management control here is to create enough order without killing the creativity that contributes to the organisation's performance, i.e., it has to be a creative order creator.

It is important to consider, in respect of Figure 8.1, that there is no ideal situation for an organisation to position themselves in. On the contrary, the employees' dialogues may exist simultaneously; for example, the steady state can be just as common as the muttering displeasure. Where the dialogue exists depends partly on the organisational level; if it is strategic, tactical, or operational. Furthermore, the dialogues may be influenced by values and events existing inside as well as outside the organisation. This may especially be the case regarding sustainability. As highlighted, the employees in the management team at the Technical Services department believed on a personal level that acting in a sustainable way is the right thing to do. Simultaneously, organisations such as Region Gotland may experience how external demands on, for example, sustainability reporting, are becoming mandatory, which in turn requires a formal internal systematisation of control systems and processes.

DISCUSSION AND CONCLUSIONS

The overall question for this chapter was: what moderating roles can management control have when organisations are to transform sustainability ambitions into actions? Based on earlier research and the empirical case of Region Gotland's Technical Services department, we have identified four different moderating roles that management control may take in order to transform strategic sustainability ambitions into tactical and operational actions.

The most common frustration in the studied organisation and most other organisations is that strategic ambitions and concepts are often decoupled from both the tactical and operational levels within organisations, i.e., sustainability aspects are almost never included in formal budgets and calculations and are seldom clearly visible in the daily operations. Management control processes and systems may here play different moderating roles depending on the level of formality in different empirical settings. Theoretically, this type of internal decoupling could be related to reasoning often used in institutional theoretical contexts. However, in studies applying institutional theory, individual professional groups seldom play a part in the analysis, which appears to be the case in this study.

The frameworks for external reporting are aiming for "one size fits all", which is the opposite of management control processes and systems that must, or at least should, be uniquely designed for every organisation in relation to their specific business model and role in society. This is especially problematic when more mandatory external reporting frameworks are implemented in relation to sustainability. The moderating roles may here be vital to adjust the external frameworks to achieve internal relevance and action within different public and private organisations. From a theoretical point of view these adjustments could be related to framing theory, where the moderating roles could enable new and more relevant internal frames for understanding different aspects of sustainability.

In addition to this mandatory trend, there have been many voluntary reporting frameworks over the years that have been competing for attention in relation to sustainability. The moderating roles for management control systems and processes will probably be important in the translation process from these voluntary frameworks to the more mandatory reporting landscape that is now taking shape through initiatives of the European Union and international standard setters. In this sense the moderating roles could be linked to actor network theory, in which translation and transformations are considered important for acceptance and legitimation in different organisational and societal contexts.

In sum, the moderating roles may initiate and enable different types of integrating, framing and transformation processes, which could have both practical and theoretical implications that could be of relevance of pursuing in future studies.

NOTE

1. The Regional Management Group consists of the heads of the six departments, together with, among others, the highest responsible official, the Regional Director.

REFERENCES

Ahrens, T. & Chapman, C.S. (2007). Management accounting as practice. *Accounting, Organizations and Society*, 32(1–2), 1–27.

Bebbington, J. & Thomsson, I. (2013). Sustainable development, management and accounting: boundary crossing. *Management Accounting Research*, 24(4), 277–283.

Beusch, P., Frisk, J.E., Rosén, M. & Dilla, W. (2022). Management control for sustainability: towards integrated systems. *Management Accounting Research*, 54, 100782.

Burritt, R.L., Hahn, T. & Schaltegger, S. (2002). Towards a comprehensive framework for environmental management accounting, links between business actors and environmental management accounting tools. *Australian Accounting Review*, 12(2), 39–50.

Cheng, M.M. and Humphreys, K.A. (2016). Managing strategic uncertainty: the diversity and use of performance measures in the balanced scorecard. *Managerial Auditing Journal*, 31 (4/5), 512–534.

Cöster, M., Isaksson, R. & Skoog, M. (2023). *Verksamhetsstyrning för hållbar utveckling [Management Control for Sustainable Development]*, Lund: Studentlitteratur.

Crutzen, N., Zvezdov, D. & Schaltegger, S. (2017). Sustainability and management control. Exploring and theorizing control patterns in large European firms. *Journal of Cleaner Production*, 143, 1291–1301.

Ferreira, A. & Otley, D. (2009) The design and use of performance management systems: an extended framework for analysis. *Management Accounting Research*, 20(4), 263–282.

Gond, J.-P., Grubnic, S., Herzig, C. & Moon, J. (2012). Configuring management control systems: theorizing the integration of strategy and sustainability. *Management Accounting Research*, 23(3), 205–223.

Guarini, E., Mori, E. & Zuffada, E. (2022) Localizing the Sustainable Development Goals: a managerial perspective. *Journal of Public Budgeting, Accounting & Financial Management*, 34(5), 583–601.

Guenther, E., Endrikat, J. & Guenther, T.W. (2016). Environmental management control systems: a conceptualization and review of the empirical evidence. *Journal of Cleaner Production*, 136(A), 147–171.

Johansson, U. & Skoog, M. (2015). *Integrerad verksamhetsstyrning [Integrated Management Control]*, Lund: Studentlitteratur.

Journeault, M., De Rongé, Y. & Henri, J.-F. (2016). Levers of eco-control and competitive environmental strategy. *The British Accounting Review*, 48(3), 316–340.

Langfield-Smith, K. (1997). Management control systems and strategy: a critical review. *Accounting, Organizations and Society*, 22(2), 207–232.

Lueg, R. & Radlach, R. (2016). Managing sustainable development with management control systems: a literature review. *European Management Journal*, 34(2), 158–171.

Malmi, T. & Brown, D.A. (2008). Management control systems as a package: opportunities, challenges and research directions. *Management Accounting Research*, 19(4), 287–300.

Pasmore, W.A., Woodman, R.W. & Simmons, A.L. (2008). Toward a more rigorous, reflective, and relevant science of collaborative management research, in A.B. Shani Rami, S. Albers Mohrman, W.A. Pasmore, B. Stymne & N. Adler (eds), *Handbook of Collaborative Management Research*, pp. 567–582, Los Angeles, CA: Sage Publications.

Pisani, J. (2006). Sustainable development – historical roots of the concept. *Environmental Sciences*, 3(2), 83–96.

Region Gotland (2023a). Vårt Gotland 2040 – regional utvecklingsstrategi [Our Gotland 2040 – regional development strategy], published 21 March 2023. Available at: https://www.gotland.se/gotland2040.

Region Gotland (2023b). Teknikförvaltningen [The department of technical services], published 25 October 2023. Available at: https://www.gotland.se/68980.

Simons, R. (1990). The role of management control systems in creating competitive advantage: new perspectives. *Accounting, Organizations and Society*, 15(1/2), 127–143.

Simons, R. (1994). How new top managers use control systems as levers of strategic renewal. *Strategic Management Journal*, 15(3), 169–189.

Steffen, W., Richardson, K., Rockström, J., Cornell, S.E. et al. (2015). Planetary boundaries: guiding human development on a changing planet. *Science*, 347(6223).

United Nations (2021). The 17 goals. https://sdgs.un.org/goals, retrieved 30 September 2021.

9. Exploring different perspectives of management control for sustainability

Chiara Crovini, Sirle Bürkland and Frederik Zachariassen

INTRODUCTION

Accounting research has devoted increased attention to sustainability over the last two decades (Hall et al., 2015; O'Dwyer and Unerman, 2016; Tregidga et al., 2018). Extensive attention has primarily been dedicated to external reporting and sustainability disclosures (see e.g. Cho et al., 2015; Bellucci et al., 2021; Dinh et al., 2023) following the regulatory initiatives, from the European Directive on non-financial information (Directive 2014/95/EU) to the international frameworks of Global Reporting Initiatives (GRI) and the Integrated Reporting Framework, which have required a considerable number of companies to report on their sustainability activities. Recently, new rules and regulations about sustainability reporting have also been issued (see the Corporate Sustainability Reporting Directive) along with the introduction of European Sustainability Reporting Standards (ESRS) that all large companies and listed SMEs in Europe will be obliged to adopt. In addition, after the creation of the Value Reporting Foundation, accounting standards have been under revision to further embed sustainability information into annual reports, potentially increasing the transparency of businesses' sustainability efforts (Afolabi et al., 2023).

The principles of relevance and materiality suggest that stakeholder engagement often determines what information is reported and made available to a broader audience (Arvidsson and Dumay, 2022). Companies have also voluntarily published sustainability reports to simplify stakeholders' access to information about various ESG-related issues (Joseph, 2012; Michelon et al., 2015; Bini et al., 2018). However, studies have identified mixed results about the meaning and relevance of such sustainability information. For example, Baboukardos and Rimmel (2016) studied South African companies after the adoption of integrated reporting and showed an increase in the value relevance of earnings, while Cordazzo et al. (2020) found that ESG information from a sample of Italian-listed companies was not value-relevant. Further, Arvidsson and Dumay (2022) investigated the reporting of Swedish companies, suggesting that the regulation is too weak to improve ESG reporting quality and usefulness, leaving a significant degree of freedom for organizations in developing their accounts of sustainability.

Consequently, from an outside-in perspective, there emerges much concern about the actual practices and motives for accounting for sustainability within companies (Gray, 2010; O'Dwyer and Unerman, 2016), how sustainability reporting is constructed and used within different organizational contexts, and how the reporting process is affected by organizational complexity, the institutional and regulatory environment, available accounting technologies and the structures of managerial decision-making (O'Dwyer and Unerman, 2016; Traxler et al., 2020; Dinh et al., 2023). Therefore, this chapter takes a look at the endeavors of management control, exploring different perspectives taken on management accounting and control of sustainability and the ways these may support the agendas of implementing a sustainability strategy in organizations. Management accounting and control systems have traditionally been focused on profit maximization and economic goals and might be limited or conflict with the broader concerns for environmental and societal well-being (Adams, 2002; O'Dwyer, 2002; Gond et al., 2012). Arguments have also been put forward as to whether these challenges will gradually dissolve as management control systems will naturally evolve for improved sustainability management (Contrafatto and Burns, 2013; Domingues et al., 2017; Adams and Frost, 2018).

Currently, there is no shared definition of "sustainability" or "corporate social responsibility", nor a common understanding of how they can be achieved (Delmas et al., 2015; Hinze and Sump, 2019). As a result, the two concepts are often used as synonyms. In this chapter, the definition of "corporate sustainability reporting" is adopted from ACCA (2016, p. 11), which is the communication of information "relevant for understanding a company's long-term economic value and contribution towards a sustainable global economy, taking account of the company's economic, environmental, social and governance performance and impacts". Consistent with this definition, sustainability reporting requires integrative measurement and management of sustainability, and therefore, management control systems are suggested as relevant for determining the reporting processes in general and, hence, forming sustainability reporting practices (Maas et al., 2016).

This chapter discusses three perspectives on management control and sustainability reporting: a compliance perspective, a critical perspective, and a managerial perspective. Within these three perspectives, research has pointed to several barriers to mobilizing and migrating management control systems towards effective sustainability reporting and management. These might pertain to matters of technical (Battaglia et al., 2016), organizational (Gond et al., 2012), or cognitive integration (George et al., 2016; Perego et al., 2016) or a lack of knowledge of best practices (Adams and McNicholas, 2007). These can also be related to the ways of integrating sustainability goals into organization-wide planning processes (Adams and McNicholas, 2007) and difficulties in choosing between different indicators and reporting guidelines (Domingues et al., 2017). These challenges may prove difficult to handle in organizations and might also partly explain the contradictory and sometimes vague conclusions about the accomplishment of sustainability reporting in organizations (Adams and Frost, 2008).

Through the three perspectives on management control, the chapter discusses different trajectories organizations may take in sustainable development and reporting. Arguments are put forward that management control practices may largely be determined by the managerial perspective and the degree of environmental complexity involved in organizational operations. The road towards internal sustainability reporting may not be straightforward, involving different managerial goals, challenges with existing reporting systems and degrees of business and environmental complexity that the management control system aims to handle. Through the analysis of existing research, a matrix is developed that identifies different characteristics of management control systems in organizations engaged in sustainability reporting. The chapter further discusses how organizations handle various degrees of complexity following the managerial agendas of sustainable development.

PERSPECTIVES OF MANAGEMENT CONTROL AND SUSTAINABILITY REPORTING

Contemporary management accounting practices are "becoming increasingly complex, being integrated within broader organizational and extra-organizational processes" (Contrafatto and Burns, 2013, p. 350). Sustainability reporting is part of these developments, in which impacts, causes, and results of the organizations' actions are difficult to isolate, let alone measure with conflicting demands for financial, social and environmental objectives (Epstein et al., 2010). Organizations *may want* or *be forced* to make possible changes to their management accounting practices to accommodate sustainability concerns (Bebbington et al., 2009; Gond et al., 2012). Research has pointed to different perspectives and managerial worldviews in relation to sustainability management and reporting (Landrum and Ohsowski, 2018; Traxler et al., 2020; Farias et al., 2024). This chapter elaborates on three perspectives (see Table 9.1) informed by different theoretical standpoints. The first perspective relates to management control and sustainability reporting that primarily strives for compliance with external regulation. This perspective is primarily seen in the light of coercive isomorphism (DiMaggio and Powell, 1983; Bromley and Powell, 2012), through which regulations and standards lead organizations to homogeneity. The second perspective relates to a more structured approach to sustainability management and accounting involving the efforts of adapting one's sustainable behaviors for the agenda of improved legitimacy and response to stakeholders' interests (O'Dwyer, 2002). The third perspective depicts more sophisticated and in-depth changes towards sustainable development, which involve integrated, flexible, and dynamic internal processes for realizing an organization's sustainable strategies. These perspectives delineate particular managerial agendas and organizational approaches to sustainability management and control. The following sections will discuss each of the three perspectives in more detail.

Further, contemporary organizations are faced with increasing complexity within the business and organizational environment (Brown et al., 2019) due to increased competition, globalization and rapid technological changes (Vasconcelos and Ramirez, 2011). Beyond daily capacity planning and operations, organizations engage in multifaceted problems of technologies and markets demanding contextual judgment and competencies across different knowledge domains. Different degrees of organizational and environmental complexity[1] need to be managed in the management control system for sustainable development to be meaningful (Contrafatto and Burns, 2013). Hence, besides the three perspectives with different organizational approaches to sustainability, management control practices are also shaped by organizational and environmental complexity that influences the ways organizations attempt to handle their processes of decision-making with internal reporting (Contrafatto and Burns, 2013; Schäffer et al., 2015; Firtin, 2023).

Organizations also increasingly engage in moral and value-based decisions possibly involving multiple social and environmental concerns that, compared to routine operating decisions, require extra processing, context building, calculation, and searching for data outside the organization's traditional boundaries. These decisions typically involve contextual complexity, as they are vulnerable to different viewpoints and interpretations. These characteristics of complexity also relate to questions of sustainability and hence may require control systems that are adaptive and less bureaucratic to understand the environmental context of the organization's value creation and the concerns of sustainability. These control systems in general develop alongside users' competencies, which continuously evolve to bridge the gap between the traditional processing of data and more complex decision-making (Vasconcelos and Ramirez, 2011).

Sharfman and Dean (1991) suggest the construct of environmental uncertainty as the breadth and depth of knowledge needed for effective interaction in the environment. For sustainability reporting purposes, this means that organizations that have greater challenges identifying the impacts of their actions on sustainability will require more knowledge in reporting those relationships. The breadth and depth of knowledge required has, in general, increased as "management accounting is becoming increasingly complex, fluid and integrated within broader organizational and extra-organizational processes", where "an important aspect of these developments is the interplay between management accounting and sustainability-related issues" (Contrafatto and Burns, 2013, p. 350). Combining the two dimensions (overall sustainability-related agendas and organizational and environmental complexity) likely relates to different management control system designs and perspectives for internal sustainability reporting (see Table 9.1).

Table 9.1   Perspectives on sustainability reporting

	Compliance perspective	Critical (decoupling) perspective	Managerial perspective
High organizational and environmental complexity	• Utilitarian approach • "Business as usual" • No/little technical development • Knowledge of sustainability reporting	• Political narratives and legitimizing of metrics • Add-ons to existing MCS (e.g., SBSC) • Exclusively incremental change • Non-integrated approaches of reporting • Loose coupling of sustainability controls • Challenges with comparability	• Potential radical MCS change • Tight coupling of sustainability controls • Close relations between sustainable development, organizational change and sustainability reporting • Embedded sustainability culture • Bottom-up approaches • MCS tailored for integrative sustainability reporting
Low organizational and environmental complexity	• Limited knowledge on sustainability reporting • Business as usual • No or little technical development	• Minimal incentives to alter MCS • Ad hoc KPI development • Peripheral and decoupled sustainability controls • Extensions to conventional management accounting techniques • Possibly limited MCS capabilities	• Moderate MCS change • MCS adapted for integrative sustainability reporting • Mainly driven by a few key individuals • Risk of MCS demobilization

The Compliance Perspective

Regulatory initiatives, from the European Directive on non-financial information (Directive 2014/95/EU) to the international frameworks of Global Reporting Initiatives (GRI) and Integrated Reporting Framework, have required a considerable number of companies to report on their sustainability activities. So far, due to the general "comply or explain" principle, these regulations and standards have been considered "soft regulations" not indicating the specific content that companies should disclose to satisfy stakeholders' information needs (La Torre et al., 2018). Therefore, new rules and regulations about sustainability reporting have been issued (see the Corporate Sustainability Reporting Directive) leading to the introduction of the European Sustainability Reporting Standards (ESRS). In addition, after the creation of the Value Reporting Foundation, where the International Integrated Reporting Council (IIRC) and the Sustainability Accounting Standards Board (SASB) were merged into the IFRS Foundation, accounting standards have been under revision to embed sustainability information into the annual reports, thus entailing a considerable shift in the format and detailedness of external sustainability reporting (Afolabi et al., 2023; Dinh et al., 2023). Such changes in the regulatory environment likely induce changes in internal reporting practices.

The *compliance perspective* involves organizations being motivated or obliged (e.g., large companies and listed SMEs) to adopt a degree of internal sustainability reporting practices as a response to the changes in the regulatory environment and the increased attention to sustainability disclosures. Hence, these organizations report on sustainability issues due to legal ramifications. In the compliance perspective, neither low nor high organizational and environmental complexity involves considerable integration of sustainability into the management agendas and control systems (Traxler et al., 2020). The reporting practices of these organizations likely follow the minimal requirements for information.

The managerial and organizational agendas within this perspective can vary. One of the reasons for this approach can be that sustainability is poorly understood, hence making sustainability agendas "flawed and simplistic" (Aras and Crowther, 2008, p. 286), or, specifically, that accountants know little about sustainability concerns (Burritt and Tingey-Holyoak, 2012). For example, based on a sample of 65 Italian companies, Passetti et al. (2014) found that companies gave little attention to sustainability accounting and that accounting tools for sustainability reporting were seldom implemented. Such organizations may use their accounting systems for legal compliance and "traditional" business objectives with no significant changes occurring in management control and internal sustainability reporting.

Other studies, for instance Gond et al. (2012), also note that when the impetus for change is only related to legal pressure, low or non-existent technical developments in the management control system occur. That is, there is a reluctance to change and retool the management control system, as it is tailored for business objectives (Contrafatto and Burns, 2013; Beusch et al., 2022), and so there are challenges in overcoming the existing orientation of the management control system. This perspective can also be adopted because of an unwillingness to create separate cost pools for "traditional" costs and environmental costs (Henri et al., 2014). Additionally, organizations might apply a utilitarian approach, in which sustainability investments are not a win–win proposition vis-à-vis economic gains (Milne et al., 2009; Thomson and Bebbington, 2013). Consequently, organizations do not seek to solve trade-offs between economic efficiency and sustainability concerns (Passetti et al., 2014; Tregidga et al., 2014). Because of this, research has even suggested that the legal corporation may simply be a wrong boundary setting for sustainability agendas and related reporting practices (Gray and Milne, 2002).

The Critical (Decoupling) Perspective

As organizations increasingly recognize that sustainable business practices can yield a competitive advantage (Porter and Kramer, 2011), these developments have spurred a great interest in and demand for sustainability reporting (Cho et al., 2015). Alongside regulations and guidelines for this type of reporting (e.g., Corporate Sustainability Reporting Directive, Directive 2014/95/EU, the UK Companies' Act, and the Danish Financial Statement Act), the need for new calculative practices (Adams and Whelan, 2009; Gray, 2010) and data collection within companies to produce these reports (Hopwood, 2009) have increased. In the *critical perspective*, sustainability reporting may be adopted for various reasons. Sustainability rhetoric in companies' reports may, for instance, be applied to repair diminished legitimacy (Banerjee, 2008) or gain an advantage in the market over competitors (Traxler et al., 2020). Sustainability issues may also be deliberately reduced to measurable and manageable problems to be able to present them to wider audiences (Larrinaga-Gonzalez and Bebbington, 2001).

Criticism of this perspective involves the arguments that sustainability reporting in these organizations may rarely reflect the actual sustainability performance (Thijssens et al., 2016). As such, the management control practices related to sustainability reporting may "remain peripheral and decoupled from core business activities and fail to reshape strategy" (Gond et al., 2012, p. 206). There is considerable research supporting these arguments, demonstrating how companies prepare corporate reports to battle eroded legitimacy without an actual altruistic intention (Banerjee, 2008; Gond et al., 2009) or have used them to restore an eroded legitimacy (Bellucci et al., 2021). Sustainability reports, in these cases, have been criticized for being misleading (Gray, 2010) and trivial (Gray, 2006) as well as being primarily shaped by powerful corporate interests (Tregidga et al., 2018). Some authors have even argued that such sustainability reporting itself is the cause and source of sustainability problems (Aras and Crowther, 2008).

When comparing the two perspectives, compliance and critical, then the degree of decoupling is different. In the compliance perspective, there can be a greater degree of forwardness by companies, meaning that companies may not intend to hide relevant information, but they do not disclose certain information, because they do not have the proper processes in place to facilitate data collection and processing. Although companies are not interested in sustainability reporting besides the bare minimum, they do not purport to a higher degree of "being sustainable". However, the critical perspective involves an instrumental use of sustainability reporting, as companies focus on sustainability performance to attain conventional profit maximization and market share (Traxler et al., 2020). Therefore, the critical (decoupled) perspective is accompanied by researchers' skepticism about the intentions of organizations and the outcome of such practices, and much suspicion is raised about the mimicking behavior of organizations (De Villiers and Alexander, 2014). Even though the notion of "environmental management control systems" is suggested as a means for assisting firms to push towards strategic sustainability goals (Gibassier and Alcouffe, 2018), management accounting and control systems have traditionally been focused on profit maximization and economic goals and might be limited, or conflict with the broader concerns for environmental and societal well-being (Adams, 2002; O'Dwyer, 2002; Gond et al., 2012).

When organizational and environmental complexity is high, organizations have to deal with more complex problems and explanations about their sustainability. Therefore, organizations may experience higher pressure to legitimize their actions with extended reporting, possibly requiring changes to reporting processes to facilitate a better sustainability "image". Management control systems may, however, be only incrementally updated, such as with add-ons to the existing systems like the sustainability balanced scorecard (SBSC) or implementation of other performance measures that may remain loosely coupled to the external disclosures (Beusch et al., 2022). In this perspective, organizations might also struggle with comparability across business units, as their management control systems are likely poorly developed (Contrafatto and Burns, 2013; Thijssens et al., 2016).

When complexity is low, there might not be enough incentive to alter the management control system (similar to the compliance perspective), since the existing management control system may be capable of supporting only a few elements of sustainability which remain decoupled and limited to a small number of incremental extensions (Lozano et al., 2016). Instead of extensive add-ons to the existing system, companies may resort to reporting on simple KPIs to extend conventional profit-based systems.

Being placed in this perspective may be intentional or non-intentional. Many organizations may also struggle with the proper integration of sustainability into overarching corporate strategy (Battaglia et al., 2016). For instance, managers report that social and financial objectives collide with several barriers to proper reporting, including the need for broad organizational change and learning (Beusch et al., 2022). Specifically, it has been argued that organizations cannot circumvent the economic incentive, and so the management control system of the organization opportunistically serves to deliver on profit optimization (O'Dwyer, 2002; Contrafatto and Burns, 2013) and therefore fails to alter the strategic corporate direction. Research has also shown other potential reasons for such modest changes in management control systems. For instance, there can be largely segregated viewpoints across the managerial interests in organizations, as top managers may be interested and keen on sustainability concerns and sustainability reporting, while middle managers remain reluctant (Beusch et al., 2022). This highlights the challenges in linking short-term profitability goals and sustainability reporting.

Accordingly, in this perspective, sustainability reporting follows a non-integrated approach, and no real sustainability culture is embedded in the organization. There is a great risk of impression management practices, leading to an intentionally distorted use of corporate reporting and visual material that can potentially misguide investors and other stakeholders (Merkl-Davies et al., 2011; Diouf and Boiral, 2017; Usmani et al., 2020). Impression management can often be seen in cases where sustainability reporting is used to restore an eroded legitimacy and to depict an organizational facade (Cho et al., 2015; Bellucci et al., 2021). This organizational hypocrisy has been more common in specific sectors, such as the tobacco industry (Bellucci et al., 2021), or, more generally, in companies unwilling to disclose certain information that might harm their image and competitive advantage (Traxler et al., 2020). These practices can be considered riskier in organizations with high organizational and environmental complexity and existing knowledge on possible sustainability risks, with management nevertheless deciding to disclose sustainability information on a superficial basis without taking into account the potential impacts and consequences to society.

In general, there are institutional pressures on organizations to change their management control systems towards sustainable development, whereas the existing systems are traditionally tailored towards profit-maximizing incentives (Contrafatto and Burns, 2013). For that reason, some organizations might be reluctant to facilitate and shape sustainability reporting practices through developments in management control systems, since they might find themselves too deeply invested in the pursuit of economic gain (O'Dwyer, 2002). Therefore, research on management control concerning sustainability involves two viewpoints: one is that the development of sustainability reporting in an organization goes against the logic of management control systems (Adams, 2002; Contrafatto and Burns, 2013), which is related to the critical perspective, and the other viewpoint is that sustainability reporting practices make management control systems evolve (Gond et al., 2012; Ligonie, 2021). The latter viewpoint relates to the managerial perspective of sustainability reporting.

The Managerial Perspective

The *managerial perspective* shows a more proactive view on sustainability reporting, involving management control frameworks and company cases devised for effective sustainability management (Maunders and Burritt, 1991; Burritt and Schaltegger, 2010). Increasing attention and concern for the social and environmental impact of businesses has led many organizations, especially large firms, to actively account for and manage their social and environmental impacts (Adams and Frost, 2008). This perspective can also be labelled as an altruistic perspective or as an integrated sustainability perspective (Weaver et al., 1999), in which sustainability accounting has been pragmatically linked and aligned with business interests (Burritt and Schaltegger, 2010; Passetti et al., 2014).

In the managerial perspective, sustainability ambitions and values become an indispensable part of a wider change process, in which ethical developments in the organization can exist outside the underlying assumptions of economic constraints (Adams and McNicholas, 2007; Contrafatto and Burns, 2013). In this way, reporting can serve both internal and external stakeholders. Research also involves cases where corporations link their sustainability data to incentive programs and performance reports, which further feed into decision-making about capacity planning and strategically aligned management actions (Koehler, 2001; Albelda-Pérez et al., 2007). Management control systems play a crucial role in this process and can contribute to developments within the organization that result in improved sustainability reporting (Gond et al., 2012). In contrast to the critical sustainability perspective, where the management control system and reporting efforts were decoupled, the managerial perspective assumes a greater degree of coupling, also labelled as "tight coupling" of sustainability reporting (Gond et al., 2012). Rather than different uses of different tools in scattered parts of the organization (Maas et al., 2016), integrated corporate sustainability involves the measurement and management of sustainability issues through more adapted management control procedures (Dyllick and Hockerts, 2002). In this way, the critical and managerial perspectives differ in that organizations have considerable diversity in their sustainability reporting processes ranging from ad hoc and informally developed KPIs in the critical perspective to more formalized KPIs related to sustainable development (Adams and Frost, 2008). This is a more proactive perspective in which organizations take actions to attain a moral and ethical obligation to contribute to sustainable development in line with a stewardship approach (Traxler et al., 2020).

As organizations in the managerial perspective follow their sustainable business strategies, the degree of complexity determines how much effort is required to mobilize and change their existing management control system to conform with the desired reporting and decision-making procedures. When complexity is high, companies have to invest more to change their existing control and reporting processes with concerns for broader cooperation between managers inside the organization (Rodrigue et al., 2013; Johnstone, 2019). Research has shown that when companies adopt a proactive and enthusiastic approach, proper sustainability reporting can go hand in hand with organizational change management, thereby creating a double-sided enabling effect (Lozano et al., 2016; Ligonie, 2021). Sustainability reporting and organizational change management processes have reciprocal reinforcing relationships, where sustainability reporting can act as a change agent for organizational change and vice versa (Lozano et al., 2016; Traxler et al., 2020). Through such double-sided relationships, management control systems naturally develop and form a tightly coupled and interactive engagement with sustainable development (Gond et al., 2012; Beusch et al., 2022), which also assists organizations in radical changes to their management control system (Burnes, 2009; Lozano et al., 2016).

When complexity is low, these changes require fewer resources or may also be less significant, since organizations are not pushed to the same degree to alter their existing systems. This can also result in a less pronounced need for the organization to be involved in change processes, being potentially driven by a few individuals (Farneti and Guthrie, 2009; Domingues et al., 2017). As the need for change is lower when complexity is lower, there might also be the risk of management control system demobilization, in which newly developed systems have a risk of sliding back to their original forms of controls due to a lack of management support (Gond et al., 2012).

DISCUSSION AND CONCLUSION

This chapter has introduced three perspectives depicting the relationship between organizational agendas and possible management control designs in the context of organizational and environmental complexity. In the *compliance perspective*, management control systems and sustainability reporting primarily strive for compliance with external regulations. In organizational contexts with either high or low environmental complexity, reporting sustainability information is considered an additional cost for the organization, and management might have limited knowledge about sustainability reporting. Research has shown that in these cases organizations are reluctant to change and adapt management control systems, which remain focused on "traditional" business objectives (Contrafatto and Burns, 2013; Beusch et al., 2022).

The *critical (decoupling) perspective* is related to a more structured approach to sustainability reporting, mainly explained by the need to improve legitimacy and respond to societal expectations (O'Dwyer, 2002). Sustainability reporting rarely reflects the actual sustainability performance (Thijssens et al., 2016), because applied controls "remain peripheral and decoupled from core business activities" (Gond et al., 2012, p. 206). This perspective also represents the crossroads between organizations that consider the development of sustainability reporting against traditional management control systems (Adams, 2002; Contrafatto and Burns, 2013), and organizations that see sustainability reporting practices as an opportunity to improve existing management control systems and integrate them into sustainable development strategies (Gond et al., 2012; Ligonie, 2021).

The latter relates to the third perspective, the *managerial perspective*, which involves a motivation to change business activities and build management control systems that could support sustainable development and related business strategies. In the managerial perspective, more sophisticated tools for management control are likely developed with more detailed internal sustainability reporting that is potentially more flexible and dynamic to accommodate the changing needs of sustainable business agendas. These three perspectives may occasionally co-exist (e.g., the reputation building and the actual agendas of sustainable development), or in some cases, it might be difficult to locate an organization in a specific dimension as they may be in a transition towards sustainable development. However, these perspectives are helpful in depicting organizational agendas related to sustainability and sustainable development that delineate a certain intention and approach to management control design and sustainability reporting.

The above-given discussion of the three perspectives shows that accounting may not be the best (although undoubtedly useful) starting point when approached from the critical perspective, potentially leading to decoupled management and reporting practices. The above-shown scholarly work in the managerial perspective of sustainability reporting indicates that a greater engagement in sustainability reporting practices evolves from strategies of sustainable development rather than regulatory requirements. The existing research also illustrates that regulatory demands may not bring about much change in sustainability management, whereas more significant changes to the management control system in terms of sustainability reporting have been found in cases where sustainability is part of an organizational strategy (Traxler et al., 2020). This raises questions about the effectiveness of existing regulatory standards (Laine et al., 2020; Afolabi et al., 2023), and the effectiveness of the prevailing outside-in approach in general, through which the behavioral changes in organizations are expected to emerge from the requirements of financial reporting (O'Dwyer and Unerman, 2016). Traxler et al. (2020), by adopting the Malmi and Brown (2008) framework, have also pointed out that cultural controls with management values and beliefs have the potential to more deeply shape and drive sustainability reporting. This type of control, together with planning, can be considered as the precondition for sustainable development and management.

Therefore, this chapter and the three perspectives offer a basis for researchers investigating the possible designs of sustainability controls within organizations. The chapter also provides a source for stimulating the debate among preparers, regulators and auditors about the different barriers and challenges to external reporting, as organizations have different starting points and implications for sustainability disclosures depending on the (lack of) management control systems and internal sustainability reporting. The chapter has discussed the perspectives that likely involve external pressures and regulation leading to impression management and distorted use of corporate reporting, potentially obfuscating useful information for external stakeholders (Merkl-Davies et al., 2011; Usmani et al., 2020) and leading to organizational hypocrisy (Cho et al., 2015; Bellucci et al., 2021). Diouf and Boiral (2017) also argued that impression management practices are related to the elastic and uncertain application of the GRI principles. On the one hand, standards are trying to promote a common language, similar indicators and more consistent reporting practices, but their adoption has been quite challenging due to the lack of knowledge and actual commitment to sustainability. This discrepancy increases the lack of comparability and transparency of the sustainability reports, also reflecting the complexity and lack of sustainability performance metrics (Diouf and Boiral, 2017). Hence, rather than developing more guidelines and frameworks for external sustainability reporting, the promotion of ethical and moral concerns about the environment with investigation into the agendas of sustainable development and management control of sustainability might effectively lead to a proper integration of sustainability into organizational strategies and business activities.

There is a need for more empirical investigation into the interplay between sustainability challenges and management control practices. Research has analyzed the impact of sustainability reporting on companies' behavior, hypothesizing only the potential effects of regulations on organizational processes, as most studies have been conceptual (e.g., Traxler et al., 2020). As mentioned above, although the role of management accounting and control within sustainability reporting has been researched to some extent, only a limited number of studies have described such management control practices in organizations. The analysis of management control systems and sustainability reporting has often been done in an isolated manner (Chenhall, 2003; Ferreira and Otley, 2009), meaning that there is yet little explanation in the literature of how management control systems affect and are affected by sustainable development agendas.

Further avenues of research could involve a deeper look into the perspectives of sustainability reporting in terms of managerial intentions and environmental complexity, the possible combinations of the perspectives that the organizations adopt as well as the transitions between them. Further research is also needed for the managerial perspective of controls, especially related to the challenges of adapting existing accounting technologies to different degrees of organizational and environmental complexity, as there is a considerable path dependency involved in developing sustainability controls and reporting processes. Research would be valuable in explaining the ways existing systems affect the possibilities of sustainability controls and organizational change, and further, how organizations could be able to shift from the compliance and critical perspectives to the managerial perspective of sustainability controls. An investigation of the possible transitions between the perspectives would be valuable because management controls for sustainability tend to be shaped by existing accounting and control practices and the efforts to materialize sustainable development are highly dependent on existing institutional settings (see e.g., Contrafatto and Burns, 2013, Traxler et al., 2020).

NOTE

1. By environmental complexity, the chapter refers to the breadth and depth of knowledge needed for effective interaction in the business environment (Sharfman and Dean, 1991).

REFERENCES

ACCA (2016), "Mapping the sustainability reporting landscape: lost in the right direction". Available at: https://www.accaglobal.com/gb/en/technical-activities/technical-resources-search/2016/may/mapping-sustainability-reporting-landscape.html.

Adams, C. A. (2002), "Factors influencing corporate social and ethical reporting: moving on from extant theories", *Accounting, Auditing and Accountability Journal*, 15(2), pp. 223–250.

Adams, C. A. and Frost, G. R. (2008), "Integrating sustainability reporting into management practices", *Accounting Forum*, 32, pp. 288–302.

Adams, C. A. and McNicholas, P. (2007), "Making a difference: sustainability reporting, accountability and organisational change", *Accounting, Auditing and Accountability Journal*, 20(3), pp. 382–402.

Adams, C.A. and Whelan, G., (2009), "Conceptualising future change in corporate sustainability reporting", *Accounting, Auditing & Accountability Journal*, 22(1), pp. 118–143.

Afolabi, H., Ram, R. and Rimmel, G. (2023), "Influence and behaviour of the new standard setters in the sustainability reporting arena: implications for the Global Reporting Initiative' s current position", *Sustainability Accounting, Management and Policy Journal*, 14(4), pp. 743–775.

Albelda-Pérez, E., Correa-Ruíz, C., and Carrasco-Fenech, F. (2007), "Environmental management systems and management accounting practices as engagement tools for Spanish companies", *Accounting, Auditing and Accountability Journal*, 20(3), pp. 403–422.

Aras, G. and Crowther, D. (2008), "Corporate sustainability reporting: a study in disingenuity?", *Journal of Business Ethics Supplement*, 87, pp. 279–288.

Arvidsson, S. and Dumay, J. (2022), "Corporate ESG reporting quantity, quality and performance: where to now for environmental policy and practice?", *Business Strategy and the Environment*, 31(3), pp. 1091–1110.

Baboukardos, D. and Rimmel, G. (2016), "Value relevance of accounting information under an integrated reporting approach: a research note", *Journal of Accounting and Public Policy*, 35(4), pp. 437–452.

Banerjee, S. B. (2008), "Corporate social responsibility: the good, the bad and the ugly", *Critical Sociology*, 34(1), pp. 51–79.

Battaglia, M., Passetti, E., Bianchi, L. and Frey, M. (2016), "Managing for integration: a longitudinal analysis of management control for sustainability", *Journal of Cleaner Production*, 136, pp. 213–225.

Bebbington, J., Higgins, C. and Frame, B. (2009), "Initiating sustainable development reporting: evidence from New Zealand", *Accounting, Auditing and Accountability Journal*, 22(4), pp. 588–625.

Bellucci, M., Acuti, D., Simoni, L. and Manetti, G. (2021), "Hypocrisy and legitimacy in the aftermath of a scandal: an experimental study of stakeholder perceptions of nonfinancial disclosure", *Accounting, Auditing and Accountability Journal*, 34(9), pp. 151–163.

Beusch, P., Frisk, J. E., Rósen, M. and Dilla, W. (2022), "Management control for sustainability: towards integrated systems", *Management Accounting Research*, 54, p. 100777.

Bini, L., Bellucci, M. and Giunta, F. (2018), "Integrating sustainability in business model disclosure: evidence from the UK mining industry", *Journal of Cleaner Production*, 171, pp. 1161–1170.

Bromley, P. and Powell, W. W. (2012), "From smoke and mirrors to walking the talk: decoupling in the contemporary world", *Academy of Management Annals*, 6, pp. 483–530.

Brown, P., Bocken, N., and Balkenende, R. (2019), "Why do companies pursue collaborative circular oriented innovation?", *Sustainability*, 11(635), pp. 1–23.

Burnes, B. (2009), "Reflections: ethics and organizational change – time for a return to Lewinian values", *Journal of Change Management*, 9, pp. 351–381.

Burritt, R. and Schaltegger, S. (2010), "Sustainability accounting and reporting: fad or trend?", *Accounting, Auditing and Accountability Journal*, 23(7), pp. 829–846.

Burritt, R. L. and Tingey-Holyoak, J. (2012), "Forging cleaner production: the importance of academic–practitioner links for successful sustainability embedded carbon accounting", *Journal of Cleaner Production*, 36, pp. 39–47.

Chenhall, R. H. (2003), "Management control systems design within its organizational context: findings from contingency-based research and directions for the future", *Accounting, Organizations and Society*, 28(2–3), pp. 127–168.

Cho, C. H., Laine, M., Roberts, R. W. and Rodrigue, M. (2015), "Organized hypocrisy, organizational façades, and sustainability reporting", *Accounting, Organizations and Society*, 40, pp. 78–94.

Contrafatto, M. and Burns, J. (2013), "Social and environmental accounting, organisational change and management accounting: a processual view", *Management Accounting Research*, 24, pp. 349–365.

Cordazzo, M., Bini, L. and Marzo, G. (2020), "Does the EU Directive on non-financial information influence the value relevance of ESG disclosure? Italian evidence", *Business Strategy and the Environment*, 29(8), pp. 3470–3483.

De Villiers, C. and Alexander, D. (2014), "The institutionalization of corporate social responsibility reporting", *British Accounting Review*, 46, pp. 198–212.

Delmas, M., Nairn-Birch, N. and Lim, J. (2015), "Dynamics of environmental and financial performance: the case of greenhouse gas emissions", *Organization and Environment*, 28(4), pp. 374–393.

DiMaggio, P. J. and Powell, W. W. (1983), "The iron cage revisited: institutional isomorphism and collective rationality in organizational fields", *American Sociological Review*, 48(2), pp. 147–160.

Dinh, T., Husmann, A., and Melloni, G. (2023), "Corporate sustainability reporting in Europe: a scoping review", *Accounting in Europe*, 20(1), pp. 1–29.

Diouf, D., and Boiral, O. (2017), "The quality of sustainability reports and impression management. A stakeholder perspective", *Accounting, Auditing & Accountability Journal*, 30(3), pp. 643–667.

Domingues, A. R., Lozano, R., Ceulemans, K. and Ramos, T. B. (2017), "Sustainability reporting in public sector organisations: exploring the relation between the reporting process and organisational change management for sustainability", *Journal of Environmental Management*, 192, pp. 292–301.

Dyllick, T. and Hockerts, K. (2002), "Beyond the business case for corporate sustainability", *Business Strategy and the Environment*, 11, pp. 130–141.

Epstein, M. J., Buhovac, A. R. and Yuthas, K. (2010), "Implementing sustainability: the role of leadership and organizational culture", *Strategic Finance*, 91(10), pp. 41–47.

Farias, G., Landrum, N. E., Farias, C. and Krysa, I. (2024), "Explorations in organized hypocrisy and a proposed direction for a sustainable future", *Sustainability Accounting, Management and Policy Journal*, 15(1), pp. 1–22.

Farneti, F. and Guthrie, J. (2009), "Sustainability reporting by Australian public sector organisations: why they report", *Accounting Forum*, 33(2), pp. 89–98.

Ferreira, A. and Otley, D. (2009), "The design and use of performance management systems: an extended framework for analysis", *Management Accounting Research*, 20(4), pp. 263–282.

Firtin, C. E. (2023), "Accountingisation of social care: the multiplicity and embeddedness of calculations and valuations in costing and caring practices", *Qualitative Research in Accounting and Management*, 20(1), pp. 144–166.

George, R. A., Siti-Nabiha, A. K., Jalaludin, D. and Abdalla, Y. A. (2016), "Barriers to and enablers of sustainability integration in the performance management systems of an oil and gas company", *Journal of Cleaner Production*, 136, pp. 197–212.

Gibassier, D. and Alcouffe, S. (2018), "Environmental management accounting: the missing link to sustainability?", *Social and Environmental Accountability Journal*, 38(1), pp. 1–18.

Gond, J.-P., Palazzo, G. and Basu, K. (2009), "Reconsidering instrumental corporate social responsibility through the Mafia metaphor", *Business Ethics Quarterly*, 19(1), pp. 55–58.

Gond, J.-P., Grubnic, S., Herzig, C. and Moon, J. (2012), "Configuring management control systems: theorizing the integration of strategy and sustainability", *Accounting Research*, 23(3), pp. 205–223.

Gray, R. (2006), "Social, environmental and sustainability reporting and organisational value creation? Whose value? Whose creation?", *Accounting, Auditing and Accountability Journal*, 19(6), pp. 793–819.

Gray, R. H. (2010), "Is accounting for sustainability actually accounting for sustainability and how would we know? An exploration of narratives of organisations and the planet", *Accounting, Organizations and Society*, 35(1), pp. 47–62.

Gray, R. H. and Milne, M. (2002), "Sustainable reporting: who's kidding whom?", *Chartered Accountants Journal of New Zealand*, 81(6), pp. 66–74.

Hall, M., Millo, Y. and Barman, E. (2015), "Who and what really counts?: stakeholder prioritization and accounting for social value", *Journal of Management Studies*, 52(7), pp. 907–934.

Henri, J., Boiral, O., and Roy, M. J. (2014), "The tracking of environmental costs: motivations and impacts", *European Accounting Review*, 23(4), pp. 647–669.

Hinze, A. and Sump, F. (2019), "Corporate social responsibility and financial analysts: a review of the literature", *Sustainability Accounting, Management and Policy Journal*, 10(1), pp. 126–156.

Hopwood, A. G. (2009), "The economic crisis and accounting: implications for the research community", *Accounting, Organizations and Society*, 34(6/7), pp. 797–802.

Johnstone, L. (2019), "Theorising and conceptualising the sustainability control system for effective sustainability management", *Journal of Management Control*, 30(1), pp. 25–64.

Joseph, G. (2012), "Ambiguous but tethered: an accounting basis for sustainability reporting", *Critical Perspectives on Accounting*, 23(2), pp. 93–106.

Koehler, D. A. (2001), "Developments in health and safety accounting at Baxter International", *Eco-Management and Auditing*, 8, pp. 229–239.

La Torre, M., Sabelfeld, S., Blomkvist, M., Tarquinio, L. and Dumay, J. (2018), "Harmonising non-financial reporting regulation in Europe: practical forces and projections for future research", *Meditari Accountancy Research*, 26(4), pp. 598–621.

Laine, M., Scobie, M., Sorola, M. and Tregidga, H. (2020), "Special issue editorial: social and environmental account/ability 2020 and beyond", *Social and Environmental Accountability Journal*, 40(1), pp. 1–23.

Landrum, N. E. and Ohsowski, B. (2018), "Identifying worldviews on corporate sustainability: a content analysis of corporate sustainability reports", *Business Strategy and the Environment*, 27, pp. 128–151.

Larrinaga-Gonzalez, C. and Bebbington, J. (2001), "Accounting change or institutional appropriation? A case study of the implementation of environmental accounting", *Critical Perspectives on Accounting*, 12(3), pp. 269–292.

Ligonie, M. (2021), "Sharing sustainability through sustainability control activities: a practice-based analysis", *Management Accounting Research*, 50, pp. 1–17.

Lozano, R., Nummert, B. and Ceulemans, K. (2016), "Elucidating the relationship between sustainability reporting and organisational change management for sustainability", *Journal of Cleaner Production*, 125, pp. 168–188.

Maas, K., Schaltegger, S. and Crutzen, N. (2016), "Reprint of Advancing the integration of corporate sustainability measurement, management and reporting", *Journal of Cleaner Production*, 136, pp. 1–4.

Malmi, T. and Brown, D. A. (2008), "Management control systems as a package: opportunities, challenges and research directions", *Management Accounting Research*, 19(4), pp. 287–300.

Maunders, K. T. and Burritt, R. L. (1991), "Accounting and ecological crisis, accounting", *Auditing and Accountability Journal*, 4(3), pp. 1–10.

Merkl-Davies, D. M., Brennan, N. M. and McLeay, S. J. (2011), "Impression management and retrospective sense-making in corporate narratives: a social psychology perspective", *Accounting, Auditing and Accountability Journal*, 24(3), pp. 315–344.

Michelon, G., Pilonato, S. and Ricceri, F. (2015), "CSR reporting practices and the quality of disclosure: an empirical analysis", *Critical Perspectives on Accounting*, 33, pp. 59–78.

Milne, M. J., Tregidga, H. and Walton, S. (2009), "Words not actions! The ideological role of sustainable development reporting", *Accounting, Auditing and Accountability Journal*, 22(8), pp. 1211–1257.

O'Dwyer, B. (2002), "Managerial perceptions of corporate social disclosure", *Accounting, Auditing & Accountability Journal*, 15(3), pp. 406–436.

O'Dwyer, B. and Unerman, J. (2016), "Fostering rigour in accounting for social sustainability", *Accounting, Organizations and Society*, 49, pp. 32–40.

Passetti, E., Cinquini, L., Marelli, A. and Tenucci, A. (2014), "Sustainability accounting in action: lights and shadows in the Italian context", *British Accounting Review*, 46, pp. 295–308.

Perego, P., Kennedy, S. and Whiteman, G. (2016), "A lot of icing but little cake? Taking integrated reporting forward", *Journal of Cleaner Production*, 136, pp. 53–64.

Porter, M. E. and Kramer, M. R. (2011), "The big idea: creating shared value", *Harvard Business Review*, January–February, pp. 62–77.

Rodrigue, M., Magnan, M., & Cho, C. H. (2013), "Is environmental governance substantive or symbolic? An empirical examination", *Journal of Business Ethics*, 114(1), pp. 107–129.

Schäffer, U., Strauss, E. and Zecher, C. (2015), "The role of management control systems in situations of institutional complexity", *Qualitative Research in Accounting and Management*, 12(4), pp. 395–424.

Sharfman, M. P. and Dean, J. W. (1991), "Conceptualizing and measuring the organizational environment: a multidimensional approach", *Journal of Management*, 17(4), pp. 681–700.

Thijssens, T., Bollen, L. and Hassink, H. (2016), "Managing sustainability reporting: many ways to publish exemplary reports", *Journal of Cleaner Production*, 136, pp. 86–101.

Thomson, I. H. and Bebbington, J. (2013), "Sustainable development, management and accounting: boundary crossing", *Management Accounting Research*, 24, pp. 277–283.

Traxler, A. A., Schrack, D. and Greiling, D. (2020), "Sustainability reporting and management control: a systematic exploratory literature review", *Journal of Cleaner Production*, 276, pp. 1–17.

Tregidga, H., Milne, M., and Kearins, K. (2014), "'(Re)presenting 'sustainable organizations'", *Accounting, Organizations and Society*, 39(6), pp. 477–494.

Tregidga, H., Milne, M. and Kearins, K. (2018), "Ramping up resistance: corporate sustainable development and academic research", *Business and Society*, 57(2), pp. 292–334.

Usmani, M., Davison, J., Napier, C. J. and Davison, J. (2020), "The production of stand-alone sustainability reports: visual impression management, legitimacy and 'functional stupidity'", *Accounting Forum*, 44(4), pp. 315–343.

Vasconcelos, F. C. and Ramirez, R. (2011), "Complexity in business environments", *Journal of Business Research*, 64, pp. 236–241.

Weaver, G. R., Trevino, L. K. and Cochran, P. L. (1999), "Integrated and decoupled corporate social performance: management commitments, external pressures, and corporate ethics practices", *Academy of Management Journal*, 42(5), pp. 539–552.

10. The evolution of internal auditing and ESG criteria compliance

Nabyla Daidj

INTRODUCTION

Since its emergence, digital transformation has been the focus of many discussions (Zaoui & Souissi, 2020) and the main concern of both academic sphere and professional world in sectors as varied as service (banking and insurance), industry, energy, transportation, retail, education and training, etc. Digitization affects all sectors of the economy and is becoming the norm for large groups, small to medium-sized businesses (SMEs/SMIs) but also for the public sector (hospitals, universities, etc.). The digital transformation implemented in companies is coupled with new challenges for the internal audit function that must both address the new risks faced by the organization and carry out its own transformation.

Since the beginning of the 2010s, changes in the economic conditions, the technological environment, the multiplicity of sources of data (structured and unstructured) and the regulatory landscape have had a great impact on the way the audit industry operates. In addition, the evolving digital transformation has started to affect internal auditing at several levels:

– on the audit sector as a whole and the major players involved;
– on internal audit function (especially within large companies) and processes;
– on internal audit methodology;
– on auditors' tools and working methods;
– on auditors' role, missions and skills.

The primary role of internal audit functions is to help decision-makers in all financial and non-financial dimensions of the organization (Ramamoorti, 2003; Kotb et al., 2020). More and more, internal auditors have to take into consideration environmental, social and governance (ESG) risks and proceed to the disclosure of ESG positions because of compliance requirements. The accelerating pace of change in both environment (climate change) and society is sharpening stakeholder focus on ESG risks that many organizations are facing.

> Organizations that aspire to go beyond minimal legal compliance need to pay particular attention to corporate governance and corporate social responsibility (CSR), as well as stakeholder pressure coming from investors, among other groups. Over the past decade, the use of environmental, social, and governance (ESG) criteria among investors has risen sharply partly as an outgrowth of CSR and, more recently, corporate sustainability discussions (Boffo and Patalano 2020). (Minkkinen et al., 2024, p. 330)

The structure of the chapter is as follows. The first part explores the evolution of internal auditing in a more complex context, focusing on several key challenges related to the development of new technologies, further risks (including ESG) and higher standards of compliance with the laws, regulations and/or mandatory guidelines. The second part focuses on the important role of internal audit in determining and executing the company's ESG activities. Internal auditors should analyze how ESG could be integrated within the existing risk assessment program and ESG assurance into the annual audit plan. Both insights from internal audit practitioners and theoretical vision by academics are presented, before the concluding remarks.

THE TRANSFORMATION OF INTERNAL AUDIT IN THE DIGITAL AGE: NEW PRACTICES AND CHALLENGES

Internal Audit versus External Audit: Definitions

At a general level, the International Organization for Standardization (ISO), a worldwide federation of national standards bodies (ISO member bodies), provides a definition of audit included in its Guidelines for auditing management systems (ISO 19011:2011, ISO (2021)). It is a

> systematic, independent and documented process for obtaining audit evidence (records, statements of fact or other information which are relevant to the audit criteria and verifiable) and evaluating it objectively to determine the extent to which the audit criteria (set of policies, procedures or requirements used as a reference against which audit evidence is compared) are fulfilled. (https://www.iso .org/obp/ui/fr/#iso:std:iso:19011:ed-2:v1:en:fr)

According to ISO, audit activities are divided into two main categories, as shown in Table 10.1.

– Internal audits are also named first party audits. They are conducted by the organization itself, or on its behalf, for management review and other internal purposes (e.g. to confirm the effectiveness of the management system or to get information for the improvement of the management system). "Internal audits can form the basis for an organization's self-declaration of conformity. In many cases, particularly in small organizations, independence can be demonstrated by the freedom from responsibility for the activity being audited or freedom from bias and conflict of interest."
– External audits include second- and third-party audits. Second party audits are conducted by parties having an interest in the organization, such as customers, or by other persons on their behalf. Third party audits are conducted by independent auditing organizations, such as regulators or those providing certification.

Internal and external auditing activities are complementary within the assurance framework and both play a critical role in the effective governance of an organization.

Table 10.1   *The distinct roles of internal and external audit*

Item	External audit	Internal audit
Recipient of reports	Shareholders, investors, banks or members	The board, the audit committee and senior managers
Employment/Report	Hired by the organisation and reporting to the shareholders or equivalent	Employed by the organisation and reporting to the board or audit committee
Scope	Financial reports and related disclosures, financial reporting risks and their management, the external auditor has some responsibility for considering the risk of material misstatement due to fraud	All categories of risks and their management including the flow of information around the company and governance. Internal audit helps a company ensure it has the proper controls, governance and risk management processes in place
Objectives	Add credibility and reliability to reports from the organisation to its shareholders by giving an opinion on them	Provide the assurance that members of the board and senior management use to fulfil their duties Specifically, the objectives of an internal audit function are to: Establish the areas of risk in the area being audited Establish the controls in place to address those risks and review their adequacy Check whether financial regulations are being followed Carry out detailed testing of the controls being relied on Make recommendations where weaknesses or inefficiencies are observed
Timing and frequency	Project(s) tied into financial reporting cycle, focused on objective of audit opinion, usually annually	Ongoing and pervasive
Focus	Mainly historical	Historic, but ideally future focussed
Responsibility for improvement	None – duty to report control weaknesses	Fundamental to the purpose of internal auditing
Status and authority	Statutory and regulatory framework	International professional standards and Corporate Governance Code
Independence	Professional ethical standards overseen by audit committee and regulatory framework	Professional ethical standards overseen by audit committee

Source: Chartered Institute of Internal Auditors (IIA) (2020a).

The Broader Scope of Internal Audit

Internal audit reports represent crucial documents that provide valuable insights and recommendations to improve an organization's operations, risk management, and governance.

Internal audit reports are often known for addressing the Five Cs reporting requirement. The Five Cs stand for:

Criterion (or criteria): What standards or controls are in place (or should be)?
Condition: What is the particular issue identified? It usually does not match the criterion or criteria. Why is the internal audit necessary?
Cause: Why did the problem occur? What is the root cause?
Consequence: What is/are the risk/s? Are issues limited to internal matters, or are there risks of external consequences for various stakeholders?
Corrective action: What are your recommendations? What should management do about the finding? What are their plans to fix things?

These areas report on why the audit was conducted, how the audit will be performed, what the auditor aims to achieve, and what steps will be taken after the presentation of the audit findings. In an audit process, follow-up audits are also performed after an initial audit to ensure that corrective action has been implemented properly.

Delivering effective and meaningful internal audit reports is not easy, as the scope of internal audits has increased considerably over the past few years, nowadays covering a vast scope, including governance, risk management and compliance.

Initially, audits mainly involved a company's accounting and financial activities (Table 10.2). Today, they can cover the organization as a whole, all activities, the different areas and/ or specific functions of the company (R&D, purchasing, production, manufacturing, supply chain, information system (IS)/information technology (IT), data quality, customer relations, etc.) and the related processes, but also all outsourced functions and all associated risks. In addition, internal audit is more and more involved in corporate social responsibility (CSR), sustainable development (SD)issues and governance assurance (see section 2).

Table 10.2   The evolving scope of internal audit

Features	Checking Up to 1960s	Compliance 1960s–1980s	System-based 1980s–1990s	Risk-based 1990s–2010s	Partnership 2010s onwards	Value-based Emerging
Independence	Independent of activities audited	Independent of activities audited	Independent of activities audited	Independent of activities audited	Independent of activities audited	Independent of activities audited
Serving	Finance	Finance	Finance/ business units	Business units	Organisation	Organisation
Reporting to	Generally CFO	Generally CFO	Generally CFO	Emerged to CEO and then Audit Committee reporting	Audit Committee for operations / CEO for administration	Audit Committee for operations / CEO for administration

Features	Checking Up to 1960s	Compliance 1960s–1980s	System-based 1980s–1990s	Risk-based 1990s–2010s	Partnership 2010s onwards	Value-based Emerging
Objective	Assurance	Assurance	Assurance	Assurance	Assurance and advisory / Value adding	Assurance and advisory / Value adding / Proactive / Offer insights / Key agent of change
Focus	Historical	Historical	Historical	Historical	Forward-looking	Forward-looking / Insights
Coverage	Controls	Controls	Controls	Controls	Governance / Risk management / Controls	Governance / Risk management / Controls
Outcome	Detect mistakes	Detect mistakes	Improve controls	Improve business unit controls	Improve business units	Improve organisation / Actively seek innovation / Help organisation achieve strategic intent
Fraud focus	Detect fraud	Detect fraud	Detect fraud	Detect fraud	Prevent fraud	Prevent fraud
Reports go to	Management	Management	Management	Management / Emerged to Audit Committee	Management and Audit Committee	Management and Audit Committee
Standards	No	Internal Audit Standards in 1978	Internal Audit Standards	Internal Audit Standards	Internal Audit Standards	Internal Audit Standards
Resourcing	In-house	In-house	In-house	In-house / Emerged to co-sourced	Co-sourced / Subject matter experts and guest auditors	Co-sourced / Subject matter experts and guest auditors
Staff qualifications	Financial	Financial	Financial	Financial	Some non-financial disciplines	Many non-financial disciplines
Planning	Cyclical annual plan	Cyclical annual plan	Cyclical 5-year plan	Risk-based 3-year plan	Risk-based 3-year or annual plan	Risk-based rolling plan
Audit types	Compliance	Compliance	System	Operational	Integrated	Service catalogue
Management requested services	No	No	No	Some	Yes	Yes – many

Source: Adapted from Institute of Internal Auditors (IIA) – Australia (2022, p. 2).

The Higher Frequency of Internal Audits

Internal audits can be conducted on a daily, weekly, monthly, or annual basis. Some departments may be audited more frequently than others. It can be the case that a manufacturing process may be audited on a daily basis for quality control requirements while the human resources department may only be audited once a year.

A number of factors are behind the increase in the frequency of internal audit operations, as follows:

1   Towards technology-enhanced audits: internal audit 3.0

Technology is more and more used to assist in auditor's decision-making. Digital transformation, combined with an increasing and faster use of new technologies, has an impact on the internal audit process and practices (Betti et al., 2021). Most new technologies (e.g. big data, data analytics, artificial intelligence (AI), robotic process automation, blockchain, etc.) are transforming auditing activities, as shown by several authors (Brown-Liburd et al., 2015; Kokina & Davenport, 2017; Rose et al., 2017; Huang & Vasarhelyi, 2019; Daidj, 2022). For example, advances in technology have expanded the data analysis capabilities that can be incorporated into the audit process. At a general level, an audit function based on new technologies and increased automation can allow faster audit cycles and more timely reporting (Daidj & Tounkara, 2021; Daidj et al., 2023).

Castka et al. (2020) make a distinction between low audit (essentially performed without technology) and high audit, relying on multiple technologies. Internal auditors are now expected to have a good understanding of the technology used by the organization and update their knowledge and expertise accordingly. Betti and Sarens (2021) consider that

> a digitalised business environment affects the internal audit function in three respects. First, it impacts its scope. The agility of the internal audit planning and the required digital knowledge are expected to increase and information technology (IT) risks gain importance, especially cybersecurity threats. Second, the demand for consulting activities performed by internal auditors is higher and third, digitalisation modifies the working practices of internal auditors in their day-to-day tasks. New technologies such as data analytics tools are being implemented progressively in internal audit departments and digital skills are considered a critical asset. (p. 872)

2   Complexity and emergence of further risks such as ESG risks (see below) in an uncertain environment

In such a context, in which strategic decision-making is made even more difficult, internal auditors and controllers once again play a fundamental role. The increasing complexity of the environment in all its dimensions (economic, legal, regulatory, digital, technological, etc.) favors the development of new analysis models and risk management strategies. Organizations are more and more concerned with risk identification, assessment, and management. The COVID-19 pandemic is a good example of emerging risk areas for internal audit to consider. This health crisis has been an unprecedented external factor, challenging internal audit in particular.

> The third line of defence is uniquely placed to play a key role in the response to the COVID-19 crisis, from a position of good organisational knowledge and with a highly relevant skill-set. As organisations adapt to dealing with the initial impact of COVID-19, IA functions have an important role to

play to continue to provide critical Assurance, help Advise management and the Board on the shifting risk and controls landscape, and help Anticipate emerging risks. (Deloitte, 2020a, p. 2)

More broadly, risk analysis consists in better understanding qualitative aspects but also in taking into account quantitative information (financial results, performance indicators, etc.). Risk-based audit methodologies have been used for years. The COSO (Committee of Sponsoring Organizations of the Treadway Commission), initially established by five major accounting associations and institutes in the U.S.A. in the mid 1980s, has developed one of the world's most widely used risk management frameworks: the Enterprise Risk Management (ERM)-Integrated Framework.

The first version of the COSO ERM framework was proposed in 2004. In an updated version issued in 2017, two new items, strategy and performance, have been added. Since then, several initiatives have been taken in order to include environmental, social and governance (ESG)-related risks into the ERM. It is designed to be used by any entity facing ESG-related risks – from startups, to not-for-profits, for-profit, large corporations or government entities – whether public or private. The COSO defines the ESG-related risks as

> the environmental, social and governance-related risks and/or opportunities that may impact an entity. There is no universal or agreed-upon definition of ESG-related risks, which may also be referred to as sustainability, non-financial or extra-financial risks. Each entity will have its own definition based on its unique business model; internal and external environment; product or services mix; mission, vision and core values and more. (COSO & WBCSD, 2018, p. 1)

More recently in March 2023, the COSO released a study with supplemental guidance for organizations to achieve effective internal control over sustainability reporting (ICSR), using the COSO Internal Control-Integrated Framework (ICIF). The ICSR guidance includes, in particular, references to the role of the internal audit function in sustainability reporting in the scope of the guidance, reflecting its integral part of ICSR.

3   Compliance requirements

Compliance is defined by the IIA (2018) as "the adherence to policies, plans, procedures, laws, regulations, contracts, or other requirements" (p. 26). The auditing profession is exposed to major challenges including compliance. Internal auditors have to ensure that the organization is meeting its compliance obligations. Compliance is one of the most important components of the well-known "three lines of defense model" defining roles, responsibilities and accountabilities for decision-making, risk and control to achieve effective governance risk management and assurance. The model has been used on a large scale for organizing governance and risk management in organizations.

Operational management (including IT) represents the first line of defense and is responsible for the implementation and maintenance of processes and controls to manage risks. Compliance functions and risk management represent the second line of defense and are responsible for monitoring risks across the organization. Internal audit represents the third line of defense and is responsible for providing independent assurance that risk management and controls are operating effectively, and for advising senior management and the board when deficiencies are identified. Internal audit functions are traditionally considered as an organization's third line of defense. The European Confederation of Institutes of Internal Auditing (ECIIA) and the Federation of European Risk Management Associations (FERMA) support the "three lines of defense" model as a benchmark for current and future regulatory guidance (Figure 10.1). From an academic angle, several authors have underlined the fact that the starting point for a value-adding internal audit is commonly offered by the three lines of defense model (Bantleon et al., 2021; Eulerich, 2021; Eulerich et al., 2022).

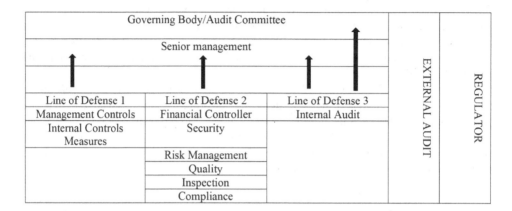

Source: Adapted from ECIIA (2021).

Figure 10.1   The three lines of defense model

In 2020, Deloitte (2020c) advocated the modernization of the three lines of defense as the internal audit function should become "more agile, nimble, and forward-looking" (Deloitte, 2020c, p. 5). The same year, the IIA updated the "three lines model" (Figure 10.2) previously known as the three lines of defense, described above.

The revised model relies on a six-step, principles-based approach which allows the governing body (i.e., the audit committee or board of directors) to provide delegation and oversight to each line, with the respective lines collaborating and providing accountability and insightful reporting (Deloitte, 2020b). First and second line roles may be mixed or distinct (Figure 10.2).

> Some second line roles may be assigned to specialists to provide complementary expertise, support, monitoring, and challenge to those with first line roles. Second line roles can focus on specific objectives of risk management, such as compliance with laws, regulations, and acceptable ethical behavior; internal control; information and technology security; sustainability; and quality assurance. (IIA, 2020b, p. 3)

The model highlights the importance and nature of internal audit independence, setting internal audit apart from other functions.

Interactions within the three lines in organizations could vary with the nature and complexity of the external environment (business, industry, regulations, etc.) and with internal constraints (resources, capabilities, competencies, organization of work, etc.).

As seen in this part, internal audit, independent from the governing body and the management, assures the reliability of internal control processes. Internal audit is concerned with fraud in all activities within the organization. Internal audits may serve various objectives and

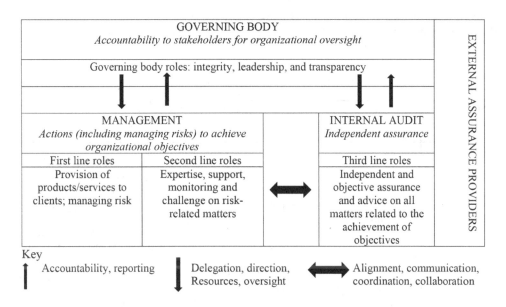

GOVERNING BODY		EXTERNAL ASSURANCE PROVIDERS

Source: Adapted from IIA (2020b, p. 4).

Figure 10.2   The IIA's three lines model

multiple stakeholders within an organization. The scope of internal audit work has broadened from strict controls to risk management, control and governance. More recently, internal auditing activities aim more and more at supporting, in particular, the growth of environmental, social and governance outcomes for stakeholders. How do ESG issues impact the company and internal auditing activities?

INTERNAL AUDITING AND ESG MATTERS

ESG Criteria, Indicators and Landscape

The acronym ESG refers to the three distinct pillars of organizational sustainability: environmental, social and governance.

> Often, this term is used synonymously or as a shorthand for sustainability or sustainable business to refer to the internal and external information value chain. More narrowly and within, this term is used generally to describe the constructs of external disclosure of categories of sustainable business information to investors and other stakeholders. (COSO, 2023, p. 8)

ESG is a framework for assessing risks to a company's operations related to environmental, social, and governance issues. ESG criteria are multiple and various (Table 10.3). The most frequently cited and most critical factors are related to mitigation of climate change (E), adaptation to climate change (E), respect for human rights (S), diversity, equity and inclusion (S), and business ethics, such as anti-bribery, anti-corruption and transparency (G).

Even if sustainability information is more qualitative than traditional financial reporting, there are key performance indicators (KPIs) and metrics measuring companies' commitments to ESG (Table 10.3).

Table 10.3   ESG criteria, scores and indicators

ESG framework	ESG criteria: main challenges (some examples)	Key scores and/or indicators & metrics (some examples)
Environment	Climate change	Annual average temperature/rainfall Renewable energy contributes to the global effort to reduce reliance on fossil fuels and mitigate climate change (renewable energy share; renewable energy intensity; renewable energy footprint)
	GHG emissions	Emission of greenhouse gases including scope 1 (direct emissions from owned or controlled source), scope 2 (indirect emissions from the generation of purchased energy consumed), and scope 3 (all other indirect emissions that occur in a company's value chain)
	Water management	Water footprint & withdrawal Total volume of water and % diverted or re-used
Social	Community relations	Number of employees volunteering in their local communities Percentage of the workforce participating in volunteer programs
	Diversity, equity, and inclusion	Percentage of men/women and salaries – labor gap Diversity within leadership ranks
	Employee engagement	Staff turnover/absenteeism
	Health and safety	Workplace injuries/illnesses by severity, type, and costs
	Human rights	Measure of a company's commitment and effectiveness towards respecting the fundamental Human Rights Convention Number of controversies published in the media linked to human rights issues and to use of child labor issues
Governance	Anti-bribery and anti-corruption	Number and percentage of members of the governance body to whom the company's anti-corruption policies and procedures have been reported, broken down by region Number and percentage of members of the governance body who have been trained against corruption, broken down by region
	Anti-fraud (tax fraud controversies)	Number of controversies published in the media linked to tax fraud, parallel imports or money laundering
	Data protection	Company's capacity to produce quality goods and services integrating the customer's health and safety, integrity and data privacy
	Executive compensation policies	Ratio of CEO compensation to median for all employees Number of controversies published in the media linked to high executive or board compensation
	Regulatory compliance	Number of reviews of corporate governance framework carried out in the period Number of corporate governance non-compliant events recorded in the period Number of actions implemented in response to corporate governance non-compliance

ESG framework	ESG criteria: main challenges (some examples)	Key scores and/or indicators & metrics (some examples)
Governance	Shareholder rights and engagement	Company's effectiveness towards equal treatment of shareholders and the use of anti-takeover devices
	Transparency, disclosure	There are several channels for ESG metrics disclosure: internal communications, annual reports, websites, social media, press, ESG ratings providers

Source: Based on Thomson Reuters (2017); Institute of Internal Auditors & Instituto de Auditores Internos de Espana (2022) and COSO (2023, p. 8).

The Evolution of the Role of Internal Audit in Relation to the Three Lines Model

In the "three lines of defense" presented previously, internal audit serves as the last line of defense, integrating ESG risk and compliance considerations into the audit plan (Figure 10.1). In the updated version called "the three lines", ESG-related risks and opportunities should be embedded into processes to ensure efficient and effective risk management (Table 10.4). As explained by the IIA and World Business Council for Sustainable Development (WBCSD) (2022), the internal audit could play a major role in providing independent and objective assurance and advice on effective governance and ESG risk management. "There is an opportunity for the governing body to recognize that internal audit can add value to the company and that integration with the sustainability function can move beyond compliance and take a more active approach to monitoring material sustainability topics" (IIA & WBCSD, 2022, p. 19).

Table 10.4   *Key actions for the three lines model roles in sustainability and ESG considerations*

Governing body	Management	Internal audit
Governing body roles:	Management roles:	Audit roles:
Establish governance mechanisms	Develop multi-capital approach	Test internal controls and accuracy of RSG data
Oversee ESG reporting strategy	Undertake materiality assessment to inform ESG risk management	Anticipate ESG disclosure regulations
Engage with stakeholders	Oversee ESG data quality and reporting	Interact regularly with other lines

Source: Adapted from IIA & WBCSD (2022, p. 14).

Internal audit could be involved in strategic missions with well-defined goals as follows: ensure reliability of internal control over ESG data collection, analysis, and reporting; identify how the different functions involved with ESG data work together and communicate on a regular basis; and monitor changes in the regulatory framework in order to anticipate ESG disclosure regulations (Table 10.5).

Table 10.5   Applying an internal audit approach to ESG

Disclosure	Frameworks and standards	Process and controls
What disclosure exists?	Are frameworks and standards used in current disclosure or internally (if so, which)?	Are process and controls formal or informal?
Who is responsible?	How can frameworks and standards enable internal audit's review?	Are process and controls documented?
Who is involved?		How can lessons from other areas of internal controls (finance and accounting, risk management) be applied to ESG?
What are the significant risks areas?		

Source: Adapted from AuditBoard and Deloitte (2022, p. 14).

Internal Audit's New Role: ESG Audit, Reporting and Independent Assurance

ESG report reliability is of particular interest to fund managers for investment decisions as well as to policymakers for regulating and monitoring purposes. What is an ESG audit? An ESG audit is an assessment of the risks an organization faces related to environmental, social and governance domains. Professionals provide several definitions that converge on certain key matters: assessment, compliance requirements (see below) and risk management. ESG audits are closely related to the degree of maturity of the organization implementing them, the type of product/service/application offered and the social and environmental context of the organization. When planning audits, internal audit should consider what ESG aspects need to be covered in the scope of work.

KPMG (2021) has shown how internal audit can play a critical role in each phase of a company's "ESG journey" (Table 10.6).

In 2021 the IIA published a White Paper on internal audit's role, describing independent assurance as a critical element of ESG reporting. As risks associated with ESG become more obvious and strategic in decision-making by the governing body and executive management, directors must have reliable assurance on the effectiveness of ESG risk management, including ESG reporting. That assurance should come from an internal audit. The IIA (2021) suggests that assurance over ESG reporting should include the following points:

– Review reporting metrics for relevancy, accuracy, timeliness, and consistency. It is crucial that all public sustainability reports provide information that accurately depicts an organization's ESG efforts. Internal audit can provide assurance on whether data (quantitative and qualitative) being reported is accurate, relevant, complete, and timely. This is particularly important as regulatory oversight increases.
– Review reporting for consistency with formal financial disclosure filings. Although sustainability reports provide non-financial data, any information that contradicts official financial information will raise questions from both regulators and investors.
– Conduct materiality or risk assessments on ESG reporting. This area can be potentially problematic because organizations sometimes struggle with understanding and reporting what is "material".

Table 10.6   A company's ESG journey

Assess Identify current state of ESG initiatives		Operationalize Design and implement tangible initiatives for specific focus areas to increase value		Report Issue consistent, comparable, reliable, and assurance ready reporting	
Deep-dive assessment		Target setting and decarbonization	ESG due diligence	Accounting	Assurance
Maturity + materiality	Roadmap	Resilience	Valuation and modeling		
GHP inventory		Reporting automation	Governance	Reporting	
ESG data		SOX-like internal controls	Data measurement		
Risk and opportunity		Transition planning	Methodology and policy creation	Disclosure	
Reporting readiness		Systems implementation	On-call services		
Key drivers					
Stakeholder opinion Stakeholders, customers, employees and other stakeholders linking climate to risk management, value creation and brand reputation			Regulations Rising regulatory expectations and/or mandates in areas of climate risk management, governance, board/management accountability and reporting		

Source: Adapted from KPMG (2021, p. 5).

- Incorporate ESG into audit plans. ESG and sustainability-related engagements currently make up about 1% of typical internal audit plans. This very low percentage must increase as ESG risks and risk management are more and more significant for organizations.

ESG Compliance Requirements

Compliance audits evaluate whether the company is following external regulations in relation to financial, technological, safety, and environmental issues; that is, compliance with laws and regulations across various country and state legislations that will govern information and transactions processed. Several regulations could be examined during compliance auditing missions. Various national, European and international regulations exist: the Sarbanes-Oxley Act (SOX), the Generally Accepted Auditing Standards (GAAS), Regulation (EU) 2016/679 of the European Parliament and of the Council of 27 April 2016 on the protection of natural persons with regard to the processing of personal data and on the free movement of such data, and repealing Directive95/46/EC General Data Protection Regulation (GDPR) and the European Payment Services Directive, second version (PSD 2).

More specifically, in recent years, a growing number of ESG laws and regulations have been passed around the world to create better consistency, transparency, and quality within corporate ESG disclosure.

There are several frameworks, broad in their scope, giving a set of principles to guide and build the understanding of a certain topic. The frameworks are elaborated by not-for-profit organizations, business groups, and others, and the recommendations and metrics can vary widely. At a general level, according to Courtnell (2022), frameworks can be divided into three categories: voluntary disclosure frameworks, guidance frameworks and third-party aggregators. The most commonly used ESG frameworks are listed in Table 10.7.

Table 10.7   Main ESG reporting frameworks and compliance requirements

Frameworks or standards	Description
Global Reporting Initiative (GRI) GRI was founded in Boston in 1997 following the public outcry over the environmental damage of the *Exxon Valdez* oil spill in Alaska in 1989. (https://www.globalreporting.org/)	The GRI offers universal standards that are designed to apply to all organizations. The GRI voluntary disclosures are broad in their aim. These disclosures address a range of ESG topics. GRI standards are divided into universal, sector (40 sectors), and topic-specific standards (for waste, occupational health and safety, tax, etc.) that can be applied to companies depending on their industry and impact. The GRI Standards are regularly reviewed
The Sustainability Accounting Standards Board (SASB) Founded in 2011 as a not-for-profit, independent standard-setting organization. SASB's mission was to establish and maintain industry-specific standards that assist companies in disclosing financially material, decision-useful sustainability information to investors. (https://sasb.org)	The aim of the SASB is to provide information to the SEC, which investors can then use to compare business performance on critical ESG issues. SASB Standards identify the subset of environmental, social, and governance issues most relevant to financial performance in each of 77 industries. They are designed to help companies disclose financially-material sustainability information to investors Disclosure topics: each SASB Standard includes a set of disclosure topics, which vary from industry to industry. The standard lists and briefly describes how management or mismanagement of various aspects of the topic may impact a company's ability to create long-term value. On average, SASB Standards include six disclosure topics per industry Accounting metrics: each SASB Standard provides companies with standardized quantitative – or, in some cases, qualitative – metrics intended to measure performance on each disclosure topic or an aspect of the topic. On average, SASB Standards include 13 accounting metrics per industry
The Task Force on Climate-Related Financial Disclosures (TCFD). Established in December 2015 following COP21. (https://www.fsb-tcfd.org)	Its goal is to develop recommendations for more effective climate-related disclosures about governance, strategy, risk management, and metrics and targets
International Integrated Reporting Council (IIRC) (https://www.integratedreporting.org/the-iirc-2/council)	The IIRC has been developed to accelerate the adoption of integrated reporting. To this end, the IIRC merged with SASB in 2021, producing the Value Reporting Foundation (VRF). The aim is to create a baseline for corporate sustainability disclosure that can be used around the world. The Integrated Reporting Framework, originally published in 2013, was accordingly updated in 2021

Source: Adapted from Courtnell (2022) and content from organizations' web sites.

As regards standards, they are specific requirements including detailed criteria explaining what needs to be reported (e.g., what data can be collected and how it can be structured. In all audits, it is critical to understand the data being relied upon. It is particularly true for ESG reporting). For example, ISO has numerous ESG-related standards, like ISO 14001 for

Environmental Management Systems and ISO 45001 for Occupational Health and Safety, which provide strategies for protecting the environment and human capital. In January 2020 ISO created a committee (ISO/TC 322) to focus exclusively on ESG in the coming years.

There is a high number of different laws and a constantly evolving ESG regulatory landscape. One of the key issues with ESG reporting is the lack of globally recognized standards and frameworks. Therefore, there is a need for more clarity and simplification in the sustainability and ESG disclosure landscape.

ESG Criteria Compliance: Evidence from Emerging and Developed Markets

ESG commitment is vital for both developed and emerging markets (Boston Consulting Group, 2023; Morgan Stanley Investment Management, 2020) even if the level of ESG disclosure compliance is still higher in developed countries. In developed countries, non-financial disclosure by companies is mandatory and regulated by statute. Various standards of disclosure have been implemented, as seen previously. In many emerging countries, frameworks are either missing or a very low level of disclosure is required (Khemir et al., 2019). The question that frequently arises also is how ESG can shape future economic growth in developing economies (Casanova et al., 2023; Fodor, 2023).

Several scholars have analyzed and/or compared regulatory frameworks for ESG disclosures in developed and developing countries (Duran & Rodrigo, 2018; Lavin & Montecinos-Pearce, 2021; Plastun et al., 2020; Singhania et al., 2024). The adoption of ESG guidelines has evolved all around the world.

In their paper, Singhania and Saini (2023) have attempted to identify similarities, differences and trends to contribute to effective and sustainable practices globally. On the basis of their own methodology on ESG disclosures, the two authors have provided a detailed analysis of ESG implementation rules in a sample of 13 developed and developing countries (Table 10.8). They have depicted and have classified these 13 countries into four different categories from well-developed ESG frameworks to ESG frameworks at an early stage. Their conclusions are very interesting regarding emerging countries in particular.

Table 10.8   Classification of ESG framework

Well-developed ESG framework	Rapidly improving ESG framework	ESG framework at developing stage	ESG framework at early stage
(Score range 28–30)	(Score range 24–27)	(Score range 24–27)	(Score range 24–27)
Norway	Germany	Singapore	Russia
Sweden	Italy	India	Indonesia
Denmark	USA	China	Thailand
Finland	Australia	Philippines	Nigeria
United Kingdom	Switzerland	Malaysia	Vietnam
Belgium	Canada	Argentina	
France	Japan		
	Brazil		
	South Africa		

Source: Adapted from Singhania & Saini (2023).

Countries that were plagued by high corruption and had low governance visibility, like Indonesia and Vietnam, focused on adopting the global framework like GRI and SASB as the initial step towards integrating ESG factors into business operations and reporting. Strengthening corporate governance measures could boost the range and depth of voluntary disclosure in these economies (Aureli et al. 2020; Elfeky 2017; Lagasio and Cucari 2019; Zhou 2019). (Singhania & Saini, 2023, p. 548)

THE GROWING IMPORTANCE OF ESG IN RESEARCH ON INTERNAL AUDIT

Internal audit's role in ESG reporting is strategic, and independent assurance is crucial to effective sustainability reporting (IIA, 2021) even if "so far, academics and practitioners have not agreed on the responsibilities of internal auditing in ESG matters" (Eulerich et al., 2022).

Indeed, at a theoretical level, research on the inclusion of new criteria such as ESG in internal auditing is still limited, as several authors have pointed out. Several topics have been explored, as summarized in Table 10.9. As mentioned previously, reporting ESG information addresses new challenges and issues. Several authors have pointed out that ESG reporting is not entirely satisfactory (Table 10.9). The integration of ESG factors into internal audit is recent and should be improved on several levels.

CONCLUSION

Internal audit has changed dramatically in the past 20 years. Several factors (in particular technology) prompted these changes in the context of the digital era. Expectations are becoming higher for value-added audits in relation to risk-based and objective assurance. Internal auditing activities are also closely linked with the value creation process. "The value is not only characterized by the internal audit function's output (e.g., number of audits, findings, recommendations), but also by the character of tasks performed by the internal audit function (e.g., focus on assurance vs. consulting activities) or the role model (e.g., watchdog vs. trusted advisor)" (Eulerich & Eulerich, 2020, p. 84).

In addition, new criteria such as ESG are becoming increasingly important to regulators, investors and other stakeholders. As mentioned by the ECIIA (2023) in its position paper, the question if Internal Audit could play a fundamental role over ESG is no longer an issue. "Boards and Top Management should ask but rather it is more of 'how' they can best benefit on this privileged view" (p. 9).

Internal auditors should provide not only advice but also independent and objective assurance on current ESG issues in the future as organizational value is going to be affected by these disclosures (Tysiac, 2021). Organizations that will be first to disclose their performance are likely to have an advantage in the marketplace, particularly from the point of view of investors and other stakeholders (IIA, 2021). Organizations most probably need to establish new processes, new projects, new teams, and new investment to reach such targets (ECIIA, 2023). The support of internal audit could also vary depending on the maturity of the organization.

This chapter has focused on an exploratory analysis of the evolution of internal auditing and ESG criteria compliance and related disclosure and assurance issues. In future research works, it will be relevant to study more specifically newly established and emerging ESG reporting frameworks.

Table 10.9   *Main insights on internal audit and ESG reporting and assessment (2003–2023)*

Topics	Authors	Insights and/or quotations
The role of internal audit in ESG reporting		
Characteristics of ESG reporting	Adams (2004) Bradford et al. (2017) Pinnuck et al. (2021)	A reporting-performance portrayal gap (Adams, 2004) A lack of completeness (Bradford et al., 2017) ESG reporting is mostly voluntary and unregulated with no generally accepted reporting principles or standards (Pinnuck et al., 2021)
Variety of ESG data, measures, KPIs/ metrics and reporting structure	Cascone et al. (2010)	"The well-known aphorism 'what gets measured gets done' has been used by business leaders for many years. As it applies to the audit function's involvement in auditing sustainability key performance indicators (KPIs), that phrase can be modified as, 'what gets measured accurately gets done more effectively.' By providing management with assurance that the measured data is accurate, internal auditing can help ensure the organization aligns its resources with the organization's long-term objectives and help management make strategic decisions based on reliable nonfinancial data." (p. 49)
Disclosure	Ackers (2016)	Although internal audit will continue to incorporate material CSR issues into its mandatory risk-based auditing approach, the results will not necessarily be publicly available. The extent of reliance that external stakeholders can place on company CSR disclosures are therefore not directly influenced by internal audit's involvement in CSR-related matters
The role of internal audit in sustainability assurance		
ESG disclosure and assurance	Eulerich et al. (2022)	The authors provide a holistic view of internal auditor's role in ESG assurance and disclosure. They "demonstrate that IAF's maturity in ESG is significantly correlated with ESG disclosure, emphasizing the unique role of the IAF in this context. [They] find that IAF involvement in ESG reporting and attributing high relevance to the environmental pillar correlate with ESG assurance and thereby expand Trotman and Trotman's (2015) study about greenhouse gas emissions and energy usage." (p. 84; see below)
A more complex role of internal auditors	Trotman & Trotman (2015)	Their paper is based on several interviews (Australian companies). It "suggests that GHG/energy assurance involves assessments by a range of stakeholders (e.g., audit committee members and senior accountants) of both in-house and outsourced internal auditors and that these internal auditors also need to assess the knowledge of a range of specialists from different disciplines, as substantial reliance is placed on their skills. This task becomes more complex in multidisciplinary teams"

Topics	Authors	Insights and/or quotations
Creation of value by internal auditors	Nieuwlands (2006; 2007) DeSimone et al. (2021)	"Internal audits of sustainability are much like internal financial audits in that internal auditors evaluate controls over reporting and suggest corrective action by communicating with management and the AC (Darnall et al. 2009). But they also have a long-term focus by continually assessing sustainability progress toward achieving desired outcomes (Darnall et al. 2009). By engaging the IAF in sustainability audits, organizations create processes and procedures aimed at improving sustainability activities, and also increase the probability of discovering sustainability issues before they become significant, thus reducing various risks (Stanwick and Stanwick 2001). IAFs may be in a position to add value to the sustainability process (Nieuwlands 2006), and have a significant role in the corporate governance process (Cohen et al. 2004)." (DeSimone et al., 2021, pp. 567–568)
Internal audit as an independent CSR assurance provider		
Internal audit and corporate social responsibility (CSR)	Tiron-Tudor & Bota-Avram (2015)	The authors examine the role of internal audit in CSR and provide practical suggestions on how internal audit practitioners should develop their audit programs in order to provide the best possible contribution in terms of corporate social responsibility
Involvement of internal audit in various ESG areas		
Environmental audit	Darnall et al. (2009)	"The landscape of environmental audits is diverse in that organizations can implement internal, external or both environmental audit types. The stakeholder influences associated with the use of these audits differs. For example, organizations that adopt internal audits are associated more with perceived influences from internal stakeholders, but not regulatory or supply chain stakeholders. However, since the results of these audits cannot be verified by external parties they may lack legitimacy with some external constituencies. By contrast, organizations that utilize external audits are more likely to be associated with greater perceived influences from internal and regulatory Stakeholders." (pp. 183–184)
Green in IT audits Indicators for Green in IT Audits	Patón-Romero, & Piattini (2016)	The authors are working on the creation of a framework for Green in IT audits, which will provide the basis for a subsequent audit framework of Green IT. They have developed an early version of this framework (based on COBIT 5), entitled "Governance and Management Framework for Green IT", through which organizations can establish governance and management of Green IT, as well as being able to audit this area

Note: IAF = internal audit function.
Source: Elaborated by the author (based on quoted papers and authors).

REFERENCES

Ackers, B. (2016). An exploration of internal audit's corporate social responsibility role – insights from South Africa. *Social Responsibility Journal, 12(*4), 719–739. https://doi:10.1108/SRJ-01-2016-0003

Adams, C. (2004). The ethical, social and environmental reporting–performance portrayal gap. *Accounting, Auditing & Accountability Journal, 17*(5), 731–757. http://dx.doi.org/10.1108/09513570410567791

AuditBoard & Deloitte (2022). *How to audit ESG risk and reporting. Key considerations for developing your environmental, social and governance audit strategy.* Retrieved October 24, 2022 from: https://www2.deloitte.com/content/dam/Deloitte/us/Documents/audit/us-how-to-audit-esg-risk-reporting.pdf

Bantleon, U., D'Arcy, A., Eulerich, M., Hucke, A., Pedell, B., & Ratzinger-Sakel, N. V. S. (2021). Coordination challenges in implementing the three lines of defense model. *International Journal of Auditing, 25*(1), 59–74. https://doi.org/10.1111/ijau.12201

Betti, N., & Sarens, G. (2021). Understanding the internal audit function in a digitalised business environment. *Journal of Accounting & Organizational Change, 17*(2), 197–216. https://doi.org/10.1108/JAOC-11-2019-0114

Betti, N., Sarens, G., & Poncin, I. (2021). Effects of digitalization of organisations on internal audit activities and practices. *Managerial Auditing Journal, 36(*6), 872–888. https://doi.org/10.1108/maj-08-2020-2792

Boston Consulting Group (2023). *Why Emerging Markets Need to Prepare for the EU's New Climate and ESG Regulations.* https://www.bcg.com/publications/2023/how-emerging-markets-can-prepare-for-the-new-esg-regulations

Bradford, M., Earp, J. B., Showalter, D. S., & Williams, P. E. (2017). Corporate sustainability reporting and stakeholder concerns: is there a disconnect? *Accounting Horizons, 31*(1), 83–102. https://doi.org/10.2308/acch-51639

Brown-Liburd, H., Issa, H., & Lombardi, D. (2015). Behavioral implications of big data's impact on audit judgment and decision making and future research directions. *Accounting Horizons, 29*(2), 451–468. https://doi:10.2308/acch-51023

Casanova, L., Miroux, A. & Bang Shah, S. (2023). *In search of an ESG framework for emerging markets. What about growth?* Working Paper. Emerging Markets Institute (EMI). http://dx.doi.org/10.2139/ssrn.4509150

Cascone, J., Derose, J., & Nefedova, A. (2010). Equipped to sustain: is your audit plan comprehensive enough to help the organization meet today's sustainability needs? *Internal Auditor, 67*(6), 49–52.

Castka, P., Searcy C., & Fischer, S. (2020). Technology-enhanced auditing in voluntary sustainability standards: the impact of COVID-19. *Sustainability, 12*(11), 4740. https://doi.org/10.3390/su12114740

COSO (2023). *Achieving effective internal control over sustainability reporting (ICSR): Building Trust and Confidence through the COSO Internal Control—Integrated Framework.* Retrieved May 29, 2023 from: https://www.coso.org/Shared%20Documents/COSO-ICSR-Report.pdf

COSO & WBCSD (2018). Enterprise Risk Management. Applying enterprise risk management to environmental, social and governance-related risks. Executive summary. Retrieved October 24, 2022 from: https://www.finchandbeak.com/documents/COSO-WBCSD%20ESGERM_Executive_Summary.pdf

Courtnell, J. (2022). *ESG Reporting Frameworks, Standards, and Requirements.* July 12. Green Business Bureau.

Daidj, N. (2022). *The Digital Transformation of Auditing and the Evolution of the Internal Audit.* London: Taylor & Francis Group.

Daidj, N., & Tounkara, T. (2021). *Le futur de l'audit IT : quelles évolutions possibles? (The future of IT auditing.* White Paper. Original work published in French). https://www.imt-bs.eu/wp-content/uploads/2021/05/Livre-blanc-audit_N.-Daidj-T.-Tounkara.pdf

Daidj, N., Bordeaux, C., & Neyrial, J. (2023). Audit, innovation et nouvelles technologies: vers l'audit augmenté avec la RPA? *(Auditing, innovation and new technologies. Towards enhanced auditing with RPA?* White Paper. Original work published in French). https://hal.science/hal-04034162/document

Darnall, N., Seol, I., & Sarkis, J. (2009). Perceived stakeholder influences and organizations' use of environmental audits. *Accounting, Organizations and Society, 34*(2), 170–187. https://doi:10.1016/j.aos.2008.07.002

Deloitte (2020a). *Internal Audit considerations in response to COVID-19.* Retrieved May 11, 2023 from: https://www2.deloitte.com/ch/en/pages/audit/articles/internal-audit-considerations-in-response -to-covid-19.html

Deloitte (2020b). *A call to action on the three lines model.* Retrieved May 11, 2023 from: https://www2 .deloitte.com/us/en/pages/advisory/articles/iia-three-lines-of-defense-risk-management.html

Deloitte (2020c). *Modernising the three lines of defense model. An internal audit perspective.* Retrieved May 11, 2023 from: https://www2.deloitte.com/uk/en/pages/risk/articles/modernising-the-three-lines -of-defence-model.html

DeSimone, S., D'Onza, G., & Sarens, G. (2021). Correlates of internal audit function involvement in sustainability audits. *Journal of Management & Governance*, *25*(2), 561–591, https://doi:10.1007/ s10997-020-09511-3

Duran, I. J., & Rodrigo, P. (2018). Why do firms in emerging markets report? A stakeholder theory approach to study the determinants of non-financial disclosure in Latin America. Sustainability, *10*(9), 3111. https://doi.org/10.3390/su10093111

ECIIA (2021). *What is internal auditing?* Retrieved January 12, 2022 from: https://www.eciia.eu/what -is-internal-auditing/

ECIIA (2023). The role of internal audit in ESG in industrial and commercial companies. Position Paper. Retrieved November 2, 2023 from: https://www.eciia.eu/wp-content/uploads/2023/10/IA-in-ESG-v3 .pdf

Eulerich, M. (2021). The new three lines model for structuring corporate governance – A critical discussion of similarities and differences. *Corporate Ownership and Control*, *18*(2), 180–187. https://doi .org/10.22495/cocv18i2art15

Eulerich, A. K., & Eulerich, M. (2020). What is the value of internal auditing? A literature review on qualitative and quantitative perspectives. *Maandblad Voor Accountancy en Bedrijfseconomie*, *94*(3/4), 83–92. https://doi.org/10.5117/mab.94.50375

Eulerich, M., Bonrath, A., & Lopez Kasper, V. I. (2022). Internal auditor's role in ESG disclosure and assurance: an analysis of practical insights. *Corporate Ownership & Control*, *20*(1), 78–86. https://doi .org/10.22495/cocv20i1art7

Fodor, K. (2023). How to instrumentalize ESG to achieve sustainable development. January 16. SciencesPo. The European Chair for Sustainable Development and Climate Transition. https://www .sciencespo.fr/psia/chair-sustainable-development/2023/01/16/how-to-instrumentalize-esgto-achieve -sustainabledevelopment/#

Huang, F., & Vasarhelyi, M. A. (2019). Applying robotic process automation (RPA) in auditing: a framework. *International Journal of Accounting Information Systems*, 35(C). https://doi:10.1016/j.accinf .2019.100433

IIA (2018). International Professional Practices Framework *Supplemental Guidance. Global Technology Audit Guide (GTAG). Auditing IT Governance.* Retrieved January 15, 2022 from: https://www.iia.nl/ SiteFiles/GTAG%2017%20Auditing%20IT%20Governance.pdf

IIA (2020a). *Internal audit's relationship with external audit.* Position paper. https://www.iia.org.uk/ resources/delivering-internal-audit/position-paper-internal-audits-relationship-with-external-audit/

IIA (2020b). *The IIA's Three Lines Model. An update of the Three Lines of Defense.* Retrieved September 23, 2022 from: https://www.theiia.org/globalassets/documents/resources/the-iias-three-lines-model -an-update-of-the-three-lines-of-defense-july-2020/three-lines-model-updated-english.pdf

IIA (2021). *Internal Audit's Role in ESG Reporting. Independent assurance is critical to effective sustainability reporting.* Retrieved September 23, 2022 from: https://www.theiia.org/globalassets/site/ content/articles/iia-white-paper---internal-audits-role-in-esg-reporting.pdf

IIA & WBCSD (2022). *Embedding ESG and sustainability considerations into the Three Lines Model.* Retrieved May 28, 2023 from: https://www.theiia.org/en/content/tools/advocacy/2022/embedding -esg-and-sustainability-considerations-into-the-three-lines-model/

Institute of Internal Auditors & Instituto de Auditores Internos de Espana (2022). *Internal Audit and ESG criteria.* Retrieved May 28, 2023 from: https://auditoresinternos.es/uploads/media_items/220221 -internal-audit-and-esg-criteria-la-f%C3%A1brica-de-pensamiento.original.pdf

Institute of Internal Auditors (IIA) – Australia (2022). *Factsheet – Internal Audit Evolution.* Retrieved September 30, 2023 from: https://iia.org.au/technical-resources/fact-sheet/iia-australia-factsheet -evolution-of-internal-audit

ISO (2021). *ISO(19011:2011). Guidelines for auditing management systems*. Retrieved November 5, 2021 from: https://www.iso.org/obp/ui/fr/#iso:std:iso:19011:ed-2:v1:en:fr

Khemir, S., Baccouche, C., & Damak Ayadi, S. (2019). The influence of ESG information on investment allocation decisions: an experimental study in an emerging country. *Journal of Applied Accounting Research, 20*(4), 458–480. https://doi.org/10.1108/JAAR-12-2017-0141

Kokina, J., & Davenport, T. (2017). The emergence of artificial intelligence: how automation is changing auditing. *Journal of Emerging Technologies in Accounting, 14*(1), 115–122. https://doi.org/10.2308/jeta-51730

Kotb, A., Elbardan, H., & Halabi, H. (2020). Mapping of internal audit research: a post-Enron structured literature review. *Accounting, Auditing & Accountability Journal, 33*(8), 1969–1996. https://doi.org/10.1108/AAAJ-07-2018-3581

KPMG (2021). Internal Audit's role in ESG. Retrieved January 17, 2023 from: https://assets.kpmg.com/content/dam/kpmg/cn/pdf/en/2021/10/internal-audit-s-role-in-esg.pdf

Lavin, J. F., & Montecinos-Pearce, A. A. (2021). ESG disclosure in an emerging market: an empirical analysis of the influence of board characteristics and ownership structure. *Sustainability, 13*(19), 10498. http://dx.doi.org/10.3390/su131910498

Minkkinen, M., Niukkanen, A., & Mäntymäki, M. (2024). What about investors? ESG analyses as tools for ethics-based AI auditing. *AI & Society, 39*, 329–343. https://doi.org/10.1007/s00146-022-01415-0

Morgan Stanley Investment Management (2020). *Diving Below the Surface: ESG Integration in Emerging Markets*. Retrieved November 5, 2023 from: https://www.morganstanley.com/im/publication/insights/investment-insights/si_diving-below-surface-esg-integration-in-emerging-markets_en.pdf

Nieuwlands, H. (2006). *Sustainability and Internal Auditing*. Altamonte Springs, FL: The IIA Research Foundation.

Nieuwlands, H. (2007). Auditing sustainable development. *Internal Auditor, 64*(2), 91–93.

Patón-Romero, J. D., & Piattini, M. (2016*). Indicators for Green in IT Audits: A Systematic Mapping Study*. [Paper presentation]. Third International Workshop on Measurement and Metrics for Green and Sustainable Software Systems (MeGSuS'16), Ciudad Real, Spain.

Pinnuck, M., Ranasinghe, A., Soderstrom, N., & Zhou, J. (2021). Restatement of CSR reports: frequency, magnitude, and determinants. *Contemporary Accounting Research, 38*(3), 2376–2416. https://doi.org/10.1111/1911-3846.12666

Plastun, A., Makarenko, I., Khomutenko, L., Osetrova, O., & Shcherbakov, P. (2020). SDGs and ESG disclosure regulation: is there an impact? Evidence from Top-50 world economies. *Problems and Perspectives in Management, 18*(2), 231–245. https://doi.org/10.21511/ppm.18(2).2020.20

Ramamoorti, S. (2003). Internal auditing: history, evolution, and prospects. In A. Bailey, A. Gramling, & S. Ramamoorti (eds), *Research Opportunities in Internal Auditing* (pp. 1–23). Altamonte Springs, FL: The Institute of Internal Auditors.

Rose, A. M., Rose, J. M., Sanderson, K.-A., & Thibodeau, J. C. (2017). When should audit firms introduce analyses of big data into the audit process? *The Journal of Information Systems, 31*(3), 81–99. https://doi.org/10.2308/isys-51837

Singhania, M. & Saini, N. (2023). Institutional framework of ESG disclosures: comparative analysis of developed and developing countries. *Journal of Sustainable Finance & Investment, 13*(1), 516–559. https://doi.org/10.1080/20430795.2021.1964810

Singhania, M., Saini, N., Shri, C., & Bhatia, S. (2024). Cross-country comparative trend analysis in ESG regulatory framework across developed and developing nations. *Management of Environmental Quality, 35*(1), 61–100. https://doi.org/10.1108/MEQ-02-2023-0056

Thomson Reuters (2017). *Thomson Reuters ESG scores.* https://www.thomsonreuters.com/en/press-releases/2017/july/thomson-reuters-and-s-network-introduce-esg-best-practices-ratings-and-indices.html

Tiron Tudor, A., & Bota-Avram, C. (2015). New challenges for internal audit: corporate social responsibility aspects. In M. M. Rahim & S. O. Idowu (eds), *Social Audit Regulation* (pp. 15–31). Cham: Springer International Publishing.

Trotman, A. J., & Trotman, K. T. (2015). Internal audit's role in GHG emissions and energy reporting: evidence from audit committees, senior accountants and internal auditors. *Auditing: A Journal of Practice and Theory, 34*(1), 199–230. https://doi.org/10.2308/ajpt-50675

Tysiac, K. (2021). Internal audit has pivotal role in ESG reporting. June 7. https://www.journalofa ccountancy.com/news/2021/jun/esg-reporting-role-of-internal-audit.html

Zaoui, F., & Souissi, N. (2020). Roadmap for digital transformation: a literature review. *Procedia Computer Science, 175*, 621–628. https://doi.org/10.1016/j.procs.2020.07.090.

11. Social entrepreneurship and performance measurement: a literature review of theoretical and empirical implications

Christoph Feichtinger

INTRODUCTION

Poverty, hunger, pollution, and a lack of education are just some of the most urgent ecological and social challenges of the 21st century, and were defined by the United Nations as part of the 2030 Agenda (Kirchgeorg, 2004). In order to meet these challenges, a new phenomenon has developed alongside traditional organizations and state institutions, which combines entrepreneurial thinking with social added value and thus introduces a change in the previous economic way of thinking (Nicholls, A., 2006; Dacin et al., 2010; Ebrahim et al., 2014; Arena et al., 2014; Ehrenberger, 2017; Peris-Ortiz et al., 2017; Metzger, 2019). Social entrepreneurship (SES) represents a modern entrepreneurial approach that is characterized by an opportunity-oriented perspective on social problems and seeks innovative approaches to solving such problems (Santos, 2012; Singh, 2016; Ehrenberger, 2017). Young entrepreneurs are considered to be a leading force in the implementation of the Sustainable Development Goals as part of the 2030 Agenda (GlobeScan & SustainAbility 2017). According to the Report on Social Entrepreneurship, one in four companies founded in Europe is already an SES (EU Commission, 2011; Terjesen et al. 2011). The economic and social potential of young companies is enormous (Ashoka Deutschland & McKinsey & Company, 2019; Metzger, 2019; Fuentes & Valenzuela-Garcia, 2019). Nine out of ten German SESs solve social problems, while 75% are highly innovative. McKinsey and Ashoka estimated the financial potential of the social entrepreneurs in the German Ashoka network to be around €18 billion per year (Ashoka Deutschland & McKinsey & Company, 2019). This underpins the dynamics of the new entrepreneurship for the sustainable development of the German economy and society (Schwarz, 2014). Internal company processes and core business disciplines are also changing as they are determined by the changed perception of companies and the pursuit of social value creation (Short et al., 2009; Fayolle & Matlay, 2010; Terjesen et al., 2011; Sassmannshausen & Volkmann, 2013; Schwarz, 2014; Peris-Ortiz et al., 2017; Zucchella et al., 2018). In this context, alternative entrepreneurship has also received increasing attention in business research and has developed into an independent research field. Despite the growing number of publications (Zahra et al. 2009; Brouard & Larivet, 2010; Sassmannshausen & Volkmann, 2013; Peris-Ortiz et al., 2017), social entrepreneurship research is in a relatively early phase of development (three stages: "pre-paradigm stage of development" [Santos, 2012, p. 336]; "stage of infancy" [Hoogendoorn et al., 2010, p. 1; Peris-Ortiz et al., 2017, p. 16f], and "embryonic state" [Pless, 2012, p. 317]). The small number of empirical investigations is considered to be the central weakness of this young research area (Hoogendoorn et al., 2010; Terjesen et al., 2011; Santos, 2012; Jansen et al., 2013; Sassmannshausen & Volkmann, 2013;

Schwarz, 2014; Peris-Ortiz et al., 2017). It should be noted that much of the literature on SES lacks substantial empirical analysis (Peris-Ortiz et al., 2017). So far, science has focused on the conceptual definition and delimitation of the term as well as the characterization and typology of SES (Dacin et al., 2010; Fayolle & Matlay, 2010; Santos, 2012; Jansen et al., 2013; Sassmannshausen & Volkmann, 2013; Peris-Ortiz et al., 2017). As a result, many aspects of new entrepreneurship are proving to be under-researched (Bielefeld, 2009; Sassmannshausen & Volkmann, 2013) In particular, this applies to the design of core business disciplines for controlling the organization (Darby & Jenkins, 2006; Bielefeld, 2009; Zahra et al., 2009; Santos, 2012; Jansen et al., 2013; Luke, 2016). In order to ensure social added value with the help of entrepreneurial skills, however, the development of suitable control mechanisms for young companies is essential (Darby & Jenkins, 2006; Bielefeld, 2009; Zahra et al., 2009; Jansen et al., 2013; Arena et al., 2014; Arogyaswamy, 2017; Olenga Tete et al., 2018; Kato et al., 2018). The transparency of social and economic performance plays a decisive role, especially when it comes to acquiring financing and scaling the business model (Achleitner et al. 2009; Schwarz, 2014; Olenga Tete et al., 2018; Ashoka Deutschland & McKinsey & Company, 2019). With regard to the purpose of the social value, traditional management accounting, which is based on the logic of the classic company, is reaching its limits (Austin et al., 2006; Darby & Jenkins, 2006; Bielefeld, 2009; Achleitner et al., 2009; Zahra et al., 2009; Fayolle & Matlay, 2010; Möller et al., 2015). In particular, the measurement of social added value is associated with numerous methodological difficulties (Austin et al., 2006; Achleitner et al., 2009; Mair, 2010; Hubers, 2017; Kato et al., 2018; Lindgreen et al., 2019). Therefore, to determine the success of SES, it is necessary to develop suitable indicators and instruments (Darby & Jenkins, 2006; Bielefeld, 2009; Zahra et al., 2009; Mair, 2010; Kato et al., 2018). At the same time, SES cannot completely turn away from classic management accounting, since SES also has to act economically (Mair & Schoen, 2007; Costa & Pesci, 2016; Metzger, 2019). The bilateral perspective and the tension between social and economic value result in new and complex requirements for management accounting, which require a new form of expression (Darby & Jenkins, 2006; Zahra et al., 2009; Bielefeld, 2009; Fayolle & Matlay, 2010; Jansen et al., 2013; Ebrahim et al., 2014; Fuentes & Valenzuela-Garcia, 2019). Management accounting must be adapted as a whole to the specific business model of the SESs and integrate the basic social idea. In this context, particular attention should be paid to performance measurement systems in order to show the performance measurement possibilities that exist for SES.

THEORY AND BACKGROUND

In the first step of this chapter, an overview of different definitions of social entrepreneurship is presented in order to create a common understanding and then a suitable one is selected. Second, general business models of social enterprises are described in order to point out the special features of these business models. Finally, a basic understanding of performance measurement systems is created.

Definition of Social Entrepreneurships

Due to the heterogeneous character of SESs, it is difficult to find an authoritative definition (Zahra et al., 2009; Dacin et al., 2010; Fayolle & Matlay, 2010; Volkmann et al., 2012;

Sassmannhausen & Volkmann, 2013; Olenga Tete et al., 2018). The term "social entrepreneurship" is said to have first appeared in the 1980s and is attributed to Ashoka founder Bill Drayton, but there is no precise evidence of this (Nicholls, A., 2006; Spiess-Knafl et al., 2013; Jansen et al., 2013; Urbano et al., 2017). Since then, scientific interest has exponentially increased and the number of articles dealing with the definition of the term has multiplied (Hoogendoorn et al., 2010; Sassmannhausen & Volkmann, 2013; Spiess-Knafl et al. 2013; Urbano et al., 2017; Harding, 2004; Weerawardena & Mort, 2006; Zahra et al., 2009; Fayolle & Matlay, 2010; Hoogendoorn et al., 2010; Brouard & Larivet, 2010; Sassmannhausen & Volkmann, 2013). Today, numerous different and sometimes conflicting definitions dominate the scientific discourse (Harding, 2004; Weerawardena & Mort, 2006; Zahra et al., 2009; Fayolle & Matlay, 2010; Hoogendoorn et al., 2010; Brouard & Larivet, 2010; Sassmannhausen & Volkmann, 2013; Mair, 2016). Therefore, it is necessary to establish a congruent understanding of the present work. Table 11.1 contains a representative selection of the most important definitions, which serves as a basis for discussion and decision making. The selection is based on the works of Dacin et al., 2010, Zahra et al., 2009, and Jansen et al., 2013, as well as on the degree of dissemination and scientific influence of the authors and works (Sassmannhausen & Volkmann, 2013; Kraus et al., 2014).

The definition's spectrum is a particular source of discussion (Peredo & McLean, 2005; Austin et al., 2006; Light, 2008; Bielefeld, 2009; Dacin et al., 2010; Huybrechts & Nicholls, 2012; Volkmann et al., 2012). Broadly speaking, SES refers to an innovative activity with a social purpose. Companies in the for-profit or non-profit sectors as well as hybrid types of companies (e.g., Austin et al., 2006 or Boschee & McClurg, 2003) can engage in these activities (Austin et al., 2006). In the context of a narrower definition, the term means the transfer of business disciplines to the third sector (e.g., Dart, 2004 or Dees et al., 2001; Alvord et al., 2004; Austin et al., 2006; Volkmann et al., 2012; Huybrechts & Nicholls, 2012). The recommendations of Pless (2012), Short et al. (2009), and Zahra et al. (2009) to follow only broad definitions should be considered here. With regard to the research interest of the chapter, the focus is thus on non-profit companies that have a financially viable income model, for-profit companies with a social purpose, and hybrid organizational forms. Basically, the definitions listed in Table 11.1 can be divided into three categories (Spiess-Knafl et al., 2013). The definitions consider (1) the person (social entrepreneur), (2) the organization (social enterprise), or (3) the phenomenon or process (social entrepreneurship; Spiess-Knafl et al., 2013). These terms are related to each other: "social entrepreneurship" is the process or the phenomenon by which different people are called "social entrepreneurs" and through which organizations emerge that are defined as "social enterprises" (Mair & Martí, 2006; Huybrechts & Nicholls, 2012). Since the personal dimension of the "social entrepreneur" appears to be of little relevance for management accounting, this approach does not go far enough for the purpose of this study. Both the institutional and process-oriented perspectives play an important role in the design of management accounting. In accordance with Nicholls, "social enterprises" are viewed as part of the phenomenon (Nicholls, A., 2006). "Social entrepreneurship" therefore represents the overarching phenomenon from which the two sub-aspects of "social entrepreneur" and "social enterprise" emerge. For this reason, a definition should be chosen from this category. According to Austin et al. (2006), all of the process-oriented definitions have the purpose of entrepreneurial activities in common, which is to create social value. This assumption is confirmed by Dacin et al. (2010), who analyzed 37 definitions and determined that the social mission is understood as the lowest common denominator. In this context, the social

Table 11.1   *Overview of the definitional approaches*

Author(s)	Definition
Leadbeater (2001)	The use of entrepreneurial behavior for social ends rather than for profit objectives, or alternatively, that the profits generated from market activities are used for the benefit of a specific disadvantaged group
Dees (2001)	Social entrepreneurs play the role of change agents in the social sector, by: (1) adopting a mission to create and sustain social value (not just private value); (2) recognising and relentlessly pursuing new opportunities to serve that mission; (3) engaging in a process of continuous innovation, adaptation, and learning; (4) acting boldly without being limited by resources currently in hand; and (5) exhibiting a heightened sense of accountability to the constituencies served and for the outcomes created
Dees et al. (2001)	Social entrepreneurs are nonprofit executives who pay attention to market forces without losing sight of their organizations' underlying missions and seek to use the language and skills of the business world to advance the material wellbeing of their members or clients
Sullivan Mort et al. (2003)	A multidimensional construct involving the expression of entrepreneurially virtuous behavior to achieve the social mission … the ability to recognize social value creating opportunities and key decision-making characteristics of innovation, proactiveness and risk-taking
Boschee & McClurg (2003)	A social entrepreneur is any person, in any sector, who uses earned income strategies to pursue a social objective …
Alvord et al. (2004)	[C]reates innovative solutions to immediate social problems and mobilizes the ideas, capacities, resources, and social arrangements required for sustainable social transformations
Dart (2004)	[Social enterprise] differs from the traditional understanding of the nonprofit organization in terms of strategy, structure, norms, [and] values, and represents a radical innovation in the nonprofit sector
Seelos & Mair (2005)	Social entrepreneurship combines the resourcefulness of traditional entrepreneurship with a mission to change society
Austin et al. (2006)	Innovative, social value creating activity that occurs within or across the nonprofit, business, or government sectors
Mair & Martí (2006)	… a process involving the innovative use and combination of resources to pursue opportunities to catalyze social change and/or address social needs
Thompson & Doherty (2006)	Social enterprises—defined simply—are organisations seeking business solutions to social problems
Nicholls, A. (2006)	Social entrepreneurships are innovative and effective activities that focus strategically on resolving social market failures and creating new opportunities to add social value systematically by using a range of resources and organizational formats to maximize social impact and bring about change
Peredo & McLean (2006)	Social entrepreneurship is exercised where some person or group … aim(s) at creating social value … shows a capacity to recognize and take advantage of opportunities … employ innovation … accept an above average degree of risk and are unusually resourceful in pursuing their social venture

Author(s)	Definition
Robinson (2006)	I define social entrepreneurship as a process that includes: the identification of a specific social problem and a specific solution ... to address it; the evaluation of the social impact, the business model and the sustainability of the venture; and the creation of a social mission-oriented for-profit or a business-oriented nonprofit entity that pursues the double (or triple) bottom line
Martin & Osberg (2007)	Social entrepreneurship is the: 1) identification of a stable yet unjust equilibrium which excludes, marginalizes or causes suffering to a group which lacks the means to transform the equilibrium; 2) identification of an opportunity and developing a new social value proposition to challenge the equilibrium; and 3) forging a new, stable equilibrium to alleviate the suffering of the targeted group through imitation and creation of a stable ecosystem around the new equilibrium to ensure a better future for the group and society

Source: Dacin et al., 2010; Zahra et al., 2009; Jansen et al., 2013.

mission can be understood as follows: "the primary mission of the social entrepreneur being one of creating social value by providing solutions to social problems" (Dacin et al., 2010, p. 42). Consequently, the social mission includes striving for a social value and, therefore, should be an elementary part of the definition in order to distinguish social from conventional entrepreneurship (Hoogendoorn et al., 2010; Singh, 2016). The definition according to Seelos and Mair (2005) is thus selected as the working definition for this chapter. This definition clearly distinguishes social entrepreneurship from existing social economy organizations (e.g., charities and third sector organizations) and focuses on the founding of organizations with a social purpose (Unterberg et al., 2015). The generic character encompasses the basic concepts and also includes the definition of the other authors (Nicholls, A., 2006). In addition, the definition emphasizes that there are similarities to traditional entrepreneurship but that the entrepreneurial purpose is fundamentally different (Austin et al., 2006; Brouard & Larivet, 2010; Carraher et al., 2016). This underlines the hybrid character of the new entrepreneurship. Therefore, SES is defined thus: "Social entrepreneurship combines the resourcefulness of traditional entrepreneurship with a mission to change society" (Seelos & Mair, 2005, p. 241).

Business Model of Social Entrepreneurship

In order to understand why the business model of SESs is special and how it differs from both classic non-profit organizations (NPOs) and traditional companies, it is necessary to define the central characteristics of the company form. In contrast to the scientific debate about the meaning of the term, there is a broad consensus in the literature with regard to essential characteristics (Lepoutre et al., 2013). Three components are particularly emphasized: sociality, innovation, and market orientation (Nicholls, A., 2006; Huybrechts & Nicholls, 2012). These dimensions correspond to what Nicholls identified as the main building blocks of social entrepreneurship (Huybrechts & Nicholls, 2012). The first dimension (sociality) relates to the social and/or environmental focus of the business activity and prioritizing social and/or environmental outcomes over financial gain (Fields, 2016; Huybrechts & Nicholls, 2012; Leadbeater, 2001; Thompson, 2002; Austin et al., 2006; Volkmann et al., 2012). "[S]ocial entrepreneurship aims for the exploitation of opportunities and for social change rather than for maximum profit in the traditional sense" (Volkmann et al., 2012, p. 12). In addition to results-related aspects, this category includes internal conditions and organizational processes, for example, employment practices, supply chain management, and energy consumption (Huybrechts & Nicholls, 2012).

The second dimension (innovation) is related to the innovative power of SESs (Leadbeater, 2001; Austin et al., 2006; Zahra et al., 2009; Huybrechts & Nicholls, 2012). The companies are highly inventive and typically combine different types of innovation, such as new organizational models, new products/services and/or new approaches and problem solutions (Nicholls, A., 2006; Huybrechts & Nicholls, 2012). However, this feature is not exclusive to SESs (Santos, 2012; Carraher et al., 2016); it also characterizes traditional entrepreneurships (Nicholls, A., 2006). The key difference, however, manifests in the business opportunity itself. When conventional market participants fail, an entrepreneurial opportunity arises for the social entrepreneur (Austin et al., 2006; Santos, 2012). They can thus be described as "change makers" who strive for a systematic change in society (Dees et al., 2001; Ashoka Deutschland, 2019).

Finally, the third dimension is the market orientation of SESs (Huybrechts & Nicholls, 2012; Arena et al., 2014). Unlike classic NPOs, SESs operate in commercial markets (Jansen et al., 2013). Their goal is to generate their own sales ("earned income") in order to ensure the economic sustainability of the company (Boschee & McClurg, 2003; Nicholls, A., 2006; Martin & Osberg, 2007; Huybrechts & Nicholls, 2012; Arena et al., 2014; Mair & Martí, 2006; Mair & Schoen, 2007). This is reflected in the production of goods and services and the associated economic risks (Huybrechts & Nicholls, 2012; Carraher et al., 2016). Consequently, SESs must act in a market-oriented manner and ensure their competitiveness. Taken together, SES represents an innovative approach that has, as its core business, market-driven solutions to societal problems (Nicholls, A., 2006; Carraher et al., 2016). This means that they not only create economic value, but also generate social added value, in particular (Costanzo et al., 2014). SESs thus combine two identities at the core of their business, which is why the boundaries between existing sectors and traditional forms of organization are blurring and new business models are emerging (Leadbeater, 2001; Nicholls, A., 2006; Evers & Ewert, 2010; Santos, 2012; Huybrechts & Nicholls, 2012; Costanzo et al., 2014).

Origins and Evaluation of Performance Measurement Systems

Arena et al. (2014) gave a brief overview of the development of performance measurement systems, which they divided into four main phases (Bititci et al., 2011; Arena & Arnaboldi, 2012; Arena et al., 2014) (see Figure 11.1). The first phase began in the 1920s and ended in the 1950s. The performance measurement systems were initially focused on the production area with a particular focus on costs and efficiency (Bititci et al. 2011; Arena et al., 2014). Between the 1950s and 1960s, the focus expanded to include the economic and financial performance of divisional and departmental budgets (Otley, 2003; Bititci et al. 2011; Arena et al., 2014). In the subsequent phase (1960s to 1980s), new performance dimensions, such as time, quality, flexibility, and customer satisfaction, were added to performance measurement systems (Hayes & Abernathy, 1980; Slack, 1983; Kaplan, 1984; Arena et al., 2014). This led to the so-called key performance indicators (KPIs), which were aimed at the long-term success factors of a company (Arena et al., 2014). The connection between strategy and performance indicators was also demonstrated in this period (Simons, 1995; Arena et al., 2014). At the same time, the idea of an integral view of company performance through non-financial and financial indicators arose (Pun & White, 2005; Arena et al., 2014), which can be supplemented by the balanced scorecard, for example, time (Kaplan & Norton, 1996; Arena et al., 2014). More recently, in the last phase, corporate boundaries have been blurred and the impact of corporate activities has been extended to larger stakeholder groups (Marchand & Raymond, 2008; Bititci et al., 2011; Arena et al., 2014). This has led to the integration of environmental and social performance (Figge et al., 2002; Bagwat & Sharma, 2007; Adams & Frost, 2008; Arena et al., 2014).

Based on Neely et al. (2002), it can be stated that performance measurement systems are seen as metrics used to quantify the effectiveness and efficiency of interventions, with the performance dimensions progressively expanding over time (Arena et al., 2014).

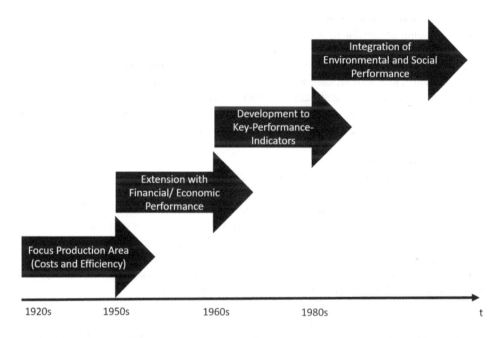

Source: Own illustration, based on Arena et al. (2014).

Figure 11.1   Overview of the development of performance measurement systems

METHODOLOGY

According to Fink (2014), a systematic literature review (SLR) describes a systematic, explicit and reproducible method for identifying, evaluating, and synthesizing the existing body of completed and recorded work produced by researchers, scholars and practitioners. It enables a transparent, comprehensible, and high-quality knowledge gain, and therefore, it is a wide-spread instrument in business administration for the aggregation of a large number of primary sources (Stamm & Schwarb, 1995; Randolph, 2009; Easterby-Smith et al., 2012; Eisend, 2014). Since the number of publications in the field of social entrepreneurship research has exponentially increased since 1990 (Short et al., 2009; Sassmannhausen & Volkmann, 2013), the SLR has proven to be a helpful tool for filtering out relevant sources, systematically analyzing them, and integrating the results.

The methodology of Ogawa and Malen (1991) was used in the qualitative literature analysis for this chapter. Gall et al. divided this approach into eight steps (Gall et al., 2007):

1st step (protocol creation)
In the first step, a protocol is created that reflects all steps of the literature analysis. Individual steps were briefly noted down as key points in order to be able to analyze them for themselves and for third parties.

2nd step (problem formulation)
When formulating the problem, the reason for the literature analysis is defined. In addition, the prerequisites are defined for an article or book to be used. This work is designed to give a state-of-the-art overview of performance management and reporting structures in social entrepreneurships. Previous articles do not provide an overview of possible performance management concepts and reporting structures for social enterprises. In this context, possible areas of research will be identified and an overview of possible concepts for use by social enterprises will be presented.

3rd step (data collection)
All data that meet the previous criteria are collected in this step. Ogawa and Malen (1991) pointed out that in addition to the qualitative and quantitative research reports, other data is also used and regarded as equivalent, for example, unranked journal articles or conceptual papers. The databases EBSCO and Web of Science were used for this purpose.

4th step (data classification)
In the next step of data classification, the documents are classified based on their type, for example, empirical study or journal article (Gall et al., 2007).

5th step (data summary)
In the fifth step, the relevant documents are summarized. Three groups of results were formed in the qualitative analysis: social enterprise balanced scorecard (SEBC), social return on investment (SROI) and other concepts of performance measurement in SES.

6th step (identification of constructs and hypothetical causal relationships)
After the data has been summarized, the main focus is placed on the essential topic of the documents and hypothetical connections to the topics are then formed. In doing so, more attention is paid to amplifying the phenomenon than to integrating the results, as is the case, for example, with the meta-analysis. In the present work, the focus is on the subject of the documents and the derivation of theses.

7th step (search for opposite results and interpretations)
Contradictory interpretations and results are sought here. At the end of the respective results of the qualitative analysis, reference is made to overlaps and differences.

8th step (cooperation with colleagues)
In the last step, colleagues should help to evaluate and question the analysis. In this context, special thanks again to the former colleagues from the Chair of Management Accounting at the University of Bamberg and the reviewer of this book for their critical scrutiny of the chapter and their support.

Analysis

Due to different geographical locations, different markets, and different technical and cultural backgrounds, the literature analysis focused on studies with application areas from the United States, Canada, the United Kingdom and Western Europe. The focus was on social entrepreneurships with a manufacturing background. The EBSCO Host and Web of Science databases were used. The following search string was used: (social entrepreneur* or social enterprise* or social venture* or social start*) and (management account* or report* or performance manag* or performance measurement or social value or social perform* or social impact). A full-text search was used to find possible matches within the text. For EBSCO Host, the search was narrowed down to the period 1980 to March 2023. In total, 1,621 articles were found. As a next step, the hits were reduced to 767 by selecting "Academic Journals". By selecting "Peer Reviewed" to meet a certain scientific standard, another ten articles could be excluded. At Web of Science, 831 articles were identified. The selection option "Review Article" enabled 52 articles to be found, and the selection option "Business" further reduced the number to 12 articles. A total of 769 articles were identified and exported to the literature management program "Citavi". Three duplicates were then excluded. A total of 18 articles were identified.

Quantitative analysis
The 18 relevant research contributions were subjected to a detailed meta-analysis (see Figure 11.2). Based on the approach of Günzel and Krause (2013), the papers were first descriptively analyzed and then analyzed in terms of content. The descriptive analysis shows that the papers were published between 2005 and 2023, with most articles published between 2015 and 2022 (44%). Thus, a slightly positive trend could be noted; in addition, no article was published at the beginning of 2023, so more articles in 2023 are possible. By analyzing the content of the articles, seven articles were also viewed and used in the respective bibliographies. In turn, these seven articles referred to 11 other articles, some of which are the basic contributions and descriptions of the respective performance measurement systems. In the end, a total of 18 articles were considered relevant.

Qualitative analysis
In the following, the content of the articles found was analyzed and summarized in three groups. It turns out that there are articles on social enterprise balanced scorecard (SEBC), social return on investment (SROI) and further concepts of performance measurement in SES.

Social enterprise balanced scorecard (SEBC)
Yang et al. (2022) and Arena et al. (2014) provided an overview of balanced scorecards, which are based on the considerations of Kaplan and Norton, and made special adjustments for SES. Somers (2005) changed the original balanced scorecard model to the social enterprise balanced scorecard (SEBC), and made three major changes to the original model. He added an

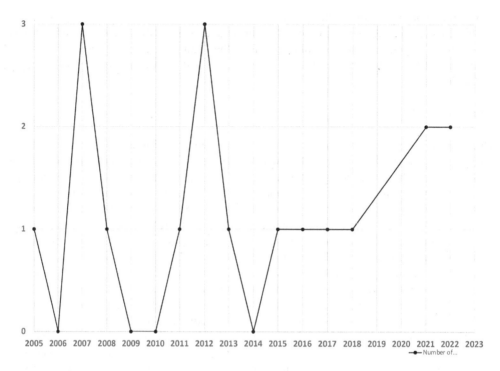

Source: Own illustration.

Figure 11.2   Overview of number of articles

extra layer, which puts social goals ahead of the financial perspective; the financial perspective was extended to focus on sustainability (to include environmental and social performance); and the customer perspective was extended to a wider range of stakeholders, distinguishing between those who pay for a service (donors, funders) and those who consume it (employees, beneficiaries, and the broader community).

Bull (2007) further adapted the original balanced scorecard model to SES by partially modifying the five original perspectives: multiple bottom line (dealing with synthetic valuation of financial, ecological, and social results), environment of the stakeholders, internal activities (for example, in relation to structure and communication and learning organization [dealing with knowledge management and employee training]) and finally, visioning (with the focus on business plans, communication, balance and mission statements) (see Figure 11.3).

The multi-bottom line was originally the "finance" area of the balanced scorecard (BSC). The previous philosophy of profit maximization and market exploitation is replaced by a strategy with a focus on social or ecological benefits. Since the goal of social enterprises is to "give something back" to society, this area was called the "multi-bottom line". The focus of this section is on social, environmental and financial sustainability. A learning organization was originally the "learning and growth" section of the BSC. This section deals with the social capital and knowledge of organizations. To this end, it aims to create the framework conditions for the organization to expose itself to continuous learning and to constantly question itself. This section was originally the "customers" section of the BSC. However, the term "stakeholders" is more appropriate for social enterprises, as they want to satisfy and serve many different target groups. Essentially, this section is about marketing. The aim here is to assess image and identity, stakeholder awareness, identification and awareness of competitors, advertising activities and their effectiveness. The focus of "internal activities" is on working methods, the structure and systems of organizations. This section was originally "internal business processes" in the BSC and has been slightly modified to focus more on open activities rather than closed processes. This is intended to create greater flexibility and adaptability and strengthen communication. In the visioning section, managers should take a critical look at the mission and business plans and communicate these precisely to the relevant stakeholders.

Additionally, Mardiono (2012) has developed a performance measurement model according to the characteristics of NPOs based on SEBC and the intellectual capital (IC) model. Lee and Moon (2008) also developed a balanced scorecard for social enterprises, which consists of the four perspectives of finance, customers, internal processes, and learning and growth.

Overall, it should be noted that the authors have based their work on the previous considerations of the BSC by Kaplan and Norton and have made individual adjustments to it. However, it can also be stated that none of the ideas have yet become established in the scientific or business world. The contributions provide good approaches for social enterprises to design their own individual BSC.

Source: Own illustration, based on Bull (2007).

Figure 11.3   *Dimensions for SEBC by Bull*

Social return on investment (SROI)

Social return on investment (SROI) was developed by Roberts Enterprise Development and was funded and tested by the New Economics Foundation (NEF, 2007). The tool is based on the idea of attributing social and monetary values to environmental outcomes, quantifying the broader social benefits in financial terms, and combining quantitative and qualitative approaches (NEF, 2007). NEF's adapted approach focuses on four areas. The first of these is stakeholder engagement, with the identified stakeholders' goals at the heart of the SROI process (Arena et al., 2014). The second area is materiality, with the analysis focusing on the areas identified as important by stakeholders. The third is the impact map, which defines cause-and-effect chains from inputs to outputs, outcomes, and impacts and develops a way to understand how the organization implements changes and thereby achieves its targeted mission. Finally, the amortization of deadweight results that would have occurred regardless of the organization's inputs is calculated. It is difficult to compare studies in this area (Arena et al., 2014) because the studies use different ratios, deadweight techniques, different discount rates, attributes, and different time periods. Millar and Hall (2013) stated that there is no "one size fits all" way to measure the performance of an SES. The authors used a mixed method with a survey of 172 participants and then in-depth qualitative interviews with 16 social entre-preneurships. The survey revealed that 40% of respondents had developed their own perfor-mance measurement system. However, 30% also stated that they use SROI as a supplement to their own performance measurement system. The majority of SESs interviewed tended to take a critical view of the SROI. The reasons given by the authors were practical problems, conflict-ing assumptions between social enterprise values and SROI practices, and the value of SROI from the perspective of the client. SESs are more inclined to measure SROI when requested by stakeholders and when they involve employees in decision making (Liston-Heyes & Liu, 2021). Beer et al. (2022) also noted that in one of their two case studies, SROI was introduced to meet stakeholder expectations. In addition, the UK government has encouraged SESs to use SROI and, in this context, has set up an investment fund to support SES (Nicholls, J., 2007; Alcock et al., 2012; Manetti, 2014). Manetti (2014) conducted a systematic literature review to show the connection between SROI and the theoretical construct "Blended Value Accounting (BVA)" and found that these two constructs fit well together. However, Manetti (2014) also presented possible negative aspects of this construct.

All in all, it can be stated that the management of social enterprises is often rather critical of the SROI or does not use it and resorts to individual solutions. However, the SROI is often requested by stakeholders in order to create a certain degree of comparability.

Further concepts of performance measurement in SES

Bagnoli and Megali (2011) used a case study to create a multidimensional controlling model that is divided into three levels (see Figure 11.4). The first dimension is the "economic–financial dimension", in which, among other things, the cash flow and "cost of activities/project and good/services" are considered. The second dimension is the "social-effectiveness dimension", in which, for example, the resources and the production method are evaluated for sustainability. In addition, the economic and social impacts are assessed. In the third dimen-sion, the "legitimacy dimension", compliance with laws and guidelines is considered. These three dimensions are connected to each other. The economic field and social-effectiveness field are linked by productivity of inputs. The economic and legitimacy fields are linked by compliance with the non-distribution constraint. The remaining fields of social effectiveness and legitimacy are linked by the involvement of workers, for example, so that all fields are connected like a triangle.

Arene et al. (2015) also used a case study to propose a performance measurements concept for SES with the following parameters: financial sustainability, efficiency, effectiveness, and impact. These should be put together with the following dimensions: resources value, product value, and results value.

Costa and Pesci (2016) developed a five-phase model to measure social impact, taking into account the perspective of the stakeholders in the multiple-constituencies approach. The phases are divided as follows: donors, managers, beneficiaries, investors, and workers. In this context, the SROI is used with other parameters in order to receive feedback from the stakeholders through feedback loops. This model has already been successfully introduced in an SES (Costa & Andreaus, 2021).

Arogyaswamy (2017) based his "time-based organizing framework" model on the "impact value chain" with five success dimensions for measuring the success of SESs: action-resources, predictors, outputs, outcomes, and impact.

André et al. (2018) went through the process of developing and using accounting tools. Instead of standard metrics, individually developed and provisional instruments were used in different case studies. To this end, social and economic aspects were integrated, and those responsible developed a system of indicators (single measurement system) based on key performance indicators (KPI).

Overall, it can be stated that there are various approaches to performance management concepts and that none of them has yet established itself in the scientific or business world. However, certain similar approaches can be found in Bagnoli and Megali (2011) and Arene et al. (2015), which focus on effectiveness and efficiency. A sustainable financial perspective is often included in the majority of concepts.

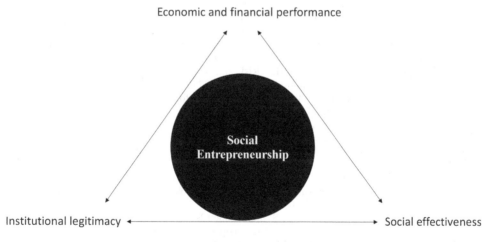

Source: Own illustration, based on Bagnoli & Megali (2011).

Figure 11.4   Dimensions for multidimensional controlling model by Bagnoli and Megali

SUMMARY

This chapter provides an overview of the term social entrepreneurship and the associated special features of the respective business models. A brief overview of the development of performance measurement was also provided, and a literature analysis was carried out with a focus on performance measurement in SES. The focus of possible empirical surveys was placed on SESs located in Europe, the United Kingdom and North America in order to enable a certain degree of comparability in a manufacturing business area. In this context, it should be noted that there are other articles from other parts of the world that were not used in this chapter, as they would have been difficult to compare on the basis of cultural and economic factors. It could be determined that there are already some considerations for the application of performance measurement in SES and that these are already being used in individual case studies. In the future, further surveys should be carried out in this research area, for example, larger surveys to gain a deeper insight. This would also provide greater comparability when using performance measurement in SES. This subject area should be considered more intensively, especially by researchers in management accounting.

REFERENCES

Achleitner, Ann-Kristin, Bassen, Alexander, Roder, Barbara, Lütjens, Lena (2009) Ein Standard für die Berichterstattung von Social Entrepreneurs, *Ökologisches Wirtschaften*, 4, 30–34. https://www .oekologisches-wirtschaften.de/index.php/oew/article/download/655/655, 12.05.2023.

Adams, Carol A., & Frost, Geoff R. (2008) Integrating sustainability reporting into management practices. *Accounting Forum*, 32(4), 288–302.

Alcock, Pete, Millar, Ross, Hall, Kelly, Lyon, Fergus, Nicholls, Alex, & Gabriel, Madeleine (2012) *Start Up and Growth: National Evaluation of the Social Enterprise Investment Fund (SEIF)*. London: Department of Health Policy Research Programme.

Alvord, Sarah H., Brown, L. David, Letts, Christine W. (2004) Social entrepreneurship and societal transformation. *Journal of Applied Behavioral Science*, 40(3), 260–282.

André, Kévin, Cho, Charles H., & Laine, Matias (2018) Reference points for measuring social performance: case study of a social business venture. *Journal of Business Venturing*, 33(5), 660–678.

Arena, Marika, & Arnaboldi, Michela (2012) Risk and budget in an uncertain world. *International Journal of Business Performance Management*, 30(4), 327–339.

Arena, Marika, Azzone, Giovanni, & Bengo, Irene (2014) Performance measurement for social enterprises. *VOLUNTAS: International Journal of Voluntary and Nonprofit Organizations*, 26(2), 649–672.

Arogyaswamy, Bernard (2017) Social entrepreneurship performance measurement: a time-based organizing framework. *Business Horizons*, 60(5), 603–611.

Ashoka Deutschland (2019) Ashoka – Heimat der Changemaker, https://www.ashoka.org/de-DE, 12.01.2023.

Ashoka Deutschland & McKinsey & Company (2019) Wenn aus klein systemisch wird: Das Milliardenpotenzial sozialer Innovationen, https://www.ashoka.org/en-gb/files/2019ashokamckinse ywennauskleinsystemischwirdpdf, 14.05.2024.

Austin, James, Stevenson, Howard, & Wei-Skillern, Jane (2006) Social and commercial entrepreneurship: same, different, or both? *Revista de Administração*, 47(3), 370–384.

Bagnoli, Luca, & Megali, Cecilia (2011) Measuring performance in social enterprises. *Nonprofit and Voluntary Sector Quarterly*, 40(1), 149–165.

Bagwat, Rajat, & Sharma, Milind K. (2007) Performance measurement of supply chain management: a balanced scorecard approach. *Computers & Industrial Engineering*, 53(1), 43–62.

Beer, Haley, Micheli, Pietro, & Besharov, Marya (2022) Meaning, mission, and measurement: how organizational performance measurement shapes perceptions of work as worthy. *Academy of Management Journal*, 65(6), 1923–1953.

Bielefeld, Wolfgang (2009) Issues in social enterprise and social entrepreneurship. *Journal of Public Affairs Education*, 15(1), 69–86.

Bititci, Umit; Garengo, Patrizia; Dörfler, Viktor; & Nudurupati, Sai (2011) Performance measurement: challenges for tomorrow. *International Journal of Management Reviews*, 14(3), 305–327.

Boschee, Jerr, & McClurg, Jim (2003) Toward a better understanding of social entrepreneurship: some important distinctions. The Institute for Social Entrepreneurs. http://www.caledonia.org.uk/papers/Social-Entrepreneurship.pdf, 12.01.2023.

Brouard, François, & Larivet, Sophie (2010) Essay of clarifications and definitions of the related concepts of social enterprise, social entrepreneur and social entrepreneurship, in Alain Fayolle & Harry Matlay (eds), *Handbook of Research on Social Entrepreneurship*. Cheltenham, UK & Northampton, MA: Edward Elgar Publishing, pp. 29–56.

Bull, Mike (2007) "Balance": the development of a social enterprise business performance analysis tool. *Social Enterprise Journal*, 3(1), 49–66.

Carraher, Shawn, Welsh, Dianne, & Svilokos, Andrew (2016) Validation of a measure of social entrepreneurship. *European Journal of International Management*, 10(4), 386.

Costa, Ericka, & Andreaus, Michele (2021) Social impact and performance measurement systems in an Italian social enterprise: a participatory action research project. *Journal of Public Budgeting, Accounting & Financial Management*, 33(3), 289–313.

Costa, Ericka, & Pesci, Caterina (2016) Social impact measurement: why do stakeholders matter? *Sustainability Accounting, Management and Policy Journal*, 7(1), 99–124.

Costanzo, Laura A., Vurro, Clodia, Foster, Doug, Servato, Flavio, & Perrini, Francesco (2014) Dual-mission management in social entrepreneurship: qualitative evidence from social firms in the United Kingdom. *Journal of Small Business Management*, 52(4), 655–677.

Dacin, Peter, Dacin, Tina, & Matear, Margaret (2010) Social entrepreneurship: why we don't need a new theory and how we move forward from here. *Academy of Management Perspectives*, 24, 37–57.

Darby, Lauren, & Jenkins, Heledd (2006) Applying sustainability indicators to the social enterprise business model. *International Journal of Social Economics*, 33(5/6), 411–431.

Dart, Raymond (2004) The legitimacy of social enterprise. *Nonprofit Management and Leadership*, 14(4), 411–424.

Dees, J. Gregory (2001) The Meaning of "Social Entrepreneurship", Original Draft: October 31, 1998. Reformatted and revised: May 30, 2001. https://centers.fuqua.duke.edu/case/wp-content/uploads/sites/7/2015/03/Article_Dees_MeaningofSocialEntrepreneurship_2001.pdf, 18.08.2023.

Dees, J. Gregory, Emerson, Jed, & Economy, Peter (2001) *Enterprising Nonprofits, A Toolkit for Social Entrepreneurs*, New York: Wiley.

Easterby-Smith, Mark, Thorpe, Richard, & Jackson, Paul (2012) *Management Research*. 4th edn. Thousand Oaks: Sage.

Ebrahim, Alnoor, Battilana, Julie, & Mair, Johanna (2014) The governance of social enterprises: mission drift and accountability challenges in hybrid organizations. *Research in Organizational Behavior*, 34, 81–100.

Ehrenberger, Marcus (2017) *Corporate Social Entrepreneurship: Prozess und Form ökonomischer Organisation zur Kreation sozialunternehmerischer Opportunitäten*. Marburg: Metropolis-Verlag.

Eisend, Martin (2014) *Metaanalyse*. Munich: Hampp.

EU Commission (2011) Opinion of the European Economic and Social Committee on the "Communication from the Commission to the European Parliament, the Council, the European Economic and Social Committee and the Committee of the Regions: Social Business Initiative – Creating a favourable climate for social enterprises, key stakeholders in the social economy and innovation", COM(2011) 682 final. https://eur-lex.europa.eu/legal-content/EN/TXT/PDF/?uri=CELEX:52012AE1292, 14.05.2024.

Evers, Adalbert, & Ewert, Benjamin (2010) Hybride Organisationen im Bereich sozialer Dienste. Ein Konzept, sein Hintergrund und seine Implikationen, in Thomas Klatetzki (ed.), *Soziale personenbezogene Dienstleistungs-organisationen: Soziologische Perspektiven*. Wiesbaden: VS Verlag für Sozialwissenschaften, pp. 103–128.

Fayolle, Alain, & Matlay, Harry (2010) Social entrepreneurship: a multicultural and multidimensional perspective, in Alain Fayolle & Harry Matlay (eds), *Handbook of Research on Social Entrepreneurship*. Cheltenham, UK & Northampton, MA: Edward Elgar Publishing, pp. 1–11.

Fields, Ziska (ed.) (2016) *Incorporating Business Models and Strategies into Social Entrepreneurship*. Hershey, PA: IGI Global.

Figge, Frank, Hahn, Tobias, Schaltegger, Stefan, & Wagner, Marcus (2002) The sustainability balanced scorecard—linking sustainability management to business strategy. *Business Strategy and the Environment*, 11(5), 269–284.

Fink, Arlene (2014) *Conducting Research Literature Reviews, from the Internet to Paper*. 4th edn. Thousand Oaks: Sage.

Fuentes, Sandrine, & Valenzuela-Garcia, Hugo (2019) A crossroads for social entrepreneurship: profits versus ethics. *Open Journal of Business and Management*, 7(2), 848–860.

Gall, Meredith D., Gall, Joyce P., & Borg, Walter R. (2007) *Educational Research, An Introduction*. 8th edn. Boston, MA: Pearson/Allyn & Bacon.

GlobeScan & SustainAbility (2017) The 2017 Sustainability Leaders: Celebrating 20 Years of Leadership. https://sustainability.com, https://sustainability.com/wp-content/uploads/2017/06/The -2017-Leaders-A-GlobeScan-SustainAbility-Survey.pdf, 12.01.2023.

Günzel, Franziska, & Krause, Juliane (2013) Die Rolle von Geschäftsmodellen im Gründungsprozess: eine Systematische Literaturanalyse. *Betriebswirtschaftliche Forschung und Praxis: BFuP*, 65(2), 175–192.

Harding, Rebecca (2004) Social enterprise: the new economic engine? *Business Strategy Review*, 15(4), 39–43.

Hayes, Robert H., & Abernathy, William J. (1980) Managing our way to economic decline. *Harvard Business Review*, 58, 67–77.

Hoogendoorn, Brigitte, Pennings, Enrico, & Thurik, Roy (2010) What do we know about social entrepreneurship? An analysis of empirical research. *International Review of Entrepreneurship*, 8(2), 1–42.

Hubers, Frank (2017) *Assessing the Impact of Social Enterprises: An Exploration of the Methods and Criteria Used by Impact Investors and Philanthropists in Asia*. Singapore: Asia Centre for Social Entrepreneurship and Philanthropy.

Huybrechts, Benjamin, & Nicholls, Alex (2012) Social entrepreneurship: definitions, drivers and challenges, in Christine K. Volkmann, Kim Oliver Tokarski, & Kati Ernst (eds), *Social Entrepreneurship and Social Business: An Introduction and Discussion with Case Studies*. Wiesbaden: Springer Gabler, pp. 31–48.

Jansen, Stephan A., Heinze, Rolf G., & Beckmann, Markus (2013) *Sozialunternehmen in Deutschland, Analysen, Trends und Handlungsempfehlungen*, Wiesbaden: Springer VS.

Kaplan, Robert (1984) The evolution of management accounting. *Accounting Review*, 59, 390–418.

Kaplan, Robert S., & Norton, David P. (1996) *The Balanced Scorecard: Translating Strategy into Action*. Boston, MA: Harvard Business School Press.

Kato, Shoko, Ashley, Shena R., & Weaver, Rasheda L. (2018) Insights for measuring social value: classification of measures related to the capabilities approach. *VOLUNTAS: International Journal of Voluntary and Nonprofit Organizations*, 29(3), 558–573.

Kirchgeorg, Manfred (2004) Vom Ökocontrolling zum Nachhaltigkeitscontrolling mithilfe der Balanced Scorecard, in Frank Bensberg, Jan Vom Brocke, & Martin B. Schultz (eds), *Trendberichte zum Controlling: Festschrift für Heinz Lothar Grob*. Heidelberg: Springer-Verlag, pp. 371–391.

Kraus, Sascha, Filser, Matthias, O'Dwyer, Michele, & Shaw, Eleanor (2014) Social entrepreneurship: an exploratory citation analysis. *Review of Managerial Science*, 8(2), 275–292.

Leadbeater, Charles (2001) *The Rise of the Social Entrepreneur*. London: Demos.

Lee, Yoeng-Taek., & Moon, Jae-Young (2008) An exploratory study on the balanced scorecard model of social enterprise. *Asian Journal on Quality*, 9, 11–30.

Lepoutre, Jan, Justo, Rachida, Terjesen, Siri, & Bosma, Niels (2013) Designing a global standardized methodology for measuring social entrepreneurship activity: the Global Entrepreneurship Monitor social entrepreneurship study. *Small Business Economics*, 40(3), 693–714.

Light, Paul C. (2008) *The Search for Social Entrepreneurship*. Washington, DC: The Brookings Institution.

Lindgreen, Adam, Vallaster, Christine, Yousafzai, Shumaila, & Hirsch, Bernhard (2019) *Measuring and Controlling Sustainability: Spanning Theory and Practice.* London/New York: Routledge.

Liston-Heyes, Catherine, & Liu, Gordon (2021) To measure or not to measure? An empirical investigation of social impact measurement in UK social enterprises. *Public Management Review*, 23(5), 687–709.

Luke, Belinda (2016) Measuring and reporting on social performance: from numbers and narratives to a useful reporting framework for social enterprises. *Social and Environmental Accountability Journal*, 36(2), 103–123.

Mair, Johanna (2010) Social entrepreneurship: taking stock and looking ahead, in Alain Fayolle & Harry Matlay (eds), *Handbook of Research on Social Entrepreneurship.* Cheltenham, UK & Northampton, MA: Edward Elgar Publishing, pp. 15–28.

Mair, Johanna, & Martí, Ignasi (2006) Social entrepreneurship research: a source of explanation, prediction, and delight. *Journal of World Business*, 41(1), 36–44.

Mair, Johanna, & Schoen, Oliver (2007) Successful social entrepreneurial business models in the context of developing economies. *International Journal of Emerging Markets*, 2(1), 54–68.

Manetti, Giacomo (2014) The role of blended value accounting in the evaluation of socio-economic impact of social enterprises. *VOLUNTAS: International Journal of Voluntary and Nonprofit Organizations*, 25(2), 443–464.

Marchand, Maria, & Raymond, Louis (2008) Researching performance measurement systems: an information systems perspective. *International Journal of Operations & Production Management*, 28(7), 663–686.

Mardiono, Lisa (2012) Development of performance model: a new measurement framework for non-profit organization. The 3rd International Conference on Technology and Operations Management, Bandung, Indonesia, 4–6 July 2012.

Martin, Roger L., & Osberg, Sally (2007) Social entrepreneurship: the case for definition. *Stanford Social Innovation Review*, Spring, 29–39.

Metzger, Georg (2019) Social Entrepreneurs in Deutschland: Raus aus der Nische – 154.000 „junge" Sozialunternehmer im Jahr 2017. *Fokus Volkswirtschaft*, 238(6).

Millar, Ross, & Hall, Kelly (2013) Social return on investment (SROI) and performance measurement. *Public Management Review*, 15(6), 923–941.

Möller, Klaus, Wirnsperger, Franz, & Gackstatter, Thomas (2015) Performance Management: Konzept, Erfahrungen und Ausgestaltung einer neuen Disziplin. *Controlling : Zeitschrift für erfolgsorientierte Unternehmenssteuerung*, 27(2), 74–80.

Neely, Andy D., Adams, Chris, & Kennerley, Mike (2002) *The Performance Prism: The Scorecard for Measuring and Managing Business Success.* London: Prentice Hall & Financial Times. https://www.academia.edu/34990359/The_Performance_Prism_The_Scorecard_for_Measuring_and_Managing_Business_Success?bulkDownload=thisPaper-topRelated-sameAuthor-citingThis-citedByThis-secondOrderCitations&from=cover_page, 14.05.2023.

NEF (2007) *Measuring Real Value: A DIY Guide to Social Return on Investment.* London: New Economics Foundation. Retrieved from http://www.neweconomics.org/, 28.02.2023.

Nicholls, Alex (2006) *Social Entrepreneurship: New Models of Sustainable Social Change.* Oxford: Oxford University Press.

Nicholls, Jeremy (2007) *Why measuring and communicating social value can help social enterprise become more competitive.* London: Cabinet Office.

Ogawa, Rodney T., & Malen, Betty (1991) Towards rigor in reviews of multivocal literature. appying the exploratory case study method. *Review of Educational Research*, 61(3), 265–286.

Olenga Tete, Paulina, Wunsch, Michael, & Menke, Charlott (2018) *Deutscher Social Entrepreneurship Monitor 2018.* Berlin: Social Entrepreneuship Netzwerk Deutschland e.V. (SEND). https://www.send-ev.de/uploads/dsem-2018_web.pdf, 21.05.2023.

Otley, David (2003) Management control and performance management: whence and whither? *British Accounting Review*, 35(4), 309–326.

Peredo, Ana María, & McLean, Murdith (2005) Social entrepreneurship: a critical review of the concept. *Journal of World Business*, 41(1), 56–65.

Peris-Ortiz, Marta, Teulon, Frédéric, & Bonet Fernandez, Dominique (eds) (2017) *Social Entrepreneurship in Non-Profit and Profit Sectors: Theoretical and Empirical Perspectives.* Cham: Springer.

Pless, Nicola M. (2012) Social entrepreneurship in theory and practice: an introduction. *Journal of Business Ethics*, 111(3), 317–320.

Pun, Kit F., & White, Anthony (2005) A performance measurement paradigm for integrating strategy formulation: a review of systems and frameworks. *International Journal of Management Reviews*, 7(1), 49–71.

Randolph, Justus (2009) A guide to writing the dissertation literature review. *Practical Assessment, Research, & Evaluation*, 14(1), 13.

Robinson, Jeffrey (2006) Navigating social and institutional barriers to markets: how social entrepreneurs identify and evaluate opportunities, in Johanna Mair, Jeffrey Robinson & Kai Hockerts (eds), *Social Entrepreneurship*. Basingstoke: Palgrave Macmillan, pp. 95–120.

Santos, Filipe M. (2012) A positive theory of social entrepreneurship. *Journal of Business Ethics*, 111(3), 335–351.

Sassmannshausen, Sean Patrick, & Volkmann, Christine (2013) *A Bibliometric Based Review on Social Entrepreneurship and its Establishment as a Field of Research*. Schumpeter Discussion Papers 2013-003. Wuppertal: Schumpeter School of Business and Economics.

Schwarz, Sabine (2014) *Social Entrepreneurship Projekte*. Wiesbaden: Springer VS.

Seelos, Christian, & Mair, Johanna (2005) Social entrepreneurship: creating new business models to serve the poor. *Business Horizons*, 48(3), 241–246.

Short, Jeremy C., Moss, Todd W., & Lumpkin, G. T. (2009) Research in social entrepreneurship: past contributions and future opportunities. *Strategic Entrepreneurship Journal*, 3(2), 161–194.

Simons, Robert (1995) *Levers of Control: How Managers Use Innovative Control Systems to Drive Strategic Renewal*. Boston, MA: Harvard Business School Press.

Singh, Archana (2016) *The Process of Social Value Creation: A Multiple-Case Study on Social Entrepreneurship in India*. New Delhi: Springer.

Slack, Nigel (1983) Flexibility as a manufacturing objective. *International Journal of Operations and Production Management*, 3(3), 4–13.

Somers, Ali B. (2005) Shaping the balanced scorecard for use in UK social enterprises. *Social Enterprise Journal*, 1(1), 43–56.

Spiess-Knafl, Wolfgang, Schüesl, Rieke, Richter, Saskia, Scheuerle, Thomas, & Schmitz, Björn (2013) Eine Vermessung der Landschaft deutscher Sozialunternehmen, in Stephan A. Jansen, Rolf G. Heinze, & Markus Beckmann (eds), *Sozialunternehmen in Deutschland*. Wiesbaden: Springer VS, pp. 21–34.

Stamm, Hansueli, & Schwarb, Thomas M. (1995) Metaanalyse, Eine Einführung. *Zeitschrift für Personalforschung*, 9(1), 5–27.

Sullivan Mort, Gillian, Weerawardena, Jay, & Carnegie, Kashonia (2003) Social entrepreneurship: towards conceptualisation. *International Journal of Nonprofit and Voluntary Sector Marketing*, 8(1), 76–88.

Terjesen, Siri, Lepoutre, Jan, Justo, Rachida, & Bosma, Niels (2011) *Global Entrepreneurship Monitor: Report on Social Entrepreneurship*. https://www.gemconsortium.org/report, 30.01.2023.

Thompson, John L. (2002) The world of the social entrepreneur. *International Journal of Public Sector Management*, 15(5), 412–431.

Thompson, John L., & Doherty, Bob (2006) The diverse world of social enterprise: a collection of social enterprise stories. *International Journal of Social Economics*, 33(5/6), 361–375.

Unterberg, Michael, Richter, Daniela, Jahnke, Thorsten, Spiess-Knafl, Wolfgang, Sänger, Ralf, & Förster, Nadine (2015) Herausforderungen bei der Gründung und Skalierung von Sozialunternehmen. Welche Rahmenbedingungen benötigen Social Entrepreneurs? Endbericht für das Bundesministerium für Wirtschaft und Energie (BMWi). https://www.bmwi.de/Redaktion/DE/Publikationen/Studien/herausforderungen-bei-der-gruendung-und-skalierung-von-sozialunternehmen.pdf?__blob=publicationFile&v=13, 12.01.2023.

Urbano, David, Ferri, Elisabeth, Peris-Ortiz, Marta, & Aparicio, Sebastian (2017) Social entrepreneurship and institutional factors: a literature review, in Marta Peris-Ortiz, Frédéric Teulon, & Dominique Bonet Fernandez (eds), *Social Entrepreneurship in Non-Profit and Profit Sectors: Theoretical and Empirical Perspectives*. Cham: Springer, pp. 9–30.

Volkmann, Christine K., Tokarski, Kim Oliver, & Ernst, Kati (eds) (2012) *Social Entrepreneurship and Social Business: An Introduction and Discussion with Case Studies*. Wiesbaden: Springer Gabler.

Weerawardena, Jay, & Mort, Gillian Sullivan (2006) Investigating social entrepreneurship: a multidimensional model. *Journal of World Business*, 41(1), 21–35.

Yang, Chang-Ling, Preechalert, Sarina, Phunnarungsi, Visit, & Huang, Kai-Ping (2022) Constructing integrated performance assessment system for social enterprises. *International Journal of Organizational Innovation*, 15(2), 95–118.

Zahra, Shaker A., Gedajlovic, Eric, Neubaum, Donald O., & Shulman, Joel M. (2009) A typology of social entrepreneurs: motives, search processes and ethical challenges. *Journal of Business Venturing*, 24(5), 519–532.

Zucchella, Antonella, Hagen, Birgit, & Serapio, Manuel G. (2018) *International Entrepreneurship*. Cheltenham, UK & Northampton, MA: Edward Elgar Publishing.

PART IV

SUSTAINABILITY REPORTING AND CAPITAL MARKETS

12. Sustainability disclosure and capital markets: a review of the literature

Michela Cordazzo, Laura Bini and Lorenzo Simoni

INTRODUCTION

Over the last two decades, firms have increasingly adopted sustainability reporting for measuring, managing, and communicating their sustainability activities and performance. Consequently, standard setters and regulators have started to get involved in several initiatives aimed at enabling a wide range of stakeholders to assess and compare sustainability reporting more effectively.

Among the most recent initiatives, the European Commission issued the Corporate Sustainability Reporting Directive (CSRD) in 2023, replacing Directive 2014/95/EU. The new Directive strengthens the rules concerning the social and environmental information that firms are required to report and involves a broader set of large firms, including non-listed firms. At the same time, the European Commission commissioned the EFRAG Technical Group to prepare the first set of draft European Sustainability Reporting Standards (ESRS), which were delivered in November 2022 and formally adopted in July 2023. In the meantime, in November 2021, at the COP26 in Glasgow, the Foundation announced its intention to propose a set of sustainability standards through the formation of an ad hoc standard setter, the International Sustainability Standards Board (ISSB). The ISSB was in charge of the development of a high-quality set of standards focusing on the needs of investors and the financial markets. Finally, in 2019 the Global Reporting Initiative (GRI) started the most important process of updating the GRI standards, to improve the quality and consistency of sustainability reporting, which resulted in the issue of the revised Universal Standards.

The growing importance of sustainability reporting and the regulatory pressures in this field drew the attention of scholars. The last 20 years have seen a significant growth of studies investigating sustainability disclosure practices, and research has made progress in evaluating the importance of sustainability reporting. Literature reviews have been conducted with the main aim of shedding light on disclosure determinants. Berthelot et al. (2003), Lee and Hutchison (2005), Fifka (2013), Hahn and Kühnen (2013), and Huang and Watson (2015) have considered empirical studies dealing with factors influencing the adoption, the extent, and the quality of sustainability reporting, as well as those affecting the decision to disclose sustainability information. Our literature review aims to enlarge previous evidence by focusing on the capital markets effects of sustainability disclosure. Although regulation initiatives address a broad range of stakeholders, shareholders and bondholders play a major role in driving sustainability disclosure practices. Considering the ongoing changes in the context, we aim to examine markets' responses to sustainability disclosure over time. Moving from the assumption that disclosure of useful information influences investment decisions (Verrecchia, 2001), we considered two main strands of research: studies on the cost of capital and value relevance studies. Firms and investors consider sustainability information to play a central role when making investments and financing decisions. Assuming that the cost of capital reflects the level of available information, sustainability disclosure is expected to have an impact on the cost of capital. On the other hand, value relevance studies aim to determine whether stock prices incorporate a certain piece of information. As investors are paying attention to firms' engagement towards sustainability, sustainability disclosure is expected to influence investment decisions.

Our literature review provides insights into how capital markets evaluate sustainability disclosure that might offer valuable suggestions for future research. Overall, our results support the view that sustainability disclosure is useful for capital market participants. However, caution is required in generalizing results. An important issue in the reviewed studies is the measurement of sustainability disclosure. Several sustainability disclosure measurements are indeed employed by researchers, focusing on different aspects. Some studies use binary measures to capture the presence of sustainability information without considering the quantity or quality of disclosure. Other studies use the level of disclosure as a proxy for disclosure quality, while still others focus on specific qualitative aspects of information. Many researchers develop their disclosure measures based on ad hoc content analysis, while others resort to ESG scores developed by financial data providers. All these differences limit the comparability of results, hampering generalization. It is worth noting that only a few studies combine the different disclosure measures to strengthen their results.

Beyond disclosure measures, two other factors seem to affect results in our sample studies. The first is represented by the investigated context. Studies focusing on developing countries seem to show a weaker effect of sustainability disclosure. As suggested by some authors, this could be related to the fact that sustainability issues receive less attention in developing countries than in Western countries. Since sustainability issues are global, a deeper focus on developing countries could offer some useful insight to governors and global standard setters. Finally, we found that SMEs seem to be excluded from the major benefits of sustainability disclosure, as SMEs disclosing more sustainability information face a higher cost of capital. Although evidence on SMEs is still limited, the extension of mandatory sustainability reporting requirements following the incoming adoption of the CSRD in Europe emphasizes the need to investigate the costs and benefits of such disclosure for SMEs.

The remainder of the chapter is structured as follows. The following section describes the methodology applied to select capital markets research works analyzing sustainability disclosure. Thereafter, we discuss existing research on the relationship between sustainability disclosure and cost of capital, as well as on the value relevance of sustainability information practices. In the conclusions, we present our main findings and some reflections for future research.

METHODOLOGY

Our literature review examines, analyses, and discusses the findings of prior relevant studies on the relationship between sustainability disclosure and capital markets. It relies on the Scopus database as it offers extensive coverage of peer-reviewed journals with an impact factor. Thus, the selection of the Scopus database was considered beneficial to the validity and objectivity of the literature review process.

We focused on articles published from 2000 to 2023, given the increasing attention researchers paid to sustainability-related topics over this period. We limited our search to specific Scopus thematic areas, including business, management, and accounting, to better identify studies of interest according to our topic. We restricted our search to articles written in English, as English is the dominant language in business, management, and accounting research.

Our research process followed three steps. The first was the collection of articles. Given the purpose of our review, we used the following search keywords to identify articles dealing with the effects on capital markets: "cost of capital*", "value relevan*", "market reaction*", and "stock pric*". These words were paired with the list of keywords defined to identify sustainability disclosure. Since several terms are used in research to refer to sustainability disclosure, we included a variety of keywords: "GRI", "ESG", "sustainability", "CSR", and "non-financial". However, as the analysis of results according to these different sustainability perspectives is beyond the scope of this chapter, we only refer to sustainability disclosure in commenting on our results. The presence of each paired keyword was searched for in an article's title, abstract, and keywords. The second step concerns the selection of articles. We read the abstract of each article to assess if it was pertinent to our objective. One of the main issues we faced in this phase was dealing with the overlaps between articles investigating the relation between sustainability performance on capital markets and those focusing on sustainability disclosure and capital markets. We excluded all articles with an explicit reference to sustainability performance. However, in a few cases, it was not clear whether a certain sustainability measure was used to assess sustainability disclosure or sustainability performance. We adopted the following rule to address these limited cases: we excluded all those articles that used a specific key performance indicator (i.e., tons of carbon emissions) regardless of how this information was collected. Conversely, we included articles that adopted sustainability ratings (i.e., Bloomberg sustainability score), albeit it was not clear which relationship they were focusing on. The third step in our process deals with the evaluation of articles. We read each article to find any interrelation between sustainability disclosure measurement and capital markets. The second and third steps of our research process were independently conducted by two co-authors to limit any reliability concerns. After discussing the selection and evaluation of each research work, a final list of articles was prepared.

THE EFFECTS OF SUSTAINABILITY DISCLOSURE ON CAPITAL MARKETS

Overall, we found 81 studies investigating the effect of sustainability disclosure on capital markets. They can be divided into two main strands of research: 16 investigating the association between sustainability disclosure and the cost of capital (see Table 12A.1 in the appendix) and 65 assessing the usefulness of sustainability information by looking at how stock prices reflect such information, i.e., value relevance studies (see Table 12A.2 in the appendix). We discuss the findings of the two strands below.

Different Sources of Financing: Cost of Capital, Cost of Debt, and Cost of Equity

Among the 16 studies investigating the effects of sustainability disclosure on the cost of capital, five focus on the overall cost of capital, seven on the cost of equity, three investigate both the cost of debt and the cost of equity, and one examines the cost of debt and the overall cost of capital.

Studies focusing on the overall cost of capital define the cost of capital as the weighted average cost of capital (WACC) and largely use the measures of sustainability disclosure provided by the Bloomberg database. Despite this consistency in the use of WACC, results are highly divergent. Gholami et al. (2023) and Kumawat and Patel (2022) report a negative relationship between sustainability disclosure and WACC in Australia and India, respectively. However, in the latter study, the negative and significant relation is limited to the total sustainability disclosure measure, while no association is found for the three measures of sustainability disclosure components, i.e., environmental, social, and governance disclosures. By contrast, Atan et al. (2018) and Gjergji et al. (2021) document a positive relationship between sustainability disclosure and WACC for Malaysian and Italian firms, respectively. Both studies provide further results by disaggregating the sustainability disclosure in the three components. Atan et al. (2018) find that, individually, none of the environmental, social, and governance disclosures are significant in influencing WACC. On the other hand, Gjergji et al. (2021) confirm a positive association between environmental disclosure and the cost of capital, while governance and social disclosure do not seem to exert any impact. Atan et al. (2018) call into question the features of the Malaysian business context among the main causes. More specifically, the authors consider that stakeholders in Malaysia still do not have high confidence in sustainability initiatives that are mainly perceived as costs for firms. Moreover, low confidence leads investors to evaluate only the total sustainability disclosure without considering the three components. Gjergji et al. (2021) identify firm size as the most meaningful influential factor on sustainability disclosure in Italy. Gjergji et al. (2021) is the only study in our literature review to investigate SMEs, including family firms. Italian SMEs reporting about sustainability seem to be penalized by investors due to the cost–benefit trade-off of disclosing such information. More specifically, SMEs' extensive use of bank financing could somehow call for the monitoring role of disclosure, and the lower diversification of these firms could amplify risks and thus increase proprietary costs. However, results also show that among SMEs, those identified as family firms benefit from a positive effect on the cost of capital when they disclose environmental information. This result is explained by bearing in mind that family firms are more sensitive to environmental strategies due to their need to be perceived as responsible corporate citizens and avoid potentially devastating public scandals. Lastly, a lack of any relationship between sustainability disclosure and WACC is reported by AlKhouri and Suwaidan (2022) in Jordan. Like Atan et al. (2018), the authors refer to contextual factors to support their results. More specifically, they consider that both managers and stakeholders perceive sustainability disclosure as a costly, burdensome activity rather than as an opportunity that leads to the sustainability of their businesses.

Studies investigating the relationship between sustainability disclosure and the cost of equity show more consistent results compared to those on WACC. Except for Clarkson et al. (2013) and Weber (2018), which do not find any significant association, all the other studies show a negative relation, supporting the idea that investors positively judge sustainability disclosure. This evidence is confirmed across countries (Australia, Germany, China, Malaysia, and the US) and industries (controversial industry sectors including alcohol, tobacco, gambling, military, firearms, nuclear power, oil and gas, cement, and biotechnology). These studies mostly use the same measure of implied cost of equity, i.e., the price–earnings–growth (PEG) model. Implied cost of equity measures provides an *ex ante* cost of equity measure that incorporates analysts' expectations about future developments of a business, as opposed to the measure based on *ex post* (realized) returns. In some cases, authors do not consider just PEG, but combine different proxies of implied cost of capital to obtain a more reliable measure (e.g., Hmaittane et al., 2019).

Among studies on the cost of equity, three studies extend the analysis to the cost of debt. The results confirm the positive effect of sustainability disclosure on a firm's creditworthiness assessment, lowering the cost of debt. The evidence involves the large, listed firms of only two countries, Australia and Malaysia. While Bhuiyan and Nguyen (2020) and Lau (2019) focus on total sustainability disclosure, Shad et al. (2020) also investigate the three sustainability disclosure components. In keeping with other results on the oil and gas industry, Shad et al. (2020) show that environmental disclosure is perceived as more relevant for lenders compared to social disclosure.

The Value Relevance of Sustainability Disclosure

We selected 65 studies using different methods to assess the value relevance of sustainability disclosure. Among these, 27 studies employ the Ohlson valuation model or its modifications and extensions (Ohlson, 1995), seven consider the market value of assets proxied by Tobin's Q, six studies use the stock return instead of market values calculated at a certain point in time, while two papers adopt methods relying on the share price volatility or change in share price. Some studies rely on more than one proxy. One study combines stock return and the firm's financial performance (Jones et al., 2007), one study uses market value and financial performance (Clarkson et al., 2013), one study jointly considers market values and shorted shares (Jain et al., 2016), one study considers market values and returns (Verbeeten et al., 2016), and one combines Tobin's Q and stock return (Li et al., 2022).

The remaining 17 studies are event studies, which evaluate market reaction in the days surrounding an announcement, such as the publication of the sustainability report. This methodology entails the calculation of abnormal stock returns in a window (typically a three- or five-day window) around the selected date, capturing market reaction to the release of a piece of information. Finally, one study assesses the usefulness of information based on the percentage of shares held by foreign investors and proves the value relevance of sustainability disclosure (Chauhan and Kumar, 2019).

In general, studies employing the Ohlson valuation model or its modified versions, Tobin's Q, or annual stock returns are those that more frequently find a positive association, with limited exceptions. Only five studies find a negative association, and three studies do not find any relationship with sustainability disclosure. Several studies explore inter-state samples (16) or the US (10), while others focus on other EU countries or the UK (nine in total). Evidence on Asian countries is limited, as we only found two studies based in Turkey and five focusing on China, Bangladesh, India, Saudi Arabia, and Iran (one for each of those countries). Almost all studies cover recent periods and refer to listed large firms, such as the top 100 in South Africa, the biggest ASX companies, the FTSE 350, or the STOXX Europe 600. The five studies showing an unexpected negative association provide different explanations for these results.

Cardamone et al. (2012) and Rehman et al. (2020) call into question the perceived cost of information included in sustainability reports, and Clarkson et al. (2013) refer to the negative content of environmental information investigated. Jeriji et al. (2023) advocate for the costs of complying with GRI guidelines. Finally, Li et al. (2022) refer to the context to explain the negative results observed. They document a negative reaction to CSR disclosure in the US, where the provision of sustainability information could be seen as costly or as an attempt at impression management.

It is worth noting that the few studies investigating the mandatory disclosure setting after the introduction of the non-financial European Directive show mixed results. Mittelbach-Hörmanseder et al. (2021) investigate the relationship between sustainability disclosure and market value in the STOXX Europe 600 before and after the Directive, showing that sustainability disclosure is value-relevant only before the Directive. These results suggest that investors negatively consider mandatory sustainability disclosure due to the implied costs of the disclosure being higher than the expected benefits. On the other hand, Cordazzo et al. (2020) find that sustainability disclosure is not value-relevant for listed Italian firms either before or after the Directive. Finally, Paolone et al. (2021) find that environmental disclosure is value-relevant after the transposition of the Directive in Italy.

Focusing on event studies based on abnormal returns around a particular event, 13 out of 17 studies show a positive market reaction to sustainability disclosure in different contexts (USA, Japan, China, and inter-state). By contrast, Clacher and Hagendorff (2012) and Mitsuyama and Shimizutani (2015) do not find any significant market reaction. Finally, Alsaifi et al. (2020) and Wang, J. et al. (2023) document a negative reaction. The authors call into question the peculiarity of the disclosure investigated to explain this negative relationship. Alsaifi et al. (2020), who focus on carbon emission information, maintain that growing pollution levels could be perceived by the market as unsustainable environmental practices. Wang, J. et al. (2023), who deal with the announcement of a reform concerning sustainability disclosure in the US, suggest that investors might consider the announced reform as costly for firms. This evidence is in line with Grewal et al. (2019) showing a negative reaction to the enforcement of the European Non-Financial Directive, which suggests that investors do not favor the introduction of mandatory sustainability disclosure requirements.

It is worth noting that the mixed results of the studies in our literature review could be influenced by the different aspects of sustainability disclosure: some studies consider total sustainability disclosure, while others focus on specific components of sustainability disclosure. Miralles-Quirós et al. (2019), Al-Hiyari and Kolsi (2021) and Lueg and Pesheva (2021) consider the three dimensions of sustainability disclosure and find that only governance disclosure is relevant for investors. Conversely, Qureshi et al. (2020) show that governance is the least significant type of disclosure among the three categories. Suttipun and Yordudom (2022) find that environmental disclosure is the most important in Thailand, while Verbeeten et al. (2016) show that only social disclosure is considered by German investors. Some studies only focus on the environmental pillar of sustainability disclosure. Beelitz et al. (2021) investigate firms subject to environmental disasters and show that environmental disclosure quality, based on the Bloomberg score, is value-relevant for such firms. Baboukardos (2018) finds that the environmental score developed by Thomson Reuters Asset4 is value-relevant for listed French firms, and the relationship between that measure and market value is moderated by environmental provisions. Similarly, Fazzini and Dal Maso (2016) document that voluntary environmental information provided by Italian firms, measured using the Bloomberg score, is value-relevant. In the same way, Paolone et al. (2021) find that mandatory environmental disclosure is value-relevant in Italy. Griffin and Sun (2013) evaluate environmental issues considering greenhouse gas emission disclosure, finding that they are value-relevant. By contrast, Jadoon et al. (2016) consider the single pillars of sustainability disclosure and find that the environmental pillar is not significant.

SUSTAINABILITY DISCLOSURE MEASURES

One of the main factors to consider in interpreting the mixed results reported above is represented by the methodological choices related to the measurement of sustainability disclosure. Several disclosure measures are proposed by the sample studies. The first distinction can be made between binary measures that capture the presence of sustainability information and measures that consider the extent of sustainability disclosure or its qualitative features.

Eighteen studies use a dichotomous variable, 14 of which refer to the publication of a sustainability report. Among these 14, Dhaliwal et al. (2011) examine the first adoption of sustainability reporting in the US, showing that firms with superior social responsibility performance enjoy a subsequent reduction in the cost of equity capital. Similar results are found by Bachoo et al. (2013) in the Australian context. Among the value relevance studies, the inter-state analysis of Aureli et al. (2020) finds that the first publication of a sustainability report is a value-relevant event across all regions/countries investigated, except for Swedish and Irish firms. Similarly, other studies find that the disclosure of sustainability reports is positively and significantly associated with market values (Berthelot et al., 2012; Wang, K. and Li, 2016; Swarnapali, 2020; Rahman et al., 2020; Alharbi et al., 2021), suggesting that the publication of sustainability reports provides investors with useful information, complementing financial information.

Three studies using dichotomous variables find partial positive effects. Carnevale et al. (2012) and Carnevale and Mazzucca (2014) document a positive relationship only in some of the investigated countries. Beelitz et al. (2021) find significant results exclusively for environmental information. Guidry and Patten (2010) show that only firms with the highest quality of sustainability reports benefit from sustainability disclosure. This latter aspect represents a crucial factor in evaluating the consequences of sustainability disclosure, as firms issuing a sustainability report or providing sustainability information in the annual report could show different levels of disclosure extension and quality, which are not captured by a dichotomous variable. Contrary to this evidence, Cardamone et al. (2012) and Rehman et al. (2020) find a negative and significant relationship between the publication of a sustainability report and market values in Italy and China, respectively.

The remaining four studies employing a dichotomous variable explore different aspects connected to sustainability disclosure. Dal Maso et al. (2017) focus on the disclosure concerning stakeholder engagement (a binary score included in the Thomson Reuters database) and find that this information is value-relevant. Kuzey and Uyar (2017), Nandy et al. (2023) and Jeriji et al. (2023) use a dichotomous classification to distinguish firms preparing their sustainability report with GRI standards. The use of GRI standards is considered a signal of good sustainability reporting practices, as they represent the most used set of standards for sustainability information. However, the results of the three studies differ considerably. Kuzey and Uyar (2017) find that firms adopting GRI standards have higher market values. Nandy et al. (2023) find that GRI standards adoption is value-relevant, but only in some of the periods investigated. Jeriji et al. (2023) document that GRI standards adoption is associated with a reduced firm value, thus considering the migration to GRI standards to be a cost for firms.

The amount and the quality of sustainability disclosure are considered crucial factors in understanding how disclosure practices affect capital markets (Guidry and Patten, 2010). Thus, it is not surprising that disclosure indices are the most adopted measures in our literature review, as 57 studies adopt a disclosure index (43 are value relevance studies, while 14 focus on the cost of financing). Among these, three combine those measures with a dummy variable (Guidry and Patten, 2010; Rehman et al., 2020; Beelitz et al., 2021).

A first relevant distinction between disclosure indexes is made between disclosure scores or ratings by third parties (the most popular for sustainability disclosure include Bloomberg and Thomson Reuters/Refinitiv) and self-constructed measures based on the content analysis of sustainability information disclosed by firms. Although self-constructed indexes may result in a more accurate assessment of disclosure quality, they suffer from scarce replicability that hampers comparability between different studies. In our literature review, 32 out of 57 studies use scores by third parties to assess sustainability disclosure. The Bloomberg scores are the most used, applied in 12 studies of our literature review. This result is not surprising, considering that this index assesses listed firms worldwide, it is based on accurate and detailed information, and it is specifically developed for assessing sustainability disclosure. Nine studies use Thomson Reuters/Refinitiv Asset4 ESG scores, while seven studies refer to the KLD score, and three studies adopt the sustainability score of KPMG. The remaining studies refer to disclosure indexes developed for a specific context, like the consensus ESG ratings proposed by the CSRHUB data service provider (Thompson et al., 2022). Many data providers offer a synthetic score that considers all three components of sustainability disclosure but also separate scores for environmental, social, and governance disclosures.

The seven studies investigating the effect of sustainability disclosure on the cost of capital by using third parties' scores show mixed results. Atan et al. (2018) document a positive relationship, Hmaittane et al. (2019), Bhuiyan and Nguyen (2020), Gholami et al. (2023), Kumawat and Patel (2022), and Tarulli et al. (2022) confirm the expected negative relationship, while Weber (2018) does not find any significant result. The fact that these studies examine different countries (Australia, India, Malaysia, and the US) could explain such differences.

With regard to the 25 value relevance studies based on sustainability indices provided by third parties, results confirm the value relevance of sustainability disclosure, with only two exceptions. Li et al. (2022) find that sustainability activities of S&P1500 firms, proxied by KLD ratings, are perceived as value-destroying in the US. This negative sign is interpreted by considering that in the US context, the provision of sustainability information might be seen as costly for firms or as an attempt to manipulate impressions, thus leading to a negative market reaction. Mănescu (2011) finds a non-significant relationship between sustainability information, proxied by KLD ratings, and stock returns for US firms. Among the studies that find a positive relationship, one relies on KPMG ratings but applies a transformation to the original variable of interest to decompose the rating in expected and unexpected sustainability disclosure[1] (Cahan et al., 2016). According to Cahan et al. (2016), the use of unexpected sustainability disclosure allows the evaluation of incremental information's effects, and also considering investors' expectations about the provision of sustainability information. These expectations are a function of different factors, such as firm- and industry-level characteristics or institutional environment.

In contrast to studies employing scores by third parties, 27 studies in our literature review use a self-developed disclosure index (in some cases in combination with third-party scores or a dummy variable). Twenty-four studies use disclosure indexes based on manual content analysis, while three rely on automated analysis. Compared to automated content analysis, manual content analysis guarantees better accuracy in contextualizing collected information. On the other hand, manual content analysis may suffer from subjectivity, reducing the reliability of data collection. The adoption of an automated coding procedure allows researchers to obtain more replicable results, as well as to analyze a wider range of documents in a relatively short time. The three studies employing automated content analysis use automated analysis based on machine learning (Michaels and Grüning, 2017; Clarkson et al., 2020; Schiehll and Kolahgar, 2021).

Among the 27 studies using a self-developed index, seven studies investigate the relationship of sustainability disclosure with the cost of debt, showing mixed results. Most of the value relevance studies employing self-developed indexes confirm a positive relationship, but the incidence of studies finding positive and significant results is lower than in the case of scores from third parties. Three studies find no association or a negative association between sustainability disclosure and market values. Cordazzo et al. (2020) find that sustainability information disclosed by listed Italian firms is not value-relevant. A similar result is found by Aras et al. (2018) in Turkish banks. Mittelbach-Hörmanseder et al. (2021) document that when European listed firms shifted from voluntary to mandatory sustainability reporting, the relationship between sustainability disclosure and share prices became negative, indicating that the market perceived this shift as costly for firms.

Other studies propose different independent variables, which are not strictly related to information disclosed by the entity in the annual or sustainability report. Sustainability disclosure is proxied by the release of certain information. For instance, some studies evaluate the capital market consequences of the inclusion in a list of socially responsible firms (Clacher and Hagendorff, 2012; Lackmann et al., 2012; Lourenço et al., 2012; Karim et al., 2016), the passing of the ESG Disclosure Simplification Act of 2021 in the US (Wang, J. et al., 2023), or carbon disclosure (Alsaifi et al., 2020). Results show that the inclusion in a list of socially responsible firms is positively considered by investors only in some cases, while events such as the passing of the ESG Act in the US or carbon disclosure spurred a negative market reaction.

DISCUSSION AND CONCLUSION

Most of the studies in our literature review support the notion that sustainability disclosure is beneficial, providing users with value-relevant information or lowering the cost of capital. However, a considerable number of studies found no significant impact of sustainability disclosure or even negative consequences of such disclosure on financial markets. In addition, among the studies that document a significant beneficial impact, some studies find that this impact holds only under some circumstances or in certain contexts. Thus, the results obtained by the different studies show a somewhat mixed picture, where sustainability disclosure may be useful to investors, depending on certain factors.

An important element that can affect the results refers to the methodological choices concerning sustainability disclosure measurement or the variable used to capture information usefulness. Only a few studies make use of different measures to assess sustainability disclosure or different proxies for evaluating information usefulness. Future research could strength this evidence, by adopting different measures in their research design. For instance, studies might combine the use of disclosure scores by third parties with self-constructed indexes or test different types of economic consequences of sustainability disclosure.

Another important aspect is related to the context investigated. For instance, studies on the relationship between sustainability disclosure and cost of capital show less pronounced results in developing countries compared to Western countries. The attention devoted to sustainability at the country level could influence this relationship. Western countries, and in particular EU countries, are promoting regulations that require certain firms to disclose mandatory sustainability information. While this is a sign of the importance attributed to sustainability disclosure, evidence shows that in many cases, investors perceive this as a cost rather than an opportunity, negatively reacting to mandatory sustainability disclosure requirements (Mittelbach-Hörmanseder et al., 2021; Wang, J. et al., 2023). These results should attract the attention of regulators, as the recent reform of mandatory sustainability disclosure with the new CSRD, effective in 2024, has introduced tighter sustainability reporting requirements. Although some studies found that mandatory sustainability disclosure has positive effects on an organization's commitment to sustainability activities (Fiechter et al., 2022), the negative consequences on investor assessment and perceived risk levels should be carefully considered by the European and national regulators. The issue of CSRD represents a unique opportunity for researchers to enrich our knowledge concerning market reactions to mandatory sustainability disclosure. Such evidence could be useful for regulators to better understand the consequences of their initiative and could also support preparers in defining their sustainability disclosure policy. An aspect of utmost importance is the extension of mandatory sustainability reporting requirements to private firms in 2026. Gjergji et al. (2021) seem to show that SMEs do not benefit from sustainability disclosure; on the contrary, the level of sustainability disclosure is associated with a higher cost of capital for these firms. Limited empirical evidence in this area does not allow generalization. Although it seems that SMEs might bear even higher costs compared to listed firms in implementing sustainability disclosure requirements, more research on this issue is needed.

NOTE

1. The authors use a first-stage regression using some determinants of sustainability disclosure to predict the level of information disclosed. The residuals of that model are used as a measure of unexpected sustainability disclosure. Hence, unexpected sustainability disclosure could signal disclosure levels that are higher (positive residuals) or lower (negative residuals) than the predicted levels.

BIBLIOGRAPHY

Abu Qa'adan, M. B. and Suwaidan, M. S. (2019), 'Board composition, ownership structure and corporate responsibility disclosure: the case of Jordan', *Social Responsibility Journal*, 15(1), pp. 28–46.
Alharbi, M. A., Mgammal, M. H. and Al-Matari, E. M. (2021), 'Sustainability report publication and bank share price: evidence from Saudi Arabia stock markets', *The Journal of Asian Finance, Economics and Business*, 8(2), pp. 41–55.

Al-Hiyari, A. and Kolsi, M. C. (2021), 'How do stock market participants value ESG performance? Evidence from Middle Eastern and North African Countries', *Global Business Review*, 09721509211001511.

Ali, A. and Jadoon, I. A. (2022), 'The value relevance of corporate sustainability performance (CSP)', *Sustainability*, 14(15), 9098.

AlKhouri, R. and Suwaidan, M. S. (2023), 'The impact of CSR on the financing cost of Jordanian firms', *Social Responsibility Journal*, 19(3), pp. 460–473.

Alsaifi, K., Elnahass, M. and Salama, A. (2020), 'Market responses to firms' voluntary carbon disclosure: empirical evidence from the United Kingdom', *Journal of Cleaner Production*, 262, 121377.

Aras, G., Tezcan, N. and Kutlu Furtuna, O. (2018), 'The value relevance of banking sector multidimensional corporate sustainability performance', *Corporate Social Responsibility and Environmental Management*, 25(6), pp. 1062–1073.

Arianpoor, A., Salehi, M. and Daroudi, F. (2023), 'Nonfinancial sustainability reporting, management legitimate authority and enterprise value', *Social Responsibility Journal*, 19(10), pp. 1900–1916.

Atan, R., Alam, M. M., Said, J. and Zamri, M. (2018), 'The impacts of environmental, social, and governance factors on firm performance: panel study of Malaysian companies', *Management of Environmental Quality: An International Journal*, 29(2), pp. 182–194.

Aureli, S., Gigli, S., Medei, R. and Supino, E. (2020), 'The value relevance of environmental, social, and governance disclosure: evidence from Dow Jones Sustainability World Index listed companies', *Corporate Social Responsibility and Environmental Management*, 27(1), pp. 43–52.

Baboukardos, D. (2018), 'The valuation relevance of environmental performance revisited: the moderating role of environmental provisions', *The British Accounting Review*, 50(1), pp. 32–47.

Bachoo, K., Tan, R. and Wilson, M. (2013), 'Firm value and the quality of sustainability reporting in Australia', *Australian Accounting Review*, 23(1), pp. 67–87.

Banke, M., Lenger, S. and Pott, C. (2022), 'ESG Ratings in the corporate reporting of DAX40 companies in Germany: effects on market participants', *Sustainability*, 14(15), 9742.

Beelitz, A., Cho, C. H., Michelon, G. and Patten, D. M. (2021), 'Measuring CSR disclosure when assessing stock market effects', *Accounting and the Public Interest*, 21(1), pp. 1–22.

Berthelot, S., Cormier, D. and Magnan, M. (2003), 'Environmental disclosure research: review and synthesis', *Journal of Accounting Literature*, 22, pp. 1–44.

Berthelot, S., Coulmont, M. and Serret, V. (2012), 'Do investors value sustainability reports? A Canadian study', *Corporate Social Responsibility and Environmental Management*, 19(6), pp. 355–363.

Bhuiyan, M. B. U. and Nguyen, T. H. N. (2020), 'Impact of CSR on cost of debt and cost of capital: Australian evidence', *Social Responsibility Journal*, 16(3), pp. 419–430.

Buallay, A. (2019), 'Between cost and value: investigating the effects of sustainability reporting on a firm's performance', *Journal of Applied Accounting Research*, 20(4), pp. 481–496.

Cahan, S. F., De Villiers, C., Jeter, D. C., Naiker, V. and Van Staden, C. J. (2016), 'Are CSR disclosures value relevant? Cross-country evidence', *European Accounting Review*, 25(3), pp. 579–611.

Cardamone, P., Carnevale, C. and Giunta, F. (2012), 'The value relevance of social reporting: evidence from listed Italian companies', *Journal of Applied Accounting Research*, 13(3), pp. 255–269.

Carnevale, C. and Mazzuca, M. (2014), 'Sustainability report and bank valuation: evidence from European stock markets', *Business Ethics: A European Review*, 23(1), pp. 69–90.

Carnevale, C., Mazzuca, M. and Venturini, S. (2012), 'Corporate social reporting in European banks: the effects on a firm's market value', *Corporate Social Responsibility and Environmental Management*, 19(3), pp. 159–177.

Chauhan, Y. and Kumar, S. B. (2019), 'The value relevance of nonfinancial disclosure: evidence from foreign equity investment', *Journal of Multinational Financial Management*, 52, 100595.

Cho, S. Y., Kang, P. K., Lee, C. and Park, C. (2020), 'Financial reporting conservatism and voluntary CSR disclosure', *Accounting Horizons*, 34(2), pp. 63–82.

Clacher, I. and Hagendorff, J. (2012), 'Do announcements about corporate social responsibility create or destroy shareholder wealth? Evidence from the UK', *Journal of Business Ethics*, 106, pp. 253–266.

Clarkson, P. M., Li, Y., Richardson, G. D. and Vasvari, F. P. (2008), 'Revisiting the relation between environmental performance and environmental disclosure: an empirical analysis', *Accounting, Organizations and Society*, 33(4–5), pp. 303–327.

Clarkson, P. M., Fang, X., Li, Y. and Richardson, G. (2013), 'The relevance of environmental disclosures: are such disclosures incrementally informative?', *Journal of Accounting and Public Policy*, 32(5), pp. 410–431.

Clarkson, P. M., Ponn, J., Richardson, G. D., Rudzicz, F., Tsang, A. and Wang, J. (2020), 'A textual analysis of US corporate social responsibility reports', *Abacus*, 56(1), pp. 3–34.

Cordazzo, M., Bini, L. and Marzo, G. (2020), 'Does the EU Directive on non-financial information influence the value relevance of ESG disclosure? Italian evidence', *Business Strategy and the Environment*, 29(8), pp. 3470–3483.

Dal Maso, L., Liberatore, G. and Mazzi, F. (2017), 'Value relevance of stakeholder engagement: the influence of national culture', *Corporate Social Responsibility and Environmental Management*, 24(1), pp. 44–56.

de Klerk, M. and de Villiers, C. (2012), 'The value relevance of corporate responsibility reporting: South African evidence', *Meditari Accountancy Research*, 20(1), pp. 21–38.

de Klerk, M., de Villiers, C. and Van Staden, C. (2015), 'The influence of corporate social responsibility disclosure on share prices: evidence from the United Kingdom', *Pacific Accounting Review*, 27(2), pp. 208–228.

Dhaliwal, D. S., Li, O. Z., Tsang, A. and Yang, Y. G. (2011), 'Voluntary nonfinancial disclosure and the cost of equity capital: the initiation of corporate social responsibility reporting', *The Accounting Review*, 86(1), pp. 59–100.

Du, S. and Yu, K. (2021), 'Do corporate social responsibility reports convey value relevant information? Evidence from report readability and tone', *Journal of Business Ethics*, 172, pp. 253–274.

Eng, L. L., Fikru, M. and Vichitsarawong, T. (2022), 'Comparing the informativeness of sustainability disclosures versus ESG disclosure ratings', *Sustainability Accounting, Management and Policy Journal*, 13(2), pp. 494–518.

European Commission (2023), 'Directive (EU) 2022/2464 of the European Parliament and of the Council of 14 December 2022 amending regulation (EU) no 537/2014, Directive 2004/109/EC, Directive 2006/43/EC and Directive 2013/34/EU, as regards corporate sustainability reporting'.https://eur-lex.europa.eu/legal-content/EN/TXT/?uri=CELEX%3A32022L2464

Fazzini, M. and Dal Maso, L. (2016), 'The value relevance of "assured" environmental disclosure: the Italian experience', *Sustainability Accounting, Management and Policy Journal*, 7(2), pp. 225–245.

Fiechter, P., Hitz, J. and Lehmann, N. (2022), 'Real effects of a widespread CSR reporting mandate: evidence from the European Union's CSR Directive', *Journal of Accounting Research*, 60(4), pp. 1499–1549.

Fifka, M. S. (2013), 'Corporate responsibility reporting and its determinants in comparative perspective: a review of the empirical literature and a meta-analysis', *Business Strategy and the Environment*, 22(1), 1–35.

Gholami, A., Sands, J. and Shams, S. (2023), 'Corporates' sustainability disclosures impact on cost of capital and idiosyncratic risk', *Meditari Accountancy Research*, 31(4), pp. 861–886.

Gjergji, R., Vena, L., Sciascia, S. and Cortesi, A. (2021), 'The effects of environmental, social and governance disclosure on the cost of capital in small and medium enterprises: the role of family business status', *Business Strategy and the Environment*, 30(1), pp. 683–693.

Grewal, J., Riedl, E. J. and Serafeim, G. (2019), 'Market reaction to mandatory nonfinancial disclosure', *Management Science*, 65(7), pp. 3061–3084.

Grewal, J., Hauptmann, C. and Serafeim, G. (2021), 'Material sustainability information and stock price informativeness', *Journal of Business Ethics*, 171, pp. 513–544.

GRI (2022), 'Our mission and history', available at: www.globalreporting.org/about-gri/mission-history/

Griffin, P. A. and Sun, Y. (2013), 'Going green: market reaction to CSRWire news releases', *Journal of Accounting and Public Policy*, 32(2), pp. 93–113.

Guidry, R. P. and Patten, D. M. (2010), 'Market reactions to the first-time issuance of corporate sustainability reports: evidence that quality matters', *Sustainability Accounting, Management and Policy Journal*, 1(1), pp. 33–50.

Hahn, R. and M. Kühnen (2013), 'Determinants of sustainability reporting: a review of results, trends, theory, and opportunities in an expanding field of research?', *Journal of Cleaner Production*, 59, pp. 5–21.

Havlinova, A. and Kukacka, J. (2023), 'Corporate social responsibility and stock prices after the financial crisis: the role of strategic CSR activities', *Journal of Business Ethics*, 182, pp. 223–242.

Hmaittane, A., Bouslah, K. and M'Zali, B. (2019), 'Does corporate social responsibility affect the cost of equity in controversial industry sectors?', *Review of Accounting and Finance*, 18(4), pp. 635–662.

Hsu, A., Koh, K., Liu, S. and Tong, Y. H. (2019), 'Corporate social responsibility and corporate disclosures: an investigation of investors' and analysts' perceptions', *Journal of Business Ethics*, 158, pp. 507–534.

Huang, X. B. and Watson L. (2015), 'Corporate social responsibility research in accounting', *Journal of Accounting Literature*, 34(1), pp. 1–16.

IFRS (2020), 'Consultation paper on sustainability reporting', London, United Kingdom, available at: https://cdn.ifrs.org/-/media/project/sustainability-reporting/consultation-paper-on-sustainability-reporting.pdf.

Jadoon, I. A., Ali, A., Ayub, U., Tahir, M. and Mumtaz, R. (2021), 'The impact of sustainability reporting quality on the value relevance of corporate sustainability performance', *Sustainable Development*, 29(1), pp. 155–175.

Jain, A., Jain, P. K. and Rezaee, Z. (2016), 'Value-relevance of corporate social responsibility: evidence from short selling', *Journal of Management Accounting Research*, 28(2), pp. 29–52.

Jeriji, M., Louhichi, W. and Ftiti, Z. (2023), 'Migrating to global reporting initiative guidelines: does international harmonization of CSR information pay?', *British Journal of Management*, 34(2), pp. 555–575.

Jones, S., Frost, G., Loftus, J. and Van Der Laan, S. (2007), 'An empirical examination of the market returns and financial performance of entities engaged in sustainability reporting', *Australian Accounting Review*, 17(41), 78–87.

Karim, K., Suh, S. and Tang, J. (2016), 'Do ethical firms create value?', *Social Responsibility Journal*, 12(1), pp. 54–68.

Kaspereit, T. and Lopatta, K. (2016), 'The value relevance of SAM's corporate sustainability ranking and GRI sustainability reporting in the European stock markets', *Business Ethics: A European Review*, 25(1), pp. 1–24.

Khanchel, I., Lassoued, N. and Gargoury, R. (2023), 'CSR and firm value: is CSR valuable during the COVID 19 crisis in the French market?', *Journal of Management and Governance*, 27, pp. 575–601.

Kumarasinghe, S., Will, M. and Hoshino, Y. (2018), 'Enhancing performance by disclosing more: some evidence from Japanese companies', *Pacific Accounting Review*, 30(1), pp. 110–128.

Kumawat, R. and Patel, N. (2022), 'Are ESG disclosures value relevant? A panel-corrected standard error (PCSE) approach', *Global Business Review*, 23(6), pp. 1558–1573.

Kuzey, C. and Uyar, A. (2017), 'Determinants of sustainability reporting and its impact on firm value: evidence from the emerging market of Turkey', *Journal of Cleaner Production*, 143, pp. 27–39.

Lackmann, J., Ernstberger, J. and Stich, M. (2012), 'Market reactions to increased reliability of sustainability information', *Journal of Business Ethics*, 107, pp. 111–128.

Lau, C. K. (2019), 'The economic consequences of business sustainability initiatives', *Asia Pacific Journal of Management*, 36(4), pp. 937–970.

Lee, T. L. and Hutchison, P. D. (2005), 'The decision to disclose environmental information: a research review and agenda', *Advances in Accounting*, 21, pp. 83–111.

Li, Y., de Villiers, C., Li, L. Z. and Li, L. (2022), 'The moderating effect of board gender diversity on the relation between corporate social responsibility and firm value', *Journal of Management Control*, 33(1), pp. 109–143.

Lourenço, I. C., Branco, M. C., Curto, J. D. and Eugénio, T. (2012), 'How does the market value corporate sustainability performance?', *Journal of Business Ethics*, 108, pp. 417–428.

Lu, Y. and Abeysekera, I. (2021), 'Do investors and analysts value strategic corporate social responsibility disclosures? Evidence from China', *Journal of International Financial Management & Accounting*, 32(2), pp. 147–181.

Lueg, R. and Pesheva, R. (2021), 'Corporate sustainability in the Nordic countries: the curvilinear effects on shareholder returns', *Journal of Cleaner Production*, 315, 127962.

Mănescu, C. (2011), 'Stock returns in relation to environmental, social and governance performance: mispricing or compensation for risk?', *Sustainable Development*, 19(2), pp. 95–118.

Michaels, A. and Grüning, M. (2017), 'Relationship of corporate social responsibility disclosure on information asymmetry and the cost of capital', *Journal of Management Control*, 28, pp. 251–274.

Miralles-Quirós, M. M., Miralles-Quirós, J. L. and Redondo-Hernández, J. (2019), 'The impact of environmental, social, and governance performance on stock prices: evidence from the banking industry', *Corporate Social Responsibility and Environmental Management*, 26(6), pp. 1446–1456.

Mitsuyama, N. and Shimizutani, S. (2015), 'Stock market reaction to ESG-oriented management: an event study analysis on a disclosing policy in Japan', *Economics Bulletin*, 35(2), pp. 1098–1108.

Mittelbach-Hörmanseder, S., Hummel, K. and Rammerstorfer, M. (2021), 'The information content of corporate social responsibility disclosure in Europe: an institutional perspective', *European Accounting Review*, 30(2), pp. 309–348.

Moalla, M. and Dammak, S. (2023), 'Corporate ESG performance as good insurance in times of crisis: lessons from US stock market during COVID-19 pandemic', *Journal of Global Responsibility*, 14(4), pp. 381–402.

Nandy, M., Kuzey, C., Uyar, A., Lodh, S. and Karaman, A. S. (2023), 'Can CSR mechanisms spur GRI adoption and restore its lost value relevance?', *Journal of Applied Accounting Research*, 24(4), pp. 609–634.

Ohlson, J. A. (1995), 'Earnings, book values, and dividends in equity valuation', *Contemporary Accounting Research*, 11(2), pp. 661–687.

Paolone, F., Granà, F., Martiniello, L. and Tiscini, R. (2021), 'Environmental risk indicators disclosure and value relevance: an empirical analysis of Italian listed companies after the implementation of the Legislative Decree 254/2016', *Corporate Social Responsibility and Environmental Management*, 28(5), pp. 1471–1482.

Qureshi, M. A., Kirkerud, S., Theresa, K. and Ahsan, T. (2020), 'The impact of sustainability (environmental, social, and governance) disclosure and board diversity on firm value: the moderating role of industry sensitivity', *Business Strategy and the Environment*, 29(3), pp. 1199–1214.

Rahman, M., Rasid, S. Z. A. and Basiruddin, R. (2020), 'Corporate social responsibility reporting and value relevance of the banking sector in Bangladesh', *Journal of Sustainability Science and Management*, 15(5), pp. 192–214.

Rehman, R. U., Riaz, Z., Cullinan, C., Zhang, J. and Wang, F. (2020), 'Institutional ownership and value relevance of corporate social responsibility disclosure: empirical evidence from China', *Sustainability*, 12(6), 2311.

Reverte, C. (2016), 'Corporate social responsibility disclosure and market valuation: evidence from Spanish listed firms', *Review of Managerial Science*, 10, pp. 411–435.

Schiehll, E. and Kolahgar, S. (2021), 'Financial materiality in the informativeness of sustainability reporting', *Business Strategy and the Environment*, 30(2), pp. 840–855.

Shad, M. K., Lai, F. W., Shamim, A. and McShane, M. (2020), 'The efficacy of sustainability reporting towards cost of debt and equity reduction', *Environmental Science and Pollution Research*, 27, pp. 22511–22522.

Suttipun, M. and Yordudom, T. (2021), 'Impact of environmental, social and governance disclosures on market reaction: an evidence of Top50 companies listed from Thailand', *Journal of Financial Reporting and Accounting*, 20(34), pp. 753–767.

Swarnapali, R. N. C. (2020), 'Sustainability disclosure and earnings informativeness: evidence from Sri Lanka', *Asian Journal of Accounting Research*, 5(1), pp. 33–46.

Tarulli, A., Morrone, D., Conte, D., Bussoli, C. and Russo, A. (2022), 'Between saying and doing, in the end there is the cost of capital: evidence from the energy sector', *Business Strategy and the Environment*, 31(1), pp. 390–402.

Thompson, E. K., Ashimwe, O., Buertey, S. and Kim, S. Y. (2022), 'The value relevance of sustainability reporting: does assurance and the type of assurer matter?', *Sustainability Accounting, Management and Policy Journal*, 13(4), pp. 858–877.

Verbeeten, F. H., Gamerschlag, R. and Möller, K. (2016), 'Are CSR disclosures relevant for investors? Empirical evidence from Germany', *Management Decision*, 54(6), pp. 1359–1382.

Verrecchia, R. E. (2001), 'Essays on disclosure', *Journal of Accounting and Economics*, 32(1–3), pp. 97–180.

Wang, J., Hu, X. and Zhong, A. (2023), 'Stock market reaction to mandatory ESG disclosure', *Finance Research Letters*, 53, 103402.

Wang, K. T. and Li, D. (2016), 'Market reactions to the first-time disclosure of corporate social responsibility reports: evidence from China', *Journal of Business Ethics*, 138, pp. 661–682.

Weber, J. L. (2018), 'Corporate social responsibility disclosure level, external assurance and cost of equity capital', *Journal of Financial Reporting and Accounting*, 16(4), pp. 694–724.

Xu, S., Liu, D. and Huang, J. (2015), 'Corporate social responsibility, the cost of equity capital and ownership structure: an analysis of Chinese listed firms', *Australian Journal of Management*, 40(2), pp. 245–276.

APPENDIX

Table 12A.1   Sustainability disclosure and cost of capital studies

Name	Period	Country/ies	Cost of capital measure	Main variable	Main results
Dhaliwal et al. (2011)	1993–2007	USA	Cost of equity	Binary variable for issuing a standalone sustainability report	Ke–
Bachoo et al. (2013)	2003–2005	Australia	Cost of equity	Binary variable for acceptable sustainability disclosure according to corporate analysis enhanced responsibility (CAER)	Ke–
Clarkson et al. (2013)	2003; 2006	USA	Cost of equity	Manually constructed environmental disclosure index (based on Clarkson et al., 2008)	NKe
Xu et al. (2015)	2009–2011	China	Cost of equity	Manually constructed sustainability disclosure index	Ke–
Michaels and Grüning (2017)	2013–2014	Germany	Cost of equity	Sustainability disclosure index (developed by artificial intelligence-based content analysis)	Ke–
Atan et al. (2018)	2010–2013	Malaysia	WACC	Bloomberg ESG disclosure score	CoC+ for combined score NCoC for individual score
Weber (2018)	2006–2015	USA	Cost of equity	GRI application levels (A, B, C)	NKe Ke– for poor CSR performers reporting
Hmaittane et al. (2019)	1991–2012	USA	Cost of equity	KLD score	Ke–
Lau (2019)	2004–2013	Malaysia	Cost of debt Cost of equity	Manually constructed sustainability disclosure index (based on Malaysia Stock Exchange's Business Sustainability Initiatives)	Ke– Kd–
Bhuiyan and Nguyen (2020)	2004–2016	Australia	Cost of debt Cost of equity	Bloomberg ESG disclosure score	Ke– Kd–

Name	Period	Country/ies	Cost of capital measure	Main variable	Main results
Shad et al. (2020)	2008–2017	Malaysia	Cost of debt Cost of equity	Manually constructed sustainability disclosure index	Ke– for combined score Ke– for economic score Kd– for environmental score NKd and NKe for social score
Gjergji et al. (2021)	2019	Italy	WACC	Manually constructed sustainability disclosure index (based on GRI items)	CoC+ CoC+ for environmental score NCoC for social and governance scores
AlKhouri and Suwaidan (2022)	2009–2019	Jordan	WACC	Manually constructed sustainability disclosure index (developed by Abu Qa'adan and Suwaidan, 2019)	NCoC
Gholami et al. (2023)	2007–2017	Australia	WACC	Bloomberg ESG disclosure score	CoC–
Kumawat and Patel (2022)	2011–2020	India	WACC	Bloomberg ESG disclosure score	CoC– for combined score NCoC for individual score
Tarulli et al. (2022)	2003–2016	Inter-state	Cost of bank debt WACC	Bloomberg ESG disclosure score	Kd– NCoC

Notes: CoC, Ke and Kd stand for cost of capital, cost of equity and cost of debt respectively; the presence of a '+' sign denotes a positive association with sustainability disclosure; the presence of a '–' sign denotes a positive association with sustainability disclosure. NCoC, NKe and NKd stand for no association with sustainability disclosure.

Table 12A.2   Value relevance studies on sustainability disclosure

Name	Period	Country/ies	Model	Main variable	Main results
Jones et al. (2007)	2004	Australia	Market adjusted returns and financial performance	Manually constructed sustainability disclosure index	VR– when considering returns; VR+ when considering firm performance
Guidry & Patten (2010)	2001–2008	USA	Abnormal returns (event study)	First-time issuance (binary variable) of a standalone sustainability report and manually constructed disclosure index	VR+ only for firms with the highest quality reports
Mănescu (2011)	1992–2008	USA	Stock return	KLD ratings	NVR
de Klerk & de Villiers (2012)	2008	South Africa	Modified Ohlson	KPMG sustainability score	VR+
Lourenço et al. (2012)	2007–2010	USA and Canada	Ohlson	Binary variable for inclusion in Dow Jones Sustainability Index	VR+
Berthelot et al. (2012)	2007	Canada	Ohlson	Binary variable for issuing a standalone sustainability report	VR+
Carnevale et al. (2012)	2002–2008	Inter-state	Ohlson	Binary variable for issuing a standalone sustainability report	NVR on the overall sample; VR+ in some countries, VR– in others
Cardamone et al. (2012)	2002–2008	Italy	Ohlson	Binary variable for issuing a standalone sustainability report	VR–
Lackmann et al. (2012)	Not defined	Europe	Abnormal return event study	The day of the DJSI STOXX publisher's press release as event day	VR+
Clacher & Hagendorff (2012)	2001–2008	UK	Cumulative abnormal result event study	The announcement that a firm has been included in the UK FTSE4Good index of socially responsible firms	NVR
Clarkson et al. (2013)	2003 and 2006	USA	Ohlson; financial performance	Manually constructed environmental disclosure index (based on Clarkson et al., 2008)	VR–
Griffin & Sun (2013)	2000–2010	USA	Market-adjusted return	Release on sustainability-related news on the CSRWire news service	VR+
Carnevale & Mazzuca (2014)	2002–2011	Inter-state	Ohlson	Binary variable for issuing a standalone sustainability report	VR+, but with differences across countries

Name	Period	Country/ies	Model	Main variable	Main results
Mitsuyama & Shimizutani (2015)	Not defined	Japan	Abnormal return event study	Inclusion in the ESG Brand list announcement by the Tokyo Stock Exchange	VR+ for environmental and social disclosures; VR− for governance disclosure
de Klerk et al. (2015)	2007–2008	UK	Ohlson	KPMG CSR disclosure score	VR+, especially for firms operating in environmentally sensitive industries
Kaspereit & Lopatta (2016)	2002–2011	European cross-country	Ohlson	SAM (S&P) rating and GRI application level	VR+; nonlinear relationship between the market value of a firm and the quantity of sustainability reporting
Jain et al. (2016)	2004–2012	US	Ohlson; shorted shares	Bloomberg ESG disclosure score and KLD ESG ratings	VR+
Fazzini & Dal Maso (2016)	2008–2013	Italy	Modified Ohlson	Bloomberg ESG disclosure scores	VR+ of environmental disclosure; assurance does not provide an incremental relevance of environmental disclosure
Reverte (2016)	2007–2011	Spain	Ohlson	Manually constructed sustainability disclosure index	VR+
Verbeeten et al. (2016)	2005–2008	Germany	Ohlson; annual stock return	Manually constructed sustainability disclosure index	VR+, but only for the disclosure of social information
Karim et al. (2016)	2007–2012	USA	Cumulative abnormal return event study	Announcement of World's Most Ethical Firms list	VR+
Wang, K. & Li (2016)	2007–2012	China	Cumulative abnormal return event study	Binary variable for first-time publication of a CSR report	VR+
Cahan et al. (2016)	2008	Inter-state	Tobin's Q	2008 KPMG rating	VR+
Dal Maso et al. (2017)	2002–2014	Inter-state	Modified Ohlson	Binary variable for stakeholder engagement disclosure (from Thomson Reuters Asset4)	VR+
Kuzey & Uyar (2017)	2011–2013	Turkey	Tobin's Q	Binary variable for GRI adoption	VR+

Name	Period	Country/ies	Model	Main variable	Main results
Kumarasinghe et al. (2018)	2006–2008	Japan	Change in market price and in EPS	Manually constructed sustainability disclosure index	VR+
Aras et al. (2018)	2013–2015	Turkey	Ohlson	Manually constructed sustainability disclosure index	NVR
Baboukardos (2018)	2005–2014	France	Ohlson	Thomson Reuters ESG scores	VR+ of environmental performance, which is moderated by environmental provisions
Buallay (2019)	2007–2016	Inter-state	Tobin's Q	Bloomberg ESG disclosure scores	VR+
Chauhan & Kumar (2019)	2007–2016	India	Percentage of outstanding shares held by foreign investors in a firm	Bloomberg ESG disclosure scores	VR+
Miralles-Quirós et al. (2019)	2002–2015	Inter-state	Ohlson	Thomson Reuters ESG scores	NVR overall; VR+ for environmental performance; VR– for social performance
Swarnapali (2020)	2012–2016	Sri Lanka	Cumulative abnormal return event study	Binary variable for issuing a standalone sustainability report	VR+
Hsu et al. (2019)	1995–2012	USA	Abnormal return event study	KLD ratings	VR+
Cordazzo et al. (2020)	2016–2017	Italy	Ohlson	Manually constructed sustainability disclosure index	NVR
Qureshi et al. (2020)	2011–2017	Inter-state	Ohlson	Thomson Reuters ESG scores	VR+, especially for firms operating in environmentally sensitive industries
Aureli et al. (2020)	2009–2016	Inter-state	Abnormal return event study	Binary variable for issuing a standalone sustainability report	VR+, except for Swedish and Irish firms; VR increases after 2013
Rahman et al. (2020)	2009–2017	Bangladesh	Ohlson	Binary variable for issuing a standalone sustainability report	VR+

Name	Period	Country/ies	Model	Main variable	Main results
Alsaifi et al. (2020)	2009–2015	UK	Abnormal return event study	Carbon Disclosure Project (CDP) report's announcement	VR– (negative information), especially for carbon-intensive industries
Cho et al. (2020)	2007–2011	Inter-state	Cumulative abnormal return event study	Voluntary disclosure of CSR news reported by newswire	VR+, reduced when the firm is more conservative
Rehman et al. (2020)	2008–2012	China	Ohlson	Binary variable for issuing a standalone sustainability report and manually constructed disclosure index	VR–
Clarkson et al. (2020)	2002–2016	USA	Ohlson	Software-based sustainability disclosure index (manually constructed)	VR+
Lueg & Pesheva (2021)	2007–2014	Inter-state	Total shareholders' return	Bloomberg ESG disclosure score	VR+, especially governance disclosure
Schiehll & Kolahgar (2021)	1999–2014	Canada	Stock return synchronicity	Software-based sustainability disclosure index (manually constructed)	VR+, especially for the social component
Al-Hiyari & Kolsi (2021)	2013–2018	Inter-state	Ohlson	Thomson Reuters ESG scores	VR+ overall; VR+ for governance and social disclosures; NVR for environmental disclosure
Paolone et al. (2021)	2017–2018	Italy	Ohlson	Manually constructed sustainability disclosure index (based on GRI standards)	VR+ for environmental disclosure
Alharbi et al. (2021)	2014–2018	Saudi Arabia	Ohlson	Binary variable for issuing a standalone sustainability report	VR+
Jadoon et al. (2021)	2012–2016	Inter-state	Ohlson	Manually constructed sustainability disclosure index (based on Asset4 and GRI data)	VR+ of overall CSR reporting; NVR for environmental dimension
Mittelbach-Hörmanseder et al. (2021)	2008–2016	Inter-state	Ohlson	Manually constructed sustainability disclosure index	VR+ or NVR before mandatory CSR disclosure requirements; VR– after the enforcement of mandatory CSR disclosure requirements

Name	Period	Country/ies	Model	Main variable	Main results
Beelitz et al. (2021)	2011	Inter-state	Cumulative abnormal return event study	Binary variable for the existence of standalone CSR report and Bloomberg ESG disclosure score	NVR of pre-negative event (disaster) presence of CSR report; VR+ of pre-negative event (disaster) environmental disclosure
Lu & Abeysekera (2021)	2013–2018	China	Cumulative abnormal return event study	Manually constructed sustainability disclosure index	VR+
Du & Yu (2021)	2002–2014	USA	Cumulative abnormal trading volume event study	KLD ratings	VR+ of disclosure readability and tone
Grewal et al. (2021)	2007–2015	USA	Stock return synchronicity	Sustainability disclosure index (based on Bloomberg ESG information and SASB information requirements)	VR+
Nandy et al. (2023)	2002–2019	Inter-state	Tobin's Q	Binary variable for GRI adoption	VR+ between 2002 and 2010, NVR between 2011 and 2019
Jeriji et al. (2023)	2010–2018	Inter-state	Tobin's Q	Binary variable for GRI adoption	VR–, especially for firms with poor CSR performance
Thompson et al. (2022)	2015–2019	South Africa	Tobin's Q	Disclosure score as reported by CSRHUB	VR+, especially in cases where sustainability assurance is present
Suttipun & Yordudom (2022)	2015–2019	Thailand	Average stock price event study	Manually constructed sustainability disclosure index	VR+ of environmental and social disclosures; VR– of governance disclosure
Li et al. (2022)	2009–2018	USA	Tobin's Q and stock return	KLD dataset	VR–, but the relationship is less pronounced when board gender diversity increases
Ali & Jadoon (2022)	2015–2020	Inter-state	Ohlson	Manually constructed sustainability disclosure index	VR+

Name	Period	Country/ies	Model	Main variable	Main results
Eng et al. (2022)	2014–2018	USA	Ohlson	Sustainability disclosure index (based on Bloomberg ESG information and SASB information requirements)	VR+ for metrics and firm-tailored narratives provide; VR− for boilerplate disclosure
Banke et al. (2022)	2021	Germany	Ohlson	Average rating score based on three scores (Carbon Disclosure Project, Morgan Stanley Capital International and Sustainalytics)	VR+
Wang, J., et al. (2023)	1 January and 31 August 2021	USA	Daily stock return (event study)	Passage of ESG Disclosure Simplification Act of 2021 in the US as event date	VR−
Arianpoor et al. (2023)	2014–2019	Iran	Tobin's Q	Manually constructed sustainability disclosure index	VR+
Moalla & Dammak (2023)	2019–2020	USA	Share price volatility	Thomson Reuters ESG scores	VR+
Havlinova & Kukacka (2023)	2007–2020	USA	Ohlson	Thomson Reuters ESG scores	VR+
Khanchel et al. (2023)	2020	France	Average abnormal return event study	Thomson Reuters ESG scores	VR+

Note: VR+ denotes a positive association between sustainability disclosure and market values; VR− denotes a negative association between sustainability disclosure and market values; NVR denotes no association between sustainability disclosure and market values.

13. Meeting the EU's Sustainability Disclosure Rules – a mission (im)possible?

Martina Macpherson

1   INTRODUCTION: FROM THE ALPHABET SOUP OF ESG TO A MISSION (IM)POSSIBLE FOR INVESTORS?

Over the last decade, investors have started to consider ESG criteria into the investment decisions to meet their varying risk, return and alpha expectations. Commonly ESG approaches such as screening, integration, active ownership or thematic investment lead to decision-making trade-offs related to investor preferences and tolerance levels.[1] These trade-offs may also be linked to a personal investment rationale as an expression of personal ethics and values.[2]

Alongside the investor trajectories for ESG as a key driver of sustainable investment growth, policymakers and regulators' demand for issuers, investors, capital markets and increasingly service providers to define, classify, and report on their sustainability risks, criteria and methods that are driving ESG adoption across jurisdictions globally.

This chapter:

- Sets out to evaluate and compare the key current policy and regulatory developments in Europe and their implications for the investment value chain. It aims to highlight the implications of the EU's Sustainable Finance Action Plan, the EU's Sustainable Finance Disclosure Regulation, the EU's Green Taxonomy, the EU's Markets in Financial Instruments Directive (MiFID) II and of pending ESG ratings regulation across European jurisdictions, and their implications for the investment value chain.
- It briefly sets out to assess, compare and map the different additional cross-EU, and national disclosure and labelling regimes with the EU's Sustainable Finance Disclosure Regulation (EU SFDR), and aims to establish if more harmonised and standardised rules, and an interoperability of these frameworks, can address the fragmentation challenges – and how.
- Ultimately, it aims to establish if the "Alphabet Soup of ESG", and an ever-increasing level of "Aggregate Confusion" is pushing ESG investing towards becoming an investor "Mission (Im)Possible?",[3] and if interoperability, through the harmonisation of reporting frameworks and metrics, can lead to better sustainability practices, can address "reporting fatigue" and may even mitigate "greenwashing" risks.

2   THE SUSTAINABLE INVESTMENT MARKET: BACKGROUND AND CONTEXT

Sustainable investing has entered the mainstream, with more than USD 35 trillion being allocated towards environmental, social and governance (ESG) approaches, according to the

Global Sustainable Investment Alliance (GSIA)'s "Global Sustainable Investment Review" (Global Sustainable Investment Alliance, 2021). The trend is clear: the adoption of ESG funds continues to grow unabated. Bloomberg Intelligence (2021) estimates that the sustainable investment market may even reach up to USD 53 trillion by 2025.

The increased emphasis on ESG considerations in investments[4] is not limited to the amount of assets that ESG-themed funds managed to attract but extends also to forward-looking considerations of such investments in the context of long-term value creation.

Meanwhile, sustainable investing continues to exist within a broad spectrum that aims to generate financial and extra-financial returns:

- At one end of the spectrum, investors adopting this approach may only wish to invest in companies that seek to maximise shareholder value and will principally focus on absolute or risk-adjusted measures of financial value. Inherent in this approach is the belief that capital markets are efficient and will effectively allocate resources to areas of the economy that maximise economic benefits.
- At the opposite end of the spectrum, philanthropy and social impact investing aim to enhance the welfare of certain or all segments of society, particularly in relation to human and workers' rights, gender equality and climate change, among other social considerations.

One of the reasons why ESG-focused funds have seen greater interest can be attributed to a change in investor mindset. Recent investor reports published by Natixis (Natixis Investment Managers, 2021), Morgan Stanley (2022) and Schroders (2023) highlight that at least 60–80% of investment managers and asset owners around the world "expect ESG issues to be considered in their investments"; some (see Natixis Investment Managers, 2021) "reject the idea that companies' only purpose is to create shareholder value" and others (see Schroders, 2023) "highlight the need for ongoing corporate engagement and active ownership to increase sustainability value". Through an increase in awareness of social issues, evolving expectations and a changing regulatory landscape, investors are committing increasing amounts of money to investments where ESG considerations are accounted for.

In choosing an investment, the prioritisation of extra-financial versus financial returns depends on the extent to which investors are prepared to balance one with the other in the pursuit of their overall objectives. One approach is social impact investing which aims to generate first and foremost a social or environmental outcome and impact. This contrasts with sustainable and responsible investing which focuses mainly on improving (extra-)financial returns by using ESG factors to assess longer-term risks and opportunities. This is achieved through an evaluation of factors beyond a company's short-term financial performance to incorporate the assessment of its longer-term environmental, social and governance challenges and developments.

Another reason for the impressive growth in ESG investments can be ascribed to the increasing demand from retail investors. Historically, ESG investing was always the preserve of institutional investors, but according to a report compiled by GlobeScan, "82% of retail investors globally expressed an interest in investing in socially and environmentally responsible companies, 72% of them would like to avoid industries that contribute to climate change" (GlobeScan, 2021). There is also a notable difference in attitude towards sustainable investments based on age. "The baby boomer generation is much less informed about sustainable investments than younger generations, such as the millennials and generation Z."

The increased emphasis on ESG considerations in investments is not limited to the amount of assets that ESG-themed funds managed to attract but extends also to the ongoing monitoring of such investments. An example of this is active ownership, where investors use their rights and position of ownership to influence the behaviour of investee companies.[5] Indeed, active ownership is closely aligned with the ambitions set out in global corporate governance and stewardship codes, and it is what shareholder and investor groups are using to put pressure on companies to further tighten their ESG objectives and positive change trajectories: in 2021, we saw a record-breaking 34 shareholder proposals on environmental and social matters receiving majority support, up from 21 in 2020.[6]

This happened against the backdrop of the COVID-19 pandemic when investors opted to focus their attention on how longer-term themes, such as public health, racial justice, and environmental matters,[7] might impact corporate performance.

3 REGULATORY DRIVERS: THE IMPLEMENTATION OF THE EU'S SUSTAINABLE FINANCE ACTION PLAN

Despite the (geo)political changes and their impact on the financial landscape over the past 48 months, and an increasingly challenging macroeconomic climate, investment focused on environmental, social and governance (ESG) factors continues to grow. Climate-related challenges, in particular, have come to the fore given the experience of unprecedented heat waves in parts of Europe, forest fires in the US and devastating floods in Pakistan during 2022–2023.

Harvard Law School has issued a series of papers, explaining how many institutional investors, including asset managers, asset owners and pension fund providers, have begun to map their impact processes and integrated screening tools into their investment protocols, incorporating ESG priorities, obligations, and expectations (Harvard Law School Forum on Corporate Governance, 2023). They outline global regulatory compliance responsibilities at a high level and assess the challenges institutional investors face given inconsistent data quality and differing national and regional approaches to ESG regulation, i.e., a lack of interoperability of approaches, frameworks and metrics for disclosure and reporting, which can be problematic for global investors and other participants in the investment decision, data and frameworks management value chain.

Alongside the growing interest in ESG investing, there have been a range of ESG regulatory efforts initiated by regulators around the world, with the Principles for Responsible Investing (PRI, n.d.) reporting in 2021 that "there are now more than 750 policy tools and guidance frameworks globally, including 159 new or revised ESG policy instruments".

Market participants such as ESGBook (2023) have also undertaken an in-depth analysis of the regulatory and policy landscape changes in ESG. They found that there is rapid growth of sustainability-based policy interventions: "1,255 ESG policy interventions have been introduced worldwide since 2011, according to ESG Book, compared to 493 regulations published between 2001 and 2010."

The pluralism of these policies and regulatory initiatives, spanning more than 1000 disclosures, reporting frameworks, different ESG standards and classifications, 45+ taxonomies, and in total more than 400 sustainability labels (as at 2023), that currently co-exist in all parts of the value chain and across markets and segments, has created a complex jungle of normative and regulatory climate risk requirements for issuers, investors and banks and hence has led to an "aggregate confusion" amongst creators, providers and users of information in relation to the material areas of scope, focus and metrics in use.

Meanwhile, most of the existing climate and sustainability risk management disclosure frameworks and the "Corporate Reporting Dialogue"[8] have focused predominantly on issuer, i.e., company-related, reporting. This is changing, however, especially since, and with the support of, the European Union's (EU) Sustainable Finance Action Plan and the European Securities Markets Authority's (ESMA) "Sustainable Finance Roadmap 2022–2024" (ESMA, 2022c). Increasingly, policies and regulations now also include dedicated investor and even service providers' sustainability disclosure rules. We will explore the interoperability of these aims, frameworks, and roadmaps in this chapter.

3.1   The EU's Green Deal and the EU's Action Plan on Financing Sustainable Growth: A Baseline for EU Disclosure Regulations

In Europe, on 11 December 2019, the European Commission launched the "Green Deal",[9] a set of policy initiatives with the overarching aim of making the EU climate neutral in 2050. The aim is:

- to review each existing European law on its climate merits,
- to introduce new legislation on the circular economy, building renovation, biodiversity, farming and innovation, and
- to make the EU's climate, energy, transport, and taxation policies fit for reducing net greenhouse gas emissions by at least 55% (= "Fit for 55") by 2030, compared to 1990 levels.

To help fund the Green Deal, on 7 March 2018 the European Commission released an "EU Action Plan on Financing Sustainable Growth".[10] The "Ten Points" Plan is a response to recommendations from the High-Level Expert Group (HLEG) on Sustainable Finance, which were submitted to the European Commission on 31 January 2018, and outlines reforms in three areas:

- moving capital flows toward sustainable investment,
- mainstreaming sustainability into risk management,
- fostering transparency and long-termism in economic activity.

Over the last five years, the EU has launched a series of policy and regulatory guidance and "Delegated Acts" defining the scope, parameters and dependencies between ESG regulations for both issuers and investors. These regulations include a broad set of company disclosure requirements and a dedicated "green" EU Taxonomy as key policies supporting the "European Green Deal" and the "EU Action Plan for Financing Sustainable Growth" – for further details, see sections 3.2 ff. below.

Together with (1) the EU's regulation (2019/2089/EU) on EU Climate Transition Benchmarks, EU Paris-Aligned Benchmarks and Sustainability-Related Disclosures for Benchmarks, (2) the newly adopted EU Green Bond Standard (2023), and most recently (3) the EU's Corporate Sustainability Due Diligence Directive (2023), they aim to improve private sector transparency and accountability around ESG impacts and risks to promote sustainable economic growth and investment in the EU.[11]

The transformation of disclosure reporting started with corporate ESG reporting, and accelerated in 2022, with the release of major proposals in the European Union and the United States, as well as globally by and through the development and alignment of normative corporate reporting standards with the newly developed reporting guidance ("S1 and S2") by the International Sustainability Standards Board (ISSB).

Although all of these recent corporate reporting developments have the potential to impact multinational companies at scale, it is probably the EU Corporate Sustainability Reporting Directive (EU CSRD – Directive 2022/2464/EU)[12] that requires most attention at present. This regulation already encompasses a series of "environmental, social and governance" criteria, and went into effect on 5 January 2023. EU Member States have until early July 2024, i.e., 18 months from the effective date, to incorporate its provisions into national law, and international companies are in scope for reporting if they meet some of the minimum reporting requirements.

The EU CSRD requires large companies and public-interest entities operating in the EU to disclose information on their ESG performance annually. The European Council approved the EU CSRD on 28 November 2022, and it was published in the *Official Journal of the European Union* (OJEU) on 16 December 2022.

- The purpose of the EU CSRD is to improve transparency and accountability around corporate ESG performance.
- This will help investors and other stakeholders have a better understanding of how these companies are addressing ESG issues, so they can make more informed decisions.
- The EU CSRD also seeks to accelerate integration of ESG considerations into corporate business practices to support the transition to a more sustainable, inclusive economy.

The EU CSRD replaces the EU's Non-Financial Reporting Directive (NFRD – Directive 2014/95/EU),[13] expanding the number of companies that will have to comply by nearly four times – from nearly 12,000 to approximately 50,000. Companies in scope will need to prepare a non-financial statement that discloses information on their policies, risks, impacts, and outcomes relating to ESG issues.

The annual statement must be audited by an independent third party and be included in the company's annual financial report.

While the EU NFRD was only applicable to public interest entities (PIEs) with more than 500 employees, the EU CSRD significantly expands the scope of applicability to:[14]

- all "large" companies, regardless of their capital market orientation, that meet two of the following three criteria: (1) an annual average of 250 employees, (2) EUR 50 million in net turnover and/or (3) EUR 25 million total assets;
- all capital market-oriented companies – including SMEs – except for micro-companies;
- non-EU companies with at least one large subsidiary or branch (certain size criteria apply) in the EU and above EUR 150 million consolidated EU revenue.

The EU CSRD will replace the EU's NFRD which has been in force since 2018, and applies to companies with over 500 employees. Companies affected by the EU NFRD had to disclose information on:

- environmental matters,
- social responsibility and the treatment of employees,

- respect for human rights,
- anti-corruption and bribery,
- diversity on company boards (age, gender, etc.).

Designed to overcome some noted shortcomings in the EU NFRD, the EU CSRD is expected to be in force for companies already subject to the EU NFRD by 2025 (reporting based on 2024 data) and 2026 for all other companies including small to medium-sized enterprises (SMEs) (reporting based on 2025 data); and in 2028 third country undertakings will also be in scope, for companies with a net turnover above EUR 150 million.

Additional requirements include:

- clarification of double materiality to identify "outside-in" (ESG impacts on business) and "inside-out" (business impacts on people and planet);
- more detailed reporting aligned with the EU Taxonomy and European Sustainability Reporting Standards (ESRS);
- integrating ESG disclosures into financial and management reporting;
- external audit of reported information;
- digitally tagging reported information so it can be fed into a central database.

Companies are required to disclose their alignment with the EU Taxonomy under the EU CSRD, a classification system that defines what "economic activities" can be considered as "environmentally sustainable". It was initially established to provide a common language and set of criteria for assessing the sustainability of investments under the EU Sustainable Finance Disclosure Regulation – for further details on the EU SFDR and EU Taxonomy classifications, see section 3.2 ff. below.

To qualify as being "sustainable", an activity must contribute to at least one of the following EU Taxonomy "six environmental objectives" and "not significantly harm" the other objectives, including:

- climate change mitigation,
- climate change adaptation,
- sustainable use and protection of water and marine resources,
- transition to a circular economy,
- pollution prevention and control,
- the protection and restoration of biodiversity and ecosystems.

Companies' business activities are "eligible for alignment assessment" under the EU Taxonomy if they are listed in these "objectives" of the EU Taxonomy. This means that specific, science-based criteria exist to evaluate their "sustainability performance". However, it does not guarantee that the company has fulfilled the criteria laid out in the regulation. In short, Taxonomy-eligibility is a necessary but not sufficient condition to prove Taxonomy-alignment.

As of 1 January 2022, companies falling under the scope of the EU NFRD have had to report the extent to which they perform Taxonomy-eligible activities, by disclosing the proportion of their "Turnover", "CapEx" and "OpEx" KPIs associated with "eligible" activities. Companies that fall under the expanded scope of the EU CSRD will also need to start doing this by 2025, at the latest.

Lastly, to comply with the EU CSRD, companies will be required to use the European Sustainability Reporting Standards (ESRS) issued by the European Financial Reporting Advisory Group (EFRAG) to prepare their ESG disclosure information:

- In April 2021, the European Commission adopted a legislative proposal for the EU CSRD that requires companies within its scope to report using a "double materiality perspective" in compliance with the ESRS adopted by the European Commission as "Delegated Acts".
- EFRAG was appointed technical adviser to the European Commission, developing the draft ESRS.
- This was confirmed by the text of 21 June 2021, resulting from the trialogue between the co-legislators, and the text of 10 November 2022 approved by the European Parliament.

The ESRS have taken existing ESG reporting frameworks and standards such as CDP, Global Reporting Initiative (GRI), Sustainability Accounting Standards Board (SASB), and others into account as part of the development process. Like many of these frameworks, the ESRS include both general and sector-specific standards and will enable companies to align their non-financial statements with the requirements of the EU CSRD. This will give stakeholders a better understanding of how these companies are addressing non-financial issues, so they can make more informed decisions. It will also help the EU advance its sustainability goals.

The ESRS "Exposure Drafts" were prepared by the EFRAG Project Task Force on European Sustainability Reporting Standards during the period from June 2021 till April 2022, and comments were invited from 30 April to 8 August 2022. The EFRAG Sustainability Reporting Board, advised by the EFRAG Sustainability Reporting Technical Expert Group, addressed the feedback of the consultation and amended accordingly the 12 draft ESRS.

On 31 July 2023, EFRAG welcomed the adoption of the "Delegated Act" on the first set of European Sustainability Reporting Standards (ESRS) by the European Commission.[15] The European Commission has now adopted the first set of ESRS.[16] These consist of:

- "ESRS 1", which sets out general principles on sustainability reporting;
- "ESRS 2", which sets out general sustainability disclosures for all entities, and those not subject to a materiality assessment are required to be reported; and
- Ten "topical standards", including five environmental, four social, and one governance standard, which are subject to a materiality assessment.

3.2   EU Sustainable Finance Disclosures Regulation (SFDR): Investors' ESG Disclosures

The EU's Sustainable Finance Disclosures Regulation (EU SFDR),[17] is the EU's core piece of disclosure regulation for investors. It introduces a range of major ambitions for financial markets in the form of a "Ten Points Plan" (EU Commission, 2018): in alignment with *the 2015 Paris Agreement and Agenda 2030 for Sustainable Development*, it aims to "reorient capital towards sustainable investment", to "manage financial risks stemming from ESG risks", and to "foster transparency and long-termism in financial and economic activity".

The EU SFDR focuses on the transparency of financial market participants, including banks, insurance companies, asset managers, and pension funds. It requires these organisations to disclose information about their ESG policies, risks, impacts and performance at both an "entity" (company) and at a "product" level.

The EU SFDR is supplemented with further details through "Regulatory Technical Standards" (RTS) that have been developed by the three European Supervisory Authorities (ESAs), including the EBA, EIOPA and ESMA. In April 2020, the ESAs issued a first consultation regarding their proposed draft "RTS" about content, methodologies and presentation of disclosures. The "Final Report" was published in December 2023[18] – see below for further details.

Under *the EU SFDR*, financial firms with investment funds must also disclose what percentage of their products are in line with the EU Taxonomy. If financial products do not comply with the criteria set out and defined in the EU SFDR under Articles 6, 8, and 9, then financial services companies must provide a rationale for their non-compliance with the EU's rules.

By requiring the EU Taxonomy to be a reference for "alignment" around "enabling" and "transitional" activities, the EU SFDR aims to encourage financial market participants to consider the ESG impacts of the products and services they offer and to grow the financing of sustainable economic activities.

At entity level, asset managers have to disclose sustainability disclosure information on their website to specify:

- how they integrate sustainability risks regarding investment decisions or advice and remuneration and engagement policies, and
- how they consider the principal adverse impacts looking at all their investments.

In practice, these disclosure requirements at entity or company level have led so far to the publication of a series of qualitative yet comprehensive statements by each asset manager.[19]

The EU SFDR sets out specific transparency requirements at the product level and makes a distinction between products with (1) "ESG characteristics" (EU SFDR – Article 8) and products with (2) "a core sustainable investment objective" (EU SFRD – Article 9). The disclosures of "sustainability risks" and (3) "Principle Adverse Impacts" (PAIs) in line with the EU SFDR will be achieved through a list of predefined metrics for assessing the environmental, social and governance (ESG) outcomes of an investment process.

Asset managers must disclose in their precontractual information, such as fund prospectuses, how a given product is classified and meets the requirements of these EU SFDR classifications categories and how the ESG characteristics and the sustainable investment objectives are being met.

Ultimately, the EU SFDR introduces three key definitions:

- *Sustainable investment* is an investment in an economic activity which (i) contributes either to an environmental or a social objective; (ii) does not significantly harm any environmental or social objectives and (iii) where the investee company follows good governance practices.
- *Sustainability risk* is an environmental, social or governance event or condition which, if it occurs, could cause a material negative impact on the value of an investment.
- *Principal adverse impacts* (PAIs) on sustainability factors are the investment's impact when considering environmental, social and employee, human rights, anti-corruption and anti-bribery matters.

The EU SFDR includes the consideration of "principal adverse impacts" (PAIs) by "Financial Market Participants" (FMPs) as defined in Article 2(1) EU SFDR, and by financial advisers, as defined in Article 2(11) EU SFDR.

Central to the EU SFDR and the "PAI Regime" is the concept of "sustainability factors", meaning "environmental, social and employee matters, respect for human rights, anti-corruption and anti-bribery matters" as set out in Article 2(24) EU SFDR.

In general terms, firms must disclose whether or not they consider such factors, for example, before making investment decisions or when giving advice, and after an investment is made, whether they monitor and mitigate relevant impacts. In short, they are mandated to disclose whether they consider the negative externalities of investments on the environment or society.

FMPs include:

- credit institutions (as defined in EU Capital Requirements Regulation) and investment firms (as defined in EU MiFID) providing MiFID portfolio management,
- manufacturers of certain types of pension products (based on definitions in EU PRIIPs (packaged retail and insurance-based investment products)); AIFMs (alternative investment fund managers),
- UCITS (undertakings for collective investment in transferable securities) management companies, and
- insurance undertakings (as defined in the EU Solvency II Directive) that make available insurance-based investment products (IBIPs), e.g., fund-linked insurance products.

Financial advisers include:

- credit institutions,
- investment firms,
- AIFMs and UCITS management companies that provide investment advice as defined in EU MiFID, and
- insurance undertakings and insurance intermediaries that provide advice (as defined by the EU Insurance Distribution Directive) with regard to IBIPs (FMPs) must score the sustainability of their investments based on a set of adverse impact indicators called the "PAI Indicators".

The "PAIs", in accordance with the EU's "Regulatory Technical Standards"[20] (RTS) issued by the European Supervisory Authorities in 2021–2023, consist of 14 "mandatory" and 31 "voluntary" indicators on environmental and employee matters, respect for human rights, and anti-corruption and anti-bribery matters.

FMPs and financial advisers must report on all 14 core "indicators", and have to choose at least two additional indicators – one climate- and environment-related and one social- and employee-related. According to Article 4 EU SFDR, FMPs are also obligated to publish and maintain certain information on their principal adverse impacts on their website through their annual "PAI Statement". In addition to releasing this "PAI Statement", FMPs are required to ensure "transparency" regarding the "PAIs" in use on a "financial product level", and it is important to note that this obligation does not extend to financial advisers.

The PAIs are to be disclosed by FMPs in the following ways:

- disclosure on an "entity level" in accordance with Article 4 EU SFDR,
- disclosure on a "product level" in accordance with Article 7 EU SFDR.

In December 2022, EU Commissioner Mairead McGuinness announced a comprehensive assessment of the EU SFDR framework "to assess potential shortcomings", focusing on legal certainty, the useability of the regulation and its ability to play its part in tackling greenwashing.[21] The open and targeted public consultations, which were open between 14 September and 22 December 2023, were an important part of this assessment.

These were complemented by workshops and roundtables, enabling stakeholders to submit further input. The industry is currently (December 2023) awaiting the outcome of the assessment, and has issued statements asking for more interoperability between ESG disclosures regulations, from a cross-jurisdictional, as well as from an investment value chain (companies versus investors) perspective.

3.3 Sustainable Investment Products: EU SFDR and (Green) EU Taxonomy Alignment

As outlined above, the EU Taxonomy[22] is a classification system for environmentally sustainable "economic activities" included in "six environmental objectives".

In the specific case of investments in activities with an environmental objective, Article 3 EU Taxonomy Regulation indicates that an "economic activity" will be considered environmentally sustainable when it:

- contributes substantially to one or more of the "six defined environmental objectives", including the mitigation and adaptation of climate change; the sustainable use and protection of water and marine resources; the transition towards a circular economy; the prevention and control of pollution; the protection and recovery of biodiversity and ecosystems;
- "does no significant harm" to the remaining objectives ("DNSH");
- complies with the "minimum guarantees" required, such as the OECD Guidelines for Multinational Enterprises and the United Nations Guiding Principles on Business and Human Rights; and
- complies with the "Technical Screening Criteria" (TSC) established by the European Commission.

The EU Taxonomy Regulation entered into force on 12 July 2020 and sets out the four overarching conditions that an "economic activity" has to meet in order to qualify as "environmentally sustainable". The EU Commission has come up with a list of "environmentally sustainable activities" by defining "technical screening criteria" for each "environmental objective" through "Delegated" and "Implementing Acts".

On 27 June 2023, the EU Commission adopted a "Taxonomy Environmental Delegated Act",[23] including a new set of EU Taxonomy criteria for economic activities making a substantial contribution to one or more of the non-climate environmental objectives, namely:

- sustainable use and protection of water and marine resources;
- transition to a circular economy;
- pollution prevention and control;
- protection and restoration of biodiversity and ecosystems.

The EU Commission has also adopted amendments to the "Taxonomy Disclosures Delegated Act" and the "Taxonomy Climate Delegated Act", covering the "environmental objectives of climate change mitigation and adaptation". The adopted texts were published in the *Official Journal of the European Union* on 21 November 2023, and will apply as of 1 January 2024.

Furthermore, Recital 6 of the EU Taxonomy Regulation establishes that complementary guidelines may be drawn up in relation to other sustainability objectives, including "social objectives", known as "Social Taxonomy", at a later stage. In this context, there is also the possibility of extending the taxonomy to cover "economic activities that significantly harm environmental sustainability".

For both Articles 8 and 9 EU SFDR, an investment manager needs to disclose information about the proportion of EU Taxonomy "alignment". Under the EU Taxonomy, an activity is considered environmentally sustainable, or "aligned", with the EU Taxonomy:

- if it makes a substantial contribution to one of "six environmental objectives", and
- "if it does not significantly harm any of the others".

Investment managers will need to indicate "the minimum share of sustainable investments that are not aligned with the EU Taxonomy", i.e., the share of their investments that satisfy the EU SFDR's definition of a sustainable investment but not the EU's (Green) Taxonomy. However, this means that an investment product can be classified as "sustainable" under Article 8 or 9 EU SFDR, without supporting "sustainable economic activities" under the EU Taxonomy.

The EU Taxonomy Regulation has been integrated into the EU SFDR, with references to EU SFDR Articles 8 or 9, as these cover and relate to definitions for "environmentally" (or socially) "sustainable investments" – for more information, see section 3.2 above.

3.4   Meeting Sustainability Preferences and the Links between EU SFDR and MiFID II

In addition to EU SFDR and the EU Taxonomy's sustainability "disclosure" and "alignment" criteria, the European regulators, led by ESMA, mandated a targeted review of MiFID II to consider a client's "sustainability preferences" when and where a financial adviser assesses a client's suitability for an investment. According to ESMA (2022b):

- The assessment of suitability is one of the most important obligations for investor protection in the MiFID II framework. It applies to the provision of any type of investment advice (whether independent or not) and portfolio management.
- In accordance with the obligations set out in Article 25(2) of Directive 2014/65/EU on Markets in Financial Instruments (MiFID II) and Articles 54 and 55 of the Commission Delegated Regulation (EU) 2017/565 (MiFID II Delegated Regulation), investment firms providing investment advice or portfolio management have to provide suitable personal recommendations to their clients or have to make suitable investment decisions on behalf of their clients.

As part of a broader EU Commission initiative on "sustainable development", the MiFID II Delegated Regulation (Commission Delegated Regulation 2021/1253/EU)[24] was updated to integrate sustainability factors, risk and preferences into certain organisational requirements and operating conditions for investment firms. The amendments entered into force on 2 August 2022.

ESMA's "Final Report on the Guidelines on Certain aspects of the MiFID II Suitability Requirements"[25] was published on 23 September 2022. ESMA's "Guidelines" will apply as from 3 October 2023. They include and reinforce the definition of "sustainability preferences" included in Article 2(7) of the MiFID II Delegated Regulation. The new definition, which finally cross-refers to the EU Taxonomy Regulation and EU SFDR, is meant to ensure that (potential) clients are recommended a broad spectrum of financial instruments with sustainability-related features that meet their sustainability preferences.

In the latest "Suitability Guidelines", ESMA has also clarified that

> in order to help clients understanding the concept of "sustainability preferences" introduced under Article 2(7) of the MiFID II Delegated Regulation and the choices to be made in this context, firms should explain the terms and the distinctions between the different elements of the definition of sustainability preferences outlined under points (a) to (c) of Article 2(7)) of the MiFID II Delegated Regulation and also between these products and products without such sustainability features in a clear manner, avoiding technical language. Firms should also explain terms and concepts used when referring to environmental, social and governance aspects.

That is, to avoid mis-selling or misrepresentation, financial advisers:

- shall first assess the broader investment objectives, time horizon(s) and individual client circumstances, before asking and determining a client's potential sustainability preferences;
- financial instruments are required to have specific features to be able to meet the client's potential sustainability preferences. The proportion of investments in sustainable investments or the consideration of "PAIs" must be determined by the client and the investment products must meet these specifications.[26]

3.5 Closing the Loops in the Investment Value Chain: New Regulation for the ESG Ratings Market

Since the introduction of the EU's mandatory disclosure rules for companies and investors, some stakeholders have expressed concerns with respect to the "transparency of ESG rating activities" and regarding the potential risks of "greenwashing" linked to ESG ratings and the role these play in the investment value chain.

The "necessity for regulation in this domain" was underlined in ESMA's "Progress Report on Greenwashing",[27] published on 31 May 2023. It identified "ESG credentials", including ESG labels, ratings or certifications as "high-risk areas for investment fund managers" and for "being a major channel of transmission for misleading sustainability related claims". To prevent conflicts of interests, ESMA's Proposal:

- provides for a "separation of business and activities", which means that ESG rating providers are not allowed to provide a list of activities, including consulting activities to investors or undertakings, the issuance and sale of credit ratings, the development of benchmarks, investment activities, audit activities and banking, insurance, or reinsurance activities;
- contains provisions with regard to the competence and independence of rating analysts. ESG rating providers must, for example, ensure that they have the knowledge and experience that is necessary for the performance of duties and tasks assigned;
- requires ESG rating providers to record their ESG rating activities for a period of at least five years, to implement complaints-handling mechanisms and to refrain from outsourcing where it would risk materially impairing the quality of the ESG rating provider's internal control policies and procedures or ESMA's ability to ensure the ESG rating provid-

er's compliance with the requirements of the proposed ESMA Regulation (tbc, status December 2023).

In addition to the foregoing organisational requirements, ESG rating providers are also subject to disclosure requirements to ensure transparency towards third parties. They are, for example, required to publish on their website certain information pertaining to the methodologies, models and key rating assumptions used. They should also disclose a minimum amount of information to subscribers and rated entities. To support smaller ESG rating providers, some exemptions are foreseen for small and medium-sized undertakings.

These "transparency provisions" will be subject to further developments by way of dedicated "Delegated Acts" to be adopted by the European Commission. Alignment with other regulatory regimes and a closer alignment of all ESG ratings regulations with the International Organisation of Securities Commission (IOSCO)'s "Final Report on Environmental, Social and Governance (ESG) Ratings and Data Products Providers" (IOSCO, 2021) are currently being mandated by various industry groups in this domain.[28]

4   THE KEY QUESTION OF INTEROPERABILITY: THE EU SFDR IN THE CONTEXT OF OTHER EU AND GLOBAL REGULATORY AND NORMATIVE RULES

Looking at the pluralism of different issuer, investor and service provider disclosure regulations in the EU alone, it is becoming clear that interoperability between aims, frameworks, and criteria in use is paramount to address key challenges in the reporting value chain.

However, a range of European countries have started to issue their own sustainability classification, labelling and disclosure frameworks. Some of these developments are not fully aligned with the expectations and requirements of the EU's regime and rules, and add additional layers of complexity for investment managers distributing investment products across multiple jurisdictions.

4.1   Additional Sustainability Disclosure Rules in the EU: Additionality versus Commonality?

Below we highlight a selection of some of the key developments in European countries, "mapping" in brief the "interactions" and "implications" between jurisdictional disclosure and labelling requirements in France, Spain, Germany and the UK versus the EU SFDR:[29]

- In *France*, the Autorité des Marchés Financiers' "AMF Doctrine DOC-2020-03",[30] issued additional sustainability disclosure requirements, which have applied, since March 2020, to asset management companies of French UCITS and French alternative investment funds that can be marketed to retail investors, and to the entities marketing such collective investment products in France, but also UCITS incorporated under foreign law. It applies to all funds that "consider non-financial criteria" and makes a distinction between funds (1) "with significantly engaging approaches", (2) "with non-significantly engaging approaches", and (3) "with an approach not meeting central or limited communication standards". These categories dictate the ability to put forward a product's sustainability characteristics/objectives via the name of the product, pre-contractual documents or marketing materials. The AMF highlights the importance of "interaction with EU SFDR" in a dedicated guidance issued on 20 January 2021:[31] in order to be able to present non-financial criteria as a key aspect of the investment product, "EU SFDR Article 8 and 9 products sold in France must meet the significant approach minimum standards defined by the position-recommendation DOC-2020-03". Non-French EU SFDR Article 8 or 9 funds that do not meet the minimum investment (and other) criteria under the AMF Doctrine "have to include a dedicated disclaimer in the pre-contractual information and product documentation".

- In *Spain*, the National Securities Market Commission (CNMV) published on 1 June 2021 (and updated on 19 July 2022) a "Q&A on EU SFDR and EU Taxonomy applicability for the Spanish Market"[32] defining expectations for EU SFDR Article 8 products, going beyond EU SFDR, when and where the promotion of "socially responsible investments" (SRIs) is concerned. Newly launched financial products pursuant to EU SFDR Article 8, "may include ESG elements in their name only if the minimum amount of investments indicated in their prospectus to achieve the environmental or social characteristics that they promote is greater than 50%". The Q&A findings indicate a need for a clear definition and "labelling regime" for investment products, in line with the parameters set out by EU SFDR Articles 8 and 9 respectively.

- In *Germany*, the German Federal Financial Supervisory Authority (BaFin) published an "EU SFDR Consultation"[33] paper on 2 August 2021, seeking views on its (draft) "Guidelines for Sustainable Funds". The "Guidelines" set forth the requirements for the structuring of investment conditions of sustainable German retail funds ("Publikumsinvestmentvermögen") to counteract "greenwashing". BaFin has been consulting on the possibility to require, among other MiFID-specific requirements, that investment products labelled as or marketed as sustainable investment products "are at least 75% invested in sustainable assets". Furthermore,

the fund's investment strategy shall ensure, e.g. through investment restrictions or additional sustainability criteria, that (I) a significant contribution is made to the realisation of one or more environmental or social objectives, (II) other environmental or social objectives are not significantly harmed and (III) good governance aspects are taken into account. Finally portfolio companies may not generate revenue from energy production from fossil fuels (excluding gas) or nuclear power exceeding 10% of their total revenue; exploration for or extraction of oil or coal exceeding 5% of their total revenue; and extraction of and services for oil sands and oil shale.

As an alternative to the minimum investment quota, funds can also pursue a sustainable investment strategy, for example in the form of a "best-in-class approach". From an investment perspective, for example, the assets that are particularly advantageous from a sustainability point of view are selected or weighted more heavily. Finally, a sustainable investment fund can also be created by replicating a sustainable index. BaFin's intention is that requirements stipulated in the EU SFDR and the EU Taxonomy Regulation will not be affected by its "Guidelines", to ensure interoperability between the frameworks, and that the Guidelines are not applicable to non-German funds which are registered for distribution in Germany.

- The *United Kingdom*, after its decision to exit the European Union in June 2016, has decided not to onshore the EU SFDR. Instead, the Financial Conduct Authority (FCA) announced on 29 November 2023[34] that it is putting in place new "Sustainability Disclosure Requirements" (SDR), and its own "Investment Labels Regime" under a dedicated

"PS23/16 package"[35] supporting its "Roadmap to Sustainable Investing"[36] published in October 2021. The UK's package of measures aims to protect consumers by helping them to make more informed decisions when investing and aims to enhance the credibility of the sustainable investment market. The FCA will introduce an "anti-greenwashing rule" for all FCA-authorised companies to make sure sustainability-related claims are "fair", "clear" and "not misleading"; meanwhile the new rules for product labels aims to guide (retail) investors based on clear "sustainability goals and criteria". Previously, on 17 December 2021,[37] the FCA announced its "PS21/24 package" of annual, climate-related financial disclosure rules, linked to the Taskforce for Climate-Related Financial Disclosures (TCFD), at company and at product level, applicable to large cap listed and public interest companies, asset managers, life insurers, non-insurer FCA-regulated pension providers, including platform firms and self-invested personal pension (SIPP) operators and FCA-regulated pension providers in the UK. The climate-related disclosure rules apply from 1 January 2022 for the largest in-scope firms and, as of 1 January 2023, to smaller firms above the GBP 5 billion exemption threshold. The first public disclosures in line with these requirements must be made by 30 June 2023. The FCA also supported a workstream convened by the International Capital Markets Association (ICMA) and the International Regulatory Strategy Group (IRSG), which has developed a voluntary "Code of Conduct for ESG Ratings and Data Product Providers",[38] which launched on 14 December 2023. Additionally, discussions have started to transform the "Code" into mandatory disclosure rules, following similar developments e.g., by ESMA,[39] as outlined above.

4.2   Fund Labelling Regimes: From Normative to Regulatory Requirements?

Investment funds in Europe apply a range of so-called SRI, ESG and sustainable finance labels, as these have been mandated by investors, even prior to the introduction of the EU's regulatory regime.

Voluntary SRI, ESG and impact labels in the EU have risen fast in volume and importance over the last few years. In its most recent overview of the market, Novethic (2020) identifies 1218 funds that fall under the nine European SRI labels that they scrutinise and registers growth figures of 79% for the volume of assets covered by labels. The fast expansion of these voluntary labels indicated the initial need for more transparency, followed now by regulatory parameters, around what type of non-financial information is used in an SRI, ESG or impact investment product.

There are already a variety of voluntary labels for SRI/ESG and impact-focused funds,[40] in brief:

● Labels centred on SRI- and ESG-focused sustainable investment funds require an ESG screening of portfolios, and some combine these screening requirements with exclusion criteria that may apply to specific sectors such as "weapons" or "tobacco", or that may limit the exposure of eligible assets to certain activities such as "fossil-fuel related activities", or that may require the conformity with international safeguards related to environmental standards or social and human rights, often with normative screening references to the UN Global Compact.
● For impact-focused funds, labels may also require adherence to internationally accepted standards and/or to market-based taxonomies. For example, LuxFLAG's "Green Bond

Label" requires that applicants follow the ICMA Green Bond Principles or the Climate Bonds Initiative's "Standard", whilst its Climate Finance Label refers to the "MDBs–IDFC Taxonomy" as part of its asset selection criteria.

In the last 24–36 months, EU regulators have become more involved in European ESG fund labels and their classifications – see, for example, the guidance of the UK's FCA (2023), outlined in section 4.1 above.

The EU proposed a voluntary fund label called the "EU Ecolabel for Financial Products" and issued some technical guidance, published in March 2021.[41] The "Report" highlighted that investment funds would need to comply with a significant level of a "Green Ratio", i.e., with a comprehensive list of "environmental" and "social" exclusion criteria, and a demanding "engagement" strategy.

However, an industry analysis from the same year, by Qontigo (2021),[42] examines the (exclusion) criteria used in the 12 most important European labels frameworks, which are setting the standards for sustainable investment products in Europe, including Belgium's "Towards Sustainability" label, the German-speaking countries' "FNG Label", and France's "ISR" and "Greenfin" labels. They provide a like-for-like comparison of exclusionary criteria and portfolio-construction techniques as applied in each individual fund label and find that:

- The EU's ESG labels landscape is "highly divergent and fragmented" as there is "very little common ground between labels as to what constitutes a sustainable investment product";
- They point towards the fact that the European Union's national regulatory rules often are in themselves a "source of divergence" and that sustainable investment rules in the various EU countries are often not interpreted uniformly when and where EU SFDR legislation is concerned (note, we come to similar conclusions in section 4.3 below).
- They also highlight that a cross-jurisdictional "consistent adoption of EU Taxonomy rules could potentially change this".

Data from an analysis by ESMA (2022)[43] came to a similar conclusion and indicates that almost no sustainable funds would be able to meet the "minimum criteria" required for the proposed "Ecolabel":

- The analysis, which sampled 3,000 ESG-focused UCITS funds with EUR 1 trillion assets under management, found just 26 funds (i.e., less than 1% of its sample) have a "portfolio greenness ratio" above 50%, including ten EU SFDR Article 8 and 16 Article 9 funds.
- The analysis, which used data from Morningstar, included exclusively funds labelled Article 8 and Article 9 under EU SFDR.
- ESMA highlighted that relaxing the 50% requirement, which it said is high compared to green fund labels that already exist in some EU countries, would boost numbers significantly, hence 69 funds would meet a 40% threshold and 136 funds would meet a 30% threshold
- On the other requirement, a portfolio's "exclusionary metric", ESMA found just 73% of funds had at least some exposure to fossil fuels, meaning they would not qualify for an ecolabel.
- ESMA said that when combining the portfolio greenness ratio and ESG exclusions, just 16 funds met the requirements of the "Ecolabel".

Most recently, and in a "Public Statement" (2023),[44] ESMA has provided an update on its "Guidelines on ESG and Sustainability-Related Terms in Fund Names", including details on the timing of their publication. The updates address some of the challenges highlighted by its analysis and include:

- A threshold for "sustainable investments": initially, ESMA had proposed the introduction of a threshold of 50% in sustainable investments for the use of sustainability-related words in funds' names that would apply, in addition to an 80% minimum threshold for investments that would be E/S investments.
- ESMA did not continue with this: instead, ESMA seeks now to (1) apply the 80% minimum proportion of investments used to meet the sustainability characteristics or objectives, (2) apply the Paris-aligned Benchmark exclusions and (3) invest "meaningfully" in sustainable investments.
- A new category for "transition-related" terms is suggested to be introduced: for fund names with such terms, ESMA suggests introducing a new category for which, in addition to the 80% E/S investments threshold, the "Climate Transition Benchmark exclusions" should be applied.
- A separation of "E" from "S" and "G" terms: funds with social or governance terms in their names promoting social/governance characteristics or objectives may be too restricted in their investment universe by fossil fuel exclusions.
- Paris-aligned Benchmark exclusions continue to be merited for funds with environmental terms in their names, as it is reasonable for investors to expect funds with environmentally related terms in their names to not significantly invest in fossil fuels; where terms are combined, ESMA considers that the future guidelines would apply cumulatively.
- "Impact and transition terms": funds using these terms in their names should also ensure that investments are made with the intention to "generate positive, measurable social or environmental impact alongside a financial return" or are on a "clear and measurable path" to social or environmental transition.

ESMA expects to adopt these "Guidelines" in Q2 2024. The "Guidelines" will then apply three months after the publication on ESMA's website in all EU languages, to meet EU transparency rules.

4.3   Challenges for the EU SFDR: Investment Feasibility and Interoperability across Jurisdictions and Segments

Investing in line with sustainable investment regulation brings some inherent challenges: as outlined above, there is a "complexity jungle" when and where an alignment between many normative and regulatory developments, at a national and an international level is concerned – too many disclosure, reporting and labelling requirements for companies and investors simply still co-exist but do not necessarily correlate, and hence lack a necessary level of interoperability.

The European Union has been bold in its ambition with the EU SFDR. But despite this, investment managers have been challenged of using the EU regulatory regime as a "labelling exercise", applying the often ambiguous and conflicting policies to brand and market their strategies as "light green" (Article 8 of EU SFDR) or "dark green" (Article 9 of EU SFDR), in a bid to attract inflows into their active and passive investment vehicles.

However, the impact of regulatory measures and classifications is already taking hold: according to research by Morningstar,[45] roughly EUR 50 billion of "Paris-Aligned Benchmark" and "Climate Transition Benchmark ETFs" have downgraded from Article 9 to Article 8 (EU SFDR) in recent months, as issuers such as BlackRock, Amundi and DWS aimed to bring their investment products in line with the updated regulation.

Additionally, research by Bloomberg (2023) is emerging that is highlighting that investing in Article 8 or 9 EU SFDR funds does not necessarily mean a new or better source for "alpha". Bloomberg assessed EU SFDR fund disclosures as a means to find "differentiated performance in an investment strategy".

They concluded that given the limited time horizon since inception:

- It is currently not possible to make a clear call if compliance with EU SFDR Articles 8 and 9 means an additional "source for alpha" – by simply investing in funds based on their EU SFDR Article.
- Running a back test using the funds' environmental score improves performance, but not enough to beat a comparable benchmark.
- They were able to observe differentiated performance, however, for the US-based holdings of EU SFDR Article 9 funds when back testing using "gross margins".

In the next months and years, it remains to be seen if and how better ESG investment labels can lead to more credibility, less "greenwashing" risk and ultimately also larger net inflows to funds, as some recent academic studies[46] have highlighted.

5 CONCLUDING REMARKS: TRANSPARENT AND TRANSFORMATIVE ESG INFORMATION MANAGEMENT GUIDED BY MULTIPLE NORMATIVE AND REGULATORY MEANS – A MISSION (IM)POSSIBLE?

Despite its complexity, the EU's ESG regulatory regime, centred around the EU SFDR for investors, has a simple objective: avoid the "greenwashing" of financial products and financial advice in the EU by providing more sustainability-related information on "risks" and "principal adverse impacts".

The EU SFDR aims to ensure that EU investors have the disclosures and education, as outlined under MiFID II Guidelines, that they need to make investment choices in line with their sustainability goals, now and for the longer term.

Ultimately, and in foreseeing the market challenges, the EU's ambitions are centred around creating more harmonisation, standardisation, and better corporate and investor disclosure standards when and where ESG frameworks, metrics and classifications are concerned:

- On the corporate side, efforts are already underway to unify a variety of reporting standards, as evidenced by the "double materiality"[47] frameworks championed by the EFRAG and the GRI as well as the financial materiality frameworks as mandated by the International Financial Reporting Standards (IFRS) Foundation & International Sustainability Standards Board (ISSB), in alignment with the SASB, the International Integrated Reporting Council (IIRC), the Carbon Disclosure Standards Board and the TCFD, among others.[48] In March and June 2022, the GRI and IFRS/ISSB announced a closer collaboration.[49] This announcement was followed by a statement from the European Commission, EFRAG and the ISSB of their intention to closely collaborate on climate risk disclosure metrics.[50] They will continue to work jointly "to optimise the interoperability of their respective standards". In addition, the joint work "will focus on the digital tagging of disclosures as a means of further facilitating interoperability".

- For investors, FinDatEx launched the "European ESG Template" (EET) for EU SFDR-compliant and labels-compliant fund reporting.[51] The EET is currently voluntary, but is already being adopted across the industry, as it covers a broad spectrum of separate ESG investment frameworks and standards, such as the EU SFDR's "principal adverse impact" (PAI) criteria, the EU Taxonomy's "alignment" criteria, as well as other national ESG disclosure requirements, the EU's leading Stewardship Codes and common EU ESG labels.

However, some challenges will remain, especially when and where differences in EU versus national disclosure regulation and labelling regimes are concerned – see sections 4.2 and 4.3 above for details. In addition, tight and "non-correlated" implementation timelines for the EU regulatory regime, when and where issuers, investors and potentially service providers are concerned, as well as reporting gaps and challenges for ESG data collection and management, can lead to reporting fatigue, reporting fragmentation and potentially to a re-classification from Articles 8 to 6, and 9 to 8 EU SFDR – as outlined in section 4.3.

We summarise a few key actions that might help address these fragmentation challenges:

- *"Higher quality" and "higher integrity" ESG data at source, and across the reporting value chain*: disclosures by companies will need to be enhanced continuously and expanded in scope internationally to allow the buy-side to comply with the full set of transparency requirements under the EU SFDR and the EU Taxonomy. With regulations applying to all actors and increasingly more binding commitments, the "Aggregate Confusion"[52] can potentially finally be addressed, for all actors.
- *Interoperability of frameworks and regimes*: the increasing competition between standard setters, policymakers and regulators when and where ESG reporting frameworks are concerned needs to be further addressed, potentially through international workstreams led by international organisations such as IOSCO, or collaboration initiatives such as the International Platform for Sustainable Finance (IPSF). Meanwhile, XBRL[53] tagging towards accounting standards and the usage of legal identifiers, LEIs,[54] will enable a more rules-based approach for reporting, accounting and auditing of ESG information.
- *Transition management alongside quantifiable metrics*: a key area of vigilance will be to manage the tensions between channelling investments into sustainable economic activities while avoiding creating a sudden price tension. ESMA's new "Fund Label Guidelines" showcase promising ideas to align transition activities with existing "Climate-Aligned" and "Paris-Aligned Benchmark" trajectories to better measure and quantify "climate action" related to traceable, environmentally sustainable business activities. Through the development of an "EU Social Taxonomy", additional socially sustainable business activities for active and passive investing could here also come into scope.
- *Asset allocation shifts towards sustainable investments*: at present, we are still in the early stages of EU SFDR and EU Taxonomy regulation, but it still remains to be seen if the adopted EU rules can significantly shift asset allocation decisions. They seem to positively influence investment flows, but do not necessarily lead to better portfolio performance

if and where only EU SFDR Articles 8 and 9 funds are considered. Globally aligned reporting regimes and "accounting rules for investors", set alongside global corporate sustainability accounting standards (i.e., an "ISSB equivalent" for investors) and auditing and assurance provisions for investor reporting, which have already come into force at an EU level through the EU SFDR, might be able to address some of the remaining challenges and inconsistencies.

Over the last five years, the EU has created an interrelated and interconnected "regulatory ecosystem for sustainable finance", providing guidance for all key actors across the investment value chain, including companies, investors and service providers. With the European Supervisory Authorities aiming to address "greenwashing" and "promoting transparency", there is hope that all these efforts combined will ultimately lead to more clarity, comparability, and consistency around ESG convictions, narratives, and definitions – across the investment value chain.

NOTES

1. For an overview of so-called trade-offs in ESG investment decision-making, please see Lehmann et al. (2022).
2. For a summary of ESG investment approaches in the fund management industry, next generation, female and high net worth investor expectations and sentiments, please see Morgan Stanley (2022) for further references.
3. Please note that a similar question has been discussed in a whitepaper by Anna Georgieva and Saumya Mehrotra (Georgieva and Mehrotra, 2021); the authors find that the criteria used in the 12 most-important pieces of European legislation, country-specific fund labels and other standards guiding SI product design are not aligned and that a full compliance with all of these parameters ultimately can lead to a very restricted portfolio and hence negative performance.
4. For a comprehensive overview on sustainable finance and investment strategies, please see Roncalli, 2023.
5. PRI, 2018.
6. See Bloomberg Green, 2021.
7. Morgan Stanley, 2021.
8. Note: The "Corporate Reporting Dialogue" was convened by the IIRC, and was designed to respond to market calls for greater coherence, consistency and comparability between corporate reporting frameworks, standards and related requirements. It aims to communicate about the direction, content and ongoing development of reporting frameworks, standards and related requirements; identify practical ways and means by which respective frameworks, standards and related requirements can be aligned and rationalised; and share information and express a common voice on areas of mutual interest, where possible, to engage key regulators.
9. EU Commission, 2019a.
10. Communication from the Commission to the European Parliament, the European Council, the Council, the European Central Bank, the European Economic and Social Committee and the Committee of the Regions Action Plan: Financing Sustainable Growth, 7 March 2018, Document 52018DC0097, link: https://eur-lex.europa.eu/legal-content/EN/TXT/?uri= CELEX:52018DC0097; for further details, see also EU Commission, 2018.
11. Note: additional, interrelated EU regulatory initiatives for sustainable finance which include (1) Regulation (2019/2089/EU) on EU Climate Transition Benchmarks, EU Paris-Aligned Benchmarks and Sustainability-Related Disclosures for Benchmarks, (2) the newly adopted

EU's Green Bond Standard (EUGB, 2023), and most recently (III) the EU's Corporate Sustainability Due Diligence Directive (EU CSDDD, 2023), which sets out the obligations for large companies regarding their "actual" and "potential" adverse impacts on human rights and the environment, with respect to their own operations, those of their subsidiaries, and those carried out by their business partners. The EU CSDDD has still not been approved at the time of publication but generally aligns in many aspects and metrics with existing supply chain regulation in the EU, such as the German Act on Corporate Due Diligence Obligations in Supply Chains (Lieferkettensorgfaltspflichtengesetz) which has already been in effect since January 2023; all these regulatory initiatives are paramount to close some of the remaining gaps in the investment value chain but are out of the scope of this chapter.

12. EU Commission, 2022.
13. European Commission, 2014.
14. For further references on the applicability of the EU CSRD and the latest development, see e.g., Skadden, Arps, Slate, Meagher & Flom LLP, 2023.
15. For reference, see EFRAG, 2023.
16. For further details, see European Commission, 2023b.
17. European Commission, 2019b.
18. European Supervisory Authorities (ESAs), 2023.
19. See e.g., AXA Investment Management, n.d.
20. European Supervisory Authorities (ESAs), 2023.
21. For reference, see EU Commission, 2023c.
22. EU Commission, 2020.
23. For further details, see EU Commission, 2023a.
24. EU Commission, 2021.
25. ESMA, 2022b.
26. Note: herein the market is already experiencing challenges when and where definitions, individual aspirations and collective expectations from sustainable and impact investment vehicles are concerned.
27. ESMA, 2023a.
28. Note: the Future of Sustainable Data Alliance (FoSDA), representing leading voices in the ESG data, ratings and products industry, has initiated multiple engagements with ESMA, the FCA and other regulators, calling for clearer definitions, and an interoperability of ratings transparency frameworks, over the course of 2023.
29. Note: Switzerland has also issued its own disclosure guidance for companies, in line with TCFD, and for investors under the newly developed "Swiss Climate Scores" (2022). For further references, please refer to Macpherson and Pavlovskis, 2023.
30. AMF, 2020.
31. AMF, 2021.
32. CNMV, 2021.
33. BaFIN, 2021.
34. FCA, 2023a.
35. FCA, 2023b.
36. FCA, 2021a.
37. FCA, 2021b.
38. ICMA and IRSG, 2023.
39. ESMA, 2023a.
40. For further references, see e.g. Novethic, 2020; Megaeva et al., 2021.
41. European Commission, Development of EU Ecolabel criteria for Retail Financial Products, Technical Report 4.0, March 2021, available online: https://susproc.jrc.ec.europa.eu/product

-bureau/ sites/ default/ files/ 2021 -03/ 2021 .03 .05 %20 - %20EUEL %20financial %20products %20-%20Technical%20Report%204%20FINAL.pdf (accessed on 16/05/2024).
42. Georgieva and Mehrotra, 2021.
43. ESMA, 2022a.
44. ESMA, 2023b.
45. For references to Morningstar's research, see ETF Stream, 2023.
46. Becker et al., 2022.
47. In financial reporting, "dual materiality" means that companies would have to report on how sustainability issues affect their business and about their own impact on people and the environment.
48. Note: "financial materiality" reporting efforts by the Value Reporting Foundation (SASB/ IIRC), CDP and CDSB are setting the scene for harmonisation and standardisation.
49. GRI, 2022.
50. IFRS, 2023.
51. FinDatEx, 2023.
52. Berg et al., 2019.
53. XBRL (eXtensible Business Reporting Language) is used for standardised reporting of business information. Currently, multiple trials are in process to utilise XBRL tagging for extra-financial information.
54. LEIs (legal entity identifiers) are a unique to a legal entity such as a limited company, fund or trust or any organisation. The LEI Code consists of a combination of 20 letters and numbers and allows each entity to be identified on a global database of entities searchable by number instead of by name, as many entities may have similar or the same name. The LEI is an ISO Standard, which is now a legal requirement for many companies and will become a key source of reference for the upcoming European Single Access Point (ESAP).

REFERENCES

AMF (2020), AMF Position Recommendation, DOC-2020-03, 11 Mar. 2020, amended on 27 July 2020, available online: https://www.amf-france.org/sites/institutionnel/files/doctrine/Position/Information %20to%20be%20provided%20by%20collective%20investment%20schemes%20incorporating %20non-financial%20approaches.pdf (accessed on 01/07/2022).

AMF (2021), Implementation of the SFDR Regulation for Asset Management Companies as of March 10, 2021, Guidance Document, 20 Jan. 2021, available online: https://www.amf-france.org/en/news -publications/news/implementation-sfdr-regulation-asset-management-companies-march-10-2021 (accessed on 13/07/2022).

AXA Investment Management (n.d.), Sustainable Finance Disclosures Regulation (SFDR), Online Blog, available online: https://www.axa-im.com/important-information/sfdr (accessed on 10/07/2022).

BaFIN (2021), Konsultation 13/2021 – Entwurf einer BaFin-Richtlinie für nachhaltige Investmentvermögen, Consultation Paper, 2 Aug. 2021 and updated on 2 Nov. 2021, available online: https://www.bafin.de/SharedDocs/Veroeffentlichungen/DE/Konsultation/2021/kon_13_21_WA4 _Leitlinien_nachhaltige_Investmentvermoegen.html (accessed on 01/12/2023).

Becker, Martin G., Martin, Fabio, and Walter, Andreas (2022), The Power of ESG Transparency: The Effect of the New SFDR Sustainability Labels on Mutual Funds and Individual Investors, *Finance Research Letters*, 47, Part B, 102708, available online: https://www.sciencedirect.com/science/article/ pii/S1544612322000332 (accessed on 01/12/2023).

Berg, Florian, Kölbel, Julian, and Rigobon, Roberto (2019), Aggregate Confusion: The Divergence of ESG Ratings, Working Paper, Forthcoming Review of Finance, 15 August 2019, available online: https://ssrn.com/abstract=3438533 (accessed on 04/08/2022).

Bloomberg (2023), Can SFDR Classifications Serve as a Signal for Generating Alpha? Blog Bloomberg Professional Services, 14 Dec. 2023, available online: https://www.bloomberg.com/professional/

blog/can-sfdr-classifications-serve-as-a-signal-for-generating-alpha/?tactic-page=571455   (accessed on 17/12/2023).

Bloomberg Green (2021), The World's Biggest Investors Get Louder About ESG, Jun. 9, 2021, available online: https://www.bloomberg.com/news/articles/2021-06-09/the-world-s-biggest-investors-get-louder-about-esg-green-insight (accessed on 31/05/2023).

Bloomberg Intelligence (2021), ESG Assets May Hit $53 Trillion by 2025, a Third of Global AUM, 23 Feb. 2021, available online: https://www.bloomberg.com/professional/blog/esg-assets-may-hit-53-trillion-by-2025-a-third-of-global-aum (accessed on 10/03/2023).

CNMV (2021), Questions and Answers on Sustainability Regulations Applicable to Financial Products: Regulation 2019/2088 (SFDR) and Regulation 2020/852 (Taxonomy), 1 June 2021, updated on 19 July 2022, available online: http://cnmv.es/docportal/Legislacion/FAQ/PyR_Sostenibilidad_pdtos_finan_en.pdf (accessed on 01/12/2023).

EFRAG (2023), Sustainability Reporting Standards: First Set of Draft ESRS, Status July 2023, available online: https://www.efrag.org/lab6?AspxAutoDetectCookieSupport=1 (accessed on 10/10/2023).

ESGBook (2023), Global ESG Regulation Increases by 155% Over the Past Decade, 19 June 2023, in Yahoo Finance, Online Blog, available online: https://finance.yahoo.com/news/global-esg-regulation-increases-155-094000127.html?guccounter=1&guce_referrer=aHR0cHM6Ly9 3d3cuZ29vZ2xlLmNvbS8&guce_referrer_sig=AQAAADUqFu0I2baodU8THey8BMK2nW8Hlk 2tlxM5h29Aqa7DYGFpwmZgizgQMUgBWt82F86Kjf-UibZ8NN6mngKPucZFU8q-pZRrcrAm0O _xqN2r4DASaSFN3-lbwg4diWoMaaZVJlmCja1uKQ3SMVBCMA4aIIAAYcx_eJTPrbjYDgdd (accessed on 11/11/2023).

ESMA (2022a), EU Ecolabel: Calibrating Green Criteria for Retail Funds, Document 50-165-2329, 21 Dec. 2022, available online: https://www.esma.europa.eu/sites/default/files/library/esma50-165-2329_trv_trv_article_-_eu_ecolabel_calibrating_green_criteria_for_retail_funds.pdf (accessed on 01/12/2023).

ESMA (2022b), Guidelines on Certain Aspects of the MiFID II Suitability Requirements, ESMA35-43-3172, 23 Sept. 2022, available online: https://www.esma.europa.eu/document/guidelines-certain-aspects-mifid-ii-suitability-requirements-1 (accessed on 16/12/2023).

ESMA (2022c), Sustainable Finance Roadmap 2022–2024, ESMA30-379-1051, 10 Feb. 2022, available online: https://www.esma.europa.eu/sites/default/files/library/esma30-379-1051_sustainable_finance_roadmap.pdf (accessed on 31/07/2022).

ESMA (2023a), Progress Report on Greenwashing, ESMA30-1668416927-2498, Report, 31 May 2023, available online: https://www.esma.europa.eu/document/progress-report-greenwashing (accessed on 16/12/2023).

ESMA (2023b), Update on the Guidelines on Funds' Names using ESG or Sustainability-Related Terms, ESMA34-1592494965-554, Public Statement, 14 Dec. 2023, available online: https://www.esma .europa.eu/sites/default/files/2023-12/ESMA34-1592494965-554_Public_statement_on_Guidelines _on_funds__names.pdf (accessed on 17/12/2023).

ETF Stream (2023), Almost No ESG Funds Meet EU's Ecolabel Criteria, ESMA Warns, 5 Jan. 2023, available online: https://www.etfstream.com/articles/almost-no-esg-funds-meet-eu-s-ecolabel-criteria-esma-warns (accessed on 04/08/2023).

EU Commission (2014), Directive 2014/95/EU of the European Parliament and of the Council of 22 October 2014 amending Directive 2013/34/EU as regards Disclosure of Non-financial and Diversity Information by Certain Large Undertakings and Groups, Document 32014L0095, 15 Nov. 2014, available online: https://eur-lex.europa.eu/legal-content/EN/TXT/?uri=celex%3A32014L0095 (accessed on 16/12/2023).

EU Commission (2018), Commission Action Plan on Financing Sustainable Growth, March 2018 (including additional updates from 2018 ff.), available online: https://finance.ec.europa.eu/publications/renewed-sustainable-finance-strategy-and-implementation-action-plan-financing-sustainable-growth_en (accessed on 01/07/2022).

EU Commission (2019a), Communication on the European Green Deal, Announcement, 11 Dec. 2019, available online: https://commission.europa.eu/document/daef3e5c-a456-4fbb-a067-8f1cbe8d9c78 _en (accessed on 01/07/2022).

EU Commission (2019b), Regulation (EU) 2019/2088 of the European Parliament and the European Council, of 27 November 2019, on Sustainability-Related Disclosures in the Financial Services Sector, Document 32019R2088, available online: https://eur-lex.europa.eu/legal-content/EN/TXT/?uri=CELEX:32019R2088 (accessed on 12/12/2022).

EU Commission (2020), Regulation (EU) 2020/852 of the European Parliament and of the Council of 18 June 2020 on the Establishment of a Framework to Facilitate Sustainable Investment, and amending Regulation (EU) 2019/2088, Document 32020R0852, 22 June 2022, available online: https://eur-lex.europa.eu/legal-content/EN/TXT/?uri=celex%3A32020R0852 (accessed on 13/12/2022).

EU Commission (2021), Commission Delegated Regulation (EU) 2021/1253 of 21 April 2021 amending Delegated Regulation (EU) 2017/565 as regards the Integration of Sustainability Factors, Risks and Preferences into Certain Organisational Requirements and Operating Conditions for Investment Firms, Document 32021R1253, 2 Aug. 2021, available online: https://eur-lex.europa.eu/legal-content/EN/TXT/?uri=CELEX%3A32021R1253 (accessed on 13/07/2022).

EU Commission (2022), Directive (EU) 2022/2464 of the European Parliament and of the Council of 14 December 2022 amending Regulation (EU) No 537/2014, Directive 2004/109/EC, Directive 2006/43/EC and Directive 2013/34/EU, as regards Corporate Sustainability Reporting, Document 32022L2464, available online: https://eur-lex.europa.eu/legal-content/EN/TXT/?uri=CELEX%3A32022L2464 (accessed on 22/07/2023).

EU Commission (2023a), Implementing and Delegated Acts – Taxonomy Regulation, Online Summary, 2023, available online: https://finance.ec.europa.eu/regulation-and-supervision/financial-services-legislation/implementing-and-delegated-acts/taxonomy-regulation_en (accessed on 17/12/2023).

EU Commission (2023b), Questions and Answers on the Adoption of European Sustainability Reporting Standards, 31 July 2023, available online: https://ec.europa.eu/commission/presscorner/detail/en/qanda_23_4043 (accessed on 01/12/2023).

EU Commission (2023c), Sustainable Finance Disclosure Regulation – Assessment, December 2023, available online: https://ec.europa.eu/info/law/better-regulation/have-your-say/initiatives/13961-Report-on-the-Sustainable-Finance-Disclosure-Regulation/public-consultation_en (accessed on 15/12/2023).

European Supervisory Authorities (ESAs) (2023), Final Report on Draft Regulatory Technical Standards on the review of PAI and financial product disclosures in the SFDR Delegated Regulation, 4 Dec. 2023, available online: https://www.eiopa.europa.eu/publications/final-report-draft-regulatory-technical-standards-review-pai-and-financial-product-disclosures-sfdr_en (accessed on 16/12/2023).

FCA (2021a), Greening Finance: A Roadmap to Sustainable Investing, Policy Paper, 18 Oct. 2021, available online: https://www.gov.uk/government/publications/greening-finance-a-roadmap-to-sustainable-investing (accessed on 13/07/2023).

FCA (2021b), PS21/24: Enhancing Climate-Related Disclosures by Asset Managers, Life Insurers and FCA-Regulated Pension Providers, Announcement, 17 Dec. 2021, available online: https://www.fca.org.uk/publications/policy-statements/ps-21-24-climate-related-disclosures-asset-managers-life-insurers-regulated-pensions (accessed on 01/12/2023).

FCA (2023a), Sustainability Disclosure and Labelling Regime confirmed by the FCA, Announcement, 29 Nov. 2023, available online: https://www.fca.org.uk/news/press-releases/sustainability-disclosure-and-labelling-regime-confirmed-fca (accessed on 15/12/2023).

FCA (2023b), Sustainability Disclosure Requirements (SDR) and Investment Labels, Policy Statement, PS23/16, Nov. 2023, available online: https://www.fca.org.uk/publication/policy/ps23-16.pdf (accessed on 15/12/2023).

FinDatEx (2023), European ESG Template (EET) Version 1.1.1, Jan.–Oct. 2023, available online: https://findatex.eu/ (accessed on 17/12/2023).

Georgieva, Anna and Saumya Mehrotra (2021), Sustainable Investment Fund Labelling Frameworks: An Apples-to-Apples Comparison, Qontigo Report, October 2021, available online: https://qontigo.com/sustainable-investment-fund-labeling-frameworks-an-apples-to-apples-comparison (accessed on 20/12/2022).

GlobeScan (2021), Investors views on ESG, Dec. 2021, available online: https://3ng5l43rkkzc34 ep72kj9as1-wpengine.netdna-ssl.com/wp-content/uploads/2021/12/GlobeScan-Radar-2021 -Retail_Investors_Views_of_ESG-Full-Report.pdf (accessed on 03/05/2023).

Global Sustainable Investment Alliance (2021), Global Sustainable Investment Review 2020, 2021, available online: https://www.gsi-alliance.org/wp-content/uploads/2021/08/GSIR-20201.pdf (accessed on 03/12/2022).

GRI (2022), GRI and ISSB Provide Update on Ongoing Collaboration, Online Blog, 23 June 2022, available online: https://www.globalreporting.org/news/news-center/gri-and-issb-provide-update-on -ongoing-collaboration (accessed on 01/12/2023).

Harvard Law School Forum on Corporate Governance (2023), Paper Series, 2023, available online: https://corpgov.law.harvard.edu (accessed on 01/12/2023).

ICMA and IRSG (2023), Code of Conduct for ESG Ratings and Data Products Providers, Guidance Document, 14 Dec. 2023, available online: https://www.icmagroup.org/assets/DRWG-Code-of -Conduct-for-ESG-Ratings-and-Data-Products-Providers-v3.pdf (accessed on 17/12/2023).

IFRS (2023), European Commission, EFRAG and ISSB Confirm High Degree of Climate-Disclosure Alignment, Announcement, 31 July 2023, available online: https://www.ifrs.org/news-and-events/ news/2023/07/european-comission-efrag-issb-confirm-high-degree-of-climate-disclosure-alignment/ (accessed on 01/12/2023).

IOSCO (2021), Environmental, Social and Governance (ESG) Ratings and Data Products Providers, Final Report, Nov. 2021, available online: https://www.iosco.org/library/pubdocs/pdf/IOSCOPD690 .pdf (accessed on 01/12/2023).

Lehmann, Marie, Macpherson, Martina, and Ung, Daniel (2022), *ESG Investing and Analysis – A Practitioner's Guide*, Risk Books, London.

Macpherson, Martina, and Pavlovskis, Alexandra (2023), Scaling Climate Risk Disclosures for Investors while Addressing Interoperability Risks: A SIX Paper Assessing the Swiss Climate Scores within the New Paradigm, SIX Whitepaper, Dec. 2023, available online: https://www.six-group.com/dam/ download/financial-information/esg-data/scs-whitepaper.pdf (accessed on 16/12/2023).

Megaeva, Karina, Engelen, Peter-Jan, and Van Liedekerke, Luc (2021), A Comparative Study of European Sustainable Finance Labels, University of Antwerp, Utrecht University, 1 Jan. 2021, available online: https://papers.srn.com/sol3/papers.cfm?abstract_id=3790435 (accessed on 15/05/2023).

Morgan Stanley (2021) Sustainable Signals: Individual Investors and the COVID-19 Pandemic, Oct. 27, 2021, available online: https://www.morganstanley.com/assets/pdfs/2021-Sustainable_Signals _Individual_Investor.pdf (accessed on 12/12/2023).

Morgan Stanley (2022), Sustainable Signals – Opportunities for Asset Managers to Meet Asset Owner Demands, Report 2022, available online: https://www.morganstanley.com/assets/pdfs/CRC-5066630 -GSF_Sustainable_Signals_AM_AO_2022_report_FINAL.pdf (accessed on 05/12/2023).

Natixis Investment Managers (2021), Natixis Investment Managers Survey Finds that Environmental, Social and Governance (ESG) Investing Momentum Builds as 60% of Investors Say Companies are Accountable to More Than Just Shareholders, 9 Nov. 2021, available online: https://www.im.natixis .com/us/press-release/natixis-investment-managers-survey-finds-that-esg-investing-momentum -builds (accessed on 15/05/2023).

Novethic (2020), Overview on European Sustainable Finance Labels, 2020, available online: https:// www.novethic.com/sustainable-finance-trends/detail/overview-of-european-sustainable-finance -labels-2020.html (accessed on 04/08/2022).

PRI (n.d.), Regulation Database, Online Database, available online: https://www.unpri.org/policy/ regulation-database (accessed on 03/05/2022).

PRI (2018), A Practical Guide to Active Ownership in Listed Equities, 2018, available online: https:// www.unpri.org/download?ac=4151 (accessed on 03/05/2023).

Roncalli, Thierry (2023), *Handbook of Sustainable Finance*, revised version January 26, 2023, Université Paris-Saclay, Paris, available online: http://www.thierry-roncalli.com/download/HSF.pdf (accessed on 03/07/2023).

Schroders (2023), Global Investor Study 2023, available online: https://www.schroders.com/en/global/ individual/global-investor-study-2023/ (accessed on 12/12/2023).

Skadden, Arps, Slate, Meagher & Flom LLP (2023), Q&A: The EU Corporate Sustainability Reporting Directive – To Whom Does It Apply and What Should EU and Non-EU Companies Consider?, 9 Oct. 2023, available online: https://www.skadden.com/insights/publications/2023/10/qa-the-eu-corporate -sustainability-reporting-directive (accessed on 16/12/2023).

14. Capital market effects of climate-related disclosure

Christian Ott

INTRODUCTION

Human activity, especially since the Industrial Revolution, has contributed significantly to the increase in greenhouse gas (GHG) emissions, causing climate change (Arias et al., 2021). Climate change, which threatens the sustainability of the global ecosystem, has become a key concern for countries, companies, investors, and the general public today (European Parliament and Council of the European Union, 2003; Kolk et al., 2008; Hart and Dowell, 2011; Krueger et al., 2020), leading the United Nations to define climate action as Sustainable Development Goal 13 (United Nations: General Assembly, 2015).

While a company contributes to climate change through its business activities, climate change, in turn, has the potential to significantly affect a company's business activities (Wasim, 2019). Companies face climate-related physical risks, such as a rise in global sea levels and an increased intensity of natural disasters, albeit affecting different industries to varying degrees of severity (Pankratz et al., 2023; Wasim, 2019). Increasingly climate-conscious customers demand more climate-friendly products and services. Countries enact policies and regulations to promote the transition to a more climate-friendly economy. Companies that fail to adequately address these challenges associated with climate change face legal consequences and reputational damage (Wasim, 2019). They are, therefore, expected to implement carbon management systems to improve their carbon performance.

At the same time, there is a growing demand for investments in companies that act in accordance with the Sustainable Development Goals. Investors acknowledge climate change as one of the most critical issues facing companies today (Krueger et al., 2020; Principles for Responsible Investment, 2022). In addition, institutional investors are increasingly being encouraged by their customers, legislators, and the general public to assume responsibility for (re-)orienting the companies they invest in, or are considering investing in, toward managing climate change (BlackRock's Big Problem, 2021; Kelly, 2021). To make informed investment decisions, investors must assess how climate change affects the company's financial performance and potential for future value creation. They require the company to provide reliable information about its exposure to climate-related risks, its strategy for managing those risks, and its efforts to take advantage of climate-related opportunities (Bassen et al., 2019; Krueger et al., 2020).

Investors are likely to perceive companies that provide more comprehensive climate-related disclosure as more transparent and less risky, which is likely to translate into a higher company value. Initiatives such as the Global Reporting Initiative (GRI), the CDP (formerly known as the Carbon Disclosure Project), and the Task Force on Climate-Related Financial Disclosures (TCFD) have developed guidelines for climate-related disclosure, thereby promoting transparency and comparability. While it used to be at the discretion of companies what climate-related information to disclose, their disclosures are now increasingly shaped by reporting standards such as the European Sustainability Reporting Standard (ESRS) E1 Climate Change or International Financial Reporting Standard (IFRS) Sustainability Standard S2 Climate-Related Disclosures. At this juncture, the extensive and steadily growing literature on the investors' perception of climate-related disclosure warrants a literature review[1] that answers the following research question: *What are the capital market effects of climate-related disclosure?*

This chapter contributes to research interested in the associations between corporate social responsibility, corporate disclosure in this regard, and corporate financial performance (Christensen et al., 2021). Well aware of the multitude of findings of related studies and to better understand the complex dynamics surrounding these variables, this chapter focuses explicitly on summarizing the research on the capital market effects of climate-related disclosure. Understanding the effects of climate-related disclosure on capital markets is vital for policymakers, standard setters, investors, and companies, as it allows for informed decision-making and promotes more climate-friendly financial markets.

The chapter is structured as follows: the following section elaborates on the conceptual underpinnings. It presents the different types of climate-related information and the potential climate-related disclosure channels. It also identifies the interests of the various capital market participants in climate-related disclosure and discusses its potential capital market effects, such as the reduction of information asymmetries and the cost of capital, as well as the increase in the company's value. The literature review section synthesizes the findings of 96 published empirical studies on the capital market effects of climate-related disclosure. The last section provides guidance for future research.

CONCEPTUAL UNDERPINNINGS

Carbon Management, Carbon Performance, and Climate-Related Disclosure

Carbon management and carbon performance

Carbon management is the consideration of the impact of a company's activities, products and services, as well as systems and processes on climate change. Even if the necessary changes initially entail considerable costs, they will hopefully be reflected in lower future climate-related costs and higher revenues (Klassen and McLaughlin, 1996; Reinhardt, 1999; Hassel et al., 2005). The effectiveness of a company's carbon management manifests in its (future) carbon performance. Following ISO 14001:2015 (International Organization for Standardization, 2015), carbon emissions are the measurable results of a company's carbon performance. Overall, a reduction in carbon emissions should be reflected in saved climate-related costs and increased revenues.

Climate-related information

Both corporate disclosure and disclosure by information intermediaries are crucial in providing investors with the information necessary to make informed investment decisions (Ott et al., 2014; Blankespoor et al., 2020). Climate-related disclosure illustrates carbon management primarily qualitatively and reports on carbon performance quantitatively. Figure 14.1 provides a comparison of climate-related information.

	Qualitative climate-related information	Quantitative climate-related information

Scope	• Focus on **carbon management**
	  • Approach to mitigating the exposure to climate change-related risks and seizing on climate change-related opportunities
	  • Contextual background information
		• Focus on **carbon performance**
		  • Scope 1 carbon emissions
		  • Scope 2 carbon emissions
		  • Scope 3 carbon emissions
		  • Other greenhouse gas (GHG) emissions

Evaluation	+ Forward-looking perspective on the company's commitment to climate change − Information subject to discretion and manipulation − Disclosure subject to misreporting and misinterpretation	+ Easy to analyze and incorporate into decision-making − Heterogeneous use of measurement methods − Oversimplification of the complexity of carbon management − Disclosure subject to misinterpretation

Figure 14.1   Climate-related information

Qualitative climate-related information
Companies typically use the textual form to outline their approach to managing their exposure to climate-related risks and seizing climate-related opportunities, and provide contextual background information. Qualitative climate-related information allows detailed insights into the complexity of carbon management, offering investors a forward-looking perspective on a company's commitment to climate change. However, qualitative information can be subject to discretion and manipulation, and its disclosure is vulnerable to misreporting and misinterpretation. Thus, investors may find it challenging to assess the company's carbon management efforts on this basis (Blankespoor et al., 2020). They risk disregarding qualitative information, especially if they must integrate it into their established quantitative analysis and decision-making models.

Quantitative climate-related information
Companies classically use numerical data to quantify their impact on climate change, i.e., its carbon performance. Quantitative climate-related information includes the amount of GHG emissions, especially carbon emissions. The GHG Protocol provides guidance on the measurement of carbon emissions (Ranganathan et al., 2004). Standardized quantitative information is particularly attractive for investors because it is easy to acquire, analyze, and incorporate into decision-making (Ilinitch et al., 1998; Blankespoor et al., 2020). It tends to be perceived as high-quality information, but the heterogeneous use of measurement methods compromises its quality (Andrew and Cortese, 2011; Ott and Schiemann, 2023). Furthermore, neglecting the context may lead to an oversimplification of the complexity of carbon management and possibly to misinterpretations.

Climate-related disclosure channels
Companies may communicate climate-related information as part of mandatory disclosure (e.g., financial reports) or voluntary disclosure (e.g., sustainability reports). While mandatory disclosure, primarily addressing the traditional information needs of investors, is characterized

by specific requirements, voluntary disclosure, considering the information needs of various stakeholders, is more flexible in terms of content, scope, and timing. The climate-related disclosure channels may differ depending on the country, the industry, and the size of the company.

For some time now, there has been (a desire for) an increasing standardization of sustainability disclosure in general and climate-related disclosure in particular (Christensen et al., 2021). Figure 14.2 provides an overview of the various disclosure initiatives. Founded in 1997, the GRI was one of the first initiatives to develop a global framework to help companies "communicate and demonstrate accountability for their impacts on the environment, economy and people" (GRI, 2023).

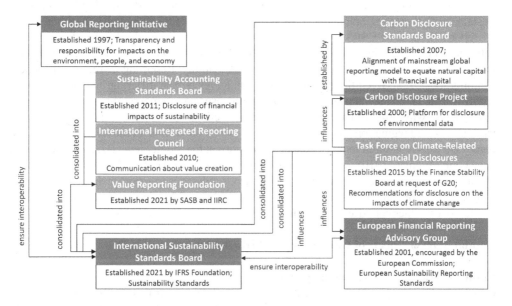

Figure 14.2   *Climate-related disclosure environment*

The CDP, established in 2000 and backed by institutional investors, collects climate-related information from companies by means of standardized questionnaires (CDP, 2023). The companies can decide whether to answer the questionnaire and make the information publicly available (Ott et al., 2017). The information collected, much of which was not previously available through other disclosure channels, is intended to help investors make informed investment decisions. The Climate Disclosure Standards Board (CDSB), established by the CDP in 2007, developed a framework for providing investors with "decision-useful environmental information" (Climate Disclosure Standards Board, 2023). In 2015, the G20 Financial Stability Board established the TCFD to give recommendations for more standardized climate-related disclosure to investors (Task Force on Climate-Related Financial Disclosures, 2023).

The Value Reporting Foundation, which emerged from the International Integrated Reporting Council and Sustainability Accounting Standards Board in 2021, and the CDSB were consolidated into the IFRS Foundation to support the work of the International Sustainability

Standards Board (ISSB) established in 2021 (IFRS Foundation, 2023b). In 2023, the ISSB issued the thematic sustainability reporting standard IFRS S2 Climate-Related Disclosures, which builds on the recommendations of the TCFD and incorporates industry-based disclosure requirements derived from Sustainability Accounting Standards Board standards (IFRS Foundation, 2023a).

With the Corporate Sustainability Reporting Directive (European Parliament and Council of the European Union, 2022) amending the Non-Financial Reporting Directive (European Parliament and Council of the European Union, 2014), the European Union wants to improve transparency and accountability on sustainability-related issues such as carbon management and carbon performance. On behalf of the European Commission, the European Financial Reporting Advisory Group brought together different stakeholders to develop the European Sustainability Reporting Standards (ESRSs). The first set of ESRSs includes the environmental reporting standard ESRS E1 Climate Change, which requires disclosure of companies' activities to manage climate change. In 2023, the European Commission adopted the ESRSs for all companies subject to the Corporate Sustainability Reporting Directive (European Commission, 2023). Even though the various initiatives pursue differing interests with their reporting standards, they appear to be interested in ensuring interoperability.

In parallel with efforts to achieve comprehensive climate-related disclosure, several countries have issued regulations on the disclosure of carbon emissions. In the United States, companies have been required to disclose GHG emissions at the facility level (U.S. Environmental Protection Agency, 2010). The European Union Emissions Trading System, a mandatory cap-and-trade system, requires companies in various industries to report their GHG emissions (European Parliament and Council of the European Union, 2003). Similar disclosure requirements exist in other countries (e.g., Australia, China, Japan, Korea, United Kingdom).

Capital Market Effects of Climate-Related Disclosure

Capital markets and their participants
Capital markets are platforms to exchange equity and debt securities, facilitating the flow of capital and efficient allocation of financial resources. While new investment securities are issued and sold on the primary capital markets, existing investment securities are traded on the secondary capital markets. Information plays a pivotal role in ensuring the functioning of the capital market.

Companies participate in the capital market by issuing investment securities, such as shares, bonds, or other investment securities, to raise financial resources. They are expected to provide relevant information, including climate-related disclosure.

Equity investors, such as asset managers, investment funds, and private equity companies, provide companies with financial resources in the form of equity securities and, thus, become their owners. The investment decisions of equity investors are based on their investment strategies and risk preferences. If they regard climate change as a critical issue facing companies today, they will invest in more climate-friendly companies (Hartzmark and Sussman, 2019; Krueger et al., 2020). They also face increasing pressure from their customers, legislators, and the general public to incorporate climate change into their investment decisions (BlackRock's Big Problem, 2021; Kelly, 2021). By analyzing climate-related disclosure, they can assess a company's carbon management and carbon performance and their impact on financial performance and future value creation.

Debt investors, such as banks, provide financial resources to companies in the form of a loan or a bond in exchange for interest and thus become their creditors. An essential criterion for a debt investor's investment decision is the company's ability to repay the debt (i.e., default risk). Debt investors may pursue a climate-friendly investment strategy voluntarily, but they also face increasing pressure to reduce the provision of financial resources to less climate-friendly companies. Climate-related disclosure can interest debt investors and credit rating agencies, as it allows them to analyze the impact of a company's carbon management and carbon performance on its default risk.

Information intermediaries, such as analysts and the media, summarize and disseminate public information and offer private information through research and interpretation (Ott et al., 2014; Blankespoor et al., 2020). Analysts enhance the investors' knowledge base for investment decisions by conducting in-depth company analyses and issuing recommendations. The media have a critical role in disseminating information to a broader audience. By summarizing and interpreting climate-related information, information intermediaries may encourage investors to consider climate-related information in their decision-making.

Other capital market participants include service providers and regulators. Service providers, such as securities exchanges or investment banks, facilitate transactions on the capital market. Regulators oversee and regulate the functioning of the capital market by ensuring investor protection and market integrity.

Capital market effects
The value of an investment security, determined on the capital market, is the result of the expected cash flows and the associated risks. Information about expected cash flows, as well as the associated risks, is of crucial importance for the functioning of the capital market. However, information asymmetries exist between the company's management and its (potential) investors (and other stakeholders) (Healy and Palepu, 2001; Verrecchia, 2001; Christensen et al., 2021). The company's management possesses private information that is useful in assessing the company's future prospects. As long as the investors lack this information, they face difficulties in distinguishing between companies with good and poor future prospects. The company's management can reduce information asymmetries by disclosing information, allowing investors to make more informed investment decisions. Climate-related disclosure may decrease information asymmetries by providing investors and other stakeholders with relevant information about a company's exposure to climate-related risks and opportunities and its efforts to manage them.

While accounting standards require the disclosure of a wide range of financial information, climate-related disclosure has long been largely voluntary. In the case of voluntary disclosure, a company's management decides at its own discretion whether to collect and disclose private information (Healy and Palepu, 2001; Verrecchia, 2001; Christensen et al., 2021). A company's management tends to disclose favorable information (e.g., a good carbon performance) because it expects it to increase the company's value and withhold unfavorable information (e.g., a poor carbon performance) because it expects it to decrease the company's value.

Adverse selection occurs when a company's management possesses private information and exercises discretion in disclosing it (Akerlof, 1970). Since investors interpret a lack of (climate-related) information as unfavorable information, the company's management is likely to fully disclose private information to make the company appear superior to other companies with less favorable information (unraveling result, e.g., Grossman and Hart, 1980; Grossman, 1981; Milgrom, 1981).

Climate-related disclosure may act as a mechanism for aligning the knowledge of management and investors about a company's carbon management and carbon performance. However, learning from (climate-related) disclosure and integrating it into their analysis and decision-making models remains an active economic choice of investors (Blankespoor et al., 2020). After learning that the disclosure exists (awareness), investors must obtain the disclosure, extract the relevant information (acquisition), and analyze the impact of the information on the company's value (analysis). Each of these three steps reflects obstacles to learning from disclosure and thus entails disclosure costs: awareness costs, acquisition costs, and analysis costs.

These theoretical foundations provide a framework for understanding the relationship between climate-related disclosure and its capital market effects. By increasing the availability of information and facilitating risk assessment, climate-related disclosure can be reflected in capital market effects, such as reduced information asymmetry, lower cost of capital, or a higher company value (Christensen et al., 2021).

Information asymmetry

Information asymmetry exists when one party involved in a transaction has superior knowledge to the other party. Corporate disclosure, including climate-related disclosure, is crucial to reduce information asymmetries between the company and its investors and among investors, thus "leveling the playing field" (Verrecchia, 2001). By increasing the availability of information, corporate disclosure facilitates the investors' estimation of future cash flows (Leuz and Verrecchia, 2000; Adhikari and Zhou, 2022). Climate-related disclosure reduces information asymmetry if investors perceive it as credible and receive information incremental to what they already know about the company's carbon management and carbon performance.

The literature discusses a variety of measures to quantify information asymmetry, including the bid–ask spread, the trading volume, and the volatility (Leuz and Verrecchia, 2000). A smaller bid–ask spread results from lower information asymmetry between buyers and sellers of investment securities, possibly due to increased climate-related disclosure. Enhanced climate-related disclosure may increase trading volume as more investors can better incorporate climate-related information into their decision-making. Climate-related disclosure may reduce price volatility by providing investors with more information and thus reducing their uncertainty.

Cost of capital

The cost of capital is the required return on an investment. Investors demand a higher (lower) return, i.e., a higher (lower) cost of capital, if an investment is associated with higher (lower) risk. Since a company's exposure to climate-related risks and opportunities increases the uncertainty of its future cash flows, it likely leads investors to integrate it into their overall risk assessment. Corporate disclosure, including climate-related disclosure, helps companies to attract the interest of investors and be included in their investment set, and makes it easier for investors to analyze the risk associated with an investment (Amihud and Mendelson, 1986; Constantinides, 1986; Cahan et al., 2016; Christensen et al., 2021). Investors who perceive a company's climate-related risks as minimal and well managed demand a lower return to compensate for it. If a growing number of investors pursue a climate-friendly investment strategy and increasingly refrain from financing less climate-friendly companies (Principles for Responsible Investment, 2022), less climate-friendly companies will face difficulties in even obtaining financial resources.

The cost of equity capital, i.e., the return that equity investors demand, is likely lower for companies with climate-related disclosure that reduces uncertainty. The literature suggests various measures of the cost of equity (Claus and Thomas, 2001; Gebhardt et al., 2001; Easton, 2004; Ohlson and Juettner-Nauroth, 2005). Enhanced climate-related disclosure may allow for more favorable debt financing terms, including lower cost of debt capital, i.e., the return that debt investors demand. A good credit rating as a result of a positive assessment of the default risk based on climate-related disclosure facilitates access to the debt capital market. The interest rate, expressed as the percentage of the borrowed amount, decreases with the decreasing risk regarding the repayment of the amount borrowed.

Company value

The company's value represents the present value of a company's expected cash flows, considering the appropriate cost of capital as the discount rate. The impact of climate-related disclosure on the company's value can arise from facilitating the prediction of future cash flows (a "numerator" effect) or reducing the cost of capital (a "denominator" effect). Higher (lower) expected cash flows and lower (higher) cost of capital increase (decrease) the company's value. Companies that provide climate-related disclosure attract greater interest from investors and are likely to trade at a premium, while companies that lack climate-related disclosure cause investors to be cautious and are, therefore, likely to trade at a discount.

The equity value (i.e., market capitalization) reflects the valuation of all information available to the equity investors. For a listed company, it can be measured by multiplying the number of shares outstanding by the share price. The entity value is the company's total market value, i.e., the sum of the market value of equity and the market value of debt. The market value is set in relation to the initial investment to assess whether there has been a creation or destruction of value. While the equity market-to-book ratio is the market value of equity divided by the book value of equity, Tobin's Q (i.e., entity market-to-book ratio) is the entity value divided by the replacement cost of its total assets (as measured by their total book value).

LITERATURE REVIEW

Review Approach

This chapter reviews the empirical literature on the capital market effects of climate-related disclosure. The search terms employed for identifying relevant research papers relate to the topic of carbon performance ("carbon", "climate change", "CO_2", "greenhouse gas"), with a focus on related disclosure ("disclosure", "report") and capital market effects (e.g., "value", "cost of equity", "cost of debt", "asymmetry", "volatility", "volume"). At least one of the search terms from each of these three groups must appear in the research paper's title, abstract, and keywords. The scientific journal databases EBSCO Business Source Premier, Emerald Journals and Book Series, ScienceDirect, SAGE Journals, Wiley Online Library, and the search engine Google Scholar are screened for relevant research papers. This literature review only includes research papers published in scientific journals. They have also been included if they were already in press by mid 2023. Findings from working papers and similar early-stage research are not considered. Additionally, the full research paper must be available (i.e., readable on a website or downloadable as a PDF file).

The research papers identified are examined for their relevance to answering the research question. While disclosure of carbon performance and other climate-related information is of interest, pure carbon management is beyond the scope of this literature review. Research papers dealing with sustainability or environmental disclosure in a broader sense are excluded to maintain a clear focus. As this chapter focuses on the capital market effects of climate-related disclosure, it does not examine other than capital market effects. In addition, only empirical studies on the topic are included; editorials, commentaries, or discussions are excluded. As a result, this literature review covers 96 research papers. A complete list of the research papers considered is available by contacting the author.

Research Papers

While the first researchers fueled interest in the topic in the 2000s (e.g., Johnston et al., 2008), the interest of researchers increased dramatically in the following decades. Empirical studies require data, so it is not surprising that the increasing availability of data from 2010 onwards has produced the first studies (e.g., Matsumura et al., 2014). Slightly less than half of the research papers included in this literature review (43 research papers) were published in the 2010s, the other half in the 2020s (52).

More than 60 different journals published research papers within the scope of this literature review. *Business Strategy and the Environment*, one of the leading sustainability research journals, published most of the research papers considered (12). Other sustainability research journals with more than three research papers are the *Journal of Cleaner Production* (five), *Corporate Social Responsibility & Environmental Management* (four), and the *Journal of Business Ethics* (three). Since the disclosure of non-financial information, such as climate-related information, is of interest to accounting researchers too, it is unsurprising that accounting research journals also published many of the research papers considered here (e.g., *European Accounting Review* (three)).

Three research papers (Matsumura et al., 2014; Bolton and Kacperczyk, 2021; Flammer et al., 2021) were published in journals classified as category 4* (*Accounting Review*, *Journal of Financial Economics*, *Strategic Management Journal*) according to the Academic Journal Guide and one (Griffin et al., 2017) in category 4 journals. With 37 research papers, category 3 journals published the vast majority. Category 2 journals published 16 research papers, and category 1 journals, 11 research papers. Twenty-eight papers were published in uncategorized journals.

Up to 1000 other research papers cite a single research paper considered in this literature review. Based on data from Google Scholar as of the end of June 2023, the seminal research paper by Matsumura et al. (2014) is the most cited one (1,088 citations). In the ranking by number of citations, Bolton and Kacperczyk (2021) follow closely behind with 986 citations. On average, the papers published in higher-ranked journals are cited much more frequently (Category 4*/4 journals: 656 citations per research paper on average; Category 3 journals: 125; Category 2 journals: 105; Category 1 journals: 59; uncategorized journals: 15).

Between one and seven authors, or an average of 2.6 authors, contribute to the research papers included in this literature review. P. M. Clarkson contributed to four research papers, L. Luo contributed to three papers, and 21 authors contributed to two papers.

Research Theory

Three-quarters of the research papers (72 research papers) included in this literature review draw on at least one explicitly stated theory. A quarter of the research papers (24) rely solely on arguments drawn from prior literature.

Half of the research papers build on socio-political theories (48), especially legitimacy theory (33), stakeholder theory (29), and institutional theory (six). Legitimacy theory suggests that companies wanting to access society's resources must demonstrate that their activities are socially acceptable (Cho and Patten, 2007). Stakeholder theory emphasizes the influence of various stakeholders besides shareholders (Freeman, 1984). Institutional theory argues that pressures of the companies' institutional context (e.g., culture) shape their activities (DiMaggio and Powell, 1983). These socio-political theories explain a company's decision to provide climate-related disclosure as a response to perceived pressure from external stakeholders other than investors (Hahn et al., 2015). They appear to provide limited guidance for explaining the capital market effects of climate-related disclosure.

Forty-one papers refer to economic-based theories such as agency theory (20), signaling theory (19), or discretionary/voluntary disclosure theory (14). Agency theory states that an information asymmetry exists between a company's managers (i.e., agents) and its investors (i.e., principals) that results from the separation of ownership and control (Akerlof, 1970; Jensen and Meckling, 1976). Signaling theory states that companies signal to investors that they are operating properly by disclosing company-related information (Ross, 1977). Discretionary disclosure theory argues that increased voluntary disclosure reduces uncertainty about future cash flows and lowers transaction costs (Verrecchia, 1983; Dye, 1985). Overall, economic-based theories suggest that investors need climate-related disclosure to reduce uncertainty in their valuation of future cash flows, particularly those that depend on a company's carbon management and carbon performance.

Other theories touched upon from time to time include the (natural) resource-based view (eight). According to resource-based theory (Barney, 1991; Hart, 1995), a company's competitive advantage depends on its resources and the capabilities resulting from their combination.

Research Setting

While companies headquartered in countries in Asia, Europe, Oceania, and North America repeatedly attract the attention of researchers, companies from countries in Africa and South America are often neglected. Most studies focus on country-specific samples, with the United States (16 research papers), Indonesia (15), China (eight), Australia (seven), India (five), Japan (four), Canada (three), and the United Kingdom (three) chosen most frequently. Other countries are occasionally studied, especially when the specific environment suggests novel insights (e.g., Griffin et al., 2021). Twenty research papers analyze global samples, and seven use regional samples (Europe: six; North America: one).

Since studies on capital market effects primarily concern listed companies, their samples are typically constructed based on major stock indices like the S&P 500 (seven). Such stock indices also serve as the basis for the CDP's survey. The resulting focus on larger companies is reinforced by the fact that smaller companies may not yet possess detailed climate-related information systems. The lack of data on smaller companies may bias sample selection.

Most studies do not restrict the sample to a specific industry. Although climate change will affect the entire global economy, it is likely to hit some industries more severely (Wasim, 2019). Nine research papers, therefore, focus on carbon-intensive industries (e.g., oil and gas, coal, electric utilities). Ten research papers analyze samples from the manufacturing industry. While 15 research papers explicitly exclude companies from the financial services industry, two studies have focused on it.

Climate-Related Disclosure

Companies disclose information about carbon management and the resulting carbon performance.

Carbon management-related disclosure

Sixty-two research papers analyze the capital market effects of disclosing information on carbon management. Climate-related disclosure analyzed in these papers is provided in the responses to the CDP (36 research papers), sustainability reports (19), annual reports (16), and other sources such as websites (six). For instance, Albarrak et al. (2019) identify tweets with carbon-related information based on a list of climate-related keywords. Surprisingly, very few papers consider multiple channels for climate-related disclosure. There is thus an implicit assumption that climate-related information is disclosed consistently across the different disclosure channels. Except for the CDP, reporting guidelines and standards are rarely referred to. However, some reporting guidelines and standards are still too nascent to have found their way into research.

To measure climate-related disclosure, the researchers focus primarily on its availability and scope. In 28 research papers, they define a dichotomous variable to distinguish between companies with and without available climate-related information. It is debatable whether the availability of individual pieces of information, such as carbon emissions, comprehensively characterizes climate-related disclosure. Some researchers draw on the participation in the CDP, which specifies a certain minimum level of climate-related disclosure, to measure its availability (e.g., Alsaifi et al., 2020). Lee et al. (2015), focusing only on CDP participants, distinguish between companies with more and less extensive climate-related disclosure.

In 40 research papers, the researchers use a score to obtain a comprehensive picture of the scope of climate-related disclosure. Most researchers conduct a content analysis to measure climate-related disclosure in sustainability reports and annual reports (26). Some researchers then develop their own disclosure scores to consider particular facets of climate-related disclosure (14). The majority opted for unweighted disclosure scores, treating all climate-related items as equally important. Other researchers replicated the disclosure score proposed by Choi et al. (2013) (12). Fourteen researchers refrain from conducting a content analysis and rely on a score provided by the CDP, which assesses the scope of a company's responses to the CDP questionnaire.

Unfortunately, only a few papers address and measure alternative dimensions of the quality of climate-related disclosure. For example, Andrus et al. (2022) assess the scope, the clarity, and the reliability as dimensions of the quality of climate-related disclosure. The reporting guidelines and standards (e.g., TCFD, ESRS E1, IFRS S2) may provide further guidance on which dimensions of disclosure quality are essential.

Carbon performance

Fifty-three research papers investigate the capital market effects of disclosing information on carbon performance. The information on carbon performance is mainly taken from the CDP (26 research papers), national emission inventories (14), or data aggregators (e.g., Bloomberg, Refinitiv; 15). The measurement of carbon performance is mainly based on actually disclosed carbon emissions, with only a few studies making estimates when carbon emissions are not available (Griffin et al., 2017; Griffin et al., 2021). Unfortunately, it is not always clear which scopes are included. If total carbon emissions are defined as the basis for measurement, it can be assumed that at least scope 1 carbon emissions are included. Fourteen papers explicitly mention that scope 2 carbon emissions are included. Only Bolton and Kacperczyk (2021) appear to consider scope 3 carbon emissions in their analyses.

Carbon performance is measured as the absolute level of carbon emissions (28) or the carbon emission intensity, i.e., the carbon emissions relative to company size (25). For the level of carbon emissions, carbon emissions are used as an absolute amount (13) or as a logarithmized absolute amount (15). For carbon emission intensity, the absolute amount of carbon emissions serves as the numerator of this ratio, and sales (18), assets (six), earnings before interest, taxes, depreciation, and amortization (EBITDA) (one), or electricity generation (one) as the denominator. The squared carbon emission intensity is used as an additional measure to capture a curvilinear relationship between carbon performance and capital market effects (Lewandowski, 2017; Trumpp and Guenther, 2017).

Capital Market Effects

Researchers use a variety of approaches to analyze the capital market effects of climate-related disclosure. Most research papers (38) examine the impact of climate-related disclosure on Tobin's Q. Its measurement is usually based on an entity market-to-book ratio. Four researchers use the equity market-to-book ratio. Bhardwaj et al. (2022) focus on the change in Tobin's Q.

Nineteen research papers use a value relevance approach that addresses the effect of climate-related disclosure on the market value. The market value of equity (total or per share) is the variable to be explained in all of these studies.

Twenty-two research papers use a cost of capital approach, with 12 focusing on the effect of climate-related disclosure on the cost of equity, 11 on the effect on the cost of debt, and one on the effect on the weighted average cost of capital as the explained variable. Two studies contrast the impact of climate-related disclosure on the cost of equity and the cost of debt (Chen and Silva Gao, 2012; He et al., 2013). The research papers focusing on the cost of equity rely on Easton's (2004) model (eight) and Ohlson and Juettner-Nauroth's (2005) model (four). Some researchers alternatively estimate the cost of equity using the capital asset pricing model, Claus and Thomas's (2001) model, and Gebhardt, Lee and Swaminathan's (2001) model. They then use these different estimates (e.g., Kim et al., 2015) or the mean of the different estimates as alternatives (e.g., Albarrak et al., 2019). For the cost of debt, the researchers use the interest rates (seven), the credit rating (three), and the loan spread (two).

Eleven research papers use an event study approach to analyze stock market reactions to carbon-related disclosure. The researchers most often use cumulative abnormal returns (eight) to measure these stock market reactions. Mora Rodríguez et al. (2021) are interested in "the fractional differencing parameter d, as it reflects the number of times the series needs to be differenced to achieve stationarity".

Six research papers examine the effects of carbon-related disclosure on information asymmetry among investors. The most often used measures are the price/return volatility (five) and the bid–ask spread (four). Several measures are typically considered simultaneously to capture information asymmetry.

Other capital market effects examined in a small subset of research papers are analyst following (two), credit risk (two), stock returns (two), and stock price crash risk (one).

Capital Market Effects of Climate-Related Disclosure

The following section will focus on the capital market effects of climate-related disclosure examined in more than three papers.

Carbon management-related disclosure

Out of the 62 research papers on the capital market effects of carbon management-related disclosure, 35 research papers provide significant results, 22 insignificant results, and five mixed results. The research papers appear to have difficulty consistently establishing the capital market effects of climate-related disclosure.

Twenty-two research papers examine the effect of carbon management-related disclosure on Tobin's Q. More comprehensive climate-related disclosure is expected to result in a higher Tobin's Q. While eight research papers identify the expected significantly positive effect of climate-related disclosure on Tobin's Q, three recognize a significantly negative effect. In addition, five research papers identify a positive but insignificant effect of Tobin's Q. The findings by Andrus et al. (2022) may provide an element of explanation. Unlike the other studies, they document a U-shaped association between the scope of climate-related disclosure and Tobin's Q, as well as an inverted U-shaped association between the clarity of climate-related disclosure and Tobin's Q.

Thirteen papers implement a value relevance approach to examine the capital market effects of carbon management-related disclosure. While five research papers provide insignificant results, eight provide significant or mixed results. In the case of significant results, the capital market appears, as expected, to assign a higher value to companies that provide (more) climate-related information than to companies that provide no or less climate-related information. Interestingly, the two papers analyzing the availability of climate-related disclosure and its scope find a negative and significant effect of the availability of climate-related disclosure and a positive effect of the level of climate-related disclosure (Griffin et al., 2017; Jaggi et al., 2018).

Twelve research papers on the capital market effects of carbon management-related disclosure examine the cost of capital. Five out of six research papers provide significant results concerning the effect of climate-related disclosure on the cost of equity. However, the results do not appear to be consistent. While the researchers using climate-related disclosure scores find the expected negative effect (He et al., 2016; Li et al., 2017; Albarrak et al., 2019; Li et al., 2019), Kumar and Firoz (2017), focusing on the availability of climate-related disclosure, find a significantly higher cost of equity. Three out of the six research papers examining the effect of climate-related disclosure on the cost of debt find the expected results in terms of significantly lower interest rates (Wang, G., et al., 2022) and significantly better credit ratings

(He et al., 2013; Khan et al., 2023). Interestingly, these researchers use scores to measure the scope of climate-related disclosure. Similarly, Lemma et al. (2019) find a significantly negative association between the climate-related disclosure score and the weighted average cost of capital. From the perspective of both equity and debt investors, it seems that it is not only the availability of climate-related disclosure that is important, but rather more its content, as measured here by its scope.

The vast majority of research papers using an event study approach examine stock market reactions to climate-related disclosure-related events (ten research papers). However, the results are inconsistent. Only four research papers provide significant results. While three research papers document negative stock market reactions to climate-related disclosure events (Alsaifi et al., 2020), Flammer et al. (2021) find a positive stock market reaction. In these studies, climate-related disclosure is usually measured on the basis of its availability, which may not sufficiently discriminate between companies.

All four research papers investigating whether and how carbon management-related disclosure influences information asymmetry show significant results. In line with expectations, both the bid–ask spread and the volatility appear lower for companies that provide (more) climate-related information. However, the results for trading volume are mixed.

Carbon performance
With regard to the 53 research papers on the capital market effects of carbon performance, 41 research papers provide significant results, three papers provide insignificant results, and nine provide mixed results. Overall, a clear pattern of a positive capital market response to an improved carbon performance seems to emerge.

In 19 research papers, researchers analyze the effect of carbon performance on Tobin's Q. With the exception of very few papers (e.g., Wang, L., et al., 2014), the vast majority of researchers find that an improved carbon performance results in a higher Tobin's Q. By including squared carbon intensity as another explanatory variable in their analyses, two studies consider that there might be a curvilinear relationship between carbon performance and Tobin's Q. While the results of Misani and Pogutz (2015) point to an inverse U-shaped relationship between carbon performance and Tobin's Q, the results of Lewandowski (2017) provide evidence for the existence of a U-shaped relationship.

Fifteen research papers use a value relevance approach to explore the association between carbon performance and market value. Almost all of these research papers point to the expected significantly positive association between carbon performance and market value. Johnston et al. (2008), in contrast to the other papers of this literature review, use data on SO_2 emission allowances to draw conclusions on the capital market effects of carbon performance. Apart from the different types of emissions used, the measurement of carbon performance based on allowances may explain their discrepant results. Interestingly, Clarkson et al. (2015) also find positive, though not significant, results for CO_2 allowances. Griffin et al. (2021), who document the "curious case" of a positive association between the carbon performance of Canadian companies and their market values, attribute their findings to the fact that Canada introduced carbon management and measurement earlier and helped companies in the transition to a more climate-friendly economy. The results of Choi et al. (2021) point to another explanation. While they find a positive effect of scope 1 carbon emissions on market value, they find negative effects of scope 2 carbon emissions. An analysis that differentiates between the scopes of carbon emissions seems to merit further consideration.

The vast majority of the 15 papers find the expected negative association between carbon performance and the cost of capital. The widely significant results of the research papers show that improved carbon performance translates into a reduction in the cost of equity (five out of seven related research papers) and the cost of debt (seven out of eight related research papers). However, Kleimeier and Viehs (2021) find a significant effect of carbon performance on the cost of debt only on the basis of direct carbon emissions. The results of Gerged et al. (2021) suggest a U-shaped association between carbon performance and the cost of equity.

Carbon management-related disclosure and carbon performance in interaction
Twelve research papers examine the capital market effects of the interaction between carbon management-related disclosure and carbon performance. The interaction effect is introduced in four research papers using a value relevance approach, six research papers analyzing the determinants of the cost of capital, and two research papers analyzing the determinants of Tobin's Q. The baseline capital market effects of carbon management-related disclosure are mostly insignificant (seven research papers), while the baseline capital market effects of carbon performance are nearly always significant (11). While all four value relevance studies point to a positive effect of the interaction between carbon management-related disclosure and carbon performance on market value, only two document a significant effect. Four of the six studies on the cost of capital identify a significant effect of the interaction between carbon management-related disclosure and carbon performance on the cost of capital. Yan et al. (2020) document a significant effect of the interaction on Tobin's Q. The interactions identified illustrate that it is crucial to distinguish between the capital market effect of carbon management, the resulting carbon performance, and the representation of both in climate-related disclosure.

DISCUSSION AND CONCLUSION

This literature review on the capital market effects of climate-related disclosure highlights the relevance of climate-related information to investors, despite a mix of different findings.

The measurement of climate-related disclosure must be critically scrutinized. The distinction between companies that disclose climate-related information and those that do not may over-simplify the analysis. This seems particularly problematic in the case of CDP data, on which many papers are based. Not all companies participating in the CDP allow their responses to the questionnaire to be made public. Ott et al. (2017) find differences between non-participating and participating companies, but also within the group of participating companies between those that make information public and those that do not. Moreover, it is important to note that the CDP has often modified the questionnaire and continues to do so today. Participation in the CDP in one year is thus not equivalent to participation the following year.

Companies disclose climate-related information through multiple disclosure channels on a voluntary and mandatory basis. Climate-related information disseminated through different channels will reach different stakeholders and be easier for them to digest, suggesting that broad dissemination will reduce awareness and acquisition costs. It is certainly an interesting question to what extent climate-related disclosure will change due to new reporting standards such as ESRS E1 and IFRS S2. Only if interoperability between different standards is achieved, will it be possible to avoid the preparation of separate climate-related disclosures. Otherwise, the question arises as to which standards will prevail as the standard for climate-related disclosure.

Single research papers go beyond measuring the completeness of reporting and include other dimensions of disclosure. A more holistic view of the quality of climate-related disclosure, i.e., measuring the fulfillment of the different dimensions of disclosure quality identified based on relevant reporting standards, could provide further insight. Which of the information published in climate-related disclosure is of primary interest to investors, i.e., which they specifically react to, is still open. The literature review indicates that emissions are of particular interest. It may also be necessary to assess whether the information reaches investors in time. It would also be worth exploring whether disclosure focusing on the changes (i.e., improvement/deterioration) would not be more interesting from the investors' perspective.

While most studies in the review seem to assume a linear relationship between carbon performance and capital market effects, only a few studies consider non-linear relationships. First, traditional studies of financial reporting are usually conducted using linear statistical models, but applying non-linear techniques may be more effective in capturing issues regarding transparency. This will help to better understand companies' behavior concerning climate-related disclosure.

The capital market will be interested in not simply being overwhelmed with information, but in receiving relevant information for investment decisions. It stands to reason that companies that disclose their carbon performance will be well regarded by investors who are concerned about this issue. At the same time, it is essential to bear in mind that the published information is not only used by capital market participants but also by competitors and the general public.

Practice can also benefit from this literature review. Companies should become aware that non-financial disclosure, such as climate-related disclosure, has capital market effects. The results confirm that investors use climate-related disclosure to assess the future prospects of companies. In conclusion, this chapter hopefully motivates managers to improve the transparency and perceived reliability of their companies' carbon management and resulting carbon performance through improved climate-related disclosure practices in order to increase their companies' value and raise financial resources from capital market participants.

NOTE

1. This literature review complements literature reviews on the capital market effects of financial disclosure (Healy and Palepu, 2001; Blankespoor et al., 2020) and non-financial disclosure (e.g., Christensen et al., 2021). It updates existing literature reviews on climate-related disclosure (e.g., Velte et al., 2020).

REFERENCES

Adhikari, A. & Zhou, H. 2022. Voluntary disclosure and information asymmetry: do investors in US capital markets care about carbon emission? *Sustainability Accounting, Management & Policy Journal*, 13, 195–220.
Akerlof, G. A. 1970. The market for "lemons": quality uncertainty and the market mechanism. *Quarterly Journal of Economics*, 84, 488–500.
Albarrak, M. S., Elnahass, M. & Salama, A. 2019. The effect of carbon dissemination on cost of equity. *Business Strategy and the Environment*, 28, 1179–1198.

Alsaifi, K., Elnahass, M. & Salama, A. 2020. Market responses to firms' voluntary carbon disclosure: empirical evidence from the United Kingdom. *Journal of Cleaner Production*, 262, 1–11.

Amihud, Y. & Mendelson, H. 1986. Asset pricing and the bid–ask spread. *Journal of Financial Economics*, 17, 223–249.

Andrew, J. & Cortese, C. 2011. Accounting for climate change and the self-regulation of carbon disclosures. *Accounting Forum*, 35, 130–138.

Andrus, J. L., Callery, P. J. & Grandy, J. B. 2022. The uneven returns of transparency in voluntary non-financial disclosures. *Organization & Environment*, 36, 39–68.

Arias, P. A. et al. 2021. Technical Summary. In: V. Masson-Delmotte et al. (eds), *Climate Change 2021: The Physical Science Basis. Contribution of Working Group I to the Sixth Assessment Report of the Intergovernmental Panel on Climate Change.* Cambridge, New York: Cambridge University Press.

Barney, J. 1991. Firm resources and sustained competitive advantage. *Journal of Management*, 17, 99–120.

Bassen, A., Gödker, K., Lüdeke-Freund, F. & Oll, J. 2019. Climate information in retail investors' decision-making: evidence from a choice experiment. *Organization & Environment*, 32, 62–82.

Bhardwaj, S., Srivastava, A. & Aggarwal, H. 2022. Do firms undertaking "green initiatives" create share holder value? *International Research Journal of Modernization in Engineering Technology and Science*, 4, 3358–3361.

Blackrock's Big Problem. 2021. *Leading NGOs call on BlackRock and Vanguard to vote for climate* [Online]. Available at: https://blackrocksbigproblem.com/leading-ngos-call-on-blackrock-and-vanguard-to-vote-for-climate/ [Accessed 30.06.2023].

Blankespoor, E., Dehaan, E. & Marinovic, I. 2020. Disclosure processing costs, investors' information choice, and equity market outcomes: a review. *Journal of Accounting and Economics*, 70, 1–46.

Bolton, P. & Kacperczyk, M. 2021. Do investors care about carbon risk? *Journal of Financial Economics*, 142, 517–549.

Cahan, S. F., De Villiers, C., Jeter, D. C., Naiker, V. & Van Staden, C. J. 2016. Are CSR disclosures value relevant? Cross-country evidence. *European Accounting Review*, 25, 579–611.

CDP. 2023. *What we do* [Online]. Available at: https://www.cdp.net/en/info/about-us/what-we-do [Accessed 30.04.2023].

Chen, L. H. & Silva Gao, L. 2012. The pricing of climate risk. *Journal of Financial and Economic Practice*, 12, 115–131.

Cho, C. H. & Patten, D. M. 2007. The role of environmental disclosures as tools of legitimacy: a research note. *Accounting, Organizations and Society*, 32, 639–647.

Choi, B. B., Lee, D. & Psaros, J. 2013. An analysis of Australian company carbon emission disclosures. *Pacific Accounting Review*, 25, 58–79.

Choi, B., Luo, L. & Shrestha, P. 2021. The value relevance of carbon emissions information from Australian-listed companies. *Australian Journal of Management*, 46, 3–23.

Christensen, H. B., Hail, L. & Leuz, C. 2021. Mandatory CSR and sustainability reporting: economic analysis and literature review. *Review of Accounting Studies*, 26, 1176–1248.

Clarkson, P. M., Li, Y., Pinnuck, M. & Richardson, G. D. 2015. The valuation relevance of greenhouse gas emissions under the European Union carbon emissions trading scheme. *European Accounting Review*, 24, 551–580.

Claus, J. & Thomas, J. 2001. Equity premia as low as three percent? Evidence from analysts' earnings forecasts for domestic and international stock markets. *The Journal of Finance*, 56, 1629–1666.

Climate Disclosure Standards Board. 2023. *About us* [Online]. Available at: https://www.cdsb.net/our-story [Accessed 30.04.2023].

Constantinides, G. M. 1986. Capital market equilibrium with transaction costs. *Journal of Political Economy*, 94, 842–862.

Dimaggio, P. J. & Powell, W. W. 1983. The iron cage revisited: institutional isomorphism and collective rationality in organizational fields. *American Sociological Review*, 48, 147–160.

Dye, R. A. 1985. Disclosure of nonproprietary information. *Journal of Accounting Research*, 23, 123–145.

Easton, P. D. 2004. PE ratios, PEG ratios, and estimating the implied expected rate of return on equity capital. *The Accounting Review*, 79, 73–95.

European Commission. 2023. Commission Delegated Regulation (EU) of 31.7.2023 supplementing Directive 2013/34/EU of the European Parliament and of the Council as regards sustainability reporting standards. Brussels: European Commission.

European Parliament and Council of the European Union. 2003. Directive 2003/87/EC of the European Parliament and of the Council of 13 October 2003 establishing a scheme for greenhouse gas emission allowance trading within the Community and amending Council Directive 96/61/EC. *Official Journal of the European Union*, L, 32–46.

European Parliament and Council of the European Union. 2014. Directive 2014/95/EU of the European Parliament and of the Council of 22 October 2014 amending Directive 2013/34/EU as regards disclosure of non-financial and diversity information by certain large undertakings and groups. *Official Journal of the European Union*, L, 1–9.

European Parliament and Council of the European Union. 2022. Directive 2022/2464 of the European Parliament and of the Council of 14 December 2022 amending Regulation (EU) No 537/2014, Directive 2004/109/EC, Directive 2006/43/EC and Directive 2013/34/EU, as regards corporate sustainability reporting. *Official Journal of the European Union*, L, 15–80.

Flammer, C., Toffel, M. W. & Viswanathan, K. 2021. Shareholder activism and firms' voluntary disclosure of climate change risks. *Strategic Management Journal*, 42, 1850–1879.

Freeman, R. E. 1984. *Strategic Management: A Stakeholder Approach*. Boston, MA: Pitman.

Gebhardt, W. R., Lee, C. M. C. & Swaminathan, B. 2001. Toward an implied cost of capital. *Journal of Accounting Research*, 39, 135–176.

Gerged, A. M., Matthews, L. & Elheddad, M. 2021. Mandatory disclosure, greenhouse gas emissions and the cost of equity capital: UK evidence of a U-shaped relationship. *Business Strategy and the Environment*, 30, 908–930.

GRI. 2023. *The global leader for impact reporting* [Online]. Available at: https://www.globalreporting .org/ [Accessed 30.04.2023].

Griffin, P. A., Lont, D. H. & Sun, E. Y. 2017. The relevance to investors of greenhouse gas emission disclosures. *Contemporary Accounting Research*, 34, 1265–1297.

Griffin, P. A., Lont, D. H. & Pomare, C. 2021. The curious case of Canadian corporate emissions valuation. *British Accounting Review*, 53, 1–21.

Grossman, S. J. 1981. The informational role of warranties and private disclosure about product quality. *Journal of Law and Economics*, 24, 461–483.

Grossman, S. J. & Hart, O. D. 1980. Disclosure laws and takeover bids. *The Journal of Finance*, 35, 323–334.

Hahn, R., Reimsbach, D. & Schiemann, F. 2015. Organizations, climate change, and transparency. *Organization & Environment*, 28, 80–102.

Hart, S. L. 1995. A natural-resource-based view of the firm. *Academy of Management Review*, 20, 986–1014.

Hart, S. L. & Dowell, G. 2011. Invited editorial: a natural-resource-based view of the firm. *Journal of Management*, 37, 1464–1479.

Hartzmark, S. M. & Sussman, A. B. 2019. Do investors value sustainability? A natural experiment examining ranking and fund flows. *The Journal of Finance*, 74, 2789–2837.

Hassel, L., Nilsson, H. & Nyquist, S. 2005. The value relevance of environmental performance. *European Accounting Review*, 14, 41–61.

He, Y., Tang, Q. & Wang, K. 2013. Carbon disclosure, carbon performance, and cost of capital. *China Journal of Accounting Studies*, 1, 190–220.

He, Y., Tang, Q. & Wang, K. 2016. Carbon performance versus financial performance. *China Journal of Accounting Studies*, 4, 357–378.

Healy, P. M. & Palepu, K. G. 2001. Information asymmetry, corporate disclosure, and the capital markets: a review of the empirical disclosure literature. *Journal of Accounting and Economics*, 31, 405–440.

IFRS Foundation. 2023a. *Climate-Related Disclosures* [Online]. Available at: https://www.ifrs.org/ projects/work-plan/climate-related-disclosures/ [Accessed 30.04.2023].

IFRS Foundation. 2023b. *International Sustainability Standards Board* [Online]. Available at: https:// www.ifrs.org/groups/international-sustainability-standards-board/ [Accessed 30.04.2023].

Ilinitch, A. Y., Soderstrom, N. S. & Thomas, T. E. 1998. Measuring corporate environmental perfor-
mance. *Journal of Accounting and Public Policy*, 17, 383–408.
International Organization for Standardization 2015. *ISO 14001:2015 – Environmental Management
Systems – Requirements with Guidance for Use*. Geneva: International Organization for Standardization.
Jaggi, B., Allini, A., Macchioni, R. & Zampella, A. 2018. Do investors find carbon information useful?
Evidence from Italian firms. *Review of Quantitative Finance & Accounting*, 50, 1031–1056.
Jensen, M. C. & Meckling, W. H. 1976. Theory of the firm: managerial behavior, agency costs and
ownership structure. *Journal of Financial Economics*, 3, 305–360.
Johnston, D. M., Sefcik, S. E. & Soderstrom, N. S. 2008. The value relevance of greenhouse gas emis-
sions allowances: an exploratory study in the related United States SO_2 market. *European Accounting
Review*, 17, 747–764.
Kelly, T. G. 2021. Institutional investors as environmental activists. *Journal of Corporate Law Studies*,
21, 467–489.
Khan, H. Z., Houqe, M. N. & Ielemia, I. K. 2023. Organic versus cosmetic efforts of the quality of
carbon reporting by top New Zealand firms. Does market reward or penalise? *Business Strategy and
the Environment*, 32, 686–703.
Kim, Y.-B., An, H. T. & Kim, J. D. 2015. The effect of carbon risk on the cost of equity capital. *Journal
of Cleaner Production*, 93, 279–287.
Klassen, R. D. & Mclaughlin, C. P. 1996. The impact of environmental management on firm perfor-
mance. *Management Science*, 42, 1199–1214.
Kleimeier, S. & Viehs, M. 2021. Pricing carbon risk: investor preferences or risk mitigation? *Economics
Letters*, 205, 1–4.
Kolk, A., Levy, D. & Pinkse, J. 2008. Corporate responses in an emerging climate regime: the institu-
tionalization and commensuration of carbon disclosure. *European Accounting Review*, 17, 719–745.
Krueger, P., Sautner, Z. & Starks, L. T. 2020. The importance of climate risks for institutional investors.
The Review of Financial Studies, 33, 1067–1111.
Kumar, P. & Firoz, M. 2017. The impact of voluntary environmental disclosure on cost of equity capital:
evidence from Indian firms. *Journal of Contemporary Management Research*, 11, 1–26.
Lee, S. Y., Park, Y. S. & Klassen, R. D. 2015. Market responses to firms' voluntary climate change
information disclosure and carbon communication. *Corporate Social Responsibility & Environmental
Management*, 22, 1–12.
Lemma, T. T., Feedman, M., Mlilo, M. & Park, J. D. 2019. Corporate carbon risk, voluntary disclosure,
and cost of capital: South African evidence. *Business Strategy and the Environment*, 28, 111–126.
Leuz, C. & Verrecchia, R. E. 2000. The economic consequences of increased disclosure. *Journal of
Accounting Research*, 38, 91–124.
Lewandowski, S. 2017. Corporate carbon and financial performance: the role of emission reductions.
Business Strategy and the Environment, 26, 1196–1211.
Li, L., Liu, Q., Tang, D. & Xiong, J. 2017. Media reporting, carbon information disclosure, and the
cost of equity financing: evidence from China. *Environmental Science and Pollution Research*, 24,
9447–9459.
Li, L., Liu, Q., Wang, J. & Hong, X. 2019. Carbon information disclosure, marketization, and cost of
equity financing. *International Journal of Environmental Research and Public Health*, 16, 1–14.
Matsumura, E. M., Prakash, R. & Vera-Muñoz, S. C. 2014. Firm-value effects of carbon emissions and
carbon disclosures. *The Accounting Review*, 89, 695–724.
Milgrom, P. R. 1981. Good news and bad news: representation theorems and applications. *Bell Journal
of Economics*, 12, 380–391.
Misani, N. & Pogutz, S. 2015. Unraveling the effects of environmental outcomes and processes on finan-
cial performance: a non-linear approach. *Ecological Economics*, 109, 150–160.
Mora Rodríguez, M., Flores Muñoz, F. & Valentinetti, D. 2021. Corporate impact of carbon disclosures:
a nonlinear empirical approach. *Journal of Financial Reporting & Accounting*, 19, 4–27.
Ohlson, J. A. & Juettner-Nauroth, B. E. 2005. Expected EPS and EPS growth as determinants of value.
Review of Accounting Studies, 10, 349–365.
Ott, C. & Schiemann, F. 2023. The market value of decomposed carbon emissions. *Journal of Business
Finance & Accounting*, 50, 3–30.

Ott, C., Schmidt, U. & Guenther, T. 2014. Information dissemination on intellectual capital in mergers and acquisitions: purchase price allocations, press releases and business press. *Accounting and Business Research*, 44, 280–314.

Ott, C., Schiemann, F. & Günther, T. 2017. Disentangling the determinants of the response and the publication decisions: the case of the Carbon Disclosure Project. *Journal of Accounting and Public Policy*, 36, 14–33.

Pankratz, N., Bauer, R. & Derwall, J. 2023. Climate change, firm performance, and investor surprises. *Management Science*, 69, 7352–7398.

Principles for Responsible Investment. 2022. *Annual Report 2021*. London: PRI Association.

Ranganathan, J., Corbier, L., Bhatia, P., Schmitz, S., Gage, P. & Oren, K. 2004. *The Greenhouse Gas Protocol: A Corporate Accounting and Reporting Standard*. Revised edition. Conches-Geneva: Greenhouse Gas Protocol Initiative.

Reinhardt, F. 1999. Market failure and the environmental policies of firms: economic rationales for "beyond compliance" behavior. *Journal of Industrial Ecology*, 3, 9–21.

Ross, S. A. 1977. The determination of financial structure: the incentive-signalling approach. *Bell Journal of Economics*, 8, 23–40.

Task Force on Climate-Related Financial Disclosures. 2023. *About* [Online]. Available at: https://www.fsb-tcfd.org/about/ [Accessed 30.04.2023].

Trumpp, C. & Guenther, T. 2017. Too little or too much? Exploring U-shaped relationships between corporate environmental performance and corporate financial performance. *Business Strategy and the Environment*, 26, 49–68.

United Nations: General Assembly. 2015. *Resolution adopted by the General Assembly on 25 September 2015 – 70/1. Transforming Our World: The 2030 Agenda for Sustainable Development*. New York: United Nations.

U.S. Environmental Protection Agency. 2010. Mandatory reporting of greenhouse gases. EPA-HQ-OAR-2008-0508. *Federal Register*, 75, 79092–79171.

Velte, P., Stawinoga, M. & Lueg, R. 2020. Carbon performance and disclosure: a systematic review of governance-related determinants and financial consequences. *Journal of Cleaner Production*, 254, 1–20.

Verrecchia, R. E. 1983. Discretionary disclosure. *Journal of Accounting and Economics*, 5, 179–194.

Verrecchia, R. E. 2001. Essays on disclosure. *Journal of Accounting and Economics*, 32, 97–180.

Wang, G., Lou, X., Shen, J., Dan, E., Zheng, X., Shao, J. & Li, J. 2022. Corporate carbon information disclosure and financing costs: the moderating effect of sustainable development. *Sustainability*, 14, 9159.

Wang, L., Li, S. & Gao, S. 2014. Do greenhouse gas emissions affect financial performance? An empirical examination of Australian public firms. *Business Strategy and the Environment*, 23, 505–519.

Wasim, R. 2019. Corporate (non)disclosure of climate change information. *Columbia Law Review*, 119, 1311–1354.

Yan, H., Li, X., Huang, Y. & Li, Y. 2020. The impact of the consistency of carbon performance and carbon information disclosure on enterprise value. *Finance Research Letters*, 37, 1–11.

15. Who signs up to the UN PRI? Evidence from the world's largest institutional investors

Paul Klumpes and Jesper Lindgaard Christensen

1   INTRODUCTION

Increasing global concern over the impact of business activities on climate change has recently led to greater levels of public scrutiny and concern about whether, and to what extent, the world's largest corporations are implementing more environmentally 'responsible' investment policies and strategies. The concern applies both to publicly listed corporations, as well as their institutional investors, 'asset owners and asset managers'.[1]

There is a substantial body of research in the corporate-oriented sustainability accounting literature that addresses a wide range of topics related to the impact of mandated disclosure and reporting standards for corporate social responsibility (CSR) and sustainability topics (e.g., Christensen, H.B. et al., 2021). However, by contrast, there is very little prior research examining such issues for their institutional investors, asset owners and asset management organisations. These legal entities range widely in organisational form and/or business purpose and range from relatively 'transparent' (investment management firms), translucent (mutual and pension funds) to opaque (sovereign wealth funds and private foundations) (Ross, 1989; Merton, 1995).

However, regardless of transparency, information from such institutional investors is only valuable and accessible if it follows commonly accepted guidelines. In the absence of standards, concerted actions, and regulation there is ample room for 'greenwashing' (Bäumlisberger, 2019; Bauckloh et al., 2023).

Following the promulgation of the more general corporate sustainability initiative (Global Compact) launched by the UN in 2000 (United Nations, 2000), the United Nations Principles for Responsible Investment (UN PRI) were launched in 2006 to facilitate the integration of environmental, social and governance (ESG) criteria into financial institutions' investment practices and reporting and to increase investor awareness of responsible investing principles (UN PRI, 2019a). Subsequently, the PRI introduced a membership fee (UN PRI, 2019b). By 2021, 3826 financial institutions had signed up to the PRI (with USD 121 trillion in assets under management, see Figure 15.1). At the time of writing, May 2024, there are 5337 signatories.

These developments raise important issues concerning the motivation and incentives facing large global asset managers and asset owners to engage with climate risk reporting, beyond a general commitment to meeting ESG targets and adhering to responsible investment principles through membership of the PRI. However, whereas asset managers are primarily legally accountable to their investor clients (which may include asset owners), asset owners themselves are accountable to their beneficiaries and more broadly to societal stakeholders. This chapter seeks to address this issue by examining alternative legitimacy and institutional theory explanations of differential incentives facing asset managers and asset owners to adhere to responsible investment principles through membership of the PRI.

The chapter provides new empirical evidence on this issue concerning the PRI membership, based on a balanced, stratified sample of the 100 globally largest asset managers and asset owner organisations, during the period of the Task Force on Climate-Related Financial Disclosures (TCFD) implementation in 2019–2020. Specifically, we address three research questions concerning incentives facing asset managers and asset owners to sign up to the PRI. Firstly, we ask whether there are different incentives facing asset managers and asset owners to sign up to the PRI. We predict that asset managers face greater incentives to sign up to the PRI than asset owner organisations, due to their desire for legitimacy in adopting responsible investment policies.

The second research question relates to the legitimation-based incentives for asset managers to sign up to the PRI. We ask if asset managers who voluntarily engage with climate change issues are more likely to be PRI signatories? By contrast, in the third research question we ask whether there are geographical differences in propensities to sign PRI. We predict that European asset owners are more likely to be PRI signatories due to institutional-related reasons, i.e., in Europe there are greater regulatory–accountability pressures on these organisations to be ethically responsible.

In addressing these research questions, we make three contributions to the existing literature. Firstly, we analyse comprehensively the determinants of PRI signatory status, through a sample of the worlds' largest asset owners and asset managers. These financial institutions are increasingly dominating the global ownership of equities and various other forms of investment (Celik and Isaksson, 2014; EFAMA, 2022) including controlling the majority of socially responsible investment assets (Majoch et al., 2017; Jansson and Biel, 2011). By contrast, prior literature on UN PRI signatories' behaviour (Majoch et al., 2017; Hoepner et al., 2021; Bauckloh et al., 2023; Slager et al., 2023; Azuma and Higashida, 2024) has used different samples (representative, pre-/after mandatory reporting and fee, early emergence period).

Secondly, the literature has been relatively silent on differentiating between different types of UN PRI signatories. Jansson and Biel (2011) argue that asset owners are more motivated to engage in climate risk investments than asset managers because of their indirect accountability to beneficiaries. Majoch et al. (2017) argue that motives for signing the UN PRI differ among asset owners, asset managers, and service providers, the latter being less inclined to sign the UN PRI.

Third, our research provides new insights into both the organisational-based ownership structure and geographical location influences over climate risk engagement by these large and increasingly important financial institutions. Our aim is to describe the UN PRI and Climate 100+ signatories in multiple dimensions, type, geography, reporting of information, whereas the underlying, detailed explanations and motivation for signing are generally outside the scope of our research.

The rest of this chapter is organised as follows. Section 2 provides the theoretical antecedents and institutional background. Section 3 overviews the main research questions. Section 4 outlines the research method, sample selection procedures, data sources and data definitions. Section 5 discusses the empirical results and findings. Section 6 concludes.

2   THEORETICAL ANTECEDENTS AND INSTITUTIONAL BACKGROUND

This section overviews the theoretical antecedents and institutional background required to understand the different accountability-related incentives facing globally large asset managers and asset owners to sign the UN PRI or not. Appendix A provides a brief overview of the development and main features of the PRI, and other related voluntary climate-related guidelines and membership organisations, which globally large asset owners and managers may choose to engage with.

2.1   Theoretical Antecedents

PRI membership offers credibility for asset managers who seek to legitimise their sustainable investment actions and policies to their stakeholder clients. Hence, an essential goal in defining corporate strategies to disclose sustainability information is to establish, maintain or repair legitimacy with regard to key stakeholders (Deegan, 2002). However, depending on their jurisdiction, asset owners may additionally face broader political, regulatory and/ or cultural pressures to engage in climate risk reporting, beyond making a more generic commitment to ESG and responsible investing principles through PRI membership. Chelli et al. (2014) propose an institutional legitimacy theory which takes the broader viewpoint of society looking 'in' and that societal norms and beliefs interpenetrate an organisation and that compliance with these institutional beliefs confers legitimacy and survival. Because globally large asset owners are financial institutions that are embedded in a broader social and institutional context, institutional-based theory predicts that their geographical origins matter for the propensity to sign up to PRI.

However, although the sustainability environmental reporting practices of corporations (of which asset managers and asset owners are major institutional investors) have received considerable attention in prior empirical literature, the equivalent challenges facing asset owner and asset manager organisations themselves have received relatively little attention, and it has primarily been on ESG reporting generally rather than their community-wide engagement through international initiatives such as the UN PRI and Climate Action 100+. Klumpes et al. (2019) provide limited evidence on this issue for a sample of large UK insurance firms and pension funds. They find that incentives facing pension schemes to engage with climate risk reporting are related to the desire to reduce information asymmetry (measured by liability risk) among their stakeholders concerning this issue. They further find that only a minority of UK pension funds reported on their actions to mitigate climate risk. However, their research was based only on a limited empirical analysis of climate change reporting by large UK pension funds during the transitional period of TCFD implementation and did not examine the degree of PRI membership of these organisations.

By contrast to asset managers, who compete globally for business that is typically based on a mix of performance fees and total assets under management, institutional theory predicts that asset owners' organisations are more idiosyncratic in nature, i.e., their governance structures and business objectives are embedded in an environment where constituencies such as regulations, norms and culture make up boundaries for organisational behaviour (Scott, 1995; Majoch et al., 2017). In this setting, organisations should communicate their values and responses to societal expectations through disclosing information, including participating in thematic initiatives like the UN PRI (Zerbini, 2017), generally instituting self-regulating initiatives.

Chelli et al. (2014) extend the 'institutional-level version' of legitimacy theory by linking the concept to the generic notion of organisations whose organisational form, objectives or cultural identity relate to the 'social contract'. Therefore, they consider 'social' organisations whose remit is linked to an express or implied social contract that is based on (1) the delivery of some socially desirable ends to society in general and/or (2) the distribution of economic, social or political benefits to groups from which it derives. Consequently, such organisations meet the twin tests by demonstrating that society both requires its services and that groups benefiting from its rewards have societal approval. Many asset owner organisations, such as pension funds, sovereign wealth funds and insurance firms, meet these social criteria for existence.

2.2   Accountability Pressures Facing Asset Managers and Owners

Defining an appropriate theoretical rationale for explaining why asset owners may or may not choose to voluntarily engage in climate risk accountability, either directly through disclosure or indirectly through membership of outside organisations such as the UN PRI or Climate 100+, is relatively more complicated than for asset managers. This is because, due to their not-for-profit legal status, the nature of their accountability relationships are more obscure than for asset managers, and furthermore differ substantially by type of asset owner.

The TCFD delineated asset owners as comprising three different types of legal entity: (a) insurance companies, which have a direct accountability for climate change engagement to their owners (i.e., shareholders and/or policyholders), (b) asset managers, who have an indirect accountability to their clients, and (c) other types of asset owners, such as pension funds and sovereign wealth funds, which have an indirect, fiduciary duty to their beneficiaries. These different accountability relationships can also be defined in terms of differences in their degree of transparency. Ross (1989) defines three different forms of transparency by financial institutions: transparent, translucent and opaque. Insurance companies are relatively transparent because of their direct agency relationship to their owners, i.e., shareholders and policyholders. By contrast, asset managers are more translucent because their transparency is limited to the legal professional relationships with their fee-paying clients. Finally, other asset owners, such as pension funds and sovereign wealth funds, are opaque institutions because of the narrowly defined fiduciary duties owed to their beneficiaries, cf. Table 15.1.

Table 15.1 shows that asset owners such as insurance companies have a first order and direct transparent relationship with their owners, shareholders and/or policyholders. Their investment objective is to maximise profit and/or meet and/or exceed the explicit policy conditions. Their reputation is also subject to efforts to mitigate conflicts of interest with their owners by demonstrating fiduciary duties of prudence and competent management of resources. By contrast, asset managers have more limited scope for accountability due to the restrictive conditions of the explicit investment contracts held with their clients, who may be other types of asset owners. These will delimit the extent of accountability to meeting the terms and conditions of the investment contract, and in fulfilling the expectations of the client in terms of meeting prescribed investment objectives. These contracts may often be legally prescribed in the form of explicit performance expectations and may involve terms for failure to meet these requirements such as legal penalties and other compensation in case of failure to deliver

Table 15.1   Accountability by asset managers and various types of asset owners

Institutional actor	Accountability relationship	Degree of transparency Ross 1989	What matters?	Why does it matter?
Insurance company	Shareholder – policyholder owner agency	Transparent	Maximise profit	Limit damage to reputation
Asset manager	Client custodian relationship	Translucent	Ensure compliance with regulations	Restitution recovery; legal entitlements
Pension fund and sovereign wealth funds	Beneficiary fiduciary duty	Opaque	Maintain ecological resilience	Preservation of beneficiaries' entitlements

these targets. Finally, other types of asset owners may have more obscure terms of reference that might be embedded either within a collective employment-related deferred compensation agreement (pension fund) or a societal-wide contract to undertake the management of public funds (e.g., sovereign wealth funds). Such organisations face greater incentives to voluntarily adhere to society-wide accountability pressures, related to climate change and/or other society-wide imperatives related to social cohesion and/or environmental laws.

3   HYPOTHESIS DEVELOPMENT

The overall research objective of this chapter is to examine various legitimacy, institutional, and voluntary public accountability theory-based incentives for globally large asset manager and asset owner organisations to voluntarily sign up to the PRI.

Our first hypothesis concerns the relative propensity of globally large asset owners and managers to engage in climate risk reporting through membership of outside organisations such as the PRI and Climate Action 100+. Consistent with the predictions of legitimacy theory, it is predicted that the propensity of asset owners and managers to be PRI signatories will be relatively higher for those organisations where there is a direct accountability relationship with their stakeholders, such as asset managers and insurance companies, than for other types of asset owners (such as pension funds and sovereign wealth funds), which have a more implicit, society-wide and implicit social contractual relationship with their major stakeholders. The first research question concerns the relative propensity of asset manager and asset owner organisations to respond to PRI-related questions compared to insurance companies or asset owners. The overview of the theoretical antecedents in section 2 implies that there will be differential incentives for asset managers, insurance companies and asset owners to voluntarily provide information to their stakeholders concerning their climate risk engagement, depending on whether or not they provide publicly available climate reports.

Due to their special legal status as social, not-for-profit organisations, common ownership and/or business relationships between various types of asset owners are a significant and material issue (Celik and Isaksson, 2013). The degree of commonality of ownership between different types of asset owners may be related to a number of factors, such as: (a) the discretion exercised by asset owners to either directly manage or outsource their investment portfolios to delegated asset management organisations; (b) the degree of commonality in ownership structure between asset owners and other types of asset owners (e.g., asset manager subsidiaries of other asset owners); (c) the investments made by asset owners in other types of asset owners (e.g., sovereign wealth funds investing in private equity and/or hedge funds); and (d) the reliance of asset owners on financial intermediary services provided by other types of asset owners and/or managers (e.g., related to brokerage, custody, investment consultancy services).

By contrast, asset managers are professional, commercial-based organisations which compete to provide professional advice and services to their retail and institutional investor clients (e.g., other types of asset owners). Furthermore, PRI signatory status provides them with organisational legitimacy in being able to show that they align their investment objectives with 'responsible investment' policies. From a legitimacy theory perspective (e.g., Deegan, 2002) disclosing information and/or joining voluntary initiatives are means for asset managers to legitimate their green credentials to their clients, who are likely to include asset owners. Consequently, they face greater peer pressure to become PRI signatories than the wider range of asset owner organisations, as summarised in Table 15.1. It is therefore predicted that asset managers have a higher propensity to sign up to the PRI than asset owner organisations.

H1: The propensity of large asset managers to be signatories of the PRI is higher than that of asset owners.

Our second hypothesis concerns what voluntary public accountability factor(s) drive asset managers and asset owners to become PRI signatories (de Boer, 2023). However, the strength of the 'legitimacy' of voluntary public accountability signals depends on whether there are adequate evaluation and enforcement mechanisms in place to maintain the credibility of the initiative. In the absence of these mechanisms and true commitment to the initiative there is a risk of greenwashing signals rather than legitimacy (Berrone et al., 2017; Bäumlisberger, 2019). Another aspect is that the credibility of voluntary disclosure can be questioned. Even if voluntary disclosure functions to increase transparency and reduce information asymmetry, effective signalling occurs when the receiver can interpret the information. To strengthen the signal associated with disclosing information, the use of standardised reporting guidelines, and membership of coordinated initiatives by outside member organisations such as Climate Action 100+, in addition to signing up to the PRI, provide this credibility and thereby reduce the risk of getting accused of greenwashing (Slager et al., 2023).

Prior empirical research (Klumpes et al., 2019; Christensen et al. (2023) shows that the degree of engagement with climate risk, defined as a combination of voluntary reporting, membership of outside organisations such as the PRI and Climate Action 100+, as well as actions taken to adopt responsible investment policies, enhances the organisational legitimacy of pension funds and insurance companies. We therefore predict that:

H2: The propensity of large global asset managers and asset owners to sign up to the PRI is related to their degree of engagement with climate change.

The third hypothesis concerns the broader societal contract between the asset owner and their primary stakeholders, which does not apply to more commercially focused asset managers, which are often subsidiaries of other financial institutions and therefore any lack public transparency. These may be subject to both organisational form and/or legal–cultural influences, consistent with the predictions of institutional legitimacy theory. Asset managers' contractual relations are primarily confined to fulfilling legal obligations to their primary stakeholders (their fee-paying clients, who might include asset owners) and are restricted by the legal form and performance incentive provisions. By contrast, asset owners may be obliged to meet broader 'duty of care'-based fiduciary duties to their primary or secondary stakeholders, which could either be explicit (e.g., insurance companies) or implicit (e.g., pension funds or sovereign wealth funds). Institutional theory therefore implies that the survival of asset owner organisations can be threatened if society has perceived that the organisation has breached its social contract (Chen, J.C. and Roberts, 2010). It also predicts that organisations are therefore likely to be subject to greater political, regulatory, cultural, and/or societal pressures to adhere to sustainability and/or climate risk reporting guidelines. Furthermore, these institutional-based pressures may be related to the geographical region in which the globally large asset manager, insurance company and/or asset owner is based. For example, the US State of California obliges pension funds based in that state to comply with climate reporting requirements. The UK government has also prescribed regulatory climate risk reporting obligations for pension funds and insurance companies. Moreover, the European Commission has set well-established accounting requirements for non-financial disclosures and has set standards for ESG reporting (European Commission, 2014) which were subsequently updated in 2022 (European Commission, 2022). Additionally, the European Commission has been active in promoting the importance of the financial sector in facilitating the green transition with a series of policy statements in 2021 (European Commission, 2021a; 2021b; 2021c). Furthermore, it has also issued guidelines for climate-related financial reporting (European Commission, 2019).

Compared to globally large asset owner organisations based in either North America or the rest of the world, it is therefore predicted that there is a greater propensity of European-based asset owners, who engage with both ESG-related sustainability directives, and with climate risk reporting guidelines, to sign up to the PRI. By contrast, asset owner and asset management organisations that are based outside the European Union have not been historically subject to such requirements, either under national or transnational law.[2] We therefore predict that:

H3: The propensity of globally large asset owner organisations to sign up to the PRI is higher in regions where mandated sustainability reporting regulation exists.

These predictions are corroborated by prior research evidence. Chen, T. et al. (2019) find that asset owners, as major institutional investors, not only generate real social impact on corporate social responsibility (CSR), but these institutions also have significantly different attitudes toward CSR-related issues and therefore face different motivations to become PRI signatories. Hoepner et al. (2021) point to a 'cultural-cognitive' factor in signing the PRI and refer to Nordic asset owners as being leading in sustainability investments during certain periods.

4   RESEARCH METHOD

4.1   Sample Selection Procedure

The sample comprises the 50 largest global asset managers and the 50 largest global asset owners in terms of assets under management, as identified in the Thinking Ahead Institute survey of the 300 globally largest asset owners and managers in 2019 (Thinking Ahead Institute, 2019a and 2019b, respectively). We have chosen to focus our research on the globally largest asset owners and asset management organisations due to their acknowledged importance in the global financial system. For example, the TCFD argued that 'large asset owners and asset managers sit at the top of the investment chain and, therefore, have an important role to play in influencing the companies in which they invest to provide better climate-related financial disclosures' (TCFD, 2017).

Likewise, the UN PRI commented, on the power of asset owners regarding directing funds to sustainable investments, that

> Asset owners set the direction of markets: the mandates they award to managers determine the objectives that the world's biggest pools of money are put to. To fulfil their duties to beneficiaries in the 2020s and beyond, asset owners will need robust approaches to investment that acknowledge the effects their investments have on the real economy and the societies in which their beneficiaries live. (Principles for Responsible Investment, 2022, p.15)

To be eligible for inclusion in our final sample, the asset owner and asset manager organisation must additionally have a publicly available website, be in continuous existence during the study period of 2019–2021, and retain its status as a large global asset owner or asset manager for the duration of the sample period. Based on a review of recent industry-based surveys of the world's largest asset owners and managers (e.g., Brigandi and Ortel, 2019; Novick et al., 2014; Asset Owners Disclosure Project, 2017; Thinking Ahead Institute, 2018; 2019a; 2019b), we define three major types of large global asset owners: pension funds, sovereign wealth funds, and insurance companies.[3] However, although many asset owners manage at least part of their investment portfolio directly, they also use asset managers for both investment and governance. Hence, 72% of the EUR 32.2 trillion assets under management administrated by European asset managers are managed on behalf of institutional investors (EFAMA, 2022). Further, some types of 'asset owners' and 'asset managers' are also either subsidiaries of, or could be alternatively classified as, 'insurers' or 'banks.[4]

This sampling criteria results in a final sample of 99 asset owners and asset managers, comprising 50 asset managers and 49 asset owners. The 49 asset owners comprise 24 life insurance companies, 12 pension funds and 13 sovereign wealth funds.

4.2 Data and Data Sources

Data was collected from both primary and secondary research sources. Primary research sources were obtained from the websites of the asset owners and asset managers of interest to this study, such as annual reports, sustainability reports and/or climate risk TCFD reports, where separately reported. Secondary data sources were obtained from two sources:

(1) The PRI website portal which includes information such as (i) the list of PRI signatories as of 2021 by type and country and (ii) climate risk questionnaires that were completed by PRI signatories for the 2019 and 2020 reporting years.

(2) The list of signatories to the CDP and to Climate Action 100+, as reported in the websites of these organisations. It should be noted that these lists of signatories only showed the names of the entities which had voluntarily signed up to these commitments as of the

data of retrieval (30 April 2022), and do not show the date on which the signatory joined the organisation.

4.3   Econometric Model Specification

The empirical model is based on the standard logistic regression model. Additionally, a probit model is used to control for econometric assumptions. The empirical tests are primarily conducted on the entire sample of 99 asset owners and asset management organisations. As a robustness check for testing H2 and H3, separate ordinal regressions are conducted for the asset management and asset owner organisation sample firms. Neither of these robustness tests shows qualitatively different findings.

4.4   Definition of Variables

The main dependent variable is the dummy variable *PRI*, indicating whether (= 1) or not (= 0) the sample asset manager or asset owner organisation was a signatory member of the PRI as of the date of the study, i.e., December 2021.

To test hypothesis H1, the dummy variable *AM* is used, indicating whether the sample organisation is an asset manager (= 1) or an asset owner (= 0).

To test hypothesis H2, we construct a categorical variable indicating the extent to which the asset owner or asset manager organisation is engaged with climate risk (from 0 to 2), ranging from voluntarily producing both a public TCFD report and being a signatory of Climate Action 100+ (= 2), undertaking either of these actions (= 1) or neither of these actions (= 0).

To test hypothesis H3, an interaction term is used to indicate whether (= 1) or not (= 0) the asset owner organisation is based within the jurisdiction of the European Union (= 1) or not (= 0) as of the study date (*EU*), i.e., AM*EU.

We additionally include three standard control variables. The first is the size of the asset owner or asset manager organisation, based on the total assets under management (expressed in billions of US dollars) at the end of the 2021 financial reporting period. For the purposes of econometric analysis, these are converted to logs (i.e., *LNSIZE*). Furthermore, there are organisational-specific factors associated with whether or not an asset manager chooses to be a member of the PRI, or whether the asset manager is independent or is controlled by other financial institutions (e.g., a subsidiary of a bank or an insurance company, which may itself be a member of the PRI). We therefore control for whether (= 1) the asset management organisation is independently controlled, or (= 0) alternatively is a subsidiary of another financial organisation (i.e., *SUBS*). The latter is presumably less able to make an independent decision as to whether or not it elects to become a signatory member of the PRI. Finally, to control for cross-country cultural dimensions, we incorporate the Hofstede (1991; 2001) 'Long term orientation' cultural dimension (*LTO*), which refers to the fostering of societal virtues oriented towards future rewards, such as retirement income saving. This may indicate whether the decision by the asset owner or asset manager sample organisation to sign up to the PRI is influenced by cross-country cultural factors.

4.5   Descriptive Statistics

Table 15.2 summarises the descriptive statistics related to each of the five major independent variables that are defined in the previous section.

Table 15.2   Descriptive Statistics – Independent variables

Variable name	Variable definition	Mean	Standard deviation
AUM	Total assets under management in billions of US dollars as at financial year ended 2020	1094.214	1195.808
LTO	Hofstede (1991; 2001) country-based cultural factor. Refers to the fostering of societal virtues oriented towards future rewards, such as retirement income saving	50.272	24.639
CE	Climate engagement with outside organisations. A categorical variable ranging from 0 to 4 indicating whether the asset owner organisation is a signatory member of up to four climate action lobby groups: (1) climate action 100+, (2) CDP, (3) Global investor action, (4) Planet One	1.283	1.196
SUBS	A dummy variable indicating whether or not the asset manager organisation is a subsidiary of another financial institution (= 1) or is independently owned (= 0)	0.242	0.431

Table 15.2 shows that the average total assets under management of the sample organisations is just over 1 trillion US dollars, although for the asset manager subsample organisations it is considerably higher (USD 1559 billion) than that for the asset owner subsample organisations (USD 669 billion). The LTO score of 50 is generally lower than that for most countries under the Hofstede (1991) classification scheme, which accounts for the considerable variation across countries in which asset owners and managers are based. The average climate engagement score of 1.3 indicates that the majority of the sample organisations are a member of at least one climate action lobby group. The *SUBS* average of 24% indicates that less than a quarter of all sample firms are subsidiaries of other organisations, although this represents nearly half of all asset manager sample organisations.

5   EMPIRICAL RESULTS

This section reports the results of empirical analysis of the sample. We first report graphical figures, which highlight the major differences in terms of PRI membership as between subsamples of asset managers and asset owners categories and by geographic region. We then provide a brief outline of the main logistic econometric test results.

5.1   Overall Trends

Figure 15.1 shows the variations in the degree of engagement with various aspects of climate risk engagement by the sample asset managers and asset owners. These trends show variations both in terms of membership of the PRI, whether the organisation produces a publicly available climate risk report, and their membership of Climate Action 100+.

Panel A: By type of entity

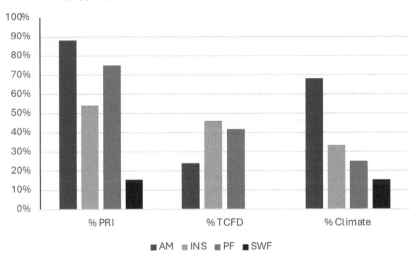

Panel B: By region

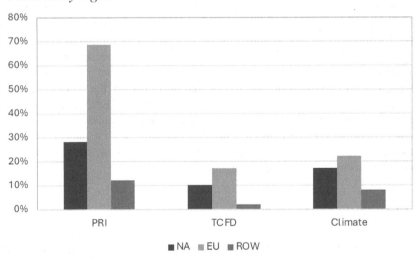

Figure 15.1   *PRI signatories, TCFD disclosures and Climate Action 100+ members as a % of total sample*

Panel A of Figure 15.1 shows the breakdown by type of business entity. While the majority of the asset manager sample are signatories of both the PRI and Climate Action 100+, only a minority (23%) produce publicly available climate risk reports following TCFD standards.

By contrast, while the majority of both the insurance company and pension fund sample organisations are PRI signatories (just over 50% and 75%, respectively), less than 50% produce publicly available reports and only a small minority (33% and 25% respectively) are signatories of Climate Action 100+. Only a small minority of sovereign wealth fund organisations are PRI and Climate Action 100+ signatories, and none produce publicly available climate risk reports.[5]

These findings are generally consistent with the predictions of research question 2, except for sovereign wealth funds. This is possibly due to the reluctance of sovereign wealth funds to engage with climate risk through membership of outside organisations such as the PRI and Climate Action 100+.[6]

Panel B of Figure 15.1 provides a breakdown of these figures by geographic region. A large proportion of the European-based asset owners are signatories of the PRI (nearly two thirds), while just under one third of the sample of large North American asset owners are PRI signatories. By contrast, only a minority of European and North American-based asset owners produce TCFD reports and are signatories of Climate Action 100+. Only a small minority of the sample asset owners based in the rest of the world are either PRI or Climate Action 100+ signatories, and only a very few of them produce publicly available climate risk reports. These findings are consistent with the predictions of research question 2, since the majority PRI members are based in Europe and are therefore subject to either EU- or UK-based compulsory climate risk reporting obligations.

5.2   Logistic Multivariate Regression Tests

Table 15.3 shows the results of the logistic regression model used to test the hypotheses.

Table 15.3   *Logistic regression of the propensity of asset owners and managers to sign up to PRI*

	Coefficient	Standard error	Z score
AM	29.831	32.324	3.13***
CE	5.726	3.054	3.27***
EU	9.506	11.253	1.90*
*EU*AM*	−0.029	0.050	2.06**
LNSIZE	1.313	0.774	0.46
SUBS	−0.555	0.576	0.57
LTO	1.030	0.015	2.02**
Constant	−0.007	0.029	1.28
Pseudo R squared	0.400		
N: observations	98		

Notes: Z statistic in parentheses. Superscripts indicate statistical significance at 0.01 (***), 0.05 (**) and 0.10 (*) percentage levels.

The overall logistical model Chi-squared statistic provides a pseudo-R-squared of 0.4, suggesting that there is a relatively good fit. The empirical results generally support the three sets of hypothesised relations concerning various incentives facing asset owners and asset manager sample organisations to sign up to the PRI. *AM* is both positive and statistically significant at the 1% level, supporting the prediction of hypothesis 1. This finding is consistent with a legitimacy theory-based explanation for why asset managers face greater incentives than asset owners to sign up to the PRI.

The categorical term *CE* is also statistically significant at the 1% level, supporting the prediction of hypothesis 2. This provides empirical support for the voluntary public accountability theory prediction that the PRI signatory status of asset manager and asset owner organisations is interrelated with their broader degree of climate change engagement through membership of other outside external organisations such as Climate Action 100+, and via producing publicly available climate change risk disclosures.

Finally, the interaction term *EU*AM* is both negative and statistically significant at the 5% level, supporting the prediction of hypothesis 3. This finding implies that there are further, institutional-level regulatory incentives facing EU-based asset owner organisations to sign up to the PRI, associated with the need to comply with EU directives related to both sustainability reporting and with climate change disclosure guidelines.

As for the control variables, although *LNSIZE* is positively associated with the propensity to sign up to the PRI, it is not statistically significant. *SUBS* is negative but is also not statistically significant. These findings suggest that neither political visibility nor lack of organisational independence are drivers of PRI signatory status. By contrast, *LTO* is positive at the 5% level of statistical significance. This suggests country-based cultural dimensions are also associated with the propensity to sign up to the PRI.

6   CONCLUSION

This chapter provides first evidence that there is a combination of organisation-specific and society-wide legitimacy factors as well as institutional-level incentives for a sample of globally large asset manager and asset owner organisations to sign up to the PRI. Our study is motivated by the growing importance of such globally large organisations in transforming capital and in addressing climate change. There is a well-established body of prior literature examining a wide range of 'sustainability accounting and reporting' issues that focuses primarily on commercial publicly listed firms, which are subject to international mandatory accounting regulations, corporate law and auditing requirements (e.g., Christensen, H.B. et al., 2021). By contrast, relatively little is known about how such issues affect their powerful institutional owners, which are diverse in organisational form and ownership–governance structure, ranging from relatively transparent public organisations (e.g., insurance firms), professional commercial asset management organisations that are often subsidiaries of financial institutions, and more opaque not-for-profit asset owners (pension funds and sovereign wealth funds). We find that asset managers face relatively greater incentives than asset owners in terms of both organisation-specific and society-wide incentives to join the PRI. Such actions both demonstrate their social credibility to their primary stakeholders as responsible investors and are interrelated with their broader climate change commitments to society generally through membership of other outside organisations and through voluntary public accountability. These results are also consistent with the findings of prior research (Majoch et al., 2017).

Consistent with the predictions of research question 1 and legitimacy theory, globally large commercial asset manager organisations face greater credibility-based incentives to become signatories of the PRI, compared to mainly not-for-profit-oriented asset owner organisations.

Our empirical results are also consistent with the predictions of research question 2, i.e., that asset managers and asset owners signing up to the PRI additionally face broader society-wide public accountability pressures by engaging with climate risk through voluntary public reporting membership of other outside organisations that lobby corporations to commit to climate change (e.g., net zero) targets.

Due to the prevalence of mandatory climate-related reporting regulations in the European Union, we also find, consistent with the predictions of research question 3 and institution-based legitimacy theory, that there is a relatively higher propensity of large European-based asset owners to sign up to the PRI, compared to those based in other geographical regions. This is likely due to the relatively more ESG-oriented EU regulatory environment, which requires them to comply with a range of ethically focused regulations, sustainability reporting directives and climate disclosure guidelines.

Our findings are subject to a few limitations and need further research. Firstly, our research was based on the publicly available information provided either by the organisation itself or via secondary sources such as the PRI website and Climate Action 100+, as of the date of publication. Because this area is rapidly evolving over time, it is likely that these findings could quickly become dated. Second, there are significant country-based and entity-based variations across these entities, which makes drawing valid inferences difficult. For example, many of the sample asset managers are subsidiaries of insurance companies and other financial institutions, which may result in gaps and/or overlaps in the analysis. Likewise, asset managers have several asset owners among their customers, some of which may have more than one of the asset managers providing services. Such services can include active ownership, which renders guidelines from owners to managers regarding, for example, requirements to sign the UN PRI. Moreover, our pension fund and sovereign wealth fund samples are based on organisations based in a wide range of jurisdictions, so that cultural–political and/or legal institutional variations may complicate the comparability of findings.

Notwithstanding these limitations, our research provides new insights into the nature and dimensions of various organisation, society-wide and institutional-level incentives facing a sample of globally large asset owners and asset managers to sign up to the PRI. Our findings have a number of implications both for research and public policy. Firstly, our research has uncovered a wide range of asset management and asset owner organisations whose transparency regarding both ESG generally and climate change specifically has lacked prior research. Further research could be undertaken regarding the motivations and reasons why these organisations choose whether to be signatories to the PRI, and more generally what other cultural, political and/or economic factors might explain this. Additionally, our research findings revealed that there are considerable overlaps between the business and/or contractual relationships between these organisations and other types of asset owners that could warrant further research, such as examining further whether the extent to which investment activities of asset owners are outsourced to professional asset managers affects the 'green credentials'. Finally, while our study has limited the scope of investigation to just a small sample of the globally largest asset owners and asset management organisations, further research could address these issues more comprehensively using a broader data set.

There are also a few important public policy implications of our research findings. Firstly, the scope of our research was limited by the publicly available PRI signatory reports and other publicly available information concerning the extent to which the sample organisations engaged with the broader public about their ESG and/or climate change engagement. Thus, our findings were reliant on the credibility of these reports, which were not audited or verified and therefore could be subject to 'greenwashing'. Furthermore, given the recent disbanding of the TCFD, there is currently a lack of publicly verifiable information as to whether these types of organisations are aligning their climate and/or ESG policies, procedures and reporting practices with evolving national and supranational rules, standards and guidelines.[7]

In terms of implications, it could be debated whether PRI signatories should be incentivised to provide a higher percentage of responses to climate report questions, for example, by making it a precondition for membership. Similarly, the UN PRI could consider continuing and enhancing the requirements to be PRI signatories, including charging fees and requiring mandatory reporting aligned with common guidelines. Moreover, international and national regulators could do more to enforce increased climate change reporting transparency by large asset owner and asset manager organisations by enhancing the already ongoing change in paradigm regarding the voluntary versus mandatory reporting requirements (spurred by the EU Commission).

Further research could expand and extend our research in several ways. For example, it would be interesting to know the entity-specific, country-level or policy-level variations that might explain the observed variations in the degree and nature of climate risk engagement. Further research could also be conducted to extend the analysis to a broader range of institutions, and to examine whether the findings are influenced by the recency of PRI signatory status. This and other issues are left for future research.

Acknowledgements and Funding

This research was funded by the Independent Research Fund Denmark, grant number 0217-00425B. We furthermore acknowledge the comments from participants at the paper development workshop organised at Audencia Business School, Nantes, France, 7–8 September 2023.

NOTES

1. In this and the next section, we use the generic term 'asset owner' to loosely include various types of major institutional investors, such as pension funds, sovereign wealth funds, as well as asset managers. We clarify these distinctions later in both the research questions and subsequent overview of the research design.
2. This situation has subsequently changed from 2024, with the implementation of the IFRS S2 Climate Change reporting standard (IFRS, 2023b), as well as the introduction of the Securities and Exchange Commission's proposed rule to enhance the climate-related disclosures for US listed corporate entities (Securities and Exchange Commission, 2022).
3. Unlike other industry sectors (e.g., classified according to Standard Industrial Classification Codes, or Global Industry Classification Standard), there is no universally consistent acceptable method of classifying various types of asset owners and asset managers. For the purposes of analysis, we combined sovereign wealth funds and foundations and endowment funds in a single category due to their similar opaqueness. We have not yet analysed 'new' forms of asset owners, such as hedge funds and private equity funds, in this chapter.

4. These two sectors were separately analysed by TCFD (2019). Since insurance firms are classified as part asset owners (e.g., Brigandi and Ortel, 2019; Blackrock, 2014) we plan to include them in our sample, as a consistency check on the TCFD's own analysis.

5. The effectiveness of Climate Action 100+ in providing climate risk and engagement and reporting by its signatory organisations has been criticised (ShareAction, 2022). Similarly, it could be debated if Climate Action 100+ is the most appropriate organisation to include in the analysis. Other, similar organisations include NetZero Asset Owner Alliance, https://www.unepfi.org/net-zero-alliance/.

6. A large number of globally large sovereign wealth funds are members of more bespoke outside organisations, such as the International Forum of Sovereign Wealth Funds and the One Planet Summit of Sovereign Wealth Funds (2021).

7. The IFRS Foundation established the International Sustainability Standard Board to develop the new IFRS S1 and S2 standards. However, in its website, the IFRS Foundation (IFRS, 2023b) refers to the ISSB as fulfilling its role in connection with 'companies' and their 'investors', rather than to broader society-based financial institutions such as asset owners. It is therefore doubtful that the prior level of monitoring of alignment with climate-related financial disclosures by the former TCFD will be continued by the ISSB.

REFERENCES

Asset Owners Disclosure Project (AODP) (2017). *Global Climate Index 2017: Rating the World's Investors on Climate Related Financial Risk.* London: AODP.

Azuma, K. and Higashida, A. (2024). Climate change disclosure and evolving institutional investor salience: roles of the Principles for Responsible Investment. *Business Strategy and the Environment*, 33(4), 3669–3686.

Bäumlisberger, D. (2019). The United Nations Global Compact as a facilitator of the Lockean social contract. *Journal of Business Ethics*, 159, 187–200.

Bauckloh, T., Schaltegger, S., Utz, S., Zeile, S. and Zwergel, B. (2023). Active first movers vs. late free-riders? An empirical analysis of UN PRI signatories' commitment. *Journal of Business Ethics*, 182, 747–781.

Berrone, P., Fosfuri, A. and Gelabert, L. (2017). Does greenwashing pay off? Understanding the relationship between environmental actions and environmental legitimacy. *Journal of Business Ethics*, 144(3), 363–379.

Blackrock (2014). *Who Owns the Assets?* Blackrock, New York. https://www.blackrock.com/corporate/literature/whitepaper/viewpoint-who-owns-the-assets-may-2014.pdf.

Brigandi, T. and Ortel, S. (2019). *The Seven Kinds of Asset Owner Institutions.* CFA Institute Blog, New York.

Celik, S. and Isaksson, M. (2014). Institutional investors and ownership engagement. *OECD Journal: Financial Market Trends*, 2013(2), 93–114.

Chelli, M., Durocher, S. and Richard, J. (2014). France's new economic regulations: insights from institutional legitimacy theory. *Accounting, Auditing & Accountability Journal*, 27(2), 283–310.

Chen, T., Dong, H. and Lin, C. (2019). Institutional shareholders and corporate social responsibility. *Journal of Financial Economics*, 135(2), 483–504.

Chen, J.C. and Roberts, R.W. (2010). Toward a more coherent understanding of the organization–society relationship: a theoretical consideration for social and environmental accounting research. *Journal of Business Ethics*, 97, 651–665.

Christensen, H.B., Hail, L. and Leuz, C. (2021). Mandatory CSR and sustainability reporting: economic analysis and literature review. *Review of Accounting Studies*, 26(3), 1176–1248.

Christensen, J., Klumpes, P., Mateus, C. and Mateus, I. (2023). Climate change risk engagement and environmental accountability of pension funds: international evidence. Working Paper, AAUBS.

De Boer, T. (2023) Updating public accountability: a conceptual framework of voluntary accountability. *Public Management Review*, 25(6), 1128–1151.

Deegan, C. (2002). The legitimising effect of social and environmental disclosures: a theoretical foundation. *Accounting, Auditing and Accountability Journal*, 15, 282–311.

EFAMA (2022). *Asset Management in Europe*. 14th edn. Brussels: European Fund and Asset Management Association.

European Commission (2014). Non-Financial Reporting Directive EU/2014/95). Brussels: European Commission.

European Commission (2019). *Guidelines on Reporting Climate-Related Information*. Brussels: European Commission.

European Commission (2021a). *Forging a Climate-Resilient Europe*. Brussels: European Commission.

European Commission (2021b). *Strategy for Financing the Transition to a Sustainable Economy*. Brussels: European Commission.

European Commission (2021c). *The Green Deal*. Brussels: European Commission.

European Commission (2022). Corporate Sustainability Reporting Directive EU/2022/2464). Brussels: European Commission.

Hoepner, A.G., Majoch, A.A., & Zhou, X.Y. (2021). Does an asset owner's institutional setting influence its decision to sign the Principles for Responsible Investment? *Journal of Business Ethics*, 168, 389–414.

Hofstede, G. (1991). *Cultures and Organizations: Software of the Mind: Intercultural Cooperation and Its Importance for Survival*. New York: McGraw-Hill.

Hofstede, G. (2001). *Cultures Consequences: Comparing Values, Behaviors, Institutions and Organizations Across Nations*. London: Sage Publications.

IFRS Foundation (2023a). IFRS S1 General Requirements for Disclosure of Sustainability-Related Financial Information. London: IFRS.

IFRS Foundation (2023b). IFRS S2 Climate-Related Disclosures. London: IFRS.

International Forum of Sovereign Wealth Funds and One Planet Summit of Sovereign Wealth Funds (2021). *Mighty Oaks from Little Acorns Grow: Sovereign Wealth Funds' Progress on Climate Change*.

Jansson, M., & Biel, A. (2011). Motives to engage in sustainable investment: a comparison between institutional and private investors. *Sustainable Development*, 19(2), 135–142.

Klumpes, P., Acharyya, M., Kakar, G. and Sturgess, E. (2019). Climate risk reporting practices by UK insurance companies and pension schemes. *British Actuarial Journal*, 24(30), 1–32.

Majoch, A.A.A., Hoepner, A.G.F. and Hebb, T. (2017). Sources of stakeholder salience in the responsible investment movement: why do investors sign the Principles for Responsible Investment? *Journal of Business Ethics*, 140(4), 723–741.

Merton, R.C. (1995). A functional perspective of financial intermediation. *Financial Management*, 24(2), 23–41.

Novick, B., Golub, B., Kushel, R., Cound, J., Medero, J. and Rosenblum, A. (2014). *Who Owns the Assets?* New York: Blackrock.

Principles for Responsible Investment, Generation Foundation and UN Environmental Programme (2022). *A Legal Framework for Impact*. London: PRI.

Ross, A. (1989). Institutional markets, financial marketing, and financial innovation. *Journal of Finance*, July, 541–556.

Scott, W.R. (1995). *Institutions and Organizations. Foundations for Organizational Science*. London: Sage.

Securities and Exchange Commission (2022). *The Enhancement and Standardization of Climate-Related Disclosures for Investors*. Washington DC: SEC.

ShareAction (2022). *Power in Numbers? An Assessment of CA100+ Engagement on Climate Change*. London: ShareAction.

Slager, R., Chuah, K. Gond, J.-P., Furnari, S. and Homanen, M. (2023). Tailor-to-target: configuring collaborative shareholder engagements on climate change. *Management Science*, 69(12), 7693–7718. https://doi.org/10.1287/mnsc.2023.4806.

TCFD (2017). *Recommendations of the Task Force on Climate-Related Financial Disclosures*. London: Task Force on Climate-Related Financial Disclosures.

TCFD (2018). *2018 Status Report*. London: Task Force on Climate-Related Financial Disclosures.

TCFD (2019). *2019 Status Report*. London: Task Force on Climate-Related Financial Disclosures.

TCFD (2020). *Third Status Report*. London: Task Force on Climate-Related Financial Disclosures.

TCFD (2021). *Fourth Status Report*. London: Task Force on Climate-Related Financial Disclosures.

TCFD (2022). *Fifth Status Report*. London: Task Force on Climate-Related Financial Disclosures.

Thinking Ahead Institute (2018). *The World's Largest 500 Asset Managers*. New York: Willis Towers Watson.

Thinking Ahead Institute (2019a). *The Thinking Ahead Institute's Asset Owner 100: The Most Influential Capital on the Planet*. New York: Willis Towers Watson.

Thinking Ahead Institute (2019b). *Pensions and Investments World 300*. New York: Willis Towers Watson.

UN PRI (2019a). About the PRI. https://www.unpri.org/pri/about-the-pri.

UN PRI (2019b). Minimum requirements for membership. https://www.unpri.org/reporting-and -assessment/minimum-requirements-for-investor-membership/315.article.

United Nations (2000). The UN Global Compact. https://unglobalcompact.org/about.

Zerbini, F. (2017). CSR initiatives as market signals: a review and research agenda. *Journal of Business Ethics*, 146(1), 1–23.

APPENDIX 15A.1: COMPLIANCE WITH TCFD RECOMMENDATIONS 2018–2023 BY ASSET OWNERS (AO), ASSET MANAGERS (AM) AND INSURERS

No	Date issued	Research approach – methodology	Key findings		
			Asset owners	Asset managers	Insurers
1	September 2018	AI review: 311 insurance companies Disclosure practices: sample of 25 reports	'Majority provided the relevant information'	'Majority provided the relevant information'	Ranged from strategy (c) to strategy (b) (unspecified)
2	June 2019	AI review: 147 insurance companies Based on 1111 PRI questionnaires issued in 2018 (asset managers) and 338 PRI asset owners)	Ranged from 4% (Metrics & Targets (c)) to 29% (Governance (a))	Ranged from 4% (Metrics & Targets (a) and (b)) to 21% (Risk management (a) and (b))	Ranged from 12% (Strategy (c)) to 39% (Strategy (a))
3	October 2020	AI review: 138 insurance companies AO & AM: PRI questionnaires, now extended to include 379 (2019) and 444 (2020) AO PRI questionnaires and 1331 (2019) and 1655 (2020) AM PRI questionnaires	2019: Ranged from 9% (Metrics & Targets (b)) to 29% (Governance (a)) 2020: Ranged from 12% (Metrics & Targets (c)) to 79% (Governance (a))	2019: Ranged from 5% (Climate (b)) to 26% (Strategy (a)) 2020: Ranged from 9% (Climate (c)) to 79% (Governance (a))	Ranged from 8% (Strategy (c)) to 49% (Strategy (a))
4	October 2021	AI review: 132 insurance companies OA & AM:538 AO and 2,182 (AM)	Ranged from 10% (Metrics & Targets (c)) to 85% (Governance (a))	Ranged from 7% (Metrics & Targets (c)) to 83% (Governance (a))	Ranged from 18% (Strategy (c)) to 52% (Strategy (a))
5	October 2022	AI review: 118 insurance companies Survey of 3000 financial institutions, 229 responses received, of which 151 AM and 78 AO	Ranged from 45% (Strategy (c)) to 75% (Metrics & Targets (a))	Ranged from 19% (Strategy (c)) to 53% (Metrics & Targets (a))	Ranged from 25% (Strategy (c)) to 58% (Strategy (a))
6	October 2023	AI review: 237 insurance companies Survey of 1300 financial institutions, 150 responses received of which 106 AM and 44 AO	Ranged from 18% Strategy (c)) to 44% (Metrics & targets (a))	Ranged from 24% (Strategy c)) to 70% (Metrics and targets (a))	Ranged from 21% (Metrics & Targets (c)) to 64% (Governance (a)). Note 0% alignment with Strategy (c))

Source: Based on TCFD Status Reports 2018 to 2023.

APPENDIX 15A.2: INSTITUTIONAL BACKGROUND: UN PRI, CLIMATE 100+, TCFD

15A.2.1 Principle of Responsible Investments (PRI)

The PRI was launched jointly by the United Nations and other sponsoring organisations in 2006 after a working party consisting of the world's largest institutional investors, experts from the investment industry, intergovernmental organisations, and civil society was brought together by the UN to formulate 'principles' for responsible investments. The resulting six principles prescribe commitments to

- incorporate ESG issues into investment analysis and decision-making processes;
- be active owners and incorporate ESG issues into ownership policies and practices;
- seek appropriate disclosure on ESG issues by the entities in which signatories invest;
- promote acceptance and implementation of the Principles within the investment industry;
- work together to enhance our effectiveness in implementing the Principles;
- report on activities and progress towards implementing the Principles.

Ways of implementing the principles are exemplified by the UN PRI,[1] and guidelines for reporting are provided. The organisation works independently of the UN to increase industry awareness on the investment implications of environmental, social and governance (ESG) factors as well as to support its international network of investor signatories in incorporating these factors into their investment and ownership decisions.

In 2018 the UN PRI implemented minimum requirements for membership such as annual reporting and membership fees. The reporting should explain responsible investment strategy, the staff and management committed to work on ESG, and the accountability procedures associated with implementation of the six principles. Failure to comply with these requirements over a two-year period will result in de-listing. The signatories are listed on the webpage of the UN PRI.

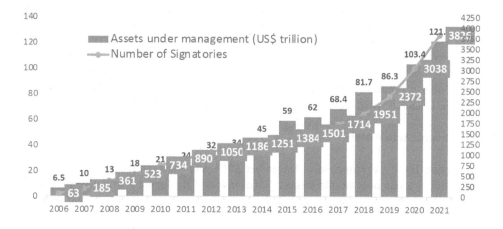

Figure 15A.1   Evolution of PRI signatories

Despite the reporting requirements and costs of membership, the number of signatories has continued to increase as depicted in Figure 15A.1, showing the number of signatories over the life of the organisation; by the end of 2021 reaching 3826 signatories, and 5337 signatories as of date of publication of this chapter.

Membership can benefit organisations in signalling to capital markets, customers, and other stakeholders, and is one way of standardisation of signals about ESG.

15A.2.2 Task Force for Climate-Related Disclosures (TCFD)

The Financial Stability Board (FSB) created the TCFD to develop recommendations on the types of information that companies should disclose to support investors, lenders, and insurance underwriters in appropriately assessing and pricing a specific set of risks – risks related to climate change.

The number of supporters of the guidelines has increased to more than 3800, companies have continued to increase their TCFD-aligned reporting, and there have been important actions by regulators, jurisdictions, and international standard-setters to use the TCFD recommendations in developing climate-related reporting requirements and standards – including but not limited to proposals released by the US Securities and Exchange Commission, the International Sustainability Standards Board, and the European Financial Reporting Advisory Group.

The TCFD (2017) issued 11 recommended disclosures across four major areas related to (a) governance (two), (b) strategy (three), (c) risk management (three), and (d) metrics and targets (three). It should be noted that these are separate from EU-specific climate-related disclosure guidelines that may be applicable to European Union-based asset owners.[2] Additionally, the International Sustainability Standards Board has issued an exposure draft which is applicable to many types of business entity, including certain types of asset owners. However, this is yet to be finalised.[3]

In 2017, the TCFD released climate-related financial disclosure recommendations designed to help companies provide better information to support informed capital allocation. The TCFD subsequently issued six status reports (TCFD, 2018; 2019; 2020; 2021; 2022; 2023), which provided an overview of the degree of alignment with its recommended disclosures by organisations based in various industry sectors. Annex 1A summarises the major findings related to various types of asset owners over the five years. Overall, the TCFD identified a gradual increase over those six years in the degree of alignment between corporate reporting of climate-related disclosures and its 11 recommended disclosures. In October 2023, the TCFD was disbanded as a result of the promulgation of new IFRS Sustainability Standards, IFRS S1 and IFRS S2, which came into effect on 1 January 2024 (IFRS, 2023a; 2023b).

15A.2.3 Climate Action 100+

Climate Action 100+ was launched in December 2017, and soon attracted worldwide attention. Since then, it has become the largest global investor engagement initiative on climate change, with growing influence and impact. It was initially meant to be a five-year initiative (2017–2022) but in 2022 it was announced that it would run to 2030. In 2023, it announced a Phase 2 strategy for 2023–2030.

Climate Action 100+ is an investor-led initiative to ensure the world's largest corporate greenhouse gas emitters take necessary action on climate change. It is made up of 700 global investors, who in 2023 were responsible for more than USD 68 trillion in assets under management. Investor participants are signatories to the initiative and are responsible for direct engagements with focus companies, individually and/or collaboratively. Investor supporters are also asset owner signatories to the initiative and publicly support the initiative's goals, but do not participate directly in engagements with focus companies. The work of the initiative is coordinated by five investor networks: the Asia Investor Group on Climate Change (AIGCC), Ceres, Investor Group on Climate Change (IGCC), Institutional Investors Group on Climate Change (IIGCC) and Principles for Responsible Investment (PRI). It is supported by a global Steering Committee.

APPENDIX NOTES

1. See https://www.unpri.org/about-us/what-are-the-principles-for-responsible-investment.
2. This section covers international guidance on climate risk reporting as issued by the TCFD. At the European level, asset owners who participate in these markets are coming under increased public scrutiny for their engagement with environment, social and governance (ESG) practices and in adhering to EU climate change adaptation initiatives (European Commission, 2021a; 2021b; 2021c), as well as EU climate change reporting guidelines (European Commission, 2019) through adopting investment strategies that seek to decarbonise their portfolios in order to achieve 'net zero'.
3. In March 2022, the ISSB published Exposure Draft IFRS S2, Climate-Related Disclosures, building on the recommendations of the Task Force on Climate-Related Financial Disclosures (TCFD) and incorporating industry-based disclosure requirements derived from SASB Standards. The ISSB redeliberated the proposals after considering the feedback on the Exposure Draft. An IFRS Sustainability Disclosure Standard was announced at the end of June 2023.

PART V

GOVERNANCE

16. Corporate governance and sustainability: an overview of the new trends in the European Union

Federica Doni and Diego Toscani

1   INTRODUCTION

Firms' corporate governance is put under the spotlight by new trends in the European Union. The commitment of firms to sustainable corporate governance is under the scrutiny of governments, supervising authorities, financial markets, the social sphere and not least, traditional and new media. A significant volume of academic and professional literature demonstrates that good corporate governance practices may increase performance by leading companies through a more sustainable value creation process.

Corporate governance is not a new issue for companies and businesses, but new trends are increasingly attracting attention to corporate governance practices within the acronym ESG (environmental, social and governance),[1] where the letter G can be considered the most important issue, as good corporate governance is a sort of precondition that is essential for achieving sustainable strategic objectives for all companies. Governance and sustainability can follow a common path within which there is a mutual relationship, as governance cannot be developed in a correct way without sustainably oriented practices. Some categorizations identify different issues that can be included in the letter G, but it is worthwhile to note that there are many different categorizations and there is no common and standardized framework on the most relevant issues related to each component. Table 16.1 shows one of the possible categorizations that have been proposed.

Table 16.1   ESG issues

Environmental	Social	Governance
Climate policies	Relationships with stakeholders	Compliance
Energy, waste & pollution prevention & control	Workplace conditions, employees' health & safety	Accurate & transparent reporting
Sustainable use & protection of water	Salary, career, pensions	Integrity & diversity in leadership selection
Transition to a Circular Economy	Diversity, equity, inclusion	No conflicts of interest in choice of
Natural resource conservation	Company holds suppliers to	board members & executives
Protection, restoration of	own ESG standards	No political contributions to obtain
biodiversity & ecosystems	Company takes no unethical	preferential treatment
	advantage of customers	No engagement in illegal conduct

Source: Authors' elaboration.

In many countries corporate governance codes are adopted by companies, particularly by large, listed organizations. At a global level, the Organisation for Economic Co-operation and Development (OECD) has recently revised (September 2023) the document entitled *G20/*

OECD Principles of Corporate Governance 2023 (OECD, 2023), in which it is possible to find an explicit recommendation to Member States for the adoption of corporate governance codes issued at the local level. Regarding issues related to sustainability, it is possible to note that the last principle (OECD, 2023, Section VI, pp. 44–50) is explicitly dedicated to the sustainability and resilience of companies. This section includes a general recommendation for developing a corporate governance framework that should incentivize companies and investors to manage their risk to contribute to the sustainability and resilience of their organizations. Different aspects are recommended, such as the importance of consistency, reliability, comparability, materiality of sustainability disclosure; the use of high-quality and internationally recognized standards; the connection between financial information and sustainability matters and other corporate reports; the need for an annual assurance attestation on sustainability disclosure by an independent auditor; a constructive dialogue between shareholders and stakeholders on sustainability matters that are relevant to the company's strategy; the corporate governance structure should ensure that boards consider sustainability risks and opportunities when carrying out their functions in reviewing governance, strategy, internal auditing, and risk management systems; and disclosure with a specific respect for climate-related physical and transition risks.

Moreover, we can refer to an interesting document published by the International Corporate Governance Network (ICGN) from 2001 and recently revised (ICGN, 2021). This document established ten Global Governance Principles: (1) Board role and responsibilities; (2) Leadership and independence; (3) Composition and appointment; (4) Corporate culture; (5) Remuneration; (6) Risk oversight; (7) Corporate reporting; (8) Internal and external audit; (9) Shareholder rights; (10) Shareholder meetings. It is worthwhile to note that the term "sustainability" is mentioned in different contexts (24 times in the document), such as within Principle 7, Corporate reporting ("approach to sustainability"), and in the "Guidance" section the term "sustainability" refers to responsibilities related to stakeholder engagement and the accountability of governance of sustainability by integrating human capital and natural capital into the company's strategy, innovation and risk (ICGN, 2021, p. 8). Sustainability is mentioned in the commitment related to the skills and knowledge of directors regarding sustainability issues. There is a specific recommendation about the establishment of committees on sustainability. The section on performance measures includes audited financial data and, where possible, assured sustainability indicators (ICGN, 2021, p. 21). Additionally, there are sections on materiality and sustainability standards that the board should integrate into corporate reporting. The Audit Committee should understand how sustainability factors are affecting the company's financial statement. Finally, Annex 2 reports the key revisions (ICGN, 2021, p. 40), which include the governance of sustainability, materiality, stakeholder relations, climate change, human rights, sustainability reporting, sustainability standards and the inclusion of sustainability-related metrics into the executive incentive plans.

In this context, most European members adopted corporate governance codes (as "soft law") in respect of issues related to boards, independence of directors, diversity and inclusion, internal control systems and remuneration policy. At European Union level, the topic of sustainability has recently been animated and stimulated, mainly by the 2022 Corporate Sustainability Reporting Directive (CSRD) and the related reporting standards, the European Sustainability Reporting Standards (ESRS), which will be illustrated below.

The rest of the chapter is organized as follows. Section 2 offers a summary of the main trends and recent changes at the European level on corporate governance and ESG issues in general. Section 3 provides an analysis of the Italian case, while Section 3.1 describes the main features of small and medium-sized enterprises (SMEs) listed on the Euronext Growth Milan (EGM) to describe the impact of ESG on their corporate governance model. Finally, Section 4 makes some concluding remarks.

2 CORPORATE GOVERNANCE AND SUSTAINABILITY IN THE EUROPEAN UNION: A NEW SCENARIO

For some years now, the European Union has been asking all the countries of the European Union to commit to the process of transition to a zero or low carbon economy. This transition is therefore requiring companies to comply with different regulations (for example, the Directive on due diligence regarding the environment and human rights, the new Directive on sustainability reporting, and sustainability regulations for financial and banking intermediaries), partially depending on the features of their business operations or the industry to which they belong. We are also witnessing multiple anticipatory actions by some companies to implement a future transition on a voluntary basis. This step undoubtedly requires a clear and defined corporate governance framework that can allow investors to consider the potential risks and opportunities resulting from these transition paths.

At EU level, the fundamental transition to sustainability governance was affirmed, albeit indirectly, by the approval of EU Directive 95/2014, the Non-Financial Reporting Directive (NFRD), which made the drafting of a sustainability report (non-financial statement) mandatory for financial institutions, public interest entities, and large, listed companies, banks and insurance companies, thus establishing very specific criteria and limiting the reporting obligation to approximately 12,000 companies. As a consequence of this new regulatory obligation, the profile of the new large European company is undoubtedly changing more and more. The business context is already being asked to adopt a "sustainable management" profile that has been significantly modified compared to the recent past, as boards of directors must identify "non-financial" risks. The fiduciary duties of directors are expanding, companies must draw up a plan for a climate strategy, and transparency obligations for sustainability reporting are further strengthened. Based on what has been established by the CSRD, listed SMEs will also gradually become involved in this scenario (starting from 2026–2028), but inevitably the profound change will also affect unlisted SMEs, which are "forced" to provide information on ESG matters for access to traditional financing channels and to be able to participate in the value chains of large companies, and are obliged to comply with European legislation (the "knock-on effect").

For the success of "good governance", the governance system will have to comply with new reporting standards which require companies to integrate financial information with details on processes and strategic choices, including issues such as corporate ethics, the fight against corruption, management of relationships with suppliers, and political influence within the company culture, increasing the importance of the ways in which this information is collected and disseminated within the company. The key role played by the governance component in the field of sustainable development is confirmed by the ESRS 2 General Principles standard, in which five general principles are listed (GOV 1–5). Regarding GOV 1, the request for information relates to the skills and abilities of each member regarding issues related to sustainability, the number of members with and without executive positions and the representation of employees and workers, in addition to the request to provide details regarding the percentage distribution of members by gender (even if the information is mandatory for the Board of Directors). GOV 2 focuses on how administrative, management and supervisory bodies are informed, and how frequently, together with their committees, about relevant impacts, risks, and opportunities, as well as the effectiveness of the policies, actions, metrics and objectives adopted. GOV 3 requires communication as to whether incentive systems related to sustainability issues are offered to the members of the administrative, management and control bodies and, if they exist, what their characteristics are. GOV 4 requires information regarding the parts of the Sustainability Statement where due diligence issues related to sustainability are addressed, to identify the actual company practices with respect to the duty of diligence. Due diligence refers to the process by which companies identify, prevent, mitigate, and report on how they address actual and potential negative impacts on the environment and people resulting from carrying out their activities. Finally, GOV 5 requires illustration of the internal control and risk management processes in relation to sustainability reporting. The regulation's detail requires an indication of the scope, characteristics, and elements of the internal control system to communicate the risk assessment and mitigation approach and the related controls. What is required by ESRS 2 must be read in conjunction with the provisions of the ESRS G1 standard to satisfy the requirements of the Commission Delegated Regulation (EU) 2023/2772 approved on 31 July 2023.

The topical standard issued by EFRAG in the field of corporate governance is analysed below.

2.1   The New EFRAG Standards on Corporate Governance

The new ESRS reporting standards dedicate significant space to corporate governance processes that are considered essential for achieving corporate success that is truly inspired by sustainable development. Within the scope of the CSRD, the Delegated Regulation approved on 31 July 2023 by the European Commission regarding the EFRAG standards has essentially indicated the ESRS G1 Business Conduct to be the main topical standard aimed at regulating and reporting the governance component within the acronym ESG.

2.2   ESRS G1 business conduct

The main aim of the standard is to make users of the Sustainability Declaration understand the company strategy, approaches, and processes as well as company performance in compliance with approved business conduct. It is worthwhile to note the seven "business conduct matters" listed in the standard (Commission Delegated Regulation (EU) 2023/2772, p. 29, https://eur-lex.europa.eu/eli/reg_del/2023/2772/oj) below:

(1)   corporate culture;
(2)   management and relationships with suppliers;
(3)   avoiding corruption and bribery;
(4)   engagement by the undertaking to exert its political influence including lobbying;
(5)   protection of whistle-blowers;
(6)   animal welfare; and
(7)   payment practices, specifically with regard to late payment to small and medium-sized enterprises (SMEs).

Table 16.2   Disclosure requirements: performance measurement

ESRS G1-9 – Composition of the administrative, management and supervisory bodies	Information about the diversity of the members of the administrative, supervisory and management bodies	Percentage of independent shareholder elected members Percentage of each diversity item: Gender Age group Any other relevant diversity indicators Average ratio of female to male board members Information on changes to the composition of the administrative, supervisory and management bodies, with the associated reasons
ESRS G1-10 – Meetings and attendance rate	Number of meetings and attendance rate for the company's administrative, management and supervisory bodies and committees	Number of meetings Number of members who participated at each meeting

Source: ESRS G1, Governance, risk management and internal control, EFRAG (2023).

The content of the standard must also be analysed keeping in mind the ESRS 1 General Principles and ESRS 2 General Requirements standards. Below is a summary of the contents relating to the disclosure requirements in relation to ESRS 2, divided into Governance (GOV), Strategy (SBM), and management of impacts, risks and opportunities (IRO), which will then be commented on in the rest of this section.

To evaluate the actual novelty of the EFRAG standards, it is useful to highlight the main differences compared to what is required by the GRI Standards. For example, regarding communication and raising awareness of corporate culture, the GRI requires describing the relevant communication methods and estimating the recipients of the "good governance" training. On the contrary, the Regulation reinforces, in terms of disclosure, the central role that must be played by corporate culture as a means of disseminating corporate conduct inspired by ESG issues, underlining their importance. Again, with reference to corporate culture, the standard offers companies the opportunity to report all the communication protection tools of corporate culture, such as whistleblowing.

As regards G1-2, i.e., the management of relationships with suppliers, the aim is to protect the supply chain by asking companies to report how the procurement process is managed and how these management methods can influence relationships with suppliers. In particular, reference to "vulnerable" suppliers, i.e., those more exposed to environmental, social and economic risks and who can have a greater impact on the supply chain, can also be included. From a comparison with the standard GRIs it emerges that EFRAG does not limit itself to asking, like the GRI, for a description of the actions to manage potential positive or negative impacts deriving from relationships with suppliers but requires that the company's strategy in managing the relationships with suppliers, both in the context of supply chain risks and in practices for implementing vulnerable suppliers to improve their performance also in environmental and social terms.

G1-3 and G1-4 are closely interrelated as the former asks the company to outline the policies adopted to prevent episodes of corruption, while the latter requires adequate communication if these cases actually occur. The main objective is to guarantee transparency regarding

Table 16.3   ESRS G1 Business conduct – disclosure requirements

Standard	Topic	Sub-topics
ESRS 2 GOV-1 Governance	The role of the administrative, supervisory and management bodies	Role Expertise
ESRS 2 IRO-1 Impact, risks and opportunities	Description of the processes to identify and assess material impacts, risks and opportunities	Relevant criteria of the assessment including: Location Activities Sector Transactions
ESRS G1-1 Corporate culture and business conduct policies	Description of the involvement of administrative, management and supervisory bodies in developing, monitoring and promoting corporate culture	Regarding business conduct: Mitigation of any negative impacts Maximization of positive impacts Management of the related risks
ESRS G1-2 Management and relationships with suppliers	Description of the management of company's relationships with its suppliers and its impacts on its supply chain	Regarding the management of the company's procurement process: Company's strategy on relationships with its suppliers Social and environmental criteria for selecting supply-side contractual partners Practices for supporting vulnerable suppliers and improving their social and environmental performance
ESRS G1-3 Prevention and detection of corruption and bribery	Description of the system to prevent and detect, investigate and respond to allegations or incidents relating to corruption and bribery, including related training	To improve transparency on the key procedures: An overview of the procedures Eventual separation between the investigating committee and the chain of management The process of reporting the outcomes to the governance bodies
ESRS G1-4 Confirmed incidents of corruption and bribery	Description of confirmed incidents of corruption or bribery	The total number and nature of confirmed incidents The number of convictions and the amount of fines Details about public legal cases Details about confirmed incidents on dismissal of company's workers Details about confirmed incidents on contracts with business partners being terminated or not renewed due to corruption

Standard	Topic	Sub-topics
ESRS G1-5 – Political influence and lobbying activities	Description of company's activities and commitments related to its political influence, including lobbying activities on its material impacts	The name of representative(s) responsible in the governance bodies Information on financial or in-kind political contributions The main topic covered by lobbying activities and their interactions with its material impacts, risks and opportunities Eventual registration in the EU Transparency Register or in an equivalent transparency register in a Member State. The appointment of any members of the governance bodies who held a comparable position in the public administration (including regulators) two years before such appointment
ESRS G1-6 – Payment practices	Description of payment practices, particularly of any late payments to SMEs	Regarding contractual payment terms: The average time for paying an invoice Company's standard payment terms in number of days The number of legal proceedings for late payments Complementary information

Source: ESRS G1, Business conduct, EFRAG (2023).

the system for preventing and reporting any corrupt behaviour, requiring provision of details on the mapping, assessment and monitoring of risks as well as the procedures and monitoring programmes relating to the fight against corruption. It is also important to point out the reasons why each stakeholder should implement the provisions contained in the anti-corruption policies and the ways in which they are informed of the tools and channels for combatting corruption. In G1-4, the company must report on cases of corruption that actually occurred during the reporting period, providing information regarding the number of convictions, the number of fines imposed for the violation of the provisions on corruption and any actions taken following the verification of violation of the rules on corruption. The fifth disclosure requirement, G1-5, concerns any political influence and lobbying activities. This information is related to direct and indirect political influence that can be exerted by a company. This information is important for respecting the reporting aims of an ESRS statement and it requires detailed information. Unlike what is required by the GRI, the Regulation requires companies to provide a greater level of detail regarding political influence activities, requiring every public statement to also include its lobbying activities.

The last of the Disclosure Requirements, G1-6, concerns payment practices and represents a completely new point of view compared to the GRI. The Regulation requires companies to highlight compliance with payment deadlines for suppliers, especially for SMEs. Detail is requested on payment terms, stability in contracts, and in particular on the effects that a delay in payments can have on businesses. The level of detail on the average time taken to pay an invoice and other types of information is high, so companies could provide the information through representative sampling: in this case the methodology must be explained.

In summary, the adoption of the ESRS G1 standard for business conduct represents a significant step towards greater transparency and responsibility in the ESG perspective. The sections dedicated to "Disclosure" and "Application requirements" offer a detailed structure for the disclosure of processes related to governance and business conduct.

3   CORPORATE GOVERNANCE AND SUSTAINABILITY: THE CASE OF ITALY

In Italy in 2011, the Corporate Governance Committee merged various business associations (ABI, ANIA, Assonime, Confindustria), the Borsa Italiana (n.d.) and the Association of Professional Investors (Assogestioni). It ensures compliance with international best practices in the field of corporate governance through the approval of the Corporate Governance Code of listed companies. The Committee also ensures annual monitoring of the implementation status of the Code. In 2020 the Corporate Governance Code introduced for the first time the term "sustainable success" which must be integrated into the business plan and which is defined as follows: "an objective that guides the action of the administrative body and which is substantiated in creating long-term value for the benefit of shareholders, taking into account the interests of other stakeholders relevant to the company" (Comitato Corporate Governance, 2020, p. 4). The term sustainable success is referred to at different points of the document and must guide the activity of the administrative body; it must constitute the purpose of the remuneration policy of the directors, the members of the control body and the top management. Additionally, the internal control system and risk management must be directed towards sustainable success.

The Corporate Governance Code does not constitute cogent or binding legislation but includes best practices at an international level, inspired by the orientation of the European Commission, although it is aimed at listed companies (Euronext Milan). It also exerts a growing influence on unlisted companies, of small to medium size. The first version of the Code dates back to 1999 and it was modified and updated several times before the last modification, which dates back to 31 January 2020. Adherence is recommended but always remains on a voluntary basis. In particular, it is strongly influenced by the new version (effective 2025) of the UK Corporate Governance Code (FRC, 2024).

Among the most innovative principles of the new version of the Code, in particular, a more marked orientation towards the sustainability of business activity is emerging, with the proposed enlightened shareholder value, i.e., the pursuit of shareholder wealth with a long-term orientation aimed at sustainable growth, paying responsible attention to the interests of all stakeholders. The concept of the corporate purpose is also proposed, which goes hand in hand with the definition of corporate values, integrity, and ethics.

For the definition of the corporate purpose, the reference to sustainability is now unequivocal, as recalled by Larry Fink in his letter to shareholders:

> Putting your company's purpose at the foundation of your relationships with your stakeholders is critical to long-term success. Employees need to understand and connect with your purpose; and when they do, they can be your staunchest advocates. Customers want to see and hear what you stand for as they increasingly look to do business with companies that share their values. And shareholders need to understand the guiding principle driving your vision and mission. (Fink, 2022)

Good corporate governance must necessarily be inspired by ethical values and business integrity. In Italy the moral responsibility of the company is delegated to the top management, who are responsible for the moral tone of the company. The Board must set an example of moral conduct and must promote and consolidate the culture of ethics in the company. They therefore have a responsibility to manage the company in an ethically correct manner by conducting management on the basis of ethical criteria. In Italy, Legislative Decree 231/2001 regulates these aspects, having introduced some time ago the "Organization, Management and Control Model", which represents the most frequently used tool to define the business model, based on the definition of risk activities and internal control principles for the achievement of corporate objectives, including those linked to sustainability.

The Decree constitutes an exemption from liability of the legal person and offers clear lines of conduct, control schemes and measures to ensure the prevention of the commission of crimes and corrupt practices. In some cases, the continuous strengthening of corporate governance leads to the definition of an integrated anti-corruption system, with the aim of further improving the level of effectiveness of anti-corruption policies. In better-structured companies, this system can also be integrated into the broader framework of the Governance Model and the Internal Control and Risk Management System (SCIGR). There is an increasingly felt need to integrate governance models, the Internal Control and Risk Management System and the sustainability process, representing a further "layer" for correct reporting in the Sustainability Statement.

In April 2023, Assonime, the association of Italian joint-stock companies, published its annual report regarding the implementation of the Corporate Governance Code and the evolution of the administrative body, in which a section was entirely dedicated to the "Governance of Sustainability". Regarding this aspect, the due diligence discipline will have a strong impact on the company's organization and the decision-making process. Administrators must therefore carefully weigh the interests involved in the decision, establishing an order of priority in the evaluation of interests. The interests of the company, as defined by all the members, remain a priority, but it becomes important to establish the tools through which it is possible to consider the interests connected to sustainability profiles. The theme of sustainability is also combined with the theme of digitalization, both considered fundamental to the sustainable development of companies. Digitalization can support, for example, the channels of dialogue with stakeholders, enhance the collegiality and competence of the board of directors towards a strategic approach to sustainability, and review the organizational structures, procedures and information flows in terms of sustainability. An interesting aspect concerns the use of sustainability and digitalization as growth factors for SMEs. Even in the absence of obligations, SMEs must seize the opportunity to undertake an ESG path aimed at using digital technologies. SME administrators will have to evaluate and manage the opportunities and risks of ESG and digital profiles with respect to their business, proportionately to the size and nature of the company, without creating inefficient and organizationally excessive structures. Two aspects are strongly recommended by Assonime: (1) investing resources for the drafting of the sustainability report, given that both as customers of financial intermediaries and as members of the value chains of large companies, SMEs will increasingly be required to provide structured information in the ESG field; (2) investment in cloud computing as a prerequisite for making the most of the opportunities of digitalization (Assonime, 2023).

3.1   Corporate Governance in the European Union SMEs: LSMEs and VSMEs Standards / Exposure Drafts

On 21 January 2024, EFRAG launched a public consultation on two draft sustainability reporting standards for small and medium-sized enterprises, with a consultation period extended until 21 May 2024. The two different documents, respectively called "ESRS LSME ED" and "VSME ED", are aimed at two different categories of SMEs. The ESRS LSME ED is oriented towards SMEs that are entities of public interest, such as companies with negotiable securities on regulated EU markets, small and non-complex Institutions (SNCIs) of the financial sector, as well as captive insurance and reinsurance companies, collectively referred to as LSME. This standard, which will be effective from 1 January 2026 with the possibility of opting for a two-year delay, aims to establish reporting requirements proportionate to the size and complexity of LSMEs, facilitating their access to finance and standardizing sustainability information. The VSME ED, however, proposes a voluntary sustainability reporting standard for unlisted SMEs. This reporting tool aims to simplify the response of unlisted SMEs to requests for sustainability information from banks, investors or large companies by concentrating this information in a single document, consequently reducing the administrative burden represented by multiple data requests ESG and facilitating the transition of SMEs towards a sustainable economy.

LSME ED (January 2024)
This standard is part of EFRAG mandatory in CSRD, Delegated Act, which will be effective on 1 January 2026 (two-years opt out). The scope focuses on SMEs with public-interest relevance, such as SMEs with bonds, shares and other securities traded in regulated markets in the EU, SNCIs, and captive insurers/reinsurers. This standard can benefit companies by supporting LSMEs in gaining better access to finance and avoiding discrimination against them on the part of financial market participants. Large undertakings ask SMEs for data requests because of business and reporting reasons, including the CSRD reporting obligations using ESRS. To limit the amount of these requests, according to CSRD, ESRS should not specify disclosures that would require large undertakings to obtain information from SMEs in their value chain that exceeds the information to be disclosed in accordance with LSME ESRS ED. EFRAG work identifies this legal requirement as "value chain cap". Beyond the legal provisions of CSRD, VSME ED is also intended to play a key role in supporting SMEs, when they prepare the information needed by large undertakings for ESRS reporting, as well as for other obligations including for business purposes. The structure of this standard includes six modules: Section 1 – General requirements; Section 2 – General disclosures; Section 3 – Policies, actions and targets (cross-cutting sections); Section 4 – Environmental disclosures; Section 5 – Social disclosures; and Section 6 – Business conduct disclosures (topical sections). The last section corresponds to ESRS G1, with some simplifications on disclosure requirements. Disclosure Requirements cover governance (GOV), strategy (SBM), impact and risk management (IR) and metrics. By considering governance disclosure requirements an LSME shall disclose the governance processes, controls and procedures used to monitor and manage impacts and risks. The standard suggests a structure of an ESRS statement within which we can find governance information in the first section on "General information" (sustainability governance) and in Section 4 on governance information (see Table 16.4).

Table 16.4   *Example of structure of an ESRS statement*

4. Governance information
Impact and risk management on business conduct topics
Policies and Action on material business conduct topics
Targets on material business conduct topics (if the undertaking has set them)
Metrics on material business conduct topics (according to Section 6)
Potential additional entity specific information

Source: EFRAG, LSMEs ED Appendix F, p. 43, available at https://www.efrag.org/News/Public-479/EFRAGs-

Regarding General Disclosures and Application Requirements, the standard includes Disclosures Requirement 3 (GOV 1), "The role of the administrative management and supervisory bodies", and Disclosurement Requirement 4 (GOV 2), "Due diligence". This standard aims to simplify and reduce governance disclosures in comparison with similar information requested by ESRS 2 and ESRS G1. For example, Disclosure Requirement 4 (GOV 2) requires a description on due diligence processes with regard to sustainability matters only if the undertaking has adopted such processes. LSME shall declare if it has adopted these processes or not.

VSME ED (January 2024)

The objective is to support micro, small and medium-sized enterprises in the following ways:

- Contribute to a more sustainable and inclusive economy
- Improve the management of the sustainability issues with which they interface, contributing to their competitive growth and increasing their resilience in the short, medium and long term
- Offer information that satisfies the demand for data from creditors and investors, help businesses in their access to financing
- Offer information that satisfies the demand for data from large companies that require information on the sustainability of their suppliers

The standard is voluntary and applies to companies whose shares are not admitted to trading on a regulated market in the European Union, and refers to micro, small and medium-sized enterprises, regulated by Art. 3 Directive 2013/34/EU.

The contents of the mouth were structured on the principle of proportionality. It includes 3 modules:

1. **Basic Module**, which constitutes the minimum requirement (only mandatory for micro-enterprises);
2. **Narrative- Policies, Actions and Targets (PAT) Module** suggested to undertakings that have formalized and implemented Policies, Actions and Objectives with respect to sustainability issues. Requires a materiality analysis similar to that of specific ESRS principles;
3. **Business Partners Module**, also to be drawn up with a prior materiality analysis, establishes the additional information that represents the information needs requested by financiers, investors and corporate customers.

In the Basic Module, the company is required to report on environmental, social and corporate business conduct issues through the information indicated in paragraphs B1–B12 of the

Standard. The information must be presented together with comparative data from the previous year, with the exception of metrics presented for the first time. The inclusion of comparative information will begin from the second year of reporting and will continue in subsequent years. The parts dedicated to corporate governance are included in the Basic Module (B12 "Convictions and sanctions for corruption and bribery"), in the Narrative PAT Module (in the essential information requirements the fifth is entitled "Governance and responsibility in relation to sustainability issues") and in the last dedicated part to the Basic Module Guidance (the section entitled "Business conduct metrics"). Below is a brief summary of the information required on corporate governance.

Table 16.5   VSMEs ED: Corporate governance information

Section	Sub-section	Content	Page
Basic Module	Basic metrics – Business Conduct	B12 Convinctions and fines for corruption and bribery *Disclosure on the number of convinctions and the total amount of fines incurred to the violation of anti-corruption and anti-bribery laws*	11
Principles for the preparation of the sustainability report	(Narrative – PAT Disclosure N. 5 – Governance: responsibilities in relation to sustainability matters	Description of governance and responsibilities that shall include roles and responsibilities of the highest governance body or of the individuals in charge of managing sustainability matters	16
Principles for the preparation of the sustainability report	Business Partners Modules Disclosure BP1 – Revenues from certain Sectors Disclosure BP2 – Gender diversity ration in governance body	BP1: statement to indicate if a company is active in 1) controversial weapons; 2) cultivation or production of tobacco; 3) fossil fuel sector; 4) chemicals production BP2: If the undetaking has a governance body it shall disclose the related gender diversity ratio	17, 18
Basic Module: Guidance	Business Conduct Metrics	Guidance on convinctions: any virdict of a criminal count against an individual or undertaking in respect of a criminal offence related to corruption or bribery	35
Business Partners Module: Guidance	Governance – Business model Metrics	BP1: A company shall disclose if it is active in certain sectors (see above on BP1) by specifying the corresponding revenues BP2: the governance body refers to the highest decision-making authority BP2: Gender diversity ratio is calculated as an average ratio of female to male board members	36

Source: EFRAG (2024). Voluntary ESRS for non-Listed Small-and Medium-sized enterprises, available at https://www.efrag.org/News/Public-479/EFRAGs-

3.2   The Challenge of Corporate Governance in the Italian SMEs Context. Empirical Evidence from the Euronext Growth Milan (EGM)

In Italy SMEs can access the financial market by listing on Euronext Growth Milan (EGM). EGM is the financial market dedicated to dynamic and competitive SMEs, which are looking for capital to finance their growth, thanks to a balanced regulatory approach, suitable for ambitious companies' needs (AssoNext, n.d.). EGM Italy offers small and medium-sized businesses the opportunity to efficiently access a selected audience of investors focused on small business capital, offering a quicker and more flexible route to listing than the main market (MTA), in line with the growth rates of SMEs. EGM is controlled by the Italian Stock Exchange, which has been controlled, in turn, by Euronext since 2020. EGM is designed to offer SMEs a combination of listing advantages as follows:

(1)   regulatory flexibility for SMEs by offering a simplified path to listing and at the same time post-listing obligations adjusted to the structure of small and medium-sized enterprises;
(2)   admission requirements are reduced compared to the requirements for listing on the main markets;
(3)   speed of access as access requirements are simplified compared to the main market and less stringent to allow a greater number of companies to be able to list;
(4)   low listing costs compared to listing on a regulated market. Lower costs are a consequence of greater regulatory flexibility and speed of quotation; in recent years a tax credit has also been confirmed;
(5)   international visibility as companies still access a global market and therefore benefit from international visibility.

Euronext Growth Milan includes SMEs that do not fall within the scope of the current NFRD, as they do not qualify as entities of public interest or do not reach certain size thresholds. The new CSRD has extended the requirements on sustainability reporting to all listed companies, included listed SMEs from 2026, excluding micro-enterprises. EGM, however, remains excluded from the extension of the scope of application of the CSRD as the extension only concerns regulated markets and not multilateral trading facilities (MTF) (Assonime & AssoNext, 2023). Despite these considerations, sustainability still represents an important challenge for the EGM sector since these companies must respond to disclosure obligations required by the financial sector and must adapt to market needs dictated by belonging to value chains subject to reporting obligations, sustainability requirements, and due diligence. This therefore requires a growing understanding of ESG issues on the part of the administrative bodies and an update on the risks and opportunities offered by ESG issues within the business model. Consequently, it is necessary to reflect on what possible changes should be made: to the governance system to be able to respond adequately; to the definition of production processes; to the provision of services; and to organizational structures. The recommendation offered by Assonime and AssoNext is not to create excessive and inefficient organizational structures that can generate excessive operating costs. A potential tool to facilitate the implementation of ESG in the business model could be to adopt the discipline of benefit companies (a particular model of social enterprises in Italy that are regulated by a specific law), which combines the economic purpose that characterizes the company with other purposes aimed at satisfying interests different from those of the shareholders.

In recent years EGM has been investigated by carrying out surveys to detect the level of awareness towards the integration of ESG issues into corporate strategy, governance and business models, although they are not subject to any regulatory obligation (Rossolini et al., 2023). In particular, with regard to the monitoring of sustainability issues at a governance level, which was measured using a "Sustainability governance index" indicator (with values from 0 to 1), quite low-level results emerged in comparison with large, listed companies, where the utilities and telecommunications sectors reach the highest values. In general, a growth in the level of awareness on ESG issues and, in particular, on issues related to governance, has been demonstrated. The most relevant issues that have seen greater growth in awareness compared to the results of the previous survey are transparency on lobbying activity, the definition of conflicts of interest, and of gifts and representations. In particular, the survey demonstrates a general improvement in terms of management of environmental and climate risks, particularly for small companies.

The analysis of the main practices of EGM companies is based on the results emerging from two main studies – IRTOP CEO Sentiment 2022 and ESG Observatory on EGM[2] – from which it emerges that companies listed on EGM demonstrate a growing sensitivity to ESG issues. With regard to governance issues, the research conducted on CEOs shows particular attention to social issues (45%), followed by environmental ones (37%), and then governance ones (36%). Another quite disappointing aspect concerns the low percentage of companies that draw up a sustainability report (29%).

The ESG Observatory on EGM, the first ESG data provider (owned by IR Top Consulting), investigated the ESG disclosure practices of the 54 companies listed as of 31 December 2022 (equal to 28% of the total) that reported their sustainability activities in 2022. The main findings can be summarized as follows regarding governance-related issues: 35% of the analysed sample declared that they adopt the risk management model to ensure correct control and identify a resolution strategy; 65% of companies do not adopt an ESG risk identification system and this part of the sample usually adopt an analysis of the internal and external business context without mapping and checking ESG risks. Among the main risks mapped are personal/economic business risks (52%), environmental (43%), corruption (28%) and social risks (22%). As regards the governance models implemented, there is a prevalence of the adoption of formal procedures, such as the adoption of the Code of Ethics (89%) and the Management, Organization and Control System pursuant to Legislative Decree 231/2001, although 89% of companies declare that they do not identify the risks linked to corruption through an anti-corruption management model. Another interesting aspect concerns the presence of ESG committees, which can represent a governance tool that allows ESG to be implemented more efficiently in strategic decisions. From the data collected, only 20% of companies have an ESG committee with the task of supervising the integration of ESG issues into the corporate strategy. This confirms that the formal aspects linked to sustainability governance are still privileged. Companies therefore tend to communicate what has already been done without offering a forward-looking vision regarding adequate medium-to-long term strategic planning.

Academic research on the EGM sector, but generally regarding SMEs, highlights that there are still many barriers and skepticism towards ESG issues. A study (Del Baldo, 2016) highlights how Italian SMEs are greatly influenced by the entrepreneur's orientation in the ESG implementation path. The analysis also demonstrates how in Italy a group of SMEs included in a specific network (which includes institutions, trade associations, non-profit organizations) manages to contribute to the dissemination of CSR issues in the territory by creating an interesting model of socially responsible orientation focused on best practices of SMEs. Moreover, interesting research on the EGM sector (Maggi et al., 2023) highlights the level of environmental disclosure in family and non-family firms. The results demonstrate a lower level of disclosure in family firms which, however, is moderated by the gender diversity of the board; this clearly reduces the gap, particularly when the number of women on the board reaches a high level.

Regarding the effects of ESG reporting in the Italian SMEs sector, a study has shown that in the opposite way to what occurs in large companies, there is a negative effect on the cost of capital in relation to environmental disclosure. However, this effect is moderated if they are family firms, which therefore generate an effect similar to that of large companies (Gjergji et al., 2021).

4   CONCLUSION

The impact of corporate governance practices on sustainable development is relevant and all governance-related issues are playing a key contribution to improving sustainability and resilience in all businesses.

There is an increasing need to inform investors about an integrated governance system capable of managing environmental and social risks and at the same time being able to disclose the relevant information in a coherent and reliable manner. In an operational respect, the roles of the administrative, management and supervisory bodies must therefore be modified, a correct flow of information on sustainability issues towards the administrative, management and supervisory bodies must be created, and the integration of sustainability strategies and performances must be foreseen in incentive systems.

The implementation of effective corporate governance becomes an essential competitive advantage in a context of ever-increasing expectations towards sustainability from investors, consumers, and communities. Corporate conduct and business integrity will therefore become the main tool for strengthening corporate reputation and promoting stakeholder trust, thus generating a positive impact on corporate sustainability and the environment in which the company operates.

NOTES

1. The acronym ESG was used for the first time in 2004 when it had been developed in a report by 20 financial institutions. In 2006 ESG issues are mentioned by the UN's Principles for Responsible Investment, as follows: "The principles were developed by investors, for investors. In implementing them, signatories contribute to developing a more sustainable global financial system." See Principles for Responsible Investment (n.d.).
2. See https://www.irtop.com/wp-content/uploads/2022/01/2022-01-12-IR-Top-Consulting-CS -CEO-SENTIMENT-SURVEY.pdf.

REFERENCES

AssoNext (n.d.). Website available at https://assonext.it/, last accessed 19 December 2023.

Assonime (2023). Rapporto di Giunta Executive Summary, L'evoluzione dell'organo amminis-
trativo tra sostenibilità e trasformazione digitale, Studi e Note 1/2023, Gruppo di lavoro della
Giunta Assonime coordinato da Corrado Passera, available at https://www.assonime.it/_layouts/
15/Assonime.CustomAction/GetPdfToUrl.aspx?PathPdf=https://www.assonime.it/attivita-editoriale/
studi/Documents/Note%20e%20Studi%201%20-%202023.pdf, last accessed 19 December 2023.

Assonime & AssoNext (2023). La sfida della sostenibilità per le PMI quotate su Euronext Growth Milan.
Evoluzione del quadro normativo e nuove opportunità, Studi e Note 3/2023, available at https://www
.assonime.it/attivita-editoriale/studi/Pagine/Note-e-Studi-3_2023.aspx, last accessed 19 December
2023.

Borsa Italiana (n.d.). Euronext Growth Milan, available at https://www.borsaitaliana.it/azioni/mercati/
euronext-growth-milan/home/caratteristiche.en.htm, last accessed 19 December 2023.

Comitato Corporate Governance (2020). Corporate Governance Code, available at https://www
.borsaitaliana.it/comitato-corporate-governance/codice/2020eng.en.pdf, last accessed 19 December
2023.

Del Baldo, M., (2016). Corporate social responsibility and corporate governance in Italian SMEs: the
experience of some "spirited businesses", *Journal of Management and Governance*, 16, 1–36. DOI
10.1007/s10997-009-9127-4.

EFRAG (2023). ESRS, available at https://www.efrag.org/lab6, last accessed 19 December 2023.

EFRAG (2024). Voluntary ESRS for non-Listed Small-and Medium-sized Enterprises, available at
https://www.efrag.org/News/Public-479/EFRAGs-

Fink, L. (2022). Larry Fink's 2022 Letter to CEOs: The Power of Capitalism, available at https://www
.blackrock.com/corporate/investor-relations/larry-fink-ceo-letter, last accessed 21 May 2024.

FRC (2024) Financial Reporting Council, UK Corporate Coucncil Code, available at https://media.frc
.org.uk/documents/UK_Corporate_Governance_Code_2024_kRCm5ss.pdf

Gjergji, R., Vena, L., Sciascia, S., & Cortesi, A. (2021). The effects of environmental, social and governance disclosure on the cost of capital in small and medium enterprises: the role of family business
status. *Business Strategy and the Environment*, 30(1), 683–693.

ICGN (2021). *ICGN Global Governance Principles*, London: International Corporate Governance
Network, available at https://www.icgn.org/sites/default/files/2021-11/ICGN%20Global
%20Governance%20Principles%202021.pdf, last accessed 19 December 2023.

Maggi, B., Gjergji, R., Vena, L., Sciascia, S., & Cortesi, A. (2023). Family firm status and environmental disclosure: the moderating effect of board gender diversity. *Business Ethics, the Environment &
Responsibility*, 32(4), 1334–1351.

OECD (2023). *G20/OECD Principles of Corporate Governance 2023*. Paris: OECD Publishing,
available at https://www.oecd-ilibrary.org/governance/g20-oecd-principles-of-corporate-governance
-2023_ed750b30-en, last accessed 19 December 2023.

Principles for Responsible Investment (n.d.). What are the Principles for Responsible Investment?,
available at https://www.unpri.org/about-us/what-are-the-principles-for-responsible-investment, last
accessed 19 December 2023.

Rossolini, M., Pedrazzoli, A., Bongini P., & Liberati, C. (2023). Rapporto sulla sostenibilità delle
imprese quotate italiane 2023, Il Sole 24 Ore. (White paper, not open access.)

17. Conceptualising climate change governance and disclosure to enhance sustainability reporting

Syed Mahfujul Alam and Ericka Costa

1   INTRODUCTION

Climate change is now regarded as a significant risk to the sustainability of firms, operations, and stakeholders (Damert and Baumgartner, 2017; Toukabri and Mohamed Youssef, 2022). The rapidly shifting attention towards climate change is stimulated by the potentially destructive consequences on ecosystems and sustainability (Depoers et al., 2016). Consequently, stakeholders and investors create a circular pressure on firms to design and disseminate effective climate change management approaches (Toukabri and Mohamed Youssef, 2022). Irrespective of firms' objectives, management faces a fundamental challenge in integrating an effective climate change management strategy to conduct organisational activities. Climate change management is thus embedded in corporate governance practice, linking governance of ESG domains (Cosma et al., 2022). Therefore, the managerial practice faces dual challenges of *governing* climate change and *disclosing* climate change-related information to stakeholders.

The extant management theories and literature indicate that competitive strategies, regulatory pressures, and social demands drive firms' attention to highlight broader environmental issues (Bui et al., 2020). Several voluntary government programmes, such as the European Union Emissions Trading Scheme, and non-governmental projects or the Carbon Disclosure Project (CDP) encouraged firms to gather data and disclose climate change-related information to stakeholders. The prior initiatives were, however, limited to greenhouse gas (GHG) emissions, which have now shifted to climate change to portray the broader set of impacts on stakeholders (Galbreath, 2009). Even though prior initiatives were intended to reduce GHG emissions, concurrent initiatives and projects are more inclined towards reducing negative impacts by investing more in green technologies. Consequently, governance practice plays a prominent role in governing green investment initiatives to manage negative impact reduction programmes of climate change and disclose how climate change management strategies reduce negative impacts (Cosma et al., 2022).

Stakeholders are also forcing firms to disclose how green investment initiatives are reducing the negative impacts of climate change (Daddi et al., 2018). Stakeholders are, therefore, demanding to receive timely and relevant climate change information (Depoers et al., 2016). Investors also demand more accountability from boards as the boards are responsible for maximising firms' values (Bui et al., 2020). The governance issue of climate change thus now deals with drawing an effective climate change *management strategy* and *disclosing data* on how firms are reducing the negative impacts of climate change.

To respond to these pressures, the 2030 Agenda for the Sustainable Development Goals (SDGs) has challenged firms' governance practices to incorporate several strategic initiatives

(United Nations, 2022). Timely achievement of this is now at stake due to the failure of managing firms' approaches to sustainability (Elsayih et al., 2020). Therefore, disclosing climate change-related information forms a major construct of sustainability reporting. In essence, sustainable business models are now dependent on climate change governance and disclosure practices (Bui et al., 2020).

The extant literature highlighted how the existing reporting guidelines and frameworks leave firms with voluntary reporting practices (Depoers et al., 2016). Voluntary adoption does not necessarily cause damage to governance and reporting practice. However, the voluntary approaches create variations between firms' governance and disclosure practices. Consequently, stakeholders and investors find inconsistent and incoherent information irrelevant and ambiguous. Since the emergence of the Kyoto Protocol, several directives, guidelines, and frameworks have existed. For example, the EU Directive, CDSB, and TCFD are a few of these that guide firms' climate governance and disclosure practices. Other initiatives, such as the CDP, voluntarily ask firms to disclose carbon data from different industries to link broader environmental disclosure to institutional investors. The broader spectrum of current practical contributions to highlight climate governance and disclosure practice symbolises the significance of climate change-related management. Conversely, the extant literature has been sluggish in developing a governance framework to manage the interests of shareholders and stakeholders in climate change management strategies and disclosure practices (Cosma et al., 2022; Toukabri and Mohamed Youssef, 2022).

Different demands and pressures have also raised the urgency of climate change governance and disclosure from shareholders, investors, and other stakeholders. Stakeholders demand the integration of carbon performance and carbon disclosure to disseminate how firms comply with socially responsible investment techniques (Bui et al., 2020). The disclosure could thus align with firms' achievement of sustainable competitive advantage (Bao and Lewellyn, 2017). Consequently, boards have a critical role in disseminating how the top management sets strategies for climate change management approaches.

The significance of the boards' roles has strengthened the exploration of the governance mechanism to link the UN 2030 Agenda to the SDGs (Toukabri and Mohamed Youssef, 2022). Therefore, the academic literature needs a broader perspective on outlining the determining factors of climate change governance. The chapter describes the general theoretical positions of climate change disclosure and corporate governance. Then, the chapter highlights theoretical perspectives of climate change governance and discusses the practical implications of existing frameworks and guidelines. It concludes by indicating nascent climate change governance and disclosure practice fields.

2   CORPORATE GOVERNANCE AND CLIMATE CHANGE DISCLOSURE – THE THEORETICAL DISPOSITIONS

Climate change disclosure refers to a wider set of information disclosures including how entities' activities impact climate change and how climate change impacts entities' activities (European Central Bank, 2023). These impacts are disclosed by identifying risks, opportunities, and climate change mitigation. Therefore, climate change disclosure is broader than just reporting and disclosing entities' carbon footprint (LSE–Grantham Research Institute, 2018). For example, the broader disclosure may contain information on how entities' GHG emissions impact biodiversity and what risks the biodiversity loss poses to entities (Nelson, 2019). Overall, climate change disclosure goes beyond reporting and disclosing emissions by encapsulating a broader picture of impacts.

The generic concept of corporate governance underlines organisations' oversight and strategic direction, and it has two fundamental dimensions: policy perspective and board structure (Toukabri and Mohamed Youssef, 2022). The policy perspective considers long-term strategic developments and specifications of recruitment and compensation policies of top management, for example, the CEO. Consequently, the policy perspective could specify how the CEO tackles strategic issues like climate change. The board structure deals with features of board size, the separation of dual roles between CEO and chairperson, the construction of various committees, and an outline of shareholdings. The board structure and composition of boards' shareholdings could form the strategic orientation of key information processing centres. The board structure is, therefore, directly linked to organisational performance (Bui et al., 2020). The two key dimensions, policy and boards, constitute how climate change disclosure would be strategised and how boards would communicate data and information to wider stakeholders.

Many different theories could be used to disentangle climate change corporate governance issues. Some of them are offered in this section. The exploration of climate change governance could be viewed from the lens of *agency theory* by underlining boards and optimal board structure. Agency theory suggests that shareholders' interests could be safeguarded by keeping the boards' independence to the fore. The board would independently monitor and control climate change management strategies and disclosure practices (Daddi et al., 2018). The board's independence could be strengthened in many different ways: first, by including a significant number of external members who have no affiliation with the firm, including any shareholding; second, by keeping a high degree of diversity among boards. The diversity could be maintained by including members of different genders, including more female representation on boards (Ben-Amar et al., 2017). Third, the board's independence is also related to including members who are not contractually connected by any material means. The assurance of an independent board member promotes new insights and perspectives on environmental and social stakeholders.

The governance issue could also be viewed from the lens of *institutional theory*, positing isomorphisms, mimetic processes, and normative pressures (Daddi et al., 2018). The three levels of coercive domains diffuse and homogenise institutional and societal impacts. Consequently, firms are coerced to demonstrate how sustainable practices are undertaken. The institutional frameworks, such as political, financial, and cultural systems, design the adoption of climate change management strategy. The institutional theory further highlights the pressure on non-governmental organisations (NGOs), educational establishments, and trade associations to frame climate change management strategy and disclosure practice. The institutional theory elucidates pressures from stakeholders, including investors, governments, suppliers, and customers, on firms to disclose climate change-related information. The variations in expectations and demands make the governance process complex, so that climate change governance requires a robust reporting practice.

The inconsistency issue could be explored via the *stakeholder theory* to see how inconsistency leads to inconsistent governance practices. The inconsistency exists at organisational levels, for example, in NGOs, the public sector, and small to medium-sized enterprises (SMEs), in assigning various climate change key performance indicators (KPIs) and measures (Gonzalez-Gonzalez and Zamora Ramírez, 2016). These climate change inconsistencies underline inconsistency in governance practice. Stakeholder theory posits the inclusion of stakeholders to avoid inconsistency in climate change governance practice (Daddi et al., 2018). The theory suggests that firms' decisions to include stakeholders are motivated by the possibility of gaining a competitive advantage by disclosing various climate change KPIs and measures. The competitive advantage motivation leads to better consistency in governance and disclosure practices (Damert and Baumgartner, 2017).

Stakeholder theory could also be explored to validate how stakeholder pressure could force firms to enhance climate change governance. Moreover, the theory could be further explored in the context of broader governance and disclosure mechanisms. Stakeholder theory posits that organisational success is inherent in addressing broader societal needs and fulfilling those needs by going beyond shareholders' concerns. In achieving societal needs through stakeholder theory, women's leadership styles are distinguished from men's, as women prioritise organisational and social needs and welfare. Furthermore, female directors have been attributed as being more likely to achieve social targets (Hossain et al., 2017). A few general qualities that separate women's from men's leadership styles are gentle, emphatic, and supportive approaches to governing activities. Women's presence, therefore, attracts more social projects and investments in which investors are more willing to invest due to positive demonstrations of long-term values in investing in social and environmental projects (Arayssi et al., 2016). Women's presence on boards thus shapes firms' board structures to become more responsible and to disclose quality climate change information.

The governance approach to climate change by firms is theoretically narrowed to avoid regulatory punishments and protect firms' reputations. Firms avoid punishments which misalign with theoretical propositions of higher levels of communications (Damert and Baumgartner, 2017). Consequently, climate change governance could further be explored via the *signalling theory*, which indicates that firms' commitments to carbon emissions are aligned with the achievement of competitive advantage, and firms are willing to invest more to gain such a competitive advantage and stay ahead in the market. Therefore, climate change governance theory has not been broadened enough to demonstrate how firms should undertake climate change strategies and disclose them to stakeholders.

The *legitimacy theory*, by contrast, could further be utilised to inform stakeholders as to how firms achieve business objectives. Stakeholders typically search for information detailing the achievement of objectives to discover how firms have used social resources and whether firms have maintained ethical principles in using those resources (Bao and Lewellyn, 2017). The legitimacy theory would justify firms' selections of ethical activities. The disclosure thus underpins a managerial technique outlining firms' communications techniques to strengthen the positive image within the social construct. Legitimacy theory simplifies boards' societal position to align business objectives with societal objectives. Governance of climate change, underlined by the legitimacy theory, forms a social contract to undertake socially responsible strategies and to disclose those strategies to stakeholders.

The application of several theories on climate change governance uncovers several constructs of climate change governance. Table 17.1 exhibits the different governance constructs of the theories discussed. Agency, institutional, stakeholder, signalling, and legitimacy theories highlight board composition, stakeholder pressure, social constructs, the inclusion of stakeholders' concerns, and boards' commitments to enhance climate change governance and disclosure practices. Table 17.1 further exhibits how those theoretical views are operationalised in climate change governance practice. The mere theoretical discussions may limit the

Table 17.1   *Theoretical highlights of climate change governance and disclosure factors*

Theoretical lens	Governance constructs	Theoretical implications
Agency theory	Independence of boards	Bringing about the diversity of boards to enhance boards' independence
Institutional theory	Homogeneous pressure on boards	Mapping stakeholders to prioritise pressure
Legitimacy theory	Boards' social contracts	Constructing socially responsible strategies
Stakeholder theory	Inclusion of broader stakeholders' concerns	Female leadership to identify broader stakeholders' concerns and prioritising those concerns to bring consistency in voluntary disclosure practices
Signalling theory	Boards' commitment to improving carbon performance (financial)	Enhancing financial and non-financial commitments by increasing the gender diversity of boards

significance of explored theories to climate change governance practice. Theoretical views could further be extended to explore factors enhancing governance and disclosure practice. The unboxing of multiple factors could broadly serve to specify board composition, communication strategy, stakeholder mapping and disclosure approaches. The present chapter thus sets the boundaries of theoretical applications to climate change governance factors.

3   ENHANCING CLIMATE CHANGE GOVERNANCE AND DISCLOSURE: UNBOXING MULTIPLE FACTORS

The prior discussions on theoretical dispositions highlighted several theoretical applications to climate change governance. The applications were inconsistent in determining how climate change governance could be enhanced to accomplish the objectives of the SDGs. Starting from the overview in the previous paragraph and the analysis of different theoretical lenses that could be used to interpret climate change corporate governance, this section will investigate multiple factors that could enhance the governance and disclosure mechanisms of climate change-related information. Drawing upon governance constructs and theoretical implications (Table 17.1), the present section discusses how multiple factors could be applied to constructing boards and enhancing climate change governance practice. Figure 17.1 highlights connections between theories and multiple factors shaping an enhanced climate change governance practice. The following section explains the implications of multiple factors and discusses the theoretical influence on practising climate change governance.

Factor 1: Information symmetry
Signalling theory indicates that managers and investors could conflict due to information asymmetry. An effective climate change governance would reduce these conflicts by enhancing information quality and availability of relevant information. Climate change governance would reduce the dependency on external factors and increase internal credibility to enhance disclosure quality. Therefore, board diversity is crucial and could provide diversified insight into climate change concerns and reveal opportunities to design governance mechanisms (Ben-Amar et al., 2017). The disclosure could further minimise management and investor

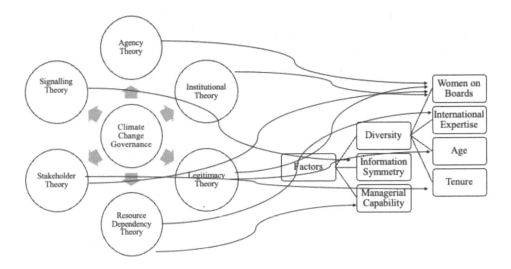

Figure 17.1   The interplay of theories and factors of climate change governance

conflicts by eliminating information asymmetry and establishing independent subcommittees solely overseeing climate change policies.

Factor 2: Managerial capability
Managerial capability could be another factor in enhancing the information quality of climate change disclosure (Daradkeh et al., 2022). Drawing upon resource dependency theory (RDT), acquiring capable managers indicates a broader skill set of managers, which enhances governance practice (Daddi et al., 2018). Capable managers outline a broader set of indicators to stakeholders, enhancing information quality to underline a strong governance practice. Capable managers would further consider variable levels of indicators rather than highlighting a limited number of indicators. Even though variable considerations would have an overlapping discourse, the broader context would enhance firms' commitments to climate change disclosure and improve governance practice. The managerial capabilities could be extended to consider firms' performance, underpinned by an effective governance mechanism. Capable managers promote socially responsible green investments to investors to positively impact firms' financial and non-financial performance.

Factor 3: Diversity
Theoretical underpinnings of climate change governance favour bringing diversity to climate change disclosure and risk committees (Jizi et al., 2022). The presence of diverse boards has positively affected sustainability reporting quality (Ben-Amar et al., 2017). Board diversity could further be discussed from the viewpoint of 'relational capital', which is crucial in attracting critical resources (Daradkeh et al., 2022). Multiple factors thus emerged from diversity factors, which could be segmented into sub-factors of diversity.

Factor 3a: Women on boards
Gender diversity has garnered such a substantial significance in the present academic literature that it has caused firms to restructure boards by recognising the positive effects of women's

presence to strategise and promote quality sustainability reporting practice (Arayssi et al., 2016). The presence of women on boards can provide dual benefits. First, women's presence would diversify a board, producing better financial performance. Following the agency theory, a diversified board including women will add value to shareholders' wealth by considering climate change-related risks. Second, the diverse boards would reduce information asymmetry in sustainability disclosure by contributing to climate change activities. The positive associations between a female presence on boards and positive financial and non-financial performance could underpin the disclosure of quality information (Galbreath, 2016). Women's presence would also support firms in ensuring a balanced governing mechanism between financial and social targets, as women's leadership is connected to increasing social awareness (Ben-Amar et al., 2017). The increased social awareness is related to the legitimacy theory by the fulfilment of social contracts (Daddi et al., 2018). The institutional theory explains the attribution of women's presence on boards to the prioritising of stakeholders' concerns in climate change strategy. Female board members would pressure top management to take account of broader stakeholders' expectations and put equal emphasis on financial and non-financial indicators in governing and disclosing climate change-related information. The equal emphasis on female board members extends the discussion to stakeholder theory by bringing broader concerns of stakeholders to bear. Women on boards are thus related to agency, legitimacy, institutional, and stakeholder theories.

Factor 3b: International expertise
In developing boards' attributes to highlight several contexts of climate change governance, national diversity within boards has also been coined as a good indicator of governance practice for disclosing sustainability information. The effectiveness of diverse international board members is grounded on resource dependence theory, positing value additions by international directors to boards in driving an effective sustainability strategy to govern climate change management (Daddi et al., 2018). The internationally expert board members enhance the quality of climate change information to disclose sustainability strategy to stakeholders. Broadening the theoretical underpinnings, the international board members are more stakeholder-oriented, as they strike a balance between stakeholders' and shareholders' needs. Consequently, climate change governance is being pushed to enhance quality and transparency in accounting and disclosure practices.

Factor 3c: Age diversity
Age diversity is another key attribute that provides new territory in climate change governance practice (Toukabri and Mohamed Youssef, 2022). Although age diversity has yet to be underlined as being as significant as other attributes, board members' expertise and varied profiles lead to positive and effective decisions to enhance climate change governance practice. Drawing upon the legitimacy theory, older directors fulfil social contracts by displaying wider concerns for sustainability issues. The seniority of directors, therefore, brings more expertise to outline the governance mechanism of climate change and enhance sustainability disclosure practices.

Factor 3d: Tenure diversity
The final board attribute that could be discussed in the climate change governance context is the tenure diversity of board members. The stakeholder theory provides a positive notion towards board tenure and socially driven strategies (Depoers et al., 2016). Applying the

theoretical view could thus indicate that boards with longer-tenured directors would produce broader sustainability disclosure indicators. Climate change-related information constitutes a significant portion of such a broader disclosure practice. Good governance practices for climate change strategies include the tenure diversity of boards as grounded on industry and practical expertise.

While climate change governance could be highlighted in several spectrums of boards' attributes, the academic literature is limited to these highlighted areas. The limitations, however, could be overcome by aligning board objectives with the broader context of social and environmental goals. Overall, the diversity of boards has been asserted as being the core attribute for bringing about effective governance practice. Therefore, the theoretical approach to climate change governance should consider achieving variety in several aspects, such as gender, nationality, age and tenure, to increase the effectiveness of climate change governance to enhance the quality of sustainability reporting. At the same time, the practical guidelines could support what the theoretical applications are positing to enhance climate governance and disclosure mechanisms. The combination of theoretical and practical guidelines would indicate whether the tensions between climate change governance and disclosure could be addressed within the present mechanism.

4   CLIMATE CHANGE GOVERNANCE – PRACTICAL IMPLICATIONS FOR DISCLOSURE

The theoretical and literature contexts underline how boards' attributes could shape a good climate change governance practice. Good governance practice ensures an enhanced sustainability disclosure and reporting practice. Indeed, boards should consider broader stakeholders' concerns in disseminating how firms tackle the impacts of climate change. While boards attempt to include stakeholders' concerns and needs in operationalising climate change governance, concerns for adopting a common baseline should not be underestimated. Consequently, industry-wide available standards, guidelines, and frameworks are crucial to designing the governance and disclosure practice. The existing leading frameworks, guidelines and standards that are currently tackling corporate governance in climate change disclosure are the Climate Disclosure Standards Board (CDSB), the Task Force on Climate-Related Financial Disclosures (TCFD) and IFRS S2, Climate-Related Disclosures. The present chapter provides insights into how these guidelines, frameworks and standards address climate change governance and disclosure mechanisms. Table 17.2 has been constructed to provide an overview of how these existing frameworks, guidelines, and standards address governance issues and ways to incorporate theoretical factors. Table 17.2 indicates the existing focuses of practitioners' platforms to highlight gaps in practising climate change governance. Based on prior theoretical discussions, Table 17.2 establishes avenues for applying theories to manifest factors in enhancing climate change governance.

The Climate Disclosure Standards Board (CDSB) outlines the link between governance and reporting, and offers several requirements for social and environmental reporting, in which governance (REQ-01) is crucial. The CDSB requires organisations to include a separate section outlining boards' strategies, policies, and approaches to tackling climate change (CDSB, 2022). The reporting should cover two aspects, i.e., an oversight committee and explanations of matters. First, the recognition of boards and committees responsible for

Table 17.2   *Highlights of existing climate change governance and disclosure guidelines and potential avenues to enhance governance and disclosure practices*

Platforms	Existing highlights	Gaps	Avenues
CDSB (REQ-01)	i. Inclusion of an independent oversight committee responsible for climate change strategies and management ii. Disclosure of committee's expertise, skills, compositions, and responsibilities	Absence of key indicators to determine the independence of boards	i. Agency theory – gender diversity, external members, and mutually non-contractual members on board ii. Stakeholder theory – older and long-tenured board members to bring wider expertise to boards
TCFD	i. Boards' oversight on climate risks and opportunities ii. Boards' roles in evaluating and managing climate risks and opportunities	Boards' compositions without diversity and weak emphasis on non-financial indicators	i. Signalling theory – capable managers to assess risks and opportunities and disseminate climate change-related information to investors ii. Legitimacy theory – women on boards to consider social and non-financial indicators to strengthen the risk and opportunity identification process
IFRS S2	Protecting shareholders' financial interests by i. Revealing an entity's exposure to climate-related physical and transition risks ii. Unfolding climate-related opportunities	Over-emphasis on financial interests	i. Resource dependency theory – an internationally diverse board would bring broader industry expertise to indicate climate-related risks and opportunities ii. Institutional theory – female participation in boards' decision-making to embed non-financially motivated risks and opportunities

climate change strategies and management should be considered. Including committees shows the significance of having an independent oversight committee for climate change disclosure. Second, an explanation of several issues related to climate change disclosure should be included, such as expertise, skills, the composition of boards, responsibilities, information processing approach, and key responsible parties. Hence, the CDSB's guidelines for framing the disclosure process emphasise boards' attributes, especially expertise and the composition of independent committees. The CDSB thus proposes the rationale behind a good governance mechanism to validate the necessity of boards' roles in enhancing climate change disclosure information quality.

The TCFD recommends specific areas for the disclosing of governance information. The TCFD prioritises governance at the top of the agenda to outline boards' responsibilities for identifying climate-related risks and opportunities. The TCFD indicates two broader areas, including *boards' oversight of climate-related risks* and *opportunities* (TCFD, 2017). Recognising risks and opportunities entails the board's responsibility for applying knowledge and expertise to deliver strategic plans for managing climate change. The context thus strengthens the argument of having a diverse board that would pull in broader industry expertise to shape climate change governance. The second TCFD area includes *detailing management roles in evaluating and managing climate change-related risks and opportunities*. Consequently, identifying and managing risks and opportunities builds the overall governance mechanisms of climate change. Even though the TCFD stresses financial dangers and options, the concerns constitute core functions of climate change governance mechanisms. Consequently, the priority of climate change governance is to have a composition of expert board members who would deliver the required information related to climate change.

The newly introduced IFRS S2, Climate-Related Disclosures, also emphasised the governance process in unpacking climate-related risks and opportunities. The broader purpose of IFRS S2 is to provide an in-depth insight into how climate-related risks affect financial positions (IFRS, 2022). Consequently, governance mechanisms require technical and industrial knowledge to disseminate climate-related risks and opportunities to protect shareholders' interests. IFRS S2 thus dominates shareholders' concerns, which are the same as the TCFD, to outline the governance mechanism for protecting shareholders' interests. While the CDSB outlines boards' general composition and attributes to manage climate change, the TCFD and IFRS S2 stress financial aspects in disclosing climate change-related information. Consequently, the effectiveness of a good governance practice, solely relying on financial indicators in managing and disclosing climate change-related information, could be questioned.

The practical implications of the CDSB, the TCFD, and IFRS S2 are limited to financial aspects, and broader stakeholders' concerns would be undermined in the current mechanisms of practising guidelines and frameworks. Even though these three guidelines incorporate risks and opportunities, their objectives are more biased towards financial aspects. The TCFD and IFRS S2 opine that it is important to highlight more investors' value-oriented matters rather than broader stakeholders' concerns. Regarding the CDSB's guidelines, they are ambiguous in prioritising stakeholders. Conversely, boards could merge the three practical guidelines and frameworks to combine financial and non-financial aspects. For example, boards could form separate committees overseeing financial and non-financial aspects of climate change. Including diversity on boards would be useful in bringing industry and international expertise to identify financial and non-financial risks and opportunities. Therefore, theoretical inputs to these guidelines would shape the formation of boards that equally prioritise financial and non-financial matters and serve broader stakeholders by disclosing various climate change-related matters to stakeholders.

An illustration is made here to show theories that could be applied to practical platforms (Table 17.2). For instance, Lahyani (2022) applied agency and stakeholder theories to propose that diversified boards tend to disclose more information and exhibit greater commitments to sustainability. Here, the advocacy of the agency theory underlines the board diversity that enhances the disclosure (Ben-Amar et al., 2017). At the same time, stakeholder theory underpins boards' commitment and independence to enhance governance (Zhang and Liu, 2020). In this way, diversity and commitments are drawn from the agency and stakeholder theories to apply to practical contexts of the CDSB (REQ-01). In a similar way, resource dependency theory could be applied to the IFRS S2 context, where the theory depicts internationally diversified and experienced boards address shareholders' interests (Khatib et al., 2020). As IFRS S2 emphasises disclosing climate-related risks, diversified and expert boards may enhance the disclosure practice by protecting the interests of shareholders and investors.

Signalling theory may also be applied to enhance boards' oversight of risk identification and management. As per the TCFD's recommendations, boards have the role of assessing risks and disclosing them to shareholders. Signalling theory supports this role by incorporating the diversity of boards with a high level of disclosure, an enhanced reputation, and a reduced agency conflict (Yan et al., 2020). The same could be explored through the legitimacy and institutional theory to bring about more diversity on boards, for instance, greater presence of women, to reduce conflicts and enhance the governance practice of identification of climate change-related risks and opportunities (Michelon and Parbonetti, 2012; Qian and Schaltegger, 2017). Overall, these theories provide frameworks, hypotheses, and propositions to explore multiple practical contexts of climate change disclosure and governance practices.

The indicated practical platforms are not exhaustive. For example, the European Sustainability Reporting Standards (ESRS) and the Global Reporting Initiative (GRI) have practical guidelines and frameworks. However, they all have a high level of interoperability/consistency to avoid double disclosure and reporting (European Commission, 2023). Therefore, the suggested theoretical applications could be applied to these practical platforms to explore climate change disclosure governance practice.

5   CONCLUSION

This chapter constructs the significance of climate change governance to enhance disclosure quality. Climate change governance has become a focal point in academic and practitioner debates and conversations (Cosma et al., 2022; Galbreath, 2016; Gonzalez-Gonzalez and Zamora Ramírez, 2016; Toukabri and Mohamed Youssef, 2022). The extant literature addressed climate change governance to explore relevant attributes of boards and the overall responsibilities of committees to manage climate change (Cosma et al., 2022; Galbreath, 2016; Gonzalez-Gonzalez and Zamora Ramírez, 2016; Toukabri and Mohamed Youssef, 2022). Good governance mechanisms are viewed through the lens of agency, institutional, legitimacy, resource dependency, stakeholder, and signalling theories (Arayssi et al., 2016; Bao and Lewellyn, 2017; Ben-Amar et al., 2017; Bui et al., 2020; Daradkeh et al., 2022; Galbreath, 2016; Hossain et al., 2017; Jizi et al., 2022). The theoretical dispositions construct multiple factors enhancing climate change governance practice.

The theoretical assumptions and literature contributions generally emphasised that boards' diversity is a core factor driving an effective corporate governance practice. Multiple factors driving boards' diversity include women on boards, age, international expertise, information symmetry, and managerial capability (Arayssi et al., 2016; Bao and Lewellyn, 2017; Ben-Amar et al., 2017; Bui et al., 2020; Daradkeh et al., 2022; Galbreath, 2016; Hossain et al., 2017; Jizi et al., 2022). While other factors are also highlighted as contributing to good governance practice, women's presence on boards has been highlighted as the core area to enhance governance mechanisms (Ben-Amar et al., 2017; Galbreath, 2016; Hossain et al., 2017). The exploration displayed several theoretical constructs, and multiple influences of women's presence on boards to enhance climate change governance practice.

Our analysis also reviewed the practical guidelines and standards on climate change, showing that they are overly biased towards financial remits. Conversely, a good governance mechanism for climate change management should equally incorporate financial and non-financial gains (Daddi et al., 2018; Hossain et al., 2017; Toukabri and Mohamed Youssef, 2022). The CDSB, the TCFD, and IFRS S2 strongly emphasised the necessity of governance practice to achieve climate change-related SDGs (CDSB, 2022; IFRS, 2022; TCFD, 2017). However, in their current forms, these frameworks are limited to protecting shareholders' financial concerns (Bao and Lewellyn, 2017). Conversely, shareholders' financial concerns will only be protected if boards bring the non-financial indicators to highlight the impact of climate change on the wider group of stakeholders (Bao and Lewellyn, 2017; Bui, et al., 2020; Cosma et al., 2022; Damert and Baumgartner, 2017). The nexus of theoretical and practical insights coincides with achieving the boards' independence in balancing financial and non-financial indicators (Damert and Baumgartner, 2017; Depoers et al., 2016; Gonzalez-Gonzalez and Zamora Ramírez, 2016; OECD, 2022).

In analysing standards, frameworks, and guidelines for climate change disclosure, we have investigated how governance structure could theoretically be explored. The future of climate governance needs to incorporate diverse board members and establish independent committees to oversee both the financial and non-financial sides of climate change (Damert and Baumgartner, 2017; Depoers *et al.*, 2016; Gonzalez-Gonzalez and Zamora Ramírez, 2016; Jizi et al., 2022; OECD, 2022; TCFD, 2017). Potential research fields thus open up for scholars to evaluate and explore how boards' expertise and independence would be enhanced. For practitioners, the potential to include non-financial metrics and indicators would improve a good governance system. Overall, the association of academic focus on non-financial indicators and a practitioners' guide on financial indicators are linked via the good governance mechanism. Success in reducing the negative impacts of climate change is dependent on the effective linkage between financial and non-financial considerations (Daradkeh et al., 2022; Depoers et al., 2016; OECD, 2022). The inclusiveness of our highlighted factors would strengthen climate change standards and guidelines and bring about consistent and enhanced climate change governance practice. Our highlights in Table 17.1 and Table 17.2 show the possible convergence of theories, standards, and guidelines to shape climate change governance practice. We mapped theoretical connections to multiple factors to indicate how several theories could be explored in linking factors to enhance governance practice. The combined approach of theories and standards will ultimately enhance sustainability reporting practice.

The chapter suggests future climate change governance practice agendas by combining theoretical views, standards, and guidelines. The future agenda could primarily include theoretical applications to practical platforms to broaden and fill out climate change disclosure governance literature. In more detail, future research could examine in practice how different factors of governance could enhance climate change disclosure. Both quantitative and qualitative empirical studies could explore how the existence of different governance mechanisms, such as those related to independence and diversity, could affect the quantity and quality of climate change disclosure.

REFERENCES

Arayssi, M., Dah, M. and Jizi, M. (2016). Women on boards, sustainability reporting and firm performance. *Sustainability Accounting, Management and Policy Journal*, 7(3), 376–401. doi: https://doi.org/10.1108/sampj-07-2015-0055.

Bao, S.R. and Lewellyn, K.B. (2017). Ownership structure and earnings management in emerging markets: an institutionalized agency perspective. *International Business Review*, 26(5), 828–838. doi: https://doi.org/10.1016/j.ibusrev.2017.02.002.

Ben-Amar, W., Chang, M. and McIlkenny, P. (2017). Board gender diversity and corporate response to sustainability initiatives: evidence from the Carbon Disclosure Project. *Journal of Business Ethics*, 142(2), 369–383. doi: https://doi.org/10.1007/s10551-015-2759-1.

Bui, B., Houqe, M.N. and Zaman, M. (2020). Climate governance effects on carbon disclosure and performance. *The British Accounting Review*, 52(2), 1–16. doi: https://doi.org/10.1016/j.bar.2019 .100880.

CDSB (2022). *CDSB Framework: for reporting environmental & social information.* Available at: https://www.cdsb.net/sites/default/files/cdsb_framework_2022.pdf (Accessed 30 June 2023).

Cosma, S., Principale, S. and Venturelli, A. (2022). Sustainable governance and climate-change disclosure in European banking: the role of the corporate social responsibility committee. *Corporate Governance: The International Journal of Business in Society*, 22(6), 1345–1369. doi: https://doi.org/ 10.1108/cg-09-2021-0331.

Daddi, T., Todaro, N.M., De Giacomo, M.R. and Frey, M. (2018). A systematic review of the use of organization and management theories in climate change studies. *Business Strategy and the Environment*, 27(4), 456–474. doi: https://doi.org/10.1002/bse.2015.

Damert, M. and Baumgartner, R.J. (2017). External pressures or internal governance: what determines the extent of corporate responses to climate change? *Corporate Social Responsibility and Environmental Management*, 25(4), 473–488. doi: https://doi.org/10.1002/csr.1473.

Daradkeh, H., Shams, S., Bose, S. and Gunasekarage, A. (2022). Does managerial ability matter for corporate climate change disclosures? *Corporate Governance: An International Review*, 31(1), 83–104. doi: https://doi.org/10.1111/corg.12436.

Depoers, F., Jeanjean, T. and Jérôme, T. (2016). Voluntary disclosure of greenhouse gas emissions: contrasting the Carbon Disclosure Project and corporate reports. *Journal of Business Ethics*, 134(3), 445–461. doi: https://doi.org/10.1007/s10551-014-2432-0.

Elsayih, J., Datt, R. and Hamid, A. (2020). CEO characteristics: do they matter for carbon performance? An empirical investigation of Australian firms. *Social Responsibility Journal*, 17(8), 1279–1298. doi: https://doi.org/10.1108/srj-04-2020-0130.

European Central Bank (2023). *What are climate disclosures?* Available at: https://www.ecb.europa .eu/ecb/educational/explainers/html/what-are-climate-disclosures.en.html#:~:text=Climate %20disclosures%20are%20documents%20that (Accessed 6 December 2023).

European Commission (2023). *The Commission Adopts the European Sustainability Reporting Standards.* Available at: https://finance.ec.europa.eu/news/commission-adopts-european-sustainability-reporting -standards-2023-07-31_en (Accessed 6 December 2023).

Galbreath, J. (2009). Corporate governance practices that address climate change: an exploratory study. *Business Strategy and the Environment*, 19(5), 335–350. doi: https://doi.org/10.1002/bse.648.

Galbreath, J. (2016). Is board gender diversity linked to financial performance? The mediating mechanism of CSR. *Business & Society*, 57(5), 863–889. doi: https://doi.org/10.1177/0007650316647967.

Gonzalez-Gonzalez, J.M. and Zamora Ramírez, C. (2016). Voluntary carbon disclosure by Spanish companies: an empirical analysis. *International Journal of Climate Change Strategies and Management*, 8(1), 57–79. doi: https://doi.org/10.1108/ijccsm-09-2014-0114.

Hossain, M., Farooque, O.A., Momin, M.A. and Almotairy, O. (2017). Women in the boardroom and their impact on climate change related disclosure. *Social Responsibility Journal*, 13(4), 828–855. doi: https://doi.org/10.1108/srj-11-2016-0208.

IFRS (2022). *IFRS S2 Climate-Related Disclosures.* Available at: https://www.ifrs.org/issued-standards/ ifrs-sustainability-standards-navigator/ifrs-s2-climate-related-disclosures/ (Accessed 30 June 2023).

Jizi, M., Nehme, R. and Melhem, C. (2022). Board gender diversity and firms' social engagement in the Gulf Cooperation Council (GCC) countries. *Equality, Diversity and Inclusion: An International Journal*, 41(2), 186–206. doi: https://doi.org/10.1108/edi-02-2021-0041.

Khatib, S.F.A., Abdullah, D.F., Elamer, A.A. and Abueid, R. (2020). Nudging toward diversity in the boardroom: a systematic literature review of board diversity of financial institutions. *Business Strategy and the Environment*, 30(2), 985–1002. doi: https://doi.org/10.1002/bse.2665.

Lahyani, F.E. (2022). Corporate board diversity and carbon disclosure: evidence from France. *Accounting Research Journal*, 35(6), 721–736. doi: https://doi.org/10.1108/arj-12-2021-0350.

LSE–Grantham Research Institute (2018). *What is climate change risk disclosure?* Grantham Research Institute on Climate Change and the Environment. Available at: https://www.lse.ac.uk/ granthaminstitute/explainers/climate-change-risk-disclosure/ (Accessed 6 December 2023).

Michelon, G. and Parbonetti, A. (2012). The effect of corporate governance on sustainability disclosure. *Journal of Management & Governance*, 16(3), 477–509. doi: https://doi.org/10.1007/s10997-010 -9160-3.

Nelson, M. (2019). *How climate change disclosures reveal business risks and opportunities*. Available at: https://www.ey.com/en_it/assurance/climate-change-disclosures-revealing-risks-opportunities (Accessed 6 December 2023).

OECD (2022). *Home*. Available at: https://www.oecd-ilibrary.org/sites/272d85c3-en/1/1/index.html ?itemId=/content/publication/272d85c3-en&_csp_=800a252d8c14910314fa8652c1e96fbb& itemIGO=oecd&itemContentType=book (Accessed 17 July 2023).

Qian, W. and Schaltegger, S. (2017). Revisiting carbon disclosure and performance: legitimacy and management views. *The British Accounting Review*, 49(4), 365–379. doi: https://doi.org/10.1016/j .bar.2017.05.005.

TCFD (2017). *Recommendations of the Task Force on Climate-Related Financial Disclosures Final Report*. Available at: https://assets.bbhub.io/company/sites/60/2021/10/FINAL-2017-TCFD-Report .pdf (Accessed 30 June 2023).

Toukabri, M. and Mohamed Youssef, M.A. (2022). Climate change disclosure and Sustainable Development Goals (SDGs) of the 2030 Agenda: the moderating role of corporate governance. *Journal of Information, Communication and Ethics in Society*, 21(1), 30–62. doi: https://doi.org/10 .1108/jices-02-2022-0016.

United Nations (2022). COP27 closes with deal on loss and damage: 'A step towards justice', says UN chief. *UN News*. Available at: https://news.un.org/en/story/2022/11/1130832 (Accessed 2 December 2022).

Yan, H., Li, X., Huang, Y. and Li, Y. (2020). The impact of the consistency of carbon performance and carbon information disclosure on enterprise value. *Finance Research Letters*, 37, 101680. doi: https:// doi.org/10.1016/j.frl.2020.101680.

Zhang, Y.-J. and Liu, J.-Y. (2020). Overview of research on carbon information disclosure. *Frontiers of Engineering Management*, 7(1), 47–62. doi: https://doi.org/10.1007/s42524-019-0089-1.

18. Sustainable corporate governance

Andrea Melis, Simone Aresu, Luigi Rombi and Mariem Khalfaoui

1   INTRODUCTION

This chapter aims to provide an overview of sustainable corporate governance. With this term, we refer to the set of mechanisms, policies, and practices that govern in whose interests a company is run, how trust and power are exercised, and how accountability is achieved (Tricker, 2022) so that a company can achieve its long-term goals, considering the social, environmental, and economic impact of its activities.

Sustainable corporate governance is not restricted to the agency relationships between a company's management, board of directors, and shareholders.[1] It also involves those relationships with a company's stakeholders, including employees, customers, suppliers, the wider community, and the natural environment. Due to these complex sets of relationships and the consequent societal pressure that derives from them, companies are facing the need to be accountable, re-think their purpose, and focus on the long-term interests of strategic and legitimate stakeholders[2] rather than on short-term shareholder value (e.g., Aguilera et al., 2008; Kaplan and Ramanna, 2021; Aresu et al., 2023).

Specifically, sustainable corporate governance comprises a set of incentive, monitoring, and advisory mechanisms that are aimed at assuring that a company is governed in a responsible way so that, being accountable to its strategic and legitimate stakeholders, strategic decision-making and daily operations take into account their interests and consider the impact of a company's operations on the natural environment and society. This chapter will examine the main corporate governance mechanisms expected to ensure sustainability integration in the governance of a company whose shares are publicly traded in the stock market. More specifically, it will focus on the following corporate governance mechanisms:

- the integration of sustainability criteria into a company's executive remuneration contracts;
- the adoption of a sustainability-related committee;
- the assurance of sustainability-related information to the public by a third auditing party;[3]
- the presence of sustainable owners in a company's shareholding structure.

The focus on these four corporate governance mechanisms is mainly due to the following reasons. The voluntary adoption of the first three mechanisms signals a company's embrace of sustainability as an essential element of its strategy (e.g., Ricart et al., 2005; Steinmeier and Stich, 2019; Bose et al., 2023). The fourth mechanism may instead represent a powerful monitoring mechanism (e.g., Dimson et al., 2015; Kavadis and Thomsen, 2023). Specifically, integrating sustainability criteria into a company's executive remuneration contract is expected to provide guidance and enable a company's executives to understand what constitutes environmental and social performance (Ittner et al., 2003) as well as incentivising executives to pursue such performance (e.g., Haque, 2017; Flammer et al., 2019). A sustainability-related committee within the board of directors should oversee a company's sustainability strategies and policies, assess and review its sustainability performance, and advise the board of directors on any sustainability-related issue (e.g., Rodrigue et al., 2013). It is, therefore, expected to help a company's executives better understand and reconcile its stakeholders' diverse and potentially conflicting interests, better monitor their executives, and enhance a company's sustainability performance. The assurance of sustainability-related information to the public by a third auditing party represents a monitoring mechanism expected to make reported performance less prone to manipulation, enhancing the reliability of the information about a company's sustainability performance and keeping a company's executives accountable for actual sustainability performance (e.g., Brown-Liburd and Zamora, 2015; Al-Shaer and Zaman, 2019). Ownership represents a key feature affecting corporate governance and purpose. The presence of sustainable owners could ensure, either by adopting 'voice' (e.g., expressing their concerns and voting during the shareholders' meeting) and/or 'exit' (e.g., selling the shares) strategies (Hirschman, 1970), the accountability of executives and directors towards the stated corporate purpose concerning sustainability, making them accountable 'to walk the talk'. For each of these corporate governance mechanisms, in the following sections of this chapter, we will illustrate their role and the main antecedents and consequences of their presence, combining relevant evidence from prior empirical academic literature, an overview of the development in practice based on data from LSEG Data & Analytics (previously Refinitiv), and anecdotal case study evidence from real-life companies.[4]

2   THE INTEGRATION OF SUSTAINABILITY CRITERIA INTO EXECUTIVE REMUNERATION CONTRACTS

The integration of sustainability criteria into executive remuneration contracts is a corporate remuneration policy that explicitly integrates the design of executive remuneration with environmental and social performance criteria. It links executive variable remuneration to the achievement of sustainability-related targets, such as improving the level of employee health and safety or reducing greenhouse gas emissions (e.g., Hong, B. et al., 2016; Flammer et al., 2019; Ikram et al., 2019; Aresu et al., 2023; Cohen et al., 2023). Companies may adopt this form of remuneration to signal their commitment and build trust with diverse stakeholders, attract long-term oriented investors, and improve their long-term overall performance (e.g., Flammer et al., 2019).

The design of this remuneration practice, which is often referred to as 'CSR contracting' (e.g., Flammer et al., 2019; Aresu et al., 2023), is characterised by the following essential elements that may substantially affect its effectiveness as an incentive mechanism:

- the rationale, nature, and measurement of the sustainability performance criteria;
- the weight of each sustainability-related performance indicator;
- the time horizon of each sustainability-related performance target;
- the target of each sustainability-related performance indicator.

The rationale for the choice of the sustainability performance criteria may depend on the different demands from a company's stakeholders (including the different types of shareholders; see Cohen et al., 2023), taking into account that these demands are addressed according to the stakeholders' relative power (Radu and Smaili, 2022) and the company's ability to measure sustainability metrics (Derchi et al., 2023). When sustainability criteria are integrated into the executive remuneration contract, the nature of performance indicators can be environmental, social, or a combination of both (e.g., health, safety and environment) (Maas and Rosendaal, 2016; Haque, 2017). These performance indicators can either be process-oriented, when they estimate a company's social and/or environmental initiatives (e.g., a carbon reduction initiative), or outcome-oriented, when they assess the outcome of a company's social and/or environmental initiative (e.g., an actual carbon reduction) (Haque, 2017). In terms of measurement, sustainability-related performance indicators can either be objective (e.g., number of work incidents) or subjective (e.g., employees' satisfaction) and either be absolute (e.g., GHG emissions) or relative (e.g., GHG emissions compared to a peer group).

The weight of each sustainability-related performance indicator is the percentage or amount of remuneration conditioned to each performance indicator. It is a critical element of the incentive plan, as adopting a given sustainability criterion can be substantive or symbolic, depending on its weight within the overall remuneration (Flammer et al., 2019).

The time horizon of each sustainability-related performance target is the period within which a specific performance target should be achieved. It generally varies from one year (in the case of short-term bonuses) to several years (e.g., in the case of long-term share-based payments) (Maas and Rosendaal, 2016). For example, in 2021, Nestlé S.A., the world's largest food and beverage company, introduced sustainability-related performance indicators in its short-term incentive plan (Nestlé, 2021). Then, in 2022, the company added these sustainability-related performance indicators to its 2023 five-year long-term incentive plan (Nestlé, 2022).

The target of each sustainability-related performance indicator refers to the amount (or percentage level) to be reached. This target can either be identified with a clear-cut quantification, a so-called 'hard target' (e.g., reduction of CO_2 emissions by 20% in the next year), or without, a so-called 'soft target' (e.g., reduction of CO_2 emissions in the next year) (Maas, 2018).

Overall, a remuneration plan may have a design that is either formulaic or non-formulaic (e.g., Ikram et al., 2019). In the case of a formulaic remuneration plan, the precise performance indicators, their relative weight, their time horizon, and the target are clearly specified (see, for example, the Shell case presented in Table 18.1). Alternatively, in a non-formulaic remuneration plan, the financial reward is conditioned to a more subjective evaluation by the board of directors, as some of the key elements of the incentive plan (e.g., the weight, target or time horizon of each performance indicator) are not clearly predefined, and the executive beneficiary of the contract is *ex ante* unaware of at least some of these elements.

Previous academic studies examined the determinants of CSR contracting (e.g., Ikram et al., 2019; Aresu et al., 2023; Derchi et al., 2023). Companies headquartered in countries with higher environmental and social regulatory pressure were found to be more likely to integrate sustainability criteria into their executive remuneration policies (Aresu et al., 2023; Cohen et al., 2023). In addition, in those countries where environmental protection is perceived as highly important, the relationship between a company's climate change strategy and this form of remuneration is stronger (Bose et al., 2023). As shown in Figure 18.1, the United States and the United Kingdom seem to have the highest number of listed companies (covered in the Asset4 database) that integrate sustainability criteria into their executive remuneration policies.

Industry characteristics were also found to drive the decision to integrate sustainability criteria into executive remuneration contracts, as companies may mimic specific peers' behaviour as a response to industry-based pressure to enhance sustainability-related performance

Table 18.1   Shell plc: the 2023 design of the CEO's annual bonus

Performance condition of the Scorecard architecture	Weight of performance condition		Performance measure adopted	Link to strategy
Cash flow from operations	35%		$bn	'Supports our financial priority to generate cash to fund shareholder distributions and capital investment'
Operational excellence	35%	Asset management excellence 15%	%	'Underpins delivery of our financial framework and ambitions to progress in the energy transition'
		Project delivery excellence 10%	%	
		Customer excellence 10%	Index	
Shell's Journey in the Energy Transition	15%	Selling lower-carbon products at 5%	Percentage of earnings from lower-carbon energy products and non-energy products	'Drives focus on the business transformations needed to succeed in the energy transition'
		Reducing operational emissions by 5%	Thousand tonnes CO_2 (Scope 1 and 2)	
		Partnering to decarbonise 5%	The number of electric vehicle charging points	
Safety	15%	SIF-F 7.5%	Serious Injury and Fatality Frequency of cases per 100 million working hours	'Drives an ongoing focus on personal and process safety'
		Tier 1 and 2 process safety 7.5%	Number of Tier 1 and 2 operational safety incidents	

Notes: SIF-F: Serious Injury and Fatality Frequency. Tier 1 and 2: A Tier 1 process safety event is an unplanned or uncontrolled release of any material from a process, including non-toxic and non-flammable materials, with the greatest actual consequence resulting in harm to employees, contract staff or a neighbouring community, damage to equipment, or exceeding a defined threshold quantity. A Tier 2 process safety event is a release of lesser consequence.
Source: Shell plc (2022), Annual Report, p. 200.

(Derchi et al., 2023). Companies operating in environment-sensitive industries (e.g., energy, mining) were more likely to adopt this remuneration design (e.g., Maas and Rosendaal, 2016; Flammer et al., 2019; Cohen et al., 2023). In recent years, CSR contracting adoption has increased in all industries, as shown in Figure 18.2. Specifically, the energy, utilities and basic materials industries have registered the highest increase.

Previous studies also documented that companies with a higher public environmental commitment, better sustainability ratings, and/or belonging to sustainability indexes are more likely to adopt CSR contracting (e.g., Cohen et al., 2023). As sustainability performance indicators and targets are complex to quantify (Hartikainen et al., 2021), sustainability-related management control systems and sustainability assurance are essential requisites for the adop-

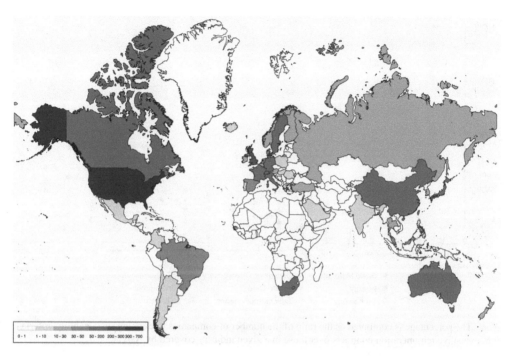

Notes: Mercator projection used. Antarctica dropped from maps. Missing values are shown in white.
Source: LSEG Data & Analytics (previously Refinitiv) database, accessed 4 December 2023. Graphical elaboration by the authors.

Figure 18.1   *The worldwide distribution of the companies that integrate sustainability criteria into their executive remuneration contracts in 2021*

tion of this form of remuneration (Abdelmotaal and Abdel-Kader, 2016; Al-Shaer and Zaman, 2019; Derchi et al., 2023).

Corporate governance mechanisms were found to play an essential positive role in integrating sustainability criteria in executive remuneration contracts. Specifically, prior academic literature (e.g., Abdelmotaal and Abdel-Kader, 2016; Radu and Smaili, 2022; Cohen et al., 2023) documented that companies characterised by a higher remuneration committee's independence, board gender diversity, the presence of board-level sustainability committees, and institutional ownership and engagement are more likely to adopt this form of remuneration. Board independence also strengthened the positive relationship between external regulatory pressures and the adoption of CSR contracting (Aresu et al., 2023).

Prior studies also documented the consequences of integrating sustainability criteria into executive remuneration contracts. CSR contracting improves the informativeness of the remuneration contract by providing, via sustainability performance indicators, additional information about executives' efforts (e.g., commitment to environmental and social initiatives). Consequently, it helps to mitigate short-term shareholder pressure on the CEO, reducing the impact of short-term financial performance on CEO dismissal decisions (Qin and Yang, 2022). Carbon-related financial incentives were also found to motivate executives and trigger their efforts towards a company's carbon emission reduction (Ott and Endrikat, 2023). In general,

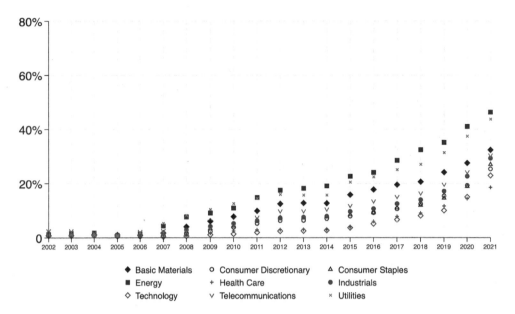

Note: The percentage is computed as the ratio of the number of companies integrating sustainability criteria into executive remuneration contracts over those in a given industry covered by Asset4.
Source: LSEG Data & Analytics (previously Refinitiv) database, accessed 4 December 2023, according to the FTSE Russell Industry Classification Benchmark. Graphical elaboration by the authors.

Figure 18.2   *The evolution of the integration of CSR contracting: industry breakdown*

the adoption of CSR contracting was found to positively affect sustainability-related performance in the medium term as companies slowly accumulate sustainability-related experience (Derchi et al., 2021).

CSR contracting is a way to persuade executives to undertake sustainability-related initiatives, enhancing process-oriented sustainability-related performance (e.g., Haque, 2017; Flammer et al., 2019). Formulaic remuneration plans were found to be more effective on environmental and social performance than non-formulaic plans (e.g., Ikram et al., 2019). Prior studies also documented that CSR contracting positively impacts green innovation (Flammer et al., 2019; Tsang et al., 2021), reduces CO_2 emissions, and improves ESG ratings (Cohen et al., 2023).

Previous literature has generally focused on the adoption or use of this form of remuneration contract, usually treating it as a 'black box'. Little or no in-depth analysis of how companies design sustainability-related incentives and complement financial-related metrics in the executive remuneration contract has been conducted. Future research might address this critical gap in the literature by examining how companies design CSR contracting (e.g., time horizon, weight), which governance and monitoring processes (e.g., remuneration committees, management control systems) may affect this design, and how the latter influences a company's performance, as companies are striving to balance sustainability and financial performance.

3   THE ADOPTION OF A SUSTAINABILITY-RELATED COMMITTEE

A sustainability-related committee (hereafter, sustainability committee) is a board committee that is expected to oversee and advise the board of directors to address the complexity of the corporate sustainability strategy and signal the board of directors' commitment towards sustainability issues.

The idea of setting up specific board subcommittees is not new and has been strongly advised by corporate governance codes of best practice (e.g., Cadbury, 1992; Zattoni and Cuomo, 2008; Financial Reporting Council, 2018) and academic literature (e.g., Aguilera and Cuervo-Cazurra, 2004; Aguilera et al., 2012) with the argument that the delegation of specific tasks to a relatively small group of directors is expected to increase the board effectiveness on the topic assigned (Spira and Bender, 2004). Companies started to voluntarily adopt sustainability committees in addition to those committees generally recommended by codes of best practices (e.g., remuneration committees). Figure 18.3 shows the evolution and industry breakdown of establishing sustainability committees on the board of directors worldwide. Overall, there has been a general increase over time in the presence of these committees on the boards of directors in different industries. Utilities, energy and consumer staples are those industries with the most significant increase in adopting this corporate governance mechanism.

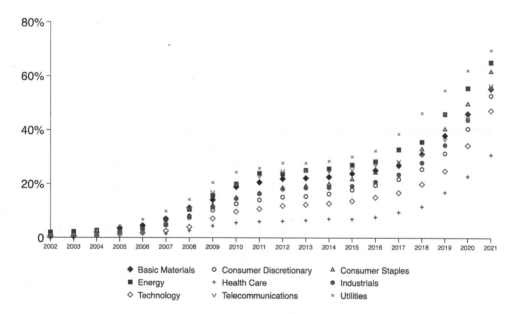

Note: The percentage is computed as the ratio of the number of companies adopting a sustainability committee over those in a given industry covered by Asset4.
Source: LSEG Data & Analytics (previously Refinitiv) database, accessed on the 4th of December 2023, according to FTSE Russell Industry Classification Benchmark. Graphical elaboration by the authors.

Figure 18.3   Evolution of the adoption of a sustainability committee: industry breakdown

As shown in Figure 18.4, the United States, China and Japan are the countries with the highest number of companies (covered in the Asset4 database) adopting a sustainability committee.

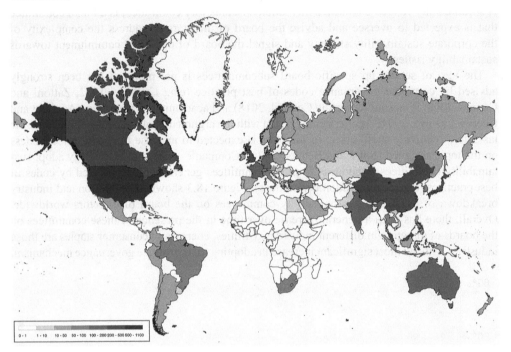

Note: Mercator projection used. Antarctica dropped from maps. Missing values are shown in white.
Source: LSEG Data & Analytics (previously Refinitiv) database, accessed 4 December 2023. Graphical elaboration by the authors.

Figure 18.4   *The worldwide distribution of the companies having a sustainability committee in 2021*

Although there is no conclusive evidence on the determinants that lead companies to adopt this corporate governance mechanism, it seems clear that, as societal pressures promote the balancing of multiple stakeholders' interests, companies have increasingly started to reflect these numerous interests in their boards' composition and structure. Integrating sustainability in the boardroom has become a necessity, and more and more board subcommittees have appeared under the titles of sustainability committees as a response to growing stakeholders' demands to monitor companies' sustainability-related activities and their outcomes (Eberhardt-Toth, 2017; Valle et al., 2019). In other words, the set-up of a sustainability committee represents an attempt by the company to manage the complexity that may come from stakeholder pressure and risk-related activities (Peters and Romi, 2015; García-Sánchez et al., 2019).

Due to the heterogeneity of corporate stakeholders' interests and the voluntary setting-up of this committee, there is no one-size-fits-all approach to the identification, composition and definition of tasks for a sustainability committee. While the purpose of a sustainability committee is relatively straightforward, identifying it is not. Sustainability committees may be titled in several ways, including ethics, sustainable development, environmental, CSR, ESG, or health and safety committees (e.g., Burke et al., 2019). There also seems to be heterogeneity in the size of this committee and its composition in terms of independence, expertise, or experience of specific sustainability-related issues. Boxes 18.1 and 18.2 provide some real-life examples of the composition and the tasks these committees are expected to do in major listed companies worldwide. Specifically, they show the case of Halliburton Inc., a US-listed company that operates in the energy industry, which set up a fully independent committee, and of Ricoh Group, a Japanese-listed company operating in the technology industry, which decided to establish a committee with a mixture of directors (executive and non-executive) and managers, chaired by the CEO.

BOX 18.1 HALLIBURTON INC.'S HEALTH, SAFETY AND ENVIRONMENT COMMITTEE

Tasks of the committee:

- reviewing and assessing our health, safety, environmental, and sustainable development policies and practices;
- overseeing the communication, implementation, and compliance with these policies, as well as applicable goals and legal requirements; and
- assisting the board with oversight of our risk-management processes relating to health, safety, the environment, and sustainability.

Committee's composition:

- five independent directors;
- average board tenure of the committee's members: eight years.

Committee's activities:

- meetings during the financial year: five.

Source: Halliburton Inc. (2015), Proxy Statements.

BOX 18.2 RICOH GROUP'S ESG COMMITTEE

Tasks of the committee:

- Respond promptly and appropriately to the expectations and needs of stakeholders by continuously discussing environmental, social, and governance issues faced by the Group at a management level and leading the discussions to the quality enhancement of the entire Group.

Committee's composition:

- CEO, Group Management Committee members, Audit and supervisory board members and an Executive Officer in charge of ESG.

Committee's activities:

- meetings during the financial year: four.

Source: Ricoh Group (2022), Integrated Report.

Sustainability committees are generally expected to oversee a company's sustainability strategies and policies and assess and review its sustainability-related performance (Ricart et al., 2005). They may also have the task of monitoring sustainability-related activities and their compliance with the company's sustainability strategy and ethical standards (Martínez-Ferrero et al., 2021). This committee could advise and encourage directors to implement sustainable management policies and systems and improve sustainability disclosure, for instance, by the assurance of sustainability-related reports (García-Sánchez et al., 2019).

While some companies choose to set up a specific sustainability committee to address these tasks (e.g., Halliburton Inc. and Ricoh Group, see Boxes 18.1 and 18.2), sustainability-related tasks may also be delegated to other board subcommittees whose functions are broader. A case in point is provided by Diasorin SpA, an Italian company that operates in the health industry, which chose to integrate sustainability-related tasks with other audit-related and risk-related tasks (see Box 18.3).

BOX 18.3   DIASORIN SPA'S CONTROL, RISKS AND SUSTAINABILITY COMMITTEE

Tasks of the committee:

- to define the guidelines of the internal control system;
- to provide advice on specific issues related to the identification of corporate risks;
- to support the board's judgement and decisions relating to risk management;
- to review the work plan and the reports submitted by the internal audit officer;
- to assess, together with the corporate accounting documents officer, the external auditors and the board of statutory auditors, the adequacy of the accounting principles used by the company;
- to report to the board of directors about the work performed and the adequacy of the system of internal control and risk management;
- to perform any additional tasks that the board of directors may choose to assign to the committee, specifically in areas related to the interaction with the external auditors and the provision of consulting support concerning related-party transactions;
- to monitor sustainability issues, to evaluate and assess sustainability matters relating to corporate activities and interactions with its stakeholders, and to supervise activities of the group concerning sustainability;
- to evaluate and assess the data collection and consolidation system to prepare the consolidated non-financial report.

Committee's composition:

- two independent directors and one non-executive director;
- average board tenure of committee's members: seven years.

Committee's activities:

- meetings during the financial year: three.

Source: Diasorin SpA (2019), Report on corporate governance and ownership structure.

Academic research documented positive implications of other board-level committees on company outcomes (audit and remuneration committees, e.g., Beasley et al., 2000; Conyon and Peck, 1998). However, prior studies did not provide strong evidence of a relationship between the establishment of a sustainability committee and its expected outcomes, such as a company's environmental performance (e.g., Berrone and Gomez-Mejia, 2009; Mallin et al., 2013; Rodrigue et al., 2013), social performance (e.g., Mallin and Michelon, 2011; Rupley et al., 2012; Hussain et al., 2018; Chams and García-Blandón, 2019), or sustainability-related disclosure (e.g., Adams, 2002; Michelon and Parbonetti, 2012; Liao et al., 2015). Although prima facie, this finding may appear to be inconsistent with the arguments highlighting board committee specialisation, it sheds some light on how the limited or no effect on board decisions of this committee may also be due to the complexity of its tasks and functions, which is due to the heterogenous stakeholders' demands (e.g., Burke et al., 2019; Radu and Smaili, 2022). Overall, setting up a sustainability committee may be substantive only in those companies that have already adopted sustainable behaviour, as it reinforces the company's attitude towards sustainability (e.g., García-Sánchez et al., 2019; Peters et al., 2019). Future studies are welcomed to examine whether and how individual characteristics of this committee's members (e.g. expertise, independence) are more effective in influencing specific corporate achievements (e.g., net-zero targets) as well as to investigate, for instance, through interviews and/or surveys, how the sustainability committee's members are engaged and cooperate with other corporate governance actors in the strategic decision-making process.

4   THE ASSURANCE OF SUSTAINABILITY-RELATED INFORMATION TO THE PUBLIC BY A THIRD AUDITING PARTY

Assurance engagement is generally considered a process in which a practitioner expresses a conclusion that helps to enhance the degree of confidence of external users about the evaluation (and/or measurement) of specific items (IFAC, 2003). Auditors are traditionally considered an essential element of corporate governance, serving as an external monitoring mechanism to safeguard shareholders' interests in the credibility of a company's financial reporting. In recent years, with the growing spread of integrated and sustainability reports, global demand for sustainability assurance services has also increased (KPMG, 2022). As shown in Figure 18.5, sustainability assurance has slowly increased in all industries (compared to the previous mechanisms described in this chapter). Specifically, utilities and telecommunications are those industries that have registered the highest increase.

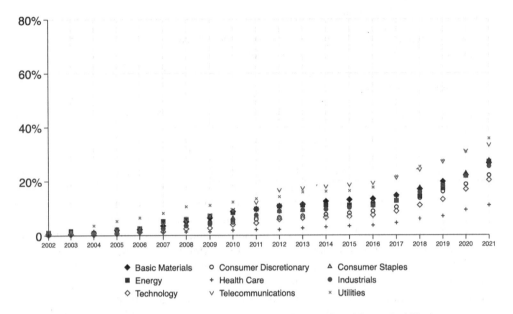

Note: The percentage is computed as the ratio of the number of companies with sustainability assurance over those in a given industry covered by Asset4.
Source: LSEG Data & Analytics (previously Refinitiv) database, accessed 4 December 2023, according to FTSE Russell Industry Classification Benchmark. Graphical elaboration by the authors.

Figure 18.5   *The evolution of sustainability assurance: industry breakdown*

Consequently, the auditors' role has expanded, no longer assuring just financial statements but also other parts of the corporate reporting package, such as the annual review and sustainability reports.

This engagement is generally called sustainability assurance and can be defined as an independent service aimed at validating sustainability reports (and similar documents, such as integrated reports). Mitigating the potential misreporting of sustainability issues is considered to be a critical element in increasing the credibility of sustainability-related information and, therefore, in increasing confidence among investors and stakeholders in the quality and completeness of this type of information (e.g., Brown-Liburd and Zamora, 2015; Al-Shaer and Zaman, 2019). Based on recent stakeholders' feedback related to sustainability reporting, it can be argued that the ultimate goal should arguably be for the audit of sustainability-related information to be as robust as financial reporting (IFRS Foundation, 2021).

The mostly voluntary nature of sustainability assurance[5] leaves room for managerial discretion related to its adoption, the choice of the provider, and the type of assurance services that range from verifying compliance with specific assurance standards to identifying life-cycle environmental impacts (e.g., Baier et al., 2022; Velte, 2021; Thompson et al., 2022).

The ISAE 3000 standard (IAASB, 2013) considers, taking into account the different engagement risk (i.e., the risk of an inappropriate conclusion when the content analysed is materially misstated), two different levels of sustainability assurance:

- A limited assurance engagement, where the assurance provider performs basic analytical procedures seeking and reviewing general sustainability-related information. The engagement risk is reduced to an acceptable level in the circumstances of the engagement. This form of assurance is typically adopted by companies entering the assurance process (KPMG, 2022). Limited assurance is generally expressed as a negatively framed conclusion (e.g., 'nothing has come to our knowledge ...'; 'we did not identify any material misstatements ...') (e.g., Sheldon and Jenkins, 2020; Zaman et al., 2021).
- A reasonable assurance engagement, where the assurance provider performs an in-depth examination that encompasses a rigorous analytical information evaluation and risk assessment, as well as an assurance of the underlying non-financial reporting and internal control systems. The engagement risk is reduced to a greater extent (compared to the limited assurance) and an acceptably low level. Reasonable assurance is generally expressed as a positively framed conclusion (e.g., 'In our opinion, the ESG information presents, in all material respects, a reliable and adequate view of ...') (e.g., Zaman et al., 2021).

Companies may decide to have limited, reasonable or no sustainability assurance at different levels, such as specific sections of a report or specific indicators. This means that certain sections or indicators can be subjected to limited assurance, others to reasonable assurance, and others may not be audited at all.

Schneider Electric SE, a French company operating in the energy industry, provides an example of the evolution from limited to reasonable sustainability assurance in specific indicators (see Box 18.4). ·

BOX 18.4   SCHNEIDER ELECTRIC SE'S ASSURANCE OF SUSTAINABILITY REPORT

In 2021, Schneider Electric obtained a limited assurance from an independent third party, EY & Associés. The limited assurance provided, in accordance with the ISAE 3000 assurance standard (IAASB, 2013), referred to most of the Schneider Sustainability Impact (SSI) and Schneider Sustainability Essentials (SSE) indicators. For example, in the 2021 sustainability report, it was written that: 'Schneider Electric updates its end-to-end carbon footprint (Scope 1, 2 and 3) annually and obtains a "limited assurance" from an independent third-party verifier on all figures' (Schneider Electric SE, 2021 Sustainable Development Report, p. 76).

In 2022, the company obtained a reasonable assurance level for some sustainability indicators, such as 'lost-time injury rate' and 'measured energy consumption by source'. Importantly, for the performance indicator carbon footprint (Scopes 1, 2 and 3 emissions), the company obtained reasonable assurance on Scopes 1 and 2's reported GHG emissions and limited assurance on Scope 3's reported GHG emissions. This shows a mixed sustainability assurance within specific performance indicators. In 2022, the external auditor reported to have relied on the International Standard on Assurance Engagements 3410 (Assurance Engagements on Greenhouse Gas Statements), issued by IAASB (Schneider Electric SE, 2022 Sustainable Development Report, p. 200). Although the company acknowledges that 'Scope 3 emissions represent more than 99% of the Group's carbon footprint' (Schneider Electric SE, 2022 Sustainable Development Report, p. 82), the lack of reasonable assurance on Scope 3 reported GHG emissions might be due to the difficulty in auditing this type of emissions.

The shift from limited to reasonable assurance has corresponded to the change in the auditing company assuring the report (from Ernst & Young to PricewaterhouseCoopers). The new auditing company has explained the more extensive work (compared to the limited assurance procedures, see Schneider Electric SE, 2022 Sustainable Development Report, p. 199) performed in the reasonable assurance engagement, such as 'evaluating the suitability in the circumstances of the Company's use of the Reporting Criteria, evaluating the appropriateness of measurement and evaluation methods, reporting policies used and the reasonableness of estimates made by the Company, and evaluating the disclosures in, and overall presentation of, the Identified Sustainability Information' (Schneider Electric SE, 2022 Sustainable Development Report, p. 201).

Source: Schneider Electric SE, 2021 and 2022 Sustainable Development Reports.

Sustainability assurance services can be provided by professional accountants or consulting companies specialising in these services. Compared to consulting companies, professional accountants, especially the Big 4, are perceived as more independent, have more assurance expertise, and can leverage their size advantage by investing in assurance technologies. However, consultants can benefit from specialising in a niche of services, a higher management knowledge, and a more creative and dynamic approach to the adopted methodologies (e.g., Farooq and De Villiers, 2017; Boiral et al., 2019).

Prior academic literature has investigated the determinants of the voluntary choice of sustainability assurance. This choice depends on a mix of country-, industry- and company-related factors (e.g., Simnett et al., 2009; Martínez-Ferrero et al., 2018; Simoni et al., 2020). In terms of country-level characteristics, companies headquartered in stakeholder-oriented (i.e., civil law-based) countries and those with stronger sustainability-related protection systems are more likely to request assurance to manage and maintain stakeholder relationships (e.g., Kolk and Perego, 2010; Datt et al., 2018). However, studies also documented substitution effects, with companies more likely to audit their sustainability-related reports when operating in countries with weaker investor protection and weaker sustainability policies, with assurance services that may be used as legitimacy-enhancing tools in those institutional contexts with less stringent protections (e.g., Zhou et al., 2016; Simoni et al., 2020).

Figure 18.6 shows that the United States, Japan, Sweden, France, the UK and Germany have the highest number of companies (covered in the Asset4 database) that have decided to audit sustainability-related information.

Concerning the industry-level characteristics, previous literature documented that adopting sustainability assurance services is more common among companies operating in socially and environmentally sensitive industries (e.g., carbon-intensive industries). Being more exposed to environmental and social risks, these companies have a stronger need to improve user confidence in the report (e.g., Simnett et al., 2009; Castelo Branco et al., 2014).

At the company level, larger and better-performing companies (either in terms of financial or social and environmental performance), those with a higher amount and quality of non-financial disclosures, or with a higher gender diversity or sustainability-related expertise in the board of directors are more likely to demand sustainability assurance services (e.g., Peters and Romi, 2015; Liao et al., 2018; Venter and van Eck, 2021).

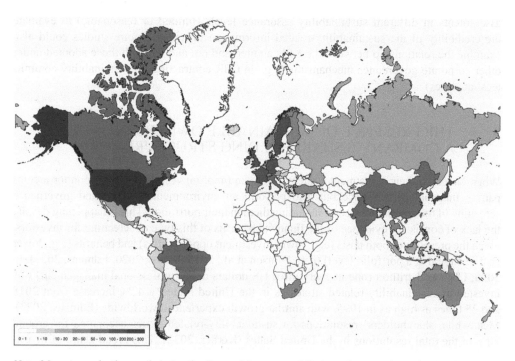

Note: Mercator projection used. Antarctica dropped from maps. Missing values are shown in white.
Source: LSEG Data & Analytics (previously Refinitiv) database, accessed 4 December 2023. Graphical elaboration by the authors.

Figure 18.6   *The worldwide distribution of the companies with sustainability assurance in 2021*

Prior studies also focused on the consequences of sustainability assurance. Sustainability assurance was found to improve the quality of the information in sustainability-related reports (e.g., Maroun, 2019), users' perception of the credibility of the disclosed information and, consequently, a company's sustainability-related reputation (Birkey et al., 2016). In general, it was found to positively affect a company's value by reducing the information asymmetry with investors and investment opportunities by enhancing the set of information available for managerial decision-making (e.g., Steinmeier and Stich, 2019; Thompson et al., 2022).

Being mostly voluntary and unregulated (e.g., Baier et al., 2022), assurance services are not yet supported by a consistent global framework and qualitative sustainability-related disclosure requirements (IFRS Foundation, 2020, p. 14; Krasodomska et al., 2021). However, important changes in sustainability assurance are expected due to the incoming IFRS standards on sustainability information,[6] which will enhance the standardisation of non-financial reporting, the IAASB project to develop an overarching principles-based standard for assurance on sustainability reporting, and the European Union Corporate Sustainability Reporting Directive (European Union, 2022), which requires a broad set of large companies to have the reported sustainability information audited. The introduction of this new regulation provides an opportunity for future research that may investigate its impact on sustainability assurance. Future research opportunities may also involve a better understanding of auditors' materiality assessments in different sustainability assurance levels (limited or reasonable) to evaluate the credibility of the sustainability-related information provided. Future studies could also examine the relationship between the KPIs audited and not audited with those adopted under other corporate governance mechanisms (e.g., in CSR contracting, in sustainability commit-tees' analyses).

5   THE PRESENCE OF SUSTAINABLE OWNERS IN A COMPANY'S SHAREHOLDING STRUCTURE

When choosing their investment strategy, more and more investors not only monitor a com-pany's financial performance but also perform an environmental, social and governance screening of the companies before including them in their portfolios. This is happening despite the lack of consistent evidence of the financial benefits of this type of screening for investors, given the presence of both costs (e.g., lower investment opportunities) and benefits (e.g., lower cost of capital at a portfolio level) (e.g., Dimson et al., 2015; Matos, 2020; Edmans, 2023). In 2020, USD 17.1 trillion (one in every three US dollars under professional management) was invested in sustainability-related strategies in the United States, a 42% increase from 2018 and 25 times as high as in 1995, with similar growth experienced worldwide (Edmans, 2023). Meanwhile, shareholders' resolutions on sustainability-related issues accounted for around 20% of the total resolutions in the United States (Kerber, 2022). This broad genre of invest-ment practices has generally been defined as ESG investing.[7]

Investors are more frequently comparing the short- and long-term costs and benefits of responsible business behaviour in terms of financial returns and reputational advantages (Villalonga, 2018). Companies' sustainability-related investments might be more suitable for investors who can wait for those projects to generate long-term returns (Matos, 2020). Institutional investors, for instance, may be interested in investing in sustainable companies to reduce the risk in their investment portfolio, as these companies are less likely to suffer from exogenous shocks (e.g., as customer loyalty is higher, see Albuquerque et al., 2019).

A company's shareholders may have different identities, including individuals, families, institutional investors (e.g., hedge, mutual and pension funds), and governments (e.g., through sovereign-wealth funds). Shareholders' identity may be associated with a company's sus-tainability-related commitment and performance (e.g., Aguilera et al., 2006; Neubaum and Zahra, 2006), depending on their investment time horizon (Faller and zu Knyphausen-Aufseß, 2018), and attitude towards the interest of corporate stakeholders (Kavadis and Thomsen, 2023). Shareholders' impact should not be considered in isolation, as investors can influence each other. For instance, individual investors seem to have a critical role in solving the free-rider problem among institutional investors. The more individuals, as clients of institutional inves-tors, care about the environmental and social attributes of their personal investment, the more likely institutional investors will care, limiting their free-riding (i.e., enjoying the investment's long-term benefits without incurring its short-term costs) (e.g., Serafeim, 2018).

A useful ownership taxonomy distinguishes investors according to their relationship with the company (Aguilera and Crespi-Cladera, 2016) as follows:

– Transactional investors, who lack any relationships with the companies in which they invest, except for obtaining financial returns (e.g., hedge funds). They tend to focus on short-term financial performance due to the competitiveness imposed by financial markets that reward them based on annual or even shorter performance. Therefore, they may avoid investing in socially responsible companies unless specific sustainable investments are value-enhancing, in financial terms, in the short term.

–   Relational investors (e.g., family and state), who have other relationships with the companies of which they are owners. Their longer-term orientation can lead to higher tolerance to short-term losses and/or greater insulation from financial market pressures, as well as long-term relationships with various stakeholders, including employees and suppliers (Rees and Rodionova, 2015; Villalonga, 2018). However, they usually also have self-interested and political motives that may conflict with a company's sustainability. For example, employees can be motivated by keeping the business running at whatever cost for the protection of their employment. Governments can invest in a particular company because it is nationally considered as being of 'strategic' importance, although operating in a highly polluting industry (e.g., oil and gas) (e.g., Klein et al., 2010; Dam and Scholtens, 2012).

Moreover, sustainable investors may affect companies' socially responsible behaviour through the use of two different strategies:[8]

–   Passive. Investors may pursue a divestment strategy, excluding companies operating in countries under public scrutiny or 'unethical' industries (e.g. gambling or weapons) from their portfolios or selling shares of less-sustainable companies that exert negative externalities. For instance, many investors have decided to wind down their holdings in Russian companies after the 2022 war in Ukraine started (e.g., Hurst et al., 2022). Alternatively, investors may pursue an investment strategy, ranking companies according to their sustainable performance and selecting only the highest-ranked companies for investment. These strategies are expected to increase less-sustainable companies' cost of capital and hinder their expansion.

–   Active. Investors may express their dissenting voice, engaging directly with the company's board of directors and senior management to encourage them to adopt more sustainable business practices. The engagement can be pursued privately (private discussions with the company's top management) or publicly (shareholders' proposals or voting during the annual general meeting). Through this strategy, investors try to influence the decision-making process in the boardroom directly.

Boxes 18.5, 18.6 and 18.7 provide real-life anecdotal cases of shareholder activism on sustainability issues. Specifically, Box 18.5 illustrates a case of successful environmental activism in AGL Ltd, Australia's largest electricity producer.

BOX 18.5   SHAREHOLDERS' ACTIVISM ON ENVIRONMENTAL-RELATED ISSUES AT AGL ENERGY LTD

In 2022, following a prolonged period of poor share price performance, AGL, the country's largest emitter of Scope 1 greenhouse gas emissions, planned to demerge into two companies to spin off its coal-fired power plants. According to the company, the split would have formed Accel Energy as a power producer and AGL Australia as an energy retailer (AGL Energy Limited, 2022a).

However, Australian billionaire activist Mike Cannon-Brookes, owning a nearly 10% stake, opposed the demerger of AGL, tweeting: 'We believe it destroys value for everyone – shareholders, employees, Australia and the planet.' (Cannon-Brookes, 2022). Following this, other shareholders, such as Hesta, one of Australia's most significant pension funds, declared they would have voted against the demerger based on environmental grounds.

Mr Cannon-Brookes, who had planned to accelerate AGL's transition away from coal and achieve net-zero emissions about a decade earlier than the company's targets, first contributed to forcing the company to withdraw the demerger proposal (AGL Energy Limited, 2022b), then contributed to reshaping AGL's corporate governance. Both the chairperson and the chief executive officer resigned, and four board members from his proposed pool of directors won support from shareholders at the annual general meeting, joining the new board of directors (The Guardian, 2022).

Box 18.6 presents an unsuccessful case of social activism in Guess Inc., a significant United States fashion company.

BOX 18.6   SHAREHOLDERS' ACTIVISM ON SOCIAL-RELATED ISSUES AT GUESS INC.

In 2022, Legion Partners Asset Management and other participants, beneficially owning a 2.5% stake in Guess Inc., filed a proxy statement in connection with a 'Vote No' campaign opposing the re-election of Paul and Maurice Marciano to the company's board of directors at the 2022 annual meeting of shareholders (SEC, 2022a). According to Legion Partners Asset Management, several sexual assault and harassment allegations, relating to a period of more than a decade, had been made against Paul Marciano, who served as the company's chief creative officer, while his brother Maurice Marciano, as a former chairman of the board, was allegedly using his power to cover up his brother's actions, and the company spent nearly USD 1 million on settlements with alleged victims (SEC, 2022a; see also Dockterman, 2018; Elan, 2022). According to Legion Partners Asset Management, this reputational damage was harming the company's brand, financial performance and stock price (SEC, 2022a). Proxy advisory firms, Institutional Shareholder Services and Glass Lewis, entered the discourse days before the 2022 annual meeting, both recommending that shareholders withhold their votes on the re-election of the Marcianos (Darmiento, 2022).

Nonetheless, this attempt failed despite the media coverage (e.g., Deveau, 2022; Barrabi, 2022; Reuters, 2022). In the 2022 annual meeting, Guess shareholders voted to re-elect all the board of directors' nominees – Anthony Chidoni, Cynthia Livingston, Maurice Marciano and Paul Marciano – to the Company's new board of directors (SEC, 2022b). Maurice Marciano and Paul Marciano, who directly and indirectly held more than 40% of common stocks (SEC, 2022c), likely played a role in this re-election. Among the four directors, Paul Marciano had the lowest consensus (nonetheless, receiving approximately 60.6% 'for' votes, see SEC, 2022b).

Box 18.7 provides a successful case of governance-related activism in Chesapeake Energy Corporation, the second-largest gas producer in the United States.

BOX 18.7   SHAREHOLDERS' ACTIVISM ON GOVERNANCE-RELATED ISSUES AT CHESAPEAKE ENERGY CORPORATION

In 2012, Chesapeake Energy was criticised over its mounting debt levels and the perks given to its co-founder Mr Aubrey McClendon, then CEO and chairman of the company, who was among the highest paid US CEOs in 2007, receiving over USD 100 million in total annual remuneration (DeCarlo, 2008), despite a significant drop in the company's stock price and financial performance during the year.

Uproar among shareholders emerged when internal documents revealed that corporate resources were used for personal benefits (e.g., to repair Mr McClendon's house, which was damaged by hailstones, and to transfer the executive's family to holiday destinations), and related-party transactions, such as advertising sponsor relationships between the company and the Oklahoma City Thunder, a National Basketball Association franchise owned by a company where Mr McClendon was a relevant shareholder (Shiffman et al., 2012). When Chesapeake Energy also started struggling with low natural gas prices and high capital expenditure, which resulted in its debt growing almost fivefold in the first quarter of 2012, two leading investors, Southeastern Management and the billionaire Carl Icahn, overall owning nearly 20% of the company, demanded changes in the company's board of directors.

In the aftermath of this pressure, in June 2012, four out of nine board members were replaced by new directors chosen by these two leading investors, and a new independent chair replaced Mr McClendon. In April 2013, Mr McClendon also resigned from the CEO position.

Few academic studies have examined the drivers of sustainable ownership. Sustainable ownership was found to be driven by corporate disclosure and societal pressure, such as that against funding operations in specific industries (e.g., Hong, H. and Kacperczyk, 2009; Serafeim, 2015). More specifically, companies that produce integrated reports were found to show a clear tendency to have more long-term institutional shareholders (Serafeim, 2015). This may be due to better information about a company's long-term prospects within integrated reports, which is useful for long-term investors when assessing the company's value and monitoring management over time (Serafeim, 2015). In terms of societal pressure, asset managers' clients are increasingly demanding sustainable investment opportunities, such as divesting from specific industries considered less responsible (e.g., the gambling industry). This pressure may lead asset managers to shift away from those industries or institutional contexts deemed controversial by society (e.g., Edmans, 2023).

More academic studies have investigated the effects of sustainable ownership than the determinants, focusing on the different owners' identities and investment time horizons. These studies generally documented a positive impact of institutional ownership on environmental and social performance, particularly for long-term institutional investors, and a positive effect of state ownership on this type of performance (see, for a review, Kavadis and Thomsen, 2023). Institutional ownership was found to positively affect environmental and social performance, especially when institutional investors come from countries where environmental and social issues are more regulated and perceived as more critical by citizens (Dyck et al., 2019). These findings show that social norms can impact institutional investors' choices, affecting the perceived reputational rewards (or penalties) due to the high (low) level of alignment with community values on sustainability issues. Also, specific types of institutional investors (e.g., pension funds, climate-conscious institutional investors) were found to have a positive role in improving sustainability reporting quality and climate risk disclosure (e.g., García-Sánchez et al., 2020; Ilhan et al., 2023). Fewer studies focused on the role of blockholders[9] (e.g., Taglialatela et al., 2024). Blockholders can play a paramount role in a company's environmental and social performance as they tend to focus on the long-term value of their investments, being unable to exit without incurring losses in their positions (e.g., Chung et al., 2019; Gloßner, 2019).

Despite the vast research on sustainable ownership (e.g., Marti et al., 2023), we encourage scholars to explore future research avenues. For instance, more studies are welcomed to understand whether and how specific corporate governance and ownership choices (e.g., the presence of CEOs with sustainability-related expertise; common institutional ownership) can trigger investors' engagement and its success in different institutional contexts (e.g., DesJardine et al., 2023). In addition, the impact of the relationship between shareholders and different stakeholders (e.g., employees, NGO associations) on driving ESG-responsible behaviours needs further investigation.

6   CONCLUDING REMARKS

This chapter has illustrated the role, determinants, and consequences of important incentive, advisory and monitoring corporate governance mechanisms that can help a company to be governed so that it achieves its purpose in a sustainable way (i.e., considering the long-term social, environmental, and economic impact of its activities). Three important caveats should be taken into consideration.

First, corporate governance mechanisms do not necessarily work in isolation. They are generally part of a corporate governance bundle, which is a combination of mechanisms that interact and influence one another, with potentially complementary and substitution effects (e.g., Aguilera et al., 2012), whose role also varies depending on their interplay with the institutional environment where a company operates (e.g., Yoshikawa et al., 2014). For example, board-level sustainability committees and sustainability assurance have been found to positively affect the choice of integrating sustainability criteria into executive remuneration contracts (Al-Shaer and Zaman, 2019). Hence, the role of these mechanisms should not be analysed independently from the organisational and institutional context in which they are embedded.

Second, due to the societal pressure and lack of clear evidence of the impact of these mechanisms on a company's value, companies may feel obliged to adopt them as symbolic legitimisation mechanisms, seeking to conform to societal demands, rather than as substantive mechanisms with an effective role in pursuing a sustainable performance. Sustainability assurance services, for example, have been criticised as 'greenwashing', i.e., symbolic tools used by a company's senior management to meet stakeholders' expectations and enhance the public image without improving a company's commitment to providing more credible and accurate sustainability-related information (Maroun, 2020). Investors could also claim to adopt sustainability-related investment strategies just to entice well-meaning clients (Flood, 2023). Sustainability committees may also result in mechanisms that resemble conformity to societal sustainability concerns, but are merely ceremonial, as they do not translate into an actual improvement in sustainable performance (Rodrigue et al., 2013). The integration of sustainability criteria into the executive remuneration contracts could serve the interests of corporate executives rather than incentivise a company's sustainability, depending on the details of the remuneration design and the level of observability by outside stakeholders (Bebchuk and Tallarita, 2022). For example, given the complexity of measuring sustainability criteria, companies could narrow down the choice of performance measures to limited dimensions of the welfare of a limited subset of stakeholders, creating distorted incentives to neglect other significant but hard-to-quantify dimensions (Bebchuk and Tallarita, 2022).

Third, we acknowledge a lack of comprehensive and accurate systematic data on sustainable corporate governance mechanisms at the international level, with some countries not covered, or covered to a lower extent. This lack of data granularity does not allow us to disentangle symbolic from substantive corporate governance mechanisms and to understand how the detailed characteristics of each specific mechanism affect its expected outcome in a given institutional context.

The overall risk is that it is still unclear what the actual contribution of these mechanisms to the aggregate stakeholder welfare is. Future research is needed to fully understand to what extent sustainable corporate governance mechanisms are either truly effective in enhancing sustainability or else could ultimately hurt rather than serve stakeholders' interests and serve just as mere legitimisation practices.

NOTES

1. In this chapter, the terms shareholder/s, owner/s, and investor/s will be used as synonyms.
2. Based on conflicting stakeholder demands, companies tend to selectively address stakeholder requirements as a function of their relative power, legitimacy, and urgency and how their combination influences a company's decision-making (e.g., Ullmann, 1985; Mitchell et al., 1997).
3. In this chapter, the terms audit, auditing and assurance will be used as synonyms.
4. Relevant case studies for the first three corporate governance mechanisms were identified via a search of the Asset4 database to identify companies that have adopted the specific corporate governance mechanism under analysis. High-profile cases of shareholders' activism were identified through their impact on prominent financial media. Then, each case was selected based on the significance of the company within its industry or country and, after an in-depth analysis of the company's relevant documents was undertaken, its potential to explain the phenomenon under analysis.
5. France and South Africa are among the few countries where sustainability assurance is mandatory (see also Krasodomska et al., 2021).
6. In June 2023, the ISSB has issued its first two Sustainability Disclosure Standards: IFRS S1 (General Requirements for Disclosure of Sustainability-Related Financial Information) and IFRS S2 (Climate-Related Disclosures).
7. Other denominations used to represent those investment strategies that include an in-depth analysis of aspects different from financial performance are, for instance, socially responsible investment, ethical investment, social investment, responsible investment, and sustainable

investment or investing (e.g., Johnsen, 2003; Eccles and Viviers, 2011; Van Duuren et al., 2016).

8. Another socially responsible initiative that combines an active and passive strategy is called tilting. Through tilting, investors may be willing to hold in their portfolio those companies operating in less sustainable industries (e.g., the energy industry) if they take corrective actions (e.g., investing in renewable energies), while selling in the opposite case (Edmans et al., 2022).

9. A blockholder can be defined as any investor who has sufficient incentive and power to monitor management (Edmans, 2014).

REFERENCES

Abdelmotaal, H. and Abdel-Kader, M., 2016. The use of sustainability incentives in executive remuneration contracts: firm characteristics and impact on the shareholders' returns. *Journal of Applied Accounting Research, 17*(3), 311–330.

Adams, C.A., 2002. Internal organisational factors influencing corporate social and ethical reporting: beyond current theorising. *Accounting, Auditing & Accountability Journal, 15*(2), 223–250.

AGL Energy Limited, 2022a. Shareholder letter in relation to AGL Energy's proposed demerger. https://www.agl.com.au/content/dam/digital/agl/documents/about-agl/media-centre/2022/220525 -shareholder-letter-in-relation-to-agls-proposed-demerger.pdf, accessed 28-05-24.

AGL Energy Limited, 2022b. AGL Energy Withdraws Demerger Proposal. https://www.agl.com.au/ about-agl/media-centre/asx-and-media-releases/2022/may/agl-energy-withdraws-demerger-proposal, accessed 28-05-24.

Aguilera, R.V. and Crespi-Cladera, R., 2016. Global corporate governance: on the relevance of firms' ownership structure. *Journal of World Business, 51*(1), 50–57.

Aguilera, R.V. and Cuervo-Cazurra, A., 2004. Codes of good governance worldwide: what is the trigger? *Organization Studies, 25*(3), 415–443.

Aguilera, R.V., Williams, C.A., Conley, J.M. and Rupp, D.E., 2006. Corporate governance and social responsibility: a comparative analysis of the UK and the US. *Corporate Governance: An International Review, 14*(3), 147–158.

Aguilera, R.V., Filatotchev, I., Gospel, H. and Jackson, G., 2008. An organizational approach to comparative corporate governance: costs, contingencies, and complementarities. *Organization Science, 19*(3), 475–492.

Aguilera, R.V., Desender, K.A. and Kabbach de Castro, L.R., 2012. A bundle perspective to comparative corporate governance. In T. Clarke and D. Branson (eds), *The SAGE Handbook of Corporate Governance*, pp. 379–405. New York: Sage Publications.

Albuquerque, R., Koskinen, Y. and Zhang, C., 2019. Corporate social responsibility and firm risk: theory and empirical evidence. *Management Science, 65*(10), 4451–4469.

Al-Shaer, H. and Zaman, M., 2019. CEO compensation and sustainability reporting assurance: evidence from the UK. *Journal of Business Ethics, 158*, 233–252.

Aresu, S., Hooghiemstra, R. and Melis, A., 2023. Integration of CSR criteria into executive compensation contracts: a cross-country analysis. *Journal of Management, 49*(8), 2766–2804.

Baier, C., Göttsche, M., Hellmann, A. and Schiemann, F., 2022. Too good to be true: influencing credibility perceptions with signaling reference explicitness and assurance depth. *Journal of Business Ethics, 178*(3), 695–714.

Barrabi, B., 2022. Investor demands Guess remove Paul and Maurice Marciano, *New York Post*, 8 February.

Beasley, M.S., Carcello, J.V., Hermanson, D.R. and Lapides, P.D., 2000. Fraudulent financial reporting: consideration of industry traits and corporate governance mechanisms. *Accounting Horizons, 14*(4), 441–454.

Bebchuk, L.A. and Tallarita, R., 2022. The perils and questionable promise of ESG-based compensation. *Journal of Corporation Law, 48*(1), 37–75.

Berrone, P. and Gomez-Mejia, L.R., 2009. Environmental performance and executive compensation: an integrated agency-institutional perspective. *Academy of Management Journal, 52*(1), 103–126.

Birkey, R.N., Michelon, G., Patten, D.M. and Sankara, J., 2016. Does assurance on CSR reporting enhance environmental reputation? An examination in the US context. *Accounting Forum, 40*(3), 143–152.

Boiral, O., Heras-Saizarbitoria, I., Brotherton, M.C. and Bernard, J., 2019. Ethical issues in the assurance of sustainability reports: perspectives from assurance providers. *Journal of Business Ethics, 159*, 1111–1125.

Bose, S., Burns, N., Minnick, K., & Shams, S., 2023. Climate-linked compensation, societal values, and climate change impact: international evidence. *Corporate Governance: An International Review, 31*(5), 759–785.

Brown-Liburd, H. and Zamora, V.L., 2015. The role of corporate social responsibility (CSR) assurance in investors' judgments when managerial pay is explicitly tied to CSR performance. *Auditing: A Journal of Practice & Theory, 34*(1), 75–96.

Burke, J.J., Hoitash, R. and Hoitash, U., 2019. The heterogeneity of board-level sustainability committees and corporate social performance. *Journal of Business Ethics, 154*, 1161–1186.

Cadbury, A., 1992. *Report of the Committee on the Financial Aspects of Corporate Governance.* London: Gee.

Cannon-Brookes, M., 2022. We believe the proposed demerger does the opposite of the above, which is why we will be voting against it. The demerger makes no sense, or cents. We believe it destroys value for everyone – shareholders, employees, Australia and the planet. 6/9. [Twitter] 2 May. https://twitter .com/mcannonbrookes/status/1521052338818977793?s=20, accessed 22-05-24.

Castelo Branco, M., Delgado, C., Ferreira Gomes, S. and Cristina Pereira Eugénio, T., 2014. Factors influencing the assurance of sustainability reports in the context of the economic crisis in Portugal. *Managerial Auditing Journal, 29*(3), 237–252.

Chams, N. and García-Blandón, J., 2019. Sustainable or not sustainable? The role of the board of directors. *Journal of Cleaner Production, 226*, 1067–1081.

Chung, C.Y., Cho, S.J., Ryu, D. and Ryu, D., 2019. Institutional blockholders and corporate social responsibility. *Asian Business & Management, 18*, 143–186.

Cohen, S., Kadach, I., Ormazabal, G. and Reichelstein, S., 2023. Executive compensation tied to ESG performance: international evidence. *Journal of Accounting Research, 61*(3), 805–853.

Conyon, M.J. and Peck, S.I., 1998. Board control, remuneration committees, and top management compensation. *Academy of Management Journal, 41*(2), 146–157.

Dam, L. and Scholtens, B., 2012. Does ownership type matter for corporate social responsibility? *Corporate Governance: An International Review, 20*(3), 233–252.

Darmiento, L., 2022. Guess founder, accused repeatedly of sexual misconduct, holds on to board seat in contentious vote, *Los Angeles Times*, 22 April.

Datt, R., Luo, L., Tang, Q. and Mallik, G., 2018. An international study of determinants of voluntary carbon assurance. *Journal of International Accounting Research, 17*(3), 1–20.

DeCarlo, S., 2008. Top Paid CEOs, *Forbes*, 30 April.

Derchi, G.B., Zoni, L. and Dossi, A., 2021. Corporate social responsibility performance, incentives, and learning effects. *Journal of Business Ethics, 173*, 617–641.

Derchi, G.B., Davila, A. and Oyon, D., 2023. Green incentives for environmental goals. *Management Accounting Research, 59*(100830), 1–21.

DesJardine, M.R., Grewal, J., & Viswanathan, K., 2023. A rising tide lifts all boats: the effects of common ownership on corporate social responsibility. *Organization Science*, 34(5), 1716–1735.

Deveau, S., 2022. Guess Investors Should Oust Marcianos After 'Insufficient' Probe, ISS Says, Bloomberg, 14 April.

Diasorin SpA, 2019. Report on corporate governance and ownership structure. https://int.diasorin.com/ sites/default/files/reports-corporate-governance/corporate_governance_report_fy_2019.pdf, accessed 22-05-24.

Dimson, E., Karakaş, O. and Li, X., 2015. Active ownership. *The Review of Financial Studies, 28*(12), 3225–3268.

Dockterman, E., 2018. 'I'm not going to let him intimidate me anymore.' Kate Upton speaks out on alleged harassment by Guess co-founder Paul Marciano, *Time*, 7 February.

Dyck, A., Lins, K.V., Roth, L. and Wagner, H.F., 2019. Do institutional investors drive corporate social responsibility? International evidence. *Journal of Financial Economics, 131*(3), 693–714.

Eberhardt-Toth, E., 2017. Who should be on a board corporate social responsibility committee? *Journal of Cleaner Production, 140,* 1926–1935.

Eccles, N.S. and Viviers, S., 2011. The origins and meanings of names describing investment practices that integrate a consideration of ESG issues in the academic literature. *Journal of Business Ethics, 104,* 389–402.

Edmans, A., 2014. Blockholders and corporate governance. *Annual Review of Financial Economics, 6*(1), 23–50.

Edmans, A., 2023. The end of ESG. *Financial Management, 52*(1), 3–17.

Edmans, A., Levit, D. and Schneemeier, J., 2022. Socially responsible divestment. European Corporate Governance Institute – Finance Working Paper No. 823/2022.

Elan, P., 2022. Guess co-founder denies sexual harassment claims after models file lawsuit, *The Guardian,* 18 March.

European Union, 2022. Corporate Sustainability Reporting Directive. Directive (EU) 2022/2464 of the European Parliament and of the Council of 14 December 2022 amending Regulation (EU) No 537/2014, Directive 2004/109/EC, Directive 2006/43/EC and Directive 2013/34/EU, as regards corporate sustainability reporting (Text with EEA relevance), PE/35/2022/REV/1, OJ L 322, 15–80.

Faller, C.M. and zu Knyphausen-Aufseß, D., 2018. Does equity ownership matter for corporate social responsibility? A literature review of theories and recent empirical findings. *Journal of Business Ethics, 150,* 15–40.

Farooq, M.B. and De Villiers, C., 2017. The market for sustainability assurance services: a comprehensive literature review and future avenues for research. *Pacific Accounting Review, 29*(1), 79–106.

Financial Reporting Council, 2018. *The UK Corporate Governance Code.* London: Financial Reporting Council.

Flammer, C., Hong, B. and Minor, D., 2019. Corporate governance and the rise of integrating corporate social responsibility criteria in executive compensation: effectiveness and implications for firm outcomes. *Strategic Management Journal, 40*(7), 1097–1122.

Flood, C., 2023. Investors warned of 'greenwashing' risk as ESG-labelled funds double, *Financial Times,* 23 April.

García-Sánchez, I.M., Gómez-Miranda, M.E., David, F. and Rodríguez-Ariza, L., 2019. Board independence and GRI-IFC performance standards: the mediating effect of the CSR committee. *Journal of Cleaner Production, 225,* 554–562.

García-Sánchez, I.M., Rodríguez-Ariza, L., Aibar-Guzmán, B. and Aibar-Guzmán, C., 2020. Do institutional investors drive corporate transparency regarding business contribution to the Sustainable Development Goals? *Business Strategy and the Environment,* 29(5), 2019–2036.

Gloßner, S., 2019. Investor horizons, long-term blockholders, and corporate social responsibility. *Journal of Banking & Finance, 103,* 78–97.

Halliburton Inc., 2015. 2015 Proxy Statement. https://ir.halliburton.com/static-files/6f93214a-4b71-4228-bba1-05d30a7444bc, accessed: 28-05-24.

Haque, F., 2017. The effects of board characteristics and sustainable compensation policy on carbon performance of UK firms. *The British Accounting Review, 49*(3), 347–364.

Hartikainen, H., Järvenpää, M. and Rautiainen, A., 2021. Sustainability in executive remuneration: a missing link towards more sustainable firms? *Journal of Cleaner Production, 324,* 1–11.

Hirschman, A.O., 1970. *Exit, Voice, and Loyalty: Responses to Decline in Firms, Organizations, and States.* Cambridge, MA: Harvard University Press.

Hong, B., Li, Z. and Minor, D., 2016. Corporate governance and executive compensation for corporate social responsibility. *Journal of Business Ethics, 136,* 199–213.

Hong, H. and Kacperczyk, M., 2009. The price of sin: the effects of social norms on markets. *Journal of Financial Economics, 93*(1), 15–36.

Hurst, D., Butler, B. and Karp, P., 2022. Australia's Future Fund to divest $200m of holdings in Russian companies, *The Guardian,* 28 February. https://www.theguardian.com/australia-news/2022/feb/28/australias-future-fund-to-divest-200m-holdings-in-russian-companies, accessed: 28-05-24.

Hussain, N., Rigoni, U. and Orij, R.P., 2018. Corporate governance and sustainability performance: analysis of triple bottom line performance. *Journal of Business Ethics, 149,* 411–432.

IAASB, 2013. *ISAE 3000 (Revised), Assurance Engagements Other than Audits or Reviews of Historical Financial Information.* New York: IAASB.

IFAC, 2003. *International Framework for Assurance Engagements*. New York: International Federation of Accountants. https://www.ifac.org/_flysystem/azure-private/publications/files/B002%202013 %20IAASB%20Handbook%20Framework.pdf, accessed 28-05-24.

IFRS Foundation, 2020. Consultation Paper on Sustainability Reporting. https://www.ifrs.org/content/ dam/ifrs/project/sustainability-reporting/consultation-paper-on-sustainability-reporting.pdf, accessed 22-05-24.

IFRS Foundation, 2021. IFRS Foundation Trustees' Feedback Statement on the Consultation Paper on Sustainability Reporting. https://www.ifrs.org/content/dam/ifrs/project/sustainability-reporting/ sustainability-consultation-paper-feedback-statement.pdf, accessed 22-05-24.

Ikram, M., Zhou, P., Shah, S.A.A. and Liu, G.Q., 2019. Do environmental management systems help improve corporate sustainable development? Evidence from manufacturing companies in Pakistan. *Journal of Cleaner Production*, 226, 628–641.

Ilhan, E., Krueger, P., Sautner, Z., & Starks, L.T., 2023. Climate risk disclosure and institutional investors. *Review of Financial Studies*, 36(7), 2617–2650.

Ittner, C.D., Larcker, D.F. and Meyer, M.W., 2003. Subjectivity and the weighting of performance measures: evidence from a balanced scorecard. *The Accounting Review*, 78(3), 725–758.

Johnsen, D.B., 2003. Socially responsible investing: a critical appraisal. *Journal of Business Ethics*, 43(3), 219–222.

Kaplan, R.S. and Ramanna, K., 2021. Accounting for climate change. *Harvard Business Review*, 99(6), 120–131.

Kavadis, N. and Thomsen, S., 2023. Sustainable corporate governance: a review of research on long-term corporate ownership and sustainability. *Corporate Governance: An International Review*, 31(1), 198–226.

Kerber, R., 2022. U.S. ESG shareholder resolutions up 22% to record level for 2022, study finds, *Reuters*, 17 March.

Klein, P.G., Mahoney, J.T., McGahan, A.M. and Pitelis, C.N., 2010. Toward a theory of public entrepreneurship. *European Management Review*, 7(1), 1–15.

Kolk, A. and Perego, P., 2010. Determinants of the adoption of sustainability assurance statements: an international investigation. *Business Strategy and the Environment*, 19(3), 182–198.

KPMG, 2022. *Big shifts, small steps. Survey of Sustainability Reporting 2022*. https://kpmg.com/xx/en/ home/insights/2022/09/survey-of-sustainability-reporting-2022.html, accessed 22-05-24.

Krasodomska, J., Simnett, R. and Street, D.L., 2021. Extended external reporting assurance: current practices and challenges. *Journal of International Financial Management & Accounting*, 32(1), 104–142.

Liao, L., Luo, L. and Tang, Q., 2015. Gender diversity, board independence, environmental committee and greenhouse gas disclosure. *The British Accounting Review*, 47(4), 409–424.

Liao, L., Lin, T. and Zhang, Y., 2018. Corporate board and corporate social responsibility assurance: evidence from China. *Journal of Business Ethics*, 150, 211–225.

Maas, K., 2018. Do corporate social performance targets in executive compensation contribute to corporate social performance? *Journal of Business Ethics*, 148, 573–585.

Maas, K. and Rosendaal, S., 2016. Sustainability targets in executive remuneration: targets, time frame, country and sector specification. *Business Strategy and the Environment*, 25(6), 390–401.

Mallin, C.A. and Michelon, G., 2011. Board reputation attributes and corporate social performance: an empirical investigation of the US best corporate citizens. *Accounting and Business Research*, 41(2), 119–144.

Mallin, C., Michelon, G. and Raggi, D., 2013. Monitoring intensity and stakeholders' orientation: how does governance affect social and environmental disclosure? *Journal of Business Ethics*, 114, 29–43.

Maroun, W., 2019. Does external assurance contribute to higher quality integrated reports? *Journal of Accounting and Public Policy*, 38(4), 1–23.

Maroun, W., 2020. A conceptual model for understanding corporate social responsibility assurance practice. *Journal of Business Ethics*, 161, 187–209.

Marti, E., Fuchs, M., DesJardine, M.R., Slager, R., & Gond, J.P., 2023. The impact of sustainable investing: a multidisciplinary review. *Journal of Management Studies, in press*.

Martínez-Ferrero, J., García-Sánchez, I.M. and Ruiz-Barbadillo, E., 2018. The quality of sustainability assurance reports: the expertise and experience of assurance providers as determinants. *Business Strategy and the Environment, 27*(8), 1181–1196.

Martínez-Ferrero, J., Lozano, M.B. and Vivas, M., 2021. The impact of board cultural diversity on a firm's commitment toward the sustainability issues of emerging countries: the mediating effect of a CSR committee. *Corporate Social Responsibility and Environmental Management, 28*(2), 675–685.

Matos, P., 2020. ESG and responsible institutional investing around the world: A critical review. *CFA Institute Research Foundation Literature Reviews*, May.

Michelon, G. and Parbonetti, A., 2012. The effect of corporate governance on sustainability disclosure. *Journal of Management & Governance, 16*, 477–509.

Mitchell, R.K., Agle, B.R. and Wood, D.J., 1997. Toward a theory of stakeholder identification and salience: defining the principle of who and what really counts. *Academy of Management Review, 22*(4), 853–886.

Nestlé, 2021; 2022. Annual Reports. Nestlé, Vevey, Switzerland.

Neubaum, D.O. and Zahra, S.A., 2006. Institutional ownership and corporate social performance: the moderating effects of investment horizon, activism, and coordination. *Journal of Management, 32*(1), 108–131.

Ott, C., & Endrikat, J., 2023. Exploring the association between financial and nonfinancial carbon-related incentives and carbon performance. *Accounting and Business Research, 53*(3), 271–304.

Peters, G.F. and Romi, A.M., 2015. The association between sustainability governance characteristics and the assurance of corporate sustainability reports. *Auditing: A Journal of Practice & Theory, 34*(1), 163–198.

Peters, G.F., Romi, A.M. and Sanchez, J.M., 2019. The influence of corporate sustainability officers on performance. *Journal of Business Ethics, 159*, 1065–1087.

Qin, B. and Yang, L., 2022. CSR contracting and performance-induced CEO turnover. *Journal of Corporate Finance, 73*, 1–24.

Radu, C. and Smaili, N., 2022. Alignment versus monitoring: an examination of the effect of the CSR committee and CSR-linked executive compensation on CSR performance. *Journal of Business Ethics, 180*, 145–163,

Rees, W. and Rodionova, T., 2015. The influence of family ownership on corporate social responsibility: an international analysis of publicly listed companies. *Corporate Governance: An International Review, 23*(3), 184–202.

Reuters, 2022. Fund wants Guess founders off board amid sexual misconduct allegations. *Reuters*, 8 February.

Ricart, J.E., Rodríguez, M.Á. and Sanchez, P., 2005. Sustainability in the boardroom: an empirical examination of Dow Jones Sustainability World Index leaders. *Corporate Governance: The International Journal of Business in Society, 5*(3), 24–41.

Ricoh Group, 2022. Integrated Report 2022. Ricoh Group, Tokyo.

Rodrigue, M., Magnan, M. and Cho, C.H., 2013. Is environmental governance substantive or symbolic? An empirical investigation. *Journal of Business Ethics, 114*, 107–129.

Rupley, K.H., Brown, D. and Marshall, R.S., 2012. Governance, media and the quality of environmental disclosure. *Journal of Accounting and Public Policy, 31*(6), 610–640.

Schneider Electric SE, 2021; 2022. Sustainable Development Report. Schneider Electric SE, Nanterre, France.

SEC, 2022a. DEFC14A, Definitive proxy statement, contested solicitations. https://www.sec.gov/Archives/edgar/data/912463/000092189522001021/defc14a09050038_03302022.htm, accessed 11-05-23.

SEC, 2022b. FORM 8 K, Current Report, https://www.sec.gov/ix?doc=/Archives/edgar/data/0000912463/000091246322000081/ges-20220422.htm, accessed 11-05-23.

SEC, 2022c. DFRN14A, Revised definitive proxy statement filed by non-management. https://www.sec.gov/Archives/edgar/data/912463/000092189522001180/dfrn14a09050038_04072022.htm, accessed 11-05-23.

Serafeim, G., 2015. Integrated reporting and investor clientele. *Journal of Applied Corporate Finance, 27*(2), 34–51.

Serafeim, G., 2018. Investors as stewards of the commons? *Journal of Applied Corporate Finance*, *30*(2), 8–17.

Sheldon, M.D. and Jenkins, J.G., 2020. The influence of firm performance and (level of) assurance on the believability of management's environmental report. *Accounting, Auditing & Accountability Journal*, *33*(3), 501–528.

Shell plc, 2022. Annual Report. Shell Plc, London.

Shiffman, J., Driver, A. and Grow, B., 2012. Special Report: The lavish and leveraged life of Aubrey McClendon, *Reuters*, 7 June.

Simnett, R., Vanstraelen, A. and Chua, W.F., 2009. Assurance on sustainability reports: an international comparison. *The Accounting Review*, *84*(3), 937–967.

Simoni, L., Bini, L. and Bellucci, M., 2020. Effects of social, environmental, and institutional factors on sustainability report assurance: evidence from European countries. *Meditari Accountancy Research*, *28*(6), 1059–1087.

Spira, L.F. and Bender, R., 2004. Compare and contrast: perspectives on board committees. *Corporate Governance: An International Review*, *12*(4), 489–499.

Steinmeier, M. and Stich, M., 2019. Does sustainability assurance improve managerial investment decisions? *European Accounting Review*, *28*(1), 177–209.

Taglialatela, J., Barontini, R., Testa, F. and Iraldo, F., 2024. Blockholders and the ESG performance of M&A targets. *Journal of Management and Governance*, *28*(2), 625–650.

The Guardian, 2022. Mike Cannon-Brookes succeeds in shaking up AGL board. *The Guardian*, 14 November.

Thompson, E.K., Ashimwe, O., Buertey, S. and Kim, S.Y., 2022. The value relevance of sustainability reporting: does assurance and the type of assurer matter? *Sustainability Accounting, Management and Policy Journal*, *13*(4), 858–877.

Tricker, B., 2022. *The Practice of Corporate Governance*. Boca Raton, FL: CRC Press.

Tsang, A., Wang, K.T., Liu, S. and Yu, L., 2021. Integrating corporate social responsibility criteria into executive compensation and firm innovation: international evidence. *Journal of Corporate Finance*, *70*, 1–27.

Ullmann, A.A., 1985. Data in search of a theory: a critical examination of the relationships among social performance, social disclosure, and economic performance of US firms. *Academy of Management Review*, *10*(3), 540–557.

Valle, I.D.D., Esteban, J.M.D. and Pérez, Ó.L.D.F., 2019. Corporate social responsibility and sustainability committee inside the board. *European Journal of International Management*, *13*(2), 159–176.

Van Duuren, E., Plantinga, A. and Scholtens, B., 2016. ESG integration and the investment management process: fundamental investing reinvented. *Journal of Business Ethics*, *138*, 525–533.

Velte, P., 2021. Determinants and consequences of corporate social responsibility assurance: a systematic review of archival research. *Society and Business Review*, *16*(1), 1–25.

Venter, E.R. and Van Eck, L., 2021. Research on extended external reporting assurance: trends, themes, and opportunities. *Journal of International Financial Management & Accounting*, *32*(1), 63–103.

Villalonga, B., 2018. The impact of ownership on building sustainable and responsible businesses. *Journal of the British Academy*, *6*(s1), 375–403.

Yoshikawa, T., Zhu, H. and Wang, P., 2014. National governance system, corporate ownership, and roles of outside directors: a corporate governance bundle perspective. *Corporate Governance: An International Review*, *22*(3), 252–265.

Zaman, R., Farooq, M.B., Khalid, F. and Mahmood, Z., 2021. Examining the extent of and determinants for sustainability assurance quality: the role of audit committees. *Business Strategy and the Environment*, *30*(7), 2887–2906.

Zattoni, A. and Cuomo, F., 2008. Why adopt codes of good governance? A comparison of institutional and efficiency perspectives. *Corporate Governance: An International Review*, *16*(1), 1–15.

Zhou, S., Simnett, R. and Green, W.J., 2016. Assuring a new market: the interplay between country-level and company-level factors on the demand for greenhouse gas (GHG) information assurance and the choice of assurance provider. *Auditing: A Journal of Practice & Theory*, *35*(3), 141–168.

PART VI

SUSTAINABILITY REPORTING
– AROUND THE WORLD

19. The compliance of Turkish listed firms with the Sustainability Principles Compliance Framework

Güler Aras, Ozlem Kutlu Furtuna and Evrim Hacıoglu Kazak

INTRODUCTION

Corporate sustainability has gained more importance after the Brundtland Report, which was a milestone in articulating a definition of sustainable development as 'Sustainable development is the development that meets the needs of the present without compromising the ability of future generations to meet their own needs' (Brundtland Commission, 1987). In encountering the diversified needs and expectations of various stakeholders, corporate sustainability practices have gained greater importance (Higgins and Coffey, 2016). Eccles et al. (2012) suggest that mandatory sustainability disclosure practices may impose pressure on firms to make more efforts to pay attention to environmental and social issues, which may tend to affect shareholder value. In most countries in the world, including Turkey, sustainability disclosure is still not mandatory, and enterprises have been dealing with various strategic implications in line with voluntary sustainability disclosure. Some firms tend to provide detailed information about their sustainability practices voluntarily, while others prefer not to disclose their sustainability approaches.

The Capital Markets Board of Turkey (CMB) amended the Sustainability Principles Compliance Framework, which contains the principles that listed firms should follow, and it was put into effect through the Capital Markets Board's Communiqué No II-17.1 and an Amendment of the Corporate Governance Communiqué No II-17.1 published in the Official Gazette dated 2 October 2020. The Amendment introduces the environmental, social and governance (ESG) principles, which are some of the most hotly debated issues in corporate law and capital markets law in developed economies, into Turkish legislation. While the principles operate only on a 'comply or explain' basis for the time being, this development shows that the firms are increasingly expected to also adopt governance strategies that take all stakeholders' interests into account in this jurisdiction. This framework enables listed firms to follow international reporting standards such as the Sustainability Accounting Standards Board (SASB), Global Reporting Initiative (GRI), International Integrated Reporting Council (IIRC) and Task Force on Climate-Related Disclosures (TCFD). Furthermore, the Sustainability Principles Compliance Framework enables Turkish firms to understand the learning process of sustainability culture. The sustainability framework is built upon three pillars: Environmental Principles, Social Principles, and Principles of Corporate Governance. Accordingly, the board of directors will determine the issues that the company prioritizes among those and form the company policies that will be disclosed to the public. The firms will also disclose the committees and units tasked with executing these policies and their short- and long-term goals.

This chapter aims to investigate comprehensive corporate sustainability disclosure approaches and also to exhibit the factors driving voluntary sustainability compliance disclosure by utilizing both quantitative and qualitative data. In order to reveal an empirical work under voluntary disclosure in an emerging country, this chapter investigates the factors driving sustainability disclosure for Turkish listed companies while comparing the various sustainability disclosure approaches. Even though several studies have explored sustainable development practices, the role of business entities to understand the level/degree of voluntary sustainability disclosure has been a crucial issue that has still received little attention in academic literature, specifically in developing countries. In line with this, this study proposes to investigate the fundamental financial indicators, in terms of firm size, asset profitability, equity profitability and market value for BIST 100 index firms during the years 2015 to 2020.

To reveal the approach of Turkish firms towards sustainability matters, the following research questions have been posed:

> RQ1. What is the extent of corporate sustainability compliance disclosures by Turkish firms?
> RQ2. What are the factors driving sustainability compliance with a voluntary sustainable framework in Turkey?

This chapter is the first empirical and comprehensive paper in the Turkish context evaluating voluntary corporate sustainability disclosure and it also exhibits the factors driving voluntary sustainability compliance disclosure by employing both quantitative and qualitative data regarding content analysis and Spearman rank correlation analysis.

The remainder of the chapter is organized as follows: the following parts highlight the theoretical framework and previous literature to reveal the approach of firms towards sustainability matters. In the methodology part, the results of two distinct methodological analyses, in terms of content analysis and Spearman correlation analysis, have been provided. The last section evaluates concluding remarks and gives a direction for future research.

THEORETICAL FRAMEWORK

Since the firms are seen as part of society, they are expected to promote social welfare and environmental justice by integrating sustainability issues into their strategies (Margolis and Walsh, 2003). Sustainability disclosures have been viewed as one of the crucial steps towards this integration. In the context of voluntary sustainability disclosure, agency theory (Spence, 1973), stakeholder theory (Freeman et al., 2004) and legitimacy theory (Meyer and Rowan, 1977) have been traced. Spence (1973) reveals that to reduce hidden information, firms have to improve transparency with the help of corporate reporting. The agency theory states that firms use various channels for mitigating the information asymmetry between managers and owners and hence, managers should disclose all relevant information available to stakeholders (Jensen and Meckling, 1976; Fama and Jensen, 1983). In this regard, sustainability reports have a significant role in reducing asymmetric information between stakeholders and managers by mitigating principal–agent conflicts (Orazalin and Mahmood, 2020).

Stakeholder theory states that firms should meet a broader range of stakeholders, in addition to creating and maximizing value for their stakeholders (Freeman et al., 2004). To ensure sustainability, corporations have to meet the stakeholders' expectations while maximizing shareholders' wealth. Corporate sustainability reports enable firms to disclose social, governance and environmental impacts of the activities with a holistic approach. In this regard, stakeholder theory is based on the notion that voluntary disclosure supports responding to stakeholders' demands.

To explain voluntary sustainability disclosure, legitimacy theory proposes an alternative theoretical framework. Meyer and Rowan's (1977) study is one of the pioneering works in that field, and states that legitimacy theory suggests that society has certain expectations from enterprises, with implicit and explicit aspects. In this respect, corporations should consider all stakeholders' expectations.

As Solomon and Lewis (2002) state, this theory gives the reasons why firms engage in corporate sustainability activities and posits an implicit social contract between society and organizations. Moreover, Hahn et al. (2015) argue that the main difference between legitimacy and stakeholder theory arises from the counterparts with which they are directly related. Legitimacy theory supports society as a whole whereas stakeholder theory is founded on the notion that firms have to encounter stakeholders' expectations in particular. In line with theoretical aspects, this chapter also clarifies the linkage between sustainability disclosure and financial indicators.

PREVIOUS LITERATURE AND HYPOTHESES DEVELOPMENT

Limited papers have revealed the voluntary sustainability disclosure methodological point of view despite the increasing role of corporations in enhancing voluntary sustainability disclosure. In this regard, this chapter proposes to extend previous results by investigating the impact of various firm-specific factors in terms of firm scale, firm profitability and market performance on the compliance with sustainability principles in Turkey. The Republic of South Africa became the first country to mandate sustainability reporting in 2002 and integrated reporting in 2010. In early 2023, the EU adopted the Corporate Sustainability Reporting Directive (CSRD), which requires EU and non-EU companies with operations in the EU to submit annual sustainability reports in addition to their financial reports (CSRD Delegated Act, 2023).

Hypotheses Development

Four firm indicators in terms of firm size, asset profitability, shareholders' equity profitability and market capitalization have been utilized as the factors driving sustainability disclosure based on theoretical and empirical literature. The related hypotheses revealing the factors driving sustainability disclosures are as follows.

Firm Size

As Hackston and Milne (1996) state, legitimacy theory and stakeholder theory both have arguments about disclosure and company size. Historical studies reveal that large-scale firms are more visible to all stakeholders and they then have to disclose more voluntary information to meet stakeholders' expectations (Sumiani et al., 2007; Kuzey and Uyar, 2017). Additionally, regarding the economies of scale theory, the cost of disclosing voluntary information is relatively lower for large-sized corporations as they have more financial resources (Matuszak et al., 2019; Spallini et al., 2021).

To investigate the firm size as a voluntary disclosure determinant, the first hypothesis of this chapter is structured as follows:

Hypothesis 1 (H1). Large firms disclose a higher volume of information about sustainability-related issues.

Firm Profitability

In the context of legitimacy theory, the profitability of companies was an important factor for voluntary sustainability in order to legitimize their activities. Roberts (1992) states that stakeholder theory proposes a significant and positive linkage between firm profitability and social disclosures. High-profit firms have to meet stakeholders' expectations and then disclose voluntary information (Waddock and Graves, 1997; Simnett et al., 2009; Branco et al., 2014). However, empirical studies present mixed findings. Some of the papers imply a negative linkage between sustainability disclosure and organization profitability (Prado-Lorenzo et al., 2009; Coffie et al., 2018; Ho and Taylor, 2007), whereas some of them posit insignificant results (Dissanayake et al., 2016; Reverte, 2009; Wachira et al., 2019), emphasizing that there is no linkage between profitability and sustainability disclosure.

To explain these inconclusive results, this chapter attempts to investigate the nexus between profitability and voluntary sustainability disclosures. In this sense, the following hypothesis is developed:

Hypothesis 2 (H2). Firms with higher profitability disclose a higher volume of information about sustainability-related issues.

Market Value

As stakeholder theory emphasizes maximizing the market capitalization of corporations and meeting shareholder expectations, voluntary sustainability disclosures can be an effective tool for the investor's decision-making process.

Empirical studies posit different results. Some of the papers reveal a positive linkage between market capitalization and sustainability disclosure (Ioannou and Serafeim 2014; Aras et al., 2018b), whereas some of them posit insignificant results (Taiwo et al., 2022).

To investigate market value as a voluntary disclosure determinant, we construct the hypothesis as follows:

Hypothesis 3 (H3). Firms with high market value disclose a higher volume of information about sustainability practices.

RESEARCH METHODOLOGY

This chapter uses two methodological approaches: first, content analysis to identify the disclosure levels, and second, the Spearman rank correlation coefficient for investigating the linkage between sustainability principles compliance scores and financial indicators between the years 2015 and 2020.

To construct sustainability principles compliance scores, this chapter utilizes the content analysis methodology, which was first used by Bowman and Haire (1975). Analysis results have been used to explore the linkage between corporate sustainability principles compliance scores and financial indicators in terms of profitability, size and market value.

Sample

This chapter covers an initial sample from the BIST 100 index. The variables related to sustainability compliance have been gathered from corporate annual reports while the financial variables have been retrieved from the Bloomberg database during the years 2015 to 2020. Sustainability principles disclosure data has been captured from corporate annual reports in 2020.

To explore the evolution of the sustainability principles compliance framework, relevant information in the 2020 annual reports of BIST 100 Index listed firms was examined. However, the study only covers 71 of the firms that were listed in the BIST 100 Index because of the non-existence of sustainability compliance disclosure in the annual reports of the others.

Table 19.1 presents the number of corporations used in the sample.

Table 19.1   Sample selection

	Number of corporations
Corporations listed in BIST 100 as of 2021	100
Corporations without sustainability compliance reports in annual reports	29
Final sample	71

Table 19.2 shows the breakdown of sample corporations by industry in the categories of education, health and sports services, electricity, gas and steam, financial institutions, manufacturing, transportation and storage, wholesale trade and restaurants and hotels. With 28 firms, financial institutions make up the highest proportion (39%), followed by the manufacturing industry (38%); whereas with just one firm, the education, health and sports service industry forms the lowest proportion of the relevant sample. The industry classification was made according to the Bloomberg Industry Classification Standard (BICS).

Table 19.2   Distribution of sampled corporations with an industry breakdown

Industry	Number of corporations	Percentage (%)
Financial institutions	28	39.44
Manufacturing	27	38.03
Wholesale trade, restaurants and hotels	7	9.86
Transportation and storage	4	5.63
Electricity, gas and steam	4	5.63
Education, health and sports services	1	1.41
Total	71	100.00

Dependent Variables – Sustainability Principles Compliance Score

The CMB has set out the sustainability principles in four pillars: general principles (strategy, policy and targets; implementation/monitoring, reporting and assurance); environmental principles; social principles (human rights and employee rights, stakeholders, international standards and initiatives), and principles of corporate governance. Accordingly, the board of directors determines issues that the company prioritizes among those and formulates the company policies that will be disclosed to the public. The companies will also disclose the committees and units tasked with executing these policies and their short- and long-term goals. All disclosure data has been manually collected from the annual reports.

Table 19.3 depicts four sustainability pillars and 60 criteria. With 26 criteria, environmental principles make up the largest group, followed by social principles (16 criteria), while corporate governance principles are the smallest group (six criteria). In the annual reports, companies should disclose '– among other things – whether the sustainability principles are applied. If not, they should disclose a reasoned explanation and the impacts on environmental and social risk management due to not fully complying with these principles.' There are four dependent variables: general principle disclosures, environmental principles, social principles and corporate governance principles. General principles have been classified as strategy, policy and targets, implementation/monitoring, reporting and assurance. The last pillar of sustainability points out how an organization accounts for corporate governance in line with transparency, accountability, fairness and responsibility.

Table 19.3   Corporate sustainability principles compliance pillars

Principles	Number of criteria
A. General principles	12
A1. Strategy, policy and targets	2
A2. Implementation/monitoring	4
A3. Reporting	5
A4. Assurance	1
B. Environmental principles	26
C. Social principles	16
C1. Human rights and employee rights	10
C2. Stakeholders, international standards and initiatives	6
D. Corporate governance principles	6
	60

Table 19.4(1) presents the dimensions, dependent variables, abbreviations and definitions.

Table 19.4(1)   Dependent variables used in Spearman rank correlation analysis

Dimensions	Variables	Abbreviations	Definitions
Sustainability principles	● Total Compliance Score	TCS	Individual dimensions of sustainability issues are based on a dichotomous approach assigning a value of 1 if the corresponding information is reported, and 0 otherwise
	● General Principles Compliance Score	GPCS	
	● Environmental Principles Compliance Score	EPCS	
	● Social Principles Compliance Score	SPCS	
	● Corporate Governance Principles Compliance Score	CPCS	

Independent Variables

Four financial indicators have been selected as the driving factors of corporate sustainability and as the possible determinants of sustainability disclosure. Total assets at the end of the current year have been used as a proxy of firm size (*lnasset*). To indicate the firm's financial profitability, return on assets (*ROA*), which is represented by net income divided by total assets at the end of the current year, has been used. This indicator will be used as a reflection of the management's perspective on profitability. Additionally, to reflect shareholders' perspective through profitability, return on equity (*ROE*) has been used as a second profitability indicator. Investor expectations have a crucial role with regard to voluntary sustainability reporting. To capture the market's perspective, market value (*lnmarket*) has been used. Table 19.4(2) presents the dimensions, related variables, abbreviations and definitions.

Table 19.4(2)   Independent variables used in Spearman rank correlation analysis

Dimensions	Variables	Abbreviations	Definitions
Company size	Total asset	lnasset	Natural logarithm of firms' total assets at the end of the current year
Financial indicators	Management's perspective – profitability	ROA	Net income divided by total assets at the end of the current year
Shareholder's perspective – profitability	Return on equity	ROE	Net income divided by total equity at the end of the current year
Market's perspective	Market capitalization	lnmarket	Natural logarithm of firms' total market capitalization at the end of the current year

EMPIRICAL RESULTS

This section first gives the extent of corporate sustainability compliance disclosures by BIST 100 index listed firms and then describes the financial indicators driving sustainability compliance with a voluntary sustainable framework in Turkey.

Content Analysis Results

To construct sustainability principles compliance scores, this chapter utilizes the content analysis methodology which was first used by Bowman and Haire (1975). In line with the CMB Amendment, listed firms refer to the Sustainability Compliance Framework in their annual reports. For BIST 100 indexed listed firms, all dimensions of sustainability mentioned before have been collected from the annual reports by using the weighted content analysis method. For coding information included in the framework, human raters are used. Table 19.5 reveals the scoring system and significance level. The sustainability principles compliance score disclosure items and the list of disclosure items are presented in the Appendix. The Sustainability Compliance Framework describes the principles in terms of general principles, environmental principles, social principles and corporate governance principles. In respect of sustainability disclosure, firms have five options through a self-assessment that reflects the fully compliant, partly compliant, low compliant, non-compliant and irrelevant. This chapter constructs individual dimensions of all sustainability issues in terms of general, environmental, social and corporate governance based on a dichotomous approach assigning a value of 1 if the corresponding information is reported and 0 otherwise. To reveal the compliance level, sub-indices have been calculated for general and social sustainability indicators. Table 19.5 reveals the scoring system and significance level.

Table 19.5   The scoring system

Compliance degree	Significance level
1.00	Full compliance with the principles
0.50–0.99	Partial compliance
0.01–0.49	Low compliance
0	Non-compliance
-	Irrelevant

Content analysis results reveal that firms that disclose information related to the corporate governance pillar have the highest compliance (0.8561), followed by the social principles (0.8147); whereas environmental principles have the lowest disclosure (0.7067). Aras et al. (2018a) analyse the multidimensional corporate sustainability implications for Turkish banks between the years 2012 and 2014, considering all sustainability reports. The content analysis results show that all the banks in the sample have the most disclosed items in the social dimension while having the fewest in the economic dimension.

Graph 1 gives the compliance percentage of sustainability compliance disclosure scores with an industrial breakdown. Education, health and sports service have the highest compliance (0,9117), followed by transportation and storage (0,8757); whereas financial institutions have the lowest disclosure (0,6650). Financial institutions cover banks, Real Estate Investment Trusts (REITs), financial leasing, holdings, venture capital, intermediary institutions, and insurance companies. Considering, financial institutions, banks have the highest compliance level (0,9875). Four of them (Garanti, Halkbank, Vakıfbank, Yapı Kredi) have full compliance (1).

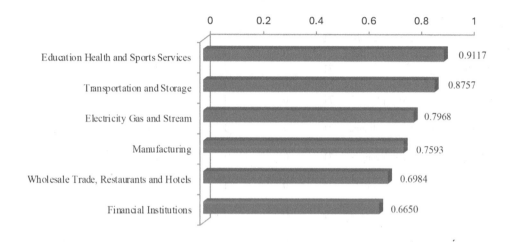

Figure 19.1   Sustainability compliance disclosure scores with an industrial breakdown

Descriptive Statistics

To investigate the inherent interrelationships between different aspects of sustainability compliance indicators, Table 19.6 gives descriptive statistics. The corporate governance principles compliance score has the highest ranked score in all sustainability disclosures whereas disclosures related to the assurance principles compliance score (under general principles compliance score) has the lowest ranked score.

Spearman Correlation Analyses Results

After content analysis, Spearman rank correlation analysis has been utilized to investigate the linkage between overall sustainability principles compliance scores and financial indicators. Table 19.7 presents the correlation analysis between all sustainability dimension scores and financial indicators. Spearman correlation coefficients reveal that Total Compliance Score (TCS), General Principles Compliance Score (GPCS), Environmental Principles Compliance Score (EPCS), Social Principles Compliance Score (SPCS) and Corporate Governance Principles Compliance Score (CGPC) have been found to significantly and positively correlate with total assets. This result is in line with expectations and indicates that larger firms are more likely to disclose sustainability practices. Additionally, the correlation between all sustainability compliance indicators and market value is positive and statistically significant. These results indicate that firms with a higher share of institutional investors tend to disclose sustainability approaches to the public.

Table 19.6   *Descriptive statistics of sustainability indicators*

Principles	N	minimum	maximum	mean	standard deviation
A. General Principles Compliance Score	71	0	1	.7230	.3030
A1. Strategy, policy and targets	71	0	1	.7680	.3090
A2. Implementation/monitoring	71	0	1	.7100	.3600
A3. Reporting	71	0	1	.8140	.2930
A4. Assurance	71	0	1	.6070	.4250
B. Environmental Principles Compliance Score	71	0	1	.7070	.3310
C. Social Principles Compliance Score	71	0	1	.8140	.2920
C1. Human rights and employee rights	71	0	1	.8420	.2790
C2. Stakeholders, international standards and initiatives	71	0	1	.7870	.3200
D. Corporate Governance Principles Compliance Score	71	0	1	.8560	.2690
	71	0	1	.7750	.2790

Table 19.7   *Correlations between sustainability principles compliance scores and financial indicators*

			lnasset	ROA	ROE	lnmarket
Spearman's Rho		Correlation coefficient	.338**	−.131	.009	.373**
	TCS	Sig. (2-tailed)	.004	.276	.941	.001
		Correlation coefficient	.362**	−.113	.039	.387**
	GPCS	Sig. (2-tailed)	.002	.349	.748	.001
		Correlation coefficient	.290*	−.097	.034	.368**
	EPCS	Sig. (2-tailed)	.014	.420	.777	.002
		Correlation coefficient	.370**	−.170	−.027	.406**
	SPCS	Sig. (2-tailed)	.001	.156	.826	.000
		Correlation coefficient	.284*	−.009	.101	.282*
	CGCS	Sig. (2-tailed)	.016	.938	.404	.017

Notes: **Correlation is significant at the .01 level (2-tailed); *Correlation is significant at the .05 level (2-tailed).

Finally, the largest correlation involves SPCS and market value (.406; $p < 0.01$). This result is in line with expectations and indicates that firms with relatively high market value are more likely to disclose social sustainability practices. On the other hand, the remaining independent variables in terms of return on assets and return on equity are not statistically correlated to the sustainability compliance scores.

Qiu et al. (2016) investigate the firms listed on the Financial Times Stock Exchange (FTSE) 350 index during the years 2005 to 2009. The authors find no relationship between environmental disclosures and profitability whereas they reveal a significant relationship between social disclosures and market capitalization. Chen et al. (2015) analysed 75 firms across America, Asia and Europe in 2012. The cross-sectional analyses reveal that human rights, society and product responsibility display a significant and positive correlation with profitability in terms of return on equity. Additionally, Farooque and Ahulu (2017) investigated 67 multinational enterprises' social and economic sustainability disclosures in Australia, the UK and South Africa; firm size was also found to be significant, indicating that large firms are closely related to high levels of management disclosures.

The findings reveal that large firms are more likely to disclose sustainability practices than small firms, to satisfy greater stakeholder scrutiny. These results are consistent with most of the previous studies carried out in Turkey (Kuzey and Uyar 2017), Sri Lanka (Dissanayake et al., 2016), Canada (Nazari et al., 2015), Spain (Spallini et al. 2021), and Ghana (Farooque and Ahulu 2017). In line with the arguments of legitimacy theory, larger firms might have more to lose due to illegitimacy, compared to small-sized firms. Notwithstanding, large-sized corporations tend to use economies of scale in a better way, have higher financial capital, and disclose more transparent information in all sustainability dimensions.

DISCUSSIONS

The growth of corporate sustainability practices in Turkey depends extensively on voluntary disclosure practices because of the lack of comprehensive and effectively enforced sustainability regulations. However, the Sustainability Principles Compliance Framework, which contains the principles that listed firms should follow, was published by the Capital Markets Board of Turkey (CMB) in 2021, enabling Turkish firms to understand the learning process of sustainability culture in recent years. According to the Sustainability Principles Compliance Framework: 'The firms should disclose – among other things – whether the sustainability principles have been applied in the annual reports. If not, they should disclose a reasoned explanation and the impacts on environmental and social risk management due to not fully complying with these principles.'

This chapter is the first empirical and comprehensive paper in the Turkish context to evaluate voluntary corporate sustainability disclosure and also demonstrates the factors driving voluntary sustainability compliance disclosure by employing both quantitative and qualitative data regarding content analysis and Spearman rank correlation analysis. This chapter contributes to the previous literature by investigating the sustainability disclosure implications of BIST 100 firms in line with the Sustainability Principles Compliance Framework published by the Capital Markets Board of Turkey.

As Waddock and Graves (1997) stated in their earlier study, profitable firms may have extra resources to report corporate sustainability disclosures. Meeting the stakeholders' expectations through sustainability reporting can bring a significant competitive advantage for profitable firms. These results are in the line with the previous studies carried out in Turkey (Aksu and Kosedag, 2006), Portugal (Branco et al., 2014), China (Liu and Anbumozhi, 2009), and Spain (Reverte, 2009). Furthermore, Orazalin and Mahmood (2020) investigate the determinants of sustainability performance reports for Kazakhstani firms during the years 2013 to 2015. The results indicate that profitable companies in Kazakhstan disclose more sustainability information when following the Global Reporting Initiative (GRI) guidelines. The results of the study failed to extricate any significant linkage between the management perspective profitability indicator, ROA and overall sustainability compliance scores. Furthermore, no significant relationship has been found between the shareholder perspective profitability indicator, ROE and overall sustainability compliance scores.

Findings generally imply that more sustainability disclosure and improvement through sustainable decision-making processes may have a positive impact on firms' financial indicators and in that way firms can meet the stakeholders' expectations. As Eccles et al. (2012) state, for long-term survival in the competitive business environment, every firm should adopt sustainability practices.

CONCLUSIONS

This chapter investigates the presence of sustainability disclosure by Turkish firms, based upon a quantitative content analysis of annual reports over the five years from 2015 to 2020. Sustainability disclosure compliance scores have been used to assess the extent of disclosures made by firms in their annual reports. Further, to analyse the factors driving sustainability compliance with voluntary sustainable disclosure and to test the hypotheses, Spearman correlation analyses have been conducted.

Concerning the possible relations of sustainability compliance scores, the findings reveal that only firm size and market performance are significantly and positively related to all dimensions of corporate sustainability disclosure for BIST 100 Index firms. These findings highlight that large-scale firms are more likely to disclose sustainability practices to the public in order to satisfy greater stakeholder scrutiny. Additionally, firms with a higher share of institutional investors tend to disclose sustainability approaches to the public and also firms with relatively high market value are more likely to disclose social sustainability practices. Hence, the results of this study will portray an exact reflection of the nexus between sustainability practices and financial indicators from emerging markets.

The findings of this chapter should be of interest to managers, investors and policymakers. All regulations towards a transparent disclosure of corporate sustainability reveal that self-regulating governance practices are valued by investors and would have a positive impact on financial indicators in the long term.

More in-depth research is needed to comprehensively analyse the dynamics of business characteristics and different industrial perspectives. This is a new step toward sustainability; expressing the extent of compliance with the principles and explaining the reasons for deviations from the new regulations is considered a crucial step for sustainability studies in Turkey. In addition, this chapter highlights some limitations arising from the fact that sustainability disclosure in Turkey is still in its infancy and data are limited. Potential further research should examine a larger population of companies and analyse the effect of regulation in a longitudinal study. Consequently, the opportunity to test the impact of sustainability compliance on sustainability performance in different institutional settings provides interesting avenues for further research.

Acknowledgement

We thank the project assistants of Yıldız Technical University Center for Finance, Governance and Sustainability (CFGS) for their assistance.

Funding

This research was supported by TUBITAK (The Scientific and Technological Research Council of Turkey, Project Number 120K901).

Conflicts of Interest

The authors declare no conflict of interest.

REFERENCES

Aksu, M. and Kosedag, A. 2006, 'Transparency and disclosure scores and their determinants in the Istanbul Stock Exchange', *Corporate Governance: An International Review*, vol. 14, no. 4, pp. 277–296.

Aras, G., Tezcan, N. and Kutlu Furtuna, O. 2018a, 'Multidimensional comprehensive corporate sustainability performance evaluation model: evidence from an emerging market banking sector', *Journal of Cleaner Production*, vol. 185, pp. 600–609.

Aras, G., Tezcan, N., and Kutlu Furtuna, O. 2018b, 'The value relevance of banking sector multidimensional corporate sustainability performance', *Corporate Social Responsibility and Environmental Management*, vol. 25, pp. 1062–1073.

Bowman, E.H. and Haire, M. 1975, 'A strategic posture toward corporate social responsibility', *California Management Review*, vol. 18, pp. 49–58.

Branco, M.C., Delgado, C., Ferreira Gomes, S. and Cristina Pereira Eugénio, T. 2014, 'Factors influencing the assurance of sustainability reports in the context of the economic crisis in Portugal', *Managerial Auditing Journal*, vol. 29, no. 3, pp. 237–252.

Brundtland Commission 1987, *Report of the World Commission on Environment and Development: Our Common Future*. Oxford: Oxford University Press.

Capital Markets Board of Turkey, Sustainability Compliance Framework in Turkey, retrieved from https://www.cmb.gov.tr/Sayfa/Dosya/166.

Chen, L., Feldmann, A. and Tang, O. 2015, 'The relationship between disclosures of corporate social performance and financial performance: evidence from GRI reports in the manufacturing industry', *International Journal of Production Economics*, vol. 170, pp. 445–456.

Coffie, W., Aboagye-Otchere, F. and Musah, A. 2018, 'Corporate social responsibility disclosures (CSRD), corporate governance and the degree of multinational activities: evidence from a developing economy', *Journal of Accounting in Emerging Economies*, vol. 8, no. 1, pp. 106–123.

CRSD Delegated Act 2023, available at: https://eur-lex.europa.eu/legal-content/EN/TXT/?uri=CELEX: 32022L2464.

Dissanayake, D., Tilt, C. and Xydias-Lobo, M. 2016, 'Sustainability reporting by publicly listed companies in Sri Lanka', *Journal of Cleaner Production*, vol. 129, pp. 169–182.

Eccles, R.G., Ioannou, I. and Serafeim, G. 2012, 'The impact of corporate sustainability on organizational processes and performance', National Bureau of Economic Research, Working Paper 17950 (previously circulated as 'The impact of a corporate culture of sustainability on corporate behavior and performance').

Fama, E.F. and Miller, M.H. 1972, 'The theory of finance', *The Journal of Finance*, vol. 29, no. 3, pp. 1031–1033, available at: https://doi.org/10.2307/2978619.

Fama, E.F. and Jensen, M.C. 1983, 'Separation of ownership and control', *Journal of Law and Economics*, vol. 26, no. 2, pp. 301–325.

Farooque, O. and Ahulu, H. 2017, 'Determinants of social and economic reportings: evidence from Australia, the UK and South African multinational enterprises', *International Journal of Accounting & Information Management*, vol. 25, no. 2, pp. 177–200.

Freeman, R.E., Wicks, A.C. and Parmar, B. 2004, 'Stakeholder theory and the corporate objective revisited', *Organization Science*, vol. 15, no. 3, pp. 364–369.

Hackston, D. and Milne, M. 1996, 'Some determinants of social and environmental disclosures in New Zealand companies', *Accounting Auditing and Accountability Journal*, vol. 9, pp. 77–108.

Hahn, R., Reimsbach, D. and Schiemann, F. 2015, 'Organizations, climate change, and transparency: reviewing the literature on carbon disclosure', *Organizational Environment*, vol. 28, no. 1, pp. 80–102.

Higgins, C. and Coffey, B. 2016, 'Improving how sustainability reports drive change: a critical discourse analysis', *Journal of Cleaner Production*, vol. 136, pp. 18–29.

Ho, L.C.J. and Taylor, M.E. 2007, 'An empirical analysis of triple bottom line reporting and its determinants: evidence from the United States and Japan', *Journal of International Financial Management & Accounting*, vol. 18, no. 2, pp. 123–150.

Ioannou, I. and Serafeim, G. 2014, 'The consequences of mandatory corporate sustainability reporting: evidence from four countries', Harvard Business School Research Working Paper No. 11-100.

Jensen, M.C. and Meckling, W.H. 1976, 'Theory of the firm: managerial behaviour, agency costs and ownership structure', *Journal of Financial Economics*, vol. 3, pp. 305–360.

Kuzey, C. and Uyar, A. 2017, 'Determinants of sustainability reporting and its impact on firm value: evidence from the emerging market of Turkey', *Journal of Cleaner Production*, vol. 143, pp. 27–39.

Liu, X. and Anbumozhi, V. 2009, 'Determinant factors of corporate environmental information disclosure: an empirical study of Chinese listed companies', *Journal of Cleaner Production*, vol. 17, no. 6, pp. 593–600.

Margolis, J.D. and Walsh, J.P. 2003, 'Misery loves companies: rethinking social initiatives by business', *Administrative Science Quarterly*, vol. 48, pp. 268–305.

Matuszak, L., Rozanska, E. and Macuda, M. 2019, 'The impact of corporate governance characteristics on banks' corporate social responsibility disclosure: evidence from Poland', *Journal of Accounting in Emerging Economies*, vol. 9, no. 1, pp. 75–102.

Meyer, J.W. and Rowan, B. 1977, 'Institutionalized organizations: formal structure as myth and ceremony', *American Journal of Sociology*, vol. 83, no. 2, pp. 340–363.

Nazari, J.A., Herremans, I.M. and Warsame, H.A. 2015, 'Sustainability reporting: external motivators and internal facilitators', *Corporate Governance: The International Journal of Business in Society*, vol. 15, no. 3, pp. 375–390.

Orazalin, N. and Mahmood, M. 2020, 'Determinants of GRI-based sustainability reporting: evidence from an emerging economy', *Journal of Accounting in Emerging Economies*, vol. 10, no. 1, pp. 140–164.

Prado-Lorenzo, J.S., Gallego-Alvarez, I. and Garcia-Sanchez, M. 2009, 'Stakeholder engagement and corporate social responsibility reporting: the ownership structure effect', *Corporate Social Responsibility and Environmental Management*, vol. 16, pp. 94–107.

Qiu, Y., Shaukat, A. and Tharyan, R. 2016, 'Environmental and social disclosures: link with corporate financial performance', *The British Accounting Review*, vol. 48, no. 1, pp. 102–116.

Reverte, C. 2009, 'Determinants of corporate social responsibility disclosure ratings by Spanish listed firms', *Journal of Business Ethics*, vol. 88, no. 2, pp. 351–366.

Roberts, R.W. 1992, 'Determinants of corporate social responsibility disclosure: an application of stakeholder theory', *Accounting, Organizations and Society*, vol. 17, pp. 595–612.

Simnett, R., Vanstraelen, A. and Chua, W.F. 2009, 'Assurance on sustainability reports: an international comparison', *Accounting Review*, vol. 84, no. 3, pp. 937–967.

Solomon, A. and Lewis, L. 2002. 'Incentives and Disincentives for Corporate Environmental Disclosure', *Business Strategy and the Environment*, vol. 11, no. 3, pp. 154–169.

Spallini, S., Milone, V., Nisio, A. and Romanazzi, P. 2021, 'The dimension of sustainability: a comparative analysis of broadness of information in Italian companies', *Sustainability*, vol. 13, no. 3, pp. 1–22.

Spence, M. 1973, 'Job market signalling', *The Quarterly Journal of Economics*, vol. 87, no. 3, pp. 355–379.

Sumiani, Y., Haslinda, Y. and Lehman, G. 2007, 'Environmental reporting in a developing country: a case study on status and implementation in Malaysia', *Journal of Cleaner Production*, vol. 15, no. 10, pp. 895–901.

Taiwo, O.J., Owowlabi, B.A., Adedokun, Y. and Ogundajo, G. 2022, 'Sustainability reporting and market value growth of quoted companies in Nigeria', *Journal of Financial Reporting and Accounting*, vol. 20, no. 3/4, pp. 542–557.

Wachira, M.M., Berndt, T. and Romero, C.M. 2019, 'The adoption of international sustainability and integrated reporting guidelines within a mandatory reporting framework: lessons from South Africa', *Social Responsibility Journal*, vol. 16, no. 5, pp. 613–629.

Waddock, S. and Graves, S. 1997, 'The corporate social performance and financial performance link', *Strategic Management Journal*, vol. 2, no. 18, pp. 303–319.

APPENDIX 19A: TURKISH SUSTAINABILITY PRINCIPLES COMPLIANCE FRAMEWORK

Principles	Principle Description
A. General Principles	
A1. Strategy, policy and targets	
A1.1	The Board of Directors determines material ESG issues, risks and opportunities and creates appropriate ESG policies. For effective implementation of these policies, internal directives and business procedures, etc. can be prepared for the company. The Board of Directors decides on these policies and discloses them publicly
A1.2	Designates the Partnership Strategy in conformance with the ESG policies, risks and opportunities. Determines its short- and long-term goals in line with the partnership strategy and ESG policies and discloses them to the public
A2. Implementation and monitoring	Determines the committees/units responsible for implementing and executing ESG policies and discloses them publicly. The responsible committee/unit reports the activities in line with policies to the Board of Directors at least once a year and in any case within the maximum periods defined in the applicable regulations of the Board for the public
A2.1	Determines the committees/units responsible for the implementation of ESG policies and discloses them to the public. The responsible committee/unit reports the activities carried out within the scope of the policies to the Board of Directors at least once a year, and in any case, within the maximum periods determined for the public disclosure of the annual activity reports in the relevant regulations of the Board
A2.2	Creates implementation and action plans in line with the short and long-term goals established and discloses them to the public
A2.3	Determines the key performance indicators (KPI) of ESR and announces them yearly. In the presence of verifiable data, it presents the KPIs with comparisons of the local and international sectors
A2.4	Discloses the innovation activities that improve the sustainability performance of business processes or products and services
A3. Reporting	Reports its sustainability performance, goals and actions at least once a year and discloses them to the public. Provides information on sustainability activities in the annual report
A4. Assurance	If verified by independent third parties (independent sustainability assurance providers), discloses its sustainability performance measurements to the public and strives to enhance such verification processes
B. Environmental Principles	Require that companies comply with environmental legislation and international standards such as ISO 14001, disclose the highest level of environmental and climate change management bodies and employees, identify incentives for environmental management, explain how environmental issues are integrated into labour-related matters and how environmental issues affect the value chain and customers, disclose measures and strategies to address the climate crisis, provide data on the use
C. Social Principles	Set standards for human and labour rights, health and safety at work, protection of personal data, ethical principles, social responsibility, customer satisfaction and transparency
C1. Human rights and employee rights	Establish a corporate human rights and employee rights policy

Principles	Principle Description
C2. Stakeholders, international standards and initiatives	Disclose its customer satisfaction policy dealing with management and disclose international standards
D. Corporate Governance Principles	Disclose the determination of measures and strategies in the sustainability field

Source: Capital Markets Board of Turkey, Sustainability Compliance Framework in Turkey, retrieved from https://www.cmb.gov.tr/Sayfa/Dosya/166.

20. Sustainability reporting model in the Malaysian palm oil industry: practices, limitations and challenges

Maizatulakma Abdullah and Gunnar Rimmel

INTRODUCTION

Over the past decades, the palm oil industry has been the subject of conflicting claims from global communities due to unsustainable palm oil production, which is believed to have contributed significantly to deforestation, open burning and biodiversity loss across the tropics. Despite the multiple counter-arguments by the producing countries, global communities, especially the European Union (EU) countries, still criticise this industry, regularly launching negative campaigns against products containing palm oil. For example, in 2018, the EU voted to ban the use of palm oil-based biofuels in their countries, with the aim of stopping rainforest deforestation.

In 2022, the EU initiated a new regulation called the 'EU Deforestation Regulation' (EUDR). Under this new regulation, all companies are required to adhere to strict due diligence requirements when selling their palm oil products or other commodities within the EU. Sri Lanka has followed the EU in limiting the use of palm oil products in its market (Potter, 2021). Furthermore, the negative aspects of palm oil use are also explicitly made aware to children and young people around the world. For example, there are many activity-based awareness programmes being conducted, especially in the developed countries, to provide the future generations with knowledge and understanding about the environmental impacts of the palm oil industry.

To counter the anti-palm oil campaign and to achieve its pledge in respect of the Sustainable Development Goals (SDGs), the Malaysian government has intervened in the palm oil industry in many aspects, including licensing, governance, a certification scheme and funding. In 2023, the Malaysian government allocated RM80 million to help the industry accelerate the pace of its sustainable development. The government also committed to promoting transparency and traceability in the palm oil industry through its national certification scheme. Furthermore, international bodies such as the Zoological Society of London (ZSL) and the World Wildlife Fund (WWF) are also committed to assisting the palm oil industry through the creation of transparency initiatives to incentivise the full disclosure of sustainability information.

This implies a developmental shift in the implementation of the sustainability reporting framework or model within the Malaysian palm oil industry, progressing from the micro level, primarily in the corporate sphere, towards a broader scope. However, explicit discussions of this model are lacking in prior studies. It is pertinent to note that there is no one-size-fits-all sustainability accounting model in practice (Abeysekera, 2022; Gokten et al., 2020; Lamberton, 2005). Nonetheless, comprehending the model's design assumes paramount importance to prevent potential manipulation by vested interests and to ensure the reported information incorporates qualitative attributes (Lamberton, 2005).

Hence, the main focus of this study is: (i) to identify the reporting entities in practice, and the reports they use to present information to stakeholders, including the forms, channels and scopes of such reports, and (ii) to explore the qualitative attributes of reported information, including the limitations of the model, as well as the challenges that can impede progress towards full transparency and traceability within this industry. It is noteworthy that this study enhances our understanding of how sustainability information is reported in the Malaysian palm oil industry. It proposes a sustainability reporting model consisting of three levels: corporate, government and international. The findings also suggest that poor sustainability reporting at the corporate level (Abdullah et al., 2020; Fanning & Spencer, 2022; Guindon, 2019; Nor Ahmad et al., 2022; Wardhani & Rahadian, 2021) can be supplemented and addressed by reporting at the government and international levels.

CONTROVERSIES LINKED TO THE PALM OIL INDUSTRY

Three decades ago, the global production of palm oil was around 10 million metric tons per year. In 2023, the United States Department of Agriculture (USDA) reported that global palm oil production had significantly increased to 77.6 million metric tons per year. This increase is due to the growing demand for palm oil, which is used in the production of various products, including foods, biofuels, cosmetics and detergents. The great demand for palm oil has prompted many tropical countries to embark on the establishment of large oil palm plantations (Vijay et al., 2016). As of April 2023, the USDA data show that palm oil is being produced in 28 tropical countries, with Indonesia and Malaysia as the top producers.

The palm oil industry started to boom in Malaysia in the 2000s. Since then, Malaysian companies' palm oil production had increased exponentially, such that the total oil palm planted area in Malaysia has expanded from 3.3 million hectares in 2000 (Ismail et al., 2003) 4.165 million hectares in 2006 (Ministry of Finance Malaysia, 2008). The total land use for oil palm cultivation in the country reached 5.67 million hectares in 2022 (Malaysian Palm Oil Board (MPOB), 2022) and is projected to continue to increase in the coming years. The expansion occurred mainly in Sabah and Sarawak – regions known for their rich biodiversity. As the industry rapidly expanded, stakeholders, especially communities and environmental activists, voiced their concerns about the negative impacts of this industry on the environment and biodiversity.

For instance, in 2007, Greenpeace issued a report entitled 'How the palm oil industry is Cooking the Climate', highlighting the issues of rainforest destruction and peatland fires in palm oil-producing countries (Greenpeace, 2007). Through satellite monitoring, Greenpeace identified millions of hectares of peat swamp forests in South East Asian countries – particularly in Indonesia – which had been converted to oil palm plantations in early 2007. According to Greenpeace (2007), the peat swamp forests store 14.6 Gt of carbon, and if the forests were destroyed, greenhouse gas (GHG) emissions would be equivalent to one year's worth of total global emissions. It was also reported that around 24 million hectares of Indonesia's forest was destroyed between 1990 and 2015 (Greenpeace, 2018) – an event that has contributed to the significant loss of orangutans, a known endangered species (Voigt et al., 2018). Such forest destruction can not only be attributed to the Indonesian oil palm companies, but also to companies from other countries, such as Malaysia and Singapore (Greenpeace, 2019), due to the structure of plantation ownership (Varkkey, 2013; Varkkey et al., 2018).

Other studies have similarly raised red flags concerning the impacts of oil palm plantations on the environment and biodiversity. For example, Koh et al. (2011) provided evidence that the conversion of peat swamp forests to oil palm plantations in Peninsular Malaysia resulted in a reduction of 46 species of forest birds. Similarly, Yudea and Santosa (2019) found a change in bird species composition in oil palm estates in Kalimantan. Brühl and Eltz (2010) proved that the conversion of forests to oil palm plantations in Sabah had caused a drastic reduction in ant species. Furthermore, the palm oil industry caused Malaysia to lose up to 60% of forest areas in Sabah and Sarawak between 1972 and 2015, threatening biodiversity (Meijaard et al., 2018) and drastically affecting the Bornean orangutan population in these areas (Seaman et al., 2019).

In Africa, Vijay et al. (2016) found that deforestation mostly occurred in Cameroon and Ghana. In Latin America, the majority of cultivated areas can be found in the Amazon rainforest, which is known for its biodiversity and rare flora and fauna (Yui & Yeh, 2013). In fact, a detailed study in the Peruvian Amazon forest found that the opening of oil palm plantations had destroyed approximately 84,500 hectares of forest areas between 2000 and 2015 (Vijay et al., 2016). Another study reported that 72% of new oil palm plantations in Peru were opened in the Amazon rainforest (Gutiérrez-Vélez et al., 2011). In Tumaco, Colombia, 60% of oil palm plantations are located in the primary forest, resulting in biodiversity loss and increased risk of extinction of the endangered animal species in the forest (Mol, 2017). These are some of the environmental and biodiversity issues that have raised ongoing disputes over palm oil production between the EU and the producing countries.

THE ASYMMETRIC INFORMATION PROBLEM

Several causes can be cited for the ongoing disputes between the EU and the producing countries regarding palm oil, and many of these have yet to find resolutions. Amongst those reasons is the asymmetric information problem (Abdullah, 2022; Abdullah & Rimmel, 2021). There is asymmetric information with respect to palm oil production, whereby producers have greater knowledge of palm oil production than the global communities. Looking at the never-ending disputes, it seems that the industry faces a huge challenge in convincing global communities as to what they have done to achieve and maintain sustainable practices.

Several studies have investigated this issue from an accounting perspective. For example, Abdullah et al. (2020) investigated environmental disclosure at the organisational level and found that palm oil companies disclose very little 'hard' information in their annual reports. Even though the study found that palm oil companies had improved their reporting drastically after receiving intense pressure from the EU, certain information lacked transparency and thus failed to convince the stakeholders. Such information include the following: (i) the location of loggings and forest clearance; (ii) environmental performance indicators, such as indicators on GHG emissions and chemical releases; (iii) environmental protection programmes, particularly on the management of peatlands; and (iv) fines and penalties for non-compliance with environmental laws. Companies seem more cautious in disclosing certain sensitive information, perhaps to avoid unwanted scrutiny by stakeholders and to reduce litigation risks, especially during 2013–2017, when the transboundary haze occurred within South East

Asia (Abdullah et al., 2020). During that period, Singapore enacted its Transboundary Haze Pollution Act 2014, which imposed criminal and civil liability on any entities (either in or outside Singapore) that caused air pollution in its territory.

The finding regarding the lack of transparency in reporting on cultivation locations by Abdullah et al. (2020) corroborates previous studies by the Zoological Society of London (ZSL). In March 2017, the ZSL issued a report entitled 'Hidden Land, Hidden Risks', which highlighted the scarcity of information on the cultivation areas that can be associated with environmental risks (ZSL, 2017). The report revealed that 70% of the 50 studied companies failed to clearly disclose information on their land use, particularly whether the areas are being planted with oil palm, unplanted, set aside for conservation, or reserved for infrastructure or other uses. The report also revealed that 56% of the 50 companies reported inconsistent figures on their land holdings.

In 2019, the ZSL released another report that highlighted the transparency issue regarding the supply chain (Guindon, 2019). Based on an analysis of 99 palm oil companies, the ZSL found that the majority of the companies failed to trace 100% of the raw materials arriving at their mills back to the plantations where they were grown. In addition, no companies were able to trace 100% of their external supplies, which usually come from smallholder farmers. In the latest assessment report of 2022, an analysis of 100 palm oil companies found that the average sustainability reporting score was 45.4%, indicating a low level of disclosures (Fanning & Spencer, 2022). Further analysis by the ZSL showed that the low disclosure score was due to the low reporting of smallholder-related information. This means that, after three years, the transparency issue still revolves around the same topic.

These transparency issues inhibit accountability and make it more difficult for stakeholders to monitor progress against palm oil companies' commitments in respect of production of sustainable palm oil products. Stakeholders do not know whether or not products containing palm oil that are sold on the supermarket shelves are free from the impacts of deforestation and open burning. For this reason, the EU is justified in taking preventive actions through the new regulation (i.e., the EUDR). Thus, it is important for palm oil companies to improve their transparency regarding the supply chain of their products, placing greater emphasis on the disclosure of smallholder-related information. At present, this kind of disclosure is at the discretion of the companies due to the limitations in current regulations in Malaysia.

In general, it is compulsory for Malaysian listed companies in all industries to adopt the Malaysian Code on Corporate Governance (MCCG), as stated under paragraph 15.25 of the Bursa Malaysia Listing Requirements. It states that:

> Listed companies must ensure that its board of directors provide an overview statement of the application of the principles set out in the MCCG, in its annual report. In addition, listed companies must disclose the application of each practice set out in the MCCG during the financial year, to Bursa Malaysia in Corporate Governance Report (CG Report) and announce the same together with the announcement of the annual report. The listed company must state in its annual report, the designated website link or address where such disclosure may be downloaded.

In 2021, the Securities Commission Malaysia issued the latest MCCG, which placed greater emphasis on the requirement for companies to address sustainability concerns. The enforcement of the new MCCG shows that Malaysia is now moving from a 'free-market' approach towards a more 'pro-regulation' approach with regard to the disclosure of sustainability information. Under Guidance G.10.2 and G.12.2 of the MCCG, all listed companies are encouraged to issue an integrated report based on a globally recognised framework to promote greater transparency and accountability, particularly regarding environmental, social and governance (ESG) issues.

Currently, there are three globally recognised sustainability-related disclosure frameworks that provide guidelines for companies to elaborate sustainability issues in their annual report: (i) the Global Reporting Initiative (GRI), (ii) the Integrated Reporting Framework by the International Integrated Reporting Council (IIRC) and (iii) the Sustainability Accounting Standards Board (SASB). One of the limitations of the GRI, however, is the omission of certain key information (Deegan, 2017), such as industry-specific information. As highlighted by Abdullah et al. (2020), the information on 'locations of logging and forest clearance' was absent from the GRI guidelines. In addition, the integrated reporting framework and SASB conceptual framework were designed based on a silo approach, in which a higher priority was placed on the needs of the capital market and investors over other stakeholders (Adams & Abhayawansa, 2022). By contrast, a company is part of a wider social system and sustainability is an issue that affect the whole system. Thus, understanding the whole picture of the sustainability reporting model implemented in the Malaysian palm oil industry is a timely endeavour, as it enables authorities to take improvement actions to help overcome loopholes and limitations.

THEORETICAL FRAMEWORK

There exist several theoretical arguments, developed in prior studies, explaining managers' motivations for voluntary or non-financial disclosures at the micro level. The most prevalent arguments stemmed from positive accounting theory, extensively discussing agency theory (Deegan, 2023). Other studies explored alternative theoretical perspectives such as legitimacy theory (Cho & Patten, 2007; Patten, 1991; Vourvachis et al., 2016; Wichianrak et al., 2022) and stakeholder theory (Nor Ahmad et al., 2022; Wardhani & Rahadian, 2021).

To understand complex phenomena, Preiser et al. (2018) suggest researchers shift focus from examining isolated characteristics of individual parts to exploring systemic properties emerging from the underlying organisation. They assert that systemic properties result from dynamic patterns of interaction. Therefore, unlike prior studies that focus on micro-level reporting phenomena, this chapter offers a distinct theoretical perspective by highlighting the more complex macro-level reporting system. As previously discussed, the Malaysian palm oil industry appears to operate under a unique and intricate reporting model that involves collaboration among entities at corporate, government and international levels. To comprehend this phenomenon, as proposed by Preiser et al. (2018), we apply complex adaptive system (CAS) theory. This theory serves as a lens for studying how a system evolves, self-organises and responds to internal and external changes, contributing to a deeper understanding of complex phenomena.

This theory is extensively used in biology, aiding in understanding biological systems' complexities and highlighting their interconnectedness, adaptability and pattern emergence. Furthermore, researchers in economics, sociology and management have employed this theory to comprehend phenomena like market behaviour and organisational dynamics (Akpinar & Özer-Çaylan, 2022; Espinosa & Porter, 2011; Palmberg, 2009; Sherif, 2006; Wollin & Perry, 2004). For instance, Sherif (2006) applies this theory to elucidate knowledge management within corporate organisations, viewing companies as complex systems comprising interrelated entities or agents – individuals, groups, processes, technology and specialised knowledge. Espinosa and Porter (2011) adopt this theory within a broader complex systems framework, recognising that the interactions among businesses, communities and governments can address socio-ecological crises and promote sustainability.

Based on the same theoretical premise, it is argued that the intense pressure in the palm oil market has compelled palm oil companies, the Malaysian government and international bodies to collaborate and engage in interactions to enhance the transparency of this industry. Consequently, a sustainability reporting model emerges as the outcome.

RESEARCH METHODS

This study adopts a qualitative approach to understand and analyse the sustainability reporting model within this industry. Data collection encompasses two primary methodologies: interviews and document analysis. In the interview phase, a list of relevant parties associated with this research topic was obtained from the MPOB. Initially, outreach was extended to 18 entities; however, only eight entities consented, leading to successful interviews with 15 representatives from these eight organisations (see Table 20.1). This inclusion of 15 participants aligns with the recommended sample size for qualitative research, as discussed in works by Guest et al. (2006; 2020).

Semi-structured interviews were conducted bilingually in English and Malay, beginning with a concise overview of the research aims. Each interview session, spanning approximately one hour, adhered to a predefined protocol. Questions covered diverse aspects, including organisational backgrounds, environmental considerations in the palm oil industry, the industry's supply chain, information reporting mechanisms, documentation pertaining to smallholder involvement, collaborative initiatives among organisations, and other relevant aspects. Participants were guaranteed confidentiality and offered the liberty to withdraw from the interview at any juncture. Subsequently, transcripts of the interviews underwent content analysis for data scrutiny.

In the document analysis phase, this study focused on scrutinising documents sourced from online repositories or shared by the interviewees. These included relevant regulations, laws, and guidelines. Additionally, information from the websites of organisations such as the MPOB, the Malaysian Palm Oil Certification Council (MPOCC), the Malaysian Sustainable Palm Oil (MSPO) Trace, the Roundtable on Sustainable Palm Oil (RSPO), WWF and ZSL was scrutinised.

Table 20.1   *Background details of the interviewees*

Interview	Organisation	Position	Department/roles
S1 (2 persons)	Government agency 1	Department managers	Strategic management department, Malaysian Sustainable Palm Oil Certification Scheme
S2 (1 person)	Government agency 2	Head of division	Smallholder Development Research Division
S3 (3 persons)	Government agency 3	High-ranking officers	Department of Environment, Ministry of Natural Resources, Environment and Climate Change
S4 (4 persons)	Government agency 4	Director and high-ranking officers	Forest management and wildlife protection in Peninsular Malaysia
S5 (2 persons)	Government agency 5	High-ranking officers	Environment Protection Department of Sabah
S6 (1 person)	Non-governmental organisation (NGO) 1	Manager	Managing biodiversity and corporate teams
S7 (1 person)	Non-governmental organisation (NGO) 2	President	Representing the community regarding environmental issues in South East Asian countries, particularly Indonesia, Malaysia, Singapore and Thailand
S8 (1 person)	Palm oil growers association	President	Social and economic welfare of oil palm farmers

FINDINGS AND DISCUSSION

Based on the interviews and document analysis, this study discovered that this industry implemented a complex reporting system, as illustrated in Figure 20.1. The mid-grey ovals (green in e-book) in Figure 20.1 represent the reporting entities within this industry. Five reporting entities have been identified: palm oil companies (at the corporate level), MPOCC (at the government level), and the RSPO, WWF, and ZSL (at the international level). The arrows in Figure 20.1 depict the interactions among these entities.

Figure 20.1 shows that there is no direct interaction between palm oil companies and smallholders. This observation sheds light on the issue raised in prior studies (Fanning & Spencer, 2022; Guindon, 2019) regarding the difficulty faced by most companies in tracing their external supplies, originating from smallholder farmers. For instance, S1 mentioned in the interview session: 'The majority of smallholders do not have their own vehicles for transporting fresh fruit bunches (FFB) to the company's factory. They sell the fresh fruit bunches to dealers or agents who visit their farm. These dealers then sell the fruit to the company' (Strategic management department, Malaysian Sustainable Palm Oil Certification Scheme).

This situation highlights the intermediary layers within the supply chain, contributing to the challenges faced by companies in tracing the origins of FFB from smallholder farmers. Consequently, this challenge restricts the information available at corporate level for reporting to stakeholders. Our document analysis further revealed that the intermediary layers may also exist in the form of cooperatives.

Figure 20.1 also illustrates the collaboration between the MPOB and the WWF, which S2 elaborated on in terms of their involvement in the MSPO Certification Scheme: 'We engage with several NGOs across various fields. One of them is the WWF, where we work within the scope of MSPO certification' (Smallholder Development Research Division).

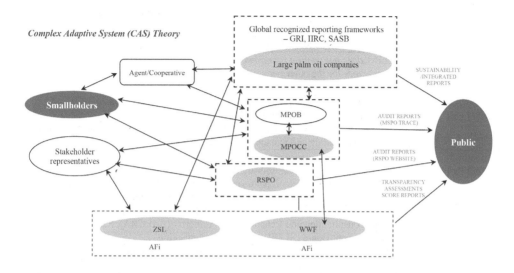

Figure 20.1 *The sustainability reporting model in the Malaysian palm oil industry*

Figure 20.1 illustrates the distinct approaches employed by each reporting entity to communicate sustainability information to stakeholders. Companies issue sustainability or integrated reports, the government discloses audit reports through its MSPO Trace website, and RSPO similarly publishes audit reports on its website. Meanwhile, ZSL and WWF provide publicly accessible transparency assessment score reports on their respective websites.

The following section will delve into the practices, limitations, and challenges of each reporting entity, excluding corporate-level reporting due to extensive prior studies in that area.

REPORTING AT THE GOVERNMENT LEVEL

The MPOCC is the governing body of the MSPO certification scheme, alongside the MPOB. The MSPO certification scheme was first launched in 2013 based on the MSPO standard, MS 2530:2013, which was developed through consensus of a special committee. This committee consists of the representatives of various stakeholders, including the government, non-governmental organisations (NGOs), the affected communities, oil palm industry associations (including smallholder associations) and academic and research institutions. The requirements in the standard are aligned with the existing national laws and regulations.

In 2022, the standard was revised and a new version was issued: MS 2530:2022. The framework for MS 2530:2022 was built based on five principles covering the following areas: (i) management commitment and responsibility; (ii) transparency; (iii) compliance with legal and other requirements; (iv) responsibility to social, health, safety and employment conditions; and (v) environment, natural resources, biodiversity and ecosystem services. The standard is split into four parts with different requirements, which are briefly presented in Table 20.2.

Each part of the standard has a different number of criteria and corresponding indicators that must be met at a satisfactory level of compliance by the certificate holders. There are two types of certificate holders under the MSPO scheme: (i) oil palm management certificate holders

Table 20.2   *The parts of the MSPO standard and its general scope of requirements*

MSPO Standard	General Scope of Requirements
MS2530-1:2022 MSPO Part 1	Part 1 *does not contain requirements* used to assess conformity. It provides the framework for the other parts and includes terms and definitions used throughout the Standards
MS2530-2-1:2022 MSPO Part 2-1	Part 2-1 contains requirements used to assess conformity for *independent smallholders* against the MSPO. These independent smallholders are categorised as individual farmers who own or lease less than 40.46 hectares (100 acres) of an oil palm smallholding and manage the smallholding themselves
MS2530-2-2:2022 MSPO Part 2-2	Part 2-2 contains requirements used to assess conformity for *organised smallholders* against the MSPO. Organised smallholders are individual farmers who own or lease less than 40.46 ha of an oil palm smallholding, and the holdings are managed by government agencies such as the Federal Land Development Authority (FELDA), the Federal Land Consolidation and Rehabilitation Authority (FELCRA), Sarawak Land Consolidation and Rehabilitation Authority (SALCRA), Sabah Land Development Board (SLDB), and other organisations
MS2530-3-1:2022 MSPO Part 3-1	Part 3-1 contains requirements used to assess conformity for *small oil palm estates* between 40.46 ha and 500 ha against the MSPO
MS2530-3-2:2022 MSPO Part 3-2	Part 3-2 contains requirements used to assess conformity for *large oil palm estates/ plantations* with areas of more than 500 ha against the MSPO
MS2530-4-1:2022 MSPO Part 4-1	Part 4-1 contains requirements used to assess conformity for *palm oil mills* against the MSPO. This standard contains requirements for sustainable management as well as supply chain requirements
MS2530-4-2:2022 MSPO Part 4-2	Part 4-2 contains requirements used to assess conformity for *palm oil processing facilities*, such as crude palm oil (CPO), palm kernel (PK), and other oil palm product processing facilities, against the MSPO. This standard contains supply chain requirements as well as introducing sustainable management practices requirements
MS2530-4-3:2022 MSPO Part 4-3	Part 4-3 contains requirements used to assess conformity for *fresh fruit bunch (FFB) dealers and palm oil traders* against the MSPO. Organisations in this category are all types of dealers under MPOB Licensing, including exporters and importers that purchase and sell oil palm products that do not change the chemical properties of the materials. This standard contains requirements for sustainable management as well as supply chain requirements

Source: Cheah (2024).

(OPMC) who have been certified to the MSPO oil palm management standard and (ii) supply chain certificate holders (SCC) who have been certified to the MSPO supply chain standard. To achieve certification, the certificate holders must be audited by a certification body accredited by the Department of Standards Malaysia.

Due to intense stakeholder pressure concerning transparency and traceability issues in the palm oil industry, the MPOCC launched MSPO Trace in 2019. Its purpose is to assist all stakeholders in tracking and tracing MSPO certification, starting from oil palm plantings and throughout the supply chain. MSPO Trace is accessible to the public through a website and an application available on the App Store and Google Play. The initiative comprises four modules: (i) certification, (ii) traceability, (iii) logo and (iv) complaints and grievances. These modules are integrated with the MSPO certification standards to facilitate the tracing of FFB from plantations throughout the supply chain, which includes milling, refining, processing and manufacturing.

Within the traceability module, MSPO Trace displays a satellite map depicting the plantation or operations location of each certificate holder. It also provides information on supplier and buyer lists, which the MPOCC claims can assist stakeholders in tracing the palm oil product to its source. However, upon reviewing MSPO Trace, it becomes evident that there is an incomplete supply chain list, particularly in the databases of smallholders and small estate certificate holders. As the system is still new, it is presumed to be under development, and information is expected to be updated periodically. Under the logo module, stakeholders are informed about the process of application for certification. Meanwhile, the complaints and grievance module caters to certificate holders, allowing them to lodge complaints or disputes through the MSPO Trace system.

As discussed earlier, stakeholders can obtain a variety of information under the certification module of MSPO Trace, especially through the reports of audit findings. The reports contain external auditors' opinions on the commitment and practices of certificate holders in the production of sustainable palm oil products. The opinion is given based on a review of relevant documents, physical site inspections and on-site interviews with all concerned parties about certificate holders' compliance with legal requirements in relation to issues regarding the environment, social responsibility, and the health and safety of employees. For example, the audit report of Sime Darby Plantation Berhad on 9 January 2023 stated the following:

> Structured worker interviews with male and female workers and staff were held in private at the workplace in the mill and the estates. Fieldworkers were interviewed informally in small groups in the field. In addition, the wives of workers and staff were interviewed in informal group meetings at their housing. Separate visits were made to each of the local communities to meet with the village head and residents. Company officials were not present at any of the internal or external stakeholder interviews. (p. 7)

Such external verification from the auditor can increase the reliability of the information reported on MSPO Trace and allows for checks and balances in the corporate reporting practices. Doing so can prevent certificate holders (amongst listed companies) from disclosing misleading information about their progress. Despite all this, MSPO Trace still has limitations in some respects, such as in the presentation and content of the disclosed information.

(i)   The Presentation of Information on MSPO Trace

Due to the asymmetric information problem between palm oil producers and global communities, it is crucial for MSPO Trace to present information that is easily understandable and comprehensible for stakeholders outside the country who have limited knowledge of the palm oil industry in Malaysia. Some of the information disclosed on MSPO Trace consists of highly technical details without sufficient explanation. These include information regarding the Sustainable Palm Oil Cluster (SPOC) for grouping smallholders within specific boundaries, as well as information on the principles, criteria and indicators of each MSPO standard. Currently, this information is scattered across other sources such as the MPOCC and MPOB websites. The usefulness of MSPO Trace could be enhanced if it consolidated all relevant information about MSPO certification in one place.

There are approximately 25 certification bodies accredited by the Department of Standards Malaysia to conduct oil palm management and supply chain certification under the MSPO certification scheme. Through document analysis, it was observed that each certification body employed a different style and format of reporting. Some apply a 'short, sharp and concise' style, while others provide comprehensive narrative information. Such reporting styles may influence stakeholders in drawing insightful conclusions about the sustainability performance of certificate holders. Information reported on MSPO Trace could be more useful if stakeholders could compare information in an audit report with similar information about other certificate holders and with information from the same certificate holder for another assessment period.

(ii)   The Scope of Information Disclosed on MSPO Trace

High carbon stock (HCS) information
Based on the interviews, it seems that the issue of HCS is given less attention than the issue of high conservation value (HCV). Document analysis also revealed that the issue of HCS has yet to be discussed in the MSPO standards. Hence, this information is not available on MSPO Trace.

Smallholder-related information
While the issue of HCV is extensively audited in larger-scale plantations, it remains unclear how this issue is addressed among smallholders, as there is no explicit information about it in their audit reports. This may be due to the complex nature of the HCV assessment process in smallholders' locations, which are often small, scattered, fragmented and remote areas, and commonly intertwined with other commodities (Pribadi et al., 2023). Assessing HCV in these areas requires auditors with specialised knowledge and skills.

Furthermore, there are limitations in the audit reports disclosed on MSPO Trace regarding the smallholders' FFB supply chain. Currently, there are no specific requirements for smallholders to record the list of buyers for their FFB. They are only obligated to record monetary information related to FFB sales transactions, as well as revenue, expenses and profit and loss statements in the Farm Record Book. It remains unclear how this current practice assists stakeholders in comprehending the entire supply chain, from smallholders to the market.

Moreover, the Farm Record Book primarily focuses on financial information and neglects the entire life-cycle activities, such as seedling operations, plantation establishment, maintenance and FFB harvesting. Each stage of these activities may have adverse environmental impacts that require consistent monitoring. For example, the slash-and-burn method used during plantation establishment causes air pollution and excessive use of chemical fertilisers and pesticides leads to water and soil pollution. It is recommended that the MPOCC consider expanding the scope of information to be recorded, maintained and disclosed by smallholders. This expansion is likely to be highly beneficial in addressing the information asymmetry problem in the palm oil industry.

REPORTING AT THE INTERNATIONAL LEVEL

(i)   Roundtable on Sustainable Palm Oil (RSPO)

Unlike the MSPO, which is a certification scheme initiated by the Malaysian government, the RSPO is a certification scheme established by a global NGO. It was formed in 2004 with inputs from stakeholders in the palm oil industry, including oil palm producers, processors or traders, consumer goods manufacturers, retailers, banks and investors, environmental conservation NGOs and social NGOs. The RSPO's global standards are built upon the RSPO theory of change framework and consist of three components: (i) RSPO Principles and Criteria (P&C), which are applied to all production-level companies (except independent mills) and all growers (except independent smallholders); (ii) the RSPO Supply Chain Certification standard (SCC standard), which is applied to all organisations in the palm supply chain that take legal ownership and physically handle RSPO-certified sustainable oil palm products at a controlled location; and (iii) the RSPO Independent Smallholder standard (ISH standard), which is applied to all independent smallholders. At a fundamental level, the RSPO covers principles similar to the MSPO, but it includes more criteria.

Regarding traceability and transparency, the RSPO appears to be superior to the MSPO as it provides two channels for these purposes, whereas the MSPO only utilises one channel, namely the audit report on MSPO Trace. The first channel for accessing information about the RSPO is through the audit report, which can be downloaded from the RSPO website under the 'search members' menu. The audit reports of RSPO P&C, SCC and ISH certificate holders contain a variety of information organised according to the criteria and indicators of each standard, including location maps of operations. Similar to the MSPO, these reports include information about auditors, which demonstrates auditor quality and the reliability of the audit work. The audit report serves as a valuable tool for enhancing transparency and traceability of palm oil companies, enabling checks and balances in corporate reporting to prevent green-washing, impression management or 'boilerplate' reports. However, it is worth noting that the document analysis reveals that each certification body issues reports with different styles and formats, which tends to reduce comparability of audit report information across different certificate holders, countries and time periods.

The second channel is the Annual Communication of Progress (ACOP) page, which is also accessible on the RSPO website. The ACOP serves as a self-reporting mechanism used by RSPO certificate holders. It aims to publicly demonstrate the progress and commitment of certificate holders towards achieving the RSPO's vision of making sustainable palm oil the norm. Stakeholders have the freedom to download all raw data from this page for decision-making or analysis purposes. The data include self-declarations from certificate holders regarding various aspects, such as operational locations, FFB production volume, certified FFB volume, buyers of their FFB and their locations, HCV and HCS areas, GHG footprint and anticipated cultivation-related pollution.

However, stakeholders must exercise caution when using information from the ACOP report, as it is a self-reporting mechanism and is not verified by an external party or the RSPO itself. Another limitation of the RSPO is the higher certification costs it imposes, which can pose a barrier to smallholder certification, particularly for independent smallholders. In this aspect, the MSPO outperforms the RSPO. With government intervention, including full subsidy of certification fees and the establishment of the SPOC, approximately 77% of smallholder-planted areas in Malaysia have been certified under the MSPO, and information about them can be found on MSPO Trace.

(ii)   The WWF Palm Oil Buyers Scorecard

In 2009, the WWF launched its initiative called the 'WWF Palm Oil Buyers Scorecard' to evaluate the commitments and progress made by palm oil buyers towards the SDGs. The WWF uses information reported by the RSPO members on the ACOP in its assessment. In addition, it also obtains first-hand data from downstream palm oil companies through a detailed questionnaire. There are five main themes that form the framework of the scorecard: (i) commitments, (ii) purchasing of sustainable palm oil, (iii) supplier accountability, (iv) sustainability platforms and (v) on the ground (including investments in smallholder producers' programmes). Each theme has several indicators that seem similar to other initiatives. These indicators are publicised on WWF's website, together with the detailed findings.

A unique aspect of this initiative is that it reports on the brands that a company sells in the market, which means its findings are very useful and relevant to consumers. However, one of the limitations of this initiative is the reliability of the data it uses, which only come from the companies and do not undergo a vetting process involving third-party verification. As reported on its website, there are no Malaysian companies who have responded to the WWF questionnaire in the latest assessment of 2021. This indicates that Malaysian companies generally lack interest in this initiative.

(iii)   The Sustainability Policy Transparency Toolkit (SPOTT)

SPOTT is a toolkit created by the ZSL in 2014 to incentivise transparency of reporting and the implementation of the best practices of companies engaged in producing three commodities: palm oil, timber and pulp, and natural rubber. SPOTT develops a different scoring framework for each commodity and annually reviews the framework through the feedback it gathers from investors and other stakeholders. This review is performed annually to ensure that the framework reflects the latest developments in ESG transparency and reporting expectations.

A unique feature of SPOTT is that it gives a different score for each piece of information disclosed according to the reliability of the data. The highest score is given to the information that can be externally verified by a third party, whereas the lowest score is given self-reported information. This scoring system can benefit stakeholders, who can efficiently retrieve additional reliable information on the progress made by oil palm companies in preserving ecosystems and biodiversity. In this system, companies are assessed against over 100 indicators (including information related to the supply chain and smallholders), which can be viewed publicly on its website. The document analysis reveals that, at present, SPOTT is the most comprehensive transparency initiative for the palm oil industry. Notably, SPOTT is the only initiative that recognises MSPO certification in its assessment. However, one limitation of this initiative is that it is difficult for stakeholders to make period by period comparisons and track improvements due to the inconsistency of the indicators used in its annual assessment.

CONCLUSION

This chapter aims to discuss the sustainability reporting model that is currently practised in the Malaysian palm oil industry. One of the novel contributions of this study that is highlighted in this chapter is the theoretical perspective used in explaining the sustainability reporting model.

CAS theory, which forms the basis of the model discussed in this chapter, suggests that sustainability reporting should not be viewed through a silo perspective, but taking the industry as a whole. The palm oil industry is a complex system of interrelated entities consisting of the government, business (represented by company) and communities (represented by independent or international bodies). Intense pressure and scrutiny in the industry over sustainability issues have prompted stakeholders to work together in order to formulate solutions that can help achieve greater traceability and transparency in the industry.

Prior studies have identified some flaws in sustainability reporting at the corporate level, especially information related to location of operations, supply chain and smallholders. This study identifies four other reporting entities, at the government and international levels: (i) MPOCC (ii) RSPO, (iii) WWF, and (iv) ZSL. These initiatives are presented in forms other than corporate level reporting practices, which are typically presented in the form of integrated or sustainability reports. Based on interviews and document analysis, it was found that some initiatives exist in the form of certification schemes while some provide disclosure scoring systems using their own methodologies. These initiatives have similarities in terms of using web technologies to channel information to the public.

In terms of the scope or contents of the reported information, all the reporting entities discuss supply chain- and smallholder-related information in their reports, and such information may complement information in integrated or sustainability reports. In particular, the MPOCC and the RSPO reveal information on the location of operations or planted areas, which can help overcome the flaws in company reporting. However, stakeholders must use the information reported with discretion because of reliability and comparability issues. For example, some initiatives have reliability issues because they only rely on companies to collect the data without third-party verification. A lack of consistency was also found in terms of the presentation format of the reports, especially when comparing audit reports between certification bodies in the MSPO and the RSPO. Such inconsistencies may hamper the comparability of the information found in these reports. Moving forward, the government and international bodies may consider enhancing transparency and traceability through improving the quality of information.

ACKNOWLEDGEMENT

This work was supported by the Malaysian Palm Oil Board – Universiti Kebangsaan Malaysia (UKM) Endowed Chair Grant (MPOB-UKM-2021-011).

REFERENCES

Abdullah, M. (2022). Mengurus Persepsi terhadap Industri Sawit Menerusi Ketelusan Maklumat. In Z. Mohd Makhbul, L.-H. Osman, M.-H. Ali, & M. R. Che-Abdul_Rahman (eds), *Pengurusan Mapan Minyak Sawit Malaysia*. 1st edn. Penerbit UKM, Bangi, Malaysia, pp. 139–148.

Abdullah, M., & Rimmel, G. (2021). Promoting sustainable palm oil through corporate transparency initiatives. In Z. Mohd Makhbul, N. Khalid, & T. Sarmidi (eds), *Management of Sustainable Palm Oil: Policies and Environmental Considerations*. 1st edn. Penerbit UKM, Bangi, Malaysia, pp. 88–99.

Abdullah, M., Hamzah, N., Mohd-Ali, H., Tseng, M., & Brander, M. (2020). The Southeast Asian haze: the quality of environmental disclosures and firm performance. *Journal of Cleaner Production*, 246, 1–11.

Abeysekera, I. (2022). A framework for sustainability reporting. *Sustainability Accounting, Management and Policy Journal, 13*(6), 1386–1409.

Adams, C. A., & Abhayawansa, S. (2022). Connecting the COVID-19 pandemic, environmental, social and governance (ESG) investing and calls for 'harmonisation' of sustainability reporting. *Critical Perspectives on Accounting, 82,* 102309.

Akpinar, H., & Özer-Çaylan, D. (2022). Achieving organizational resilience through complex adaptive systems approach: a conceptual framework. *Management Research, 20*(4), 289–309.

Brühl, C. A., & Eltz, T. (2010). Fuelling the biodiversity crisis: species loss of ground-dwelling forest ants in oil palm plantations in Sabah, Malaysia (Borneo). *Biodiversity and Conservation, 19*(2), 519–529.

Cheah, C. E. (2024). *Overview of the Revised MSPO Standards (MS2530:2022),* 30 March. https://mspo .org.my/mspo-blogs/overview-of-revised-mspo-standards-ms25302022

Cho, C. H., & Patten, D. M. (2007). The role of environmental disclosures as tools of legitimacy: a research note. *Accounting, Organizations and Society, 32*(7–8), 639–647.

Deegan, C. (2017). Twenty-five years of social and environmental accounting research within Critical Perspectives on Accounting: hits, misses and ways forward. *Critical Perspectives on Accounting, 43,* 65–87. https://doi.org/10.1016/j.cpa.2016.06.005

Deegan, C. (2023). *Financial Accounting Theory.* 5th edn. Cengage, Andover, UK.

Espinosa, A., & Porter, T. (2011). Sustainability, complexity and learning: insights from complex systems approaches. *Learning Organization, 18*(1), 54–72.

Fanning, I., & Spencer, E. (2022). *ZSL research shows palm oil industry must increase transparency to combat deforestation.* https://www.spott.org/news/zsl-research-shows-palm-oil-industry-must -increase-transparency-to-combat-deforestation/?dm_i=6UDP,C7QP,1IQEOU,1HGG2,1

Gokten, S., Ozerhan, Y., & Gokten, P. O. (2020). The historical development of sustainability reporting: a periodic approach. *Zeszyty Teoretyczne Rachunkowości, 107*(163), 99–118.

Greenpeace (2007). *How the palm oil industry is Cooking the Climate.* https://www.greenpeace.org/usa/ research/how-the-palm-oil-industry-is-c/

Greenpeace (2018). *World Orangutan Day: Numbers in decline despite Indonesian government's claims.* https://www.greenpeace.org/international/press-release/18064/world-orangutan-day-numbers -in-decline-despite-indonesian-governments-claims/

Greenpeace (2019). *Burning down the House: How Unilever and other global brands continue to fuel Indonesia's fires.* https://storage.googleapis.com/planet4-international-stateless/2019/11/5c8a9799 -burning-down-the-house-greenpeace-indonesia-fires-briefing.pdf

Guest, G., Bunce, A., & Johnson, L. (2006). How many interviews are enough? An experiment with data saturation and variability. *Field Methods, 18*(1), 59–82.

Guest, G., Namey, E., & Chen, M. (2020). A simple method to assess and report thematic saturation in qualitative research. *PLoS ONE 15*(5), e0232076.

Guindon, M. (2019). *ZSL report finds majority of companies don't know origin of their palm oil.* Zoological Society of London. https://www.spott.org/news/zsl-report-finds-majority-of-companies -dont-know-origin-of-their-palm-oil/

Gutiérrez-Vélez, V. H., DeFries, R., Pinedo-Vásquez, M., Uriarte, M., Padoch, C., Baethgen, W., Fernandes, K., & Lim, Y. (2011). High-yield oil palm expansion spares land at the expense of forests in the Peruvian Amazon. *Environmental Research Letters, 6*(4), 044029.

Ismail, A., Simeh, M.-A., & Noor, M.-M. (2003). The production cost of oil palm fresh fruit bunches: the case of independent smallholders in Johor. *Oil Palm Industry Economic Journal, 3*(1), 1–8.

Koh, L. P., Miettinen, J., Liew, S. C., Ghazoul, J., & Ehrlich, P. R. (2011). Remotely sensed evidence of tropical peatland conversion to oil palm. *Proceedings of the National Academy of Sciences, 108*(12), 5127–5132.

Lamberton, G. (2005). Sustainability accounting: a brief history and conceptual framework. *Accounting Forum, 29*(1), 7–26.

Malaysian Palm Oil Board (MPOB) (2022). *Oil Palm Planted Area 2022.* https://bepi.mpob.gov.my/ images/area/2022/Area_summary2022.pdf

Meijaard, E., Garcia-Ulloa, J., Sheil, D., Wich, S. A., Carlson, K. M., Juffe-Bignoli, D., & Brooks, T. M. (2018). *Oil Palm and Biodiversity: A Situation Analysis by the IUCN Oil Palm Task Force.* IUCN Oil Palm Task Force, Gland.

Ministry of Finance Malaysia (2008). *Economic Report 2007/2008*. https://www.mof.gov.my/portal/arkib/economy/ec2008.html

Mol, H. (2017). Colombia's contested grounds. In H. Mol, *The Politics of Palm Oil Harm: A Green Criminological Perspective*. Palgrave Macmillan, Cham (pp. 91–122).

Nor Ahmad, S. N. H. J. N., Amran, A., & Siti-Nabiha, A. K. (2022). Symbolic or substantive change? How a Malaysian palm oil company managed sustainability issues in words and deeds. *Qualitative Research in Accounting and Management, 19*(4), 473–510.

Palmberg, K. (2009). Complex adaptive systems as metaphors for organizational management. *Learning Organization, 16*(6), 483–498.

Patten, D. M. (1991). Exposure, legitimacy, and social disclosure. *Journal of Accounting and Public Policy, 10*(4), 297–308.

Potter, M. (2021). Sri Lanka bans palm oil imports. *Reuters*, 6 April. https://www.reuters.com/article/idUSKBN2BS1GD/

Preiser, R., Biggs, R., De Vos, A., & Folke, C. (2018). Social-ecological systems as complex adaptive systems: organizing principles for advancing research methods and approaches. *Ecology and Society, 23*(4), article 46.

Pribadi, D. O., Rustiadi, E., Syamsul Iman, L. O., Nurdin, M., Supijatno, Saad, A., Pravitasari, A. E., Mulya, S. P., & Ermyanyla, M. (2023). Mapping smallholder plantation as a key to sustainable oil palm: a deep learning approach to high-resolution satellite imagery. *Applied Geography, 153*, 102921.

Seaman, D. J. I., Bernard, H., Ancrenaz, M., Coomes, D., Swinfield, T., Milodowski, D. T., Humle, T., & Struebig, M. J. (2019). Densities of Bornean orang-utans (*Pongo pygmaeus morio*) in heavily degraded forest and oil palm plantations in Sabah, Borneo. *American Journal of Primatology, 81*(8), e23030.

Sherif, K. (2006). An adaptive strategy for managing knowledge in organizations. *Journal of Knowledge Management, 10*(4), 72–80.

Varkkey, H. (2013). Malaysian investors in the Indonesian oil palm plantation sector: home state facilitation and transboundary haze. *Asia Pacific Business Review, 19*(3), 381–401.

Varkkey, H., Tyson, A., & Choiruzzad, S. A. B. (2018). Palm oil intensification and expansion in Indonesia and Malaysia: environmental and socio-political factors influencing policy. *Forest Policy and Economics, 92*(July), 148–159.

Vijay, V., Pimm, S. L., Jenkins, C. N., & Smith, S. J. (2016). The impacts of oil palm on recent deforestation and biodiversity loss. *PLoS ONE, 11*(7), 1–19.

Voigt, M., Wich, S. A., Ancrenaz, M., Meijaard, E., Abram, N., Banes, G. L. ... Kühl, H. S. (2018). Global demand for natural resources eliminated more than 100,000 Bornean orangutans. *Current Biology, 28*(5), 761–769.e5.

Vourvachis, P., Woodward, T., Woodward, D. G., & Patten, D. M. (2016). CSR disclosure in response to major airline accidents: a legitimacy-based exploration. *Sustainability Accounting, Management and Policy Journal, 7*(1), 26–43.

Wardhani, R., & Rahadian, Y. (2021). Sustainability strategy of Indonesian and Malaysian palm oil industry: a qualitative analysis. *Sustainability Accounting, Management and Policy Journal, 12*(5), 1077–1107.

Wichianrak, J., Wong, K., Khan, T., Siriwardhane, P., & Dellaportas, S. (2022). Soft law, institutional signalling – Thai corporate environmental disclosures. *Social Responsibility Journal, 18*(2), 205–220.

Wollin, D., & Perry, C. (2004). Marketing management in a complex adaptive system: an initial framework. *European Journal of Marketing, 38*(5–6), 556–572.

Yudea, C., & Santosa, Y. (2019). How does oil palm plantation impact bird species diversity? A case study from PKWE Estate, West Kalimantan. *IOP Conference Series: Earth and Environmental Science, 336*(1), 012026.

Yui, S., & Yeh, S. (2013). Land use change emissions from oil palm expansion in Pará, Brazil depend on proper policy enforcement on deforested lands. *Environmental Research Letters, 8*(4), 044031.

ZSL (2017). *Hidden Land, Hidden Risks?* http://www.spott.org/wp-content/uploads/sites/3/2017/05/Hidden-Land_Hidden-Risks.pdf

21. The extent and quality of sustainability-related reporting: evidence of integrated thinking in South Africa?

Dusan Ecim and Warren Maroun

1 INTRODUCTION

Given concerns about the limitations of traditional financial reporting, the state of the environment and ongoing social challenges, organisations are coming under increasing pressure to apply an integrated thinking philosophy (Atkins et al., 2020a; Tirado-Valencia et al., 2020; Malafronte & Pereira, 2021). Integrated thinking should be embedded in an organisation's decision-making, operations and management control systems with results presented clearly to stakeholders (Stubbs & Higgins, 2014; Rinaldi, 2020).

Integrated thinking is defined as: "the active consideration by an organization of the relationships between its various operating and functional units and the capitals that the organization uses or affects. Integrated thinking leads to integrated decision-making and actions that consider the creation, preservation or erosion of value over the short, medium and long term" (International Integrated Reporting Council (IIRC), 2021, p. 3).

This chapter is concerned with assessing the extent of integrated thinking by South African listed companies. The choice of jurisdiction is informed by the fact that South Africa is regarded as a pioneer in different types of environmental and social reporting, stakeholder-centric governance and the concurrent management of economic and extra-economic considerations among its private sector firms (De Villiers et al., 2014). Examining integrated thinking in South Africa is also important given that much of the prior research dealing with sustainable development overlooks developing economies, especially those in Africa.

An integrated thinking schematic, adapted from Maroun et al. (2023), is applied to evaluate integrated thinking by a sample of firms listed on the Johannesburg Stock Exchange (JSE). The analysis complements studies dealing with the quality of sustainability (e.g. Michelon et al., 2015; Wiseman, 1982) or integrated reports (e.g. Malola & Maroun, 2019; Maroun, 2019) and their value relevance (e.g. Beck et al., 2015; Zhou et al., 2017) but which have not specifically focused on an underlying integrated thinking logic (Ecim & Maroun, 2023; Malafronte & Pereira, 2021). Findings should be useful for academics concerned with the development, application and consequences of integrated and similar types of reporting and for stakeholders wanting to evaluate an organisation's progress with integrated thinking implementation.

2   INTEGRATED REPORTING AND THINKING IN SOUTH AFRICA

The "King IV Report on Corporate Governance for South Africa" (King IV) is South Africa's most recent code on corporate governance. It identifies integrated thinking and reporting as central to the achievement of effective internal control, the generation of responsible returns for investors, the creation of value for the broader community of stakeholders and long-term sustainable development (Institute of Directors (IOD), 2016). According to King IV and the IIRC's 2021 framework, an integrated report should provide: "concise communication about how an organization's strategy, governance, performance and prospects, in the context of its external environment, lead to the creation, preservation or erosion of value over the short, medium and long term" (IIRC, 2021, p. 10).

Integrated reporting is a principles-driven process informed by the need to explain how an organisation relies on and impacts multiple types of capitals at the strategic, risk-management and operational levels (De Villiers et al., 2020). Financial imperatives need to be balanced by considering the interdependencies among economic, environmental and social factors to promote both financial stability and sustainable development (IIRC, 2021). However, integrated reporting must be genuine. It cannot be treated as a compliance-driven exercise or a tool for managing impressions (Haji & Anifowose, 2016; Atkins & Maroun, 2015).

Figure 21.1 summarises features of high-quality reports based on technical reviews of South African integrated reports and select academic research.

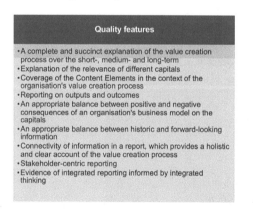

Quality features	Quality indicators
•A complete and succinct explanation of the value creation process over the short-, medium- and long-term •Explanation of the relevance of different capitals •Coverage of the Content Elements in the context of the organisation's value creation process •Reporting on outputs and outcomes •An appropriate balance between positive and negative consequences of an organisation's business model on the capitals •An appropriate balance between historic and forward-looking information •Connectivity of information in a report, which provides a holistic and clear account of the value creation process •Stakeholder-centric reporting •Evidence of integrated reporting informed by integrated thinking	•Coverage or 'density' of disclosures •Content integration •Absence of repetition •Language and tone •Ease of interpretation (including conciseness) •Presentation of information (including use of graphs, tables and images) •Emphasis on policies and actions •Methods/processes for identifying and engaging with stakeholders •Number of stakeholders accessing and engaging with the company on its integrated reports •Balance between positive and negative information; forward-looking and historical information; narrative and qualitative disclosures •External assurance and other sources of internal assurance •Rankings in independent reviews/competitions

Source: Developed from IRCSA, 2018; Malola & Maroun, 2019; PwC, 2015; Haji & Anifowose, 2016; Eccles et al., 2019.

Figure 21.1   Features and indicators of high-quality integrated reports

South Africa has played a leading role in advancing integrated thinking under an "apply and explain" model (see IOD, 2016). Organisations are expected to adopt governance principles which espouse integrated thinking and explain how these are operationalised. The financial and extra-financial benefits are expected to drive widespread use of integrated thinking and reporting with the result that these are not statutory requirements for South African firms.

Ernst & Young (EY) annually assess the top 100 Johannesburg Stock Exchange (JSE)-listed companies' integrated reports (see EY, 2022). EY evaluates reporting quality based on how well companies have applied the guiding principles and reported on the content elements outlined by the IIRC Framework (for details, see IIRC, 2021; EY, 2022). Overall, EY's reviews suggest that South Africa's most prominent organisations are committed to preparing high-quality integrated reports characterised by balanced accounts of financial and extra-financial performance. In support of this position is a growing body of academic research which finds that some organisations use integrated reporting as an impression management tool (Haji & Anifowose, 2016) but that integrated reporting goes hand-in-hand with improvements to internal management processes (McNally & Maroun, 2018), reduced information asymmetry (Barth et al., 2017), lower levels of risk for investors (Zhou et al., 2017) and more robust governance systems (Maroun & Cerbone, 2020). South African organisations are also ahead of their international peers when it comes to the adoption and application of integrated reporting. See Figure 21.2.

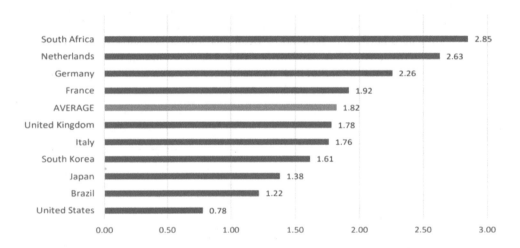

Source: Eccles et al. (2019).

Figure 21.2   Comparison of integrated report quality

Integrated thinking and reporting often develop in tandem. In some cases, an organisation may prepare an integrated report before it has fully developed and implemented an integrated thinking philosophy (Bridges & Yeoman, 2020). Irrespective of whether integrated reporting or thinking comes first, the quality features and indicators in Figure 21.1 point to a sophisticated reporting environment which, in practical terms, can only be achieved if integrated reports are supported by an underlying commitment to integrated thinking (Chartered Institute of Management Accountants (CIMA), 2017).

Integrated thinking does not require a complete overhaul of the business model and strategy (McNally et al., 2017) and can be achieved in incremental stages which includes embedding a sustainability imperative in internal processes (Adams et al., 2020). Despite the IIRC coining the term "integrated thinking", the concept has been found in sustainability literature since the 1990s (see Gray, 1992) and has continued to gain prominence over the last two decades (Ecim & Maroun, 2023). Integrated thinking promotes a sustainable approach to business management that considers the triple context of economic, environmental and social performance (Baboukardos et al., 2021).

Addressing environmental issues promotes the long-term viability of a company and maximises benefits for shareholding and non-shareholding stakeholders (Atkins & Macpherson, 2019). Concurrently, social issues must be addressed to mitigate adverse impacts on communities, ensure the development of essential skills and maintain access to human capital (Helm, 2020). While providers of financial capital play a critical role in the broader integrated thinking framework, the legitimate needs of a broader group of stakeholders must also be considered (IIRC, 2021). Integrated thinking ensures that there is a holistic process to gauge risks, capitalise on opportunities and improve internal processes. Financial stability, social and environmental responsibility and legitimacy in the eyes of key stakeholders is the result (Beck et al., 2015).

Key features of integrated thinking include:

(1) responding to stakeholders' legitimate needs and interests;
(2) evaluating, managing and capitalising on risks and opportunities in the external environment;
(3) assessing the interdependencies among activities and capitals together with the resulting trade-offs and outcomes; and
(4) a multi-timeframe analysis of activities, performance and outcomes (adapted from IIRC, 2021).

The benefits of, and barriers to, integrated thinking are summarised in Figure 21.3.

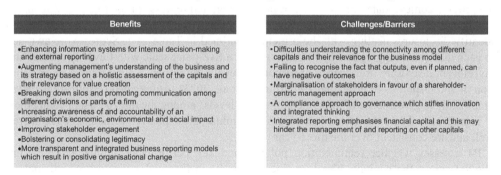

Benefits	Challenges/Barriers
•Enhancing information systems for internal decision-making and external reporting •Augmenting management's understanding of the business and its strategy based on a holistic assessment of the capitals and their relevance for value creation •Breaking down silos and promoting communication among different divisions or parts of a firm •Increasing awareness of and accountability of an organisation's economic, environmental and social impact •Improving stakeholder engagement •Bolstering or consolidating legitimacy •More transparent and integrated business reporting models which result in positive organisational change	•Difficulties understanding the connectivity among different capitals and their relevance for the business model •Failing to recognise the fact that outputs, even if planned, can have negative outcomes •Marginalisation of stakeholders in favour of a shareholder-centric management approach •A compliance approach to governance which stifles innovation and integrated thinking •Integrated reporting emphasises financial capital and this may hinder the management of and reporting on other capitals

Source: Developed from Dumay & Dai, 2017; Oliver et al., 2016; Rinaldi, 2020; Ecim & Maroun, 2023; Stubbs & Higgins, 2014; Velte & Stawinoga, 2017.

Figure 21.3   The benefits of, and barriers to, integrated thinking

While the format and content of integrated reports have been examined in detail, there has been less emphasis on integrated thinking (Tweedie & Martinov-Bennie, 2015). The latter cannot be observed directly but it is possible to draw inferences based on:

- companies' awareness and understanding of different types of capitals on which their business models are dependent;
- leadership commitment to, and capability of operationalising strategies which balance economic, environmental and social goals;
- the establishment of structures to achieve sustainable development;
- the development of performance management goals which integrate financial and extra-financial considerations; and
- the quality of external communication (Maroun et al., 2023; Malafronte & Pereira, 2021; Busco et al., 2021).

Each point is explored in more detail below.

2.1   An Integrated Thinking Schematic

Table 21.1 outlines five principles and related indicators associated with integrated thinking.

The principles are based on the guidance provided by the IIRC and prior academic literature, complemented by proprietary data collected from one-on-one interviews with corporates, investors and environmental, social and governance (ESG) analysts. Additional details on how the instrument in Table 21.1 is validated are provided in Maroun et al. (2023).

2.2   Levels of Integrated Thinking

To provide context, data are collected from the integrated reports[1] of the top 100[2] JSE-listed companies by market capitalisation over a three-year period. The reports were examined to identify disclosures dealing with the principles outlined in Table 21.1. Scores were awarded to each disclosure (aggregated by indicator) using a five-point scale with Level 1 representing no relevant disclosure or evidence of response. Level 5 represents a comprehensive explanation of and responses to principles (see Maroun et al., 2023). Aggregated results are depicted graphically to give a sense of integrated thinking "levels" among the top 100 listed companies.

Figure 21.4 shows the scores per integrated thinking principle. All principles have scored well and are consistent over the three-year period.

P4 assesses whether remuneration policies and key performance indicators (KPI) are aligned across the capitals, blending financial and non-financial indicators which include setting sustainability targets (Dumay & Dai, 2017; Oliver et al., 2016). However, performance incentives prioritise financial metrics. Marginalising environmental and social dimensions is detrimental to outcomes-based governance rooted in the integrated thinking necessary for mitigating risk, managing crises and capitalising on opportunities (see Atkins et al., 2020a). As a result, P4 has the lowest score (average = 70%). Emphasis is being placed on a more holistic approach to managing financial and extra-financial performance indicators by the Global Reporting Initiative (GRI), the Task Force on Climate-Related Financial Disclosures (TCFD), the International Integrated Reporting Council (IIRC) and, most recently, the International Sustainability Standards Board (ISSB). That companies' KPIs may not include a balanced

Table 21.1   *Integrated thinking schematic*

Principle	Indicator
Principle 1 (P1): Integrated awareness and understanding The organisation demonstrates clear awareness and understanding of the connectivity and interdependence of matters material to its ability to create value over time	1.1 Awareness and understanding of external factors impacting the organisation's operating context 1.2 Awareness and response to the legitimate needs and interest of stakeholders 1.3 Awareness and understanding of risks and opportunities 1.4 Awareness and understanding of material themes 1.5 Articulation of business rationale for sustainability and integrated thinking as a driver of long-term value creation
Principle 2 (P2): Integrated leadership commitment and capability Leadership provides the mandate for integrated thinking and makes a deliberate and coordinated effort to connect and integrate matters material to organisational sustainability	2.1 Leadership ambition and commitment to an integrated approach to sustainability 2.2 Diversity of leadership experience 2.3 Strategic positioning of sustainability 2.4 Values and ethics 2.5 Conscious and relevant adoption of codes and standards
Principle 3 (P3): Integrated structures Organisational structures and systems are conducive to integrated decision-making and reporting	3.1 Integrated governance 3.2 Integrated accountability for sustainability 3.3 Integrated business model 3.4 Integrated and devolved stakeholder engagement processes 3.5 Integrated systems, technologies and processes
Principle 4 (P4): Integrated organisational performance management Performance management of targets and KPIs is balanced and integrated to express the holistic and comprehensive performance of the organisation over the short, medium and long term	4.1 Non-financial metrics 4.2 Targets and contextualised performance metrics 4.3 Response to performance 4.4 Integrated assurance
Principle 5 (P5): Integrated External Communication Communication to external stakeholders offers an accurate, holistic, balanced and integrated view of the organisation's performance and ability to create value over the short, medium and long term.	5.1 Integrated marketing and communication 5.2 Integrated external reporting

Source: Maroun et al., 2023.

focus on economic, environmental and social factors is an important consideration for stakeholders and an area of improvement for those charged with governance to consider.

P3 reported the second lowest score. Many companies have yet to implement integrated structures fully with 28% of companies scoring below 70% (not tabulated). Disclosures dealing with ESG metrics are not consistently integrated with the explanation of how value is being generated over the short, medium, and long term. The disclosures are detailed but they are usually qualitative and exclude a review of actual outcomes versus planned objectives. Exactly how governing bodies and executives ensure a multi-capital approach to business management is not consistently explained in the integrated reports.

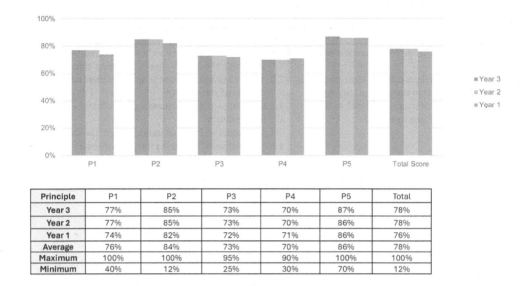

Principle	P1	P2	P3	P4	P5	Total
Year 3	77%	85%	73%	70%	87%	78%
Year 2	77%	85%	73%	70%	86%	78%
Year 1	74%	82%	72%	71%	86%	76%
Average	76%	84%	73%	70%	86%	78%
Maximum	100%	100%	95%	90%	100%	100%
Minimum	40%	12%	25%	30%	70%	12%

Figure 21.4   Average integrated thinking scores

For P1, ESG issues may be identified as strategic considerations or business risks but how the respective business models and internal controls are operated or changed could not be determined. Similarly, the sampled companies did not consistently explain how material issues are identified. Materiality is being framed primarily in monetary terms (see also Cerbone & Maroun, 2020).

P2 has an average score of 84%. According to non-tabulated results, only 8% of the entities in the study group score below 70%. This is most likely because entities' leadership structures are well developed and aligned with codes of corporate governance that emphasise board diversity, leadership commitment and ethics (IOD, 2016).

Consistent with EY's findings, the sampled companies score well when it comes to communication with external parties (P5 = 87% average). Although not a statutory requirement, most listed companies have been preparing integrated reports from 2009/2010, which accounts for the high scores (Atkins & Maroun, 2015). Figure 21.5 reports the average score for the five principles with companies grouped by integrated report quality according to EY.[3]

Companies which have the lowest EY integrated report quality scores (progress to be made; quality = 1) also have the lowest integrated thinking scores (71%). When integrated report quality scores are highest (excellent (score = 4) and top ten (score = 5)), so too are the integrated thinking scores (82%, 81%).

3   DETERMINANTS AND OUTCOMES OF INTEGRATED THINKING

Figure 21.6 summarises potential determinants of integrated thinking.

Certain organisational features are identified as determinants of higher quality integrated thinking. Examples include firm size, industry type, governance structures and the levels

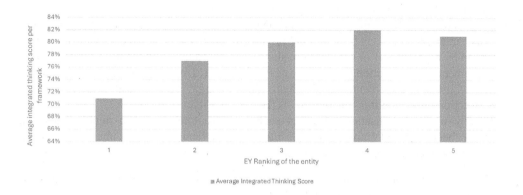

Figure 21.5   Report quality calibration

of institutional shareholdings (Tirado-Valencia et al., 2020). In general, the results suggest that stakeholder scrutiny, resource availability and complex business models promote the development of the accounting and management systems necessary for preparing high-quality integrated reports and, by inference, developing a culture of integrated thinking (Rodríguez-Gutiérrez et al., 2019). Conversely, organisations with limited resources and relatively simple business models may not appreciate the benefits of integrated reporting and an underlying philosophy of integrated thinking (Rinaldi, 2020; Velte & Stawinoga, 2017; Tirado-Valencia et al., 2020).

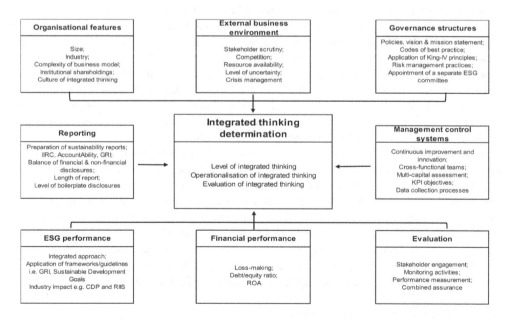

Source: Adapted from Atkins et al., 2020b; IRCSA, 2018.

Figure 21.6   Summary of integrated thinking determinants

An integrated approach to managing economic, environmental and social considerations can be a strategic advantage (De Villiers & Dimes, 2020; De Villiers et al., 2020). If this is the case, integrated thinking may be more prominent where the business environment is characterised by higher levels of competition, significant uncertainty and the need for continuous improvement and innovation (Malafronte & Pereira, 2021; Dumay & Dai, 2017). Put simply, well-established management control systems allow an organisation to collect the data necessary to action integrated thinking objectives (Bui & De Villiers, 2018).

Exactly which organisational features enable or promote integrated thinking has not, however, been resolved empirically. The integration of financial, environmental and social factors is an inherently complex and iterative process which depends on:

- incorporating economic, environmental and social factors (mindful of the sustainability development goals) into strategic decisions;
- assessing the trade-offs, opportunities and risks across the value chain and capitals;
- making the relevant changes to operating practices and management control systems to achieve business objectives; and
- communication of the organisation's value in terms of the relevant capitals (developed from IIRC, 2021; Barth et al., 2017).

Integrated thinking needs to be an integral part of the governance framework that informs the values, culture and mission statements of the organisation (King et al., 2022; IOD, 2016). The governance structure must support responsible value creation over the short, medium and long term by enabling strategy development, risk management and refinement of business models that take the different capitals and the legitimate expectations of shareholding and non-shareholding stakeholders into consideration (IIRC, 2021; IOD, 2016).

To be effective, integrated thinking must also be accepted as a valid approach for dealing with operational issues and must be applied by managers at each level of the organisation (Rinaldi, 2020; Stubbs & Higgins, 2014; IRC, 2018). This will require a comprehensive system of data collection, multi-capital performance metrics, monitoring systems, stakeholder engagement and multidisciplinary teams to support decision-making (Rinaldi, 2020; Stubbs & Higgins, 2014; IRC, 2018). Business models will need to be refined to ensure that the overall objective of sustainable development is embedded into an organisation's policies and practices (CIMA, 2017; Alrazi et al., 2015; Büchling & Maroun, 2021).

To ensure that integrated thinking has substance, organisations would rely on a battery of performance indicators which cover environmental, social and governance metrics. These may be informed by industry standards, codes of best practice, reporting frameworks and past experiences (Oliver et al., 2016). ESG performance measures would evaluate environmental and social outcomes directly but also consider associated financial implications. An organisation's ability to generate financial returns and lower investment risk are closely related to how social and environmental matters affecting the business model are managed and assessed (Alrazi et al., 2015; Baboukardos et al., 2021; Maroun & Atkins, 2018). Post-implementation review is essential to identify emerging risks, update assessments and drive continuous improvement.

3.1   Examining Select Determinants

The relationship between integrated thinking levels and select determinants (summarised in Table 21.2) are evaluated using non-parametric tests.

Table 21.2   *Summary of variables used in the statistical analysis*

Grouping variable	Assessment[a]	Statistical approach[b]
Size	Entities are allocated to a size quartile based on the natural log of total assets	H statistic & J-T statistic
Financial performance	Entities are allocated to a quartile based on return on assets (ROA)	H statistic & J-T statistic
Leverage	Entities are allocated to quartiles based on the debt/equity ratios	H statistic & J-T statistic
Industry	Entities are allocated scores based on environmental and social impact from highest to lowest impact: mining/industrial (3); financial (2); other industries (1)	H statistic & J-T statistic
CDP	Entities are allocated to quartiles based on their ESG performance scores per the Carbon Disclosure Project. These are ordinal scores developed independently by the CDP. The scores are allocated to each company over the study period with a one-year lag	H statistic & J-T statistic
RISS/SRI	The JSE Socially Responsible Development Index (SRI) index includes companies based on their ESG performance. Companies are scored based on whether or not they are included as part of the index (Yes = 1 or No = 0)	U statistic
Separate ESG committee	It was determined whether each entity had a separate ESG committee (Yes = 1 or No = 0)	U statistic
Separate sustainability report or King IV report prepared	It was determined whether each entity had a separate sustainability report or King IV report (Yes = 1 or No = 0)	U statistic
Other reports	It was determined whether each entity had other reports issued dealing with ESG issues (Yes = 1 or No = 0)	U statistic
Pages	The number of pages in the integrated report was recorded. Companies were assigned to quartiles based on the length of their integrated reports	H statistic & J-T statistic

Notes: [a] 1 is allocated to the lowest quartile (i.e. smaller size/weaker financial performance/higher leveraging/ weaker ESG scores) and 4 to the highest quartile (higher performing metrics).
[b] Integrated thinking scores are evaluated among companies grouped by the grouping variables using either a Kruskal–Wallis H-test (H statistic) or a Mann–Whitney U test (U statistic). The sign and statistical significance of the variable is evaluated using the standardised Jonckheere–Terpstra (J-T statistic) test.

The results are presented in Table 21.3.

Table 21.3   Statistical association of integrated thinking principles and variables

Principle	P1		P2		P3		P4		P5		Total	
Grouping variable	H- or U-statistic	Std J-T statistic	H- or U-statistic	Std J-T statistic	H- or U-statistic	Std J-T statistic	H- or U-statistic	Std J-T statistic	H- or U-statistic	Std J-T statistic	H- or U-statistic	Std J-T statistic
Size	9.113*	1.756	2.116	1.210	8.632*	0.483	5.578	1.552	12.348*	-0.559	7.355	1.275
Financial performance	7.491	0.853	0.378	-0.228	5.650	0.260	4.962	-1.008	4.504	-1.309	5.521	-0.090
Leverage	9.182*	n/a	16.971**	n/a	5.255	n/a	4.114	n/a	11.541**	n/a	10.403*	n/a
Industry	18.068**	3.744**	12.758**	3.652**	15.200**	2.039*	9.480**	3.045**	8.003*	2.743**	16.477**	3.607**
CDP	39.545**	3.259**	43.887**	3.876**	13.909	2.015*	20.366**	2.026*	18.198**	0.788	40.448**	3.333**
Pages	2.706	0.009	1.858	-1.193	3.987	1.161	1.053	0.444	10.961*	-2.851*	1.934	-0.511
SRI Index	6.264	n/a	4.15*	n/a	4.47*	n/a	3.502	n/a	6.343*	n/a	8.272*	n/a
Separate ESG committee	2.886	n/a	8.016**	n/a	7.326**	n/a	2.486	n/a	3.616	n/a	4.059*	n/a
Separate SR prepared	10.566**	n/a	10.787**	n/a	16.494**	n/a	10.234**	n/a	116.77**	n/a	22.191**	n/a
Other reports	9.987**	n/a	11.345**	n/a	2.561	n/a	10.652**	n/a	11.504**	n/a	17.608**	n/a
King IV report	8.987**	n/a	3.658	n/a	14.483**	n/a	11.697**	n/a	94.733**	n/a	18.645**	n/a

Notes: **Significant at the 1% level (2-tailed). *Significant at the 5% level (2-tailed).

Integrated thinking is not the domain of only the largest (H total = 7.355, p > 5%) and most profitable (H total = 5.521, p > 5%) firms. Smaller organisations and those with a lower return on assets are also able to leverage their human capital, structures and communication channels to manage value creation. In contrast, higher levels of financial risk (H total = 10.403, p < 5%) and a greater social or environmental impact of the industry (H total = 16.477, p < 1%; J-T = 3.607, p < 1%) are associated with higher integrated thinking scores. This suggests that integrated thinking forms an integral part of an overall approach to risk mitigation in financial and extra-financial terms, albeit that causal relationships will need to be established by future researchers.

In support of the fact that the integrated thinking scores are not just capturing impression management, consider the relationship between these and the CDP scores or inclusion on an SRI Index. Both the latter proxy for the sophistication of internal management processes, systems and reporting dealing with climate change and related issues. They provide, at least, some insight into the infrastructure necessary for ensuring that organisations are managing extra-financial issues proactively and are not just engaged in high-level reporting. The same logic applies to integrated thinking. Those entities which have a more sophisticated accounting and management structure (gauged by the CDP scores or inclusion on the SRI Index) also have higher integrated thinking scores (H total = 40.448, p < 1%; U total = 8.272, p < 5%; J-T total = 3.333, p < 1%). The possibility of impression management cannot be precluded but it is unlikely that an organisation would invest extensively in systems to support extra-financial performance and not rely on these to ensure substantive reporting to stakeholders.

Better integrated thinking is not the result of companies including more information in their communication to stakeholders (H total = 1.934, p > 5%; J-T total = −0.511, p > 5%) but is influenced by compliance with South Africa's codes of corporate governance (U total = 18.645, p < 1%) and the use of the GRI (U total = 22.191, p < 1%) or other frameworks (U total = 17.608, p < 1%) to inform management and reporting of extra-financial issues. Having a separate ESG committee also influences positively the levels of integrated thinking. Natural, social and other capitals can be more effectively addressed as part of an integrated business model when suitable ESG experts form part of the governing body (U total = 4.059, p < 5%).

4   CONCLUSION

This chapter uses an integrated thinking schematic to evaluate the levels of integrated thinking among JSE-listed entities. The schematic provides an easy-to-apply tool which can be used by organisations and their stakeholders to define and evaluate integrated thinking. It does not provide a scientific "measure" of the level of integrated thinking but can be used to compare organisations, identify limitations and inform improvements to business processes.

Evaluating an organisation's commitment to and application of integrated thinking is not simple. The internal mechanisms which simultaneously support and are changed by the application of integrated thinking cannot be observed directly by external stakeholders. Organisations' integrated and sustainability reports can, however, provide insights. In particular, the execution of integrated thinking enhances the management of and reporting on value creation as well as stakeholder awareness and accountability. Findings show that entities in South Africa are scoring well on integrated thinking principles, primarily because of the strong governance and reporting structures in place. Integrating performance management with sustainability-related targets has, however, been identified as a weakness.

An integrated report may not illustrate the full extent to which integrated thinking takes place in an organisation (IRC, 2018). There may be a disconnect between what is disclosed and how an underlying integrated thinking philosophy is applied (Oliver et al., 2016). As a result, weaknesses in the application of integrated thinking do not mean that integrated thinking is absent. The organisations under review may follow a comprehensive approach for developing strategies, mitigating risks and maximising value for stakeholders but are not including the details in their integrated reports. It must also be remembered that it will take time to develop appropriate integrated thinking frameworks and report these effectively to stakeholders. In addition, the possibility that integrated reports are used to manage impressions or to acquiesce to the expectation of certain stakeholders cannot be precluded (Haji & Anifowose, 2016).

This research offers a practical means for stakeholders to evaluate integrated thinking application by an organisation when they have only publicly available information. Practitioners and those charged with governance can also use the principles and determinants of integrated thinking to identify areas of weakness that need to be addressed by management.

Pragmatically, the operationalisation of integrated thinking, particularly in developing economies where environmental and social implications can have a greater impact, is relevant. Integrated thinking will assist organisations with holistic decision-making, the development of sustainable policies and strategies by incorporating environmental, social and economic factors, promoting social inclusion and interdisciplinary collaboration and improving stakeholder engagement. By adopting a comprehensive approach to complex problems, organisations can better address their unique challenges and develop towards a more sustainable future.

Future research needs to explore the role played by corporate governance mechanisms in advancing the extent and quality of sustainability-related reporting and how this can support integrated thinking. For example, how can boards of directors drive integrated thinking and the achievement of the Sustainable Development Goals? What key performance indicators are best suited to advancing integrated thinking and what types of management control and accounting systems are required to support integrated thinking? These practices can be compared across jurisdictions and industries to provide broader insights into the levels and development of integrated thinking and the approach to achieving sustainability. The evidence emerging from developed and developing economies can be contrasted to evaluate whether any practices can be adopted universally.

Finally, there are important questions for management and governing bodies to consider, such as whether the organisation's strategy, risk assessment and business model have been aligned and updated to include the relevant economic, environmental and social issues (IFAC, 2020). A related concern is whether or not the necessary systems, policies, controls, KPI measures and engagement channels are in place and incorporated into the value creation process (ibid.).

NOTES

1.   Separate sustainability reports, ESG checklists, interim results, investor presentations and companies' webpages are not included in the analysis. This is because an integrated report

should encapsulate underlying ESG, financial and other metrics and summarise these reports succinctly (Zhou et al., 2017).

2. Three reports were excluded as the entities formed part of another group of companies for which the report had already been assessed and included for analysis.

3. The scale used by EY ranges from lowest to highest quality: "Progress to be made" (1), "Average" (2), "Good" (3), "Excellent" (4), "The Top 10" (5).

REFERENCES

Adams, C. A., Druckman, P. B. & Picot, R. C. 2020. *Sustainable Development Goals Disclosure (SDGD) Recommendations*. ACCA, Chartered Accountants Australia and New Zealand, ICAS, IFAC, IIRC, WBA.

Alrazi, B., De Villiers, C. & van Staden, C. J. 2015. A comprehensive literature review on, and the construction of a framework for, environmental legitimacy, accountability and proactivity. *Journal of Cleaner Production*, 102, 44–57. DOI: http://dx.doi.org/10.1016/j.jclepro.2015.05.022.

Atkins, J. & Macpherson, M. 2019. Developing a Species Protection Action Plan – An Integrated Approach for Taxonomies, Reporting and Engagement for the Financial Services Sector. Concept Paper circulated and presented at Investec Bank's Natural Capital, Species Extinction & Sustainable Financial Markets Event, 30 May.

Atkins, J. & Maroun, W. 2015. Integrated reporting in South Africa in 2012: perspectives from South African institutional investors. *Meditari Accountancy Research*, 23(2), 197–221. DOI: http://www.emeraldinsight.com/doi/abs/10.1108/MEDAR-07-2014-0047.

Atkins, J., Buchling, M., Cerbone, D., Lange, Y., Maroun, W., Kok, M., Ram, A., Sebastian, A., Wadee, Z. & van Zijl, W. 2020a. Accounting, Governance and Integrated Thinking in the Context of COVID-19. University of the Witwatersrand's School of Accountancy. Available at: https://www.wits.ac.za/media/wits-university/faculties-and-schools/commerce-law-and-management/accountancy/documents/Accounting%20governance%20and%20integrated%20thinking%20in%20the%20context%20of%20COVID-19%20(FInal).pdf (Accessed 21 May 2020).

Atkins, J., Buchling, M., Cerbone, D., Lange, Y., Maroun, W., Kok, M. & van Zijl, W. 2020b. Integrated report quality. A review of South African-specific research. Centre for Critical Accounting and Auditing Research, University of the Witwatersrand. Available at: https://www.wits.ac.za/media/wits-university/faculties-and-schools/commerce-law-and-management/accountancy/documents/Factors%20associated%20with%20better%20quality%20integrated%20reporting%20(final).pdf (Accessed 21 May 2020).

Baboukardos, D., Mangena, M. & Ishola, A. 2021. Integrated thinking and sustainability reporting assurance: international evidence. *Business Strategy and the Environment*, 30, 1580–1597. DOI: https://onlinelibrary.wiley.com/doi/epdf/10.1002/bse.2695.

Barth, M. E., Cahan, S. F., Chen, L. & Venter, E. R. 2017. The economic consequences associated with integrated report quality: capital market and real effects. *Accounting, Organizations and Society*, 62, 43–64.

Beck, C., Dumay, J. & Frost, G. 2015. In pursuit of a "single source of truth": from threatened legitimacy to integrated reporting. *Journal of Business Ethics*, 141(1), 191–205.

Bridges, C. & Yeoman, M. 2020. Integrated thinking or integrated reporting, which comes first? In C. De Villiers, P.-C. K. Hsiao & W. Maroun (eds), *The Routledge Handbook of Integrated Reporting*. Abingdon: Routledge, pp. 241–250.

Büchling, M. & Maroun, W. 2021. Accounting for biodiversity and extinction: the case of South African national parks. *Social and Environmental Accountability Journal*, 41, 66–97. DOI: https://doi.org/10.1080/0969160X.2021.1889385.

Bui, B. & De Villiers, C. J. 2018. Management control systems to support sustainability and integrated reporting. In C. J. De Villiers (ed.) *Sustainability Accounting and Integrated Reporting*. Abingdon: Taylor & Francis, pp. 121–148.

Busco, C., Granà, F. & Achilli, G. 2021. Understanding integrated thinking: evidence from the field, the development of a framework and avenues for future research. *Meditari Accountancy Research*, 29(4), 673–690. DOI: https://doi.org/10.1108/MEDAR-04-2021-1263.

Cerbone, D. & Maroun, W. 2020. Materiality in an integrated reporting setting: insights using an institutional logics framework. *The British Accounting Review*, 52(3), 2–18. DOI: https://doi.org/10.1016/j.bar.2019.100876.

CIMA 2017. Aligning purpose and the business model to market opportunities and sustainable performance: how the finance organization helps understand, enhance, and report strategies for long-term value creation. *Integrated Thinking*, 13(3), 1–28. Available at: https://www.aicpa-cima.com/resources/download/integrated-thinking (Accessed 3 June 2024).

De Villiers, C. & Dimes, R. 2020. How management control systems enable and constrain integrated thinking. *Meditari Accountancy Research*, 29(4), 851–872. DOI: https://doi.org/10.1108/MEDAR-05-2020-0880.

De Villiers, C., Rinaldi, L. & Unerman, J. 2014. Integrated reporting: insights, gaps and an agenda for future research. *Accounting, Auditing & Accountability Journal*, 27(7), 1042–1067. DOI: https://doi.org/10.1108/AAAJ-06-2014-1736.

De Villiers, C., Hsiao, P.-C. K. & Maroun, W. 2020. *The Routledge Handbook of Integrated Reporting*. Abingdon: Routledge.

Dumay, J. & Dai, T. 2017. Integrated thinking as a cultural control? *Meditari Accountancy Research*, 25(4), 574–604.

Eccles, R. G., Krzus, M. P. & Solano, C. A. 2019. A comparative analysis of integrated reporting in ten countries. Available at: http://dx.doi.org/10.2139/ssrn.3345590 (Accessed 1 April 2020).

Ecim, D. & Maroun, W. 2023. A review of integrated thinking research in developed and developing economies. *Journal of Accounting in Emerging Economies*, 13(3), 589–612. DOI: http://dx.doi.org/10.1108/JAEE-02-2022-0046.

EY 2022. EY Excellence in Integrated Reporting 2022. Press release. Available at: https://www.ey.com/en_za/news/2022/09/excellence-in-integrated-reporting-awards-2022.

Gray, R. 1992. Accounting and environmentalism: an exploration of the challenge of gently accounting for accountability, transparency and sustainability. *Accounting, Organisations and Society*, 17(5), 399–425.

Haji, A. A. & Anifowose, M. 2016. The trend of integrated reporting practice in South Africa: ceremonial or substantive? *Sustainability Accounting, Management and Policy Journal*, 7(2), 190–224. DOI: https://doi.org/10.1108/SAMPJ-11-2015-0106.

Helm, D. 2020. The environmental impacts of coronavirus. *Environmental & Resource Economics*, 76, 21–38.

IFAC 2020. *Creating Value with Integrated Thinking: The Role of Professional Accountants*. New York: IFAC. Available at: https://www.ifac.org/knowledge-gateway/contributing-global-economy/publications/creating-value-integrated-thinking (Accessed 21 February 2020).

IIRC 2021. The International Integrated Reporting Framework. Available at: https://integratedreporting.org/wp-content/uploads/2021/01/InternationalIntegratedReportingFramework.pdf.

IOD 2016. *King IV Report on Corporate Governance in South Africa*. Johannesburg: Lexis Nexus South Africa.

IRC 2018. Achieving Balance in the Integrated Report: An Information Paper. Available at: https://integratedreporting.org/resource/irc-achieving-balance-in-the-integrated-report-an-information-paper/ (Accessed 28 April 2020).

IRCSA 2018. Achieving Balance in the Integrated Report: An Information Paper. Available at: http://integratedreportingsa.org/achieving-balance-in-the-integrated-report/ (Accessed 28 April 2020).

King, M., Atkins, J. & Maroun, W. 2022. Establishing a framework for extinction accounting, accountability and finance. In J. Atkins & M. Macpherson (eds), *Extinction Governance, Finance and Accounting*. Abingdon: Routledge, pp. 56–78.

Malafronte, I. & Pereira, J. 2021. Integrated thinking: measuring the unobservable. *Meditari Accountancy Research*, 29(4), 805–822. DOI: https://doi.org/10.1108/MEDAR-12-2019-0640.

Malola, A. & Maroun, W. 2019. The measurement and potential drivers of integrated report quality: evidence from a pioneer in integrated reporting. *South African Journal of Accounting Research*, 33(2), 114–144. DOI: https://doi.org/10.1080/10291954.2019.1647937.

Maroun, W. 2019. Does external assurance contribute to higher quality integrated reports? *Journal of Accounting and Public Policy*, 38(4), 106670. DOI: https://doi.org/10.1016/j.jaccpubpol.2019.06.002.

Maroun, W. & Atkins, J. 2018. The emancipatory potential of extinction accounting: exploring current practice in integrated reports. *Accounting Forum*, 42(1), 102–118. DOI: https://doi.org/10.1016/j.accfor.2017.12.001.

Maroun, W. & Cerbone, D. 2020. *Corporate Governance in South Africa*. Berlin: Walter de Gruyter GmbH & Co KG.

Maroun, W., Ecim, D. & Cerbone, D. 2023. Refining integrated thinking. *Sustainability Accounting, Management and Policy Journal*, 14(7), 1–25. DOI: http://dx.doi.org/10.1108/SAMPJ-07-2021-0268.

McNally, M.-A. & Maroun, W. 2018. It is not always bad news: illustrating the potential of integrated reporting using a case study in the eco-tourism industry. *Accounting, Auditing & Accountability Journal*, 31(5), 1319–1348. DOI: https://doi.org/10.1108/AAAJ-05-2016-2577.

McNally, M.-A., Cerbone, D. & Maroun, W. 2017. Exploring the challenges of preparing an integrated report. *Meditari Accountancy Research*, 25(4), 481–504. DOI: https://doi.org/10.1108/MEDAR-10-2016-0085.

Michelon, G., Pilonato, S. & Ricceri, F. 2015. CSR reporting practices and the quality of disclosure: an empirical analysis. *Critical Perspectives on Accounting*, 33, 59–78. DOI: https://doi.org/10.1016/j.cpa.2014.10.003.

Oliver, J., Vesty, G. & Brooks, A. 2016. Conceptualising integrated thinking in practice. *Managerial Auditing Journal*, 31, 228–248.

PwC 2015. Integrated reporting. Where to next? Available at: http://www.pwc.co.za/en/assets/pdf/integrated-reporting-survey-2015.pdf (Accessed 16 February 2016).

Rinaldi, L. 2020. Integrated thinking for stakeholder engagement. A processing model for judgments and choice in situations of cognitive complexity. In C. De Villiers, P.-C. K. Hsiao & W. Maroun (eds), *The Routledge Handbook of Integrated Reporting*. Abingdon: Routledge, pp. 280–292.

Rodríguez-Gutiérrez, P., Correa, C. & Larrinaga, C. 2019. Is integrated reporting transformative? An exploratory study of non-financial reporting archetypes. *Sustainability Accounting, Management and Policy Journal*, 10(3), 617–644. DOI: https://doi.org/10.1108/SAMPJ-12-2017-0156.

Stubbs, W. & Higgins, C. 2014. Integrated reporting and internal mechanisms of change. *Accounting, Auditing & Accountability Journal*, 27(7), 1068–1089.

Tirado-Valencia, P., Cordobés-Madueño, M., Ruiz-Lozano, M. & De Vicente-Lama, M. 2020. Integrated thinking in the integrated reports of public sector companies. Evidence and contextual factors. *Sustainability Accounting, Management and Policy Journal*, 12(2), 330–352. DOI: https://doi.org/10.1108/SAMPJ-11-2019-0387.

Tweedie, D. & Martinov-Bennie, N. 2015. Entitlements and time: integrated reporting's double-edged agenda. *Social and Environmental Accountability Journal*, 35(1), 49–61.

Velte, P. & Stawinoga, M. 2017. Integrated reporting: the current state of empirical research, limitations and future research implications. *Journal of Management Control*, 28(3), 275–320.

Wiseman, J. 1982. An evaluation of environmental disclosures made in corporate annual reports. *Accounting, Organizations and Society*, 7(1), 53–63.

Zhou, S., Simnett, R. & Green, W. 2017. Does integrated reporting matter to the capital market? *Abacus*, 53(1), 94–132.

22. Sustainability reporting in Central and Eastern European countries

Cătălin-Nicolae Albu, Nadia Albu, Mădălina Dumitru, Maria-Silvia Fota and Raluca Gina Guşe

1   INTRODUCTION

The objective of this chapter is to offer an overview of sustainability reporting practices in countries based in Central and Eastern Europe[1] (CEE) by summarizing prior literature findings, and to indicate avenues for future research. For the purpose of this chapter, we look at sustainability reporting[2] practices in CEE, a group of countries deserving to be subject to academic inquiry for several reasons. First, CEE is a region with "collective geographical significance" (Krivogorski et al., 2023, p. 1), and research on this setting is emerging, but still scarce in leading accounting journals. This region entered Soviet influence after the Second World War, being imprinted with socialist values at all economic, political, and social levels. The CEE countries started to transition toward a market-based economic model in the late 1980s to early 1990s but the transition seems an unfinished process, given that macroeconomic indicators show that these countries still lag behind developed countries (Albu et al., 2017).

Second, as a result of these historical developments, the institutional context of CEE countries provides both strong catalysts and inhibitors for sustainability reporting. Sustained (but still incomplete) reforms intended to implement Western standards and models and a strong desire to belong to the West support sustainability reporting, while a secrecy culture and the limited incentives for and use of disclosures counterbalance progress in this respect. Therefore, this is a very fruitful setting to investigate how sustainability reporting requirements and practices unfold over time, and the outcomes of opposing factors and conditions on the development of sustainability reporting.

Our analysis distinguishes three sustainability reporting phases (Albu et al., 2021; Horváth et al., 2017; Witek-Crabb, 2019). We were able to identify the time boundaries of these periods, given the regulatory developments and overall sustainability reporting practices in the country/region.[3] The first period after the fall of communism (1990s, early 2000s) is characterized by the lack of interest and even opposition to sustainability issues, mainly because of the communist past and the emergence of wild capitalism.

The second period is one of familiarization, when corporate social responsibility (CSR) practices, including their reporting, are selectively introduced (either by multinational corporations – MNCs, or through regulations) but locally filtered. As such, CSR is mainly perceived as charity actions, and sustainability reporting is perceived as a public relations exercise when it is voluntary and as compliance when it is mandatory. This period debuts in the 2000s when the first social and environmental reports are prepared, voluntarily, by the local subsidiaries of MNCs, and when some CEE countries develop and implement sustainability strategies and various regulations regarding CSR and sustainability reporting (UNDP, 2007). The legal environment in this period is "vigilant and challenged" (UNDP, 2007), with some pressure for CSR and sustainability reporting but also with major obstacles (lack of capacity or experience). Therefore, few large companies engage in sustainability reporting, or are internalizing the management of sustainability issues. The last event in this period is the adoption of and familiarization with the European Directive 2014/95/EU (NFRD) (European Union, 2014). The NFRD required public-interest companies with more than 500 employees to include a non-financial statement in the management report or to prepare a stand-alone report including environmental, social and employee matters, respect for human rights, anti-corruption, and bribery matters. The directive was further transposed in the legislation of the member states, and it became effective in 2017.

The third period, located after the implementation of the NFRD, implies awareness, acceptance, and assimilation of sustainability principles, resulting in organizational changes (in strategy, processes, etc.). Thus, while sustainability reporting is mainly related to and investigated through related disclosures, its internal operationalization (i.e., management control) (e.g., Traxler et al., 2020) is equally and perhaps more important. Therefore, we take a wider view, going beyond the focus on disclosure by looking at the organizational actions for assembling and communicating sustainability reporting.

The next section introduces the review approach. The most salient features for sustainability reporting of the CEE institutional environment are presented next. Then, we summarize the sustainability reporting literature regarding the extent of disclosures, the determinants, and the consequences of such reporting. Afterwards, we move to the organizational realm to discuss the implementation and communication of sustainability information. We conclude the chapter by providing a wide agenda for future research on sustainability reporting in the CEE setting.

2   REVIEW APPROACH

We followed a review approach that allowed us not only to account for the current state of knowledge, but also to provide a synthesis for researchers to identify new research topics and approaches. Given this ambition and the variability of CEE research in terms of quality and credibility, we did not aim at taking a full inventory of prior studies. Instead, we opted to follow a less systematic approach, "allowing for critical scrutiny and insight generation rather than aiming for vacuum cleaning" (Alvesson and Sandberg, 2020, p. 1298). This approach is generally known as traditional and/or narrative review (Hiebl, 2023; Massaro et al., 2016; Paré et al., 2015). Therefore, while aiming to identify what was written in relation to sustainability reporting in CEE countries, we do not "attempt to seek generalization or cumulative knowledge from what is reviewed" (Paré et al., 2015).

We conduct our analysis by taking a longitudinal stance and a wide organizational approach. We searched for and selected relevant literature in line with this approach, starting from a "more limited and careful set of readings" (Alvesson and Sandberg, 2020, p. 1298) selected based on the topic studied (i.e., sustainability reporting), context of research (i.e., CEE) and relevance (e.g., reliable publishers, acknowledged authors, reputable journals). The data was synthesized in the form of a narrative summary. While not having a predefined review protocol and rigid rules, our review follows the existent recommendations for conducting literature reviews (Alvesson and Sandberg, 2020; Hiebl, 2023; Massaro et al., 2016; Paré et al., 2015).

3   INSTITUTIONAL CONTEXT

Sustainability reporting does not occur in a vacuum, and the understanding and mobilization of the institutional context, particularly outside the developed West (Tilt, 2016) is necessary to move from describing practices to an in-depth understanding of the phenomenon. CEE countries represent a geographical group sharing many similarities and differences in their institutional environment (Albu et al., 2017). For instance, they are generally smaller in size than many other developed or developing countries and have smaller and less influential capital markets (Albu et al., 2017). The top CEE companies are also of smaller dimensions compared to their Western European counterparts, many of them still being unlisted and with a significant state ownership (Horváth et al., 2017). The countries' communist past offers a common ideological background for (and a deterrent to) the transition to democracy (e.g., Albu et al., 2021; Dragomir et al., 2022; Krasodomska et al., 2020; Krivogorsky et al., 2023; UNDP, 2007). Several rounds of reforms took place in all areas of political, economic, and social life, including management and accounting (MacLullich and Gurău, 2004). These countries generally represent a good destination for foreign investment and for expansion of MNCs, and engagement in these forms of globalization is considered to be closely linked to practices aligned to Western norms. Like other emerging economies (Belal and Momin, 2009), the CSR/ sustainability reporting agenda in CEE countries has been driven by external pressures, including regulatory requirements (i.e., NFRD), MNCs and their practices, and international actors (e.g., consultancy firms, including the Big 4, foreign investors, and international agencies) (Dyczkowska et al., 2016; Guşe et al., 2016). This Western-driven framework was adopted in addition to international models and standards. Studies show that, in general, reforms "resulted in hesitations and difficulties" (Albu et al., 2017, p. 251).

These countries differ in terms of their cultural background and religious stances (Horváth et al., 2017). Moreover, they differ in economic growth (Horváth et al., 2017; UNDP, 2007), their development and liquidity of the local capital market (Krivogorsky et al., 2023), tax rates and state control (Farkas, 2011). Different reform strategies were followed across the CEE region after the fall of communism, and consequently their local development differed in the transitioning years (UNDP, 2007).

Therefore, even if the local infrastructure for accounting is currently modeled after international norms, standards, and patterns, this is achieved in a spirit owing much to the pre-communist geographical and cultural influences, communist ideology, and post-communist allegiances. As such, sustainability-related concepts and practices were interpreted through the lenses of the local culture, combining a communist heritage and "wild capitalism" following the fall of communism (Albu et al., 2021). On the one hand, several CSR concepts or practices were perceived as "a type of socialist renaissance" (Cho et al., 2021, p. 142), locally interpreted as philanthropy or charity (Aureli et al., 2020; Albu et al., 2021). On the other hand, CSR and more recently mandatory sustainability reporting implied a cost and an additional burden (Albu et al., 2021; Krasodomska et al., 2020). The desire to obtain quick profits impeded a long-term sustainability desideratum (Dagilienė and Nedzinskienė, 2018). The recent positive attitude toward sustainability reporting is determined by the regulatory and public/media support (Witek-Crabb, 2019), but, overall, this attitude is "still ambiguous" (Krasodomska et al., 2020, p. 753). Finally, studies conducted in the CEE region evidence the difficulties in increasing the (initially financial) reporting quality and transparency over time

(Albu et al., 2017; Dumitru et al., 2017) in this setting, which is paramount for sustainability reporting.

The CEE institutional context is therefore rather unfavorable to sustainability reporting, but improvements have manifested over time. These improvements are, as yet, uneven and fragmentary across countries and companies, which provides a fruitful basis for research.

4   KNOWLEDGE GAINED FROM EXISTING RESEARCH ON SUSTAINABILITY REPORTING

This section includes the extent of sustainability reporting in CEE, its determinants and consequences, operationalization of sustainability reporting at organizational level, and its channels of communication.

4.1   Extent of Sustainability Reporting

Companies in CEE started to be engaged later and to a smaller degree in sustainability reporting relative to their counterparts from more developed countries. Sustainability reporting is generally inferior in these countries, both in terms of quantity and quality of disclosures (e.g., Aluchna et al., 2023; Arraiano and Haţegan, 2019; EUKI, 2020; UNDP, 2007). However, engagement with sustainability reporting has intensified exponentially in recent years in the region (Beleneşi et al., 2021), particularly due to mandatory reporting requirements, but it still lags behind that in developed countries. For example, KPMG (2022) finds that only 72% of the top 100 companies in CEE report on sustainability, compared to 85% in Western Europe.

A small percentage of companies in a group of CEE countries provide useful disclosures (i.e., Poland, Croatia, Romania, the Czech Republic, Slovakia), while the companies based in another group of countries show "a complete lack of awareness of the expected quality and purpose of non-financial reporting" (i.e., Bulgaria, Hungary, Slovenia) (EUKI, 2020, p. 51). Some companies provide specific information, for instance on climate change, but the number of targets is low and not science-based (EUKI, 2020). Their ambitions refer mostly to environmental sustainability and technological empowerment, while employees represent the main target group for their environmental, social and governance (ESG) efforts, followed by consumers and suppliers (Kearney, 2022).

The extent of sustainability reporting also varies across the CEE region. For instance, Romania showed a higher concern for the environment, being the first European country to ratify the Kyoto Protocol (Aureli et al., 2020). Estonian companies improved on the ethics and accountability dimensions. Most disclosures provided on Hungarian companies' websites refer to environmental protection, education, and health.

The effects of the NFRD in terms of disclosure practices also vary. For example, while the NFRD had a positive effect on the social and environmental dimensions in Poland and Romania, it had no effect on governance (Aluchna et al., 2023; Beleneşi et al., 2021). This may be a result of the fact that corporate governance disclosure is subject to a previous directive (Directive 2006/46/EC).

The extent of information may depend on the characteristics of the companies. The environmentally sensitive,[4] state-owned, or listed companies (Dumitru et al., 2017) are more careful about sustainability reporting. The degree of transparency varies across CEE industries

(Jindrichovska and Purcărea, 2011; Dumitru et al., 2017; Lääts et al., 2017; Tiron-Tudor et al., 2019) and research has documented the biased use of disclosures, with a view toward framing a favorable image of corporate performance (Jindrichovska and Purcărea, 2011).

4.2   Determinants of Sustainability Reporting

Research identified multiple catalysts and inhibitors of the institutionalization of sustainability reporting[5] in various settings. We summarize the factors of influence in three categories: conceptual and regulatory aspects; macroeconomic and societal aspects; company-level particularities. Table 22.1 includes an overview of the literature. We provide some details about the role of these factors in sustainability reporting below.

The conceptual and regulatory aspects

The conceptual and regulatory context of sustainability reporting in CEE countries consists of specific instruments, including European Union (EU) directives, national legislation, and conceptual frameworks. Most contributions to literature identify these instruments as catalysts. For instance, the acceptance of the Global Reporting Initiative (GRI) guidelines improves sustainability reporting in CEE (Cho et al., 2021). The NFRD is the act that has brought the most sustainability reporting improvements to CEE. Yet, there was a "delay in [ESG] performance improvement suggest[ing] that companies require time to introduce transparency principles into organisational structures" (Aluchna et al., 2023).

The regulatory context can also act as an inhibitor, as it conditions the companies to report information using the same format, limited to minimal compliance (Aluchna et al., 2023). The vague definition of concepts (e.g., "CSR" – Cho et al., 2021; "social impact" – Peršić and Halmi, 2018; "materiality" – Fiandrino et al., 2022) can act as an inhibitor, too. There is a regulatory void for the companies that do not reach the thresholds set by the European directives (Ali et al., 2017; Guşe et al., 2016), such as the small and medium-sized enterprises (SMEs). This may hinder proper sustainability reporting, as companies are not held responsible for the consequences of their actions without regulation or penalties for their lack of compliance (Horváth et al., 2017).

Macroeconomic and societal aspects

The weak development of sustainability reporting in CEE countries relative to Western countries is influenced by the region's historical development (Steurer et al., 2012). A catalyst is the international pressure (especially from the EU), which improved sustainability reporting. The literature identifies MNCs, international buyers, foreign investors, and the media as the most influential factors for sustainability reporting development (Ali et al., 2017; Cho et al., 2021). Yet, the democratic institutions (e.g., the media) are weakly developed in the CEE countries (Cho et al., 2021).

Governmental initiatives and public policies contributed to the development of sustainability reporting as well. For instance, the Ministry of Economy in Poland offers financial support to SMEs for their CSR initiatives (Dyczkowska et al., 2016). Awards granted by the authorities may represent a catalyst (i.e., Sustainable Brand Index). However, in many cases, the government attitude toward sustainability in general and sustainability reporting in particular was uneven over time, inconsistent, and offered limited support for its translation in practice (Cho et al., 2021; Krasodomska et al., 2020).

Table 22.1   *Sustainability reporting catalysts and inhibitors*

Aspect	Catalysts	Inhibitors
Conceptual and regulatory aspects		
Conceptual understanding	Conceptual frameworks acceptance (Barbu and Ienciu, 2019; Cho et al., 2021; Dumitru et al., 2017)	Vague definitions (Cho et al., 2021; Peršić and Halmi, 2018) Difficulties in understanding the guidelines (e.g., GRI – Barbu and Ienciu, 2019; EU developments – Camilleri, 2015)
Legal system	Code law, implying a stakeholder-oriented model (e.g., Poland – Cho et al., 2021)	
Legislation	EU directives (Aluchna et al., 2023; Arraiano and Haţegan, 2019; Cho et al., 2021; Guşe et al., 2016) Local laws (Albu et al., 2021; Barbu and Ienciu, 2019; Dumitru et al., 2017; Guşe et al., 2016; Peršić and Halmi, 2018)	Lack of penalties for non-compliance (Guşe et al., 2016) or consequences of companies' actions (Horváth et al., 2017) Lack of regulation for a significant part of the companies (Ali et al., 2017; Guşe et al., 2016)
Macroeconomic and societal aspects		
Macroeconomic development	Internationalization (Cho et al., 2021) Globalization level (Horváth et al., 2017) Government initiatives and public policies (Arraiano and Haţegan, 2019; Dyczkowska et al., 2016)	Economic-, government- and society-related factors of each country, generating differences in national business systems (Aureli et al., 2020)
Major/influential/ powerful stakeholders	International stakeholders: buyers, media, regulatory bodies (e.g., the World Bank) (Ali et al., 2017; Aureli et al., 2020) Investors (Ali et al., 2017; Cho et al., 2021) MNCs (Cho et al., 2021; Guşe et al., 2016) Stock exchange (Dyczkowska et al., 2016)	Institutions and systems (e.g., media) with weaker development in CEE than in Western countries (Kemp, 2001, cited by Cho et al., 2021)
National culture and civil society	Civil society (Apostol, 2015; Horváth et al., 2017) Trade unions – for social reporting (Arraiano and Haţegan, 2019) Academic environment (Guşe et al., 2016) Training (Krasodomska et al., 2020)	National culture dimensions measured by Hofstede (2020) (e.g., Poland – Cho et al., 2021) Weak civil society pressure toward CSR (Cho et al., 2021; Line and Braun, 2007) Less demanding stakeholders (Ali et al., 2017; Cho et al., 2021) and investors (Cho et al., 2021) Lack of appropriate training (Barbu and Ienciu, 2019)
Company-level particularities		
Company size and group structure	Companies' turnover, assets, number of employees (Ali et al., 2017; Dagilienė and Nedzinskienė, 2018; Radu et al., 2023)	Distant and detached subsidiary managers (Cho et al., 2021) Lack of knowledge and experience in SMEs (Cho et al., 2021)

Aspect	Catalysts	Inhibitors
Corporate governance	Managers' age, experience, and level of education (Arraiano and Haţegan, 2019), behavior (Cho et al., 2021), main values they share with the companies (Arraiano and Haţegan, 2019) Independent directors (Barbu and Ienciu, 2019; Radu et al., 2023); number of board members (Dagilienė and Nedzinskienė, 2018; Radu et al., 2023); auditor (Dumitru et al., 2017; Guşe et al., 2016)	Weak institutional support for CSR reporting (Cho et al., 2021) Lack of understanding of the real impact of CSR (Dagilienė and Nedzinskienė, 2018) Managers' reluctance (Barbu and Ienciu, 2019)
Ownership structure	State ownership (Dagilienė and Nedzinskienė, 2018; Dumitru et al., 2017) Foreign ownership (Baskin, 2006; Radu et al., 2023)	State's block holding (Dragomir et al., 2022)
Financial performance	Financial efficiency (Fijałkowska et al., 2017) Market capitalization (Barbu and Ienciu, 2019 – Romania)	Poor corporate performance (Ali et al., 2017)
Reporting tools		Underdeveloped metrics and models (Peršić and Halmi, 2018) Lack of electronic systems (Barbu and Ienciu, 2019)
Market characteristics	Market status (Barbu and Ienciu, 2019) Presence in a global value chain (Ali et al., 2017) Industry sector (Dumitru et al., 2017), including environmentally sensitive domains (Arraiano and Haţegan, 2019; Dagilienė and Nedzinskienė, 2018; Dragomir et al., 2022) Monopolistic position and the state's strategic interest (Dragomir et al., 2022) Competitive advantage (Baskin, 2006)	
Financing	Stock exchange listing, multiple listing firm, listing in social investment funds (Ali et al., 2017; Cho et al., 2021; Dumitru et al., 2017; Arraiano and Haţegan, 2019)	
Cost		(Ali et al., 2017; Aluchna et al., 2023; Cho et al., 2021)

The lack of civil consciousness and the communist remnants represent inhibitors of sustainability reporting, as national culture was found to have a negative impact on sustainability reporting in CEE (Cho et al., 2021). The mere word "social" engendered a reluctance from the public, as it was a reminder of the communist period (Albu et al., 2021; Cho et al., 2021). Traditionally, social responsibility belonged to the government, while companies limited their actions to the legal requirements (Line and Braun, 2007). During the communist years, the government was the sole decision maker, adjusting resource consumption (e.g., through providing a limited offer of goods and services) and distributing rationed resources (including food), focusing on savings (e.g., by turning off the energy for a few hours in the evenings during the winter). Everybody worked on an eight-hour schedule and had a place to live. Most of the houses were similar. The lack of transparency, which still impacts the reporting process, was a characteristic of communist societies (Albu et al., 2021).

Civil society may stimulate sustainability reporting "by placing greater societal demands and expectations on businesses" (Cho et al., 2021, p. 151), through NGOs and trade unions. Yet, civil society in these countries is weak (Aureli et al., 2020; Horváth et al., 2017) (with few exceptions, see Apostol, 2015). Stakeholders are less demanding as well (Ali et al., 2017), leading to low pressure on the government and businesses (Line and Braun, 2007).

Company-level particularities

Sustainability reporting quality was associated in previous studies with company size (measured as the value of assets, turnover, number of employees) or group structure. Headcount is also used by the EU to define thresholds for sustainability reporting. Large companies, which are subject to stricter regulations, have the knowledge, experience, and funds to prepare better reports than the small ones. The cost of sustainability reporting is generally an inhibitor in CEE (Aluchna et al., 2023). Subsidiaries of MNCs, even though theoretically benefiting from the group's experience with sustainability reporting, do not copy the reporting practices of their parent companies, their sustainability reporting being driven by other logics (Cho et al., 2021).

Corporate governance characteristics such as independent directors (Barbu and Ienciu, 2019), number of board members (Dagilienė and Nedzinskienė, 2018), and auditor type (Dumitru et al., 2017; Guşe et al., 2016) influence the quality of sustainability reporting. Previous studies showed an association between manager characteristics (such as age, experience, education, behavior, main values) and sustainability reporting. The studies also investigate the role of ownership structure, such as government and foreign ownership (Baskin, 2006; Dagilienė and Nedzinskienė, 2018; Dumitru et al., 2017), institutional ownership, and managerial ownership, in relation to the quantity and quality of sustainability reporting.

Stock exchange listing, cross listing and listing in social investment funds (Ali et al., 2017; Dumitru et al., 2017) represent a catalyst for sustainability reporting in CEE. Stock market rankings and indexes (such as Vektor in Romania and Respect in Poland) are drivers of better reporting (Dyczkowska et al., 2016). The presence of a local company in international markets represents a catalyst for reporting too (Kearney, 2022).

4.3 Consequences of Sustainability Reporting

We classified the consequences of sustainability reporting as positive and negative. A positive consequence of the increase in the quantity and quality of sustainability reporting disclosures (Aluchna et al., 2023; Arraiano and Haţegan, 2019) might be higher ESG performance (Aluchna et al., 2023), but this outcome must be better documented (Hahn et al., 2020). Other positive consequences of sustainability reporting are improved financial performance (measured by market value) (Fijałkowska et al., 2017) and superior investment risk appraisal, which lead to better capital allocation (Aluchna et al., 2023). Visibility on the market and transparency generated by sustainability reporting (Barbu and Ienciu, 2019) will attract new foreign and local investors (Cho et al., 2021), generating a reduction in the financing costs and an increase in the long-term value for stakeholders (Fiandrino et al., 2022).

The internal processes of the entities are improved through sustainability reporting (Barbu and Ienciu, 2019) and the adoption of sustainability reporting guidelines. An increase in investments made considering ESG factors will improve the company's performance and stability during crisis periods (Chiaramonte et al., 2022). More responsible companies will have social benefits, such as attracting and retaining talented employees (Fiandrino et al., 2022).

There are, however, negative consequences of sustainability reporting in CEE, making the companies reticent. One of them is that its adoption generates costs: for example, the political cost for regulatory harmonization (Kinderman, 2020) or the cost of preparing such reports (Ali et al., 2017; Aluchna et al., 2023; Kinderman, 2020). The expected corporate cost might generate a negative market reaction (Grewal et al., 2015) because the investors expect an associated decrease in profits. A difficult switch from "business as usual practices" must be made at the management level (Kinderman, 2020). The benefits perceived by the companies, such as the investments attracted, may lag behind the sustainability reporting effort (Arraiano and Hațegan, 2019). A balance must be found between the mandatory and voluntary sustainability reporting in order to mitigate the stakeholders' concerns. Finally, uniform, regulation-based reporting will determine a loss of reputational reporting advantages obtained by being leaders in sustainability reporting (Kinderman, 2020).

4.4   Operationalization of Sustainability Reporting at the Organizational Level

CSR and sustainability reporting represent organizational projects, involving employees from various professional fields, unlike financial reporting, which is owned by the accounting department. This new business practice shifts professional boundaries, and new professions (e.g., sustainability managers/consultants) emerge. While previous studies at the international level acknowledge the role of accounting systems and accounting knowledge in orchestrating sustainability reporting (e.g., Traxler et al., 2020), and have begun to investigate the potential role for the accounting profession (e.g., Egan and Tweedie, 2018), little is known about these topics in the context of CEE countries.

Professional accounting associations are ambassadors of the accountants' involvement in sustainability reporting, and many provide the necessary knowledge in this respect. While international professional bodies have championed this movement for many years (e.g., Albu et al., 2011; Krasodomska et al., 2020), prior studies on CEE countries indicate that local bodies had a minimal and delayed involvement with this new professional area (e.g., Guşe et al., 2016; Krasodomska et al., 2020). In this context, there seems to be a divide between the members of the local professional bodies and those educated and certified by international associations (e.g., Krasodomska et al., 2020). The latter might be more inclined to be involved in sustainability reporting, and to have the appropriate skills.

Research investigates this either from a demand side (the role ascribed by companies), or from a supply side (the accountants' attitude toward sustainability reporting). The organizational demand for accountants to occupy a role in sustainability reporting is varied. Albu et al. (2011) investigate the demand for CSR-related competencies in the job offer advertisements in Romania between 2007 and 2009. They find a very low but increasing demand year on year. As such, in 2009, one advertisement "requires competencies in environmental taxation, two make reference to social and environmental aspects within performance measurement, and one mentions the elaboration of policies regarding the evaluation and control of environmental and social implications" (Albu et al., 2011, p. 229). These competencies refer less to sustainability reporting but testify to a potential role for accountants in the process of managing CSR-related information internally. Horváth et al. (2017) is based on a survey administered in 2015–2016 to the largest 300 companies in ten CEE members of the EU (out of 11; Bulgaria had no respondents), yielding 368 responses. Two thirds of respondents are MNCs. The study reports that only 15% of respondents in CEE have a CSR department where sustainability reporting is located, compared to 55% in Western Europe. Frequent locations for sustainability report-ing roles are public relations/communications (22%), but also finance departments (23%, compared to 3% of respondents from Western Europe). However, there are significant vari-ations between countries. For example, sustainability reporting is located within the finance department in only 9% of cases in Romania (Sucală and Sava, 2017), but in 30% of the Polish companies investigated by Kochalski et al. (2017).

From a supply side, a few studies investigate the accountants' intention to engage in this new professional role. Krasodomska et al. (2020) investigate the attitude of Polish accountants toward sustainability reporting and find a generally low level of knowledge of the concept and a reluctance to become engaged. Professionals with international certifications or working in MNCs are better equipped to take on this new role. The rest of the profession is mainly engaged in financial and particularly tax reporting. This limited commitment to sustainability reporting is also found in Romania by Sofian (2021). The study, conducted in 2018, investi-gates the perception among Romanian professionals of integrated reporting. Most respondents consider that the finance department should not have a leading role in producing reports incor-porating non-financial information.

4.5   Channels of Communication for Sustainability Reporting

Companies employ various channels for sustainability reporting. While some of them are issued on an annual basis, because of the legal requirement, the others reflect the companies' intention to address the informational needs of stakeholders and to better engage with them. However, several concerns were raised related to the reliability, comparability, and timeframe of online disclosures (Carrots and Sticks, 2020). We summarize below the extant research in CEE by following the typology proposed by Tregidga and Laine (2021). We acknowledge that social media disclosures are under-researched, but we identified some work which focuses on press releases.

Annual reports
In the early stages of sustainability reporting in CEE, annual reports were used to a higher extent than in developed countries as the main communication tool (Jindrichovska and Purcărea, 2011; Horváth et al., 2017; Lääts et al., 2017; Wagner and Petera, 2017). For example, Horváth et al. (2017) find that 26% of the CEE companies use the annual report, relative to 7% in Western Europe. However, CEE companies generally make more vague dis-closures mainly by including a paragraph with a brief description of the required aspects in the management report (Tiron-Tudor et al., 2019). The lack of images, graphs and the descriptive style of the text negatively impacted the readability and understandability of the data. As such, researchers documented a low qualitative level of non-financial disclosures (Dumitru et al., 2017; Peršić and Halmi, 2018).

Sustainability reports
Sustainability reports are stand-alone publications with an increased length and complexity. This communication tool is employed less by CEE companies (21%) relative to Western Europe (52%) (Horváth et al., 2017). However, this finding depends on the jurisdiction. For example, 60.3% of Polish companies publish a separate non-financial report, whereas in Romania only 40% do so (EUKI, 2020). The research found that this tool is mainly used by the largest companies listed on the stock exchange or MNCs' subsidiaries, given the considerable costs of preparing such an extended report (Horváth et al., 2017).

CEE entities issuing sustainability reports generally employ GRI standards to frame their reports (Horváth et al., 2017), but to a smaller extent than in developed countries (Arraiano and Haţegan, 2019; Cho et al., 2021). Moreover, sustainability reporting in CEE may be characterized as uneven in terms of quantity and types of activities (Cho et al., 2021; EUKI, 2020). In addition, this tool can be used to favorably portray corporate image (Săndulescu, 2021).

Integrated reports
Integrated reports can address the disruptions caused by an overload of information in large and complex reports (Tiron-Tudor et al., 2019), data duplication across several channels, and the lack of correspondence between financial and non-financial stand-alone reports (Matuszczyk and Rymkiewicz, 2018). Following the current trend in non-financial reporting (Tregidga and Laine, 2021), but at a slower pace than in developed countries (Horváth et al., 2017), CEE companies started to publish integrated reports (3% relative to 9%). The highest number of integrated reports was found in Slovakia. This form of communication might help CEE companies "to build a business card that is internationally recognized and universally comparable" (Sofian, 2016).

Web pages
The acknowledgement of a more diverse group of stakeholders gave rise to web page sustainability disclosures (Adams and Frost, 2006). This tool can allow for real-time communication that is inexpensive and fast, as users can easily select the information they need (Wanderley et al., 2008). Moreover, companies can choose to display videos or external links to better disseminate the information (Wanderley et al., 2008; Matuszak and Różańska, 2020). However, these advantages are less used by CEE companies relative to Western practice (Băleanu et al., 2011), as some companies do not update the information or choose to present only a general view of their sustainability approach. Moreover, the incremental value of the information is generally low, as it reflects a summarized version of the above-mentioned reports (Tregidga and Laine, 2021). Finally, some researchers suggest that websites are mainly used to highlight positive events and achievements (Băleanu et al., 2011; Dimante and Alksne, 2017).

Press releases
Non-financial performance can also be disseminated through ad hoc press releases. This way of communication complements the traditional forms of reporting by providing updated information prior to the publication of stand-alone or integrated reports. Moreover, it can be used by those companies that are not within the scope of the mandatory requirement to publish such a report, to signal their contribution to the current sustainability trend. As press releases are an important information source used by journalists for their news articles (Kiousis et al., 2007), companies may report on their sustainable actions for increased visibility. However,

Săndulescu (2021) documented the use of impression management strategies in press releases, both prior and after a negative event related to occupational safety, by analyzing the corporate narratives of a Romanian company. This represents an under-researched field in CEE, which should be further explored in forthcoming studies.

Table 22.2 gives an overview of prior findings by reporting phase.

Table 22.2   *Overview of research on CEE by stage of development of sustainability reporting*

Studies investigating, or speaking to the investigation of:	Stage 1 – lack of interest in sustainability reporting	Stage 2 – familiarization with sustainability reporting	Stage 3 – engagement with/ localization of sustainability reporting
the context	Albu et al., 2021; Arraiano and Hațegan, 2019; Aureli et al., 2020; Horváth et al., 2017; Line and Braun, 2007; UNDP, 2007	Albu et al., 2021; Arraiano and Hațegan, 2019; Horváth et al., 2017	Albu et al., 2021; Aluchna et al., 2023
the extent and forms of sustainability reporting	Albu et al., 2021; UNDP, 2007	Albu et al., 2021; Dumitru et al., 2017; Horváth et al., 2017	Albu et al., 2021; Cho et al., 2021; Dragomir et al., 2022
the determinants of sustainability reporting	Ali et al., 2017; Dagiliene and Nedzinskiene, 2018; Dyczkowska et al., 2016; Guşe et al., 2016; UNDP, 2007	Ali et al., 2017; Dyczkowska et al., 2016; Dumitru et al., 2017; Guşe et al., 2016	Cho et al., 2021; Dragomir et al., 2022; Radu et al., 2023
the consequences of sustainability reporting		Barbu and Ienciu, 2019; Camilleri, 2015; Cho et al., 2021	Aluchna et al., 2023; Fiandrino et al., 2022
the operationalization of sustainability reporting	Albu et al., 2011	Horváth et al., 2017; Krasodomska et al., 2020; Peršić and Halmi, 2016, 2018; Sofian, 2021	EUKI, 2020
the channels for sustainability reporting	Jindrichovska and Purcărea, 2011	Horváth et al., 2017; Tiron-Tudor et al., 2019	EUKI, 2020; Săndulescu, 2021

5   CONCLUSION AND FUTURE RESEARCH AVENUES

Literature on sustainability reporting is emerging but it is still limited in the CEE context and offers a fragmented knowledge of practices (Dagilienė and Nedzinskienė, 2018; Dinh et al., 2023; Horváth et al., 2017). Our overview offers a condensed understanding of prior findings from CEE and opens spaces for additional research.

First, our review points out that there are few comparative studies at the level of the region (e.g., Dagilienė and Nedzinskienė, 2018; Dumitru et al., 2017; Horváth et al., 2017; Korca and Costa, 2021). Additional studies are needed to offer a more general understanding of sustainability reporting practices. Moreover, comparative studies could capture the influence of the similarities and differences in the institutional context of CEE countries on sustainability reporting practices. In this regard, research teams of academics from different countries could be formed, as they will know the local realities and overcome the language barrier, in order to analyze a large number of reports or conduct local interviews and case studies.

Second, most studies are placed at a certain moment in time, particularly immediately before or after the implementation of the NFRD. Therefore, there is a limited understanding of the evolution of sustainability reporting (e.g., Albu et al., 2021). It is reported, for example, that the overall extent and quality of disclosures has increased over time, but there are also cases of discontinued disclosure. Moreover, it is acknowledged that the first phase in sustainability reporting is one of acceptance, then compliance, followed by a qualitative stage of engagement with CSR, including through strategic and organizational activities. Little is known about what triggers companies to engage in more significant sustainability reporting. Research might also investigate the role of various policy instruments and their effectiveness over time (see Steurer et al., 2012 for a typology of various policy instruments, and a discussion of their application in the field of CSR in Europe). There are differences, for example, in the way regulations (pre-NFRD, NFRD, and subsequent regulations) are adopted at the national level (CSR Europe and GRI, 2017). However, few studies (e.g., Dumitru et al., 2017) investigate the role of these differences on sustainability reporting practices, particularly with a longitudinal approach.

Third, calls were made to consider context (e.g., Korca and Costa, 2021), or "the crucial role of societal cultures" (Krivogorsky et al., 2023, p. 8) in the localization of sustainability reporting. The institutional factors that influence sustainability reporting might be mobilized more in future research. For example, two significant institutional features of CEE countries are the presence of MNCs (through subsidiaries) and the importance of state-owned enterprises. Research offers some puzzling findings regarding their influence on sustainability reporting. As such, prior studies show that sustainability reporting is performed mostly by MNCs (Arraiano and Hațegan, 2019), which were the pioneers and the drivers of sustainability reporting (Albu et al., 2021; Dyczkowska et al., 2016; Krasodomska et al., 2020). However, studies also show that local subsidiaries disclose less and in a different manner than their parent companies, and that MNCs do not necessarily impose their practices on CEE subsidiaries (Cho et al., 2021; Dumitru et al., 2017). In some cases (Albu et al., 2021), MNCs subsidiaries were pioneers in initiating sustainability reporting under a voluntary regime and discontinued it later when it was mandatory for other industry players. More research is thus needed to understand how MNCs' subsidiaries balance adherence to the group's practices and their local reporting behavior, especially in the context of the new CSR Directive, which provides exemptions from reporting for affiliated entities under certain circumstances. Additionally, the role of the state and state ownership is puzzling. Several industries in CEE continue to showcase significant state ownership and control (Dragomir et al., 2022). Together with listed companies, state-owned enterprises are subject to more scrutiny and may be more willing to engage in sustainability reporting (Dumitru et al., 2017). On the other hand, many state-owned enterprises are affected by corruption, political interference, and poor management practices, and therefore are less inclined to be engaged in sustainability reporting. Studies emerge in this area (e.g., Dragomir et al., 2022) but additional research is needed to understand the role and implications of state ownership.

Fourth, we call for additional research employing a variety of methodological approaches, particularly moving beyond the content analysis of sustainability reporting, which seems to prevail (Korca and Costa, 2021; Lungu et al., 2016). Little is known about the role of various organizational actors, including managers, accountants, sustainability employees, and external consultants in the operationalization of sustainability reporting. Operationalization of sustainability reporting is related to management culture since the top management support, personal values and CSR training influence organizational practices (Witek-Crabb, 2019), and these are not visible in the sustainability reports. With some notable exceptions (e.g., Albu et al., 2021; Krasodomska et al., 2020), there are few studies based on stakeholders' perception in CEE countries, the same as for other emerging economies (Belal and Momin, 2009). Moreover, studies focusing on disclosure and compliance tend to ignore what is omitted in disclosures; and studies are needed to understand not only the presence but also the absence of CSR and sustainability reporting (Belal and Momin, 2009). Therefore, interviews, surveys, and case studies have the potential to shed additional light on sustainability reporting practices.

Fifth, we call for more theorized studies mobilizing a variety of theories to explain sustainability reporting practices. Even if some progress has been made since the study of Belal and Momin (2009), we still share their concern that research in CEE is under-theorized and with a limited engagement of the local context's features. From a theoretical perspective, prior studies mostly do not explicitly follow a "traditional" theory (Lungu et al., 2016) and fewer papers employ less common theoretical approaches (Korca and Costa, 2021). We therefore join Filatotchev et al. (2022) in calling for more contextualized theoretical framing of investigations on sustainability reporting. In this respect, researchers interested in CEE countries should consider the applicability of Western-issued theories and an adaptation of such theories to the local context of emerging economies.

Sixth, including larger samples in the studies should be considered. The CEE companies are not well-represented in databases such as Refinitiv, which makes it difficult to collect large volumes of data for research purposes. Considering another approach (such as the use of robots or artificial intelligence for data collection) can facilitate the process.

Seventh, the observance of reporting principles such as materiality, reliability, completeness, and comparability of information is not explored in relation to sustainability reporting in CEE.

Finally, the implementation of the new CSR Directive and the switch from non-financial to sustainability reporting open the space for additional research, particularly in terms of the extent to which CEE countries are prepared for the implementation of stricter requirements and how various actors will respond to these requirements. Important changes to internal systems are triggered by an internalization of sustainability reporting, and CEE companies may not have the required resources, nor may management be convinced to allocate such resources. The effects of such scarcity on sustainability reporting of CEE companies may also be subject to academic inquiry.

NOTES

1. We focus on the countries located in CEE which are members of the European Union (like other studies, e.g. Horváth et al., 2017). The list includes Bulgaria, Croatia, Czech Republic, Estonia, Hungary, Lithuania, Latvia, Poland, Romania, Slovenia and Slovakia.

2.   We adopt the term sustainability reporting but acknowledge the terminological variation existent in prior regulations and studies (including such terms as non-financial reporting, and social
and environmental reporting, among others).
3.   These phases are relevant for the micro level as well. Sustainability reporting for each company
may be placed in one of these phases, given its CSR organizational culture and sustainability
reporting practices (e.g., even if a country now is in the third stage, given the regulatory progress and the increase in the overall number of companies engaged in sustainability reporting,
some companies may still be in earlier stages).
4.   Those companies that act in metal mining, coal and lignite mining, oil exploration, paper,
chemical and allied products, petroleum refining, glass, metals, and air transport (Barbu et al.,
2014).
5.   The type of influence (positive or negative) might vary in some cases between the reporting
aspects considered (e.g., environmental, social or governance).

REFERENCES

Adams, C.A. and Frost, G.R. (2006). Accessibility and functionality of the corporate web site: implications for sustainability reporting. *Business Strategy and the Environment*, 15(4): 275–287.
Albu, N., Albu, C.N., Gîrbină, M.M. and Sandu, M.I. (2011). The implications of corporate social
responsibility on the accounting profession: the case of Romania. *Amfiteatru Economic*, XIII(29):
221–234.
Albu, N., Albu, C.N. and Filip, A. (2017). Corporate reporting in Central and Eastern Europe: issues,
challenges and research opportunities. *Accounting in Europe*, 14(3): 249–260.
Albu, N., Albu, C.N., Apostol, O. and Cho, C.H. (2021). The past is never dead: the role of imprints
in shaping social and environmental reporting in a post-communist context. *Accounting, Auditing &
Accountability Journal*, 34(5): 1109–1136.
Ali, W., Frynas, J.G. and Mahmood, Z. (2017). Determinants of corporate social responsibility
(CSR) disclosures in developed and developing countries: a literature review. *Corporate Social
Responsibility and Environmental Management*, 24: 273–294.
Aluchna, M., Roszkowska-Menkes, M. and Kamiński, B. (2023). From talk to action: the effects of the
Non-Financial Reporting Directive on ESG performance. *Meditari Accountancy Research*, 31(7):
1–25.
Alvesson, M. and Sandberg, J. (2020). The problematizing review: a counterpoint to Elsbach and Van
Knippenberg's argument for integrative reviews. *Journal of Management Studies*, 57(6): 1290–1304.
Apostol, O. (2015). A project for Romania? The role of the civil society's counter-accounts in facilitating
democratic change in society. *Accounting, Auditing & Accountability Journal*, 28: 210–241.
Arraiano, I.G. and Haţegan, C.D. (2019). The stage of corporate social responsibility in EU-CEE coun-
tries. *European Journal of Sustainable Development*, 8(3): 340–353.
Aureli, S., Salvatori, F. and Magnaghi, E. (2020). A country-comparative analysis of the transposition
of the EU non-financial directive: an institutional approach. *Accounting, Economics, and Law:
A Convivium*, 10(2): 1–30.
Băleanu, T.E., Chelcea, L. and Stancu, A. (2011). The social responsibility of the top 100 Romanian
companies: an analysis of corporate websites. *Amfiteatru Economic*, 13: 235–248.
Barbu, E.M. and Ienciu, N.M. (2019). Social responsibility and treatment of employees: how to improve
reporting among European companies? *Revue Management & Avenir*, 108: 83–106.
Barbu, E.M., Dumontier, P., Feleagă, N., and Feleagă, L. (2014). Mandatory environmental disclo-
sures by companies complying with IASs/IFRSs: the cases of France, Germany, and the UK. *The
International Journal of Accounting*, 49: 231–247.
Baskin, J. (2006). Corporate responsibility in emerging markets. *Journal of Corporate Citizenship*, 24:
29–47.
Belal, A.R. and Momin, M. (2009). Corporate social reporting (CSR) in emerging economies: a review
and future directions. *Research in Accounting in Emerging Economies*, 9: 119–143.

Beleneşi, M., Bogdan, V. and Popa, D.N. (2021). Disclosure dynamics and non-financial reporting analysis: the case of Romanian listed companies. *Sustainability*, 13, 4732.

Camilleri, M.A. (2015). Environmental, social and governance disclosures in Europe. *Sustainability Accounting, Management and Policy Journal*, 6(2): 224–242.

Carrots and Sticks (2020). Sustainability reporting policy: global trends in disclosure as the ESG agenda goes mainstream. Available at https://www.carrotsandsticks.net/media/zirbzabv/carrots-and-sticks -2020-june2020.pdf.

Chiaramonte, L., Dreassi, A., Girardone, C. and Piserà, S. (2022). Do ESG strategies enhance bank stability during financial turmoil? Evidence from Europe. *The European Journal of Finance*, 28(12): 1173–1211.

Cho, C., Krasodomska, J., Ratliff-Miller, P. and Godawska, J. (2021). Internationalization and CSR reporting: evidence from US companies and their Polish subsidiaries. *Meditari Accountancy Research*, 29(7): 135–162.

CSR Europe and GRI (2017). Member state implementation of Directive 2014/95/EU. A comprehensive overview of how member states are implementing the EU Directive on non-financial and diversity information. Available at https://www.accountancyeurope.eu/wp-content/uploads/1711 -NFRpublication-GRI-CSR-Europe.pdf.

Dagilienė, L. and Nedzinskienė, R. (2018). An institutional theory perspective on non-financial reporting: the developing Baltic context. *Journal of Financial Reporting and Accounting*, 16(4): 490–521.

Dimante, D. and Alksne, A., 2017. Sustainability reporting in Latvia: management views. In P. Horváth and J.M. Pütter (eds), *Sustainability Reporting in Central and Eastern European Companies: International Empirical Insights*. Cham: Springer, pp. 77–85.

Dinh, T., Husmann, A. and Melloni, G. (2023). Corporate sustainability reporting in Europe: a scoping review. *Accounting in Europe*, 20(1): 1–29.

Dragomir, V.D., Dumitru, M. and Feleagă, L. (2022). The predictors of non-financial reporting quality in Romanian state-owned enterprises. *Accounting in Europe*, 19(1): 110–151.

Dumitru, M., Dyduch, J., Guşe, R.G. and Krasodomska, J. (2017). Corporate reporting practices in Poland and Romania – an ex-ante study to the new non-financial reporting European Directive. *Accounting in Europe*, 14(3): 279–304.

Dyczkowska, J., Krasodomska, J. and Michalak, J. (2016). CSR in Poland: institutional context, legal framework and voluntary initiatives. *Accounting and Management Information Systems*, 15: 206–254.

Egan, M. and Tweedie, D. (2018). A "green" accountant is difficult to find. Can accountants contribute to sustainability management initiatives? *Accounting, Auditing & Accountability Journal*, 31(6): 1749–1773.

EUKI (2020). 2020 Research Report. An analysis of the climate-related disclosures of 300 companies from Central, Eastern and Southern Europe pursuant to the EU Non-Financial Reporting Directive. European Climate Initiative.

European Union (2014). Directive 2014/95/EU of the European Parliament and of the Council of 22 October 2014 amending Directive 2013/34/EU as regards disclosure of non-financial and diversity information by certain large undertakings and groups. Available at http://eur-lex.europa.eu/legal -content/EN/TXT/PDF/?uri=OJ:L:2014:330:FULLandfrom=EN (accessed 20 September 2018).

Farkas, B. (2011). The Central and Eastern European model of capitalism. *Post-Communist Economies*, 23(1): 15–34.

Fiandrino, S., di Trana, M.G., Tonelli, A. and Lucchese, A. (2022). The multi-faceted dimensions for the disclosure quality of non-financial information in revising Directive 2014/95/EU. *Journal of Applied Accounting Research*, 23(1): 274–300.

Fijałkowska, J., Zyznarska-Dworczak, B. and Garsztka, P. (2017). The relation between the CSR and the accounting information system data in Central and Eastern European (CEE) countries – the evidence of the Polish financial institutions. *Journal of Accounting and Management Information Systems*, 16(4): 490–521.

Filatotchev, I., Ireland, R.D. and Stahl, G.K. (2022). Contextualizing management research: an open systems perspective. *Journal of Management Studies*, 59(4): 1036–1056.

Grewal, J., Riedl, E.J., and Serafeim, G. (2015). Market reaction to mandatory non-financial disclosure. Harvard Business School Working Paper, No. 16-025.

Guşe, R.G., Almăşan, A., Circa, C. and Dumitru, M. (2016). The role of the stakeholders in the institutionalization of the CSR reporting in Romania. *Accounting and Management Information Systems*, 15(2): 304–340.

Hahn, R., Reimsbach, D., Wickert, C. and Eccles, R. (2020). Special Issue of Organization and Environment on "Non-financial disclosure and real sustainable change within and beyond organizations: mechanisms". *Organization & Environment*, 33(2): 311–314.

Hiebl, M.R.W. (2023). Literature reviews of qualitative accounting research: challenges and opportunities. *Qualitative Research in Accounting & Management*, 20(3): 309–336.

Hofstede, G. (2020), "Hofstede insights". Available at https://www.hofstede-insights.com/.

Horváth, P., Pütter, J., Haldma, T., Lääts, K., Dimante, D. et al. (2017). Sustainability reporting in Central and Eastern European companies: results of an international and empirical study. In P. Horváth and J.M. Pütter (eds), *Sustainability Reporting in Central and Eastern European Companies: International Empirical Insights*. Cham: Springer, pp. 109–127.

Jindrichovska, I. and Purcărea, I. (2011). CSR and environmental reporting in the Czech Republic and Romania: country comparison of rules and practices. *Accounting and Management Information Systems*, 10(2): 202–227.

Kearney (2022). Robust awareness of ESG in CEE must now be reflected in levels of aspiration and execution. Available at https://www.kearney.com/sustainability/article/-/insights/esg-is-climbing-the -corporate-and-societal-agenda-in-cee.

Kemp, M. (2001). Corporate social responsibility in Indonesia: Quixotic dream or confident expectation? Technology, Business and Society Program Paper No. 6, United Nations Research Institute for Social Development, Geneva.

Kinderman, D. (2020). The challenges of upward regulatory harmonization: the case of sustainability reporting in the European Union. *Regulation and Governance*, 14: 674–697.

Kiousis, S., Popescu, C. and Mitrook, M. (2007). Understanding influence on corporate reputation: an examination of public relations efforts, media coverage, public opinion, and financial performance from an agenda-building and agenda-setting perspective. *Journal of Public Relations Research*, 19(2): 147–165.

Kochalski, C., Mikołajewicz, G., Nowicki, J. and Ratajczak, P. (2017). Sustainability reporting in Poland: an in-depth analysis with reference to the Respect index companies. In P. Horváth and J.M. Pütter (eds), *Sustainability Reporting in Central and Eastern European Companies: International Empirical Insights*. Cham: Springer, pp. 11–49.

Korca, B. and Costa, E. (2021). Directive 2014/95/EU : building a research agenda. *Journal of Applied Accounting Research*, 22(3): 401–422.

KPMG (2022). Big shifts, small steps. Survey of Sustainability Reporting 2022. Available at https://kpmg.com/xx/en/home/insights/2022/09/survey-of-sustainability-reporting-2022.html.

Krasodomska, J., Michalak, J. and Swietla, K. (2020). Directive 2014/95/EU. Accountants' understanding and attitude towards mandatory non-financial disclosures in corporate reporting. *Meditari Accountancy Research*, 28(5), 751–779.

Krivogorsky, V., Mintchik, N. and Alon, A. (2023). Accounting research in former Soviet bloc countries: past trends and current and future developments. *Journal of International Accounting, Auditing and Taxation*, 50, 100529.

Lääts, K., Gross, M. and Haldma, T. (2017). Sustainability reporting in Estonia: patterns of sustainability information disclosure in Estonian companies. In P. Horváth and J.M. Pütter (eds), *Sustainability Reporting in Central and Eastern European Companies: International Empirical Insights*. Cham: Springer, pp. 63–76.

Line, M., and Braun, R. (2007). *Baseline Study on CSR Practices in the New EU Member States and Candidate Countries*. UNDP and the European Commission. Retrieved from www.acceleratingcsr.eu/uploads/docs/BASELINE_STUDY_ON.pdf.

Lungu, C.I., Caraiani, C., Dascălu, C., Turcu, D. and Turturea, M. (2016). Archival analysis of corporate social responsibility research: the Romanian perspective. *Accounting and Management Information Systems*, 15(2): 341–371.

MacLullich, K., and Gurau, C. (2004). *The Relationship between Economic Performance and Accounting System Reform in the CEE Region: The Cases of Poland and Romania*. Edinburgh: Heriot-Watt University.

Massaro, M., Dumay, J. and Guthrie, J. (2016). On the shoulders of giants: undertaking a structured literature review in accounting. *Accounting, Auditing & Accountability Journal*, 29: 767–801.

Matuszak, Ł. and Różańska, E. (2020). Online corporate social responsibility (CSR) disclosure in the banking industry: evidence from Poland. *Social Responsibility Journal*, 16(8), 1191–1214.

Matuszczyk, I. and Rymkiewicz, B. (2018). Integrated reporting and sustainable development reporting: comparison of guidelines IIRC and GRI G4. *Central and Eastern European Journal of Management and Economics*, 6(1): 31–43.

Paré, G., Trudel, M.-C., Jaana, M. and Kitsiou, S. (2015). Synthesizing information systems knowledge: a typology of literature reviews. *Information & Management*, 52(2), 183–199.

Peršić, M. and Halmi, L. (2018). Exploring the quality of social information disclosed in non-financial reports of Croatian companies. *Economic Research – Ekonomska Istraživanja*, 31(1): 2024–2043.

Radu, O.M., Dragomir, V.D. and Hao, N. (2023). Company-level factors of non-financial reporting quality under a mandatory regime: a systematic review of empirical evidence in the European Union. *Sustainability*, 15(23): 16265.

Săndulescu, M.S. (2021). Sustainability reporting and impression management: a case study in the oil and gas industry. *Journal of Accounting and Management Information Systems*, 20(2): 264–289.

Sofian, I. (2016). The adoption of integrated reporting principles by the Romanian companies listed at the Bucharest Stock Exchange. *Audit Financiar*, 14(144): 1335–1335.

Sofian, I. (2021). Perspectives of Romanian accounting professionals on Integrated Reporting. *Accounting and Management Information Systems*, 20(1): 651–681.

Steurer, R., Margula, S., and Martinuzzi, A. (2012). *Public policies on CSR in Europe: Themes, instruments, and regional differences*. Institute of Forest, Environmental and Nature Resource Policy, Discussion Paper 2-2012. Retrieved from https://boku.ac.at/fileadmin/data/H03000/H73000/H73200/InFER_Discussion_Papers/InFER_DP_12_2_Regional_differences.pdf.

Sucală, V.I. and Sava, A.M. (2017). Sustainability reporting in Romania: is sustainability reporting enough? In P. Horváth and J.M. Pütter (eds), *Sustainability Reporting in Central and Eastern European Companies: International Empirical Insights*. Cham: Springer, pp. 167–179.

Tilt, C.A. (2016). Corporate social responsibility research: the importance of context. *International Journal of Corporate Social Responsibility*, 1(2): 1–9.

Tiron-Tudor, A., Nistor, C.S., Ştefănescu, C.A. and Zanellato, G. (2019). Encompassing non-financial reporting in a coercive framework for enhancing social responsibility: Romanian listed companies' case. *Amfiteatru Economic*, 21(52): 590–606.

Traxler, A.A., Schrack, D. and Greiling, D. (2020). Sustainability reporting and management control – a systematic exploratory literature review. *Journal of Cleaner Production*, 276: 1–17.

Tregidga, H. and Laine, M. (2021). Stand-alone and integrated reporting. In J. Bebbington, C. Larrinaga, B. O'Dwyer and I. Thomson (eds), *Routledge Handbook of Environmental Accounting*. Abingdon: Routledge, pp. 108–124.

UNDP (2007). *Baseline Study on CSR practices in the New EU Member States and Candidate Countries*. New York: United Nations Development Programme.

Wagner, J. and Petera, P. (2017). Sustainability reporting in the Czech Republic. In P. Horváth and J.M. Pütter (eds), *Sustainability Reporting in Central and Eastern European Companies: International Empirical Insights*. Cham: Springer, pp. 129–142.

Wanderley, L.S.O., Lucian, R., Farache, F. and de Sousa Filho, J.M. (2008). CSR information disclosure on the web: a context-based approach analysing the influence of country of origin and industry sector. *Journal of Business Ethics*, 82: 369–378.

Witek-Crabb, A. (2019). CSR maturity in Polish listed companies: a qualitative diagnosis based on a progression model. *Sustainability*, 11(1736): 1–28.

23. SDG water disclosure around the globe

Md Alamgir Jalil, Silvia Gaia and Chaoyuan She

1   INTRODUCTION

With the 2030 Agenda, the United Nations (UN) introduced a set of 17 Sustainable Development Goals (SDGs) and 169 targets with the aim of improving social and environmental sustainability around the globe (UN, 2015). As outlined by the UN, "the SDGs represent a major opportunity for businesses to shape, steer, communicate and report their strategies, goals and activities, allowing them to capitalize on a range of benefits" (UNDP, n.d.). Despite extensive evidence existing of how companies discharge their accountability toward society in relation to ESG practices and on their corporate reporting choices (see Andrew & Baker, 2020 for a review of these studies), limited evidence exists on how businesses around the world are engaging with the SDGs and are reporting the relevant information to the public (e.g., Bose & Khan, 2022; Pizzi et al., 2021; Zampone et al., 2023).

This chapter aims to contribute to this research stream by focusing on water-related SDGs (SDG 6 and SDG 14) and exploring how companies disclose their commitment to the achievement of water-related SDGs in terms of the quantity and quality (tone, readability and length) of the related narrative disclosures. We analyse the water-related SDGs disclosures, in terms of quality and quantity, published in the corporate reports of 143 international companies operating in the period 2016–2020 in sectors characterised by high or medium operational sensitivity to water. SDG water-related disclosures were identified using the SDG 6 and SDG 14 keyword lists developed by Wang et al. (2023). We define a sentence as SDG water-related disclosure if the sentence contains at least one of the keywords from this dictionary. Results indicate a low engagement with these types of disclosures, which is concerning, considering the importance that water management has for sustainable development and the water risk that firms may face. They also indicate that firms seem to be keener to discuss more environmental aspects of water disclosure (SDG 14) than social aspects (SDG 6), contrasting with the results of previous studies (e.g., Bose & Khan, 2022). Our results also reveal that disclosures on water-related SDGs are biased, as firms tend to highlight more positive aspects of their water-related performance, and use texts that are more complex and difficult to understand. Overall, this evidence is in line with the impression management literature (Brennan et al., 2009; Muslu et al., 2019), which highlights that companies use more optimistic and complex disclosures to conceal information and confuse information users.

The remainder of the chapter is organised as follows. First, a brief description of the SDGs and water-related issues will be provided, together with an overview of the main studies on the associated reporting practices. This will be followed by a description of the research methodology of the study and a discussion of the main findings. Comments and conclusions will conclude the chapter.

2   AN OVERVIEW OF THE UN SDGS AND WATER MANAGEMENT REPORTING

In 2015, the UN member states adopted the 2030 Agenda for Sustainable Development, at the core of which there is the need "for action to tackle growing poverty, empower women and girls, and address the climate emergency" (UN, 2015). At the heart of this Agenda there are 17 Sustainable Development Goals (SDGs), which set 169 targets that aim to promote social prosperity while protecting the environment, by calling for action to end hunger, poverty and inequality; improve education, gender equality, water management, and clean energy uses; fight climate change and protect biodiversity (UN, 2015).

The UN emphasised that achieving the SDGs would require collaboration across governments, private and public sector organisations and civil society (Bebbington & Unerman, 2018). Companies have a big role to play in this. They are expected to reassess their purpose and look beyond the financial bottom line. Companies that align their strategy and purpose with the SDGs are likely to get competitive advantages since the SDGs are becoming increasingly important to investors (Paetzold et al., 2022). Disclosing information about the SDGs is therefore crucial for companies to show to investors and corporate stakeholders their commitment to social and environmental sustainability and the achievement of the SDGs. Despite this importance, a study conducted by KPMG (2017) found that only 43% of the world's 250 largest companies by revenue, based on the Fortune 500 ranking of 2016, explicitly reported on their contribution to the SDGs in the period 2016–2017. By contrast, PwC (2019) reported that nearly 72% of 1,141 large corporations across 31 countries and seven sectors mentioned the SDGs in their 2018 corporate reports. The study, however, also outlined that very few companies provide more specific disclosure on how they are aligning their strategy to the SDGs or on the specific SDG targets that they plan to achieve (PwC, 2019). Bose and Khan (2022), who examined SDG reporting over the period 2016–2019, found that companies' engagement with SDG disclosure is shallow. Only 8.40% of the 6,941 firm-year observations analysed disclosed information on SDG targets over the sample period, and most of this disclosure started in 2019. By contrast, the studies of Pizzi et al. (2021) and Zampone et al. (2023), which measured the engagement of companies with SDGs disclosure, using a disclosure index based on the GRI, provide a more positive picture showing that companies disclose relevant information for around one-third of the SDGs.

Interestingly, the study conducted by Bose and Khan (2022) also shows that social-related SDGs, such as SDG 8: Decent work and economic growth, SDG 5: Gender equality, SDG 3: Good health and well-being and SDG 2: Zero hunger, were the SDGs disclosed by the highest number of companies. However, environmental-related SDGs and water-related SDGs, such as SDG 6: Clean Water and Sanitation and SDG 14: Life Below Water were disclosed the least. This is despite the management of water-related natural resources, including oceans, seas and freshwater, being considered to be one of the major challenges faced globally to achieve sustainable development (UNGA, 2015). Access to water is at the centre of sustainable development: it is critical for supporting the processes that support all life on Earth, including human beings, industrial production and economic growth, and it is at the core of the adjustments in ecological, social and economic systems in response to climate change (UN, n.d.). Evidence on corporate water management disclosure is also limited. The few studies conducted in this area show that companies operating in the water industry tend to disclose more extensive information, which tends to be in line with water regulators' guidelines (Stray,

2008), whereas companies operating outside the water industry tend to provide more limited disclosure (Zeng et al., 2020; Zhang et al., 2021).

To our knowledge, studies on SDGs and water-related disclosure have focused mostly on evaluating the quantity of the information disclosed. No evidence has been provided in relation to the qualitative characteristics of these disclosures. This chapter aims to fill this gap by analysing the extent, tone, readability and length of water-related disclosures in relation to SDG 6 and SDG 14.

3   RESEARCH METHODOLOGY

3.1   Sample Selection

A sample of 143 international companies operating in sectors characterised by high or medium operational sensitivity to water[1] was selected from the list of ASSET4 global companies to investigate the characteristics of water-related information disclosed in relation to the UN SDGs in the period 2016–2020. This selection criterion has resulted in a total of 715 firm-year observations. We have chosen to focus on companies operating in sectors with high or medium operational sensitivity as these companies are expected to engage more heavily in water-related actions and, consequently, to disclose relevant information concerning such actions (Zeng et al., 2020; Zhang et al., 2021).

3.2   Extent and Quality of SDG Water-Related Disclosures

We examine both the quantity and quality of SDG water-related disclosures. To identify and prepare firms' SDG water-related disclosures for variable constructions, we first use textual analysis packages such as Quanteda and tokenizers to parse firms' sustainability texts into sentences. Next, we employ the SDG 6 and SDG 14 keyword lists developed by Wang et al. (2023) to identify water-related disclosures. We define a sentence as an SDG water-related disclosure if the sentence contains at least one of the keywords from our dictionary. Finally, we pool all identified sentences from each report to generate our main variables of interest.

3.2.1   Extent of water-related disclosures
We use two alternative measures to capture the extent of water-related disclosures. Our first variable (*WATER_DIS_NUM*) captures the absolute extent of water-related disclosures. It is defined as the number of sentences mentioning SDG 6 or SDG 14 keywords in a firm's sustainability report. Our second variable (*WATER_DIS_PERC*) captures the relative extent of water-related disclosures, which is defined as the percentage of water-related sentences over total sentences of disclosure in a sustainability report. To provide further insights into the specific information related to individual SDGs, we also split disclosures into SDG 6 and SDG 14 -related disclosures.

3.2.2   Disclosure tone
Disclosure tone is the presentation of content which can be used by businesses to manipulate users' beliefs and perceptions about corporate performance (Muslu et al., 2019). Firms that use an abnormally optimistic tone to disclose poor performance in sustainability reports are likely

to exaggerate their sustainability performance, hence resulting in lower disclosure quality. Alternatively, firms that use a pessimistic tone in the sustainability reports are likely to indicate a lower likelihood of opportunistic behaviour by management , thus indicating a higher disclosure quality (Muslu et al., 2019). Following prior studies, we employ the Loughran and McDonald (2011) list of "positive" and "negative" words to measure the tone or sentiment of corporate water disclosures (*TONE*). This list is widely used in accounting studies to measure the tone of both financial and non-financial disclosures (Loughran & McDonald, 2016; Muslu et al., 2019). We measure disclosure tone as the ratio of the difference between the number of positive (optimistic) and negative (pessimistic) words over the total number of words in the water-related disclosures, as identified in our first stage of analysis.

3.2.3   Disclosure readability

Similarly, firms may obfuscate their negative actions by making their qualitative disclosure less readable and hiding negative aspects of sustainability performance (Cho et al., 2012; Diouf & Boiral, 2017). Firms that use more readable sentences are less likely to hide or obfuscate negative activities and are more transparent in non-financial voluntary disclosure such as sustainability reporting (Li, 2008). Studies on syntactic manipulation use several methods such as FOG, SMOG (Simple Measure of Gobbledygook), and Flesch-Kinkaid to measure the readability of a text (Brennan et al., 2009). Although the FOG index is the most popular measure of readability, it is likely to be an inappropriate and poorly specified measure for measuring the readability of business documents as complex business terms can be easily understood by the investors (Brennan et al., 2009; Loughran & McDonald, 2014; 2016). Following Muslu et al. (2019), we use the SMOG index, which is more effective for assessing the readability of high-quality reports. The SMOG index is calculated as SMOG = $1.043 \times$ [(number of polysyllables) $\times$ (30/number of sentences)]$^{1/2}$ + 3.129. A higher index indicates the length of formal education (number of years) required for a reader of average intelligence to understand the qualitative disclosure (i.e., lower readability).

3.2.4   Disclosure length

Last, firms may use more wording and lengthier texts to increase the complexity of disclosures (Li, 2008; Loughran & McDonald, 2014). Therefore, we also use the average length of water disclosure as another indicator of water disclosure quality. We define the average length of disclosures (*LENGTH*) as the average number of words in each relevant sentence (Leung et al., 2015). This measure is different from the extent of water disclosures as it captures the overall complexity of sentences reported.

4   MAIN FINDINGS AND DISCUSSIONS

4.1   SDG Water Disclosures by Country and Industry

In this section, we present descriptive statistics of the main measures used to evaluate the quantity and quality of water-related disclosures and show how firms are disclosing water-related information around the world.

Table 23.1 Panel A presents the sample distribution by country. As indicated in the table, most of the firms that report water-related disclosures come from Japan, followed by

Table 23.1   Composition of the sample

Panel A – Country-based segment of the sample					
Country name	No. of companies	Country name	No. of companies	Country name	No. of companies
Japan	69	Sweden	4	Austria	1
Germany	9	Switzerland	4	Greece	1
South Korea	9	Taiwan	3	Hong Kong	1
China	6	Thailand	3	Hungary	1
France	6	Belgium	2	Ireland	1
UK	5	Canada	2	Italy	1
USA	5	Netherlands	2	Luxemburg	1
Finland	4	Norway	2	Russia	1
Panel B – Industry-based segment of the sample					
Industry sector	No. of companies	Industry sector	No. of companies	Industry sector	No. of companies
Basic materials	43	Technologies	17	Energy	7
Industrials	22	Health care	14	Utilities	7
Consumer discretionary	20	Consumer Staples	13		

Germany, South Korea, China, France, the UK, and the US. By contrast, we found very few firms reporting water-related disclosures in countries including Austria, Greece, Hong Kong, Hungary, Ireland, Italy, Luxembourg, and Russia.

Table 23.1 Panel B presents our sample distribution as classified by eight major industry sectors based on the Industry Classification Benchmark. As shown in the table, most of the sample firms come from the basic materials industry (30%), industrials (15%) and consumer discretionary (14%). These results are consistent with the identification by the CEO Water Mandate (2014) where firms coming from high water-sensitive industries are more likely to report water-related information.

4.2   The Extent of SDG Water-Related Disclosures

Table 23.2 Panel A reports the descriptive statistics of the extent of water-related disclosures. As indicated in the table, there is a large variation in how firms disclose water-related information, ranging from 22 sentences in the lower quantile to 87 sentences in the upper quantile. The average number of sentences referring to water-related information is approximately 67 sentences. When converting them to percentages, firms on average allocate 4.6% of spaces discussing water-related issues, which is remarkably low given the potential water risk firms may face. This result is consistent with prior studies that find that firms, even though they are from high water risk industries, tend to disclose minimal SDG water-related information in their sustainability reports (Zeng et al., 2020). These findings seem to indicate that firms are acting slowly in response to the increasing demand from stakeholders for nature-related disclosures (Zeng et al., 2020; Zhang et al., 2021).

We further examine differences between the SDG topics that firms tend to focus on by splitting SDG water-related disclosures into SDG 6-related and SDG 14-related information. As shown in Table 23.2 Panel B, firms on average disclose 23 sentences on SDG 6 and 63

Table 23.2   *Findings of the extent of water disclosures*

Panel A. Descriptive statistics of the extent of water disclosures						
	N	Mean	SD	P25	P50	P75
WATER_DIS_NUM	715	67.33	75.88	22.00	45.00	85.00
WATER_DIS_PERC	715	4.60	5.05	1.85	3.39	5.27

Panel B. T-test between SDG6 and SDG14 disclosures						
	N	Mean	Std Error	SD	Diff	t stats
SDG6_DIS_NUM	715	22.67	0.82	21.98	−40.8	
SDG14_DIS_NUM	715	63.47	2.78	74.29		−17.05***
SDG6_DIS_PERC	715	1.60	0.06	1.72	−2.74	
SDG14_DIS_PERC	715	4.34	0.19	4.95		−18.33***

Panel C. Trends of the average extent of water disclosures						
	Stats	2016	2017	2018	2019	2020
WATER_DIS_NUM	Mean	59.81	62.28	66.92	69.22	78.43
WATER_DIS_PERC	Mean	4.69	4.80	4.32	4.64	4.54

Note: *** $p < 0.01$.

sentences on SDG 14, which constitute 1.6% and 4.3% of total sentences disclosed in sustainability reports, respectively. A further T-test in Table 23.2 Panel B confirms that the extent of SDG 14 disclosures is significantly larger than that of SDG 6 disclosures. These results suggest that firms consider the environmental aspect of water resources, i.e., the conservation and sustainable use of oceans, seas and marine resources, to be more financially material than its social aspect, i.e. ensuring availability and sustainable management of water and sanitation for all. One possible explanation for this difference is that, given the increasing demand for nature-related financial disclosures from the market, firms that rely heavily on water resources are more likely to discuss the risks and opportunities of water use to meet investors' information needs. In contrast, clean water and sanitation would require more community contributions, hence the market may respond less favourably when firms over-invest in this area, consistent with the findings in Afrin et al. (2022).

We also investigate the trends of firms' SDG water-related reporting over the sample period. Table 23.2 Panel C shows that there is an upward trend for firms reporting SDG water-related information in their sustainability reports, with a jump from approximately 60 sentences in 2016 to more than 78 sentences in 2020. There are two possible drivers behind this trend. First, there is a strong market demand for firms to disclose natural capital information due to the increasing attention of investors to climate change and its associated environmental issues. With the growing population and the acceleration of global warming, it has been forecast that global demand for clean water will exceed the available supply by 40% by 2030 (CEO Water Mandate, 2008). Consequently, investors are calling for more water-related financial disclosures from firms that heavily rely on water resources. This demand is also reflected in the ongoing development of the Taskforce on Nature-Related Financial Disclosures (TNFD). Second, the wide adoption of/participation in the Global Reporting Initiatives (GRI), the EU Corporate Sustainability Reporting Directive (CSRD), the Sustainability Accounting Standards Board (SASB) Standards, and the Carbon Disclosure Project (CDP) also provide more guidelines on how firms should disclose water-related information. As a result, firms increase such disclosures to comply with these standards. Despite the number of sentences increasing over the sample period, we also find a downward trend for the proportion of water-related

Table 23.3   Findings of the textual characteristics of water disclosures

Panel A. Descriptive statistics of the textual characteristics of water disclosures

	N	Mean	SD	P25	P50	P75
TONE	715	0.05	0.22	-0.07	0.05	0.19
SMOG	715	24.31	6.52	20.26	23.23	27.19
POS_SENTENCE	715	16.69	19.83	4.00	10.00	20.50
NEG_SENTENCE	715	11.74	12.00	4.00	8.00	16.00
LENGTH	715	163.64	106.01	108.62	136.18	186.38

Panel B. Trends of the textual characteristics of water disclosures

	Stats	2016	2017	2018	2019	2020
TONE	Mean	0.08	0.06	0.05	0.06	0.03
SMOG	Mean	24.02	24.56	24.24	24.65	24.08
LENGTH	Mean	160.24	164.91	158.97	180.26	153.80

information in sustainability reports. For example, the percentage of water-related disclosures dropped from 4.8% in 2017 to 4.54% in 2020. This is probably due to the increasing amount of information being reported in the sustainability reports, reflecting the increasing market and regulatory pressures for sustainability transparency.

4.3   Tone, Readability, and the Average Length of SDG Water-Related Disclosures

Next, we examine the textual characteristics of SDG water-related disclosures by examining their tone, readability, and length. Table 23.3 Panel A reports the descriptive statistics of the tone, readability, and average number of words of water disclosures. The results show that firms tend to disclose SDG water disclosures in a more positive tone as the mean sentiment of sentences is 0.05, but the tone is close to neutral. However, the statistics also reveal a wide difference between tone in the lower quantile (−0.07) and the upper quantile (0.19). We further separate sentences into positive and negative ones and the results show that firms tend to highlight the positive aspects of their sustainability performance. These results are consistent with prior studies arguing that firms adopt impression management strategies to manage stakeholder perceptions about water performance (Diouf & Boiral, 2017).

To illustrate how tone varies in water-related disclosures, we present two text extracts of water disclosures found in our sample. The first text extract is found in the Evonik AG Sustainability Report 2017. The second text extract is disclosed in the AUO Corporation 2020 Sustainability Report. As we can see from the texts, Evonik AG highlights the increases in wastewater loads and provides further explanations for the reasons behind such increases in its water disclosures, suggesting the firm is presenting a neutral picture of its water performance. By contrast, AUO Corporation uses several impressive phrases, such as *continued to promote*, and *successfully decrease*, to highlight the positive side of its water performance without mentioning any negative aspects or potential challenges faced. Therefore, Extract 2 is considered to portray a more positive nature of the firm's water performance than Extract 1.

BOX 23.1 TEXTS WITH NEGATIVE AND POSITIVE SENTIMENT

Extract 1: Texts with Negative Sentiment

Chemical oxygen demand (COD) accounts for the highest proportion of wastewater loads. This is the concentration of all substances in the wastewater that can be oxidized under certain conditions. About half of the increase in COD is due to the initial consolidation of the businesses acquired from Air Products. In addition, there was an increase in wastewater loads in some cases due to higher production output. The slight rise in heavy metal emissions was essentially within the analytical variation for the measuring method because in many cases the values obtained are only slightly above the detection threshold.

Source: Evonik AG Sustainability Report 2017.

Extract 2: Texts with Positive Sentiment

AUO has continued to promote production water reduction, circulating water reuse, and increasing the recycling of production water, we have successfully decreased production water in 2020 by 1.19 million tonnes. In terms of production water recycling, AUO has recycled 158.46 million m^3 of water in 2020, an increase of 13.05 million m^3 from 2019. Production recycles rate also rose from 92.29% to 93.81%. In terms of water use intensity, due to the lowering of water consumption, a total of 21.69 million m^3 of water was used in 2020, and water consumption per unit was decreased from 0.35 tonne/m^2 to 0.32 tonne/m^2.

Source: AUO Corporation Sustainability Report 2020.

Next, we examine whether firms manage impressions by making SDG water-related information more difficult to understand. The results show that the average value of the SMOG index is 24.31, which indicates that people would need a graduate education level to read and understand the texts. This finding suggests that managers obfuscate water disclosures by using more complicated and less readable sentences, consistent with the impression management literature (Brennan et al., 2009; Muslu et al., 2019). To demonstrate how the readability varies among reports, we present two text extracts with high and low SMOG indexes. The first one is disclosed in Indorama Ventures Sustainability Report 2017 with a SMOG index of 18.77. The second text extract is found in the Huntsman International Sustainability Report 2017, with a SMOG index of 12.16. As we can see from the texts, Extract 1 has lengthy sentences with excessive use of commas. The text also uses more complicated words to explain water-related actions. By contrast, Extract 2 uses relatively shorter sentences and limited use of commas; the text is also well structured by using ordinal adverbs. Consequently, Extract 2 is easier to read and more understandable than Extract 1.

BOX 23.2 TEXTS WITH HIGH AND LOW SMOG

Extract 1: Texts with High SMOG

IVL Dhunseri Petrochem Industries Private Limited, an IVL subsidiary in Panipat, Haryana, India, established a rainwater harvesting system at its plant in 2017 to supply surface water to subsurface aquifers (before it's lost as surface runoff). The amount of rainwater estimated to percolate into the ground is over 41,500 m^3/year, which amounts to approximately over 30% of 2017 annual fresh water withdrawn by the plant. This water will be free of pollutants as well as salts, minerals and other man made contaminants, and will help in reducing soil erosion and contamination of surface water with pesticides and fertilizers by replenishing groundwater. We have plans to extend this system to additional sites in future.

Source: Indorama Ventures Sustainability Report 2017.

Extract 2: Texts with Low SMOG

Huntsman's discharges to water have decreased since 2010 through 2015, remained nearly flat in 2016, and decreased again in 2017. There are two reasons for this trend. First, we are complying with – and in many cases exceeding – increasingly strict water quality standards. Second, we understand water quality's direct connection with water scarcity. Keeping water clean goes hand in hand with the efficient use of water. Huntsman's improvements on water quality strengthen the company's commitment to conserving water.

Source: Huntsman International Sustainability Report 2017.

Furthermore, we examine whether firms use lengthier sentences to increase the complexities of disclosures. As we can see from Table 23.3, the average number of words in a sentence is 163 which is significantly higher than the average words per sentence (approximately 23 words) in a 10-K report (Loughran & McDonald, 2014). This finding is consistent with prior studies showing that managers would use lengthier sentences to confuse users of the information. We also present two text extracts with shorter and lengthier sentences to show how managers may adopt this technique to conceal certain information. The first text is extracted from the Agfa-Gevaert Annual Report 2019 while the second one is found in the LG Household CSR Report 2018. In terms of the average number of words in a sentence, Extract 1 has, on average, 13.86 words per sentence, while Extract 2 has 22.25. Although Extract 1 has relatively more words in total (i.e., 97) compared to Extract 2 (i.e., 89), it uses fewer words per sentence to report water performance. Extract 2, by contrast, uses more words per sentence, which makes information rather disjointed and difficult to understand. Overall, these two examples demonstrate how lengthy sentences can be used to confuse readers about firms' water-related activities.

BOX 23.3 TEXTS WITH LENGTHY AND SHORT SENTENCES

Extract 1: Texts with Short Sentences

Total water consumption decreased by 8.6% in 2019. Specific water consumption rose slightly by 2.1% to 31.3 m^3 per tonne of product produced. Water consumption excluding cooling water fell by 18.3% in 2019. Specific water consumption excluding cooling water fell by 8.7% to 10.6 m^3 per tonne of product produced. This is the result of continued efforts to use water sparingly. The specific process water consumption could once again be further reduced to 4.5 m^3 per tonne of product produced. The continuous efforts we are making to optimize the production processes therefore result in a considerable reduction.

Source: Agfa-Gevaert Annual Report 2019

Extract 2: Texts with Lengthy Sentences

In 2018, our overall water consumption decreased from the previous year. The consumption of surface water and water supply increased by 3.7% and 3.9%, respectively, while that of groundwater decreased by 20.5%. This was because HAITAI htb switched its water source for CIP1) at its business site in Cheonan from groundwater to water supply. To reduce water consumption, our business sites continue to manage the amount of water use for each purpose, find appropriate usage of recycled water, and develop improvement measures for areas that require high water consumption.

Source: LG Household CSR Report 2018

Lastly, we examine the trends of water disclosure textual characteristics over the sample period. Table 23.3 Panel B reports the mean values of tone, readability, and average length between 2016 and 2020. We find a downward trend for the tone of water-related disclosures, suggesting that firms have started discussing negative aspects of water performance, largely due to the increasing demand for water risk information. Regarding readability and the average length, we, however, do not observe a clear trend over the sample period. The readability of water disclosures is largely consistent while the average length has fluctuated over the years. Such fluctuation may be caused by changes in the writing/formatting style of the sustainability reports.

5   CONCLUSIONS

In this chapter, we investigate how companies disclose their commitment to the achievement of water-related SDGs in terms of the quantity and quality (tone, readability and length) of the related narrative disclosures. By analysing water-related SDGs disclosures reported by 143 international companies in the period 2016–2020, our results highlight two major concerns in relation to firms' SDG reporting practices. First, they reveal a low engagement in reporting SDG water-related information and an over-emphasis on reporting information related to water risk (SDG 14) with limited information regarding improving water hygiene and providing clean water to less developed economies (SDG 6), which may impede the achievement of SDG goals by 2030. While this chapter does not examine the possible causes behind this phenomenon, we speculate that the market and regulatory demands for more water transparency may be one of the factors driving the provision of more information related to SDG 14 than SDG 6. We believe that it is important for firms to report information in relation to both SDGs since the two goals are interconnected and it is against the ethos of the UN SDG framework to advance one goal while downplaying the others (Bebbington & Unerman, 2018; Nilsson et al., 2016). Second, our results also reveal that disclosures on water-related SDGs are biased, as firms tend to highlight more positive aspects of their water-related performance, and use texts that are more complex and difficult to understand. In fact, these findings are not new, as extensive studies have shown that firms employ impression management strategies when reporting sustainability-related information (Brennan et al., 2009; Muslu et al., 2019). However, our results suggest that there is a downward trend for using an optimistic tone in SDG water-related disclosures, suggesting that it may be increasingly difficult for firms to engage in impression management strategies when stakeholders are increasingly concerned with environmental issues. Furthermore, the implementation and adoption of stringent sustainability reporting standards, such as European Sustainability Reporting Standards (ESRS), SASB, GRI, and ISSB standards, may also force firms to report metrics of their (positive and negative) water performance. Future studies could certainly explore the impact of sustainability reporting standards on the quality of SDG disclosures as well as its role in mitigating the use of impression management strategies when reporting.

While this chapter only provides an overview of how firms report SDG water-related information, future studies could also explore the impact of SDG water reporting beyond the capital market. For example, while it is important for firms to assess and report risks related to water scarcity, it is equally important to understand the impact of firms' operations on local water sources and the impact of water use on sanitation and water accessibility in water-scarce regions. This research question is in line with the notion of double materiality adopted by the EU Corporate Sustainability Reporting Directive (CSRD), according to which firms should account for both inward and outward sustainability impacts. Scholars could explore these research questions using interdisciplinary theories and perspectives, and some recent examples including Gaia theory (Rodrigue & Romi, 2022), planetary boundaries (Rockström et al., 2009), and an Anthropocene perspective (Bebbington et al., 2020). A greater understanding of these questions could also be achieved by introducing novel environmental science datasets to accounting research. Although the SDGs are largely set at the country level, accounting scholars also play a major role in converting these national indicators into firm-level metrics. Therefore, we believe that there are ample research opportunities that could potentially be exploited during this conversion and accounting process. At the same time, we should also be aware that the clock is ticking and there is not much time left for us to meet these goals by 2030.

NOTE

1. The following industries are considered as industries with high priority for exposing significant water-related business risks: agriculture, beverage producers, biomass power production, chemicals, clothing and apparel, electric power production, food producers, food retailers, forestry and paper, freshwater fishing and aquaculture, hydropower production, mining, oil and gas, pharmaceuticals and biotech, technology hardware and equipment, semiconductors, water utilities, and services sectors. However, construction and materials, gas distribution and multi-utilities, manufacturing of industrial goods, household goods, home construction, leisure goods, media (printed), real estate (asset owners), transportation and travel, and leisure sectors are listed as the medium priority (CEO Water Mandate, 2014).

REFERENCES

Afrin, R., Peng, N., & Bowen, F. (2022). The wealth effect of corporate water actions: how past corporate responsibility and irresponsibility influence stock market reactions. *Journal of Business Ethics*, *180*, 105–124.

Andrew, J., & Baker, M. (2020). Corporate social responsibility reporting: the last 40 years and a path to sharing future insights. *Abacus*, *56*(1), 35–65.

Bebbington, J., & Unerman, J. (2018). Achieving the United Nations Sustainable Development Goals: an enabling role for accounting research. *Accounting, Auditing & Accountability Journal*, *31*(1), 2–24. https://doi.org/10.1108/AAAJ-05-2017-2929

Bebbington, J., Österblom, H., Crona, B., Jouffray, J.-B., Larrinaga, C., Russell, S., & Scholtens, B. (2020). Accounting and accountability in the Anthropocene. *Accounting, Auditing & Accountability Journal*, *33*(1), 152–177.

Bose, S., & Khan, H. Z. (2022). Sustainable Development Goals (SDGs) reporting and the role of country-level institutional factors: an international evidence. *Journal of Cleaner Production*, *335*, 130290.

Brennan, N. M., Guillamon-Saorin, E., & Pierce, A. (2009). Methodological insights: impression management: developing and illustrating a scheme of analysis for narrative disclosures–a methodological note. *Accounting, Auditing & Accountability Journal*, *22*(5), 789–832.

CEO Water Mandate (2008). The CEO water mandate transparency framework (phase one). Pacific Institute, Oakland, CA.

CEO Water Mandate (2014). Corporate water disclosure guidelines: Toward a common approach to reporting water issues. Pacific Institute, Oakland, CA.

Cho, C. H., Guidry, R. P., Hageman, A. M., & Patten, D. M. (2012). Do actions speak louder than words? An empirical investigation of corporate environmental reputation. *Accounting, Organizations and Society*, *37*(1), 14–25. http://dx.doi.org/10.1016/j.aos.2011.12.001

Diouf, D., & Boiral, O. (2017). The quality of sustainability reports and impression management: a stakeholder perspective. *Accounting, Auditing & Accountability Journal*, *30*(3), 643–667. https://doi.org/doi:10.1108/AAAJ-04-2015-2044

KPMG (2017). *The Road Ahead. The KPMG Survey of Corporate Responsibility Reporting*. https://assets .kpmg.com/content/dam/kpmg/xx/pdf/2017/10/kpmg-survey-of-corporate-responsibility-reporting -2017.pdf

Leung, S., Parker, L., & Courtis, J. (2015). Impression management through minimal narrative disclosure in annual reports. *The British Accounting Review*, *47*(3), 275–289.

Li, F. (2008). Annual report readability, current earnings, and earnings persistence. *Journal of Accounting and Economics*, *45*(2), 221–247. https://doi.org/10.1016/j.jacceco.2008.02.003

Loughran, T. I. M., & McDonald, B. (2011). When is a liability not a liability? Textual analysis, dictionaries, and 10-Ks. *The Journal of Finance*, *66*(1), 35–65. https://doi.org/10.1111/j.1540-6261.2010 .01625.x

Loughran, T. I. M., & McDonald, B. (2014). Measuring readability in financial disclosures. *The Journal of Finance*, *69*(4), 1643–1671. https://doi.org/10.1111/jofi.12162

Loughran, T. I. M., & McDonald, B. (2016). Textual analysis in accounting and finance: a survey. *Journal of Accounting Research*, *54*(4), 1187–1230. https://doi.org/10.1111/1475-679X.12123

Muslu, V., Mutlu, S., Radhakrishnan, S., & Tsang, A. (2019). Corporate social responsibility report narratives and analyst forecast accuracy. *Journal of Business Ethics*, *154*(4), 1119–1142. https://doi .org/10.1007/s10551-016-3429-7

Nilsson, M., Griggs, D., & Visbeck, M. (2016). Map the interactions between Sustainable Development Goals. *Nature*, *534*(7607), 320–322.

Paetzold, F., Busch, T., Utz, S., & Kellers, A. (2022). Between impact and returns: private investors and the Sustainable Development Goals. *Business Strategy and the Environment*, *31*(7), 3182–3197.

Pizzi, S., Rosati, F., & Venturelli, A. (2021). The determinants of business contribution to the 2030 Agenda: introducing the SDG Reporting Score. *Business Strategy and the Environment*, *30*(1), 404–421.

PwC (2019). *SDG Reporting Challenge. Creating a Strategy for a Better World: How the Sustainable Development Goals Can Provide the Framework for Business to Deliver Progress on Our Global Challenges*. https://www.pwc.com/gx/en/sustainability/SDG/sdg-2019.pdf

Rockström, J., Steffen, W., Noone, K., Persson, Å., Chapin, F. S., Lambin, E. F., Lenton, T. M., Scheffer, M., Folke, C., & Schellnhuber, H. J. (2009). A safe operating space for humanity. *Nature*, *461*(7263), 472–475.

Rodrigue, M., & Romi, A. M. (2022). Environmental escalations to social inequities: some reflections on the tumultuous state of Gaia. *Critical Perspectives on Accounting*, *82*, 102321.

Stray, S. (2008). Environmental reporting: the U.K. water and energy industries: a research note. *Journal of Business Ethics*, *80*(4), 697–710. https://doi.org/10.1007/s10551-007-9463-8

UN (n.d.). *Water and Sustainable Development*. https://www.un.org/waterforlifedecade/water_and _sustainable_development.shtml

UN (2015). *The Sustainable Development Agenda*. https://www.un.org/sustainabledevelopment/ development-agenda/

UNDP (n.d.). *Sustainable Development Goals. Business and the SDGs*. https://www.undp.org/sdg -accelerator/business-and-sdgs

UNGA (2015). *Transforming Our World: The 2030 Agenda for Sustainable Development*. https://sdgs .un.org/2030agenda

Wang, W., Kang, W., & Mu, J. (2023). *Mapping research to the Sustainable Development Goals (SDGs)*. Research Square. Unpublished. https://doi.org/10.21203/rs.3.rs-2544385/v2

Zampone, G., García-Sánchez, I., & Sannino, G. (2023). Imitation is the sincerest form of institutionalization: understanding the effects of imitation and competitive pressures on the reporting of Sustainable Development Goals in an international context. *Business Strategy and the Environment*, *32*(7), 4119–4142.

Zeng, H., Zhang, T., Zhou, Z., Zhao, Y., & Chen, X. (2020). Water disclosure and firm risk: empirical evidence from highly water-sensitive industries in China. *Business Strategy and the Environment*, *29*(1), 17–38. https://doi.org/10.1002/bse.234

Zhang, L., Tang, Q., & Huang, R. H. (2021). Mind the gap: is water disclosure a missing component of corporate social responsibility? *The British Accounting Review*, *53*(1), 100940. https://doi.org/10 .1016/j.bar.2020.100940

PART VII

SUSTAINABILITY REPORTING – METHODS, THEORIES AND OUTLOOK

24. Stakeholders in sustainability research: a review of the literature using a topic modeling approach

Emmeli Runesson and Niuosha Samani

1   INTRODUCTION

Enhancing the disclosure of sustainability information by companies and financial institutions is believed to play an important role in directing financial and capital flows towards sustainable investments. This includes information related to environmental impact, social and employee matters, human rights, and efforts to combat corruption and bribery. With higher-quality disclosures, it becomes easier to assess, track, and manage companies' performance and their societal influence.

The introduction of Directive 2014/95/EU, also known as the "Non-Financial Reporting Directive" (NFRD), has implied significant progress towards promoting transparency and accountability in the European Union (EU) regarding social and environmental concerns. This directive has become a tool in advancing the EU's corporate social responsibility (CSR) agenda. However, while there is evidence that the NFRD has increased social and environmental disclosures in affected jurisdictions (Agostini et al., 2022; Cuomo et al., 2024; Samani et al., 2023), criticisms remain concerning corporate transparency and information comparability (Agostini et al., 2022; Fiandrino et al., 2022).

In response to these concerns, the European Union (EU) has developed the Corporate Sustainability Reporting Directive (CSRD-2022/2464, effective in 2024). The CSRD covers a larger number of companies and increases requirements for comprehensive reporting standards and audits. Notably, the CSRD emphasizes the double materiality perspective, which highlights the need for companies to disclose their impact on the environment and society, beyond the consequences of environmental and social matters for company value.

Achievement of double materiality requires understanding stakeholders, i.e., those who can affect or are affected by an organization's objectives. According to stakeholder theory (Freeman, 1984), organizations are in continuous relationships with various actors in the social and political process. The stakeholder perspective emphasizes the importance of managers building connections and links with external stakeholders, including the government, customers, the community, the media, and NGOs (Clarkson, M., 1995).

In this chapter, we present a comprehensive literature review on stakeholder-related topics and findings related to the role of various stakeholder groups in driving companies' accountability and responsibility. Our aim is to give a summary of the research field on an aggregate level as well as on a stakeholder group level. First, based on analyses of the abstracts, titles and (author-) provided keywords, we identify top publication outlets, the methods and theories applied, and the topics covered (topics are generated using latent Derichlet allocation, a natural language processing model). Second, we classify papers through an iterative process based on pre-identified stakeholder groups and keywords found in the literature. For each group, we highlight topics and trends and provide some examples of key research findings.

2   BIBLIOMETRIC ANALYSIS

In this section, we describe the articles in our literature review. We present top journals in terms of the number of citations and publications, the methods applied in the articles, and the theories covered.

To generate the sample, we target all publications in accounting journals ranked 2 or higher in the Academic Journal Guide (AJG) and with a presence in Scopus. Scopus is considered a suitable sampling frame as it has extensive coverage of the journals in the AJG list (57 of 61 journals with an AJG-2 ranking or higher). We apply three search criteria:[1]

(1)   the word "stakeholder" appears in any searchable field (including title, abstract, keywords and references);
(2)   the article relates to sustainability reporting; the search terms applied to all searchable fields were "sustainability report*", "csr report*", "corporate social responsibility report*", "non-financial report*", "non financial report*", "social report*", "integrated report*", "environmental report*", "esg report*", "environmental, social and governance report*";
(3)   to limit the sample to original research, the word "review" should not appear in the title, keyword or abstract field.

We thus obtained 1,657 papers from 52 unique journals (see Table 24.1).[2] The first paper in the sample was published in 1986, with an exponential increase in the number of papers published over time.

A few journals may be said to dominate the stakeholder literature both in terms of output and influence (*Accounting, Auditing and Accountability Journal, Sustainability Accounting, Management and Policy Journal, Critical Perspectives on Accounting,* and *Accounting Forum*); however, there is still a significant spread in publications across outlets. Table 24.2 presents the top 15 journals by citation and article counts (which shows a considerable overlap between the number of citations and the number of articles in a given journal).

Turning to the applied methods, we analyze the abstracts to classify papers based on method type – whether they are empirical or non-empirical, and if empirical, whether they use quantitative, qualitative, or mixed methods. Our results show that a clear majority of papers (84%) make explicit reference to words indicating an empirical approach. A manual review of the remaining 16% shows that these, with few exceptions, aim to develop ideas or theories deductively. Figure 24.1(a) shows the distribution of papers with respect to method type, indicating that a majority of papers are quantitative (41%), 19% are qualitative, 16% make reference to empirical results or methods (but we cannot confidently determine whether qualitative or quantitative methods are applied), and 9% make reference to both qualitative and quantitative methods. A further look at the keywords (Figure 24.1(b)) shows, unsurprisingly, that most quantitative papers fit within a statistical/archival data framework (678 papers); 406 papers mention interviews or case studies; a large number of papers refer to text analysis (275, of which 20 refer to discourse analysis, 21 refer to sentiment/tone analysis, and 75 papers refer to thematic, topic, and content analysis); 127 papers refer to surveys or questionnaires; and 55 papers refer to experiments.

Table 24.1   Sample overview

	Obs.
Articles in journals with an AJG-ranking of 2 or higher with the word "stakeholder" in any field according to Scopus *and* that refer to sustainability reporting	8023
Of which are classified as accounting journals	1830
Of which are not review articles	1657
Final sample	1657
Number of unique journals	52
Yearly breakdown	
–1999	15
2000–2004	30
2005–2009	128
2010–2014	244
2015–2019	529
2020–2022	711
Total	1657
Citation counts (Scopus)	
Mean	43
Median	14

Notes: This table describes the sample selection, the distribution of articles over time, and the average number of citations.

Table 24.2   Top-occurring journals

Source title	Citations	Articles
Accounting, Auditing and Accountability Journal (AAAJ)	13777	269
Accounting, Organizations and Society (AOS)	9653	44
British Accounting Review (BAR)	6458	76
Critical Perspectives on Accounting (CPA)	5754	129
Accounting Forum (AF)	4092	96
Journal of Accounting and Public Policy (JAPP)	3754	29
Sustainability Accounting, Management and Policy Journal (SAMPJ)	3624	183
Accounting Review (TAR)	3527	
European Accounting Review (EAR)	2406	39
Managerial Auditing Journal (MAJ)	2191	58
Accounting and Business Research (ABR)	1578	
Australian Accounting Review (AAR)	1566	52
Journal of Business Finance and Accounting (JBFA)	1406	
Accounting and Finance (AF)	1298	63
Journal of Applied Accounting Research (JAAR)	1246	79
Journal of Accounting in Emerging Economies (JAEE)		48
International Journal of Disclosure and Governance (IJDG)		35
Accounting Research Journal (ARJ)		29

Notes: This table presents the top 15 journals by the number of citations and articles, respectively, sorted by citations. Blank cells in the Citations (count) column mean the journal is not among the top 15 in terms of the count (Citations).

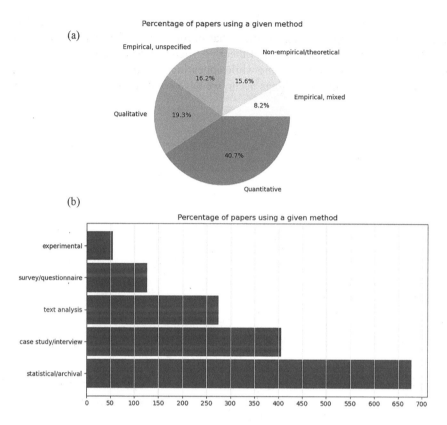

(a)

Percentage of papers using a given method

(b)

Percentage of papers using a given method

Notes: Figure 24.1(a) shows the distribution of papers with respect to five mutually exclusive categories: papers that (1) are strictly quantitative, (2) are strictly qualitative, (3) use mixed methods, (4) are empirical but not categorizable (based on our applied keywords), and (5) non-empirical.

Key words used for each category (plurals, hyphenated variations and tense variations are omitted for brevity):

Quantitative: "associate", "association", "bag of word", "bibliographic", "bibliometric", "computerized", "correlate", "correlated", "correlation", "lda", "machine learning", "quantitative", "questionnaire", "regress", "regression", "positive relationship", "negative relationship", "sample of", "sentiment", "statistical", "statistics", "survey", "text analysis", "textual analysis", "tone", "topic model", "topic modeling", "wordlist", "experiment", "experimental".

Qualitative: "case study", "cases", "discourse analysis", "interview", "interviewee", "interviewer", "qualitative", "thematic", "theme".

Empirical, mixed: see key words under Quantitative and Qualitative.

Empirical, unspecified: "content analysis", "descriptive", "empirical", "results", "findings".

Non-empirical/theoretical: no key words found.

Figure 24.1   Percentage of papers using a given method

We also provide an overview of the references made to explicit theories in the abstracts. Figure 24.2 shows the top theories. Theories that occur three or fewer times are shown in the Table 24.3. Not all theories are actual theories, such as "accounting theory", and some theories may also be considered the same while appearing with different labels. Except for in cases where obvious variants or spellings occur, we have retained the terminology used in the original texts.

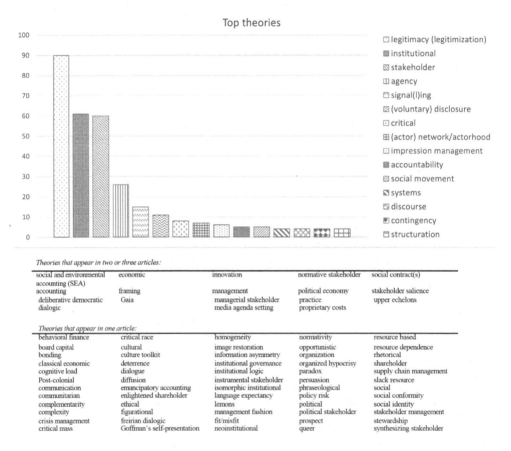

Theories that appear in two or three articles:

social and environmental accounting (SEA)	economic	innovation	normative stakeholder	social contract(s)
accounting	framing	management	political economy	stakeholder salience
deliberative democratic	Gaia	managerial stakeholder	practice	upper echelons
dialogic		media agenda setting	proprietary costs	

Theories that appear in one article:

behavioral finance	critical race	homogeneity	normativity	resource based
board capital	cultural	image restoration	opportunistic	resource dependence
bonding	culture toolkit	information asymmetry	organization	rhetorical
classical economic	deterrence	institutional governance	organized hypocrisy	shareholder
cognitive load	dialogue	institutional logic	paradox	supply chain management
Post-colonial	diffusion	instrumental stakeholder	persuasion	slack resource
communication	emancipatory accounting	isomorphic institutional	phraseological	social
communitarian	enlightened shareholder	language expectancy	policy risk	social conformity
complementarity	ethical	lemons	political	social identity
complexity	figurational	management fashion	political stakeholder	stakeholder management
crisis management	freirian dialogic	fit/misfit	prospect	stewardship
critical mass	Goffman's self-presentation	neoinstitutional	queer	synthesizing stakeholder

Figure 24.2   Top theories

3   TOPIC MODELING

To identify the topics covered by the articles in our sample, we turn to computerized topic modeling. Topic modeling is a subfield in natural language processing (NLP) that has gained some attention lately due to the increasing availability of digitized texts. The specific model or algorithm we adopt is known as latent Dirichlet allocation (LDA) (Blei et al., 2003). LDA employs unsupervised machine learning to uncover latent patterns in the data and define topics based on the likelihood of words appearing together. With LDA, each document is seen as

Table 24.3   Topic terms

Top 30 most salient terms in the corpus				
disclosure	board	integrate	responsibility	standard
sustainability	report	social	director	audit
csr	accountability	legitimacy	biodiversity	account
environmental	reporting	carbon	annual	political
assurance	performance	corporate	process	materiality
accounting	financial	bank	governance	risk

Topic	Top-20 most relevant terms
CSR and valuation	[CSR] corporate responsibility disclosure social investor performance earning level value high governance use activity information market risk country relationship voluntary
Assurance/audit and integrated reporting	assurance report sustainability reporting integrate audit [IR] information financial use practice auditor internal stakeholder quality adoption provider [SDG] integrated governance
Public accountability, NGOs and social values	accountability social accounting [NGO] public stakeholder account profit value movement corporate organization society power debate economic democratic critical context transparency
Environmental and social disclosure and firm characteristics	environmental disclosure performance financial annual use report risk governance size corporate quality information industry level extent determinant relationship characteristic voluntary
Organizational practices and social/environmental accounting	accounting social account organizational practice change management accountant critical field organization logic discourse system environmental charity perspective explore [SEA]
Environmental and social disclosure and legitimization strategies	disclosure legitimacy carbon climate_change report change reporting annual use climate stakeholder medium legitimation response strategy extinction practice social regulatory narrative
Materiality and stakeholder engagement	sustainability materiality stakeholder accountability report boundary process practice tool development [SME] reporting [TBL] concept materiality_assessment sustainable user engagement transparency material
Diversity in corporate boards	board gender bank director family woman gender_diversity standard hybrid_organization female [IASB] female_director diversity [EER] banking graph financial board_gender_diversity composition certification
Critical perspectives on sustainability and socio-political processes	sustainability diffusion counter_account compensation reporting digital animal social assurance report state fair normativity attractiveness innovation process [PM] political job adopter

Notes: This table shows the most salient terms in the entire corpus and describes the nine topics in terms of the most representative words in each topic. The selection of topic words is based partly on the overall term frequency within a given topic, and partly on the relative frequency of a term in the topic compared to the entire corpus. This means a word that is not so common overall can receive a greater weight and be included among the top words if its uniqueness to the topic makes it relevant or informative about the topic content.

a distribution over a finite number of topics, and each topic is represented as a distribution over words. The document–topic and the topic–word distributions are updated through an iterative algorithm that ideally passes through the corpus (collection of documents) multiple times.

The first step in topic modeling, after obtaining the documents to be analyzed, is to prepare the text for analysis by (1) tokenizing the texts (creating units of analysis, i.e., individual words and occasionally word pairs or triplets), (2) lemmatizing the tokens (grouping words based on their parts of speech; e.g., the lemma of "engagements" is "engagement" and the lemma of "reading" is "read"), and (3) removing stop words (common words that do not carry meaning in a topic context, typically articles, conjunctions and prepositions, such as "this", "do", "in", "a") and other words that are either too common or too rare. Specifically, we drop terms that occur only once in the corpus, and terms that occur in more than 90% of the documents.

The second step in topic modeling is the training of the LDA models. We train a number of models and compare their attributes to arrive at the model we believe best describes the data. Specifically, we considered topic models with five through 30 topics and compared model interpretability based on calculated coherence scores (where high scores indicate greater inter-pretability of topics). Using an intertopic distance map, we identified the model that produced the least amount of overlap among topics. Overall, we found that the model with nine topics generated the clearest topics. The nine topics are shown in Table 24.3, sorted by size (i.e., based on how common the words of a given topic are in relation to the entire corpus).

The most salient topic overall (1: CSR and valuation) includes papers on CSR disclosure in the context of shareholders, firm performance and value. The second largest topic (2: Assurance/audit and integrated reporting) contains words related to assurance, audits and integrated reports. The next topic (3: Public accountability, NGOs and social values) focuses on societal values and includes terms such as civil society, power, democracy, transparency, debate, and process. The fourth largest topic (4: Environmental and social disclosure and firm characteristics) shares some features with the first topic as it relates on performance, but its focus is on firm characteristics as determinants of CSR disclosure. Key terms include environ-mental, disclosure, performance, determinant as well as size and governance. The fifth topic (5: Organizational practices and social/environmental accounting) reflects a management accounting focus on management control and organizational practices and change, both in a social and environmental context, with references to additional theoretical concepts such as critical, logic and discourse. The sixth topic (6: Environmental and social disclosure and legitimization strategies) includes papers that focus on corporate disclosures and strategies to achieve legitimacy, both in the environmental (climate, biodiversity) and social domain. The seventh topic (7: Materiality and stakeholder engagement) is the topic that most explicitly concerns stakeholders and the question of broader materiality and accountability. The eighth topic (8: Diversity in corporate boards) is relatively small but also very specific and well delin-eated. Keywords are clearly governance-focused, with words such as board, directors, and governance, and the concern in particular is gender diversity. Finally, the last topic (9: Critical perspectives on sustainability and socio-political processes) is the most heterogeneous, but with multiple references to words such as diffusion, counter-account, social and political.

Each article has a probability of belonging to each topic, with the average probability ranging from 1% to 21% (Table 24.4). The distribution of the dominant topic (based on the calculated probability) across the ten and 20 most-cited papers shows that *CSR and valuation* is not only most popular among authors, it is also most often cited by other researchers. However, Environmental and social disclosure and firm characteristics (Topic 4), despite being a smaller topic, comes up equally often among the ten most-cited papers and much more often among the 20 most-cited papers. Conversely, large topics that do not generate much interest in the research community in terms of citations appear to be Assurance/audit and integrated reporting (Topic 2) and Public accountability, NGOs and social values (Topic 3).

Next, we turn to the evolution of topics over time. We have grouped the articles in five-year intervals to avoid drawing misleading conclusions as a result of having few articles in the early

Table 24.4   Topic overview

Topic #	The nine topics of the corpus	Top 10 articles	Top 20 articles	Average prob. (%)
1	CSR and valuation	4	4	21.1
2	Assurance/audit and integrated reporting	1	1	16.7
3	Public accountability, NGOs and social values		1	13.4
4	Environmental and social disclosure and firm characteristics	4	7	14.1
5	Organizational practices and social/environmental accounting	1	2	11.6
6	Environmental and social disclosure and legitimization strategies		2	11.2
7	Materiality and stakeholder engagement		1	7.1
8	Diversity in corporate boards		1	3.8
9	Critical perspectives on sustainability and socio-political processes		1	1.0
	Total	10	20	100

Note: This table presents the nine topics identified in the corpus (ordered by size), the number of articles among the top ten and 20 cited that are assigned to a given topic (based on the dominant topics), and the average probability of any given article belonging to a given topic.

years, and these receiving undue weight (see Table 24.1 for a sample distribution over time). We can see from Figure 24.3 that Topic 1 and Topic 2 have not only grown the most over the years, but Topic 1 has also become relatively more dominant since 2010 (crowding out other topics), and, prior to 2005, Topic 2, Assurance/audit and integrated reporting, did not figure at all. This is consistent with assurance and integrated reporting being relatively recent concepts.

As for how topics vary by journal, we focus on the top ten journals in terms of citation counts (Figure 24.4). Consistent with the overall focus of the journal, and unsurprisingly, the top journals in this context (AAAJ and AOS) place comparatively less weight on the largest topic (CSR and valuation) and relatively more weight on the topic related to public accountability and social values (Topic 3) and stakeholder engagement (Topic 7). Valuation issues (i.e., Topic 1) receive more attention in BAR, JAPP, EAR and TAR. None of the top four journals (AAAJ, AOS, BAR and CAP) focus on audit and assurance (Topic 2), while the remaining six all do. AOS and CPA stand out in their focus on organizational practices (Topic 5) while AAAJ and BAR are leading in terms of articles focusing on legitimization strategies (Topic 6).

We conclude this section by examining the top ten most-influential papers in this field, based on their citation counts. These papers were published in highly ranked journals including TAR, AOS, EAR, and BAR. Most of these papers employ empirical research methods and statistical analysis. Their primary focus lies on voluntary disclosures, as the time frame pre-dates any requirements for non-financial disclosures. Considering that our literature review centers around the role of stakeholders, these papers are built on the underlying assumption that the extent of non-financial disclosures is influenced by public pressures and the relative significance of stakeholder groups. Consequently, legitimacy theory, along with theories of public pressure and stakeholder engagement, is frequently employed as the main theoretical framework. Moreover, we observe a clear alignment between the primary focus of these papers and the predominant topic addressed in each one, which serves to validate our topic modeling approach. Papers such as Dhaliwal et al. (2011; 2012), Haniffa and Cooke

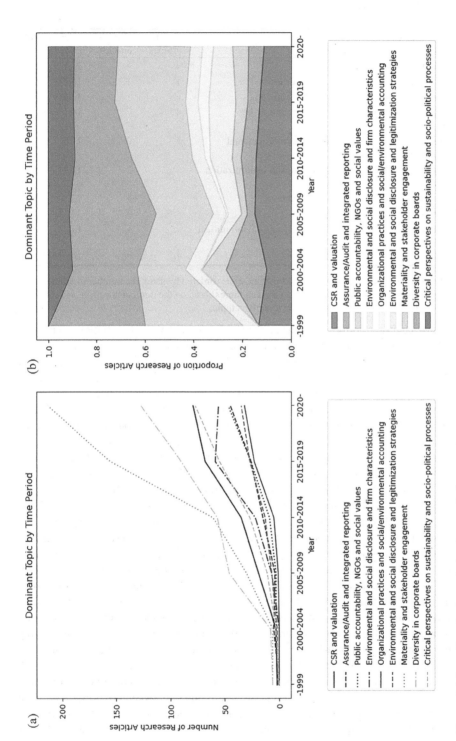

Figure 24.3   Dominant topic by time period

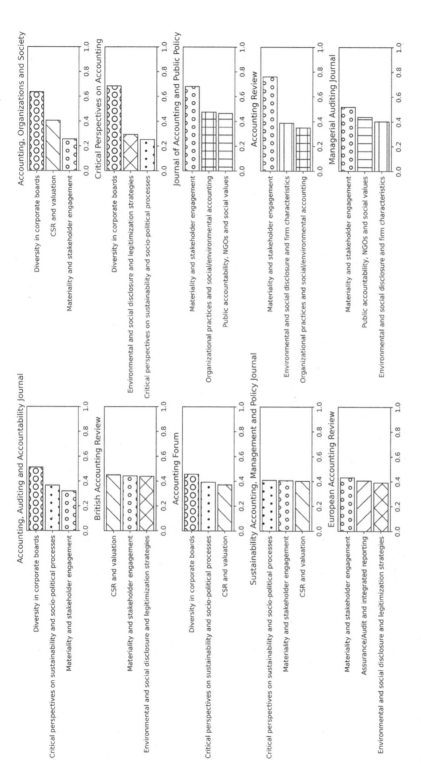

Figure 24.4   Topics by journal

Table 24.5   Top ten articles based on number of citations

Authors	Titles	Source title	Cited by	Method type	Theory used	Dominant topic
Dhaliwal et al. (2011)	Voluntary nonfinancial disclosure and the cost of equity capital: the initiation of corporate social responsibility reporting	Accounting Review	1648	statistical/archival	Voluntary disclosure theory	CSR and valuation
Neu et al. (1998)	Managing public impressions: environmental disclosures in annual reports	Accounting, Organizations and Society	1015	meso-level empirical illustration	Public pressure and legitimacy theory	Environmental and social disclosure and firm characteristics
Cho & Patten (2007)	The role of environmental disclosures as tools of legitimacy: a research note	Accounting, Organizations and Society	1002	statistical/archival	Legitimacy theory	Environmental and social disclosure and firm characteristics
Haniffa & Cooke (2005)	The impact of culture and governance on corporate social reporting	Journal of Accounting and Public Policy	984	statistical/archival	Legitimacy theory	CSR and valuation
Dhaliwal et al. (2012)	Nonfinancial disclosure and analyst forecast accuracy: international evidence on corporate social responsibility disclosure	Accounting Review	788	statistical/archival	Stakeholder theory/disclosure theory	CSR and valuation
Simnett et al. (2009)	Assurance on sustainability reports: an international comparison	Accounting Review	715	statistical/archival	Agency theory	Assurance/audit and integrated reporting
Gray (2010)	Is accounting for sustainability actually accounting for sustainability … and how would we know? An exploration of narratives of organisations and the planet	Accounting, Organizations and Society	657	Non-empirical/theoretical		Organizational practices and social/environmental accounting
Liao et al. (2015)	Gender diversity, board independence, environmental committee and greenhouse gas disclosure	British Accounting Review	583	statistical/archival	Stakeholder theory	CSR and valuation
Cormier et al. (2005)	Environmental disclosure quality in large German companies: economic incentives, public pressures or institutional conditions?	European Accounting Review	576	statistical/archival	Public pressure and institutional theory	Environmental and social disclosure and firm characteristics
Adams et al. (1998)	Corporate social reporting practices in western Europe: legitimating corporate behaviour?	British Accounting Review	520	content analysis, statistical/archival	Legitimacy theory	Environmental and social disclosure and firm characteristics

Note: This table provides the top ten publications in our literature review, based on the number of citations.

(2005), and Liao et al. (2015) distinctly concentrate on aspects such as profitability, firm value, analysts, shareholders, and board of directors. In these cases, the dominant topic is CSR and valuation. Another prevalent topic is Environmental and social disclosure and firm characteristics, which covers papers that focus on environmental disclosures and the driving incentives for providing them in companies (see Neu et al., 1998; Cho and Patten, 2007; Cormier et al., 2005). Finally, Simnett et al. (2009) specifically address how assurance on sustainability reporting enhances credibility of reporting and corporate reputation, making Assurance/audit and integrated reporting the dominant topic associated with their study.

4   STAKEHOLDER GROUPS

Stakeholders can be classified into different categories based on their level of involvement and impact on the organization. Here, we focus on the appearance of stakeholders in the abstracts and keywords of articles in our sample review.[3] The main categories of stakeholders are shown in Table 24.6, along with examples of keywords used to identify the stakeholder groups. Additionally, we report the number of articles corresponding to each stakeholder category. As anticipated, most of the papers concentrate on capital providers (with a primary focus on investors) and regulatory bodies. Social stakeholders, such as communities, local organizations, and non-governmental organizations (NGOs), follow closely in terms of the frequency of their mentions. Lastly, internal stakeholders, including employees, management, customers, and suppliers, rank lower on the list in terms of their representation within the corpus.

In the last column, we present the two dominant topics based on the classification of papers into stakeholder groups. We observe that in the management group, the dominant topic focuses on organizational practices, with literature primarily examining the role of top executives in promoting sustainability practices within organizations. Regarding capital providers, the dominant topic is CSR and valuation, encompassing findings that highlight the importance of CSR in valuation models and credit decisions made by capital providers. For the customers and suppliers, the topics of CSR and valuation and legitimization strategies are at the forefront. For mediating groups, such as the media and employees, CSR and valuation once again remains a core topic, alongside a focus on Environmental and social disclosure and firm characteristics. Notably, for stakeholder groups indirectly involved in organizational practices, such as NGOs and public communities, there is no emphasis on valuation. Instead, topics such as public accountability and integrated reporting emerge as the primary themes.

Figure 24.5 shows the publication trend for each stakeholder group. There is a relatively greater increase in the number of papers referring to capital providers and policymakers, and to a more modest extent, NGOs. The stakeholder groups represented by the lowest number of articles in our sample are employees and customers and suppliers.

Subsequently, we present a selection of findings from recent papers under each group of stakeholders.

Capital Providers

Investors
The association between investors' valuation and CSR disclosures and performance has been extensively studied in sustainability research. Previous studies have demonstrated that inves-

Table 24.6   Stakeholder groups

Stakeholder group	#Papers	Example of stakeholders	First two dominant topics
Capital providers	507	Institutional investors, analysts, board of directors, family owners, mutual funds, venture capitalist, foreign investors, financial institutions, banks	CSR and valuation Environmental and social disclosure and firm characteristics
Policymakers	480	Government, regulator, public sector, ministry, state, politician, authority, municipal, standard-setters	Assurance/audit and integrated reporting CSR and valuation
Non-governmental organizations (NGOs)	228	NGO, IPCC, IIRC, GRI, WWF, UNICEF, Greenpeace, Amnesty, nonprofit, non-governmental, charity	Public accountability, NGOs and social values Assurance/audit and integrated reporting
Communities and people	167	Community, indigenous, resident, society, people	Public accountability, NGOs and social values Organizational practices and social/environmental accounting
Mediating institutions (media)	161	Media, web, public forum, press, news	Environmental and social disclosure and firm characteristics CSR and valuation
Management	150	CEO, CFO, accountant, entrepreneur, senior managers, top executives, accounting professional	Organizational practices and social/environmental accounting Assurance/audit and integrated reporting
Employees and labor organizations	93	Employee, union worker, whistleblower	CSR and valuation Environmental and social disclosure and firm characteristics
Customers and suppliers (business partners)	59	Customer, supplier, producer, competitor, subsidiary, retailer	CSR and valuation Environmental and social disclosure and legitimization strategies

tors have social preferences and use ESG information to value their investments (Dhaliwal et al., 2011; 2014; Qiu et al., 2016). Dhaliwal et al. (2014) show a negative correlation between CSR disclosures and the cost of capital, particularly in stakeholder-oriented countries. This is because larger stakeholder groups demand high-quality non-financial information, and management is more likely to provide it. In a recent study, He et al. (2022) highlight the need to explore the influence of country-specific climate policies on investors' perceptions, and show that in countries with no solid climate change policy, minimizing carbon emission investments is perceived to be value destroying.

In addition to the value implications of CSR disclosures, there is another body of research that investigates how various types of investors drive CSR strategies in companies. In this context, the role of large shareholders is often examined, as they may have power vis-à-vis the board and management. For instance, Zhang et al. (2021) examine the role of institutional investors in corporate decisions in promoting voluntary water disclosures and how such disclosures can be used as a tool for implementing self-regulation. In another study, Muniandy et al. (2023) examined the role of state ownership and found that firms with governmental

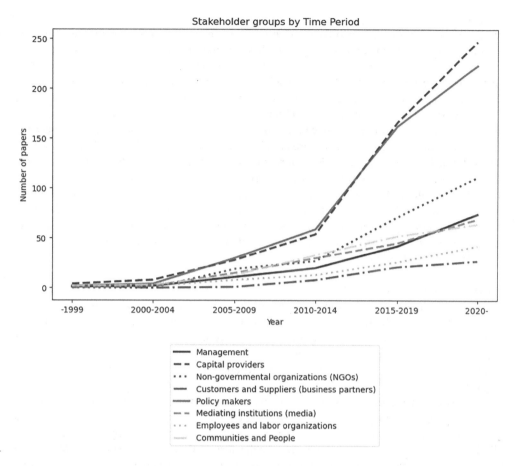

Figure 24.5   Stakeholder groups by time period

shareholdings are associated with a higher level of ESG disclosures than those without governmental shareholdings.

Corporate boards

The board of directors and its structure have long been the focus of accounting and finance research. Boards, as representatives of investors, not only play an important role in addressing governance issues but also advise management in promoting CSR practices. Haque (2017) focuses on board independence and gender diversity and provides evidence for favorable practices regarding carbon reduction efforts. They show that an ESG compensation policy is a way for the board to incentivize managers to follow carbon reduction initiatives. Khoo et al. (2022) show that a higher proportion of independent directors is associated with better CSR performance. This association is particularly significant for firms that are more visible and face greater external CSR pressure. In another study, Khoo et al. (2023) indicate that CSR committee members receive more support from shareholders, through their votes, compared to other directors.

Banks

While financial institutions and banks have faced much scrutiny in evaluating the long-term stability of firms, little is known about how they integrate ESG performance and disclosures into their lending decisions. Eliwa et al. (2021) provide supporting evidence that lending institutions use ESG performance and disclosure as inputs for their credit decision models. However, they could not find any differences between the effects of ESG performance and ESG disclosures on lowering the cost of debt. They argue that while these institutions value ESG practices, a distinction between companies' "symbolic" practices and "substantive" ones may be difficult, as disclosures are largely discretionary. Nevertheless, Wei et al. (2023) suggest that firms with better CSR performance have better access to trade credit, as better CSR performance reduces firms' systematic risk, making them more attractive to lenders. In addition to the influence of banks on credit decisions, sustainability issues within banks are also examined. Moufty et al. (2021) investigate various sustainability dimensions of US banks and find a significant positive relationship between the internal social dimensions of sustainability and bank performance. However, they did not find any effect with respect to these environmental dimensions.

Analysts and auditors

As CSR information becomes more relevant in investors' decision-making, the role of assurance and audits of such information becomes prevalent. Clarkson, P., et al. (2019) demonstrate that firms with a strong commitment to CSR are more inclined to provide independent CSR reports and adopt a more comprehensive assurance scope. Furthermore, it appears that capital market participants value the provision of a CSR report when it is assured by a Big 4 accounting firm.

Other studies have examined the role of analysts in relation to CSR information. Bernardi and Stark (2018a) show that integrated reporting (IR) has a positive impact on users' perceptions, including analysts' forecasts. This is primarily driven by the extent of environmental disclosure and, to a lesser degree, governance disclosure. Bernardi and Stark (2018b) further explore the connection between the levels of disclosure on environmental and social activities and performance and the subsequent analyst following, supporting a correlation between these disclosures and their value relevance. Overall, these studies suggest that environmental and social disclosures can play a significant role in shaping analysts' perceptions.

Policymakers and Regulators

Previous papers on the role of regulation provide evidence for both the costs and benefits of mandatory CSR policies. As for the benefits, Liu et al. (2017) find that a regulation stipulating the disclosure of greenhouse gas emissions in Australia had a positive impact on the voluntary disclosure of climate change-related information. Regarding potential costs, Rajgopal and Tantri (2023) examine CSR requirements newly imposed by the government in India and find that firms that engaged in CSR voluntarily before the mandate reduced their CSR spending after the mandate. The lost signaling value of voluntary CSR led to a decline in stock prices and operating performance for these firms. There is also evidence of firms meeting minimum requirements under mandatory regimes. Adler et al. (2022) note that while there was a significant increase in waste management reporting by Indian companies following a national waste management campaign in 2014, the initial level of reporting was notably low. Furthermore,

Appiagyei and Donkor (2024) find that although there is a positive relationship between the quality of integrated reporting and sustainability performance under the mandatory regime in South Africa, this relationship is weaker among environmentally sensitive firms.

Stolowy and Paugam (2018) point out that stakeholders are also concerned with the rise of too much irrelevant non-financial information, also known as "information overload", in the disclosure literature. Accordingly, they explore the diversity in definitions and practices of non-financial reporting (NFR) and highlight that considerable heterogeneity exists in how NFR concepts are defined among regulators, standard-setters, and leading sustainable firms. Linked to the lack of convergence in definitions of NFR, they also show that the NFR practices of leading sustainable firms vary substantially. Furthermore, the extent to which regulatory bodies in developing countries can influence CSR practices is relatively unexplored in previous accounting research. Lauwo et al. (2022) find that Tanzania's hierarchical and dysfunctional national-level meta-governance structures dominated the localization of the Sustainable Development Goals (SDGs), blocking achievement of the SDGs due to a lack of coordination mechanisms.

Apart from the effects of regulations and standards, the changes in CSR practices due to changes in the political environment of countries is an interesting topic of research. Antonini et al. (2021) analyze the climate change disclosures of large US firms in standalone CSR reports during the pre-Trump (2014–2015) and Trump (2017–2018) eras. The results indicate that, on average, the extent of climate change disclosures did not change significantly between the two eras, indicating that policy interventions may not significantly affect firms and their policies regarding CSR disclosures. However, cross-sectional analysis reveals that companies headquartered in states that strongly supported Trump in the 2016 election had more negative changes in disclosures compared to other firms. Studying the Chinese setting, Situ et al. (2021) shed light on the relationship between the Chinese government's political ideology and the CSR practices of Chinese companies, based on the role of symbolic power. They show how devotion to political ideology can help companies accumulate symbolic and economic capital, resulting in Chinese companies symbolically providing corporate environmental reporting.

Non-Governmental Organizations (NGOs)

The role of NGOs is growing in significance as they shape the CSR practices of firms. The Global Reporting Initiative (GRI) is arguably the most influential non-governmental organization that has impacted CSR disclosures. The GRI is commonly adopted voluntarily, especially among large firms. According to KPMG's (2022) survey, 78% of G250 firms (the world's 250 largest companies based on the Fortune 500 ranking) and 68% of N100 firms (top 100 firms with the highest revenue in 58 countries) apply GRI standards. However, the question remains whether GRI guidelines have been adopted and implemented effectively or if they are merely used for impression management. For example, Moussa et al. (2022) examine a sample of UK firms and show that particularly those in environmentally sensitive sectors tend to disclose soft or semi-hard environmental targets as a symbolic gesture to manage stakeholder perceptions and legitimize their existence. Additionally, positive associations are observed between environmental target disclosures and GRI guidelines, indicating that such voluntary practices may be a symbolic action rather than a genuine one. In another study, Parsa et al. (2018) examine the effectiveness of GRI guidelines pertaining to labor and human rights reporting and find limited evidence of corporations fulfilling their accountability towards their workforce.

Other than the GRI, the role of other NGOs in various institutional settings has been examined. In Malaysia, Ang and Wickramasinghe (2022) conducted a study over a nine-month period of fieldwork at a river-care program run by an NGO. Their study indicates that in cases of conflict, coordination efforts by NGOs have provided opportunities for dialogic accounting practices and transformed "perceived accountability" into "adaptive accountability". In another study, Sidhu and Gibbon (2021) investigate the ways in which accounting practices for sustainable development in Malaysian organizations contribute to decoupling economic growth from ecological impacts, and demonstrate how the organizational approach to sustainable development is institutionalized and mediated.

Communities and People

Sustainability issues, whether environmental or social, are ultimately linked to people. A significant question is therefore how corporations engage with people, especially considering that people often lack power in the decision-making processes of corporations. In a cross-country comparison study, Eliwa et al. (2021) find that firms with higher ESG performance have lower costs of debt, particularly in countries where the community plays a more influential role (i.e., stakeholder-oriented countries). Specifically, they provide evidence that the impact of ESG performance and disclosure on the cost of debt is more prominent in stakeholder-oriented countries where the community has a stronger presence. Gaia and Jones (2017) discuss the perception and raising of awareness of biodiversity among local councils in the UK and show that these councils primarily view biodiversity in terms of its instrumental value, emphasizing how biodiversity is useful to humans, such as for human welfare or resource conservation. The authors stress the importance of raising awareness among key local stakeholders, including landowners, residents, visitors, businesses, and industries, as they can contribute to biodiversity conservation efforts.

Focusing on social dimensions, Goncharenko (2023) studies the impact of the #MeToo movement on how organizations are held accountable for sexual misconduct in the workplace. The study highlights the role of community activists in raising public awareness and shaping organizational accountability for sexual misconduct. Overall, this study emphasizes the importance of community activism arising from social movements and how it translates into increased demands for organizational accountability.

Mediating Institutions (Media)

The role of the media in pressuring firms to be more forthcoming with transparent information has been documented in research. When corporations receive media coverage, it can increase public awareness of their activities. If corporations do not address the issues raised by the media, it can lead to reputational damage and negatively impact the value of the company.

Paananen at al. (2021) show that firms' disclosures of environmental liabilities become more specific when they face more media exposure. Despite the mandatory nature of disclosures of environmental liabilities (as required under IAS 37), the authors observe diversity in disclosure practices across industries and regions, and thus argue that print media can exercise an important supervisory role by putting pressure on firms. Manetti and Bellucci (2016) examine social media platforms, such as Facebook, Twitter, and YouTube, and how effective they are as tools for stakeholder engagement. The study focuses on online interactions between organizations and their stakeholders and finds that while some organizations use social media to engage stakeholders in defining the contents of their sustainability reports, the level of interaction is generally low. In a similar study, Landi et al. (2021) provide evidence that social media has been extensively used as a public engagement tool in Italy, the United Kingdom, and New Zealand, but only in New Zealand has it been used as a dialogic accounting tool. This suggests that there may be legitimacy threats and resource scarcity that are preventing other countries from using social media in this way.

Although there is plenty of evidence indicating that the media can act as a potential watchdog to companies and their wrongdoing regarding CSR practices (e.g., Elijido-Ten, 2011; Islam and Deegan, 2010), there is also evidence of manipulation of the media by large influential companies. For example, Cao et al. (2022) examine Chinese companies with high CSR rankings in the media and find that these firms pay higher advertising expenses while also having poorer environmental performance. Their results point to the use of the media to greenwash their image to gain economic benefits.

Management

Top executives, particularly CEOs, play a significant role in defining the CSR policies of their companies and the institutionalization process of sustainability practices (Higgins et al., 2014). Previous research shows that CEOs' power, their ethical ideology, and their attitudes towards CSR practices are among the factors that explain variations in companies' CSR. Li et al. (2018) find that CEOs' power strengthens the association between environmental, social, and governance (ESG) disclosure and firm value. This indicates that stakeholders perceive ESG disclosures from firms with more powerful CEOs as a sign of greater commitment to ESG practices. CEOs' power is also shown to be associated with a higher proportion of non-financial performance targets (Bachmann et al., 2020). Other studies that focus on the role of CEOs provide evidence for CSR performance improving upon the arrival of CSR champions (executives with superior CSR practices) (Feng and Malik, 2020), and higher CSR scores in firms run by non-materialistic CEOs (Davidson et al., 2019).

A change in the attitudes of CEOs towards taking a broader stakeholder group into consideration is also found to improve CSR practices. Agoglia et al. (2022) show that in firms that consider a broader range of stakeholders, including communities and the environment, managers are not only committed to CSR practices but also have a lower level of upward and downward earnings management. This is explained by CSR considerations influencing individuals' decisions to minimize self-serving interests. However, there is also evidence of a lack of accountability as ESG disclosures are subject to a great deal of discretion. For instance, Barkemeyer et al. (2014) reveal that the rhetoric used by CEOs in sustainability reports is primarily geared towards impression management rather than accountability, despite the growing standardization of sustainability reporting.

Employees

Among studies that examine employees, there are those that focus on employees' perception of CSR, treating them similarly to other corporate insiders, and those that consider employees as a specific stakeholder group within the social domain. Belonging to the first group, Wang and Yan (2022) examine how employee "quality" is associated with CSR engagement and find that firms with a high-quality workforce have greater CSR engagement, particularly among firms with high-value human capital. Additionally, the study identifies employees' bargaining power and monitoring role as potential channels through which employee quality affects CSR. Presley et al. (2018) investigate the impact of a company's sustainability practices on job seekers' perceptions of the company as a potential employer. The results suggest that sustainability and its underlying dimensions have a significant influence on the attractiveness of a company to potential employees.

Disclosures about employees in corporate reports are at times found to be inadequate or misleading. For instance, narratives about employees in CEOs' letters are studied by Mäkelä (2013), who examines the largest 25 Finnish companies. The analysis reveals that CEOs' letters often provide a limited view of employees, depicting them as having a narrow, mechanistic role in achieving growth and development that is of instrumental value to the companies, rather than recognizing them as complex individuals with diverse qualities and needs.

On the other hand, mediating organizations that support the interests of employees, such as labor unions and media, are shown to drive changes with respect to employee well-being, as well as reporting them. The presence of union or employee representatives on the board, which is a common practice among Swedish firms, is studied by Samani et al. (2023). They find that the presence of employee representation on the board and the implementation of the NFRD have a positive impact on the extent and quality of employee-related disclosures by companies, while firms with employee representatives also have more precise disclosures. In examining the role of the media in providing employee-related information in reports, Coetzee and Van Staden (2011) investigate safety disclosures made by South African mining companies in their annual reports, sustainability reports, and reactive corporate press releases following two significant mining accidents. The study finds that organizations respond to perceived legitimacy threats by increasing their safety disclosures.

Customers and Suppliers

Attracting customers is an important matter for firms when it comes to achieving sustainability goals. Prior research illustrates how CSR is used as a marketing tool to differentiate firms and gain a competitive advantage in a crowded marketplace. However, whether CSR reporting is only used as a marketing tool or is representative of actual changes in sustainability practices remains a question. The findings of a recent study by Yu and Zheng (2022) support the notion that CSR reporting can lead to economic benefits for firms, in addition to the potential social and environmental benefits.

Regarding the role of suppliers, there is a consensus that suppliers' engagement in sustainable development can drive significant changes in firms and in shaping their CSR practices. Wei et al (2023) show that higher CSR performance enhances trust from suppliers, who may be more willing to provide trade credit to firms they trust. Darendeli et al. (2022) examine the effect of a CSR information shock on suppliers' business relationships with corporate customers. The study finds that suppliers with lower CSR ratings experienced negative effects, including reductions in the number of contracts and corporate customers. The authors suggest that this effect could be explained by two mechanisms: benchmarking of suppliers' CSR by corporate customers and public pressure on customer–supplier contracting related to CSR. Furthermore, Roy et al. (2023) show that when subsidiaries of multinational corporations operate in regions with weak institutional pressures and low stakeholder awareness, they have more autonomy to apply global CSR practices that may not necessarily align with local needs and values. The study highlights the importance of considering the role of local stakeholders and institutions in shaping CSR practices.

5   SUMMARY AND CONCLUSIONS

With this literature review, we have aimed to provide researchers with a comprehensive overview of the literature on sustainability reporting for a variety of stakeholders. In this chapter, we presented the results from a bibliometric analysis of accounting publications related to sustainability reporting and stakeholders; the topics that are commonly addressed in this literature; and key research findings for each pre-identified stakeholder group.

In the bibliometric analysis, we identified the journals with the most numerous and most cited publications in the field, which included primarily *Accounting, Auditing and Accountability Journal* (AAAJ), *British Accounting Review* (BAR), *Critical Perspectives on Accounting* (CPA), *Accounting Forum* (AF), and *Sustainability Accounting, Management and Policy Journal* (SAMPJ). The methods applied in the literature were examined, revealing that only 16% of the papers were non-empirical. Among the empirical papers, approximately half utilized quantitative methods, a quarter used qualitative methods, and the remainder applied mixed methods or did not specify the empirical method in the abstract. It was found that prominent theories in the accounting literature include legitimacy, institutional, and stakeholder theories. Additionally, there are nearly 100 variations of less commonly used theories, such as "culture toolkit theory", "Gaia theory", "social contract theory", and "social identity theory".

In the topic analysis, we identified nine topics in the literature (in descending order of size): CSR and valuation, Assurance/audit and integrated reporting, Public accountability, NGOs and social values, Environmental and social disclosure and firm characteristics, Organizational practices and social/environmental accounting, Environmental and social disclosure and legitimization strategies, Materiality and stakeholder engagement, Diversity in corporate boards, and Critical perspectives on sustainability and socio-political processes. A trend analysis shows that CSR and valuation is an area in the sustainability literature that is not only dominant, but growing in popularity. Emerging areas of interest include integrated reporting and assurance of sustainability reporting, consistent with regulatory developments. From some of the topics it is possible to make connections to stakeholder groups.

Finally, we systematically categorized papers based on which stakeholder groups were concerned. The eight stakeholder groups were inductively generated based on a keyword search of stakeholder-related terms from our sampled papers. These groups (in descending order based on the number of publications) are Capital providers (507), Policymakers (480), Non-governmental organizations (NGOs) (228), Communities and people (167), Mediating institutions (media) (161), Management (150), Employees and labor organizations (93), and Customers and suppliers (business partners) (59). The stakeholder groups partly echo the findings of the topic analysis, where capital providers are a dominant group, followed by NGOs and the general public. Policymakers, though an important stakeholder group, do not appear in any particular topic but are likely spread over multiple topics.

In our presentation of key findings from the literature, we have grouped the literature based on stakeholder focus. Overall, these papers show the mechanisms under which stakeholders can exert pressure on companies to change CSR practices. For example, CEOs' power and attitudes towards CSR, institutional investors, employee representation on the board, community activism, reporting guidelines (e.g., GRI) and other initiatives from NGOs, are all shown to influence ESG performance and disclosure. Some studies also discuss that CSR reporting has been used as a marketing tool to differentiate firms, gain a competitive advantage, attract customers, and build trust with suppliers. The heterogeneity implied by the many and varied determinants of CSR outcomes has triggered a call for mandatory ESG disclosures. It remains to be seen whether initiatives such as the EU's Corporate Sustainability Reporting Directive (CSRD) can harmonize practices, especially with many potential standards and regulatory bodies contending for the position as top player.

Based on the analysis presented in this chapter, we propose three avenues for future research. Firstly, in alignment with the principle of double materiality, researchers should furnish additional empirical evidence demonstrating how various stakeholders, extending beyond investors, exert influence on information outcomes and accountability. The ultimate expectation is that, if companies embrace responsibility, observable shifts in organizational practices towards more sustainable approaches should follow. That is, while disclosures based on single materiality assessments have been examined by referring to market reactions, disclosures based on double materiality assessments must be evaluated in terms of their effectiveness in contributing to sustainable development within the organization.

Secondly, drawing from our examination of existing studies, we challenge future research to assess the cost-effectiveness of disclosures and the regulation thereof, recognizing that disclosure alone may not ensure substantial changes in organizational practices. As the volume of sustainability reporting increases (following recent regulatory developments), future research should undertake cost–benefit analyses and explore the broader economic implications of expanded reporting and regulatory frameworks. The absence of cost–benefit analyses for sustainability information underscores the challenges in conducting such assessments. However, it would be wasteful to allow such complexities to impede progress.

Thirdly, our bibliometric study highlights the dominance of a limited number of established theories from management and finance (legitimacy theory, institutional theory, and stakeholder theory). We contend that these theories primarily focus on the preparer's perspective, explaining reporting choices, and may not be the most fitting for understanding how stakeholders interpret sustainability disclosures. Future work should strive to go beyond these familiar frameworks, either by employing other theories identified in our review or by attempting to develop new theories. The consideration of stakeholders has historically been lacking in a reporting context, but in this new era, it is imperative to foster new ways of thinking.

NOTES

1. We recognize that the evolving terminology in this field over time may lead to the potential exclusion of relevant papers from our research. Therefore, we acknowledge this as a limitation.
2. A comprehensive list of papers may be obtained upon request.
3. We exclude the last sentence of the abstract in our keyword search, as it is likely that this sentence refers to stakeholders, but merely includes generic information regarding the implication of the study, rather than being about those stakeholders.

REFERENCES

Adams, C. A., Hill, W. Y., and Roberts, C. B. (1998). Corporate social reporting practices in Western Europe: legitimating corporate behaviour? *British Accounting Review*, *30*(1), 1–21.

Adler, R., Mansi, M., and Pandey, R. (2022). Accounting for waste management: a study of the reporting practices of the top listed Indian companies. *Accounting & Finance*, *62*(2), 2401–2437.

Agoglia, C. P., Beaudoin, C. A., Kuselias, S., and Tsakumis, G. T. (2022). Can corporate social responsibility counteract managers' incentives to manage earnings? *Journal of Accounting, Auditing & Finance*, 0148558X221110672.

Agostini, M., Costa, E., and Korca, B. (2022). Non-financial disclosure and corporate financial performance under Directive 2014/95/EU: evidence from Italian listed companies. *Accounting in Europe*, *19*(1), 78–109.

Ang, S. Y., and Wickramasinghe, D. (2022). Ethical disputes, coordinating acts and NGO accountability: evidence from an NGO river-care programme in Malaysia. *Critical Perspectives on Accounting*, 102416.

Antonini, C., Olczak, W., and Patten, D. M. (2021). Corporate climate change disclosure during the Trump administration: evidence from standalone CSR reports. *Accounting Forum*, *45*(2), 118–141.

Appiagyei, K., and Donkor, A. (2024). Integrated reporting quality and sustainability performance: does firms' environmental sensitivity matter? *Journal of Accounting in Emerging Economies*, *14*(1), 25–47.

Bachmann, R. L., Loyeung, A., Matolcsy, Z. P., and Spiropoulos, H. (2020). Powerful CEOs, cash bonus contracts and firm performance. *Journal of Business Finance & Accounting*, *47*(1–2), 100–131.

Barkemeyer, R., Comyns, B., Figge, F., and Napolitano, G. (2014). CEO statements in sustainability reports: substantive information or background noise? *Accounting Forum*, *38*(4), 241–257.

Bernardi, C., and Stark, A. W. (2018a). Environmental, social and governance disclosure, integrated reporting, and the accuracy of analyst forecasts. *British Accounting Review*, *50*(1), 16–31.

Bernardi, C., and Stark, A. W. (2018b). On the value relevance of information on environmental and social activities and performance – some evidence from the UK stock market. *Journal of Accounting and Public Policy*, *37*(4), 282–299.

Blei, D. M., Ng, A. Y., and Jordan, M. I. (2003). Latent Dirichlet allocation. *Journal of Machine Learning Research*, *3*, 993–1022.

Cao, J., Faff, R., He, J., and Li, Y. (2022). Who's greenwashing via the media and what are the consequences? Evidence from China. *Abacus*, *58*(4), 759–786.

Cho, C. H., and Patten, D. M. (2007). The role of environmental disclosures as tools of legitimacy: a research note. *Accounting, Organizations and Society*, *32*(7–8), 639–647.

Clarkson, M. B. (1995). A stakeholder framework for analyzing and evaluating corporate social performance. *Academy of Management Review*, *20*(1), 92–117.

Clarkson, P., Li, Y., Richardson, G., and Tsang, A. (2019). Causes and consequences of voluntary assurance of CSR reports: international evidence involving Dow Jones Sustainability Index inclusion and firm valuation. *Accounting, Auditing & Accountability Journal*, *32*(8), 2451–2474.

Coetzee, C. M., and Van Staden, C. J. (2011). Disclosure responses to mining accidents: South African evidence. *Accounting Forum*, *35*(4), 232–246.

Cormier, D., Magnan, M., and Van Velthoven, B. (2005). Environmental disclosure quality in large German companies: economic incentives, public pressures or institutional conditions? *European Accounting Review*, *14*(1), 3–39.

Cuomo, F., Gaia, S., Girardone, C., and Piserà, S. (2024). The effects of the EU Non-Financial Reporting Directive on corporate social responsibility. *European Journal of Finance*, *30*(7), 726–752.

Davidson, R. H., Dey, A., and Smith, A. J. (2019). CEO materialism and corporate social responsibility. *The Accounting Review*, *94*(1), 101–126.

Darendeli, A., Fiechter, P., Hitz, J. M., and Lehmann, N. (2022). The role of corporate social responsibility (CSR) information in supply-chain contracting: evidence from the expansion of CSR rating coverage. *Journal of Accounting and Economics*, *74*(2–3), 101525.

Dhaliwal, D. S., Li, O. Z., Tsang, A., & Yang, Y. G. (2011). Voluntary nonfinancial disclosure and the cost of equity capital: the initiation of corporate social responsibility reporting. *The Accounting Review*, *86*(1), 59–100.

Dhaliwal, D. S., Radhakrishnan, S., Tsang, A., and Yang, Y. G. (2012). Nonfinancial disclosure and analyst forecast accuracy: international evidence on corporate social responsibility disclosure. *The Accounting Review, 87*(3), 723–759.

Dhaliwal, D., Li, O. Z., Tsang, A., and Yang, Y. G. (2014). Corporate social responsibility disclosure and the cost of equity capital: the roles of stakeholder orientation and financial transparency. *Journal of Accounting and Public Policy, 33*(4), 328–355.

Elijido-Ten, E. (2011). Media coverage and voluntary environmental disclosures: a developing country exploratory experiment. *Accounting Forum, 35*(3), 139–157.

Eliwa, Y., Aboud, A., and Saleh, A. (2021). ESG practices and the cost of debt: evidence from EU countries. *Critical Perspectives on Accounting, 79*, 102097.

Feng, N. C., and Malik, M. (2020). Carryforward effects of CSR champions. *Accounting Horizons, 34*(3), 113–128.

Fiandrino, S., Gromis di Trana, M., Tonelli, A., and Lucchese, A. (2022). The multi-faceted dimensions for the disclosure quality of non-financial information in revising Directive 2014/95/EU. *Journal of Applied Accounting Research, 23*(1), 274–300.

Freeman, R. E. (1984). *Strategic Management: A Stakeholder Approach*. London: Pitman.

Gaia, S., and Jones, M. J. (2017). UK local councils reporting of biodiversity values: a stakeholder perspective. *Accounting, Auditing & Accountability Journal, 30*(7), 1614–1638.

Goncharenko, G. (2023). The# MeToo legacy and "the Collective Us": conceptualising accountability for sexual misconduct at work. *Accounting, Auditing & Accountability Journal, 36*(7/8), 1814–1838.

Gray, R. (2010). Is accounting for sustainability actually accounting for sustainability … and how would we know? An exploration of narratives of organisations and the planet. *Accounting, Organizations and Society, 35*(1), 47–62.

Haniffa, R. M., and Cooke, T. E. (2005). The impact of culture and governance on corporate social reporting. *Journal of Accounting and Public Policy, 24*(5), 391–430.

Haque, F. (2017). The effects of board characteristics and sustainable compensation policy on carbon performance of UK firms. *British Accounting Review, 49*(3), 347–364.

He, R., Luo, L., Shamsuddin, A., and Tang, Q. (2022). The value relevance of corporate investment in carbon abatement: the influence of national climate policy. *European Accounting Review, 31*(5), 1233–1261.

Higgins, C., Stubbs, W., and Love, T. (2014). Walking the talk(s): organisational narratives of integrated reporting. *Accounting, Auditing & Accountability Journal, 27*(4), 1090–1119.

Islam, M. A., and Deegan, C. (2010). Media pressures and corporate disclosure of social responsibility performance information: a study of two global clothing and sports retail companies. *Accounting and Business Research, 40*(2), 131–148.

Khoo, E. S., Lim, Y., Lu, L. Y., and Monroe, G. S. (2022). Corporate social responsibility performance and the reputational incentives of independent directors. *Journal of Business Finance & Accounting, 49*(5–6), 841–881.

Khoo, E. S., Chen, L., and Monroe, G. S. (2023). Shareholder election of CSR committee members and its effects on CSR performance. *Journal of Business Finance & Accounting, 50*(3–4), 716–763.

KPMG (2022). *Big Shifts, Small Steps: Survey of Sustainability Reporting 2022*. Available at: https://assets.kpmg.com/content/dam/kpmg/xx/pdf/2022/10/ssr-small-steps-big-shifts.pdf.

Landi, S., Costantini, A., Fasan, M., and Bonazzi, M. (2021). Public engagement and dialogic accounting through social media during COVID-19 crisis: a missed opportunity? *Accounting, Auditing & Accountability Journal, 35*(1), 35–47.

Lauwo, S. G., Azure, J. D. C., and Hopper, T. (2022). Accountability and governance in implementing the Sustainable Development Goals in a developing country context: evidence from Tanzania. *Accounting, Auditing & Accountability Journal, 35*(6), 1431–1461.

Li, Y., Gong, M., Zhang, X. Y., and Koh, L. (2018). The impact of environmental, social, and governance disclosure on firm value: the role of CEO power. *British Accounting Review, 50*(1), 60–75.

Liao, L., Luo, L., and Tang, Q. (2015). Gender diversity, board independence, environmental committee and greenhouse gas disclosure. *British Accounting Review, 47*(4), 409–424.

Liu, Z., Abhayawansa, S., Jubb, C., and Perera, L. (2017). Regulatory impact on voluntary climate change–related reporting by Australian government-owned corporations. *Financial Accountability & Management, 33*(3), 264–283.

Manetti, G., and Bellucci, M. (2016). The use of social media for engaging stakeholders in sustainability reporting. *Accounting, Auditing & Accountability Journal*, *29*(6), 985–1011.

Moussa, T., Kotb, A., and Helfaya, A. (2022). An empirical investigation of UK environmental targets disclosure: The role of environmental governance and performance. *European Accounting Review*, *31*(4), 937–971.

Moufty, S., Clark, E., and Al-Najjar, B. (2021). The different dimensions of sustainability and bank performance: evidence from the EU and the USA. *Journal of International Accounting, Auditing and Taxation*, *43*, 100381.

Muniandy, B., Ali, M. J., Huang, H., and Obeng, V. A. (2023). Board generational cohorts, gender diversity and corporate environmental and social disclosures: evidence from China. *Journal of Accounting and Public Policy*, 107066.

Mäkelä, H. (2013). On the ideological role of employee reporting. *Critical Perspectives on Accounting*, *24*(4–5), 360–378.

Neu, D., Warsame, H., and Pedwell, K. (1998). Managing public impressions: environmental disclosures in annual reports. *Accounting, Organizations and Society*, *23*(3), 265–282.

Paananen, M., Runesson, E., and Samani, N. (2021). Time to clean up environmental liabilities reporting: disclosures, media exposure and market implications. *Accounting Forum*, *45*(1), 85–116.

Parsa, S., Roper, I., Muller-Camen, M., and Szigetvari, E. (2018). Have labour practices and human rights disclosures enhanced corporate accountability? The case of the GRI framework. *Accounting Forum 42*(1), 47–64.

Presley, A., Presley, T., and Blum, M. (2018). Sustainability and company attractiveness: a study of American college students entering the job market. *Sustainability Accounting, Management and Policy Journal*, *9*(4), 470–489.

Qiu, Y., Shaukat, A., and Tharyan, R. (2016). Environmental and social disclosures: link with corporate financial performance. *The British Accounting Review*, *48*(1), 102–116.

Rajgopal, S., and Tantri, P. (2023). Does a government mandate crowd out voluntary corporate social responsibility? Evidence from India. *Journal of Accounting Research*, *61*(1), 415–447.

Roy, T., Burchell, J., and Cook, J. (2023). Playing to the audience? Multilevel interactions between stakeholders and institutions around CSR in Bangladesh. *Accounting, Auditing & Accountability Journal*, *36*(2), 464–493.

Samani, N., Overland, C., and Sabelfeld, S. (2023). The role of the EU Non-Financial Reporting Directive and employee representation in employee-related disclosures. *Accounting Forum*, *47*(2), 278–306.

Sidhu, A. M., and Gibbon, J. (2021). Institutionalisation of weak conceptions of sustainability in the United Nations Clean Development Mechanism: empirical evidence from Malaysian organisations. *Accounting, Auditing & Accountability Journal*, *34*(5), 1220–1245.

Simnett, R., Vanstraelen, A., and Chua, W. F. (2009). Assurance on sustainability reports: an international comparison. *The Accounting Review*, *84*(3), 937–967.

Situ, H., Tilt, C., and Seet, P. S. (2021). The influence of the Chinese government's political ideology in the field of corporate environmental reporting. *Accounting, Auditing & Accountability Journal*, *34*(9), 1–28.

Stolowy, H., and Paugam, L. (2018). The expansion of non-financial reporting: an exploratory study. *Accounting and Business Research*, *48*(5), 525–548.

Wang, M., and Yan, W. (2022). Brain gain: the effect of employee quality on corporate social responsibility. *Abacus*, *58*(4), 679–713.

Wei, Y., Liu, Q., and Luo, J. (2023). How does corporate social responsibility have influence on firms' access to trade credit. *Accounting & Finance*, *63*(S1), 1321–1349.

Yu, W., and Zheng, Y. (2020). The disclosure of corporate social responsibility reports and sales performance in China. *Accounting & Finance*, *60*(2), 1239–1270.

Zhang, L., Tang, Q., and Huang, R. H. (2021). Mind the gap: is water disclosure a missing component of corporate social responsibility? *British Accounting Review*, *53*(1), 100940.

25. Analysing discourse in corporate sustainability reporting: linguistic insights

Emre Parlakkaya and Renata Stenka

1   INTRODUCTION

In this chapter, our main objective is to provide an overview of methodological developments and trends in the discourse-analytical accounting research,[1] with a specific focus on the accounting research studying language use in corporate sustainability disclosures. The discourse-analytical research is characterised by its breadth and a lack of precision (Loughran & McDonald, 2016). Furthermore, a substantial body of literature studies accounting-related language use in accounting journals, and this research area has been rapidly growing (Bochkay et al., 2023).

The data for such studies encompass a wide range of texts related to accounting and accountability, including, but not limited to, annual corporate reports, corporate press releases, earning announcements, and various media and social media publications (Bae et al., 2023). Recently, corporate sustainability disclosures, in particular corporate sustainability reports,[2] have garnered significant attention from accounting researchers.

The primary driver of this popularity is, firstly, the increasing significance and proliferation of sustainability reports over the last two decades (KPMG, 2020). The publication of corporate sustainability reports, occasionally under varying titles such as sustainable development reports and corporate social responsibility reports, has become a common practice among business organisations in both developed and developing countries (Buhr et al., 2014). It is important to note that while national and supra-national policies and regulations have played a vital role in this, companies have been publishing sustainability reports primarily on a voluntary basis, as an acknowledgment of an increasing importance to be, or at least be seen to be, 'sustainable' (A4S, 2021; Tregidga et al., 2014).

Secondly, sustainability reports, due to their more extensive narrative, represent a valuable data source for discourse studies when compared to more conventional, numerically oriented financial reports. In fact, a significant amount of accounting discourse research uses corporate sustainability disclosures as a main data source, with a particular focus on corporate sustainability reports. In addition, the advances in computational technologies further contributed to the convenience of studying language use (El-Haj et al., 2019). Thanks to the powerful yet user-friendly software tools, the retrieval, storage, and consistent analysis of textual data have become more feasible.

Here we attempt to contribute to the development of accounting discourse research on corporate sustainability disclosures by discussing the key methodological trends with their strengths as well as shortcomings. We then propose that the corpus linguistics approach be used in accounting discourse research by demonstrating how it could help address the shortcomings of existing methodological approaches that we have identified (McEnery & Hardie, 2012). The corpus linguistic approach to discourse has been acknowledged as a valuable method, and has been frequently applied to study language in other fields, such as communication and media studies (Baker, 2006; Baker et al., 2008). Nevertheless, it remains underutilised in accounting research, despite its recognised validity in other scholarly fields (Beattie, 2014; Stenka & Jaworska, 2019).

We will proceed by reviewing the relevant existing research within the extensive and rich discourse-analytical accounting literature, with a special emphasis on the studies that centre around corporate sustainability reporting. Afterwards, we will demonstrate the shortcomings of the methodological approaches used and suggest how novel (in accounting research) tools and techniques adopted from the corpus linguistics can address them (Baker, 2006). We will showcase corpus linguistics applications with some examples within the context of corporate sustainability reporting (Beattie, 2014). Finally, we will conclude our discussion by outlining potential future research directions for accounting scholars interested in utilising these novel linguistic insights in their work, particularly focusing on corporate sustainability disclosures or accounting texts in general.

2   EXISTING LITERATURE AND TRENDS IN ACCOUNTING LANGUAGE RESEARCH

In line with the 'narrative turn' in the social sciences, there has been an interest in studying language within the field of accounting (Lupu & Sandu, 2017). Considering accounting research that studies language and language use, two main methodological approaches become evident, namely the quantitative and qualitative strands of research. Each of these strands is guided by distinct analytical paradigms and is informed by different philosophical and theoretical foundations (Tregidga et al., 2012). It ought to be noted that they also occasionally intersect in the studies conducted.

2.1   Quantitative Approach in Discourse-Analytical Accounting Research

The first strand, namely the quantitative approach, has its roots in the positivistic tradition and principally relies on statistical calculations (Tregidga et al., 2012). Quantitative language research in accounting is generally market-oriented (Bae et al., 2023). Its main objective is to explore, and contribute to, the functioning of capital markets and observe the impact of information on the behaviour of the capital market participants, including investors, companies, and regulators. The quantitative approach investigates the correlations and causal relationships between the language used in the specific texts and other various numerical metrics or characteristics, such as company performance. The textual data considered could be any accounting or accounting-related texts. However, corporate reports, and in fact certain sections of corporate reports, are usually the primary text genre utilised by the studies.

The initial step in these studies involves quantifying the language used in texts to generate numerical linguistic variables (Loughran & McDonald, 2020). That is, numerical values are assigned to specific textual properties, which pertain to the content or form of the text (Beattie, 2014). The linguistic variables generated in this way can vary depending on the purpose of the studies. Some of the common variables employed in the quantitative research include word frequencies (Chen & Bouvain, 2009), readability scores (Li, 2008), sentiment scores (Cho et al., 2010), as well as text size and disclosure index scores (Melloni et al., 2017).

Such linguistic variables are then further examined in relation to other non-linguistic variables to explore statistical associations and relationships. The non-linguistic variables would typically be related to the indicators of a company's performance. These performance variables can serve as proxies for a company's financial performance, including measures such as profitability, level of earnings, future profitability or earning prospects (Bozanic & Thevenot, 2015; Melloni et al., 2017). Alternatively, they may represent the sustainability performance of the company under scrutiny. Sustainability performance measures often include environmental, social or governance scores, or, in some instances, combined sustainability scores based on all three of these dimensions (Matsumura et al., 2014; Melloni et al., 2016). The non-linguistic variables are generally sourced from online databases such as Compustat, Thomson Reuters or Bloomberg. Interestingly, non-linguistic variables other than company performance measures are relatively less frequently employed. When they are used, they would include country-specific variables based on institutional and cultural factors or sectoral variables based on the industry sector (Chen & Bouvain, 2009; Purda & Skillicorn, 2015).

Once the variables are identified, researchers build econometric models to analyse the statistical significance and nature of relationships between the generated linguistic and collected non-linguistic variables. Finally, an evaluation and discussion based on the relevant literature and theories are presented to provide insights and explanations for the findings, for example to determine the correlational or causational nature of statistically significant relationships. Such analysis could also facilitate theory development. Having briefly outlined the process of employing the quantitative approach for studying language use in accounting research, we will now proceed to discuss the strengths and limitations of this approach. Our intention, in particular, is to propose a way in which the limitations of the quantitative methodological approach that we identify could be addressed by the application of the tools offered by corpus linguistics.

It is reasonable to assert that word frequency is a commonly employed linguistic variable (Pollach, 2012). The word frequency scores are typically obtained by counting the occurrences of individual words or groups of words. Occurrence frequencies of a pre-determined word or a group of words are generally used as linguistic variables. In some instances, the most frequently occurring words are initially identified within the text and then their frequencies are used as linguistic variables, which are subsequently examined in relation to non-linguistic variables. The use of word frequency as a linguistic variable represents the so-called bag of words view of language (Bochkay et al., 2023; El-Haj et al., 2019).

The bag of words view regards language as a series of slots to be filled by words, thus not taking into account the textual context. In other words, it does not consider the syntax, grammatical relations or co-occurring words surrounding the individual words, all of which provide for the meaning embedded in language (El-Haj et al., 2019). This view offers only a partial understanding of language, as it does not fully align with how language functions in real life (Sinclair, 1991). The co-occurring words, grammatical relationships, and syntactic variations have an impact on the semantics of the individual word occurrences. Therefore, it is important to recognise that we cannot treat a word occurrence in isolation from its textual context (Firth, 1968). While examining word frequency scores would serve as a good starting point for language analysis, relying solely on word frequency scores as linguistic variables might lead to an incomplete and potentially inaccurate perspective (Jaworska, 2017; Stenka & Jaworska, 2019).

Similar to the word frequency scores, sentiment scores are also derived based on the bag of words view of language. Sentiment scores are typically computed using software tools, such as DICTION and Harvard-IV (Cho et al., 2010; Davis et al., 2012; Tetlock, 2007). These software tools assess the sentiments associated with individual words in texts using predefined dictionaries and calculate overall sentiment scores for the entire text under consideration (Loughran & McDonald, 2016). These dictionaries group words based on their sentiments, like certainty, positivity or negativity.

When text is input into software tools, the words within the text are first retrieved and then categorised, and their sentiment values are measured (per dictionaries), ultimately yielding sentiment scores for the entire text. Since sentiment analysis categorises and counts words in isolation, adhering to the bag of words view of language, there is a potential issue of obtaining misleading results given that the context of the word use is not considered (Stenka & Jaworska, 2019). Moreover, in principle the sentiment dictionaries were designed for general use, and thus do not consider the specific context of accounting texts. Consequently, these dictionaries might not be particularly suitable for assessing sentiment in the context of corporate reports (Loughran & McDonald, 2011). A word with positive connotations in the corporate reporting setting might be classified as negative by these general-use sentiment dictionaries, leading to incorrect inferences.

Another frequently used linguistic variable in quantitative discourse-analytical accounting research is readability scores (Clatworthy & Jones, 2001; Stone & Lodhia, 2019), often calculated using measures like the fog index. Readability scores aim to measure the complexity of the language used. They are computed based on factors such as the number of syllables in words, the length of sentences and the number of passive constructions in the text (Ben-Amar et al., 2021; Jones, M., & Shoemaker, 1994). The readability scores nevertheless may not always be reliable indicators for assessing the complexity of the language used in accounting and accounting-related texts. Note, these scores were originally developed to evaluate texts intended for children's literature (Bailin & Grafstein, 2001) and thus in principle could be problematic as reliable indicators for assessing the complexity of the language in professional texts such as accounting and accounting-related documents. For instance, in the case of technical texts like corporate reports, and accounting standards and guidelines, lengthy sentences or complex words might not necessarily hinder the readability of the texts given the profile of the audience (Brennan et al., 2009). As a result, readability scores may not be a suitable proxy for text complexity in an accounting context, and therefore, the statistical associations between the readability scores of corporate reports and corporate performance measures might not always carry significant meaning.

As already mentioned, some research also employs text size and disclosure index scores as variables derived from textual data. Text size may take various numeric values related to the length of the corporate reports. For instance, the total number of pages, the number of paragraphs, or the number of sentences can and have been used as linguistic variables (Beattie, 2014; Beattie et al., 2004). On the other hand, disclosure index scores are determined based on the presence and/or absence of specific elements within corporate reports.

A disclosure index, comprised of specific disclosure elements, is constructed in accordance with a corporate reporting framework or guidelines, such as the Integrated Reporting Framework (Kilic & Kuzey, 2018; Rivera-Arrubla et al., 2017). The contents of corporate reports are manually analysed to detect the presence and absence of the disclosure items specified in the created index, such as external risks, business model and carbon emissions

(Robb et al., 2001). In the corporate reports under examination, binary values (zero or one) or rankings (e.g., ranging from zero to five) are assigned to each disclosure item. These values are then aggregated to establish an overall disclosure index score for a company's reports (Beattie et al., 2004). Afterwards, the companies' disclosure index scores, derived from their report content, are compared with each other or further scrutinised in relation to specified non-linguistic variables, such as the country, industry, or performance of the company.

We can argue that disclosure index scores serve as meaningful proxies, depending upon the specific research questions being addressed. Nevertheless, it is important to acknowledge that the manual and labour-intensive nature of such investigations often poses constraints that restrict the data size to a limited number of reports. On the other hand, using the report length is an appropriate approach, but it might give very preliminary insights, as the length alone does not tell us much about the informational content of the corporate reports.

Finally, in quantitatively oriented accounting discourse research, there are also several other linguistic and non-linguistic variables used (e.g., Purda & Skillicorn, 2015). The central message we aim to convey here is that despite their valuable implications, there are generally drawbacks to using such linguistic variables. The quantitative approach allows for relatively large textual data sets to be examined in a less-biased way, but it arguably has the inherent drawback of simplifying the language use, overlooking 'the aspects of the textual context' (Stenka & Jaworska, 2019). After reviewing the second main research strand in accounting discourse research below, we will introduce a novel methodological approach that could be harnessed to address these drawbacks to a certain extent.

2.2 Qualitative Approach in Discourse-Analytical Accounting Research

Qualitative discourse studies are situated mainly within the interpretive (and critical) research tradition (Tregidga et al., 2012). They predominantly rely on qualitative coding (Beattie et al., 2004). These studies normally involve in-depth textual investigation to uncover attributed meanings within social contexts. Qualitative accounting discourse research places a strong emphasis on the semantics and contextual embeddedness of the language use and is usually informed by various conceptual and theoretical frameworks that very often originate from other social science fields, such as, sociology, psychology, economics, and political studies (Beattie, 2014; Brennan et al., 2009).

The conceptual and theoretical lenses that underpin qualitative discourse-analytical accounting research encompass various perspectives, including impression management (Merkl-Davies & Brennan, 2011; Merkl-Davies et al., 2011), legitimation (Lupu & Sandu, 2017; Stenka, 2022), the use of metaphors and figurative language (Merkl-Davies & Koller, 2012; Milne et al., 2006), prevailing understandings of significant concepts or identities (Tregidga et al., 2014; Tregidga et al., 2018), and wording (Nwagbara & Belal, 2019). In these studies, researchers examine an individual text or series of texts to reveal, for example, impression management or legitimation strategies employed by text producers, i.e., corporate report producers. The investigations are in general conducted manually (Bryman & Bell, 2015).

Additionally, some research makes use of qualitative data analysis software, such as NVivo and ATLAS.ti (Beattie et al., 2004; Cho et al., 2015). These software tools are used for the qualitative or thematic coding of texts, aiding in the systematic identification and classification of textual instances related to the phenomena under investigation. For example, in studies focusing on impression management techniques, researchers look for factors such as the selectivity of performance measures presented, emphasis of visual elements included, or rhetorical strategies employed in corporate reports (Nwagbara & Belal, 2019). They also analyse the order of information, whether positive statements are foregrounded, and time orientation of statements, distinguishing between forward-looking and backward-looking content within corporate reports (Beattie et al., 2004; Brennan et al., 2009).

The legitimation studies are also widespread in qualitative discourse-analytical accounting research. Accounting researchers endeavour to identify the legitimation strategies, such as moralisation and authorisation, used in corporate reports or other accounting-related texts (Lupu & Sandu, 2017; Peda & Vinnari, 2020; Price et al., 2018). Similarly, certain metaphors, such as the journey metaphor for the sustainability concept (Milne et al., 2006) and the self-representation of sustainable organisations (Tregidga et al., 2014), are scrutinised in accounting literature. These investigations seek to reveal the motivations behind the meaning conveyed through corporate reports or other accounting-related texts in circulation. Subsequently, an evaluation and discussion of the findings are presented, concerning the underlying meanings, which may pertain to the production of public consent, reputation management, and the justification of decisions and actions. The conceptual and theoretical lenses play a crucial role in interpreting the findings and guiding the discussions (Tregidga et al., 2013; Unerman & Chapman, 2014).

These qualitative studies are valuable in that they touch upon issues that might otherwise go unnoticed, contribute to raising awareness, and provide fresh perspectives on the processes of meaning making and meaning transmission. However, like any methodological approach, the qualitative approach, with its main pillar of qualitative coding, has its drawbacks (Stenka & Jaworska, 2019). First and foremost, qualitative research is subjective, especially when compared to quantitative research, making it prone to researcher bias (Baker et al., 2012). The pre-existing assumptions (e.g., prior thoughts) of researchers, confirmation bias and primacy effect (primacy bias) can influence the research process and findings (Baker, 2006). These pre-assumptions, often present before a research project begins, can lead to confirmation bias. Confirmation bias is the human tendency to seek and interpret information in a way that aligns with and confirms researcher's pre-assumptions, prior expectations, and existing beliefs. The primacy effect is another cognitive bias, referring to the human tendency to place greater emphasis on and pay more attention to the information encountered early, particularly at the outset[3] (Baker, 2006; Stenka & Jaworska, 2019).

In addition to subjectivity and bias issues, the qualitative research has several other constraints. Qualitative coding is a labour-intensive and time-consuming process that demands substantial resources and involves multiple stages. In such research, firstly, a coding template with predefined codes is created, based on the research objectives. These coding templates are informed by the relevant existing literature and the adopted theoretical framework (Higgins & Walker, 2012). Alternatively, a preliminary study may be conducted on a small subset of data to identify emerging themes, which are then incorporated into the coding template. Afterwards, researchers meticulously go through corporate reports page by page, assigning relevant codes to text content from the coding template (Higgins & Coffey, 2016). These codes are then grouped into broader themes, ultimately leading to the main research findings for discussion (Bryman & Bell, 2015).

Qualitative coding software programs like NVivo might be used to facilitate the process of assigning, categorising, and organising codes. Nevertheless, it is still the researchers themselves who need to carry out manual coding. Thus, it does not make a significant difference with regard to the labour-intensive and time-consuming nature of qualitative research (Baker et al., 2008). For this reason, the number of texts that are analysed is often limited in these studies. For instance, researchers may investigate the corporate reports of a single company or a few companies, as the research questions are formed to accommodate these limitations (Buhr & Reiter, 2006; Livesey & Kearins, 2002; Milne et al., 2009). In general, the data focused on in qualitative discourse-analytical accounting research remains limited, making it challenging to generalise findings. Moreover, the limited data set might raise questions about the validity of arguments made based on research findings (Baker, 2006).

Having briefly discussed the shortcomings of qualitative discourse-analytical accounting research, we once again emphasise its value. Similar to the quantitative accounting discourse research reviewed in the previous section, the qualitative research has some methodological drawbacks. Whilst the qualitative approach allows in-depth and contextual exploration of the text, it generally has the data size constraints and issues of bias (Stenka & Jaworska, 2019). These drawbacks could be addressed, to some extent, with a novel (in accounting research) methodological approach borrowed from the linguistics field (Jaworska, 2017; Pollach, 2012).

2.3 Summary and a Novel (in Accounting Research) Approach

Thus far, we have provided an overview of the two main methodological approaches in discourse-analytical accounting research. We have also highlighted their drawbacks. We believe that using the corpus linguistics approach, adopted from the linguistics field, can address some of the above-discussed shortcomings associated with traditional qualitative and quantitative research methods (Baker et al., 2008; Stenka & Jaworska, 2019). Furthermore, we argue that the corpus linguistics approach can enhance the depth of insights achievable in accounting discourse research (Pollach, 2012).

Before moving into a discussion of the corpus linguistics approach, it is worth acknowledging other methodological trends being developed and holding promise for improvement of the existing accounting discourse research. Notably, natural language processing techniques, machine learning algorithms, and artificial intelligence tools have become recent developments within the social sciences (Bae et al., 2023; El-Haj et al., 2019). They appear to have an impact on the future of discourse-analytical accounting research. Nonetheless, we will concentrate only on the corpus linguistics approach within the scope of this chapter. If you are interested in exploring these emerging trends and their potential applications in accounting, we recommend referring to the works of Anand et al. (2020) and Bochkay et al. (2023).

3 CORPUS LINGUISTICS APPROACH

Following the lead of few others (Beattie, 2014; Stenka & Jaworska, 2019), we propose that discourse-analytical accounting research can significantly benefit from adopting the novel (in accounting) corpus linguistics approach. It has the potential to help address several of the limitations associated with existing methodologies, as discussed above. The corpus linguistics approach offers a range of advantages. Firstly, it provides a rich set of innovative tools and techniques that could be effectively utilised. These include collocation, concordance, keywords (keyness), semantic tagging, grammatical tagging, and N-grams (multiword expressions)[4] – see Table 25.1 (Baker, 2006; Jaworska, 2017).

Table 25.1   *Main corpus linguistics tools that could be utilised in accounting research*

Corpus linguistics tool	Tool's function
Collocation	Identifying and providing the statistically significant co-occurrences of words in a running text
Concordance	Identifying and providing the occurrences and co-occurrences of a word or group of words within their textual context
Keywords (keyness)	Identifying and providing list of keywords that occur significantly more frequently in a corpus (than in a large reference corpus)
Semantic tagging	Labelling and categorising the words or word groups based on their semantics
Grammatical tagging	Labelling and categorising the words or word groups based on their grammatical/syntactic function in a phrase (within part-of-speech tagging)
N-grams (multiword expressions)	Identifying and providing multiword expressions in a text

Corpus linguistics tools are operationalised through the use of specialised software and programs, commonly referred to as corpus linguistics software. Many of the corpus linguistics software options are readily accessible and easy to use. For instance, widely used corpus linguistics software programs such as LancsBox (developed by Lancaster University), Corpus Query Processor (Lancaster University), WMatrix (Lancaster University), and AntConc (Anthony, 2022) are freely available and have user-friendly interfaces. Additionally, there is the Sketch Engine software (https://www.sketchengine.eu), which is frequently used by researchers (Jaworska, 2017).

Moreover, research employing the corpus linguistics approach utilises both quantitative and qualitative insights without compromising on either. It facilitates striking 'the balance between purely quantitative ... and purely qualitative methods providing both a bird's eye and street level view [of text] combining simultaneously breadth and depth of analysis' (Stenka & Jaworska, 2019, p. 8). This dual perspective allows for a more comprehensive examination, drawing on both quantitative computational techniques and qualitative analysis procedures (Gray & Biber, 2011; Mahlberg, 2007). Consequently, applying a corpus linguistics approach enriches the traditional quantitative-only research with additional qualitative insights, and qualitative-only research with additional quantitative insights.

The corpus linguistics approach allows the data to take the lead, before the involvement of the researcher's subjective input (Stenka & Jaworska, 2019). Specifically, in the early stage of analysis, textual patterns and certain linguistic variables emerge from the data with only minimal researcher intervention. Then, these emerging insights are further examined qualitatively within their textual context (Mautner, 2016; McEnery & Hardie, 2012). The researcher's gaze is guided by the computational processes embedded in linguistics software. Therefore, the corpus linguistics approach helps mitigate researcher bias, including the impact of pre-existing assumptions, confirmation bias, and the primacy effect. This leads to a reduced level of researcher bias, compared to studies relying purely on manual qualitative coding (Baker, 2006).

As asserted by Baker et al. (2008, p. 277), corpus linguistics 'methods offer the researcher a reasonably high degree of objectivity; that is, they enable the researcher to approach the texts (or text surface) (relatively) free from any preconceived or existing notions regarding their linguistic or semantic/pragmatic content'. Furthermore, the corpus linguistics approach allows researchers to move beyond and above the bag of words view of language to which quantitative research often adheres. In the computational processes, the contextual surroundings of individual word occurrences, that is, co-occurring words, and the grammatical and syntactic variations associated with those individual word occurrences, are taken into account.

Thanks to the advanced computational algorithms, the corpus linguistics approach enables us to effectively process and analyse large amounts of textual data at once (Mautner & Learmonth, 2020; Sinclair, 1991). It points us to the textual properties (Baker et al., 2008) that may not be apparent to the naked eye (Jaworska, 2017). Textual properties can be reliably accounted for using corpus linguistics tools, regardless of the data set size (Baker, 2006; Baker et al., 2008). In this sense, corpus linguistics tools enable researchers to avoid (to some extent) the trade-off between the volume (size of the data) and richness (depth of the investigation) of their analysis. This is achieved by leveraging both computational tools and in-depth qualitative examination techniques (Baker et al., 2008; Jaworska, 2017). As a result, this approach offers deeper insights than traditional qualitative approaches, and significantly enhances our understanding of language use (Baker, 2006; Jaworska, 2017).

In this regard, it facilitates a systematic examination of text in which 'the incremental effect of discourse' can be observed (Baker, 2006, p. 13), by allowing us to study larger data sets than traditional solely qualitative discourse research. Along the same lines, the corpus linguistics approach helps address a major shortcoming of quantitative discourse research, which often adopts a partial view of language. In this approach, word occurrences are not treated in isolation, as is the case in the bag of words view. Instead, the syntactic, grammatical, and lexical context of individual word occurrences is considered and explored, both in the initial and, particularly, in the further steps of the analysis (Jaworska, 2017).

Finally, corpus linguistics is recognised as a valid methodological approach for the study of language and language use (Wodak & Meyer, 2016), and esteemed as a valuable 'linguistic toolbox' for discourse research (Baker et al., 2008; Mautner, 2016). In fact, corpus linguistics has become a firmly established approach in linguistics, and has been widely applied to study texts across various contexts (Baker, 2006; Mautner, 2016).

Corpus Linguistics Approach in Accounting Research

Despite its acknowledged validity, usefulness and the research calls, the corpus linguistics approach is underutilised in the accounting literature (Beattie, 2014; Stenka & Jaworska, 2019). To the best of our knowledge, only one study explicitly employs the corpus linguistics approach to investigate language use in accounting journals. That is the work of Stenka and Jaworska (2019), which analyses the concept of users in comment letters submitted to the International Accounting Standards Board. Also, there are a limited number of studies that apply the corpus linguistics methodology to explore language use in corporate reports, but these studies are published in journals outside the accounting domain (Fuoli, 2018; Jaworska, 2018; Lischinsky, 2011; O'Kelly, 2019; Rutherford, 2005; Zappettini & Unerman, 2016). For example, O'Kelly (2019), published in the *Social & Legal Studies* journal, examines the construction of the human rights concept in corporate sustainability reports by using the corpus linguistics approach. Fuoli (2018), published in the *Applied Linguistics* journal, investigates the representation of companies' self-identity in corporate reports through the corpus linguistics tools and techniques.

Overall, the usage of the corpus linguistics approach in accounting is limited, with only a small amount of research utilising the corpus linguistics tools and techniques within the accounting literature (Stenka & Jaworska, 2019). Furthermore, there are research calls for accounting scholars to benefit from the corpus-based approach, as it facilitates a more linguistically informed analysis (Beattie, 2014; Stenka & Jaworska, 2019). In response to this methodological gap in accounting literature and the research calls, we have a series of studies that apply the corpus linguistics approach to accounting text, more specifically the corporate sustainability reporting context.

In the next section, we will provide a concise introduction to our research series. We will illustrate the application of corpus linguistics tools, emphasising their relevance for accounting language research. In doing so, we will also briefly describe some of the main corpus linguistics tools and discuss their application. Our goal is to raise awareness among accounting scholars about the novel corpus linguistics approach and its usefulness for the analysis of corporate sustainability reports and other accounting-related texts.

4   EXEMPLARY APPLICATIONS OF THE CORPUS LINGUISTICS APPROACH IN ACCOUNTING RESEARCH

We can present our work as three separate papers,[5] each of which uses a data set (corpus) comprising 105 exemplary integrated reports. The data size stands at nearly 5 million words, and all the reports within the data set are sourced from the International Integrated Reporting Council's Exemplary Reports Database (https://examples.integratedreporting.org). Our research focuses on, respectively, analysing the sustainability concept within the context of integrated reporting, examining the stakeholder concept in the integrated reporting context, and exploring the six capitals within integrated reporting.

4.1   Analysing the Sustainability Concept in Integrated Reports

In this work, we analysed the construction of the sustainability concept in integrated reports to reveal how the notion of sustainability is represented and interpreted in the corporate world. Traditionally, such an investigation would involve qualitative coding of the relevant report sections (Laine, 2010; Tregidga & Milne, 2006). Or in a quantitative study, the instances of the word 'sustainability' would be counted and used as a linguistic variable (Gatti & Seele, 2014). However, we went beyond traditional approaches, and utilised corpus linguistics tools for a more linguistically informed and enriched analysis (Baker, 2006). In particular, we employed collocation and concordance tools with the assistance of the corpus linguistics software, Sketch Engine.

Collocation simply refers to statistically significant tendency of two words to co-occur together within a predetermined span, typically five words to the left and five words to the right, in a text (Baker, 2006). It represents the habitual lexical patterns, or in other words, recurrent word combinations in a given text (Stubbs, 2001). To identify the collocates (collocations) of the word 'sustainability', we used the embedded counting algorithms in Sketch Engine, which counted every occurrence of sustainability and the words co-occurring in its vicinity for each instance of sustainability. Subsequently, statistically significant co-occurring words, which appear in the vicinity of sustainability consistently (and not by chance), were derived as collocates through Sketch Engine (Baker et al., 2008). In line with the linguistics theory of meaning (Firth, 1957; Sinclair, 1991), the collocates of the sustainability concept in integrated reports provide valuable insights into the meaning that is attributed to this notion by the report producers.

In this sense, our initial focus was on examining the collocations of the sustainability concept within our corpus to understand how this concept is constructed and represented in integrated reports. The software automatically derives the collocates of sustainability, reducing researcher intervention and potential researcher bias in this phase of the analysis (Baker, 2006). These collocates, calculated through statistical metrics, offer us preliminary insights about the construction of the sustainability concept in our corpus (Jaworska, 2018). Then, to gain deeper insights, we conducted an analysis of all the co-occurrences of sustainability and its collocates using the concordance tool (Baker & McEnery, 2005; Gabrielatos & Baker, 2008).

The concordance tool is designed to identify and provide all occurrences and co-occurrences of any inputted word or words, enabling in-depth qualitative investigation within their textual context (Baker, 2006; Mahlberg, 2007). This tool thus allows us to account for the semantically meaningful grammatical and lexical context surrounding each word occurrence (Baker et al., 2012; Orpin, 2005). In our case, the concordance tool played an important role in helping us identify and further investigate the collocational co-occurrences of the sustainability concept. For example, we extracted the adjective and noun collocates of the sustainability concept and qualitatively analysed these collocational co-occurrences one by one within their co-text in the second stage of our analysis. This provided us with additional qualitative insights into how the sustainability concept is represented in integrated reports.

Owing to the collocation and concordance tools of the corpus linguistics approach, we believe we have achieved both quantitative and qualitative insights without sacrificing one for the other. This has resulted in more nuanced analysis and findings (Baker et al., 2008; Stenka & Jaworska, 2019). We also argue that our analysis of the sustainability concept is more linguistically informed, less biased, and more comprehensive compared to what can be attained through purely qualitative or purely quantitative investigations.

4.2   Analysing the Stakeholder (versus Shareholder) Concept in Integrated Reports

The second research in our series focuses on the comparison of the discursive representations of the stakeholders vis-à-vis shareholders in integrated reports. In this study, we once again departed from traditional qualitative coding and individual word counting approaches. Instead, we employed the corpus linguistics tools of grammatical tagging and concordance. Grammatical tagging is a component of part-of-speech tagging, and marks (and counts) words and word groups based on their grammatical functions within a phrase or sentence (Lexical Computing, 2023).

Using the grammatical tagging tool, we drew every instance of the stakeholder and shareholder concepts when they appeared in the subject and object positions within phrases in integrated reports. This approach enabled us to identify and observe whether stakeholders and shareholders are depicted as active and agential identities or passive and patient-like identities (Berk, 1999). That is, it allowed us to determine whether they are predominantly represented as acting or being acted upon in the context of integrated reporting (Fairclough, 1992; Jones, R., et al., 2021; Iwamoto, 1995). During this phase of our analysis, our input was limited, as the software tool guided us, thus minimising the impact of researcher bias (Baker, 2006).

Afterwards, we employed the concordance tool to complement our analysis with in-depth qualitative investigation. Informed by Halliday's transitivity framework (Fowler, 1991; Halliday & Mathiessen, 2014), we examined each instance of stakeholder and shareholder when they appeared in a subject, that is, an active position, in a phrase, in order to observe the types of acts they were portrayed to carry out in integrated reports.

The use of grammatical tagging and concordance tools allowed us to derive more enriched findings regarding the representations of stakeholders and shareholders in integrated reports, in contrast to a traditional qualitative or quantitative only approach (Mautner, 2016). Also, these tools helped us reduce the subjectivity, as the software guided us in investigating the lexical, grammatical, and syntactic patterns surrounding the textual occurrences of the concepts under our focus (Stenka & Jaworska, 2019). Lastly, we managed to conduct an in-depth investigation of the representations of stakeholders and shareholders in our relatively large data set, without excluding relevant content and meaning embedded in the data from our scrutiny.

4.3 Analysing the Six Capitals in Integrated Reports

In the third paper of our research series, we turned our attention to the six capitals concept of integrated reporting. This concept was proposed by the Integrated Reporting Framework of the International Integrated Reporting Council (IIRC, 2013). It represents an extension of the conventional financial capital and encourages companies to account not only for financial capital but also for other, non-financial, capitals. The six capitals specified by the framework are financial capital, manufactured capital, human capital, intellectual capital, social and relationship capital, and natural capital. Integrated reports are expected to centre around these six capitals, telling us the story of how they are affected by the operations of business organisations (Adams, 2015; Aras & Williams, 2022).

Our work aims to shed light on how various types of the six capitals are regarded in the context of integrated reporting. Thus, we explored the extent to which these different capital types are considered in our corpus of integrated reports. In a traditional study, such an analysis would primarily rely on the frequency of word occurrences related to the six capitals. However, our investigation went further; we conducted a keywords analysis with the corpus linguistics tools, specifically keywords, collocation, and concordance.

The keywords tool essentially provides a list of keywords that appear significantly more frequently in the focus corpus than in a larger reference corpus. It is a valuable tool for revealing what a corpus is about, showing the predominant themes and trends in a corpus (Baker et al., 2008; Jaworska, 2017). In our study, we conducted a quantitative investigation by comparing our focus corpus of integrated reports with a large English Language corpus from the Sketch Engine TenTen Corpus Family, representing the English language use (https://www.sketchengine.eu/documentation/tenten-corpora/). Directed by the software, we extracted the keywords of our corpus in this manner. Then, we performed a further qualitative analysis to categorise these extracted keywords in relation to the six different types of capitals.

To validate our classification, we carefully scrutinised randomly selected concordance lines of these keywords, as provided by Sketch Engine. Additionally, we explored the strongest collocates of the term 'capital' within their textual context. This comprehensive approach allowed us to uncover the extent and consideration of the different types of six capitals in integrated reporting. We believe that we substantially enriched our findings through the use of corpus linguistics tools, which enabled us to simultaneously obtain more objective quantitative and deeper qualitative insights (Baker, 2006; Mautner, 2016).

5   CONCLUSION AND FUTURE RESEARCH AVENUES

In this chapter, our primary aim was to promote the usefulness and benefits of the corpus linguistics approach for discourse-analytical accounting research (Baker, 2006; Beattie, 2014). We sought to contribute to the advancement of accounting discourse research by bringing innovative corpus linguistics tools to the attention of accounting scholars, who are interested in studying corporate sustainability reports and other accounting-related text. Throughout the chapter, we commenced with reviewing the conventional methodological approaches in this research body; and we highlighted their inherent limitations. We then discussed how these drawbacks could be addressed, to some extent, through the application of corpus linguistics tools and techniques. Finally, we briefly showcased some illustrative applications of the corpus linguistics approach within the context of corporate sustainability reporting.

We reiterate the value of existing discourse-analytical accounting research, while presenting this chapter as an attempt to introduce an innovative methodological approach from the linguistics field to accounting researchers. Before concluding this chapter, we want to suggest some potential future research avenues that could greatly benefit from the application of corpus linguistics tools and techniques. Firstly, future research could look at prominent and currently debated concepts related to corporate sustainability reporting to unveil how they are understood in the corporate world, as we have done with sustainability and stakeholder concepts. For instance, the representation of materiality, double materiality, integrated thinking, and responsible investment concepts within the corporate sustainability reports and related regulatory documents could be investigated using the corpus linguistics tools of collocation and concordance.

Exploring the portrayal of individual stakeholder groups' identities in corporate sustainability reports through the utilisation of grammatical tagging, collocation and concordance tools might be worthy research paths to follow. Specifically, future research could investigate the construction of different stakeholder groups separately, such as employees, management, accountants, clients, regulators, and the public. Then, the findings could be compared to observe how representations of various stakeholder groups differ within the corporate arena.

In a more market-oriented study, one could explore the correlations and causal relationships between the keywords (in reference to a large corpus of corporate reports) of sustainability reports published by companies with good sustainability performance and of those by companies with poor sustainability performance. This analysis would allow for a comparative investigation to identify significant similarities and differences. Furthermore, it may be feasible to develop a model that estimates a company's sustainability performance based on the keywords tool. Such a model would hold great value for both the literature and capital markets.

NOTES

1. In this chapter, discourse refers to the language use, and discourse-analytical accounting research encompasses any accounting research studying the language and language use within the accounting area.
2. In this chapter, we employ the term 'corporate sustainability reports' as an umbrella term, referring to all types of corporate reports addressing social, environmental and governance issues. Corporate sustainability reports are referred to differently across the corporate arena, e.g., sustainability reports, sustainable development reports, corporate social responsibility reports.
3. It is important to note here that pre-assumptions held by the researcher, confirmation bias, and primacy bias are not exclusive to researchers or solely sourced from the research environment. These are natural human tendencies that arise from the way the human mind processes information.
4. We will discuss the four main tools of corpus linguistics within section 4, titled 'Exemplary applications of the corpus linguistics approach in accounting research'. Those tools are concordance, collocation, grammatical tagging and keywords. If you are interested in exploring other corpus linguistics tools or seeking further information, you can refer to the book, *Using Corpora in Discourse Analysis* by Baker (2006).
5. In these research projects, we have co-authors: Sylvia Jaworska, in the projects discussed in section 4.1 and section 4.3, and Omiros Georgiou, in the project discussed in section 4.2. The papers are still in the process of being published.

REFERENCES

A4S. 2021. *Navigating the Reporting Landscape: An Introduction to Sustainability-Related Reporting for Finance Professionals.* London: Accounting for Sustainability Project. https://www.account ingforsustainability.org/content/dam/a4s/corporate/home/KnowledgeHub/Guide-pdf/Navigating %20the%20Reporting%20Landscape.pdf.downloadasset.pdf

Adams, C. A. 2015. The international integrated reporting council: a call to action. *Critical Perspectives on Accounting, 27,* 23–28.

Anand, V., Bochkay, K., Chychyla, R., and Leone, A. 2020. Using Python for text analysis in accounting research. *Foundations and Trends in Accounting, 14*(3–4), 128–359.

Anthony, L. 2022. *AntConc.* https://www.laurenceanthony.net/software/antconc/

Aras, G., and Williams, P. F. 2022. Integrated reporting and integrated thinking: proposing a reporting model that induces more responsible use of corporate power. *Sustainability, 14*(6), 3277.

Bae, J., Yu Hung, C., and van Lent, L. 2023. Mobilizing text as data. *European Accounting Review, 32*(5), 1085–1106.

Bailin, A., and Grafstein, A. 2001. The linguistic assumptions underlying readability formulae: a critique. *Language & Communication, 21*(3), 285–301.

Baker, P. (2006). *Using Corpora in Discourse Analysis.* London: Continuum.

Baker, P., and McEnery, T. 2005. A corpus-based approach to discourses of refugees and asylum seekers in UN and newspaper texts. *Journal of Language and Politics, 4*(2), 197–226.

Baker, P., Gabrielatos, C., Khosravinik, M., Krzyżanowski, M., McEnery, T., and Wodak, R. 2008. A useful methodological synergy? Combining critical discourse analysis and corpus linguistics to examine discourses of refugees and asylum seekers in the UK press. *Discourse & Society, 19*(3), 273–306.

Baker, P., Gabrielatos, C., and McEnery, T. 2012. Sketching Muslims: a corpus driven analysis of representations around the word 'Muslim' in the British press 1998–2009. *Applied Linguistics, 34*(3), 255–278.

Beattie, V. 2014. Accounting narratives and the narrative turn in accounting research: issues, theory, methodology, methods and a research framework. *The British Accounting Review*, *46*(2), 111–134.

Beattie, V., McInnes, B., and Fearnley, S. 2004. A methodology for analysing and evaluating narratives in annual reports: a comprehensive descriptive profile and metrics for disclosure quality attributes. *Accounting Forum*, *28*(3), 205–236.

Ben-Amar, W., Bujaki, M., McConomy, B., and McIlkenny, P. 2021. Gendering merit: how the discourse of merit in diversity disclosures supports the gendered status quo on Canadian corporate boards. *Critical Perspectives on Accounting*, *75*, 102170.

Berk, L. M. 1999. *English Syntax: From Word to Discourse*. Oxford: Oxford University Press.

Bochkay, K., Brown, S. V., Leone, A. J., and Tucker, J. W. 2023. Textual analysis in accounting: what's next? *Contemporary Accounting Research*, *40*(2), 765–805.

Bozanic, Z., and Thevenot, M. 2015. Qualitative disclosure and changes in sell-side financial analysts' information environment. *Contemporary Accounting Research*, *32*(4), 1595–1616.

Brennan, N. M., Guillamon-Saorin, E., and Pierce, A. 2009. Methodological insights – impression management: developing and illustrating a scheme of analysis for narrative disclosures – a methodological note. *Accounting, Auditing & Accountability Journal*, *22*(5), 789–832.

Bryman, A., and Bell, E. 2015. *Business Research Methods*. 4th edn. Oxford: Oxford University Press.

Buhr, N., and Reiter, S. 2006. Ideology, the environment and one world view: a discourse analysis of Noranda's environmental and sustainable development reports. *Advances in Environmental Accounting and Management*, *3*, 1–48.

Buhr, N., Gray, R., and Milne, M. J. 2014. Histories, rationales, voluntary standards and future prospects for sustainability reporting: CSR, GRI, IIRC and beyond. In: J. Bebbington, J. Unerman, and B. O'Dwyer (eds), *Sustainability Accounting and Accountability*. 2nd edn. Abingdon: Routledge, pp. 51–71.

Chen, S., and Bouvain, P. 2009. Is corporate responsibility converging? A comparison of corporate responsibility reporting in the USA, UK, Australia, and Germany. *Journal of Business Ethics*, *87*(1), 299–317.

Cho, C. H., Laine, M., Roberts, R. W., and Rodrigue, M. 2015. Organized hypocrisy, organizational façades, and sustainability reporting. *Accounting, Organizations and Society*, *40*, 78–94.

Cho, C. H., Roberts, R. W., and Patten, D. M. 2010. The language of US corporate environmental disclosure. *Accounting, Organizations and Society*, *35*(4), 431–443.

Clatworthy, M., and Jones, M. J. 2001. The effect of thematic structure on the variability of annual report readability. *Accounting, Auditing & Accountability Journal*, *14*(3), 311–326.

Davis, A. K., Piger, J. M., and Sedor, L. M. 2012. Beyond the numbers: measuring the information content of earnings press release language. *Contemporary Accounting Research*, *29*(3), 845–868.

El-Haj, M., Rayson, P., Walker, M., Young, S., and Simaki, V. 2019. In search of meaning: lessons, resources and next steps for computational analysis of financial discourse. *Journal of Business Finance & Accounting*, *46*(3–4), 265–306.

Fairclough, N. 1992. *Discourse and Social Change*. Cambridge: Polity Press.

Firth, J. R. 1957. *Papers in Linguistics 1934–1951*. Oxford: Oxford University Press.

Firth, J. R. 1968. Linguistic analysis as a study of meaning. In: F. R. Palmer (ed.), *Selected Papers of J. R. Firth 1952–1959*. London: Longman, pp. 12–26.

Fowler, R. (1991). *Language in the News: Discourse and Ideology in the Press*. Abingdon: Routledge.

Fuoli, M. 2018. Building a trustworthy corporate identity: a corpus-based analysis of stance in annual and corporate social responsibility reports. *Applied Linguistics*, *39*(6), 846–885.

Gabrielatos, C., and Baker, P. 2008. Fleeing, sneaking, flooding: a corpus analysis of discursive constructions of refugees and asylum seekers in the UK press, 1996–2005. *Journal of English Linguistics*, *36*(1), 5–38.

Gatti, L., and Seele, P. 2014. Evidence for the prevalence of the sustainability concept in European corporate responsibility reporting. *Sustainability Science*, *9*(1), 89–102.

Gray, B., and Biber, D. 2011. Corpus approaches to the study of discourse. In: K. Hyland and B. Paltridge (eds), *Continuum Companion to Discourse Analysis*. London: Continuum, pp. 138–154.

Halliday, M., and Matthiessen, C. M. 2014. *An Introduction to Functional Grammar*. 4th edn. Abingdon: Routledge.

Higgins, C., and Coffey, B. 2016. Improving how sustainability reports drive change: a critical discourse analysis. *Journal of Cleaner Production, 13*, 18–29.

Higgins, C., and Walker, R. 2012. Ethos, logos, pathos: strategies of persuasion in social/environmental reports. *Accounting Forum, 36*(3), 194–208.

IIRC, 2013. *The International <IR> Framework.* https://www.integratedreporting.org/wp-content/uploads/2013/12/13-12-08-THE-INTERNATIONAL-IR-FRAMEWORK-2-1.pdf

Iwamoto, N. 1995. The analysis of wartime reporting: patterns of transitivity. *Edinburgh Working Papers in Applied Linguistics, 6*, 58–68.

Jaworska, S. 2017. Corpora and corpus linguistics approaches to studying business language. In: G. Mautner, and F. Rainer (eds), *Handbook of Business Communication: Linguistic Approaches.* Berlin: Walter de Gruyter, pp. 583–606.

Jaworska, S. 2018. Change but no climate change: discourses of climate change in corporate social responsibility reporting in the oil industry. *International Journal of Business Communication, 55*(2), 194–219.

Jones, M. J., and Shoemaker, P. A.,1994. Accounting narratives: a review of empirical studies of content and readability. *Journal of Accounting Literature, 13*, 142–184.

Jones, R. H., Jaworska, S., and Aslan, E. 2021. *Language and Media: A Resource Book for Students.* 2nd edn. London: Routledge.

Kilic, M., and Kuzey, C. 2018. Assessing current company reports according to the IIRC Integrated Reporting Framework. *Meditari Accountancy Research, 26*(2), 305–333.

KPMG. 2020. *The time has come: The KPMG Survey of Sustainability Reporting 2020.* https://assets.kpmg/content/dam/kpmg/xx/pdf/2020/11/the-time-has-come.pdf

Laine, M. 2010. Towards sustaining the status quo: business talk of sustainability in Finnish corporate disclosures 1987–2005. *European Accounting Review, 19*(2), 247–274.

Lexical Computing. 2023. *POS tags.* https://www.sketchengine.eu/blog/pos-tags/

Li, F. 2008. Annual report readability, current earnings, and earnings persistence. *Journal of Accounting and Economics, 45*(2–3), 221–247.

Lischinsky, A. 2011. In times of crisis: a corpus approach to the construction of the global financial crisis in annual reports. *Critical Discourse Studies, 8*(3), 153–168.

Livesey, S. M., and Kearins, K. 2002. Transparent and caring corporations? A study of sustainability reports by The Body Shop and Royal Dutch/Shell. *Organization & Environment, 15*(3), 233–258.

Loughran, T., and McDonald, B. 2011. When is a liability not a liability? Textual analysis, dictionaries, and 10-Ks. *Journal of Finance, 66*(1), 35–65.

Loughran, T., and McDonald, B. 2016. Textual analysis in accounting and finance: a survey. *Journal of Accounting Research, 54*(4), 1187–1230.

Loughran, T., and McDonald, B. 2020. Textual analysis in finance. *Annual Review of Financial Economics, 12*, 357–375.

Lupu, I., and Sandu, R. 2017. Intertextuality in corporate narratives: a discursive analysis of a contested privatization. *Accounting, Auditing & Accountability Journal, 30*(3), 534–564.

Mahlberg, M. 2007. Lexical items in discourse: identifying local textual functions of sustainable development. In: M. Hoey, M. Mahlberg, M. Stubbs, and W. Teubery (eds), *Text, Discourse and Corpora: Theory and Analysis.* London: Continuum, pp. 191–218.

Matsumura, E. M., Prakash, R., and Vera-Munoz, S. C. 2014. Firm-value effects of carbon emissions and carbon disclosures. *The Accounting Review, 89*(2), 695–724.

Mautner, G. (2016). Checks and balances: how corpus linguistics can contribute to CDA. In: R. Wodak and M. Meyer (eds), *Methods of Critical Discourse Studies.* 3rd edn. London: Sage, pp. 154–179.

Mautner, G., and Learmonth, M. 2020. From administrator to CEO: exploring changing representations of hierarchy and prestige in a diachronic corpus of academic management writing. *Discourse & Communication, 14*(3), 273–293.

McEnery, T., and Hardie, A. 2012. *Corpus Linguistics: Method, Theory and Practice.* Cambridge: Cambridge University Press.

Melloni, G., Stacchezzini, R., and Lai, A. 2016. The tone of business model disclosure: an impression management analysis of the integrated reports. *Journal of Management & Governance, 20*(2), 295–320.

Melloni, G., Caglio, A., and Perego, P. 2017. Saying more with less? Disclosure conciseness, complete-ness and balance in integrated reports. *Journal of Accounting and Public Policy*. *36*(3), 220–238.

Merkl-Davies, D. M., and Brennan, N. M. 2011. A conceptual framework of impression manage-ment: new insights from psychology, sociology and critical perspectives. *Accounting and Business Research*, *41*(5), 415–437.

Merkl-Davies, D. M., and Koller, V. 2012. 'Metaphoring' people out of this world: a critical discourse analysis of a chairman's statement of a UK defence firm. *Accounting Forum*, *36*(3), 178–193.

Merkl-Davies, D. M., Brennan, N. M., and McLeay, S. J. 2011. Impression management and retrospec-tive sense-making in corporate narratives: a social psychology perspective. *Accounting, Auditing & Accountability Journal*, *24*(3), 315–344.

Milne, M. J., Kearins, K., and Walton, S. 2006. Creating adventures in wonderland: the journey metaphor and environmental sustainability. *Organization*, *13*(6), 801–839.

Milne, M. J., Tregidga, H., and Walton, S. 2009. Words not actions! The ideological role of sustainable development reporting. *Accounting, Auditing & Accountability Journal*, *22*(8), 1211–1257.

Nwagbara, U., and Belal, A. 2019. Persuasive language of responsible organisation? A critical discourse analysis of corporate social responsibility (CSR) reports of Nigerian oil companies. *Accounting, Auditing & Accountability Journal*, *32*(8), 2395–2420.

O'Kelly, C. 2019. Human rights and the grammar of corporate social responsibility. *Social & Legal Studies*, *28*(5), 625–649.

Orpin, D. 2005. Corpus linguistics and critical discourse analysis: examining the ideology of sleaze. *International Journal of Corpus Linguistics*, *10*(1), 37–61.

Peda, P., and Vinnari, E. 2020. The discursive legitimation of profit in public–private service delivery. *Critical Perspectives on Accounting*, *69*, 102088.

Pollach, I. 2012. Taming textual data: the contribution of corpus linguistics to computer-aided text anal-ysis. *Organizational Research Methods*, *15*(2), 263–287.

Price, M., Harvey, C., Maclean, M., and Campbell, D. 2018. From Cadbury to Kay: discourse, intertextu-ality and the evolution of UK corporate governance. *Accounting, Auditing & Accountability Journal*, *31*(5), 1542–1562.

Purda, L., and Skillicorn, D. 2015. Accounting variables, deception, and a bag of words: assessing the tools of fraud detection. *Contemporary Accounting Research*, *32*(3), 1193–1223.

Rivera-Arrubla, Y. A., Zorio-Grima, A., and García-Benau, M. A. 2017. Integrated reports: disclosure level and explanatory factors. *Social Responsibility Journal*, *13*(1), 155–176.

Robb, S. W. G., Single, L. E., and Zarzeski, M. T. 2001. Nonfinancial disclosures across Anglo-American countries. *Journal of International Accounting, Auditing and Taxation*, *10*(1), 71–83.

Rutherford, B. A. 2005. Genre analysis of corporate annual report narratives: a corpus linguistics-based approach. *The Journal of Business Communication*, *42*(4), 349–378.

Sinclair, J. 1991. *Corpus, Concordance, Collocation*. Oxford: Oxford University Press.

Stenka, R. 2022. Beyond intentionality in accounting regulation: habitual strategizing by the IASB. *Critical Perspectives on Accounting*, *88*, 102294.

Stenka, R., and Jaworska, S. 2019. The use of made-up users. *Accounting, Organizations and Society*, *78*, 101055.

Stone, G. W., and Lodhia, S. 2019. Readability of integrated reports: an exploratory global study. *Accounting, Auditing & Accountability Journal*, *32*(5), 1532–1557.

Stubbs, M. (2001). *Words and Phrases: Corpus Studies of Lexical Semantics*. Oxford: Blackwell.

Tetlock, P. C. 2007. Giving content to investor sentiment: the role of media in the stock market. *Journal of Finance*, *62*(3), 1139–1168.

Tregidga, H., and Milne, M. J. 2006. From sustainable management to sustainable development: a longitudinal analysis of a leading New Zealand environmental reporter. *Business Strategy and the Environment*, *15*(4), 219–241.

Tregidga, H., Milne, M., and Lehman, G. 2012. Analyzing the quality, meaning and accountability of organizational reporting and communication: directions for future research. *Accounting Forum*, *36*(3), 223–230.

Tregidga, H., Kearins, K., and Milne, M. 2013. The politics of knowing 'organizational sustainable development'. *Organization & Environment*, *26*(1), 102–129.

Tregidga, H., Milne, M., and Kearins, K. 2014. (Re)presenting 'sustainable organizations'. *Accounting, Organizations and Society*, *39*(6), 477–494.

Tregidga, H., Milne, M., and Kearins, K. 2018. Ramping up resistance: corporate sustainable development and academic research. *Business & Society*, *57*(2), 292–334.

Unerman, J., and Chapman, C. 2014. Academic contributions to enhancing accounting for sustainable development. *Accounting, Organizations and Society*, *39*(6), 385–394.

Wodak, R., and Meyer, M. 2016. Critical discourse studies: history, agenda, theory and methodology. In: R. Wodak and M. Meyer (eds), *Methods of Critical Discourse Studies*. 3rd edn. London: Sage, pp. 1–22.

Zappettini, F., and Unerman, J. 2016. 'Mixing' and 'bending': the recontextualisation of discourses of sustainability in integrated reporting. *Discourse & Communication*, *10*(5), 521–542.

26. Sustainability reporting and communication in new media

Charles H. Cho, Dorota Dobija, Chaoyuan She and Ewelina Zarzycka

1 INTRODUCTION

Sustainability reporting guidelines challenge organizations to provide fair, accurate, transparent and balanced reports by disclosing their sustainable efforts in one-way communications on a regular basis. However, communication between businesses and their stakeholders has evolved because of the advent of new media outlets. The spread of the Internet, particularly social media (SM) platforms, not only makes it possible for sustainability information to reach different stakeholders more quickly, but it also makes it possible for stakeholders to take part in this dissemination more easily; stakeholders can disclose, engage, and even challenge businesses about their sustainability-related (non-)actions. As a result, SM has become a "public arena of citizenship" (Whelan et al., 2013, p. 777); yet the usage of new media brings some threats to businesses since stakeholders could disclose information against the will of companies, posing risks to their reputation and financial stability.

In this study, we provide a reflection on the use of new media by different types of organizations – private sector; public sector; and NGOs. This reflection is mainly derived from our own research findings as well as the relevant literature that we identified from prior research. We argue that the development of new media communication inherently varies across different types of organizations. More specifically, we highlight that new media expose private and public organizations to more reputational risks as they have made it easier for stakeholders and citizens to engage with and criticize these sectors on sustainability issues. In order to manage potential reputational damage that arises from such exposure, new media are often used by private and public organizations as a tool for one-way communication and stakeholder impression management. NGOs, in contrast, benefit the most in the rise of new media communication as digital platforms have become an effective arena in which grassroot NGOs can initiate social activism and disseminate counter accounts to hold private and public organizations accountable for irresponsible activities. Different usage of new media by organizations would also lead to potentially divergent implications for future development in new media on organizations' sustainability reporting practices. Therefore, we discuss how future development of new media may impact different types of organizations and suggest future avenues of research.

The remainder of the chapter is organized as follows. Section 2 gives an overview of the use of new media in sustainability reporting by the private sector. Sections 3 and 4 provide the same for public sector organizations and NGOs, respectively. Section 5 suggests avenues for future research.

2 USE OF NEW MEDIA IN SUSTAINABILITY REPORTING BY PRIVATE SECTOR

Traditionally, most companies provide sustainability information through officially published annual sustainability reports – interpreting the data against previous years, drawing conclusions and communicating the results to stakeholders – most commonly in a static document in print and/or online (Reimsbach & Hahn, 2015). Corporate websites are also considered an effective channel to provide stakeholders with non-financial information. However, the development of new communication technologies has had a profound impact on how companies disclose sustainability information and communicate with stakeholders (Dumay, 2016). The Internet, which offers global discussion forums (Unerman & Bennett, 2004), has been, and continues to be, used to facilitate simultaneous online discussions involving a wide range of people. New Internet-based channels of communication, such as SM, mainly have the potential to substantially change the process of stakeholder engagement and dialogue (for literature review on SM and sustainability see: Nerantzidis et al., 2023). SM are defined as "a group of Internet-based applications that build on the ideological and technological foundations of Web 2.0, and that allow the creation and exchange of user generated content" (Kaplan & Haenlein, 2010, p. 61). Recent studies provide evidence that firm size, board structure and companies' position in corporate social responsibility (CSR) rankings determines the use of SM platforms for sustainability disclosures (Amin et al., 2021; Xiang & Birt, 2021).

The use of SM leads to the production of *more* information, its *quicker* diffusion and new ways to access, evaluate and use it (Dumay & Guthrie, 2017). SM thus entails that firms are pressured to pay more attention to the opinions of their individual stakeholders and to change and adapt their legitimation strategies accordingly (Castelló et al., 2016). By allowing companies to interact with large groups of people, especially external stakeholders, SM is particularly well suited for stakeholder engagement (Bellucci & Manetti, 2017). It mainly enables companies to communicate with stakeholders and establish a dialogue with them about sustainability issues (Bebbington et al., 2007; Bellucci et al., 2019). Some companies create digital space in SM where individual citizens can discuss CSR problems and even voice their concerns about corporate practices (Whelan et al., 2013). As a result of these interactions, companies may identify material topics for stakeholders, which they should account for, as well as providing supplementary sustainability information required by different stakeholder groups (Lodhia & Stone, 2017). Moreover, SM makes it possible for stakeholders to "initiate and discuss any issue of their interest and engage in dialogue about and with the company, in a media characterized by almost immediate and worldwide diffusion" (Gómez-Carrasco & Michelon, 2017, p. 855). As such, SM may act as the "public arena of citizenship" (Whelan et al., 2013, p. 777), where stakeholders disseminate content though Facebook, Instagram or Twitter, frequently against the will of companies (Dumay & Guthrie, 2017). Through such involuntary disclosures, stakeholders may fight for the right to have some impact on companies' decisions regarding CSR strategies and practices (Lyon & Montgomery, 2013; Saxton et al., 2021; Wenzel et al., 2021; Whelan et al., 2013). Via SM, stakeholders demonstrate their increased collective power by voicing their ethical and broader social concerns regarding companies' activities (Kim & Young, 2017; Saxton et al., 2021). Specifically, Twitter constituted an important opinion-voicing arena; stakeholder messages can be morally and ethically persuasive, impacting corporate actions (Neu et al., 2020). The use of repetition and persuasion techniques (Hossain et al., 2019; Suddaby et al., 2015) in tweets aims to force companies to respond to the actions that are advocated by stakeholders. Stakeholder disclosures can be positive as well as negative for a company and are not subject to any regulations and/or company control, which may pose a threat to a firm's reputation if not managed properly (Dumay & Guthrie, 2017). However, recent research finds that companies are not willing to respond to involuntary disclosures made by stakeholders (Dobija et al., 2023a).

Prior research also documents that companies generally fail to engage in two-way dialogues with stakeholders, focusing on one-way communications and mere disclosure of sustainability information for legitimacy purposes (e.g., Ardiana, 2019; Gómez-Carrasco et al., 2021; Manetti & Bellucci, 2016). Manetti and Belluci (2016) find that companies interact with stakeholders through SM mainly in order to define the sustainability content, while Okazaki et al. (2020) report that firms' online communication is limited to broadcasting general announcements addressed mainly to customers. The latter is confirmed by Ardiana's (2019) study of Australian companies that engage with stakeholders on SM to boost market share. Companies' strategies aimed at impression management or legitimacy building can have diverse effects on stakeholder perception. According to She and Michelon (2019), actions-related disclosures may generate both positive as well as negative reactions of stakeholders, while Maniora and Pott (2020) find that the number of social posts on Facebook is negatively associated with the company's reputation.

Thus, it is particularly important to understand *what* strategies companies need to develop to engage stakeholders in more meaningful two-way communication (Dobija et al., 2023a; Gómez-Carrasco et al., 2021; Okazaki et al., 2020) to bring real sustainable change (Hahn et al., 2020), improve their sustainability performance (Dube & Zhu, 2021) and increase organizational accountability (Neu et al., 2020). However, it is still unclear whether companies should address all stakeholders in SM in the same way regardless of their power and status, or ignore some less salient ones (Saxton et al., 2021). Moreover, it is crucial to understand how companies draft their messages on SM and what topics should be discussed to attract shareholders' reactions. Finally, some authors claim that both companies and stakeholders should play a symmetric role in converting SM communication into sustainability-related outcomes (Hahn et al., 2020). According to Dillard and Roslender (2011) dialogic, or polygonic, accounting conducted on SM platforms may play an important role in enhancing a two-way dialogue between a company and its stakeholders. In dialogic accounting, stakeholders are encouraged to express their own views and expectations towards a company (Bellucci et al., 2019) – not only as a reaction to corporate communication but also as a form of independent information disclosure about a company.

3   ROLE OF NEW MEDIA IN SUSTAINABILITY REPORTING BY PUBLIC SECTOR ORGANIZATIONS

Digital technologies are also changing the relationship between public administration and citizens, improving the possibilities for greater transparency and accountability (Gesuele, 2016). As in the case of private sector companies, public sector organizations (both independent agencies and/or national and local governments) can also use new media in order to directly connect, but also interact, with citizens (Agostino, 2013). Sustainability development is certainly one of the important aspects communicated through these new channels.

A growing number of public sector organizations worldwide engage in sustainability reporting, both voluntarily and in response to legal pressures (Giacomini et al., 2021; Niemann & Hoppe, 2018) in the hope of better policymaking and citizen engagement. Pan-national organizations such as the OECD or the World Bank have advocated the adoption of socially responsible practices by public sector organizations (Fox et al., 2002; OECD, 2006). Also, the UN's Agenda 21 action plan recognizes in particular the role of local government organizations in promoting sustainable development because of their proximity to citizens' daily lives. At the same time, citizens are also calling for greater transparency and accountability in relation to sustainable practices of public sector organizations (Argento et al., 2019), as the public expects public organizations to manage the limited resources in a sustainable manner (Lynch, 2010). However, unlike in the private sector, the practice of issuing sustainability reports has yet to be fully adopted (Giacomini, 2020; MacDonald et al., 2020). Prior research on sustainability disclosure of public sector organizations focused mainly on reports, documents and website analysis (Alcaraz-Quiles et al., 2014; Che Ku Kassim et al., 2019; 2020; Niemann & Hoppe, 2018; Ortiz-Rodríguez et al., 2015).

New media also becomes increasingly important in the case of the public sector as governments experiment with such concepts as e-government, e-services, e-management, e-citizen and e-democracy. However, research on how public sector organizations use new media channels to communicate on social and environmental aspects is still rare and mainly focuses on the use of websites. Navarro et al. (2014), for instance, analyze local government websites and found that while they do not publish sustainability reports, they do report significant information about sustainability on their websites and suggest that there is a need to make managers and politicians more aware of the significance of providing sustainability information to citizens, as well as the importance of having a strategy for online communications on sustainability. At the same time, to increase the use of new media, additional investments are needed in online and broadband services to make the information available to the public. Che Ku Kassim et al. (2020) analyzed the environmental disclosures of local governments in the context of developing countries and document that the public sector has taken initiatives to provide such disclosures on its websites even in the absence of any regulatory framework, although the scope of information provided is limited and varies considerably. Alcaraz-Quiles et al. (2014) investigated the determinants of online sustainability reporting by local governments and suggest that population size and financial autonomy may have a positive impact on sustainability reporting by local governments, while fiscal pressures negatively influence the scope of sustainability reporting.

While a growing field of research discussing the use of new media in the public sector exists, studies mentioning sustainability are very limited so far. Digital technologies, especially SM, provide opportunities for instant sharing of information about actions and interactions between public sector organizations and citizens (de Boer, 2023). SM may also influence the role citizens may play in public accountability (Vanhommerig & Karré, 2014). However, public sector organizations do not use the full potential of the new media and focus on passive communication directed more at informing rather than interacting and engaging (Chen et al., 2020; Falco & Kleinhans, 2018; Mergel, 2012; 2013; Neely & Collins, 2018). Prior research also focused on attributes of public communication that can enhance public engagement, investigating how communication styles and the use of more participatory approaches by information providers may affect public engagement (Agostino, 2013; Agostino & Arnaboldi, 2016; Bonsón et al., 2015; Meijer & Thaens, 2013; Mergel, 2013). Additionally, several studies investigated public engagement, focusing on a specific context of communication such as Covid-19 communication or a crisis situation (Mansoor, 2021; Padeiro et al., 2021; Tang et al., 2021; Tursunbayeva et al., 2017).

However, prior research suggests that governments generally fail to use SM to engage with citizens (Faber et al., 2020; Landi et al., 2021; Trencher, 2019; Warren et al., 2014; Zavattaro & Sementelli, 2014). Dobija et al. (2023b) suggest, however, that the topic of the conversation requires the adoption of different communication strategies in order to create engagement. When it comes directly to sustainability reporting in new media, Giacomini et al. (2021) investigated environmental disclosures by local governments and find that despite a general decrease in other sustainability reporting practices, the use of new media (particularly Facebook) for sustainability purposes increases. In addition, citizens become more active when it comes to sustainability matters as compared with other posts. However, the communication between the governments and citizens can be still described as one way on both sides. How public sector organizations get involved with communication on sustainability and whether they are able to conduct two-way communications, or even a dialogue with citizens, is still to be investigated.

4   USE OF SOCIAL MEDIA BY NGOS AND DISSEMINATION OF COUNTER ACCOUNTS

The use of new media by NGOs is not a new phenomenon. In fact, long before the widespread popularity of social networking sites, NGOs have been using Web 1.0 technologies such as blogs and e-mails to communicate with members and promote campaigns (Seo et al., 2009). With the rise of Web 2.0 technologies and social networks, communications have moved from one-way messaging to two-way interactions (Kaplan & Haenlein, 2010). In contrast to private and public sectors that continue using new media as a one-way communication mechanism, NGOs quickly adapted to this new fashion and incorporated new media into their communication strategy to expand audience size and improve campaign effectiveness (Guo & Saxton, 2013). According to the 2018 Global NGO Technology Report (Nonprofit Tech for Good, 2018), in 2017 93% of NGOs worldwide had a Facebook page, 77% had a Twitter page, and 56% had a LinkedIn page. While extensive academic literature has provided supporting evidence that the use of social media by NGOs can increase the effectiveness of fundraising (Saxton & Wang, 2014), building social capital (Saxton & Guo, 2020), organizing social movements (Karpf, 2010), and educating the public (Seo et al., 2009), what fascinates accounting scholars is its potential use to disseminate counter accounts and bring emancipatory actions in respect of irresponsible corporate practices that the private sector often tries to greenwash in its social media communications (Gallhofer et al., 2006).

Counter accounts are defined as "accounting information produced by external individuals and/or organizations on their representation of the social and environmental impacts of others" (Dey & Gibbon, 2014, p. 109). In contrast to the conventional notion of accounting information reported by corporations in their annual reports, counter accounts aim to portray an alternative picture of corporations' social and environmental impacts that allow stakeholders to make not only economic decisions but also moral and political ones (Vinnari & Laine, 2017). In other words, counter accounts can be considered "an illustration of the low epistemological threshold of accounting" (Vinnari & Laine, 2017, p. 12). Due to their unique nature, counter accounts may exist in various formats, ranging from traditional reports – such as shadow reports and social audits (Apostol, 2015; Thomson et al., 2015; Tregidga, 2017) that disclose both quantitative and qualitative financial and non-financial information – to innovative formats such as maps (Denedo et al., 2017), videos (Laine & Vinnari, 2017; Vinnari & Laine, 2017), website blogs (Irvine & Moerman, 2017), and social media messages (Denedo et al., 2019).

There are two main streams of accounting literature examining the use of SM by NGOs. The first stream focuses on the co-production process of counter accounts via SM. The key cornerstone behind this process is the notion of dialogic accounting. Dialogic accounting is defined as a process where stakeholders are engaged and empowered during the dialogue process to promote transformative actions (Brown & Dillard, 2013; Unerman & Bennett, 2004). By engaging with stakeholders from diversified backgrounds, NGOs can promote mutual learning processes, stimulate conversations, and better develop a relationship between NGOs and their stakeholders (Bellucci & Manetti, 2017). Consequently, insightful counter accounting information can be produced as an outcome of the dialogic process and such information can be further engaged with stakeholders via social media to problematize the exposed issues. Several studies have examined how NGOs use SM to facilitate the co-production of counter accounts from a dialogic accounting perspective. For example, Bellucci and Manetti (2017) examine how Facebook is utilized as an instrument for dialogic accounting by a sample of US non-profit organizations and they find that, while only a minority of the organizations employ Facebook to engage with stakeholders, those that have SM profiles use the platforms to create a system of dialogic interaction on social, environmental and financial topics with stakeholders. Denedo et al. (2019) examine how local NGOs perceive the usefulness of counter accounts in protecting the human, economic and environmental rights of indigenous communities in the Niger Delta and they find that Facebook, Twitter, Blogs, YouTube and Instagram are extensively used by these NGOs to problematize irresponsible corporate practices and to support community and coalition building in different arenas. In a similar vein, Vinnari and Laine (2017) analyzed video clips that are filmed by animal activists and go viral on SM and find that activists make visual messages appeal to stakeholders' morality to shorten the distance between audiences and the distant suffering "others" – in their case, pigs on Finnish farms. As a result, using SM messages as a form of moral and political education, counter accounts can evoke audiences' sympathy towards the oppressed group and present practical options on how to act on the suffering.

SM may also facilitate the creation of a new wave of conversations which could be different from the counter accounts that are initially exposed. For example, when examining Twitter users' reactions to the Panama Papers, Neu et al. (2020) find that social activist groups (including NGOs) employ SM to expose previously private financial information to the public and initiate accountability conversations on social media. However, in a subsequent study, Neu and Saxton (2024) find that, while the initial Panama Papers information released mainly targets politicians and their business allies, the Twitter conversation stream that occurred (either immediately or years) after the event no longer focused on politicians and corporate social responsibility. Instead, the Twitter conversation sparked a new debate on the notion of social accountability and the demands for such accountability.

The second stream of accounting literature examines whether counter accounts that are disseminated by NGOs (or other grassroots activist groups) via social media may generate any impacts on stakeholders' behaviors and corporate sustainability activities. The argument behind this research question is that SM can create a public arena of citizenship where stakeholders can be empowered to comment on and publicize a firm's sustainability activities and to hold firms accountable for their irresponsible practices (Lyon & Montgomery, 2013; Whelan et al., 2013). For example, using a case study of Action on Smoking and Health UK (ASH) and their use of counter accounts during the period 1999–2010, Thomson et al. (2015) find that ASH disseminates counter accounts via Facebook and YouTube to reduce the demand for smoking and confronts the social responsibility claims of British American Tobacco. Similarly, by employing Castells' network-making perspective, She (2023) argues that social media dissemination of counter accounts would strengthen NGOs' network-making power; thus a large group of corporate stakeholders can be engaged, and a strong network can potentially be formed to enhance the effectiveness of NGOs' campaigns. By analyzing Greenpeace's "Save The Arctic" (STA) campaign, She (2023) finds that stakeholder interactions with disseminated counter accounts, and the number of Facebook accounts connected in disseminating such information, lead to more stakeholders signing up the petitions. Furthermore, Greenpeace's social media dissemination of counter accounts can also attract policymakers' attention and influence public opinions towards climate change.

Some studies also find that counter accounts disseminated by NGOs via SM indirectly influence corporate activities by mobilizing shareholders. For example, by examining Twitter messages posted by large non-governmental organizations (NGOs) targeting companies from the S&P500, Dupire et al. (2021) find that NGO tweets stating a positive message about the sustainability activities of the firm have a positive effect on stock prices, while negative tweets have a negative effect. In the same vein, using a sample of over 1.5 million tweets referring to Spanish-listed banks, Gómez-Carrasco and Michelon (2017) find that tweets published by trade unions have negative effects on both stock price and trading volume. By contrast, tweets published by civic and consumer associations can only have negative effects on the share price when these tweets are reacted to by many Twitter users. However, there is still little understanding of whether and how NGOs' SM communication can affect corporate sustainability reporting practices, considering the increasing societal demand for greater transparency on sustainability issues.

5   AVENUES FOR FURTHER RESEARCH IN SUSTAINABILITY REPORTING AND NEW MEDIA

Based on previous and current research, we note that while some skepticism about the usage of new media for sustainability reporting is documented, there is a lack of depth on such analyses. The implications of the usage of new media may also differ depending on the type of organizations we examine. Furthermore, literature does not seem to clearly connect the dots with other pressing areas of research related to the advent of technology.

First, the development of new media, such as SM, can provide more opportunities for NGOs to enhance their ability to speak truth to power. Given the high autonomy and interactivity of SM communication, the co-production of counter accounts can move from an NGO-led approach – where NGOs prepare and disseminate counter accounts and stakeholders share such information – to a crowdsourced one, where information is gathered and contributed solely by stakeholders via social media. Perkiss et al. (2019) refer to this co-production process as "spotlight accounting" , in which crowdsourced information, including data on sustainability, is systematically collated in a central, public database for shared utility. However, we believe that the spotlight accounting process can be further categorized into two different forms: (1) the production of accounting information takes place completely on social media; and (2) production of accounting information is based on data that are physically counted and collected by contributors, but the initiation, collation, and dissemination are done via social media. WikiRate, as discussed in Perkiss et al. (2019), is a typical example of the first case, in which contributors search for sustainability information in companies' reports and input relevant information into an online datasheet. #BreakFreeFromPlastic (BFFP) is a good example of the second form. BFFP is a global movement, initiated on social media, which works to achieve a future free from plastic pollution.[1] Every year, BFFP conducts a brand audit that involves counting and documenting brands found in plastic waste to help identify companies that are responsible for plastic pollution. By the end of 2022, BFFP has organized 2,373 brand audit events and audited 2,125,414 items of plastic waste with the help of 206,895 volunteers in 87 countries – all initiated and organized via social media. As a result, we believe that scholars could further explore both forms of spotlight accounting to shed light both on how stakeholders are coordinated during the co-production process and on the potential implications of spotlight accounting on corporate sustainability activities.

However, new media also comes with a "dark side" – there are recent occurrences where such media have been used and abused to spread "fake news" and misinformation (e.g., the 2016 US presidential elections; Covid-19) and have endangered society in many ways. Therefore, the role and use of new media in sustainability reporting also comes with threats – whether they are triggered by the organizations or the stakeholders. Examining such "dark side" risks and dangers, as well as the impact of this new communication channel on society, seems to be warranted in this area.

Next, an issue closely related to new media is the advent of Web 3.0 technologies, such as blockchain, virtual reality (VR), "bots", and the exponential growth of artificial intelligence (AI). Blockchain and AI can be powerful tools for sustainability reporting as the production and dissemination of information is becoming decentralized, so that information is no longer stored and monitored by organizations. Consequently, there might be no need for organizations to create a centrally administered database to store sustainability information as such information could be computed, recorded, and published by AI into the blockchain. Indeed, whether sustainability reports would still exist in the future is also questionable since corporate sustainability-related transactions would be automatically recorded and updated by suppliers and customers (without manipulations by corporations) in a blockchain ledger (Tapscott & Tapscott, 2016). As a result, we believe that understanding the impact of Web 3.0 technologies on sustainability reporting and what roles private, public, and NGO sectors could play during this process would be a promising topic to be investigated.

At the same time, we think that the advent of these new technologies, especially AI, also creates news risks for organizations. Whenever technology interferes with how humans decide, live and act, there is systematically a potential problem – and risk (Boulianne et al., 2023). This is well documented from an ethics perspective by considering "the ethical challenges raised by big data analytics and artificial intelligence" (Brivot & Cho, 2023, p. xxiv). More specifically, Boulianne et al. (2023) post that artificial intelligence has the capacity to carry out sophisticated tasks typically performed by humans, including speaking and writing, and tries to mimic how the human brain works. However, systematic biases and concerns about data privacy provide unanticipated ethical problems; therefore AI has a flip side and is prone to human error and prejudice. If we transpose this issue to the context of sustainability and sustainability reporting, the same concerns persist, therefore warranting further research to investigate the many issues related to new media communication on sustainability generated by AI and bots.

Finally, one important future research avenue remains the *effectiveness* of new media communication – does, or will, this bring real change, or will we remain at the stage of more sustainability talk and less action (Cho et al., 2012)?

NOTE

1. More information can be found on BFFP website: https://www.breakfreefromplastic.org/.

REFERENCES

Agostino, D. (2013). Using social media to engage citizens: a study of Italian municipalities. *Public Relations Review*, 39(3), 232–234.

Agostino, D., & Arnaboldi, M. (2016). A measurement framework for assessing the contribution of social media to public engagement: an empirical analysis on Facebook. *Public Management Review*, 18(9), 1289–1307.

Alcaraz-Quiles, F.J., Navarro-Galera, A., & Ortiz-Rodríguez, D. (2014). Factors determining online sustainability reporting by local governments. *International Review of Administrative Sciences*, 81(1), 79–109.

Amin, M.H., Mohamed, E.K., & Elragal, A. (2021). CSR disclosure on Twitter: evidence from the UK. *International Journal of Accounting Information Systems*, 40, 100500.

Apostol, O.M. (2015). A project for Romania? The role of the civil society's counter-accounts in facilitating democratic change in society. *Accounting, Auditing & Accountability Journal*, 28, 210–241.

Ardiana, P.A. (2019). Stakeholder engagement in sustainability reporting: evidence of reputation risk management in large Australian companies. *Australian Accounting Review*, 29(4), 726–747.

Argento, D., Grossi, G., Persson, K., & Vingren, T. (2019). Sustainability disclosures of hybrid organizations: Swedish state-owned enterprises. *Meditari Accountancy Research*, 27(4), 505–533.

Bebbington, J., Brown, J., Frame, B., & Thomson, I. (2007). Theorizing engagement: the potential of a critical dialogic approach. *Accounting, Auditing and Accountability Journal*, 20(3), 356–381.

Bellucci, M., & Manetti, G. (2017). Facebook as a tool for supporting dialogic accounting? Evidence from large philanthropic foundations in the United States. *Accounting, Auditing and Accountability Journal*, 30(4), 874–905.

Bellucci, M., Simoni, L., Acuti, D., & Manetti, G. (2019). Stakeholder engagement and dialogic accounting: empirical evidence in sustainability reporting. *Accounting, Auditing and Accountability Journal*, 32(5), 1467–1499.

Bonsón, E., Royo, S., & Ratkai, M. (2015). Citizens' engagement on local governments' Facebook sites. An empirical analysis: the impact of different media and content types in Western Europe. *Government Information Quarterly*, 32(1), 52–62.

Boulianne, E., Fortin, M., & Lecompte, A. (2023). Artificial intelligence and data analytics: ethical implications for accounting. In M. Brivot & C.H. Cho (eds), *Research Handbook on Accounting and Ethics*. Cheltenham, UK, and Northampton, MA: Edward Elgar Publishing, pp. 168–190.

Brivot, M., & Cho, C.H. (2023). *Handbook on Accounting and Ethics*. Cheltenham, UK, and Northampton, MA: Edward Elgar Publishing.

Brown, J., & Dillard, J. (2013). Critical accounting and communicative action: on the limits of consensual deliberation. *Critical Perspectives on Accounting*, 24(3), 176–190.

Castelló, I., Etter, M., & Nielsen, F.A. (2016). Strategies of legitimacy through social media: the networked strategy. *Journal of Management Studies*, 53(3), 402–432.

Che Ku Kassim, C., Ahmad, S., Mohd Nasir, N., Wan Mohd Nori, W., & Mod Arifin, N. (2019). Environmental reporting by the Malaysian local governments. *Meditari Accountancy Research*, 27(4), 633–651.

Che Ku Kassim, C.K.H., Ahmad, S., Mohd Nasir, N.E., Mod Arifin, N.N., & Wan Mohd Nori, W.M.N. (2020). Environmental disclosures on local governments' websites: a Malaysian context. *International Journal of Public Sector Management*, 33(6/7), 663–679.

Chen, Q., Min, C., Zhang, W., Wang, G., Ma, X., & Evans, R. (2020). Unpacking the black box: how to promote citizen engagement through government social media during the COVID-19 crisis. *Computers in Human Behavior*, 110, 106380.

Cho, C.H., Guidry, R.P., Hageman, A.M., & Patten, D.M. (2012). Do actions speak louder than words? An empirical investigation of corporate environmental reputation. *Accounting, Organizations and Society*, 37(1), 14–25.

de Boer, T. (2023). Updating public accountability: a conceptual framework of voluntary accountability. *Public Management Review*, 25(6), 1128–1151.

Denedo, M., Thomson, I., & Yonekura, A. (2017). International advocacy NGOs, counter accounting, accountability and engagement. *Accounting, Auditing & Accountability Journal*, 30(6), 1309–1343.

Denedo, M., Thomson, I., & Yonekura, A. (2019). Ecological damage, human rights and oil: local advocacy NGOs dialogic action and alternative accounting practices. *Accounting Forum*, 43(1), 85–112.

Dey, C., & Gibbon, J. (2014). External accounts. In J. Bebbington, J. Unerman, & B. O'Dwyer (eds), *Sustainability Accounting and Accountability*. 2nd edn. Abingdon: Routledge, pp. 108–123.

Dillard, J., & Roslender, R. (2011). Taking pluralism seriously: embedded moralities in management accounting and control systems. *Critical Perspectives on Accounting*, 22(2), 135–147.

Dobija, D., Cho, C.H., She, C., Zarzycka, E., Krasodomska, J., & Jemielniak, D. (2023a). Involuntary disclosures and stakeholder-initiated communication on social media. *Organization and Environment*, 36, 69–97.

Dobija, D., Grossi, G., Staniszewska, Z., & Mora, L. (2023b). Adaptive social media communication for web-based accountability. Working paper, Kozminski University.

Dube, S., & Zhu, C. (2021). The disciplinary effect of social media: evidence from firms' responses to glassdoor reviews. *Journal of Accounting Research*, 59(5), 1783–1825.

Dumay, J. (2016). A critical reflection on the future of intellectual capital: from reporting to disclosure. *Journal of Intellectual Capital*, 17(1), 168–184.

Dumay, J., & Guthrie, J. (2017). Involuntary disclosure of intellectual capital: is it relevant? *Journal of Intellectual Capital*, 18(1), 29–44.

Dupire, M., Filbien, J.-Y., & M'Zali, B. (2021). Non-governmental organization (NGO) tweets: do shareholders care? *Business & Society*, 61(2), 419–456.

Faber, B., Budding, T., & Gradus, R. (2020). Assessing social media use in Dutch municipalities: political, institutional, and socio-economic determinants. *Government Information Quarterly*, 37(3), 101484.

Falco, E., & Kleinhans, R. (2018). Beyond information-sharing. a typology of government challenges and requirements for two-way social media communication with citizens. *Electronic Journal of E-Government*, 16(1), 32–45.

Fox, T., Ward, H., & Howard, B. (2002). *Public Sector Roles in Strengthening Corporate Social Responsibility. A Baseline Study*. New York: World Bank. Available at: https://www.iied.org/16017iied.

Gallhofer, S., Haslam, J., Monk, E., & Roberts, C. (2006). The emancipatory potential of online reporting: the case of counter accounting. *Accounting, Auditing & Accountability Journal*, 19(5), 681–718.

Gesuele, B. (2016). Municipalities and Facebook use: which key drivers? Empirical evidence from Italian municipalities. *International Journal of Public Administration*, 39 (10), 771–777.

Giacomini, D. (2020). Debate: should there be rules governing social media use for accountability in the public sector? *Public Money Management*, 40(6), 471–472.

Giacomini, D., Rocca, L., Zola, P., & Mazzoleni, M. (2021). Local governments' environmental disclosure via social networks: organizational legitimacy and stakeholders' interactions. *Journal of Cleaner Production*, 317, 128290.

Gómez-Carrasco, P., & Michelon, G. (2017). The power stakeholders' voice: the effects of social media activism on stock markets. *Business Strategy and the Environment*, 26(6), 855–872.

Gómez-Carrasco, P., Guillamón-Saorín, E., & Garcia Osma, B. (2021). Stakeholders versus firm communication in social media: the case of Twitter and corporate social responsibility information. *European Accounting Review*, 30(1), 31–62.

Guo, C., & Saxton, G.D. (2013). Tweeting social change: how social media are changing nonprofit advocacy. *Nonprofit and Voluntary Sector Quarterly*, 43, 57–79.

Hahn, R., Reimsbach, D., Wickert, C., & Eccles, R. (2020). Special issue of Organization and Environment on "Nonfinancial disclosure and real sustainable change within and beyond organizations: mechanisms". *Organization and Environment*, 33(2), 311–314.

Hossain, M., Islam, M.T., Momin, M.A., Nahar, S., & Alam, M.S. (2019). Understanding communication of sustainability reporting: application of symbolic convergence theory (SCT). *Journal of Business Ethics*, 160, 563–586.

Irvine, H., & Moerman, L. (2017). Gambling with the public sphere: accounting's contribution to debate on social issues. *Critical Perspectives on Accounting*, 48, 35–52.

Kaplan, A.M., & Haenlein, M. (2010). Users of the world, unite! The challenges and opportunities of social media. *Business Horizons*, 53(1), 59–68.

Karpf, D. (2010). Online political mobilization from the Advocacy Group's perspective: looking beyond clicktivism. *Policy & Internet*, 2, 7–41.

Kim, E., & Young, Y.N. (2017). How do social media affect analyst stock recommendations? Evidence from SandP 500 electric power companies' Twitter accounts. *Strategic Management Journal*, 38, 2599–2622.

Laine, M., & Vinnari, E. (2017). The transformative potential of counter accounts: a case study of animal rights activism. *Accounting, Auditing & Accountability Journal*, 30(7), 1481–1510.

Landi, S., Costantini, A., Fasan, M., & Bonazzi, M. (2021). Public engagement and dialogic accounting through social media during COVID-19 crisis: a missed opportunity? *Accounting, Auditing & Accountability Journal*, 35(1), 35–47.

Lodhia, S.K., & Stone, G. (2017). Integrated reporting in an Internet and social media communication environment: conceptual insights. *Australian Accounting Review*, 27, 17–33.

Lynch, B. (2010). An examination of environmental reporting by Australian state government departments. *Accounting Forum*, 34, 32–45.

Lyon, T.P., & Montgomery, A.W. (2013). Tweetjacked: the impact of social media on corporate greenwash. *Journal of Business Ethics*, 118(4), 747–757.

MacDonald, A., Clarke, A., Ordonez-Ponce, E., Chai, Z., & Andreasen, J. (2020). Sustainability managers: the job roles and competencies of building sustainable cities and communities. *Public Performance Management Review*, 43(6), 1–32.

Manetti, G., & Bellucci, M. (2016). The use of social media for engaging stakeholders in sustainability reporting. *Accounting, Auditing and Accountability Journal*, 29(6), 985–1011.

Maniora, J., & Pott, C. (2020). Does firms' dissemination of corporate social responsibility information through Facebook matter for corporate reputation? *Journal of International Accounting Research*, 19(2), 167–196.

Mansoor, M. (2021). Citizens' trust in government as a function of good governance and government agency's provision of quality information on social media during COVID-19. *Government Information Quarterly*, 38(4), 101597.

Meijer, A., & Thaens, M. (2013). Social media strategies: understanding the differences between North American police departments. *Government Information Quarterly*, 30(4), 343–350.

Mergel, I. (2012). *Social Media in the Public Sector: A Guide to Participation, Collaboration and Transparency in the Networked World*. San Francisco, CA: John Wiley & Sons.

Mergel, I. (2013). A framework for interpreting social media interactions in the public sector. *Government Information Quarterly*, 30(4), 327–334.

Navarro Galera, A., de los Ríos Berjillos, A., Ruiz Lozano, M., & Tirado Valencia, P. (2014). Transparency of sustainability information in local governments: English-speaking and Nordic cross-country analysis. *Journal of Cleaner Production*, 64, 495–504.

Neely, S.R., & Collins, M. (2018). Social media and crisis communications: a survey of local governments in Florida. *Journal of Homeland Security and Emergency Management*, 15(1), 20160067.

Nerantzidis, M., Tampakoudis, I., & She, C. (2023). Social media in accounting research: a review and future research agenda. *SSRN Electronic Journal*.

Neu, D., & Saxton, G.D. (2024). Twitter-based social accountability callouts. *Journal of Business Ethics*, 189, 797–815.

Neu, D., Saxton, G., Everett, J., & Shiraz, A. (2020). Speaking truth to power: Twitter reactions to the Panama Papers. *Journal of Business Ethics*, 162, 473–485.

Niemann, L., & Hoppe, T. (2018). Sustainability reporting by local governments: a magic tool? Lessons on use and usefulness from European pioneers. *Public Management Review*, 20(1), 201–223.

Nonprofit Tech for Good (2018). *2018 Global NGO Technology Report*. Available at: http://techreport.ngo/.

OECD (2006). *Digital Broadband Content: Public Sector Information and Content*. Paris: OECD.

Okazaki, S., Plangger, K., West, W., & Menéndez, H. (2020). Exploring digital corporate social responsibility communications on Twitter. *Journal of Business Research*, 17, 675–682.

Ortiz-Rodríguez, D., Navarro-Galera, A., & Alcaraz-Quiles, F. (2015). The influence of administrative culture on sustainability transparency in European local governments. *Administration and Society*, 50(4), 555–594.

Padeiro, M., Bueno-Larraz, B., & Freitas, Â. (2021). Local governments' use of social media during the COVID-19 pandemic: the case of Portugal. *Government Information Quarterly*, 38(4), 101620.

Perkiss, S., Dean, B., & Gibbons, B. (2019). Crowdsourcing corporate transparency through social accounting: conceptualising the "Spotlight Account". *Social and Environmental Accountability Journal*, 39(2), 81–99.

Reimsbach, D., & Hahn, R. (2015). The effects of negative incidents in sustainability reporting on investors' judgments – an experimental study of third-party versus self-disclosure in the realm of sustainable development. *Business Strategy and the Environment*, 24(4), 217–235.

Saxton, G.D., & Guo, C. (2020). Social media capital: conceptualizing the nature, acquisition, and expenditure of social media-based organizational resources. *International Journal of Accounting Information Systems*, 36, 100443.

Saxton, G.D., & Wang, L. (2014). The social network effect: the determinants of giving through social media. *Nonprofit and Voluntary Sector Quarterly*, 43, 850–868.

Saxton, G.D., Ren, C., & Guo, C. (2021). Responding to diffused stakeholders on social media: connective power and firm reactions to CSR-related Twitter messages. *Journal of Business Ethics*, 172, 229–252.

Seo, H., Kim, J.Y., & Yang, S.-U. (2009). Global activism and new media: a study of transnational NGOs' online public relations. *Public Relations Review*, 35(2), 123–126.

She, C. (2023). Social media dissemination of counter accounts and stakeholder support – evidence from Greenpeace's "Save the Arctic" campaign on Facebook. *Accounting Forum*, 47(3), 390–415.

She, C., & Michelon, G. (2019). Managing stakeholder perceptions: organized hypocrisy in CSR disclosures on Facebook. *Critical Perspectives on Accounting*, 61, 54–76.

Suddaby, R., Saxton, G., & Gunz, S. (2015). Twittering change: the institutional work of domain change in accounting expertise. *Accounting, Organizations and Society*, 45, 52–68.

Tang, Z., Miller, A.S., Zhou, Z., & Warkentin, M. (2021). Does government social media promote users' information security behavior towards COVID-19 scams? Cultivation effects and protective motivations. *Government Information Quarterly*, 38(2), 101572.

Tapscott, D., & Tapscott, A. (2016). *Blockchain Revolution: How the Technology Behind Bitcoin Is Changing Money, Business, and the World*. New York: Penguin.

Thomson, I., Dey, C., & Russell, S. (2015). Activism, arenas and accounts in conflicts over tobacco control. *Accounting, Auditing & Accountability Journal*, 28(5), 809–845.

Tregidga, H. (2017). "Speaking truth to power": analysing shadow reporting as a form of shadow accounting. *Accounting, Auditing & Accountability Journal*, 30(3), 510–533.

Trencher, G. (2019). Towards the smart city 2.0: empirical evidence of using smartness as a tool for tackling social challenges. *Technological Forecasting and Social Change*, 142, 117–128.

Tursunbayeva, A., Franco, M., & Pagliari, C. (2017). Use of social media for e-Government in the public health sector: a systematic review of published studies. *Government Information Quarterly*, 34(2), 270–282.

Unerman, J. and Bennett, M. (2004). Increased stakeholder dialogue and the internet: towards greater corporate accountability or reinforcing capitalist hegemony? *Accounting, Organizations and Society*, 29(7), 685–707.

Vanhommerig, I., & Karré, P. M. (2014). Public accountability in the Internet age: changing roles for governments and citizens. *International Review of Public Administration*, 19(2), 206–217.

Vinnari, E., & Laine, M. (2017). The moral mechanism of counter accounts: the case of industrial animal production. *Accounting, Organizations and Society*, 57, 1–17.

Warren, A., Sulaiman, A., & Jaafar, N.I. (2014). Social media effects on fostering online civic engagement and building citizen trust and trust in institutions. *Government Information Quarterly*, 31(2), 291–301.

Wenzel, M., Trittin-Ulbrich, H., Edinger-Schons, L.M., Castelló, I., & de Bakker, F. (2021). Special issue Call for Papers: Stakeholder engagement: Opening up participation, inclusion, and democracy. *Business and Society*. Available at: https://journals.sagepub.com/pb-assets/cmscontent/BAS/CfP _Stakeholder_Engagement-1611936667513.pdf.

Whelan, G., Moon, J., & Grant, B. (2013). Corporations and citizenship arenas in the age of social media. *Journal of Business Ethics*, 118, 777–790.

Xiang, Y., & Birt, J.L. (2021). Internet reporting, social media strategy and firm characteristics – an Australian study. *Accounting Research Journal*, 34(1), 43–75.

Zavattaro, S., & Sementelli, A. (2014). A critical examination of social media adoption in government: introducing omnipresence. *Government Information Quarterly*, 31(2), 257–264.

27. Sustainability reporting in light of the European Union regulations: integrating theory and policy

Maria Aluchna

INTRODUCTION[1]

The ability of a company to grow and develop is determined by its capacity to forge sound relations with its constituencies. While social and environmental performance used to be an additional, voluntary, non-core business activity (Chan et al., 2014; Huang & Kung, 2010), it has now become one of the key aspects of strategy and an important metric of company operation. Since stakeholders recognize the importance of firms' social and environmental impacts, they expect companies to provide disclosure of non-financial performance (Ceulemans et al., 2015; Fernandez-Feijoo et al., 2014; Hooghiemstra, 2000). With a variety of terms in use, non-financial reporting is part of sustainability reporting, corporate social reporting, ESG reporting or integrated reporting, defined as information about the social, environmental and economic impact of business activities (Baboukardos & Rimmel, 2016; Boiral, 2013). Adopting the framework offered by different theoretical concepts, studies attempt to understand firm motivations, and the patterns and practice of sustainability disclosure (Bartolacci et al., 2022).

Prior literature has focused on the organizational and institutional determinants of voluntary reporting, as well as its development and institutionalization in the organizational context (Cho et al., 2012; Melloni et al., 2017; Stacchezzini et al., 2016). The existing research shows that many large companies that remain in the spotlight of public opinion have a history of issuing sustainability reports. The extensively explored corporate practice on non-financial reporting predominantly refers to the voluntary approach. Driven by the intention to respond to stakeholder pressure or to differentiate themselves from competitors, companies have been engaging in voluntary disclosure of their social and environmental activities. However, the voluntary reports revealed numerous shortcomings related to their narrative character, the lack of comparability across sectors and countries, and the absence of any verification by an external audit. Moreover, there remains a substantial number of firms, particularly small and medium-sized companies, as well as companies operating in less developed economies, that publish very limited non-financial information or none at all.

By introducing legislation on mandatory sustainability disclosure, countries are attempting to react to these limitations – firstly, they are addressing the weaknesses of the voluntary approach and seeking to improve the quality of reports, and secondly, they are exerting pressure on a large number of companies by demanding disclosure of their impact on society and the environment. Greater environmental, social and governance (ESG) transparency promotes social responsibility and provides information to a wide group of stakeholders (Esteban-Arrea & Garcia-Torea, 2022; Ottenstein et al., 2022). It is also meant to influence consumer choices, as well as having an impact on financing policy. In particular, investors, driven by arguments of risk mitigation, are expected to invest in sustainable companies, whereas banks are encouraged to offer loans to these firms (Hoepner & Schneider, 2022). As a result, increasing sustainability disclosure is presumed to stimulate growth of sustainable ventures while inhibiting investment in sectors that are harmful for society and the environment.

The goal of the study is to provide answers to two research questions on (1) what the actual limitations of sustainability disclosure are, and (2) how the EU regulation on sustainability reporting addresses these limitations. In addressing these research questions, the chapter outlines the conceptual frameworks adopted in the prior studies and current European Union regulation, centered around the concept of sustainability disclosure and the transition toward sustainable low emissions and a resource-efficient economy. In particular, the chapter outlines the EU legislation concerning sustainability reporting (SR) within the framework of stakeholder, institutional and legitimacy theories. The coercive mechanisms offered in the relevant regulations and directives mentioned above are also discussed here. Furthermore, this chapter positions the EU regulation within the existing literature, integrating theory, empirical evidence and policy recommendations.

The chapter is organized as follows. The next section presents the concept of non-financial reporting, presenting its definitions and origins, alongside its embodiment in corporate practice. The following section outlines the evolution from voluntary to mandatory reporting, succeeded by a discussion of the EU legislation centered around the Green Deal in the next section. Final remarks are presented in the concluding section.

THE CONCEPT OF NON-FINANCIAL REPORTING

Definition and Purpose

Sustainability/non-financial reporting (Manes-Rossi et al., 2018; Stolowy & Paugam, 2018) is understood as information about the social, environmental and economic impact of business activities (Boiral, 2013), presented under a voluntary or mandatory regime (Chelli et al., 2018) and disseminated according to selected standards, such as the GRI (Global Reporting Initiative) or IIRC (International Integrated Reporting Council) principles, the TCFD (Task Force on Climate-Related Financial Disclosures), the CDP (Carbon Disclosure Project) framework, TRI (toxic release inventory) or labor standards. It encompasses a variety of terms, such as social reporting (Gond & Herrbach, 2006), environmental reporting (Brammer & Pavelin, 2006), ESG reporting (Bernardi & Stark, 2018) or integrated reporting (Flower, 2015). There are also some specific terms commonly used in the literature, such as triple bottom line reporting (Norman & MacDonald, 2004), climate reporting (Pellegrino & Lodhia, 2012) or carbon disclosure (Matisoff et al., 2013). In addition, company membership in ratings databases (such as MSCI (formerly KLD) or ESG) can be interpreted as a proxy for sustainability disclosure. The data sets are based on non-financial information collected or accessed and (in certain cases) audited by consulting companies, which is subsequently used to calculate a rating or score index denoting the scope of reporting.

According to Gray et al. (1987), social and environmental reporting is defined as the process of communicating the social and environmental effects of organizational economic actions addressed to particular stakeholder groups and society at large. Christensen et al.

(2021) emphasize that sustainability reporting includes the measurement, disclosure and communication of information on ESG activities, risks and policies. Companies are expected to disclose social and environmental performance and policies and activities in response to the expectations of regulators, non-governmental organizations, social and environmental activist groups, customers, communities, investors and other stakeholders (Chan et al., 2014; Huang & Kung, 2010; Baboukardos et al., 2023). With regard to the format, the literature uses the terms of disclosure, reporting, report publishing and dissemination. It recognizes standalone and integrated reports published under voluntary or mandatory legal regimes and distinguishes different measures of reporting quality.

Non-financial reporting is viewed as the manifestation of a fundamental change in understanding company responsibility and accountability, replacing the traditional shareholder-focused approach with a stakeholder perspective (Kolk & Pinkse, 2010; La Torre et al., 2020). The scope of company responsibilities broadens to include its impact on society and the environment, and consequently a greater transparency in ESG activities is demanded by stakeholders (Baumüller & Sopp, 2022). Therefore, company performance is not solely based on the financial dimension but also incorporates the social and environmental impacts. Sustainability reporting is expected to develop company practice from "accounting-based accountability to accountability-based accounting" (La Torre et al., 2020, p. 711).

Accounting scholars emphasize that the development of non-financial disclosure represents the extension of reporting value related to ESG, which used to be neglected in traditional financial statements (Mio & Venturelli, 2013). Including non-financial measures allows the measuring of the financial value of a company to be augmented with recognition of its social and environmental progress and innovation. It also decreases information asymmetry for investors and other stakeholders (Coffee, 2021), offering a more precise picture of company activities in providing a set of measures to operationalize sustainable development.

Finally, non-financial disclosure is expected to broaden executives' horizons. With the incorporation of ESG components into firm performance, the assessment of corporate strategy gains a forward-looking perspective (Gray, 2010) that incorporates potential long-term costs and damage to society and the environment (Ballou et al., 2012). The rise in non-financial disclosure is expected to improve social and environmental performance, enhance the company's reputation and decrease ESG risks. Ultimately, sustainability reporting is presumed to stimulate a transition toward a sustainable economy, leading to positive social impacts and improved ESG performance.

Conceptual Frameworks for Explaining Corporate Practice

Studies on sustainability disclosure reveal significant differences in practice with respect to the scope, content and quality of corporate reports. Such differences arise from the voluntary approach to SR, the lack of imposed standards, and company discretion in respect of the extent and form of disclosure. Bartolacci et al (2022) emphasize the non-existence of universal theory and the pluralism of conceptual approaches to explain the practice of sustainability disclosure that recognizes the importance of stakeholder theory, legitimacy theory, resource dependency theory and institutional theory. In addition, agency theory and signaling theory have also been adopted to study differences in sustainability reporting.

The conceptual approaches offer various assumptions as to why and how companies are motivated to performing sustainability disclosure (Christensen et al., 2021). According to stakeholder theory, companies are accountable not only to shareholders but are also expected to address the interests of different stakeholders, including employees, suppliers, customers, regulators or communities (Freeman & Cavusgil, 1984). Therefore, the sole focus on creating shareholder value should be replaced with a more balanced approach, assuming that the company also engages in improving social and environmental performance. By extension, company reporting is expected not only to include financial statements but also sustainability disclosure. Within the concept of ESG disclosure, the tasks of corporate governance are being broadened (Kolk & Pinkse, 2010), with a more enlightened approach calling for "a balanced focus between short-term profits and long-term sustainability benefits" (Amran et al., 2014, p. 219; Baldini et al., 2018), alongside the integration of shareholder and stakeholder perspectives. In line with reporting standards and the concept of managing stakeholder relations, companies are expected to address the materiality principles and organize sustainability reporting according to the areas their stakeholders deem important. Stakeholder engagement remains the key part of this process, helping identify materials topics which are to be addressed in the corporate report.

Institutional theory explains company behavior as a reaction to pressures in the institutional environment (Oliver, 1991; Roberts & Greenwood, 1997) and argues that companies need to accommodate pressure from their constituencies in order to survive. Efficiency seeking may not be the goal – companies adjust to certain pressures resulting from isomorphic process (coercive, mimetic and normative) to demonstrate value commitment and to attain legitimacy among their constituencies (DiMaggio & Powell, 1983). In this stream of research, sustainability reporting is viewed as a corporate response to different pressures in the environment, indicating the key role of coercive mechanisms in the form of mandatory reporting regulations.

According to legitimacy theory, company activity is in line with societal rules, beliefs and expectations (Suchman, 1995). Companies strive to address norms and rules recognized by their constituencies to gain legitimacy, and within the construct of the social contract they try to mitigate the risk of losing their reputation or license to operate (Cho, 2009). Legitimacy theory is widely adopted to explain sustainability reporting, as companies are often found to engage in symbolic practice. Using different strategies of selective disclosure, companies seek to uphold the image of a legitimate business. Interestingly, these strategies can range from a proactive approach, aimed at preventing legitimacy concerns related to sustainability performance, to a reactive approach in dealing with social and environmental controversies that may arise (Bartolacci et al., 2022). In order to attain legitimacy from their constituencies, firms are also likely to engage in impression management or greenwashing practice.

Alternative approaches are offered by agency theory and signaling theory. Agency theory focuses on the identification of the conflicts between principal and agents (Fama & Jensen, 1983) that arise due to information asymmetry, different risk exposure and different investment horizons. This can be adopted for sustainability reporting, showing that greater ESG disclosure is likely to lower information asymmetry and to attract investors who can help in building company value. Greater transparency can also serve as an additional mechanism for monitoring managerial behavior. On the other hand, signaling theory assumes that company behavior is driven by motivation to communicate outperformance, so as to gain legitimacy and build value (Mahoney et al., 2013). SR is viewed as an element of managing reputational risk and signaling a firm's commitment to sustainability (Rosati & Faria, 2019).

As the number of corporate sustainability reports has been growing exponentially, stakeholders are expected to have access to a variety of information on corporate activities, data on

Table 27.1   *Limitations of sustainability reporting*

Topics	Identified limitations of SR
Population	Low number of companies that disclose sustainability information
Scope of reporting	Limited scope of disclosure
	Choice of reporting scope and standards at managerial discretion
Quality of reporting	Information disclosure by companies with no or limited engagement of stakeholders
	Lack of information materiality
Reporting standards and comparability	Choice of reporting scope and standards at managerial discretion
	Low reporting comparability across time and sectors
	Standard changes, lack of continuity
Reliability of reporting	Limited assurance, limited impact on access to financing
	Selective disclosure, impression management, greenwashing
Integration with company practice	Instrumental approach, decoupling between means and ends

financial and non-financial performance, and measures of the company's impact on society and the environment. The existing literature reveals numerous limitations and concerns relating to previous reporting practice, while the number of companies reporting sustainable performance remains low in comparison to the overall population of companies and other organizations. Moreover, the evidence from existing studies indicates the limitations of voluntary disclosure, as well as some constraints in the mandatory reporting introduced by regulations.

With regard to voluntary disclosure, the criticism was mainly related to insufficient transparency (Matisoff et al., 2013) and the limited usefulness of company reports (Boiral, 2013; Chaidali & Jones, 2017) in terms of assessing firms' social and environmental performance (Archel et al., 2008). Contrary to the propositions of stakeholder theory, the engagement of stakeholders in the reporting process remains marginal. This has led to disclosure being aimed more at meeting shareholder interests and addressing principal–agent conflicts than responding to non-market stakeholders such as employees or communities. As hypothesized by legitimacy theory, studies also reveal ample evidence showing that companies adopt an instrumental approach to non-financial reporting, engaging in selective disclosure and a search for acceptance amongst their constituencies (Laufer, 2003). Sustainability reporting suffers from limited comparability (Vuontisjärvi, 2006) and low clarity (Baumüller & Sopp, 2022; Diouf & Boiral, 2017), while the information disclosed by companies lacks balance (Boiral, 2013) and materiality (Mio, 2010). The practice reveals evidence of symbolic disclosure and impression management, which remains consistent with concerns raised in studies drawing upon signaling theory. In addition, companies are found to disclose information required by investors and salient stakeholders while neglecting non-economic constituencies (Aluchna el al., 2022). Finally, as suggested by the institutional perspective, the reporting practice leads to policy–practice decoupling due to a low level of stakeholder inclusiveness in the reporting process (Manetti, 2011; Mio, 2010). Table 27.1 summarizes the overview of the limitations of sustainability reporting identified in the practice of voluntary disclosure.

Furthermore, in line with notions of institutional theory on the importance of coercive mechanisms, regulations that impose a legal requirement to publish certain data have the strongest impact on the practice of non-financial reporting (Agyei & Yankey, 2019; Herbohn et al., 2014). The obligation of disclosures, along with the determination of the form, scope and standards of reporting, is aimed at eliminating the limitations of the voluntary approach. It is intended to introduce more universal reporting standards and formats that should ensure the continuity and comparability of non-financial results between different companies and various sectors and across periods of time. Many studies indicate that the introduction of mandatory non-financial reporting has a positive and lasting impact on both the quantity (Fontana et al., 2015; Tsagas & Villiers, 2020) and the quality (Frost, 2007) of information disclosed. The existing studies emphasize that the effective enforcement of the law remains the essential requirement for actual sustainability disclosure improvement. Consequently, poor enforcement neither translates into the implementation of new practices (Acerete et al., 2019) nor improves ESG transparency. Moreover, reporting under the regime of mandatory regulation increases compliance, but does not translate into corporate strategy (Stubbs et al., 2013).

NON-FINANCIAL REPORTING REGULATION

Initiating Non-Financial Disclosure

The concept of non-financial reporting is associated with the publication of the 1962 book *Silent Spring* by Rachel Carson (Gokten et al., 2020), which documents the impact of the uncontrolled use of pesticides from chlorinated hydrocarbons and organic phosphorus compounds on the natural environment. This book became a stimulus for the development of the ecological movement, drawing attention to the impact that companies have on the environment. It was followed by the report of the Committee on Environmental Effects of Organizational Behavior by the American Accounting Association in 1973 and the UK Corporate Report (Renshall, 1976) on the social and environmental implications of measuring and reporting non-shareholder information. The Brundtland Commission of 1987, which defined the concept of sustainable development and provided information on the degradation of the natural environment globally, is perceived as a milestone for non-financial reporting. With the formulation of the first Global Reporting Initiative (GRI) standards in 1999, a taxonomy of the impact of enterprises on society in individual non-financial categories was proposed. Next, Denmark was the first country to implement the non-financial reporting obligation in 1995, covering about 3,000 companies (Tschopp & Huefner, 2015). In the following years, similar regulations, albeit with different solutions, were adopted in the Netherlands, Norway, Sweden and Spain (Holgaard & Jørgensen, 2005). Later, the obligation of non-financial reporting was introduced successively in France and the UK. In the UK, listed companies have been required to submit a report disclosing their annual greenhouse gas emissions, diversity policy and human rights records under the Companies Act 2006 (Strategic Report and Directors' Report) Regulations 2013. An influential 2016 'Carrots and Sticks' study found around 400 sustainability reporting instruments in 64 countries, 65% of which are mandatory (KPMG, 2016). In 2022, regulation on mandatory climate-related reporting was also introduced in the US (Sulkowski & Jebe, 2022).

The European Union has been the most active region in formulating the regulatory framework for reporting ESG information. The first provisions were introduced in 2013 via directives concerning annual financial statements, consolidated financial statements and related reports of certain types of entities, followed in 2014 by the Non-Financial Reporting Directive (NFRD). Subsequent regulations include the Sustainable Finance Disclosure Regulation (SFDR), the Corporate Sustainability Reporting Directive (CSRD), and the EU Taxonomy and the Corporate Sustainability Due Diligence Directive (CSDDD). In addition, the regulations of the European Green Deal provide a framework for the development of society and the economy to achieve climate neutrality (net zero greenhouse gas emissions).

Non-Financial Reporting Directive

The Non-Financial Reporting Directive 2014/95/EU (NFRD) formally amended Directive 2013/34/EU with regard to the disclosure of non-financial and diversity information by certain large entities and groups (Monciardini et al., 2020). According to the directive (European Commission, 2014; Tsagas & Villiers, 2020), the non-financial reporting obligation applies to large public-interest companies with more than 500 employees or whose total balance sheet assets are over EUR 20 million or with a net turnover over EUR 40 million (European Commission, 2014). It includes listed companies, banks, insurance companies and other companies designated by national authorities as public-interest entities.

In June 2017, the European Commission published its non-mandatory guidelines to help companies disclose environmental and social information (European Commission, 2017). Two years later, in June 2019, the European Commission published guidelines on reporting climate-related information, offering a new supplement to the existing guidelines on the NFRD (European Commission, 2019). The non-financial report (in the form of a statement on non-financial information as part of the report on activities or in the form of a separate report) should include (European Commission, 2014): (1) a brief description of the entity's business model; (2) key non-financial performance indicators related to the entity's operations; (3) a description of the policies applied by the entity in relation to social issues, employment, the environment, respect for human rights and counteracting corruption, as well as a description of the results of applying these policies; (4) a description of due diligence procedures, if the entity applies them as part of its policies in relation to the above-mentioned issues; and (5) a description of significant risks related to the entity's operations. Since the NFRD does not impose an obligation to apply specific standards, companies report in accordance with any selected standards or norms (European Commission, 2014). They may also use their own rules or propose a combination of different standards. Moreover, the NFRD does not introduce the obligation to audit published non-financial reports by third parties.

The NFRD has contributed to a significant increase in the number of companies publishing non-financial reports, enhancing ESG disclosure throughout the EU. The European Commission report on the effects of the NFRD (CEPS, 2021) indicates that about 2,000 companies (excluding subsidiaries) in the EU are directly subject to the directive. However, in practice, about 10,000 other entities (excluding subsidiaries) are required to prepare reports that take into account the provisions of the NFRD and national legislation. It is estimated that another 9,000 other public interest entities (PIEs) and large entities other than PIEs report non-financial information in accordance with the NFRD guidelines without a legal requirement. At the same time, according to the calculations of the report (CEPS, 2021), the annual administration costs related to the provision of non-financial statements in accordance with the NFRD amount to EUR 82,000 on average, of which approximately 40% can be fully attributed to the law. These costs depend on the size of the company and industry, as well as the complexity and type of reporting and any optional audit. In addition, around two-thirds of the companies surveyed incur insurance costs, which average EUR 76,000 per year (CEPS, 2021).

Sustainable Finance Disclosure Regulation

The Sustainable Finance Disclosure Regulation (SFDR) is Regulation (EU) 2019/2088 of the European Parliament and of the Council of 27 November 2019 on sustainability-related disclosures in the financial services sector. It aims to achieve greater transparency regarding how to analyze the risks to sustainable development that occur as part of the activities carried out by financial market participants and financial advisors (Regulation (EU) 2019/2088, 2019). The SFDR regulation applies to EU-based financial market participants (FMPs) with 500+ employees, such as investment firms, pension funds, asset managers, insurance companies, banks, venture capital funds, and credit institutions offering portfolio management. According to the Regulation, new disclosures should cover at least:

- information on the adopted strategy regarding the risk to sustainable development when making investment decisions (SR – sustainability risks), taking into account: (1) a description of the method for identifying the list of risks and prioritizing the main adverse effects on sustainable development and indicators, (2) a description of the main adverse effects on sustainable development and a description of any measures taken to address them, and (3) information on compliance with codes of responsible business conduct and internationally recognized standards in the field of due diligence and reporting;
- disclosures regarding the negative impact of investment decisions on sustainability impacts (ASI – adverse sustainability impacts);
- information on the remuneration policy, in terms of including information on how to ensure the coherence of these policies with the introduction of risks for sustainable development into the activity.

In the case of no information being forthcoming on the impact of investment decisions on sustainable development, the "comply or explain" principle is applied. However, this rule does not apply to entities which, as at the balance sheet date, exceeded the average number of 500 employees during the financial year from 30 June 2021. Detailed technical standards have been developed by European financial market regulators (the European Banking Authority, the European Securities and Markets Authority and the European Insurance and Occupational Pensions Authority). The SFDR classifies funds as grey (financial products with sustainability risks integrated into investment decisions, without promoting environmental or social characteristics or targeting sustainable investment), light green (financial products which promote environmental or social characteristics) and dark green (financial products with sustainable investment or reductions in carbon emission as objectives).

EU Taxonomy

EU Taxonomy is represented by Regulation 2020/852 of the European Parliament and of the Council of 18 June 2020 on establishing a framework to facilitate sustainable investments. The purpose of the taxonomy regulation is to standardize the definition of what can be considered as sustainable economic activity, supporting the achievement of climate neutrality and the implementation of harmonized rules in the EU (European Parliament, 2020). Developing such a definition adds to transparency with regard to the nature of company activities, so as to increase the level of environmental protection by redirecting capital from environmentally damaging to more ecological investments. In addition, the precise definition of sustainable economic activity is intended to limit the abuse of terms associated with the ecological or responsible operation of enterprises known as greenwashing (European Parliament, 2020). The first disclosures by targeted companies, according to the provisions of the taxonomy regulation, were published in 2022 and include data from 2021. Companies are required to disclose three key percentage performance indicators: turnover, capital expenditure (CapEx) and operating expenditure (OpEx).

Economic activities to be defined as sustainable activities need to meet four requirements: (1) contribute to the achievement of at least one of the environmental objectives specified in the document; (2) do no damage to other environmental goals; (3) comply with the technical criteria according to the division presented in the regulation; and (4) comply with social security and governance guarantees. The taxonomy lists six environmental goals, which include (European Parliament, 2020):

1. climate change mitigation;
2. adaptation to climate change;
3. sustainable use and protection of water and marine resources;
4. transition to a circular economy;
5. pollution prevention and control;
6. protecting and restoring biodiversity and ecosystems.

The existing regulation offers a set of indicators for the first two environmental objectives, i.e., climate change mitigation and climate change adaptation, while work on the remaining goals is in progress. In addition, a given activity qualifies as making a significant contribution to the implementation of at least one of the above-mentioned environmental goals if it directly helps other activities to make a significant contribution when: (1) it does not lead to dependence on assets that undermine long-term environmental goals, and (2) it has significant positive effects on the environment (European Parliament, 2020).

The information disclosed by financial institutions will help assess the direction of capital flow to investments in environmentally sustainable projects. According to the regulation, high taxonomic indicators should enable easier raising of funds for new investments. It is expected that capital will be more easily available to sectors with higher ratios, and within the same industry, to entities that disclose higher values of taxonomic ratios (European Parliament, 2020). The taxonomy does not prohibit investing in activities that harm the environment, but grants additional preferences for ecological solutions. However, projects that do not fit the definition of sustainable activity will have difficulty in accessing financing – the funds will either be more expensive or will not be available.

Corporate Sustainability Reporting Directive

The regulation of non-financial reporting has been further developed with the Corporate Social Reporting Directive (CSRD, 2022/2464), which amends Regulation 537/2014, Directive 2004/109/EC, Directive 2006/43/EC and Directive 2013/34/EU. The replacement of the NFRD with the CSRD introduces more detailed reporting requirements and increases the number of companies reporting (European Parliament, 2022). The goal of the CSRD is to enhance stakeholder access to information on a company's impact on society and the environment, and to eliminate loopholes in the regulations introduced by the NFRD. In particular, the CSRD (European Parliament, 2022) extends the scope of application of the requirements to all large entities and all entities listed on a regulated market (except listed micro-entities). It also requires certification of sustainability reports and standardizes the requirements of information that must be published by enterprises according to the European Sustainability Reporting Standards (ESRS). Finally, the CSRD improves the accessibility of information by requiring it to be published in a separate section of the management reports submitted by companies. According to the CSRD's provisions, listed companies or companies with more than 250 employees will disclose their environmental, social and management policies by means of standardized, motivated and certified documents. Across the European Union, the number of regulated companies is estimated to increase from 11,000 for the NFRD to around 50,000 for the CSRD.

The CSRD introduces the obligation to audit non-financial information, which should translate into greater credibility of published reports (European Parliament, 2022). In addition, the CSRD regulations introduce digitization and tagging solutions, according to which the activity report will be available in the XTML format, with a separate section on sustainable development in the form of XBRL. The CSRD will require that the company's sustainability data be provided in a single digital format compliant with the ESEF (European Single Electronic Format) Regulation. Digitization will facilitate machine reading and data analysis.

Moreover, the CSRD provisions set a standard according to which EU companies will have to disclose their climate and environmental impact, and not only in the area of their direct operations, but also throughout the entire value chain. In addition, reporting will be based on the double materiality rule, which means that the identification of all potential negative and positive impacts on people and the environment related to the activities of the company and its value chain should consider the sustainability materiality and the financial materiality (Deloitte, 2022). The sustainability materiality of the impact includes sustainability issues relating to a company's direct operations or impacting through its value chain. Impact materiality also means that information concerning sustainability is impact relevant if a project is associated with actual or potential significant impacts on people or the environment and is related to the aspect of sustainability in the short, medium or long term. Financial materiality means the disclosure of sustainability/ESG issues that affect or may significantly affect the financial health and operating results of the company and therefore the value for investors. Financial materiality refers to sustainability issues that are financially significant if they have a financial impact on companies, i.e., they generate risks or opportunities that affect or may affect future cash flows and thus the value of the company in the short, medium or long-term, but are not included in financial reporting.

Reporting will be carried out according to the European Sustainability Reporting Standards. The structure is based on a standard system (EFRAG, 2023). Firstly, three layers of standards cover (1) sector-agnostic information that include issues common to all companies; (2) sector-specific information on issues common to all companies in a given sector; and (3) entity-specific information on issues specific to a given company. Secondly, the standards refer to three areas of general description (ESRS1) and more detailed information (ESRS2) on strategy (such as the business model, strategy and organizational issues), on implementation (including policies and goals set), and on performance measurement, such as measurement of the effects of implemented policies and the status of achieving goals. Thirdly, standards cover three ESG themes, including:

- environmental – natural environment (ESRS E1 – climate change, ESRS E2 – pollution, ESRS E3 – water and marine resources, ESRS E4 – biodiversity and ecosystems, ESRS E5 – resource use and circular economy);
- social – society (ESRS S1 – own workforce, ESRS S2 – workers in the value chain, ESRS S3 – affected communities, ESRS S4 – consumers and end-users);
- governance – corporate governance and organization management (ESRS G1 – business conduct).

Corporate Sustainability Due Diligence Directive

On February 23, 2022, the European Commission adopted a proposal for a Directive on Corporate Sustainability Due Diligence (CSDDD) (European Commission, 2022), setting out the obligations of companies to audit whether they comply with environmental and human rights law. According to the approach proposed by the UN and OECD in 2018, due diligence is a process that companies should carry out to identify the actual and potential negative impacts of their activities, as well as to prevent negative impacts arising (or likely to arise) as a result of their activities (in the company's core business, the supply chain and other business relationships), and to mitigate these negative impacts. The CSDDD aims to support sustainable and responsible business behavior across global value chains. According to the CSDDD draft, companies will be required to perform due diligence and to prevent or reduce, as well as taking responsibility for, the company's such impacts in this context. The proposal incorporated results of responses from the public consultation on the Sustainable Corporate Governance Initiative and the study on Directors' Responsibilities and the Sustainable Corporate Governance and Supply Chain Due Diligence Requirements.

DISCUSSION OF THE EVOLUTION OF NON-FINANCIAL REPORTING LEGISLATION

The implementation of the NFRD is viewed as a milestone in access to information on sustainability practice and performance. Researchers have observed positive effects in terms of the quantity and quality of sustainability reporting (Ottenstein et al., 2022), indicating a rise in the number of reporting companies. However, others remain skeptical about its factual impact on company practice in terms of the scope and quality of reporting (Chelli et al., 2018; Criado-Jiménez et al., 2008; Dumitru et al., 2017), pointing to the relatively poor quality of disclosed information (Monciardini et al., 2020). The criticism of the NFRD relates to the following aspects. Firstly, stakeholders, including investors, require more data than companies are currently obliged to publish. Secondly, the directive covers a relatively small number of companies and mainly includes the largest entities, thereby leaving out the majority of companies from its purview. Next, the directive does not impose specific reporting standards and allows for a high degree of flexibility regarding the form of presentation of non-financial information, which significantly inhibits comparison of ESG performance across companies, sectors and periods of time. Moreover, the regulatory discretion of member states also makes

Table 27.2   Practice of voluntary reporting and solutions by mandatory disclosure

Reporting aspect	Practice of voluntary reporting	Solution in the EU regulation
Population	Only companies which choose to report	NFRD – obligatory for large companies and entities of public interest CSRD – obligatory as above, followed by other listed companies Taxonomy/SFDR – companies and financial institutions
Materiality	Depending on company approach	NFRD – focus on specified areas but decisions left up to individual companies CSRD – double materiality (importance to stakeholders and financial impact on company)
Scope	Recommended, voluntarily chosen by companies	NFRD – voluntarily chosen by companies but in specified areas CSRD – obligatory (ESRS) CSDDD – adding impact on human rights and environment
Reporting standards/ comparability	Voluntarily chosen by companies, limited comparability	NFRD – voluntarily chosen by companies CSRD – obligatory (ESRS), enhanced comparability
Assurance	Voluntary	NFRD – voluntary audit chosen by companies CSRD – obligatory assurance by an external auditor
Digital form / machine reading	No	NFRD – not required CSRD – obligatory
Greenwashing	Difficult to control	NRFD/ CSRD – not specified but difficult to maintain in the subsequent years of reporting Taxonomy – defined areas of sustainable activity
Access to external finance	Not regulated but depending on investor perception of reputation risk	Taxonomy – defined areas of sustainable activity SFDR – with classification of financial assets

it difficult to compare data at the EU level (Aureli et al., 2020). The lack of an auditing requirement for non-financial information hinders verification of published reports, rendering them less credible. Finally, the lack of a digital reporting standard inhibits the ability to access information in a consistent manner. These issues are addressed by the implementation of the CSRD. Table 27.2 summarizes this discussion, presenting the practice of voluntary reporting and solutions offered by mandatory disclosure.

As shown in Table 27.2, the EU regulation addresses the concerns and limitations inherent in voluntary reporting. As argued by Sulkowski & Jebe (2022), the progress in reporting legislation is rooted in the institutional setting and remains subject to path-dependence. While the NFRD introduced parameters for mandatory disclosure, the CSRD imposes fundamental changes in corporate practice by increasing the number of reporting companies, setting standards to improve comparability, and enhancing the credibility of published non-financial information by mandating external audits of sustainability reports. In addition, since the CSRD is based on double materiality, it offers a balance of financial and stakeholder considerations, whereas the CSDDD adds the component of human rights to corporate due diligence. The

SFDR sets a framework for financial institutions to report and classify assets held. The taxonomy regulation lowers the likelihood of greenwashing, forcing companies to conform to definitions of sustainable activity, and is expected to play a crucial role in redirecting funds to sustainable business activities. As shown in Table 27.2, these regulations in some way address the shortcomings of voluntary reporting as identified in the prior literature. The regulations are part of a bigger framework known as the Green Deal, which is an initiative of the European Commission consisting of a package of legislative proposals to align the EU's climate, energy, transport and tax policies to meet the goal of reducing net greenhouse gas emissions by at least 55% by 2030 (compared to 1990 levels). The green transformation in the EU is based on the eight foundations of the Green Deal.[2]

CONCLUSION

The goal of the chapter was to provide answers to the following two research questions: (1) what are the actual limitations of sustainability disclosure? (2) How does EU regulation on sustainability reporting address these limitations? To address these questions the chapter offers an overview of the conceptual frameworks used in prior research on voluntary sustainability disclosure and presents a discussion concerning EU regulations centered around the concept of ESG transparency, with such regulations viewed as mechanisms for strengthening the transition towards a sustainable economy. While the introduction of financial reporting has enabled measurement of company performance and influenced determined strategic decision-making, the recent implementation of mandatory non-financial reporting is expected to provide a broad picture of company activity, assessing its impact on society and the environment. The set of regulations enacted in the EU increases the scope of disclosures (NFRD, CSRD, CSDDD) and introduces the classification of sustainable economic activity (Taxonomy, SFDR). The legislation exerts pressure on companies to report ESG performance and consequently to incorporate sustainability goals into their corporate strategy. The set of EU regulations addresses the corporate practice of voluntary reporting, exposing the widespread limitations in this practice with reference to a variety of conceptual frameworks.

In addressing the two main research questions, the study offers implications for further research. Firstly, the implementation of regulations raises questions regarding the effectiveness of these coercive mechanisms for improving transparency, particularly with respect to stakeholder engagement, materiality of information and reliability of reporting. Such analyses are sorely needed to verify how effectively the means of regulation relate to their desired ends. Secondly, given the regulatory efforts underway, there is a call for studies on the link between sustainability reporting and sustainability performance. It is important to analyze whether the EU regulatory framework for sustainability reporting, which remains in line with the European Green Deal policy and focuses on the principles of company operation and consumer behavior, will indeed stimulate actions to be taken to contribute to the EU's climate neutrality.

NOTES

1. This paper was prepared within the Polish National Science Center (NCN) Beethoven Classic Grant, "The effect of non-financial reporting legislation on human resource management prac-

tices and corporate governance in Germany and Poland, The case of Directive 2014/95/EU",
in cooperation with Germany, no. 2018/31/G/HS4/02504.
2.   These are: (1) clean, cheap and safe energy, (2) climate goals of achieving climate neutrality
by 2050, (3) sustainable and intelligent transportation, (4) protection of ecosystems and biodiversity, (5) eliminating pollution, (6) energy-efficient building sector, (7) circular economy
and (8) sustainable agriculture and food system.

REFERENCES

Acerete, B., Gasca, M., & Llena, F. (2019). Analysis of environmental financial reporting in the Spanish
toll roads sector. *Revista Espanola de Financiacion y Contabilidad*, *48*(4), 430–463. https://doi.org/
10.1080/02102412.2019.1591880

Agyei, S. K., & Yankey, B. (2019). Environmental reporting practices and performance of timber firms
in Ghana: perceptions of practitioners. *Journal of Accounting in Emerging Economies*, *9*(2), 268–286.
https://doi.org/10.1108/JAEE-12-2017-0127

Aluchna, M., Roszkowska-Menkes, M., Kamiński, B., & Bosek-Rak, D. (2022). Do institutional investors encourage firm to social disclosure? The stakeholder salience perspective. *Journal of Business
Research*, *142*, 674–682. https://doi.org/10.1016/j.jbusres.2021.12.064

Amran, A., Lee, S. P., & Devi, S. S. (2014). The influence of governance structure and strategic corporate
social responsibility toward sustainability reporting quality. *Business Strategy and the Environment*,
23(4), 217–235. https://doi.org/10.1002/bse.1767

Archel, P., Fernández, M., & Larrinaga, C. (2008). The organizational and operational boundaries of
triple bottom line reporting: a survey. *Environmental Management*, *41*(1), 106–117. https://doi.org/10
.1007/s00267-007-9029-7

Aureli, S., Del Baldo, M., Lombardi, R., & Nappo, F. (2020). Nonfinancial reporting regulation and
challenges in sustainability disclosure and corporate governance practices. *Business Strategy and the
Environment*, *29*(6), 2392–2403. https://doi.org/10.1002/bse.2509

Baboukardos, D., & Rimmel, G. (2016). Value relevance of accounting information under an integrated
reporting approach: a research note. *Journal of Accounting and Public Policy*, *35*(4), 437–452. https://
doi.org/10.1016/j.jaccpubpol.2016.04.004

Baboukardos, D., Gaia, S., Lassou, P., & Soobaroyen, T. (2023). The multiverse of non-financial reporting regulation. *Accounting Forum*, *47*(2), 147–165. https://doi.org/10.1080/01559982.2023.2204786

Baldini, M., Maso, L. D., Liberatore, G., Mazzi, F., & Terzani, S. (2018). Role of country- and firm-level
determinants in environmental, social, and governance disclosure. *Journal of Business Ethics*, *150*(1),
79–98. https://doi.org/10.1007/s10551-016-3139-1

Ballou, B., Casey, R. J., Grenier, J. H., & Heitger, D. L. (2012). Exploring the strategic integration of
sustainability initiatives: opportunities for accounting research. *Accounting Horizons*, *26*(2), 265–288.
https://doi.org/10.2308/acch-50088

Bartolacci, F., Bellucci, M., Corsi, K., & Soverchia, M. (2022). A systematic literature review of theories
underpinning sustainability reporting in non-financial disclosure. In: L. Cinquini & F. De Luca (eds),
Non-Financial Disclosure and Integrated Reporting. Cham: Springer, pp. 87–113. https://doi.org/10
.1007/978-3-030-90355-8_4

Baumüller, J., & Sopp, K. (2022). Double materiality and the shift from non-financial to European
sustainability reporting: review, outlook and implications. *Journal of Applied Accounting Research*,
23(1), 8–28. https://doi.org/10.1108/JAAR-04-2021-0114

Bernardi, C., & Stark, A. W. (2018). Environmental, social and governance disclosure, integrated reporting, and the accuracy of analyst forecasts. *British Accounting Review*, *50*(1), 16–31. https://doi.org/10
.1016/j.bar.2016.10.001

Boiral, O. (2013). Sustainability reports as simulacra? A counter-account of A and A+ GRI reports.
Accounting, Auditing & Accountability Journal, *26*(7), 1036–1071. https://doi.org/https://doi.org/10
.1108/AAAJ-04-2012-00998

Brammer, S., & Pavelin, S. (2006). Voluntary environmental disclosures by large UK companies. *Journal of Business Finance and Accounting*, *33*(7–8), 1168–1188. https://doi.org/10.1111/j.1468 -5957.2006.00598.x

CEPS (2021). *Study on the Non-Financial Reporting Directive*. Luxembourg: Publications Office of the European Union.

Ceulemans, K., Lozano, R., & Alonso-Almeida, M. del M. (2015). Sustainability reporting in higher education: interconnecting the reporting process and organisational change management for sustainability. *Sustainability*, *7*(7), 8881–8903. https://doi.org/10.3390/su7078881

Chaidali, P., & Jones, M. J. (2017). It's a matter of trust: exploring the perceptions of integrated reporting preparers. *Critical Perspectives on Accounting*, *48*, 1–20. https://doi.org/10.1016/j.cpa.2017.08.001

Chan, M. C. C., Watson, J., & Woodliff, D. (2014). Corporate governance quality and CSR disclosures. *Journal of Business Ethics*, *125*(1), 59–73. https://doi.org/10.1007/s10551-013-1887-8

Chelli, M., Durocher, S., & Fortin, A. (2018). Normativity in environmental reporting: a comparison of three regimes. *Journal of Business Ethics*, *149*(2), 285–311. https://doi.org/10.1007/s10551-016-3128 -4

Cho, C. H. (2009). Legitimation strategies used in response to environmental disaster: a French case study of total SA's Erika and AZF incidents. *European Accounting Review*, *18*(1), 33–62. https://doi .org/10.1080/09638180802579616

Cho, C. H., Guidry, R. P., Hageman, A. M., & Patten, D. M. (2012). Do actions speak louder than words? An empirical investigation of corporate environmental reputation. *Accounting, Organizations and Society*, *37*(1), 14–25. https://doi.org/10.1016/j.aos.2011.12.001

Christensen, H. B., Hail, L., & Leuz, C. (2021). Mandatory CSR and sustainability reporting: economic analysis and literature review. *Review of Accounting Studies*. https://doi.org/10.1007/s11142-021 -09609-5

Coffee, J. 2021. The future of disclosure: ESG, common ownership, and systematic risk. *Columbia Business Law Review*, 602. https://scholarship.law.columbia.edu/faculty_scholarship/2680

Criado-Jiménez, I., Fernández-Chulián, M., Husillos-Carqués, F. J., & Larrinage-González, C. (2008). Compliance with mandatory environmental reporting in financial statements: the case of Spain (2001–2003). *Journal of Business Ethics*, *79*(3), 245–262. https://doi.org/10.1007/s10551-007-9375-7

Deloitte (2022). Rewolucja w sprawozdawczości środowiskowej w UE. Dyrektywa CSRD a łańcuch dostaw. https://www2.deloitte.com/pl/pl/pages/risk/articles/rewolucja-w-sprawozdawczosci -srodowiskowej-w-UE.html

DiMaggio, P. J., & Powell, W. W. (1983). The iron cage revisited: institutional isomorphism and collective rationality in organizational fields. *American Sociological Review*, *48*(2), 147. https://doi.org/10 .2307/2095101

Diouf, D., & Boiral, O. (2017). The quality of sustainability reports and impression management: a stakeholder perspective. *Accounting, Auditing and Accountability Journal*, *30*(3), 643–667. https://doi.org/ 10.1108/AAAJ-04-2015-2044

Dumitru, M., Dyduch, J., Guşe, R. G., & Krasodomska, J. (2017). Corporate reporting practices in Poland and Romania – an ex-ante study to the New Non-Financial Reporting European Directive. *Accounting in Europe*, *14*(3), 279–304. https://doi.org/10.1080/17449480.2017.1378427

EFRAG (2023). Implementation guidance. Draft EFRAG IG 1, Materiality assessment. https://efrag.org/ Assets/Download?assetUrl=%2Fsites%2Fwebpublishing%2FSiteAssets%2FDraft%2520EFRAG %2520IG%25201%2520MAIG%2520231222.pdf

Esteban-Arrea, R., & Garcia-Torea, N. (2022). Strategic responses to sustainability reporting regulation and multiple stakeholder demands: an analysis of the Spanish EU Non-Financial Reporting Directive transposition. *Sustainability Accounting, Management and Policy Journal*, *13*(3), 600–625. https://doi .org/10.1108/SAMPJ-07-2021-0292

European Commission (2014). Directive 2014/95/EU of the European Parliament and of the Council of 22 October 2014 amending Directive 2013/34/EU. https://eur-lex.europa.eu/legal-content/EN/TXT/ HTML/?uri=CELEX:32014L0095&from=EN

European Commission (2017). Communication from the Commission — Guidelines on non-financial reporting (methodology for reporting non-financial information). *Official Journal of the European Union*, *C*(4234), 1–20. http://ec.europa.eu/finance/company-reporting/non-financial_reporting/index

_en.htm#related-documents%0Ahttps://eur-lex.europa.eu/legal-content/EN/TXT/PDF/?uri=CELEX: 52017XC0705(01)&from=EN

European Commission (2019). Communication from the Commission: Guidelines on non-financial reporting: Supplement on reporting climate-related information (2019/C 209/01). *Official Journal of the European Union*, C 209/1–30. https://eur-lex.europa.eu/legal-content/EN/TXT/PDF/?uri= CELEX:52019XC0620(01)&from=EN

European Parliament (2020). Regulation (EU) 2020/852 of the European Parliament and of the Council of 18 June 2020 on the establishment of a framework to facilitate sustainable investment, and amending Regulation (EU) 2019/2088. *Official Journal of the European Union*, *2019*(L198), 1–31.

European Parliament (2022). Directive (EU) 2022/2464 of the European Parliament and of the Council of 14 December 2022, as regards corporate sustainability reporting. https://eur-lex.europa.eu/legal -content/EN/TXT/?uri=CELEX:32022L2464

Fama, E. F., & Jensen, M. C. (1983). Separation of ownership and control. *Journal of Law & Economics*, *26*(2), 301–325.

Fernandez-Feijoo, B., Romero, S., & Ruiz-Blanco, S. (2014). Women on boards: do they affect sustainability reporting? *Corporate Social Responsibility and Environmental Management*, *21*(6), 351–364. https://doi.org/10.1002/csr.1329

Flower, J. (2015). The international integrated reporting council: a story of failure. *Critical Perspectives on Accounting*, *27*, 1–17. https://doi.org/10.1016/j.cpa.2014.07.002

Fontana, S., D'Amico, E., Coluccia, D., & Solimene, S. (2015). Does environmental performance affect companies' environmental disclosure? *Measuring Business Excellence*, *19*(3), 42–57. https://doi.org/ 10.1108/MBE-04-2015-0019

Freeman, S., & Cavusgil, S. T. (1984). Strategic management. A stakeholder approach. *Journal of International Marketing*, *15*(4), 1–40.

Frost, G. R. (2007). The introduction of mandatory environmental reporting guidelines: Australian evidence. *Abacus*, *43*(2), 190–216. https://doi.org/10.1111/j.1467-6281.2007.00225.x

Gokten, S., Ozerhan, Y., & Gokten, P. O. (2020). The historical development of sustainability reporting: a periodic approach. *Zeszyty Teoretyczne Rachunkowości*, *107*(163), 99–118. https://doi.org/10.5604/ 01.3001.0014.2466

Gond, J.-P., & Herrbach, O. (2006). Social reporting as an organisational learning tool? A theoretical framework. *Journal of Business Ethics*, *65*, 359–371. https://doi.org/https://doi.org/10.1007/s10551 -006-6405-9

Gray, R. (2010). Is accounting for sustainability actually accounting for sustainability … and how would we know? An exploration of narratives of organisations and the planet. *Accounting, Organizations and Society*, *35*(1), 47–62. https://doi.org/10.1016/j.aos.2009.04.006

Gray, R., Owen, D., & Maunders, K. (1987). *Corporate Social Reporting – Accounting and Accountability*. London: Prentice-Hall.

Herbohn, K., Walker, J., & Loo, H. Y. M. (2014). corporate social responsibility: the link between sustainability disclosure and sustainability performance. *Abacus*, *50*(4), 422–459. https://doi.org/10 .1111/abac.12036

Hoepner, A. G. F., & Schneider, F. I. (2022). EU Green Taxonomy data – a first vendor survey. *Economists' Voice*, *19*(2), 221–234. https://doi.org/10.1515/ev-2022-0022

Holgaard, J. E., & Jørgensen, T. H. (2005). A decade of mandatory environmental reporting in Denmark. *European Environment*, *15*(6), 362–373. https://doi.org/10.1002/eet.397

Hooghiemstra, R. (2000). Corporate communication and impression management: new perspectives why companies engage in corporate social reporting. *Journal of Business Ethics*, *27*, 55–68. https://doi.org/ 10.1023/A:100640070775755–68

Huang, C. L., & Kung, F. H. (2010). Drivers of environmental disclosure and stakeholder expectation: evidence from Taiwan. *Journal of Business Ethics*, *96*(3), 435–451. https://doi.org/10.1007/s10551 -010-0476-3

Kolk, A., & Pinkse, J. (2010). The integration of corporate governance in corporate social responsibility disclosures. *Corporate Social Responsibility and Environmental Management*, *17*(1), 15–26. https:// doi.org/10.1002/csr.196

KMPG (2016). *Carrots & Sticks. Global Trends in Sustainability Reporting Regulation and Policy*. KPMG, GRI, UNEP and Centre for Corporate Governance in Africa at the University of Stellenbosch

Business School. https://assets.kpmg.com/content/dam/kpmg/pdf/2016/05/carrots-and-sticks-may -2016.pdf

La Torre, M., Sabelfeld, S., Blomkvist, M., & Dumay, J. (2020). Rebuilding trust: sustainability and non-financial reporting and the European Union regulation. *Meditari Accountancy Research, 28*(5), 701–725. https://doi.org/10.1108/MEDAR-06-2020-0914

Laufer, W. S. (2003). Social accountability and corporate greenwashing. *Journal of Business Ethics, 43*(3), 253–261. https://doi.org/10.1023/A:1022962719299

Mahoney, L. S., Thorne, L., Cecil, L., & LaGore, W. (2013). A research note on standalone corporate social responsibility reports: signaling or greenwashing? *Critical Perspectives on Accounting, 24*(4–5), 350–359. https://doi.org/10.1016/j.cpa.2012.09.008

Manes-Rossi, F., Tiron-Tudor, A., Nicolò, G., & Zanellato, G. (2018). Ensuring more sustainable report- ing in Europe using non-financial disclosure – de facto and de jure evidence. *Sustainability, 10*(4), 1162. https://doi.org/10.3390/su10041162

Manetti, G. (2011). The quality of stakeholder engagement in sustainability reporting: empirical evi- dence and critical points. *Corporate Social Responsibility and Environmental Management, 18*(2), 110–122. https://doi.org/10.1002/csr.255

Matisoff, D. C., Noonan, D. S., & O'Brien, J. J. (2013). Convergence in environmental reporting: assess- ing the carbon disclosure project. *Business Strategy and the Environment, 22*(5), 285–305. https://doi .org/10.1002/bse.1741

Melloni, G., Caglio, A., & Perego, P. (2017). Saying more with less? Disclosure conciseness, complete- ness and balance in integrated reports. *Journal of Accounting and Public Policy, 36*(3), 220–238. https://doi.org/10.1016/j.jaccpubpol.2017.03.001

Mio, C. (2010). Corporate social reporting in Italian multi-utility companies: an empirical analysis. *Corporate Social Responsibility and Environmental Management, 17*(5), 247–271. https://doi.org/10 .1002/csr.213

Mio, C., & Venturelli, A. (2013). Non-financial information about sustainable development and environ- mental policy in the annual reports of listed companies: evidence from Italy and the UK. *Corporate Social Responsibility and Environmental Management, 20*(6), 340–358. https://doi.org/10.1002/csr .1296

Monciardini, D., Mähönen, J. T., & Tsagas, G. (2020). Rethinking non-financial reporting: a blueprint for structural regulatory changes. *Accounting, Economics and Law: A Convivium, 10*(2), 14–35. https://doi.org/10.1515/ael-2020-0092

Norman, W., & MacDonald, C. (2004). Getting to the bottom of "triple bottom line". *Business Ethics Quarterly, 14*(2), 243–262. https://doi.org/10.5840/beq200414211

Oliver, C. (1991). Strategic responses to institutional processes. *The Academy of Management Review, 16*(1), 145. https://doi.org/10.2307/258610

Ottenstein, P., Erben, S., Jost, S., Weuster, C. W., & Zülch, H. (2022). From voluntarism to regulation: effects of Directive 2014/95/EU on sustainability reporting in the EU. *Journal of Applied Accounting Research, 23*(1), 55–98. https://doi.org/10.1108/JAAR-03-2021-0075

Pellegrino, C., & Lodhia, S. (2012). Climate change accounting and the Australian mining industry: exploring the links between corporate disclosure and the generation of legitimacy. *Journal of Cleaner Production, 36*, 68–82. https://doi.org/10.1016/j.jclepro.2012.02.022

Regulation (EU) 2019/2088 (2019). Regulation (EU) 2019/2088 of the European Parliament and of the Council of 27 November 2019 on sustainability-related disclosures in the financial services sector. *Official Journal of the European Union*, 1–16. https://eur-lex.europa.eu/legal-content/EN/TXT/PDF/ ?uri=CELEX:32019R2088&from=EN

Renshall, J. M. (1976). Changing perceptions behind the corporate report. *Accounting, Organizations and Society, 1*(1), 105–109. https://doi.org/10.1016/0361-3682(76)90013-1

Roberts, P. W., & Greenwood, R. (1997). Integrating transaction cost and institutional theories: toward a constrained-efficiency framework for understanding organizational design adoption. *Academy of Management Review, 22*(2), 346–373. https://doi.org/10.5465/AMR.1997.9707154062

Rosati, F., & Faria, L. G. D. (2019). Business contribution to the sustainable development agenda: organizational factors related to early adoption of SDG reporting. *Corporate Social Responsibility and Environmental Management, 26*(3), 588–597. https://doi.org/10.1002/csr.1705

Stacchezzini, R., Melloni, G., & Lai, A. (2016). Sustainability management and reporting: the role of integrated reporting for communicating corporate sustainability management. *Journal of Cleaner Production, 136*, 102–110. https://doi.org/10.1016/j.jclepro.2016.01.109

Stolowy, H., & Paugam, L. (2018). The expansion of non-financial reporting: an exploratory study. *Accounting and Business Research, 48*(5), 525–548. https://doi.org/10.1080/00014788.2018.1470141

Stubbs, W., Higgins, C., & Milne, M. (2013). Why do companies not produce sustainability reports? *Business Strategy and the Environment, 22*(7), 456–470. https://doi.org/10.1002/bse.1756

Suchman, M. C. (1995). Managing legitimacy: strategic and institutional approaches. *The Academy of Management Review, 20*(3), 571. https://doi.org/10.2307/258788

Sulkowski, A., & Jebe, R. (2022). Evolving ESG reporting governance, regime theory, and proactive law: predictions and strategies. *American Business Law Journal, 59*(3), 449–503. https://doi.org/10.1111/ablj.12210

Tsagas, G., & Villiers, C. (2020). Why "less is more" in non-financial reporting initiatives: concrete steps towards supporting sustainability. *Accounting, Economics and Law: A Convivium, 10*(2), 20180045. https://doi.org/10.1515/ael-2018-0045

Tschopp, D., & Huefner, R. J. (2015). Comparing the evolution of CSR reporting to that of financial reporting. *Journal of Business Ethics, 127*(3), 565–577. https://doi.org/10.1007/s10551-014-2054-6

Vuontisjärvi, T. (2006). Corporate social reporting in the European context and human resource disclosures: an analysis of Finnish companies. *Journal of Business Ethics, 69*(4), 331–354. https://doi.org/10.1007/s10551-006-9094-5

28. A new era of sustainability reporting research on the horizon: an outlook

Gunnar Rimmel, Güler Aras, Diogenis Baboukardos, Joanna Krasodomska, Christian Nielsen and Frank Schiemann

1   INTRODUCTION

The main purpose of the *Research Handbook on Sustainability Reporting* is to present the multifaceted, complex, and multilayered aspects of research on sustainability reporting. All the previous chapters reflect an ongoing evolution of sustainability reporting, which is shaped by a combination of voluntary international initiatives, regulatory developments, and the increasing recognition of sustainability as a fundamental aspect of corporate reporting and governance. As businesses continue to navigate complex global challenges, sustainability reporting remains a crucial tool for communicating their impact and progress towards a more sustainable future. Research on sustainability reporting is inherently interesting for several compelling reasons, reflecting its multidimensional nature and its intersection with various academic disciplines.

As the structure of the *Research Handbook on Sustainability Reporting* shows, possible areas of research interest can be located within broader, overarching topics. Therefore, the chapters in this book covered the changing regulatory landscape of sustainability reporting, research on sustainability reporting practices, the capital markets context, and corporate governance issues, exemplary insights into diverse approaches to sustainability reporting (regulation) around the world, the methods and theories underlying sustainability reporting research, as well as prospects for future advances. It is indicative that, during the preparation of the book, new developments emerged which led authors to amend their chapters accordingly. This reflects that sustainability reporting is a fast-paced and dynamic field which, not surprisingly, has attracted much attention from the accounting research community.

These new developments were largely related to the ongoing standardization of sustainability reporting practices. The EU has led the way in this area by introducing substantial changes regarding sustainability disclosure regulations, which live up to the aims of the EU Green Deal.

The imposition of stringent sustainability reporting requirements under the EU Green Deal precipitates a paradigm shift for corporations operating within the EU. EU regulations have the ambition not only to increase the quality and comparability of the ESG disclosures but also to use it to encourage a shift in firms' behaviour toward achieving sustainable development. The ensuing corporate response involves not only meeting regulatory compliance but also necessitates a recalibration of internal reporting mechanisms, data collection processes, and strategic sustainability initiatives. The challenges inherent in this transition include resource constraints, data quality assurance, and the integration of sustainability metrics into core business strategies.

A critical aspect of the impact lies in the recalibration of the regulatory landscape governing sustainability reporting. The CSRD, as a legislative cornerstone, introduces enhanced reporting obligations for a broader spectrum of entities, extending beyond listed companies to include large non-listed companies and certain small and medium-sized enterprises. The interoperability of the ESRS with international frameworks, most importantly with ISSB and GRI standards, reinforces the commitment to global harmonization and facilitates cross-border comparability.

The impact of the EU Green Deal on sustainability reporting reverberates beyond EU borders. The ambitious targets set by the EU, coupled with the ripple effect on global supply chains, signal a broader commitment to catalyse global sustainable development. The spillover effect of intensified reporting standards may influence corporate practices globally, fostering a more concerted and standardized approach to sustainability disclosure.

In the next section of this chapter, we present the main reasons behind the trend indicated above, namely the shift from voluntary sustainability reporting to mandatory standards. We then outline how the phenomena discussed will affect sustainability reporting research, differentiating such key areas as comparability, new technologies, holistic reporting approaches, corporate behaviour, stakeholders' engagement with sustainability reporting, cultural and contextual dimensions, promoting innovation and collaboration, and ethical and social implications.

2   MOVING FROM STUDYING VOLUNTARY SUSTAINABILITY REPORTING TO STUDYING THE MULTIFACETED PERSPECTIVES OF MANDATORY SUSTAINABILITY REPORTING

The transition in sustainability reporting from a voluntary practice to a mandatory one with the introduction of local and international standards is a significant development that holds substantial implications for global sustainable development. This shift marks a crucial step towards achieving a more consistent, comparable, and accountable approach to corporate sustainability reporting. Various reasons have been proposed for the necessity of such development both from EFRAG and the ISSB. These reasons provide a starting point for future research endeavours.

Standardization Enhances Comparability

Mandatory sustainability reporting can, especially at a global level through international standards, ensure a uniform frame of reference for all companies and the users of this information. This facilitates the comparability of performance metrics across companies, industries, and regions, allowing stakeholders to make informed decisions. A standardized approach mitigates the risk of 'greenwashing', where companies may present misleading or superficial sustainability information. Mandatory reporting standards would provide a baseline for assessing the impact of corporate activities more reliably.

Increased Accountability and Transparency

Mandatory reporting instils a sense of accountability among corporations. It compels organizations to disclose essential sustainability information, fostering transparency in their operations and supply chains. Standardized reporting requirements level the playing field, reduce the possibility of selective disclosure and ensure that all relevant aspects of a company's sustainability performance are adequately addressed.

Global Consistency for Investors

Investors increasingly consider ESG factors in their decision-making process. Mandatory sustainability reporting can ensure that investors receive consistent and comparable data, allowing them to allocate capital more efficiently to sustainable and responsible businesses. Standardization reduces the information asymmetry between investors and companies, enabling better risk assessment and more accurate valuation of companies based on their sustainability performance.

Alignment with Global Agendas

The transition to mandatory reporting can align companies' activities with global sustainability goals, such as the UN SDGs. This alignment reinforces the commitment of businesses to contribute meaningfully to broader societal and environmental objectives. It fosters a collaborative and integrated approach towards achieving global sustainability targets, as companies worldwide adhere to a common set of reporting principles and indicators.

Regulatory Compliance and Legal Certainty

Mandatory reporting standards can provide legal clarity and a regulatory framework for organizations. This ensures that companies are aware of their obligations and can plan and implement sustainability measures with confidence. Regulatory compliance also reduces the risk of legal action against companies that fail to meet their sustainability reporting obligations, fostering a culture of adherence to responsible business practices.

The degree to which the above-mentioned consequences of mandatory disclosure materialize crucially depends on the content and character of the respective regulation. While even rather general and ambiguous disclosure mandates can create measurable effects, the regulation that is more specific arguably should lead to even stronger improvements in comparability, accountability, mitigation of greenwashing, regulatory compliance, and legal certainty.

To summarize, the transition from voluntary sustainability reporting to mandatory standards is imperative for advancing global sustainable development. It establishes a foundation for consistency, accountability, and transparency, aligning corporate practices with international sustainability goals and facilitating more informed decision-making by stakeholders. This evolution in sustainability reporting reflects that the field is maturing, and recognizes that companies have an integral role to play in addressing global environmental and social challenges. Consequently, the transition to mandatory sustainability reporting will also impact sustainability reporting research.

3   A NEW ERA OF SUSTAINABILITY REPORTING RESEARCH ON THE HORIZON WITH MULTITUDES OF PROMISING AVENUES FOR FUTURE SUSTAINABILITY REPORTING RESEARCH

Over the last few years, sustainability reporting has undergone unprecedented changes, with many companies around the world facing regulatory pressures to disclose more and better information than they used to do on a voluntary basis. Sustainability reporting research is a rapidly developing field, and there are many promising avenues for future research. In the following, we identify some of the key areas that are likely to be of interest to researchers in the coming years.

Comparability

What comparability means and how it can be ensured are open questions. Researchers can contribute by studying sustainability reporting standard setters' initiatives to make sustainability reports more comparable and consistent across companies and industries. The development of standardized metrics and frameworks for measuring and reporting on ESG performance, the quality of data and the interoperability across different reporting frameworks can be informed by such research endeavours. Evaluating the effectiveness of these measures in achieving their intended improvement in sustainability reporting quality can also be explored, for example through pre- and post-implementation studies.

New Technologies

Future research endeavours can analyse sustainability reports and sustainability information disclosed through other channels (e.g., websites, news articles, social media), through the use of new technologies. This includes exploring the use of data analytics, blockchain technology, and other innovative approaches to enhance the transparency and trustworthiness of sustainability reporting. To this end, artificial intelligence (AI) and machine learning (ML) can provide useful tools for improving the efficiency and effectiveness of sustainability reporting and sustainability reporting research. To be clear, the use of new technologies is not an end in itself. Instead, researchers should carefully consider the opportunities, but also the limits, of the research tools they apply, to ensure a good fit between research question and research design.

Holistic Reporting Approaches

Researchers may examine the process of integrating sustainability reporting with other forms of business reporting for external use (such as financial statements and annual reports) as well as for internal use (such as budgeting and costing). We are already witnessing a shift in the information demand from capital markets and stakeholders for better and more complete information. How this can be achieved is an open empirical discussion. Further, much less is known about the design and implementation of management control systems that align with sustainability goals and objectives. Future research can focus on how sustainability can be integrated into budgeting, forecasting, costing, and controlling processes. This includes developing sustainability-based budgeting models, incorporating ESG criteria into strategic planning, and aligning resource allocation with sustainability goals. Researchers can study how corporate performance measurement systems will incorporate ESG metrics, designing incentive-based structures to motivate sustainable behaviour, and establishing risk management frameworks that address ESG-related risks.

Corporate Behaviour

Future research can assess the impact of sustainability reporting on corporate behaviour, including decision-making, risk management, and investment strategies. This will help to understand how sustainability reporting can be most effectively used to drive positive change in business practices and promote sustainable development. Research can investigate whether sustainability reporting leads companies to make more sustainable decisions and to explicitly address emerging and existing challenges such as climate change, biodiversity loss, renewable energy, reducing waste, inequality, and improving working conditions.

Stakeholders' Engagement with Sustainability Reporting

Stakeholder engagement has been identified as a key issue for the success of sustainability reporting and is in fact emphasized by standard setters as being crucial to the process. Although extant literature has examined this issue, more evidence is needed on how various stakeholder groups affect companies' sustainability reporting. This includes developing more user-friendly reporting formats, communicating sustainability information in a more accessible way, and fostering dialogue between companies and their stakeholders.

Cultural and Contextual Dimensions

As we are moving towards standardization of sustainability reporting worldwide, the role of local traits, cultures, and behaviours can be seen as being of major importance. As is the case with the International Financial Reporting Standards, the mere adoption of the same sustainability reporting standards cannot ensure similar application. Future research can explore the role of cultural and contextual dimensions of the application of sustainability reporting.

Promoting Innovation and Collaboration

Researchers can promote innovation and collaboration in sustainability reporting by fostering dialogue among academics, practitioners, and standard setters. Researchers can continue to engage in bridging the gap between management accounting theory and practice in the area of sustainability reporting. This includes developing practical tools and frameworks for sustainability management accounting, conducting case studies based on real-world experiences, disseminating research findings to practitioners to identify practical challenges, and encouraging collaboration on the development of new reporting frameworks and standards.

Ethical and Social Implications

Researchers can further explore the ethical and social implications of sustainability reporting and the impact of reporting on marginalized communities. This includes research on ethical issues in sustainability reporting, examining the role of sustainability reporting in promoting social justice, and conducting research on the experiences of various stakeholders with sustainability reporting.

4   CONCLUDING REMARKS

For some sustainability reporting academics who have been working in this field for many years, the current explosion of interest from the 'mainstream' accounting research community is surprising and even upsetting. It is understandable that some researchers might be apprehensive about their niche research becoming mainstream. After all, niche research often attracts a small but dedicated community of researchers who are deeply invested in the field. If 'mainstream' research disregards the insights of earlier niche research and generally narrows the research focus, for example to an overly strong focus only on financial consequences for firms while ignoring non-financial consequences or the connections between sustainability reporting and stakeholders, societal developments or other environmental or social policy regulations, then the concerns of the experienced sustainability accounting researcher are warranted. However, there are also many potential benefits of the current strong interest in sustainability reporting, such as increased visibility and impact, more research projects with a wider focus overall and, consequently, more reliable insights and fruitful exchanges as well as many new research opportunities.

This comprehensive *Research Handbook on Sustainability Reporting* can serve as a valuable resource for aspiring researchers interested in exploring this burgeoning field. By providing a comprehensive overview of the current state of knowledge, identifying key research gaps, and offering insights into methodological approaches, this handbook aims to inspire more researchers to embark on their research journeys and make meaningful contributions to the area.

By demonstrating the breadth and depth of sustainability reporting research, the handbook highlights the contributing researchers' curiosity and enthusiasm for this dynamic field. More importantly, this handbook identifies key research gaps and emerging trends providing insights into areas that require further investigation and can serve as a roadmap for future research endeavours. The *Research Handbook on Sustainability Reporting* showcases a variety of methodological approaches for engaging in sustainability reporting research, which should encourage other researchers to think creatively and develop innovative methodologies. This methodological diversity can lead to the development of new tools and frameworks that advance the field and provide more nuanced insights into sustainability issues. The handbook contains independent inquiry and contributes to the advance of sustainability reporting knowledge.

Sustainability reporting research is a complex and challenging field as it is interdisciplinary by nature. Conducting research in this domain of inquiry requires creative thinking and innovative solutions to complex problems. Despite the challenges, exploring this field is not only highly relevant, but it offers valuable insights and is also rewarding.

Without any doubt, sustainability reporting research is an essential part of accounting research. As the world strives to become more sustainable, accountants will need to be able to collect, analyse and report information on sustainability-related issues, and to provide guidance and support decision-making processes based on such information. Sustainability reporting research will help the profession to develop the skills and knowledge needed to address these challenges. Consequently, sustainability reporting research has the potential to make a real difference in the world by helping companies to become more sustainable and by promoting a more sustainable future for all.

Index